The Ways of Byzantine Philosophy

The Ways of Byzantine Philosophy

Edited by **Mikonja Knežević**

Sebastian Press
Alhambra, California

THE WAYS
OF BYZANTINE PHILOSOPHY

Published by
Sebastian Press
Western American Diocese of the Serbian Orthodox Church
in collaboration with the Faculty of Philosophy,
Kosovska Mitrovica

Prepress & printing
Interklima—grafika, Vrnjacka Banja
Contemporary Christian Thought Series, № 32

Address all correspondence to:
Sebastian Press
1621 West Garvey Avenue
Alhambra, California 91803

Email: westsrbdio@gmail.com
Website: http://www.westsrbdio.org

The ways of Byzantine philosophy / Mikonja Knežević, editor. — Alhambra, California: Sebastian Press, Western American Diocese of the Serbian Orthodox Church, Faculty of Philosophy, Kosovska Mitrovica, 2015.

476 pages ; 23 cm.

(Contemporary Christian thought series ; no. 32)

ISBN: 978-1-936773-25-1

1. Philosophy—Byzantine Empire. 2. Philosophy, Ancient. 3. Philosophy, Medieval. 4. Christian philosophy. 5. Christianity—Philosophy. 6. Orthodox Eastern Church—Byzantine Empire—Doctrines—History. 7. Orthodox Eastern Church—Theology. 8. Philosophy and religion—Byzantine Empire. 9. Theologians—Byzantine Empire. 10. Christian saints—Byzantine Empire—Philosophy. 11. Byzantine empire—Church history. 12. Byzantine empire—Civilization. I. Knežević, Mikonja, 1978– II. Series.

Contents

Introduction

Mikonja Knežević

When in 1949 Basil Tatakis published his *La philosophie byzantine*[1], as a supplementary volume of E. Brehier's *Histoire de la philosophie*, he set foundations of the study of an – up to then, and unfortunately even today – mainly neglected and unexplored period of medieval philosophical heritage[2]. By the time of the publication of this remarkable, but now rather outmoded, volume, Byzantine philosophy was barely recognized as a field of *possible* research, being often reduced exclusively to its theological component and deprived of any autonomy with regards to the wider corpus of research on "Byzantine literature." Even when authors who could be qualified as "Byzantine philosophers" gained more significance, it was because they were treated as carriers of ancient ideas, so it seemed that Byzantine writers lived and wrote only to please, in due time, the intellectual needs of western authors.

The reasons of such treatment of the Byzantine philosophical heritage are many and they certainly need an exhaustive historical analysis. These can be recognized in the fact that many works of Byzantine thinkers were unpublished, as well as in some factors of ideological nature. Among such ideological factors one can surely count an anachronistic determination of the nature of philosophy, together with a conspicuous inclination towards a general and uncritical defamation of anything marked as "Byzantine," an idea long present in the Western academic circles. In that sense, it is indicative to quote an assessment of Byzantium which Hegel, similarly to Voltaire and Gibbon, gave in his *Philosophy of History*: "Its general aspect presents a disgusting picture of imbecility; wretched, nay, insane passions, stifle the

1. B. Tatakis, *La philosophie byzantine*, É. Bréhier, *Histoire de la philosophie*, fascicule supplémentaire № II, Paris: Presses Universitaires de France 1949, ^{2}1959. This Tatakis' book has been translated into the following languages: *Filosofia bizantina*, Buenos Aires: Editorial Sudamericana 1952; *Ἡ βυζαντινὴ φιλοσοφία*, μτφρ. Ἐ. Καλπουρζή, ἐποπτεία καὶ βιβλιογραφικὴ ἐνημέρωση Λ. Μπενάκη, Βιβλιοθήκη γενικῆς παιδείας № 5, Ἀθήνα: Ἑταιρεία Σπουδῶν Νεοελληνικοῦ Πολιτισμοῦ καὶ Γενικῆς Παιδείας 1977; *Историја византијске философије*, Никшић: Друштво философа и социолога Црне Горе 1996 = *Византијска философија*. Прилози: К. Елер, Л. Бенакис. Библиографије: Р. В. Поповић, Б. Б. Брајовић. Друго издање приредио Б. Шијаковић, Београд, Никшић: Српско друштво за хеленску философију и културу/Σερβικὴ ἑταιρεία ἑλληνικῆς φιλοσοφίας καὶ πολιτισμοῦ: Јасен ^{2}2002; *Byzantine Philosophy*, translated by N. Moutafakis, Indianapolis, Cambridge, Mass.: Hackett Publishing Co., Cambridge University Press 2001; *Bizantinska srednjeveška misel*. Prevedla V. Velkovrh Bukilica, Celje: Mohorjeva družba 2001.
2. Cf. A. de Libera, *La philosophie médiévale*, Paris: PUF 1993, 9.

growth of all that is noble in thoughts, deeds, and persons."[3] Whichever might be the reasons in question, Byzantine philosophical heritage was for a long time viewed as utterly uncompetitive and incomparable to the philosophical achievements of Western scholastics, despite the undeniable fact that many insights of Western medieval philosophers were formed under the influence of Byzantine thinkers. In that vein, it is perhaps sufficient to mention John Scotus Eriugena, whose ideas were largely formed under the influence of Dionysius the Pseudo-Areopagite and Maximus the Confessor, or Thomas Aquinas, some of whose theoretical insights were undoubtedly inspired by John Damascene[4]. However, while the works of Eriugena and Aquinas were extensively studied within Medieval philosophy courses, the works of the Dionysius Pseudo-Areopagite, John Damascene or Maximus the Confessor – named *Maximum monachum, divinum philosophum* by Eriugena himself – were mostly bypassed and (dis)qualified as exclusively theological.

In the second half of the twentieth century – thanks to Klaus Oehler, who attempted to interpret Byzantine philosophy as a continuation of ancient Greek philosophy[5], and to Linos Benakis, who accentuated the autonomy of Byzantine philosophical thought with regards to the theological thinking[6] –

---

3. G. W. F. Hegel, *The Philosophy of History*. With Prefaces by Charles Hegel and the Translator, J. Sibree, M.A., Kitchener, Ontario: Batoche Books 2001, 358. The history of Byzantine Empire, affirms Hegel several pages earlier (355), "exhibits to us a millennial series of uninterrupted crimes, weaknesses, basenesses and want of principle; a most repulsive and consequently a most uninteresting picture." However, G. Arabatzis, "Hegel and Byzantium (With a notice on Alexandre Kojève and Scepticism)," *Philosophical Inquiry* XXV, 1–2 (2003) 31–39, strove to demonstrate that this "negative" view of Hegel on Byzantium could be interpreted differently; according to him, "[t]he search for the hegelian perception of byzantine thought seems to open new perspectives for the study of byzantine philosophy."
4. Cf. e. g. M. Frede, "John of Damascus on Human Action, the Will, and Human Freedom," in: K. Ierodiakonou, ed., *Byzantine Philosophy and its Ancient Sources*, Oxford: Oxford University Press 2002, 63–95.
5. Cf. K. Oehler, "Die Kontinuität in der Philosophie der Griechen bis zum Untergang des byzantinischen Reiches," in: K. Oehler, *Antike Philosophie und byzantinisches Mittelalter*, München: Verlag C. H. Beck 1969, 15–37. This thesis has been further emphasized by K. Boudouris, "'Η ἔννοια καὶ τὸ περιεχόμενο τῆς ἑλληνικῆς φιλοσοφίας,", in: Μ. Δραγώνα-Μονάχου, Γ. Ρουσόπουλου, ed., *Ἡ ἐπικαιρότητα τῆς ἀρχαῖας ἑλληνικῆς φιλοσοφίας*, Ἀθήνα 1997, 39–53: 44: "[...] ἡ ἑλληνικὴ φιλοσοφία ὁρίζεται ὡς διανοητικὴ παραγωγὴ τῶν Ἑλλήνων ἀπὸ τῆς ἐποχῆς τῶν Προσωκρατικῶν μέχρι σήμερα, δηλαδὴ δεχόμαστε ὅτι περιλαμβάνει τὴν Ἀρχαία Ἑλληνικὴ φιλοσοφία, τὴ Βυζαντινή, τὴ Μεταβυζαντινὴ καὶ τὴν Νεοελληνικὴ φιλοσοφία." Oehler' thesis on the continuity of hellenic philosophy till the fall of Constantinople is based on the permanent presence of "hellenic" factor in byzantine philosophical thinking and insofar it can be advocated; however, this kind of approach can relativize "particularity of philosophical thought in Byzantium," as it was noticed by K. Ierodiakonou, "Byzantine Philosophy Revisited (a decade after)," in: B. Bydén, K. Ierodiakonou, ed., *The Many Faces of Byzantine Philosophy*. Papers and monographs from the Norwegian Institute at Athens, series 4, 1, Athens: Norwegian Institute at Athens 2012, 1–21: 7.
6. L. Benakis, "Die theoretische und praktische Autonomie der Philosophie als Fachdisziplin in Byzanz," in: *Knowledge and the Sciences in Medieval Philosophy. Proceedings of the Eight International Congress of Medieval Philosophy*, vol. 1, ed. by M. Asztalos, J. E. Murdoch, I. Niiniluoto, Acta Philosophica Fennica 48, Helsinki 1990, 223–227.

the study of Byzantine philosophy, inaugurated by Tatakis, gained a new momentum. Byzantine philosophy, slowly but steadily, started to appear as a legitimate subject of historical and philosophical endeavors, a trend confirmed by several indicators. Firstly, there is an increased number of encyclopedias and histories of philosophy which contain entries dealing with Byzantine philosophy[7]. Similarly, there is a noticeable number of younger researchers who, without any ideological prejudices[8], decide to dedicate themselves precisely to this understudied period of Medieval philosophical inheritance. A significant step in this direction is represented by an increasing number of critical editions of Byzantine authors' works, among which one can point to the *Corpus Philosophorum Medii Aevi - Philosophi Byzantini*, published by the Academy of Athens, under the direction of Linos Benakis.

Such a tendency in modern scholarship had as its consequence appearance of two monographs, published in the last fifteen years, which dealt with Byzantine philosophy, in an attempt to supplement – if not replace – Tatakis' pioneering study. The first was written by a renowned scholar of Byzantine philosophical tradition, Georgy Kapriev. Initially published in Bulgarian under the title *Byzantine Philosophy: Four Centers of Synthesis*, and subsequently in German as *Philosophie in Byzanz*, this book represents an important breakthrough compared to Tatakis' book, due to its novel approach, as well as to the use of the bibliographical material that appeared in the meantime[9]. Especially significant is the second, revised, edition of this book in Bulgarian, which doubtlessly represents the most solid review of Byzantine philosophy available[10]. This monograph is unavoidable reading for both experts and general audience. The second book that offers an overview of Byzantine philosophy is the study of Basil Lourié, entitled *History of Byzantine Philosophy: Formative Period.* This publication gives an important contribution to the investigation of philosophy in Byzantine period, despite the fact that it leaves untreated many authors belonging to the Byzantine philosophical corpus[11].

Besides these two monographs which, each in its own way, explore Byzantine philosophy through its "centers of synthesis," an important contribution is presented by two edited volumes, published thanks to efforts of

7. See: K. Ierodiakonou, "Byzantine Philosophy Revisited (a decade after)," in: B. Bydén, K. Ierodiakonou, ed., *The Many Faces of Byzantine Philosophy*, Athens 2012, 1–21: 1.
8. Cf. K. Ierodiakonou, "Introduction," in: K. Ierodiakonou, ed., *Byzantine Philosophy and its Ancient Sources*, Oxford: Oxford University Press 2002, 1–13: 8: "What we still need to do is to take their [i.e. of Byzantine philosophers] works seriously as philosophical writings; putting aside our prejudices and misconceptions, we need to make a renewed effort to reconstruct and to do justice to Byzantine philosophy."
9. Г. Каприев, *Византийската философия. Четири центра на синтеза*, София: Лик 2001 = *Philosophie in Byzanz*, Würzburg: Königshausen & Neumann 2005.
10. Г. Каприев, *Византийската философия. Четири центра на синтеза.* Второ допълнено издание, София: Изток-Запад 2011.
11. В. М. Лурье, *История византийской философии. Формативный период*, Санкт-Петербург: Axiōma 2006.

Katerina Ierodiakonou. The first attempts "to shed light on Byzantine philosophy against the background of ancient philosophical thought", that is, to answer the question "whether and in which ways the Byzantines were able to appropriate and to develop the philosophical tradition they had inherited from antiquity."[12] The second volume, published in 2012, is a continuation of the first one, in terms of the selection of themes and problems treated. Both volumes are accompanied by extensive editor's prefaces, elaborating on main methodological, semantic and historical questions pertaining to the study of Byzantine philosophy. Certainly, some of those issues are those addressing the periodization of Byzantine philosophy, its relationship with the theological thought *sensu stricto*, its specific characteristics, identification of philosophers in Byzantium, etc.

The understanding according to which it is more appropriate to talk about a "polyprismatic character" or "many faces of Byzantine philosophy," rather than about its certain "essence" – which would transform it into a monolithic and undifferentiated phenomenon[13] – is present in this volume as well, through a total of twenty four original contributions. A considerable number of contributors can be regarded as established scholars, while some belong to the younger generation, very enthusiastic in their approach to the study of Byzantine philosophical heritage. The texts here presented are mainly focused on philosophical aspects of Byzantine thinkers' works, and use different interpretative methods and hermeneutic standpoints. Specific issues addressed belong to different academic disciplines, such as history of ideas, anthropology, logic, metaphysics, etc. As for the authors treated in this volume, one can freely state that they belong to all periods of Byzantine philosophical thought, starting with the creation of Byzantine empire, up to its collapse in the fifteenth century.

It goes without saying that, despite a great number of contributions, this volume does not pretend to offer a comprehensive overview of Byzantine philosophy, or an "introduction" to Byzantine philosophy. Its main intention is not even of a protreptic character, in sense of convincing the reader

12. K. Ierodiakonou, "Introduction," in: K. Ierodiakonou, ed., *Byzantine Philosophy and its Ancient Sources*, Oxford 2002, 1–13: 1.

13. This is particularly emphasized by M. Trizio, "Byzantine Philosophy as a Contemporary Historiographical Project," *Recherches de Théologie et Philosophie Médiévales* 74, 1 (2007) 247–294. Quite reasonably, Trizio indicated the difficulties that encounters the endeavour to establish the "essence" of Byzantine philosophy, since the concept "philosophy" was understood completely differently in some Byzantine authors, such as e. g. Symeon the New Theologian and Michael Psellos (p. 250–257). Trizio, therefore, concludes that "[t]he aim should not be to provide at all costs an image of Byzantine philosophy as a whole, but to point out the different Byzantine philosoph*ies*, the different social practices and the different manifestations of the term 'philosophy' in Byzantium" (286). However, in this respect I prefer, together with K. Ierodiakonou, "Byzantine Philosophy Revisited (a decade after)," in: B. Bydén, K. Ierodiakonou, ed., *The Many Faces of Byzantine Philosophy*, Athens 2012, 1–21: 9–10, to speak about "many faces" or "many ways" of Byzantine philosophy, than about "Byzantine philosoph*ies*," as Trizio does.

"that Byzantine philosophy is worth investigating". If this volume has any "tendency" at all, then this tendency could be seen in showing that the facticity of Byzantine philosophy cannot be questioned today[14], as well as in underlining the *polyvalent* character of the Byzantine philosophical tradition, which – even through its representatives that identified themselves as strictly theologians – contains a variety of insights which can be stimulating not only for historians of philosophy but for today's philosophical speculation itself. Maximus the Confessor's ideas on the notion of *thelēsis* on a strictly theoretical level, quite authentic and *original* in the philosophical thought since Homer to the seventh century[15], are just one of the indicators towards this viewpoint. Despite the fact that Byzantine philosophy does not represent a uniform theoretical phenomenon, but it moves through the different paths of intellectual considerations and life attitude (just as philosophy was in ancient times considered as a way of life as well[16]), it certainly contains certain specific characteristics which may differentiate it not just with regards to the Latin Medieval philosophy but also in comparison to the later philosophical currents in western Europe. In that sense, the fact that the Byzantine philosophy lacks a systematic character not only does not represent a deficiency but can even be an advantage: for, when one tradition of thought is not encircled in a "system," its capacities are not completely exhausted, but on the contrary, such a tradition offers insights that are distinctively different from those to which our own philosophic reasoning is accustomed. This fact suggests that Byzantine philosophy might have certain repercussions also to the contemporary philosophical streams. Some of the contributions in the present volume attempted to show precisely that some of "the ways of Byzantine philosophy" might lead even to the modern age.

In the very end, I would like to express my deepest gratitude to those who helped in shaping this book. First of all, thanks are due to Maksim Vasiljević, Bishop of the Western American Diocese of the Serbian Orthodox Church, who showed his readiness to publish the volume with Sebastian Press, and to Fr. Daniel Kirk, who, within the limits of possibility, improved the linguistic aspect of the texts contained here. The typesetting and technical preparation was done by Boban Stanojević; also, special thanks I owe to prominent scholars such as John Demetracopoulos, Michele Trizio and Grigory Benevich

14. Cf. F. Ivanović, "Byzantine Philosophy and its Historiography," *Byzantinoslavica* LXVIII (2010) 369–380: 376.
15. Cf. F. Heinzer, "Anmerkungen zum Willensbegriff Maximus' Confessors," *Freiburger Zeitschrift für Philosophie und Theologie* 28 (1981) 372–392; J. D. Madden, "The Authenticity of Early Definitions of Will (thelēsis)," in: *Maximus Confessor. Actes du Symposium sur Maxime le Confesseur, Fribourg, 2–5 septembre 1980*, édités par F. Heinzer et Chr. Schönborn, Paradosis. Études de littérature et de théologie ancienne № 27, Fribourg, Suisse: Éditions Universitaires 1982, 61–79.
16. This is particularly emphasized by P. Hadot, *Qu'est-ce que la philosophie antique?*, Paris: Editions Gallimard 1995; *La Philosophie comme manière de vivre.* Entretiens avec Jeannie Carlier et Arnold I. Davidson, Paris: Éditions Albin Michel S.A. 2001.

for their kind support regarding this volume. I wish also to thank Bogdan Lubardić, Filip Ivanović, as well as Anita Janković; last, but not least, I am grateful for the patience and diligence to my colleagues and friends who published their research results in this volume and who earnestly supported me in the efforts to bring this project to end, despite many difficulties encountered. I do hope that this project shall not be the last of our cooperation.

Belgrade, October 2015

Philosophy in Byzantium and Byzantine Philosophy

Georgi Kapriev

In[1] his largely positive 2006 review[2] of my book *Philosophie in Byzanz*, Peter Schreiner points out that while my trailblazing article of 2002 is entitled "Is There Such a Thing As Byzantine Philosophy"[3], my book seeks to build up a narrative of "philosophy in Byzantium". If the reviewer could read in Bulgarian, he would have found out that the much more modest 2001 preliminary version of the book also features the collocation "Byzantine Philosophy" in its title. The distinction between the two concepts, which I have subsequently delineated, is not fully explicit in the book of 2005 either.

In a paper which I presented in 2010 in Schreiner's presence, I referred briefly to the distinction that I envisage between the two terms. On that occasion, my statement amounted to the following: "When I speak of 'philosophy in Byzantium', I usually mean the conglomerate of all philosophical projects in Byzantine culture. In contrast, by 'Byzantine philosophy' I mean those philosophical tendencies that set themselves apart from Western traditions, mainly by laying particular emphasis on the dynamic of being. These tendencies do not bring to the fore essence, substance or whatever is in itself, but rather foreground its actuality, its actions, and its motions, i.e. its existence, whereby its essence comes to be known. It is this peculiar nuance added to the mainstream set of metaphysical problems that I consider a peculiar contribution of Byzantium's philosophical culture".[4] Now I want to discuss this position in more detail and to describe more meticulously what I refer to as Byzantine philosophy.

To the best of my knowledge, insignificant is the number of those voices that still attribute some kind of "essential character" to philosophy in Byzantium. Comparably few are also those who would envision some kind of

1. This text was created in the course of my work as a fellow of the Morphomata International College at the University of Cologne; it was presented at the opening session of the Philosophy in Byzantium scholarly circle, affiliated with the German Society of Ancient Philosophy. The session was held on April 19th, 2013 in Bonn.
2. P. Schreiner, "Georgi Kapriev, Philosophie in Byzanz," *Historische Zeitschrift* 282 (2006) 464.
3. G. Kapriev, "Gibt es eine byzantinische Philosophie?," *Ostkirchliche Studien* 1 (2002) 3–28.
4. G. Kapriev, "Was hat die Philosophie mit der Theologie zu tun? Der Fall Byzanz," in: A. Rigo, P. Ermilov, M. Trizio, eds., *Byzantine Theology and its Philosophical Background*, Studies in Byzantine History & Civilization 4, Turnhout 2011, 8.

monolithic form or unequivocal continuity of this philosophy. Some time ago, I was reproached (without much justification, I should say) for advocating such a view.[5] At this point, I would also like to dissociate myself from the tendency to designate as "philosophy" a certain way of life, viz. the ascetic and pious life of the monk, although this designation, which dates back to Late Antiquity, did have validity in Byzantium. My interest is mostly focused on speculative and discursive philosophy; my subject is the rational and rationalist discourse in the Byzantine tradition: philosophy as investigation of the logos of being qua being, or to put it in Latin, metaphysics. However, metaphysics was interpreted and practiced by Byzantine thinkers, too, in more ways than one. In this sense, it is worth reminding that in the Eastern Roman Empire creative philosophy was predominantly taught at private schools and was pursued as a private endeavor. Besides, it should be noted that there were no philosophical schools to speak of in Byzantium. The Thomists are the only exception to the rule, and this fact is symptomatic enough. The well known claim, frequently reiterated by philosophers, that they "have no teachers" does not mean to imply that they did not study philosophy with a mentor, but rather that they do not follow in the footsteps of any predecessors.

In this context, it is quite appropriate to lay the emphasis on the diversity of philosophical programs within Byzantine culture. It would then be safe to insist that each of the philosophical "projects" (and ideally, each particular philosophical position), should be considered by its own measure and in its own unique set of circumstances, as Michele Trizio does.[6] Eventually, I said I was willing to accept, in this train of thought, that it is possible to assert that there were as many philosophies in Byzantium as there were philosophers, each of whom deserves to be studied in his own right.[7] At the same time, I feel compelled to warn that it is relatively easy to lose the conceptual perspective on the field of philosophical culture. There is a danger for the specifics of the historical-philosophical study to be sacrificed.

This must be the rationale behind K. Ierodiakonou's "revised" position of 2012. Like myself, she highlights the fact that Byzantine philosophical thought incorporates a number of different teachings and different ways of philosophical life. What is more, she concurs with the thesis that the peculiarity of this thought should be identified – the peculiarity which distinguishes it from ancient and contemporary philosophy and from the respective concepts of what philosophy is. She also dismisses – quite rightly so – the

5. M. Trizio, "Byzantine Philosophy as a Contemporary Historiographical Project," *Recherches de Théologie et Philosophie médiéval* 1 (2007) 272–277.
6. Cf. Ibid., 288–294.
7. G. Kapriev, "Was hat die Philosophie mit der Theologie zu tun? Der Fall Byzanz," in: A. Rigo, P. Ermilov, M. Trizio, eds., *Byzantine Theology and its Philosophical Background*, Studies in Byzantine History & Civilization 4, Turnhout 2011, 8.

assertion of some kind of "essence" of philosophy in Byzantium, which, to cap it all, should be perceived as unique, immutable and constant.

(Let me say in parentheses that theoretical philosophy is a method, a method of thinking, and it is always about reflection, critical reflection. This means that it could not be a substance or an essence, nor could it possess anything like that. For philosophy to become an "essence", a reification of the method should be undertaken. Should this be done, philosophy will evolve into ideology in the bad sense of the word, i.e. into "false consciousness", if we choose for once to resort to Marxist terms).

Ierodiakonou upholds the diversity of forms in this tradition and its discontinuity. (Let me just point out that the discontinuity issue is rather complex in that "the history of influences" and "the history of receptions" are not identical notions – I am quoting Theo Kobusch here). She accepts neither the thesis of the only "genuine face" of philosophy in Byzantium nor "the many philosophies" thesis. She makes a point of referring merely to the "many faces of Byzantine philosophy". Besides, she quite aptly poses the question whether this philosophy is different in its ethos from Latin, Arab, or Judaic medieval philosophy.[8] On the whole, I concur with this position.

The painstaking non-essentialist and non-arbitrary identification of the general borders and constitutive elements of a particular tradition, as well as the even more painstaking and non-ideological foregrounding of typological traits, which makes it possible to differentiate among disparate tendencies within this tradition, is not in itself a historical and philosophical sin, but is, rather, an integral part of our profession.

First and foremost, one should mention the bolster of the underlying worldview which moulds the so called Abrahamite philosophies (to borrow a term from Tzvi Langerman)[9]. They share a perception of God, man, and the world which is definitely different from the polytheistic one. The transcendent and personal God creates of His own free will a work that has an absolute beginning and unfolds in a vectorial time. It is in this dimension that world history evolves, and in it the universal human being has her place – a human being conceived in her psychosomatic unity as the bearer of a universal natural reason and an autonomous free will. The emphasis in this perspective on the personal, rather than on the general and the special, makes for a new anthropological vision constituting not only the ethical views, but also the perception of natural and supernatural knowledge, both of which are closely bound up with the altered interpretation of being as a whole. Besides, it should be noted, reiterating a thesis put forward by Ludger Honnefelder, that in this tradition life was structured in accordance with a universal truth,

8. K. Ierodiakonou, "Byzantine Philosophy Revisited (a decade after)," in: B. Bydén, K. Ierodiakonou, eds., *The Many Faces of Byzantine Philosophy*, Athens 2012, 1–21.
9. Here I refer to the theses put forward in Tzvi Langerman's paper "The Soul in Ibn Kammuna's Ethical Writings," presented on 22. 02. 2012 at the conference "Die Seele im Mittelalter. Von der Substanz zum funktionalen System" (21.–23. 02. 2012, Hanover).

and respectively, in accordance with universal principles that could never indeed be attained in and of themselves. These positions, as well as the ones that they entail, constitute an axiomatic system which not only lies at the core of the philosophical culture of the Romaioi and of Christians at large, but also shapes the views of the philosophical representatives of Islam and Judaism, far beyond the Middle Ages at that.

Besides, Christian philosophers drew upon the teachings of the New Testament, which extended the axiomatic basis. Paradigmatic to their thought is the thesis, brilliantly formulated by Maximus the Confessor, according to whom "the Son remains in theological unity with the Father".[10] Theology and economy are inextricably connected in Christ's hypostasis, and it is the economy that is to be regarded as the sphere of philosophy per se[11]. This position is the pivotal point that enables and even demands a Trinitarian and Christological speculative reflection. Discursive speculation on the theological, conducted with philosophical methods, belongs in the realm of philosophy or stands in a necessary connection with it.

I am often tempted to explain a certain peculiarity of the Eastern tradition of Christianitas, i.e. of what was to become Europe, with an example that sounds somewhat extravagant at first. I maintain that the Latin *res* does not render without residue the Greek πρᾶγμα. And vice versa. I am suggesting this not because I want to give philologists a hard time, but because I want to show in the simplest possible way something obvious. Πρᾶγμα and *res* are *concreta*, which in principle have the same signified, i.e. "an object," "a thing." Their *abstracta*, however, unequivocally bring to light the character of "objects" and "things" in the respective cultural circle. *Realitas* articulates the unity of objects exactly in terms of their substantial autonomy and their mutual relationship. This unity is what is considered as "reality". And yet the *abstractum* of πρᾶγμα is πρᾶξις, and it articulates something far different from the reality so conceived. It signifies "doing", "acting". At this point, I must make the qualification that no polar distinctions will come out of this observation, but only nuances indeed. Whereas Western culture first poses the question of the thing in its substantiality, and only then does it turn to its actions, Eastern culture first identifies the actions, after which it asks itself about the generator of these actions and about its character. The first known is the dynamic of being, whereby the perspective on being things takes shape.

This circumstance has been remarkably articulated by Michael Psellos in his paraphrasis of Aristotle's *On Interpretation*. Psellos insists that in the sentence, the predicate has "a natural priority" over the subject and is more perfect than it. He points out that the subject signifies only the substance whereas the predicate signifies both, i.e. apart from signifying the substance,

10. *Expositio orationis dominicae*, PG 91, 348CD.

11. Cf. G. Kapriev, "Zeitlichkeit und Geschichtlichkeit als Grundelemente der byzantinischen Philosophie," in: G. Kapriev, G. Mensching, hrsg., *Die Geschichtlichkeit des philosophischen Denkens*, Sofia 2004, 58–71.

it points to something else as well. The noun signifies only the οὐσία while the verb refers both to the οὐσία and to its action (ἐνέργεια). Thus, upon articulating the predicate, one also means the thing articulated by the verb, along with its action. The verb, too, articulates the essence, and along with its cognitive primary action at that. The verb is therefore the "container" of the noun and has a natural priority over it. It should be noted that as far as its principle is concerned, this position is far from a lonely voice in the Byzantine tradition; it is supported by many interpreters, mostly speculative grammarians.[12]

The peculiarity not only of philosophical, but also of quotidian thought moulds Byzantium's discourse, even if only on the basis of the simple fact that it makes use of the Greek language. This circumstance applies even to Byzantine Thomists because they follow Thomas Aquinas through the Greek translations of his texts, and it is worth noting that their reading is not fundamentally alien to the Thomist type of philosophizing. This peculiarity is a distinctive trait of all philosophical programs in Byzantium.

Within this thematic context, I define as "Byzantine philosophy" the platforms that consciously place action at the center of the philosopher's attention, their pivot being constituted by the so called doctrine of energies. I dub them thus, not because these programs express the "essence" of Byzantine philosophizing – such an essence never existed in the first place. I dub them thus, not because their representatives philosophize in a most consistent manner; I refrain from such sports classifications when it comes to inherently consequential philosophizing. I dub them thus, not because these programs prevail in number, although, statistically speaking, this is the case. I dub them thus, because they manifest, in a manner more radical than that of the rest, the abovementioned "peculiar contribution of philosophical culture in Byzantium" in the context of European thought.

It is high time, I believe, we put an end to the tradition that has transformed the doctrine of energies into a shibboleth. I am referring here to three tendencies. On one side of the divide, there was the so called Neo-Palamism. The representatives of this movement, who are now few and far between, have transformed the doctrine of energies into an absolute and have attached to it the stylized form of an ideology. As is typical of ideologies, the doctrine was presented a-historically in the sense of its being the only truthful system, which resulted in ignoring exactly its philosophical merits. The adepts of this school of thought brought to the fore the doctrine's anti-rationalism, its general untranslatability into the terms of the Western tradition, etc. The Neo-Palamites took almost no interest in the philosophical

12. Cf. K. Ierodiakonou, "Psellos Paraphrasis on Aristotle's 'De interpretatione'", in: K. Ierodiakonou, ed., *Byzantine Philosophy and its Ancient Sources*, Oxford 2002, 169 sqq.

program of this doctrine; instead, they were focused on its use as a theological and ecclesiological tool. Thus, for the sake of ideological applications and misapplications, the doctrine was philosophically compromised.

On the other side, there were those mostly Catholic theologians, predominantly Dominicans and Jesuits, who fought the ideological battle against the Neo-Palamites in the 1960s and 1970s. I am referring to a trend that should be practically traced back to Hans-Georg Beck, who developed a trailblazing school of thought; however, the tendency owes its true origin to Albert Ehrhard. Resting their claims on predictably repetitive yet impressively strong premises, these ideologues portrayed the proponents of the doctrine as champions of a "mystical theology", relentlessly identified with some kind of "Orthodoxy hostile to education". The doctrine of energies was placed on a par with Palamism, which was in turn branded as obscurantist and philosophically impotent; it was then pitted against a certain, fuzzily defined yet definitely progressive, "Byzantine humanism". The all-encompassing canonization advocated by the Palamites was countered with an all-encompassing demonization.

Related, albeit not identical, to this trend are the Enlightenment and pseudo-Enlightenment attempts to suggest that there exists "a Palamite Counter-Reformation"[13] (whatever this is supposed to mean), as well as the attempts to contrive some kind of "Spinozism before Spinoza" in Plethon's work[14] and other misconceptions of this sort. These endeavors were aimed at discovering some rudimentary traces of modern philosophical programs in the Byzantine tradition, and such traces can undoubtedly be foretasted there, too. Thus, in the good old style of the 19th century, the Romaioi philosophers, whom these authors thought of as heroes, were proclaimed narrow-minded, inept thinkers who had, however, their moments of empowering epiphany; this made them fit for the role of proud predecessors of the great philosophers of modernity. As a result, the very peculiarity of Byzantium's cultural and intellectual achievement goes down the drain. All these tendencies and the accompanying trends related to them should be considered historically dead.

As a matter of fact, the philosophical doctrine of energies does not begin with Palamas, nor does it end with him and his followers. I could point to at least three books, published in the last ten years, whose authors prove that in the 4th century and even before that period, there existed such a doctrine in the Christian context of the East: Bradshaw's, Larchet's, and my own book.[15] In the closing part of his study of 2010 *La théologie des énergies divines. Des origines à saint Jean Damascène*, Jean-Claude Larchet formulates thirty key arguments of the doctrine of energies, which had established themselves by

13. Cf. N. Siniossoglou, *Radical Platonism in Byzantium*, Cambridge 2011, 122.
14. Ibid., 418 sqq.
15. D. Bradshaw, *Aristotle East and West. Metaphysics and the Division of Christendom*, Cambridge 2004; G. Kapriev, *Philosophie in Byzanz*, Würzburg 2005; J.-Cl. Larchet, *La théologie des énergies divines. Des origines à saint Jean Damascène*, Paris 2010.

the 8th century.[16] In a sort of summary, published in 2008, he draws attention to the fact that these arguments "account for quite a few constitutive elements in the theology of divine energies, developed by St. Gregory Palamas in the 14th century"[17]. The doctrine of energies lies at the core of the diverse manifestations of Byzantine philosophy, one of which is Palamism. It should be noted, of course, that Palamas did transform the doctrine into the one and only center of his theological-philosophical system.

As is well known, the doctrine of energies was first formulated by Aristotle in Book IX of his *Metaphysics.* The specifically Byzantine contribution consists in going beyond the limits set by the Peripatetics and the Neo-Platonists. The key signposts here are "the concept of hypostasis" (as opposed to the concept of person, which applies only to rational beings), "the concept of the absolute free will of God and of man", "the concept of hexis", "the concept of perichoresis", etc. I believe I have written and spoken extensively on these matters[18], so here I will confine myself to delineating the horizon.

I could be reproached, if anyone would like to do so, for being interested mainly in that part of the Byzantine tradition which I designate as "Byzantine philosophy". This would be no rumor; it is a fact. And it is no reproach at all. Let me provide some justification for this preoccupation of mine.

Over the last 200 years or so, there has hardly been an academic who has chosen to present Byzantine philosophy in all its scope as her own philosophical program. After the fall of Constantinople in 1453, the philosophical tradition in Byzantium began to fall into decline. The middle of the 18th century saw its last manifestations. Since the closing decades of the 18th century, even in the region structured culturally by Byzantium, the forms of Western thought cater to the need for philosophical knowledge. Today it would be hard, or downright impossible, to identify a specific pattern that we associate with philosophizing in the European East.

It is exactly the developments in Western philosophy and science since the last decades of the 20th century that have added validity to a renewed interest in certain views and positions of Byzantine philosophy. There have been worthwhile attempts to apply particular motifs, methods, and concepts from this philosophy to contemporary research, not necessarily within the confines of philosophical disciplines[19]. Quite symptomatically, all these projects are related to the pivotal concept of Byzantine philosophy – the doctrine of energies. The Byzantine form of this doctrine has proved to be quite productive in contemporary models of thought and research.

16. J.-Cl. Larchet, *La théologie des énergies divines. Des origines à saint Jean Damascène*, Paris 2010, 455–460.
17. J.-Cl. Larchet, "La théologie des énergies divines des origines à saint Jean Damascène", in: P. Ladoceur, ed., *The Wedding Feast*, Montreal 2010, 34.
18. Cf. e.g. the relevant chapters and paragraphs in G. Kapriev, *Philosophie in Byzanz*, Würzburg 2005.
19. I know of such projects in the fields of physics (especially quantum physics), medicine, psychology, and sociology.

It is most necessary to stress the differences between the ideological – whether theological or related to the Enlightenment – uses of this doctrine and the abovementioned modes of application. First of all, the doctrine of energies is not to be refashioned as an extra-philosophical (e.g. theological) weapon. Secondly, it is not made use of because of the elements of conceptual correspondence with the historically available Western models, but because of its peculiarity and its immanent creativity. The philosophical programs drawing upon the doctrine of energies are characterized by their relevance to the contemporary agenda, and this is not achieved at the expense of the doctrine's originality and specifics.

We do history of philosophy, but history of philosophy is not some kind of an auxiliary discipline fit for the archivist. The rather controversial distinction between "historians of philosophy" and "philosophers" has not had a leg to stand on for quite some time now. There are only philosophers, Albert Zimmermann used to say on this topic, some of whom are better aware of the history of their trade. History of philosophy is philosophizing on philosophizing. It is a live palimpsest, a dense dialog, an intense concerted intellectual effort, which, importantly, is not diaphonic but polyphonic. In this process, however, the voice of the interlocutor who has received the first question must be clearly audible. Otherwise the whole thing makes no sense at all.

On these grounds, I have chosen, in my practice, to designate as "Byzantine philosophy" the tendency, or the face, of philosophy in Byzantium that I have delineated above. This does not mean, of course, that I view all other programs in the field of Romaioi culture as irrelevant to it, and therefore as, say, Latin, pagan, or Inuit.

Translated by Lubomir Terziev

Hexaemeral Anthropology of St. Gregory of Nyssa: "Unarmed Man" (ἄοπλος ὁ ἄνθρωπος)

Dušan Krcunović

1. (Non)Contemporary Considerations

If the famous treatise by St. Gregory of Nyssa (c. 335–394) *On the Making of Man* (379)[1] was to be assessed by contemporary epistemic criteria, it would equally belong to the genres of both philosophical and theological anthropology. The author of this famous treatise, quite expectantly, takes Biblical cosmogony and anthropogony as the ultimate starting point of his anthropological speculations, but on the other side, he also shows an interest in the results of empirically oriented sciences of man (such as anatomy, physiology, psychology) in order to boldly dive into their theological and philosophical interpretation.[2] Such an approach justifies the twofold genre classification of the treatise *On the Making of Man* which exemplifies the author's thoughtful endeavor to understand the dynamic and antinomic corporeal-spiritual structure of human nature in its unity and entirety.

Contemplating on "Moses' mystical anthropogony (ἀνθρωπογονία)"[3] St. Gregory of Nyssa was able to uncover the secret of man's corporeity that was looked on by radical platonising Origenistic spirituality with an unhidden aversion, advocating the position of irreconcilable antagonistic dualism

1. Gregor. Nyss., *De hominis opificio*, PG 44, 124D–256C.
2. Gregory's interpretation of scientific knowledge had important implications for the science itself. Se more in: F. M. Young, "Adam and Anthropos: A Study of the Interaction Science and the Bible in Two Anthropological Treatises of the Fourth Century," *Vigiliae Christianae* 37 (1983) 110–140, 118–121.
3. Gregor. Nyss., *De hominis opificio*, PG 44, 256B. Otherwise, the term "anthropology" does not exist in the vocabulary of Gregory, but it is represented, *avant la lettre*, precisely by the term "anthropogony." The term "anthropology" comes into the conceptual history only around the year 1600, and in the middle of the 18th century (around 1750) gets its philosophical context. See: O. Marquard, "Zur Geschichte des philosophischen Begriffs 'Anthropologie' seit dem Ende des 18. Jahrhunderts," in: O. Marquard, *Schwierigkeiten mit der Geschichtsphilosophie*, Frankfurt a. M. 1973, 122–144; 213–247; also see the same authors's entry "Anthropologie", in: J. Ritter, hrsg., *Historisches Wörterbuch der Philosophie*, Bd. 1, Basell, Stuttgart 1971, 362–374.

between the corporeal and the spiritual in man. Following that dualism, to put it in contemporary language, a rigid pattern of essentialist anthropology was established, functioning as a kind of metaphysical Procrustes' bed for anything that was not conformable. Man's corporeal dimension could simply not fit in such a metaphysical pattern. However, as each dualism has two sides; the empirical science of man laid claim to anthropological truth with equal toughness on man's opposite side, the corporeal one. Handling arguments *ad oculum*, naturalistically inclined empiric anthropology reduced higher intellectual powers of man down to physiological phenomena and processes, i.e. to a lower corporeal stratum of human nature.

Hence, St. Gregory of Nyssa found himself facing two challenges: apart from the fact that his brother St. Basil the Great never succeeded in completing his *Hexaemeron* by contemplating on man, in his time there were also two already mentioned influential conflicting anthropological conceptions, in the form of metaphysical dualism and naturalistic reductionism.

One of the fundamental traits of Cappadocian intellectual standpoints was articulated out of the demand to take positions within the polemic context of polarized attitudes. What St. Basil the Great had achieved with his *Hexaemeron* within Cappadocian cosmology – defending the Biblical idea of creation of the world, in contrast to Plotinus' metaphysical derivationism and Aristotelian teachings on world's eternity, advocating the proper attitude toward the world as God's creation, between pagan cosmolatric divinization of the world and Gnostic devaluation and demonization of the world – was what St. Gregory was striving to achieve in anthropology with his treatise *On the Making of Man.* Following his brother's *Hexaemeron* with the intention of supplementing and completing the glorious cosmologic piece of work, Gregory of Nyssa carefully searched for *via media*[4] between the metaphysical and naturalistic interpretations of human nature. St. Gregory had set off on such studious "middle road" – which, hand in hand with Nemesius of Emesa, has brought him reputation of one of the most profound and most systematic classical Christian anthropologists – with a clear task: to overcome the "contradiction" between the perfection authentic creation of man "by the image and likeness of God" and the present state of man's imperfection. To fulfill the task meant to defend the integrity of the image of God in man in the wholeness of man's corporeal-spiritual nature, that is, in its hierarchically structured "synthetic dualism."

4. It has already been noted that Gregory "worked assiduously to carve out a middle position between the Platonism that he knew from reading Plotinus and Origen, and the materialism that he acquired from his acquaintance with Galen and the medical writers, thereby reconciling two seemingly opposed concepts: i) that the intelligible mind existed, and ii) that it interacted with a corporeal body that did not limit its capacities, but somehow fulfilled them." See: S. Wessel, "The Reception of Greek Science in Gregory of Nyssa's De hominis opificio," *Vigiliae Christianae* 63 (2009) 24–46, 26.

His working hypothesis had to be that man's corporeity as such was not a repercussion of transcendent transgression and Fall of the initially spiritual man, as Origen claimed, but that the corporeal, along with all other in man, had actually suffered their repercussions. In relation to this, the tacit assumption would be that in the primordial moment of his historic dimension, man made no progress from his biological and physical condition "similar to animality" (θηριώδης) towards gradual humanization, as the advocates of the "anthropological theories of progress," reflected in the works of ancient pre-Socratic philosophers and Sophists, claimed.[5] After all, there had to be a kind of positive connection, a certain correlation between "the image of God" in man – who due to Fall had lost his original "likeness"– and the biological condition of man's fragile corporeity. Most simply put, man's corporeal constitution indeed contains something unconformable to Godlikeness – mortality, passion, suffering, and ephemeralness – which causes tragic "compassion" (ἔλεος)[6], but within the same corporeal constitution there has been, since the very beginning, something deiform, certain "empirical" indicators of man's higher origin and "dignity" (τιμή).

The procedure following which an appropriate correlation between man's God-likeness and corporeity was to be demonstrated, is proclaimed at the beginning of the treatise *On the Making of Man*[7]. There, St. Gregory clearly stresses his intention to connect in the ensuing research the three experientially different and ostensibly contradictory – but for the concept and reality of human nature constitutive – dimensions.

1) Past events as "something we believe" (τῶν πεπιστευμένων) had happened, i.e. creation of man by "the image and likeness of God". St. Gregory especially accentuates the difference between cosmogony, which was developing according to God's "commandment" (πρόσταγμα), and anthropogony which came only after God's "council" (βουλή)[8] as an additional mark of man's idiosyncrasy. A feature of Gregory's understanding of the famous *theologoumenon* from Biblical anthropogonic narrative is the striking identification of God's "image" (εἰκῶν) and "likeness" (ὁμοίωσις), by which he deviates from the tradition of differentiating between the two designations established by Irenaeus of Lyons, more than two centuries earlier.[9]

5. See: W. K. C. Guthrie, *The Sophists*, Cambridge: Cambridge University Press 1971, 14ff; 60ff. The standpoint on man's primordial imperfection promoted by the Ionian philosophers of nature clashed with the mythical idea of "golden age" of man's prehistory after which the degeneration appeared. See: Th. Cole, *Democritus and the Sources of Greek Anthropology*, Atlanta: Scholars Press 1990, 1.
6. Gregor. Nyss., *De hominis opificio*, PG 44, 180C.
7. Gregor. Nyss., *De hominis opificio*, PG 44, 128AB.
8. Gregor. Nyss., *De hominis opificio*, PG 44, 133C.
9. G. B. Ladner, "The Philosophical Anthropology of Saint Gregory of Nyssa," *Dumbarton Oaks Papers* 12 (1958) 59–94, 63–66: "Gregory is the first of the Fathers to attribute to man full

2) The existing condition of human things or "what we perceive now" (τῶν νῦν θεωρουμένων) on the empirical man, under circumstances of sorrowful loss of his original perfection. This existing man is in the narrow focus of empirical human sciences, which abstract the unempirical fields of τῶν πεπιστευμένων. That is why these sciences put an emphasis on objective descriptions of human nature and renounce any other axiological and normative statements on man. "Anthropological theories of progress" depart from empirical results obtained by human sciences and put forward hypotheses concerning primitive natural condition of man which man abandons over time due to his "innate" technical intelligence.
3) Future or "what we expect" (τῶν προσδοκωμένων) to happen in terms of man's aspirations, since "no other being, other than this creation, i.e. man, has been made like to God"[10]. This dimension of theological anthropology is accounted for by educational theory and ascetic practice. The mystical paideutic dimension presumes an orientation towards the ideal of likeness to God, which man realizes due to his original Godlikeness, freedom of will and "plasticity" of his φύσις.

It is quite obvious that none of the above mentioned dimensions are themselves sufficient to wholly comprehend human being and that Gregory's notion of "human nature" (ἡ ἀνθρωπίνη φύσις) encompasses all three of them. In other words, to answer the anthropological question means to state not only "what man *is*", but also "what man *needs* to be"[11]. Starting from "what we perceive now" about man (2), Gregory had implicitly put before himself and his refined audience questions which allow anachronistic formulations within the context of contemporary philosophical and theological anthropology:[12] in what kind of a relation do the idea of man as "image of God" and his biological sphere stand? Since the description of the sphere comprises only enumeration of man's "deficits," in what way, then, can the Godlikeness of humankind – in its biological circumstances – be expressed? No doubt that no matter how hypothetical these questions might be, they concern man's

ὁμοίωσις Θεῷ not only at the end, but at the beginning of his history" (*ibid.*, 64). – Gregory's brother Basil also differentiated εἰκῶν and ὁμοίωσις. On this subject see: M. A. Orphanos, *Creation and Salvation according St. Basil of Caesarea*, Athens 1975, 80–81. When he announces that he is going to speak on man, Basil adds that this subject will be related to "Ἐν τίνι μὲν οὖν ἔχει τὸ κατ' εἰκόνα Θεοῦ ὁ ἄνθρωπος, καὶ πῶς μεταλαμβάνει τοῦ καθ' ὁμοίωσιν"; see: *In. Hex. hom.*, IX, 6, PG 29, 208A. On the basis of this standpoint it is clear that he considers the characteristic of κατ' εἰκόνα as an absolute property of human nature: "ἔχει," i.e., man "possesses it", while "καθ' ὁμοίωσιν" is only partial, i.e. man only "participates" (μεταλαμβάνει) in it (*ibid.*, 81).

10. Gregor. Nyss., *De hominis opificio*, PG 44, 128A.
11. So U. Volp, *Die Würde des Menschen. Ein Beitrag zur Anthropologie in der Alten Kirche*, Supplements to Vigiliae Christianae, Leiden: Brill 2006, 174.
12. For this work inspiring were the insights of W. Pannenberg, *Anthropologie in theologischer Perspektive*, Göttingen: Vandenhoeck und Ruprecht 1983, 36 and further.

imperfection, a topic elaborated in one of the most remarkable fragments of *The Making of Man.* The weakness of human nature has become the "central anthropological topos" in the history of anthropological ideas in general,[13] and thus "anachronistic" speculations on Gregory of Nyssa's Christian anthropology become hermeneutically legitimate, and even obligatory.[14]

In his debate with Celsus, who denied God's providential plan by appealing to man's weakness – Origen claimed that man's corporeal imperfection itself is a part of God's plan by which man's flaws along with the "inability to survive" were to "encourage his mental activity and technological achievements that will make up for his physical deficiencies."[15] Still, Origen does not deliberate on man's physical weakness in relation to the idea of his Godlikeness, and that fact could easily have been one of the main reasons why Gregory of Nyssa restores this controversial anthropologic motif or "topos."

Mysterious human biological and physical incompleteness, helplessness and vulnerability has sparked off ancient anthropological debates on the origin of man and culture. Centuries before Gregory of Nyssa but also after him, this topic has been undergoing phases of hibernation and revival. Its contemporary actualization almost coincides with the birth of anthropology as a new philosophical discipline.[16] A problem which belongs to the domain of empirically oriented scientific bio-anthropology has become a point of meeting (or of clash) of theological, philosophical, naturalistic and cultural anthropology. Or, in Marquard's words, one anthropological term has "gained amphibious status between metaphysics and the empirical"[17] where such status is also professed by contemporary philosophical anthropology which takes man's problematic biological situation as the starting point. Philosophical anthropology has been formed along of the route of development of the "philosophy of life" (*Lebensphilosophie*) the slogan of which *Vivo, sum* was a reaction to the Cartesian formula *Cogito, sum.* Man, as a corporeal living creature, and no longer Cartesian "bodiless" *ens cogitans*, becomes a supreme philosophical subject among the doyens of philosophic anthropology – Max

13. So W. Schmidt-Biggemann, *Philosophia perennis. Historical Outlines of Western Spirituality in Ancient, Medieval and Early Modern Thought*, Dodrecht: Springer, 2004, chapter: "The Inner Man and the Aim of Creation: Gregory of Nyssa's 'Oratio de Creatione Hominis'," 143–150: 146–148.
14. "Self-justification" for nominating another "postmodern" theme in Gregory of Nyssa we find in S. Coakley, "Re-thinking Gregory of Nyssa: Introduction: Gender, Trinitarian Analogies, and the Pedagogy of The Song," *Modern Theology* 18, 4 (2002) 431–443.
15. Th. Cole, *Democritus and the Sources of Greek Anthropology*, 51[12].
16. Marquard emphasizes that the restoration of the motive of human biological deficiency occurred against the background of modern theodicy that includes "the relief of God from guilt" for man's shortcomings. See: O. Marquard, "Homo compensator. Zur anthropologischen Karriere eines metaphysischen Begriffs," in: O. Marquard, *Philosophie des Stattdessen. Studien*, Stuttgart: Philipp Reclam jun. GmbH &: Co. 2000, 11–29, especially 15–18.
17. O. Marquard, "Homo compensator. Zur anthropologischen Karriere eines metaphysischen Begriffs," 11. Helmuth Plessner, Arnold Gehlen, Michael Landmann and Hans Blumenberg share the same motive: man as a "creature of deficiencies" (*Mängelwesen*).

Scheler, and even more so for his followers Helmuth Plessner and Arnold Gehlen who using the "means of modern science" had modernised Herder's anthropological insights into human bio-morphological incompleteness and deficiency.[18] The term "deficient being" (*Mängelwesen*) becomes a synonym for man. The new philosophical discipline thus strived to distance and isolate itself from the naturalistic reductionism of bio-anthropology, rediscovering man's uniqueness, his ambiguous "dystopian" position inside a world that was no longer the Judeo-Christian universe, but the universe of modern science – foreign to man almost as much as the demonized world of Gnostics was.

Man's specific biological condition, singled out from the milieu of Christian tradition and considered outside it, loses its original sense. Thus human life – deprived of the origin in and orientation toward God's reality – is interpreted by contemporary philosophical "anthropocentric anthropologies" as "an escape from the flaws" into different compensations.[19] Fleeing from the "metaphysical escapism" which allegedly does not allow man to be a man, man falls victim to "anthropocentric escapism." For that reason, going back to the treatise *On the Making of Man*, in which we find contemplation on today's central anthropological topos on the "weakness" of human nature, could well be a corrective of the contemporary philosophical and anthropological theories. Although Arnold Gehlen takes Herder as a "forerunner" of the contemporary philosophical anthropology, whose deliberations on man's biological circumstances should be normative,[20] the pre-history of the problem goes a much longer way back.

We find first such reflections on man within Plato's elaboration of ancient mythological anthropogony by which man, because of forgetfulness of reckless Epimetheus, had remained the "unarmed nature" (ἄοπλος φύσις). The organic insufficiencies of the primordial, biologically unspecialized human φύσις, according to the ancient myth, were compensated for by Prometheus, who had gifted man with fire which is the eternal symbol of man's technical skills, of man as a *homo faber* and of culture as a whole. The abundant Prometheus' gifts were conditioned with the primordial "deficiencies" of the human nature.

18. A. Gehlen, *Čovjek: njegova priroda i njegov položaj u svijetu*, Sarajevo: Veselin Masleša 1990, 73 and further. [A. Gehlen, *Man: His Nature and Place in the World*, trans. C. McMillan, K. Pillemen, New York: Columbia University Press 1988] – See also Pannenberg's contrasting Herder and Gehlen on the basis of the Christian idea of man's image of God; W. Pannenberg, *Anthropologie in theologischer Perspektive*, Göttingen 1983, 40–71.

19. For the term "anthropocentric anthropology" and its context see in: Б. Лубардић, „Шта је то људско биће? – савремена православна антропологија: просополошки правац", *Боїословље*, 1–2 (2010) 145–202, 151ff. [= B. Lubardić, "What is a Human Being? – Modern Orthodox Anthropology"]

20. A. Gehlen, *op. cit.*, 86: "Herder has achieved what is required of every philosophical anthropology, even the one that pressuposes the theological concept of man: to percieve the intelligence of man within his biological situation [...]."

However, pre-historic philosophical contemplation of man's unusual corporeal constitution does not end there. Plato's idea of man as ἄοπλος was taken over and further developed by St. Gregory of Nyssa.

That said, our intention here is to affirm one of many testimonies of the continuity of Hellenic philosophy in Byzantium, while emphasizing, on the other side, its contribution to the later progress of a significant anthropological idea, in the historical development of which Gregory's treatise represents an important link, missing, however, in contemporary philosophical-anthropologic considerations.[21] An opinion that going back to the patristic inheritance can in no way be a regressive turn has already been voiced in the introduction of this paper. Gregory of Nyssa had linked the idea of man's biological "defenselessness" and "nakedness" as well as the idea of man's uprightness that is particularly highlighted by Basil the Great, with Biblical definition of man as "the image of God" (εἰκόνα τοῦ Θεοῦ). Biological "defenselessness" and "uprightness" as corporeal aspects of Godlikeness represent with the Cappadocians one of the important signs of the ultimate goal of human life: "to become similar to God as much as it is possible to human nature" (Ὁμοίωσις Θεῷ κατὰ τὸ δυνατὸν ἀνθρώπου φύσει)[22]. In other words, St. Gregory's anthropology is the "anthropology of deification" (P. Evdokimov).

Before we dive into St. Gregory's elaboration of man's corporeal organization, let us first take a look at a possible Platonist background of the problem.

2. Plato: Anthropologic Aporia

The historic trajectory of the idea of man as a being with "innate" biological flaws has its source in Plato's "remake" of the myth of Prometheus which appears in the dialogue *Protagoras*. We remember the beginning of the myth narrated by Plato's (or historic?)[23] Protagoras: "There was a time when there were gods, and mortal breed." After this "pre-temporal" time, there was a "particular time" for the creation of "mortal breeds" made of earth and fire by gods. At that time, the gods commanded brothers Prometheus

21. Pannenberg does not go beyond Herder in trying to establish the connection between the Christian idea of man's godlikeness and the ideas of contemporary philosophical anthropologies on man's lack of biological specialization, reduction of instincts, freedom of the environment, openess to the world... Therefore, as much succinct as it may be, the suggestion on the place of Gregory of Nyssa in the history of philosophy of man given by here quoted W. Schmidt-Biggemann, *Philosophia perennis. Historical Outlines of Western Spirituality in Ancient, Medieval and Early Modern Thought*, Dodrecht: Springer 2004 (chapter: "The Inner Man and the Aim of Creation: Gregory of Nyssa's 'Oratio de Creatione Hominis,'" 143–150) is yet very valuable.

22. Basil., *De Spiritu Sancto, PG* 32, 69B; see, e. g., Gregor. Nyss., PG 44, 273D. Cf. Plato, *Theaetetus*, 176a–b.

23. Guthrie believes that Plato reproduce Protagoras' understandings; W. K. C. Guthrie, *The Sophists*, 64.

and Epimetheus to adequately "equip" (κοσμῆσαί) the living creatures and "assign them abilities" (νεῖμαι δυνάμεις) essential for life (320 d5–6). Note that the νεῖμαι refers to *nemesis*, the idea of fateful predetermination.

Epimetheus, whose name represents the omen of human fate,[24] had asked and received Prometheus' consent to allocate biologically purposeful abilities. Being deeply involved in his task, however, the "foolish" Epimetheus had used up all the biological resources on "irrational creatures" (εἰς τὰ ἄλογα) forgetting about the "human kind" (τὸ ἀνθρώπων γένος; 321 c1–2).

The second part of the myth is much more well-known, as in it Prometheus himself comes onto the stage. Seeing the man "naked (γυμνόν), barefoot (ἀνυπόδητον), uncovered (ἄστρωτον) and unarmed" (ἄοπλον; 321c5–6), philanthropically inclined Prometheus takes care of human salvation. Famous for his sacrifice for human kind, Prometheus had stolen fire from Hephaestus and Athens, handing down to man the prerequisite of "technical knowledge" (ἔντεχνος σοφία; 321d–322a).

Due to the imbalance in the use of artificial knowledge which does not remove but encourage the antisocial and mutually destructive character of the primordial man, the third act of anthropogonic play presents Zeus who sends Hermes to share "political skills" among people: the virtues of "shame and righteousness" which make the basis of a *polis* (322c–d).

In this short reminiscence of hermeneutically pregnant myth, man's biological deficiency appeared as a matter of incidental recklessness, and not divine intention, as if man's biological deficiency was understood as negativity and mishap. Whatever the conclusion on these two implications of the story, for now we are to note that the genuine but unrecognized hero of the anthropogonic episode of the myth is actually not Prometheus but Epimetheus – the personification of man's biological incompleteness and lack of proper skills. If that is what makes a man a man, then "Epimetheus is not foolish," as Karel Thein observed, adding that "one kind should have remained in its genuine form and condition,"[25] this kind being no other but the human kind. This "original form and condition" of human corporeity indicates that he had "taken part in the divine" (θείας μετέσχε μοίρας) "through the kinship with gods" (διὰ τὴν τοῦ θεοῦ συγγένειαν) somehow before the gift of fire. Only one such being, unequipped for the life in its immediate environment and open to the world, could have received "from above" the gift of hubristic technical skill, from Prometheus' hands. Supposing that this unorthodox interpretation of the myth is correct, man's genuine "kinship" (συγγένεια) with the

24. Ἐπυμηθεύς – "the one who realizes too late," "the one who thinks with regret after the committed act," unlike his brother Προμηθεύς – "the one who is deliberate," "the one who looks to the future."

25. K. Thein, "Teleology and Myth in the Protagoras," in: A. Havlíček, F. Karfík, eds., *Plato's "Protagoras". Proceedings of the Third Symposium Platonicum Pragense*, Prague: OIKOYMENH 2003, 60–70, 64.

divine was reflected in his "theomorphic"[26] constitution which had been a prerequisite of "piety" – the original openness to the divine world. Should that be so, then *homo religiosus* "precedes" the *homo faber* who had not become "akin" to gods subsequently by means of technical skills, he had been akin to gods much before he had even mastered these skills. Technical skills enable humans, among else, to express their primordial piety through material sacraments, by building temples and altars, and by creating sculptural and pictorial images of their "anthropomorphic" divinities.

The craftiness of Plato's anthropological aporia, "the craftiness of the myth" of anthropogony, is in Epimetheusian oblivion of man's unarmed, naked, helpless and vulnerable corporeity. Human body, in its biological lack of equipment, has remained the most original and most universal indicator of man's "theomorphicity" which contains the variety of man's abilities. The body, man's ἄοπλος φύσις in general, is a sign of man's "godlikeness" or συγγένεια with the divine, an anthropological presumption of religiosity before any conventionalism of the Sophists.

3. St. Gregory of Nyssa: Godlikeness in the "Biological Sphere" of Man

It is a well-known fact that Gregory's treatise *De hominis opificio* is a continuation of Basil's *Hexaemeron*. St. Gregory would replace the missing part of *Hexaemeron* with his considerations representing a synthesis of Biblical hermeneutics and scientific discussion on human nature.[27] St. Gregory thus attempted to establish consistency between the Biblical account of man's creation by the image of God, and the actual state of human nature.

In his anthropological considerations Gregory departs from the anthropocentric character of creation: the world was created *because* of man and *for* man. Man's position in that world is envisaged by the metaphor of God's hospitality towards man who comes into the world as to a "feast" prepared in the honour of ceremonial enthronization of the new emperor of the world – the man.[28] Here, anthropogony coincides with the "ceremony" of enthronization of man as an emperor whose empire is the world itself. The whole arsenal of unusual "symposiastic" metaphors (home, hospitality, the dining table, feast) would represent a naive rhetoric and mere verbal iconography, should all this would not (un)intentionally remind of the famous story about Pythagoras who had compared man's life in the world to coming to a feast. To this feast, as observed by the doxographer, some are drawn by vainglory, others by trading benefits, while "only the best ones come as spectators"

26. Here we follow insightful observations of K.Thein, "Teleology and Myth in the Protagoras," 64–65.
27. See: F. M. Young, "Adam and Anthropos: A Study of Interaction Science and the Bible in Two Anthropological Treatises of the Forurth Century," 111.
28. Gregor. Nyss., *De hominis opificio*, PG 44, 133AB.

(βέλτιστοι ἔρχονθαι θεαταί) that is to say – with philosophical motives.[29] Be the similarity of the texts accidental or intentional, the story gets a whole new dimension with Gregory: man as such, by his "double" nature, sensually enjoys the fruits of the created world, while "theoretically" enjoying the Creator of that world. The two dimensions of religious pleasure, the sensory and the contemplative, are the two sides of man's, why put it any differently, Eucharistic manner of existence.

Gregory's lavishing metaphors for man's utterly primordial authoritative attitude towards the world could be conceptualised and condensed in terms of genuine "openness to the world" (*Weltoffenheit*), exactly as contemporary philosophical anthropology describes man.[30] Openness to the world comes from the fusion of man's original Godlikeness and his authoritative attitude in relation to the world. Unlike in Plato's cosmogony in which world as a whole is but a sensory "image" of a super-sensory divine "paradigm", in Mosaic cosmogony only man is created "by the image" of the Creator. Numerous answers to the question what makes man's constitution as "the icon of God" usually emphasized man's intellectual powers as prerogatives of Godlikeness or pointed to one element of man as to their primary setting.[31] However, in Biblical quotes (Gen 1, 26) Gregory of Nyssa searches and finds a firm foothold for his claims that the primal prerogative of Godlikeness is manifested through man's authority over the world, whilst he sees the empirical confirmation of authoritative designation in man's "corporeal appearance"[32]. As a likeness of God's creative authority over the creation, man's dominion does not display itself as an outer imperial glamour or insignias of power, but is manifested in a manner worth of the dignity of ethic virtue, righteousness and blessedness of immortality.[33] With its looks and posture, body manifests the soul which is "self-governed" (αὐτεξούσιον) and "swayed autocratically by its own will" (θελήμασιν αὐτοκρατορικῶς), "detached" (κεχωρισμένον) from material world and therefore "unsubordinated" (ἀδέσποτον).[34] In St. Gregory's descriptive-normative explanation of the secret of success of the living portrait of deiform human nature – the portrait made by the hand of God, of course – we easily notice the anthropological basis of man's freedom

29. Diogen Laertije, *Životi i mišljenja istaknutih filozofa*, preveo A. Vilhar, Beograd: BIGZ 1979, VIII, 8. [See the edition of M. Marcovich, Diogenes Laertius, *Vitae philosophorum*]
30. Starting from its doyen M. Scheler, *Položaj čovjeka u kosmosu*, Sarajevo: Veselin Masleša 1987 [M. Scheler, *Man's Place in Nature*, trans. H. Meyerhof, New York, Fefrar, Straus, and Giroux 1961.] – See: W. Pannenberg, *Anthropologie in theologischer Perspektive*, 73: "Handelt es sich nun bei der Zusammengehörigkeit von Gottebenbildlichkeit und Berufung zur Weltherrschaft in Vertretung Gottes selber um einen Sachzusammenhang, der auch im Phänomen der sog. Weltoffenheit des Menschen wiederzuerkennen ist?." Pannenberg's answer is a positive one.
31. See: В. Лоски, *Оглед о мистичком богословљу Источне цркве*, Света Гора Атонска: Манастир Хиландар 2003, 90–93.
32. Gregor. Nyss., *De hominis opificio*, PG 44, 136B.
33. Gregor. Nyss., *De hominis opificio*, PG 44, 136CD.
34. Gregor. Nyss., *De hominis opificio*, PG 44, 136BC.

and ethics as a possibility and reality of his true mastering of the created and ephemeral world. Beside ethical virtues, this portrait of human nature contains also "the mind and the word" as traits of intellectual virtues which faithfully preserve man's Godlikeness, since "Divinity is mind and word." Accordingly, other than ethics, man masters the world both cognitively and linguistically, since he inquires and examines beings, getting ideas about them. Finally, St. Gregory adds love which creates a unity between ethical and intellectual virtues in man,[35] thus ascertaining the unity of human nature as a harmonious and beautiful entirety which becomes "the likeness of the Divine imperial authority."

If we looked at St. Gregory's analysis of man's ethical-cognitive relation to the world from a contemporary perspective, then his non-technically understood mastering of the world could become rather confusing. It should particularly be kept in mind that, according to Gregory, man's power over the world is conditioned by an absence of passion and by catharsis as preconditions of the detachment from matter, while in modern technical civilization mastering the nature implies a will for power which is then materialised by technology. St. Gregory could answer by pointing out that exactly this perverted urge to conquer and exploit the nature is telling of a deformed trait of man's Godlikeness.[36] This particular way of mastering the nature nails the man to the material world and distorts the genuine Godlike character of such mastery. Technology is not a manner in which to actualize man's potentials to become similar to God. We have already seen that according to the "orthodox" interpretations of the Protagoras' myth on the creation of man and culture, only Prometheus' "demiurgic skill" enables the man to be "akin" to the divine reality, and that before this gift man belonged to the animal world. Anthropological theories of progress claim exactly the same, at times explicitly at that. Plato, according to the suggested alternative interpretation of Protagoras' myth on the origins of man and the *Kulturgeschichte*, had pointed to the aporia (the hidden "craftiness of the myth") that, even before technical inventions, man, as an authentic "unarmed nature", could realize his Godlikeness.

35. Gregor. Nyss., *De hominis opificio*, PG 44, 137BC.

36. It is a kind of irony of our postmetaphysical and postanthropological age that man is still definable only in terms of image. Yet Herman Broch noticed that "man can deny God's existence, but he will never deny that he is his own true image"; H. Broh, *Misli o politici*, 187. – A similar observation is put forward by K. P. Liessmann, "Das, was nicht sein soll," in: D. Ganten, V. Gerhardt, J. Nida-Rümelin, hrsg., *Was ist der Mensch?*, Berlin: Walter de Gruyter 2008, 166–169: 166–167: "Die Frage nach dem Menschen ist eine Frage nach dem Bild, das der Mensch von sich schäfft und nach dem er sich schaffen möchte. Der biblische Satz: 'Und Gott schuf den Menschen ihm zum Bilde, zum Bilde Gottes schuf er ihn' behält seine Gültigkeit auch und gerade nach der Abdankung des Schöpfergottes: Das Bild, die Imagination bleibt das entscheidende Moment in der Selbstschaffung des Menschen. Nicht: Wer sind wir? ist die Frage, sondern: Wie sehen wir uns?"

It is quite possible that somewhere inside this aporia one should look for St. Gregory's motivation to re-introduce the traditional anthropological question relating to the flaws or imperfections of man's nature. The relation between the creation of man by God's image, embodies in the commandment "[...] and let them have dominion over the fish of the sea, and over the fowl of the air, and over the cattle, and over all the earth [...]" (Gen 1, 26), and current state of human nature, its dramatic biological situation, is what creates contradiction. In comparison with other forms of life on earth, man's biological incapacity is usually explained by a simple allusion to the difference between prelapsarian and postlapsarian conditions of human nature which, through Fall and Sin, found itself in a world to which it was not accustomed. The mind and the language, which are linked to man's inventiveness, are usually derived from man's biological deficiency. Biological deficiency is "compensated" by the technology without which man could not survive in a world that is no longer Paradise. It seems that St. Gregory of Nyssa was not satisfied with the variety of similar answers coming from philosophical and Christian traditions.

St. Gregory had announced the removal of contradiction between the man as created at the beginning of time and the man we now look at, in relation to what he may again become in his attempts to achieve likeness to God. Thus the question should be reiterated: Can man's biological situation be observed independently from the Biblical narrative of the Fall? If yes, what is the relation between this biological situation and man's Godlikeness? Finally, is not man's bio-morphological characteristic itself already a manifestation of his Godlikeness?

Textual confirmation of the affirmative answer to these questions is found in the seventh and the eighth chapters of the treatise *On the Making of Man*. There, corporeal dimension of human nature is considered. Departing from what we now see on man, the youngest Cappadocian shoots two vectors of questions in the direction of the Biblical text which offers answers contrary to both the traditional philosophical-theological solutions and the empirical science on man. "Why need for the upright shape" of the human body? Why is the body deprived of innate forces that preserve its life?, St. Gregory asks. We have already seen in the fourth chapter that the bodily appearance is singled out as a bearer of man's special status, of his imperial dignity – it is the primal and the most remarkable aspect of man as the image of God.

Like Plato before him or even more like philosophical anthropologists of the 20th century after him, St. Gregory points to the man's biological situation and underlines that man is "without natural covers," "naked" (γυμνός), "unarmed" (ἄοπλος) and that he lacks all that which is necessary to keep him alive.[37] Such "Epimethean" man reveals his fundamental biological situation from which one is to understand man's likeness to God through the

37. Gregor. Nyss., *De hominis opificio*, PG 44, 140D.

aspect of his "mastery over the whole world." That St. Gregory initially speaks of the "uprightness of the form" (τοῦ σχήματος ὄρθιον) of human body points to the "theoretical" stance, stemming from man's original openness to the world, which precedes the biologically pragmatic stance realized through technical intelligence. At the beginning of chapter eight, St. Gregory clarifies that the upright position actually denotes man's striving "towards heaven," suggesting that the very etymology of "man" (ἄνθρωπος) comes from "the one who looks upwards" (ἄνω βλέπει).[38] The whole man's bodily figure, his unique corporeal-spiritual composition, discloses his intellectual and rational nature. Fascination with God and the created world, or the relation towards Godlike reality, has primacy in comparison to pragmatic relations to the world coming from the self-relating urge for self-preservation. The absence of organs and instincts adequate for self-preservation determines man's peculiar bio-morphologic situation which draws St. Gregory's attention.

One of the most influential exponents of German school of philosophical anthropology, Michael Landmann has coined the expression "*anthropina*" denoting the fundamental, almost "timeless" or, in historic dimensions, permanently present, ontological structures of human existence. A synoptic overview of different epochs in human history – during which the emphasis shifted from one to another *anthropinon* (creativity, wit, work, culture...) – uncovers the whole "system of *anthropina*" to which man owes what he is in comparison to other beings.[39] This constantly open, dynamic, system of mutually implicative anthropological constancies rests on peculiarities and exclusivity of life circumstances of man as a biologically inadaptable and unspecialized being, deprived of instincts and organs necessary for self-preservation. From a biological viewpoint, man is a being incapable of living and is therefore in need to master the conditions of his existence creating himself these conditions mysteriously denied to him. Landmann himself hesitates to define man's biological incompleteness as a fundamental *anthropinon*, both for its negativity and its origins in comparing man and animal. Man's bio-morphological features appear in comparative biology as a deficiency which stimulates biologically necessary surrogates of compensation; however, if a human being is looked at as a being *per se* those "deficiencies" become advantages of a creative being.[40] Contemporary philosophical anthropologies build their anthropological narratives departing from man's

38. See: Gregor. Nyss., *De hominis opificio*, PG 44, 144B. Also: Basil., *Hom. Attende tibi ipsi*, PG 31, 216C and *In. Hex. hom.*, PG 29, 192A. – The ultimate source of the theory of man's upright posture is Plato, *Timaeus* 90a–b, 91e. An interesting discussion on the relationship between the upright posture and the ability of thinking see in P. Gregorić, "Plato's and Aristotle's Explanation of Human Posture," *Rhizai* 2 (2005) 183–196.
39. See: M. Landmann, "The System of Anthropina," in: D. M. Weiss, ed., *Interpreting Man*, Aurora, Colorado: The Davis Group Publishers 2002, 123–142.
40. M. Landmann, "The System of Anthropina," 125.

bio-morphological situation in which man is looked at as a "poor or rich being."[41] Whichever alternative philosophical anthropology chooses, "man himself becomes an anthropomorphism in it" – to use Schnädelbach's wording.[42] Because of his biological deficiency, man's not belonging to the world lost its theological dimension due to which the self-preservation interweaves with salvation through the concept of "compensation" (Odo Marquard).

For Christian anthropology, the most fundamental of all ἀνθρωπίνα – the expression found in St. Gregory of Nyssa[43] – is, doubtlessly, that only man is created "by the image and likeness of God." This most meticulous *anthropinon* is with Gregory in an emphasized connection to man's biological situation as ἄοπλος, and thus this feature bears positive connotations. Fragility and weakness of man's corporeal constitution is not the consequence of the Fall, but the indicator of Godlikeness itself. "The insufficiency of man's nature" he calls "illusion" (τὸ δοκοῦν) because it is precisely where man's rule over the world is based. St. Gregory notices that if man's body was "naturally armed" then man would be "theriomorphic", that is – "beast-like (θηριώδης) and truculent".[44] Bio-morphological specialization would neither make man the master of the natural world, nor make him godlike. Instead, Gregory says that precisely because of his biological insufficiencies and his physical vulnerability has man been made the master of all other beings. According to Gregory's theory of human biological deficiency, man is "unarmed" because he is the "image of God" and that initial phase encloses not only "anthropological presumptions of technology" but presumptions of "attaining the likeness of God" as well. Thus, there can be no contradiction between the prelapsarian and the postlapsarian man; in both cases man is godlike and one of the omens of his godlikeness lies exactly in his biological unspecialization.

St. Gregory's widening of the classic Biblical *theologoumenon* about man's Godlikeness to man's biological situation makes him a real Christian thinker who considers the situation in terms or functions of Godlikeness, independently of the balance of losses that man had suffered through the Fall. At the same time, the inclination toward deification of human nature is surely understood as more principal than his urge for self-preservation. The two inclinations are confronted in man due to his "intermundane" position as the

41. H. Blummenberg, "Anthropologische Annäherung an die Aktualität der Rhetorik," in: H. Blumenberg, *Ästhetische und metaphorologische Schriften*, Suhrkamp 2001, 406–434, 406. According to Blumenberg, the fact that man is not biologically fixed for the environment (*Umwelt*) can be understood negatively, as a consequence of the deficiency (*Mangel*) of the means for self-preservation, or again can be understood positively, as a wealth of openness (*Offenheit*) for the fullness of the world towards which man does not show only an interest of a vital kind.
42. H. Schnädelbach, "The Face in the Sand: Foucault and the Anthropological Slumber," in: A. Honneth, et al., eds., *Philosophical Interventions in the Unfinished Project of Enlightenment*, Cambridge, MA: MIT Press 1992, 314.
43. Gregor. Nyss., *De hom. Opif.*, PG 44, 181B.
44. Gregor. Nyss., *De hom. Opif.*, PG 44, 141B.

"middle between two extremes" (τὸ ἀκρότατων [...] μέσον)[45] – the divine incorporeal nature and animal-irrational life. The position between the two realities makes human existence both magnificent and risky. Orientation toward the divine reality through the ideal of attaining the likeness to God liberates man, while the lack of that orientation through "attaining the likeness to God to the world" leads him to humiliation and subordination. Anthropological self-awareness is reflected in that antinomy of man's position, in his having a home in the world, and his not having it.

Finally, in the background of each anthropology there is a cosmology. Gregory's philosophical-theological anthropology is the continuation of the Cappadocian "teleological" cosmology that culminates in the creation of man. The creation of man is the *telos* of the creation of world, and God the Creator becomes man's *telos*. *Fabula docet* of the most systematic work of the Cappadocian anthropology is that the true progress of man, in the direction of realizing his utmost abilities and his freedom, is the one that, at least for a step, brings him closer to the "likeness to God" in both ethical and existential-ontological senses. One of the central ideas of Gregory's anthropology is that man's "unarmedness and nakedness" is understood positively as a gift from God and as an aspect of his godlikeness itself, and not negatively as a deprivation and insufficiency from which man flees into compensating. The main anthropological question in the context of hexaemeral anthropology should not be "what is man" or "how man, with all his biomorphological insufficiencies, has been or is able to survive" but "how can man regain his Godlikeness?" One part of the answer is contained in man's biological sphere itself, where the absence of specialization and the lack of instincts for self-preservation, fragility and vulnerability, biological inadaptability, detachment from the environment and openness to the world, are all testimonies to man's godlikeness and dignity, as well as to the freedom of his creative self-determination.

45. Gregor. Nyss., *De hom. Opif.*, PG 44, 181B.

St. Gregory the Theologian on Divine Energeia in Trinitarian Generation

Torstein Theodor Tollefsen

In this paper I discuss *energeia* in St. Gregory the Theologian's anti-Anomoean doctrine of divine generation. It is important to note that I am concerned with a *concept*, not with a *term*. Gregory does not seem to make extensive use of the word *energeia*, but he obviously moves into a restrictive application of conceptual schemes to highlight divine generation. The application is restrictive since it is part of a strategy that does not claim to develop any kind of scientific doctrine of the Trinity. We return to the way the application is restricted below. I translate the term *energeia* provisionally as *activity*. In Plotinus we find, behind the metaphors of emanation, a doctrine we may call the doctrine of double activity.[1] This doctrine is designed to highlight how the hypostases of the Neoplatonic system are eternally generated. There is an "activity of the essence," i.e. an internal activity, and an "activity out of the essence," i.e. an external activity. I adopt the terms internal and external activity in order to highlight other systems of thought as well, for instance the Church Fathers. The topic of this article is, then, St. Gregory Nazianzus' doctrine of internal divine activity, which in this case means the activity that structures the divinity as a Triad. As a matter of fact, I'll show that Gregory does not develop any detailed doctrine in his so-called *Theological Orations*, which are the primary focus of my attention. In this regard he acts rather unlike St. Gregory of Nyssa, as we shall see below. Gregory Nazianzus has, however, his reasons, and it seems to me that methodologically he follows his convictions in a quite consequent manner. I shall first make some preliminary remarks on the historical context for the application of a concept of divine activity.

Gregory's five *Theological Orations* were preached in Constantinople, probably during the summer or the autumn of 380.[2] They were preached at a crucial moment of the Trinitarian controversy.[3] In February that year em-

1. For this doctrine in Plotinus, see Rist (1967), chapter 6; Emilsson (2007), chapter 1; Bradshaw (2007), chapter 4; Tollefsen (2008), 195–197.
2. Norris (1991), 9.
3. I prefer the term Trinitarian controversy instead of Arian controversy. The theology of Arius became the catalyst of several theological positions that in different respects differed from the Nicene conception as received by for instance St Athanasius and the Cappadocians.

peror Theodosius had declared in an edict that Nicene orthodoxy would be the official teaching of the Empire, and in November he visited the capital and forced the Arian bishop either to accept the Nicene faith or to go into exile. He chose exile, and the scene was cleared for the Ecumenical Council of 381.

The *Theological Orations* were preached against a renewed kind of Arianism that may be called Anomoeanism, since a distinctive feature of its teaching was that God the Son is *unlike* (ἀνόμοιος) God the Father.[4] In 361 Eunomius, then bishop of Cyzikus, in the heat of controversy published an *Apologia*, the arguments of which were answered by St. Basil in his *Contra Eunomium* (c. 365). Eunomius answered Basil in his *Apologia apologiae* (about 379), and St. Gregory of Nyssa attacked Eunomius in return in his own *Contra Eunomium*. The first and second parts were finished in 380, while the third part was written between 381 and 383.[5] St. Gregory Nazianzen's five *Theological Orations* from 380 are his primary contribution to the fight against the Anomoean theology of Eunomius and the "Eunomians."

What, then, are the distinctive features of Eunomius' Trinitarian doctrine? According to the fragments of Eunomius' *Apologia apologiae*, preserved in Gregory of Nyssa's *Contra Eunomium*, there is a hierarchy of three essences.[6] The first essence is the Unbegotten and perfect God, next comes the essence that is made by the first, and third follows the essence that is made by the second. The first is by its *activity* the cause of the second essence; the second is by its activity the cause of the third. Each essence is simple (ἁπλῆς). The activities that follow each being are circumscribed (συμπεριγραφομένων) by their works, as are the works commensurate with (παραμετρουμένων) the activities. The first, second, and third essences are what traditional terminology calls the Father, the Son, and the Holy Spirit. The Son, obviously, is a created being, in fact something as strange as a created God. The Holy Spirit, which the Son makes on behalf of the Father, cannot be called divine at all. Eunomius says in his *Liber apologeticus* that the unbegotten Godhead does not share His being with anything else.[7]

Eunomius, unlike Plotinus, does not distinguish between internal and external activities of God. He only talks of divine activities out of the essence of the first being. Since what is made by them have beginning and end, the activities themselves have beginning and end.[8] The activity that made the Son is God's will (βούλησις). The Son, therefore, results from the will of the

4. Kopecek (1979) has published a comprehensive study of "Neo-Arianism" in two volumes. For a more recent discussion of the controversy, cf. Behr (2004). Cf. Bradshaw (2007), Chapter 7, for a philosophical evaluation of the controversy.
5. Mateo-Seco and Maspero (2010), 307.
6. *CE*, GNO 1, 72.
7. *Liber apologeticus*, Vaggione (1987), 62/63.
8. *Liber apologeticus*, Vaggione (1987), 64/65.

Unbegotten. At this point Eunomius seems to be the victim of some inconsistency. He speaks of a divine foreknowledge prior to the existence of the first-born, i.e. the Son.[9] If there is a "before" the existence of the Son, and if the activity that made the Son has a beginning, and the Son himself has a beginning, does not this mean that *time* intrudes into the eternal being of God? Eunomius, of course, sees this problem, and claims that the Son was made before all things, and that He was "genuinely begotten before the ages" (ἀληθῶς γενηθέντα πρὸ αἰώνων).[10] Even so, this does not dissolve the problem, since Eunomius still has to explain the exact meaning of the beginning of the divine activity of making of the Son. We shall not dwell further on this problem, but rather turn to the making of the Son as such.

Gregory of Nyssa makes us aware of a rather strange aspect of the Eunomian doctrine of the divine activities. In his *Contra Eunomium* he says Eunomius speaks of the activities as following alongside (the verb is παρέπομαι) or following or coming after (the verb is ἕπομαι) the essence.[11] Here we definitely may speak of a *real distinction* between God's essence and activity, even if this in the present context means something quite different than what the same term means in Meyendorff's interpretation of St. Gregory Palamas.[12] The reason for this radical distinction is, of course, that Eunomius wants to avoid bringing the created being of the Son into the eternal sphere of the divinity as such. Gregory of Nyssa, on the contrary, obviously thinks the divine activity is something more closely attached to the being of God. We return to this in connection with St. Gregory Nazianzus' Trinitarian doctrine.

There is one more, rather essential thing that should be noted before we turn to the discussion of divine activity in Gregory's anti-Anomoean theology. Eunomius taught a doctrine of the knowability of the divine nature. There is a well known Eunomian fragment preserved in Socrates Scholasticus claiming that God knows no more of His essence than we do.[13] There is no doubt that Eunomius believed we have access to God's being in such a way that a rather distinctive kind of theology would be possible. In my opinion, St. John Chrysostom catches the note precisely in his homilies *On the Incomprehensible Nature of God*, the first five of which were delivered from about 386–387 in Antioch. Chrysostom asks, apropos of the Anomoeans, what the angels do in heaven: do they ask one another questions about the divine essence?[14] Surely not! They glorify God. They adore Him and sing mystical

9. *Liber apologeticus*, Vaggione (1987), 64/65.
10. *Liber apologeticus*, Vaggione (1987), 48/49; *Expositio fidei*, Vaggione (1987), 152/153.
11. *CE*, GNO 1, 72.
12. Cf. Meyendorff (1974), 216.
13. *Historia ecclesiastica* 4. 7. Vaggione (1987), 167–70, believes it is genuine, and I think it fits well into the epistemology of Eunomius' *Liber apologeticus*. The fragment, it could be claimed, also fits well into the kind of philosophical mentality that characterizes Aetius' *Syntagmation*, cf. the analysis by Kopecek (1979), chapter 4.
14. *De incomprehensibili Dei natura homiliae*, Homily 1, 308–12, 321 in the edition in the Sources chrétiennes 28, Jean Chrysostome, *Sur l'incompréhensibilité de Dieu*, Paris 1951.

hymns with much religious awe. They stand before the mystery in holy fear. It seems to me that there is a major difference between the God of St. Athanasius, of the Cappadocian fathers, and of St. John Chrysostom on the one hand, and the God of Aetius and Eunomius on the other. According to the Anomoeans, in addition to being an adorable being, God is a subject of accurate theological discourse, while in contrast to this, the God of the orthodox is a terrifying, transcendent mystery that condescends in love to human beings. This God is beyond human grasp and the proper way to adhere to Him is in hymns and praise. This God is beyond discursive reasoning and accurate predication. If there shall be predication, and surely there must be, it will be of another kind, in the consciousness that what we talk of should be addressed respectfully and in proper words. Of course, one does not deny that theology needs accuracy. Even so, this is another kind of accuracy than the Anomoean one. This, I think, is the topic of Gregory Nazianzus' *First Theological Oration*.

Gregory attacks the Eunomians who "pride themselves on their eloquence," who conducts a discourse that is "excessive and superfluous," and who apply dialectical techniques that make the *mystery* into something of little moment.[15] According to Vaggione, almost every Nicene author who attacked Aetius and Eunomius accused them of applying extra-biblical authorities to the interpretation of Scripture, "and by striving for *akribeia* they subjected the Word of God to the analysis of the schools."[16] Eunomius, it was said, was nothing other than a "logic chopper," not a Christian.[17] Gregory obviously experiences the Eunomian eagerness in theological argument as presumptuous. It is a violation of prudence to conduct discourse on divine topics in the way the Anomoeans do. In his famous words Gregory says not everyone should philosophize about God, nor should one talk of such matters to everyone, nor to all kinds of audiences, nor on all occasions, nor on all points. Rather, one should choose the times and the persons carefully and observe the proper limits.[18] His concern is the preservation of the mystery, and it is not safe, he says, for the unclean to touch the pure.[19] One should only philosophize on subjects within our reach and to the degree that the mental power of the audience may extend.[20]

After this introductory homily, Gregory next turns to theological questions (*Homily* 28). He describes the theologian, what his character should be like and how he should proceed. Then he himself acts like a theologian – or does he? He rather performs a rhetorical scene when he plays the role of Moses in Exodus (24, 1–2): "Now He said to Moses, 'Come up to the Lord, you and Aaron, Nadab and Abihu, and seventy of the elders of Israel, and worship

15. *Oratio* 27, 1.
16. Vaggione (2000), 91.
17. Vaggione (2000), 93.
18. *Oratio* 27, 3.
19. *Oratio* 27, 3.
20. *Oratio* 27, 4.

from afar. And Moses alone shall come near to the Lord, but they shall not come near; nor shall the people go with him.'" Here one cannot play the part of a clever dialectician who claims knowledge of God as God is in Himself, rather one must preserve the defined limits in sight of the fearful majesty (Exodus 24, 17–18): "The sight of the Lord was like a consuming fire on the top of the mountain in the eyes of the children of Israel. So Moses went into the midst of the cloud and went into the mountain." I suppose what Gregory wants to say is something like "is there a theologian greater than Moses, and what did he see?" Gregory's explicit answer is:[21] "And when I looked up, I scarce saw the back parts of God." This culmination of the story is, of course, based on the sequence where Moses asks to see God's Glory (Exodus 33,18–20): "And he said, 'Please, show me your glory.' Then He said, 'I will make all my goodness pass before you, and I will proclaim the name of the Lord before you. I will be gracious to whom I will be gracious, and I will have compassion to whom I will have compassion.' But He said, 'You cannot see my face; for no man shall see me and live.'" Moses stands in the cleft of the rock and in a dramatic theophany sees God's back (Exodus 33, 23).

What did the greatest of theologians see when God revealed Himself? Gregory, playing the part of Moses, says:[22] "And when I looked a little closer, I saw, not the first and unmingled Nature, known to itself – to the Trinity, I mean; not that which abides within the first veil, and is hidden by the cherubim; but only that Nature, which at last reaches even to us." Gregory interprets this "Nature which reaches even to us" as the divine Majesty or, in accordance with David (cf. Psalm 8, 1), the Glory, "which is manifested among creatures, which It has produced and governs." This is what God has left behind Him, as tokens of Himself, comparable to reflections of the sun in water. We cannot look directly at the sun itself, since its unmixed light is too strong for our power of perception. Gregory is clearly making the familiar Cappadocian and anti-Anomoean point that the being of God in Himself is beyond our reach, while even so God is manifest in certain ways for us. He refers to the famous words of Plato's *Timaeus*, where it is said that it is *difficult* to discover God, but *impossible* to declare Him in words, and corrects Plato saying it is impossible to express Him, and even more impossible to conceive of Him.[23] Even a heavenly mind, higher in nature and nearer to God than we, is yet more distant from God and from the complete comprehension of His nature, than it is above our natural composition.[24]

It is quite obvious that the distinction made by Gregory above is similar and probably identical with the distinction made by St. Basil the Great and St. Gregory of Nyssa in a different and more philosophical language, viz. between God's essence (οὐσία) and His activities (ἐνέργειαι). In his *Letter* 234,

21. *Oratio* 28, 2.
22. *Oratio* 28, 3.
23. *Timaeus* 28c and Gregory, *Oratio* 28, 4.
24. *Oratio* 28, 3.

Basil finds it ridiculous to claim knowledge of the divine essence, and says that even if we don't have access to the essence, we do not admit ignorance of God. Our thoughts of God are gathered from attributes which we know, such as greatness, power, wisdom, goodness, providence, and justness. Basil also mentions philanthropy and creative power. We know such attributes because of God's activities:[25] "His activities come down to us, but His essence remains unapproachable (αἱ μὲν γὰρ ἐνέργειαι αὐτοῦ πρὸς ἡμᾶς καταβαίνουσιν, ἡ δὲ οὐσία αὐτοῦ μένει ἀπρόσιτος)." Gregory of Nyssa applies the same distinction in a lot of places, and he even turns the terminology and the distinction into an important piece of ontology that he applies to internal and external divine actions and processes. We return to this below.

For our purpose there is no reason to enter into Gregory Nazianzen's subtle rhetoric in *Oration* 28.[26] His main thesis is that our earthly mode of existence makes it an impossibility to claim knowledge of the divine essence, and the exercise of reason in theological matters, even if allowed, is beset by difficulties if the topic is God. It is at the beginning of next *Oration* (29) that what concerns us here turns up.

Even if we cannot attain scientific knowledge of God, the Anomoean controversy of course challenged the defenders of Orthodoxy to talk about divine generation. Gregory starts from the notion of divine *monarchia* and speaks of equality of nature, harmony of mind, identity of motion, and convergence towards unity of that which springs from it (i.e. from unity).[27] Though there is numerical distinction, there is no division of the essence. Then follows a potent dictum: διὰ τοῦτο μὸνας ἀπ' ἀρχῆς, εἰς δυάδα κινηθεῖσα, μέχρι τριάδος ἔστη. "Therefore the monad, having from the beginning arrived by motion at the dyad, found its rest in triad." Gregory adds: "And this is for us the Father, the Son, and the Holy Spirit." The question is how these words shall be interpreted. There is definitely talk of movement in the divine, i.e. of a kind of internal divine activity that constitutes the triad which, obviously is the Trinity. The Father is the Begetter and the Emitter of the hypostases of the Son and the Spirit without, Gregory says, passion, in a non-temporal and incorporeal way. He declines to highlight this like one of the Greek philosophers did, and speak of an "overflow of goodness" as if it were "a bowl overflowing."[28] However, he says explicitly, indicating that the Greek philosopher had taught some kind of necessary generation, that the generation is not to be thought of as involuntary. We shall return to the topic of will below.

This sentence is commented on by St. Maximus the Confessor.[29] He says Gregory does not offer a causal explanation (αἰτιλογία) of the cause of

25. In Saint Basil, *The Letters*, by R. J. Deferrari, Loeb Classical Libraray, London 1972.
26. For a convincing analysis, see Narkevics (2006), 83–112.
27. *Oration* 29, 2.
28. Who said this? Cf. Norris (1991), 134–135.
29. *Ambigua ad Thomam*, CCSG 48, 6–9.

beings, itself beyond being (τῆς ὑπερουσίου τῶν ὄντων αἰτίας).[30] In other words, Gregory does not talk of the internal causal activity of the Godhead as such. Rather, what is offered is an ἀπόδειξις of the "reverent glory that surrounds it. The term ἀπόδειξις may be taken in the strict sense of a *proof* or in the less strict sense as a *showing forth*. It should probably be understood in the less strict sense. Maximus says further:[31] "If hearing of movement, you wonder how the Godhead that is beyond infinity is moved, understand that what happens is happening to us and not to the Godhead."

Is this a sound interpretation of Gregory? There are two things to take notice of here, first that the sentence in Gregory is a *showing forth* of the "reverent glory that surrounds it," and secondly, that this is not a causal explanation, but rather concerns something that happens to us and not to God. First, we should take Gregory's constant insistence on the unknowability of the divine nature seriously, and it then becomes natural to refer back to what he said at the beginning of *Oratio* 28 (28, 3). Gregory speaks of going up into the mountain with Moses, but the *theophany* one experiences there, gives no access to the first Nature, that is to the Trinity. What one experiences is "that Nature, which at last reaches even to us," what Gregory himself interprets as the divine Majesty or Glory. Secondly, even though there has to be presupposed kinds of internal activity in the Godhead, activities of generation and procession, these are data we believe in, but cannot develop into a set of philosophical explanations. When Maximus says this is something happening to us, it could be understood to indicate something like "this is the way we may think of it in our own minds, this is how we figure it out."[32] If we take into consideration something said by St. Gregory of Nyssa in his *Ad Ablabium* this may be made even clearer:

> We, on the other hand, following the councils of Scripture, have learnt that that nature is unnameable and unspeakable, and we say that every term either invented by the custom of men, or handed down to us by the Scriptures, is indeed explanatory of conceptions of the Divine Nature, but does not include the signification of that nature itself.[33]

Gregory of Nyssa's idea is quite radical: theological terms do not disclose the divine nature in itself, but rather, if I may put it that way, they disclose the "image" we form of God in our minds. The question that turns up now is, of course, where we find the criteria for this "image" or such a conception or set of propositions.

30. *Ambigua ad Thomam*, CCSG 48, 7.
31. Ibid.
32. This is the way Maximus is understood by Louth as well, in a comment on *Ambiguum* 1 in Louth (1996), 169.
33. *Ad Ablabium*, GNO 3, 1: 42–43.

Gregory of Nyssa points definitely to the tradition of the Church.[34] The criteria by which theological conceptions should be measured, are to be taken from the Fathers. This notion, of course, needs a lot more elaboration in order to be transparent, but we shall turn to Gregory Nazianzus and ask if he may enlighten us with his understanding of such criteria. This question, of course, brings with it the whole topic of theological method, which cannot be discussed extensively here.[35] In *Oratio* 27 Gregory has displayed what he considers the proper way to speak of God, and the proper marks of the theologian. All of it directed against talkative people fond of the dialectical method (27, 8). In *Oratio* 28 he tries to show the limitations of dialectical procedures, and in *Oratio* 29 he tries to reduce the privileged status of the Anomoean concept of the "unbegotten" to absurdity. On what *ground*, then, is the proper theologian to philosophize on God, if we are not to apply dialectical methods?

Aetius claims, in the introduction to his *Syntagmation* that what he says is in accordance with the Scriptures, but even so, the way he reasons is not directly from a Scriptural basis, rather the analysis he makes of certain concepts seems to become for him the key to the reading of Scripture itself.[36] If we turn to Eunomius' *Liber apologeticus*, we find an explicit statement about theological method that coincides with what was just said of Aetius:

> There are two roads marked out to us for the discovery of what we seek – one is that by which we examine the actual essences and with clear and unadulterated reasoning about them make a judgement on each; the other is an enquiry by means of the actions (διὰ τῶν ἐνεργείων), whereby we distinguish the essence on the basis of its products and completed works – and neither of the ways mentioned is able to bring out any apparent similarity of essence.[37]

It is in a special sense the first road that invites the dialectical method as we see it demonstrated in Aetius' *Syntagmation*. The second road, of course, may be conducted in a more "Scriptural" way, since it should probably start from the biblical witness to divine activities. The principle of philosophizing from activities to essence, seems to have been adopted as a common Cappadocian principle as well, even if applied in slightly different ways by the three theologians, and even if the methodological context of the application differs from the Anomoean one.

What, then, of Gregory's method? On what basis are we to philosophize on God? He refers to the parable of the sower who went out to sow (Matt 13, 3–9). Gregory thinks he has prepared the ground in *Oratio* 27, and then he speaks of being impressed and impressing it with Holy Scripture.[38] Further,

34. *Ad Ablabium*, GNO 3, 1: 39.
35. Once more I recommend the reader to consult Narkevics (2006).
36. Cf. Kopecek (1979), chapter 4.
37. *Liber apologeticus*, Vaggione (1987), 58/59. Greek term inserted by me.
38. *Oratio* 28, 1.

when he follows Moses into the mountain and sees the back parts of God, he speaks of being "sheltered by the rock" (Ex 33, 21–23), which, in accordance with St. Paul, he interprets as Christ (cf. 1 Cor 10, 4). In other words, he keeps to the Scriptures and what they reveal. However, the proper vantage-point is the rock, which, on the authority of St. Paul, is Christ.

Christ is the key to the perception of Scriptural meaning. Gregory, however, does not discard human reason, but one's mental powers should be prepared like the fallows to receive the seed. In *Oratio* 28 Gregory plays the play of his adversaries and demonstrates the philosophically uncontroversial thesis that God is incorporeal. However, innocent as this may seem, in the next *Oratio* (29), immediately after the potent proposition on the monad, the dyad, and the triad, he claims, as mentioned above, that what goes on in the structuring of the Triad is without passion, without time, and in a non-corporeal manner (ἀπαθῶς, καὶ ἀχρόνως, καὶ ἀσωμάτως).[39] This might, of course, be controversial, since the Anomoeans do not admit such internal activities of generation in the Godhead. However, one might claim hypothetically that *if* there is such generation, *then* it should be qualified thus, which, of course, all Neoplatonists would have accepted, even if they had not accepted the kind of Triad Gregory argues for. On the other hand, these three adverbs immediately assist Gregory in his argument against the Anomoeans: if they claim that divine generation *qua* activity begins and ends, which intrudes time into the sphere of the Godhead and make divine generation impossible, then Gregory may boldly say that the Son and the Spirit came into being *when the Father did*, and "there never was when the He was not" – the οὐκ ἦν ὅτε οὐκ ἦν, turning the original Arian dictum ἦν ποτε ὅτε οὐκ ἦν against his adversaries.[40] The Anomoeans may further argue that since the three are co-eternal, why are they not all alike unoriginate, by implication *unbegotten*, which would be impossible? – Aetius had argued against the idea that what is begotten might be unbegotten, as had Eunomius.[41] – Gregory answers that one must distinguish between being unoriginate (ἄναρχον) and being eternal (ἀΐδιον). Once more we find a dictum that would have been accepted by any Neoplatonist. Gregory says that what is unoriginate is eternal, but what is eternal might not be unoriginate, if it has the unoriginate as its cause: generation, we should remember, is to be conceived as non-corporeal and atemporal. Gregory makes the claim that the cause is not necessarily (temporally) prior to its effects. This, once more, would have found agreement with the Neoplatonists. The point is illustrated with the sun and its light. At this point, Gregory has, even if hypothetically, made several important philosophical claims of which none is unreasonable.

39. *Oratio* 29, 2.
40. *Oratio* 29, 3.
41. Cf. Kopecek (1979), 232, Eunomius, *Liber asceticus*, Vaggione (1987), 44–47.

So far there is not much to be gathered of any doctrine of divine activity, if by that we mean an elaborate ontology of Trinitarian generation. However, there is one more relevant point to be considered in this regard, viz. Gregory's answers to his opponent's polemical questions about the divine will in the so-called generation.[42]

The Anomoean argument is that if the Son is begotten, He is begotten either voluntary or involuntary. If He is begotten involuntary, then the Father is under some kind of external constrain, if He is begotten voluntary, then the Son is the Son of will, and not of the Father. This sounds like a kind of *reductio ad absurdum*, but there is more to it than that. Eunomius has a rather strange doctrine that the term Father denotes, not an essence nor a hypostasis, but precisely the creative *activity of will* that made the Son, who for that reason is a creature.[43] As we have seen above, this activity is then set up as a kind of "thing in between" the hypostases of the first God and His Son. Gregory, however, does not swallow the hook. At this point he argues along the same lines as St. Gregory of Nyssa: he does not accept the concept of a "will" as something "in the middle," i.e. between God and His creatures. Even so, he thinks it would be stupid not to distinguish between the one who wills and the act of willing, the one who begets and the act of begetting, and the one who speaks and the act of speaking (ἀλλ' ἕτερον ἐστίν, οἶμαι, θέλων καὶ θέλησις, γεννῶν καὶ γέννεσις, λέγων καὶ λόγος, εἰ μὴ μεθύομεν).[44] This amounts to making a distinction between the being (essence) of something and its activity. In short, it is one thing to be *someone who wills* and another ontological category to be *an act of willing*. Gregory says on the one hand that there is the mover, on the other the motion. What is begotten (the effect) is not the result of begetting (the activity), but rather of the person who begat (the substance). When Gregory, on this background, is tempted to say something about divine will in divine generation, he sticks to his basic conception of God as beyond objects of knowledge: "The things with God is beyond all this [...]" Even so he makes a non-committed statement: perhaps (ἴσως), he says, the divine *will* to beget is begetting. At this point St. Gregory of Nyssa feels more secure.[45] He argues that even if our experience is that a wish and what we wish for are not present at the same time, things are rather different with God. To God, to will and to possess the object of will is immediately realized. The Father willing the Son, therefore, is the immediate possessing of the Son. One might, of course, ask the critical question if not the Father could have begun to will the Son. Gregory would have answered that the Father's will is always directed towards the Good, and since the Son is the Good by nature, He cannot fail to be the immediate object of the Father's will, and,

42. *Oratio* 29, 6–7.
43. *Liber asceticus*, Vaggione (1987), 66/67.
44. *Oratio* 29, 6. For Gregory of Nyssa, cf. *Contra Eunomium*, GNO 1, 87.
45. *Contra Eunomium*, GNO 1, 191–194.

by implication, the Son is eternally with the Father.[46] Gregory even tries to lessen the distance between the Father and the Son still more, when he says the Son is the will of the Father.[47]

Even if Gregory of Nyssa is more explicit than Gregory Nazianzus at this point, there is no reason to believe that Gregory of Nyssa thinks we have any philosophical access to the divine being. As we saw above, God remains for him as well beyond human comprehension. Gregory Nazianzus, as we have now seen, claims to contemplate divine revelation from the Rock, and he may also claim that reasoning brings us hypotheses about God that would be counted rather sound even by non-Christian thinkers. From this double standpoint he moves, in the next *Oratio* (30), to the analysis of several texts deployed in the Trinitarian controversy, and tries convincingly to dissolve what seem to be their inherent difficulties. It all culminates in the exegesis of divine and Christological titles, which he calls to "sketch Him by attributes that surrounds Him."[48] The best theologian is not he who has discovered the whole, but he who, to quote the translation of Wickham and Williams, "has gathered in his mind a richer picture, outline, or whatever we call it, of the truth."[49] When he argues in *Oratio* 31 for the divinity of the Holy Spirit, he does something similar, viz. contemplates a lot of titles.[50]

One might say that even if Gregory Nazianzus does not develop a detailed ontology of divine generation – something he cannot do given that the object is inaccessible for investigation – he still has sketched an ontology. This ontology makes a restrictive use of a distinction between God's essence and His activities. However, the God of Gregory is not the same kind of being as the God of Eunomius. God is the dreadful mystery, to be adored and not spoken of excessively. For this reason Gregory says the begetting of God should be honored in silence.[51]

Abbreviations

CCSG: Corpus Christianorum Series Graeca, Turnhout, Leuven.
GNO: Gregorii Nysseni Opera, Leiden.

Bibliography

Basil, *The Letters*, ed. Deferrari, R. J., Loeb Classical Library, London 1972.
Behr, J. (2004), *Formation of Christian Theology*, vol. 2, *The Nicene Faith*, part 1–2, New York.

46. *Contra Eunomium*, GNO 2, 192; NPNF 5, 202.
47. *Contra Eunomium*, GNO 1, 288.
48. *Oratio* 30, 17–21.
49. *Oratio* 30, 17.
50. *Oratio* 31, 29.
51. *Oratio* 29, 8.

Bradshaw, D. (2007), *Aristotle East and West*, Cambridge.

Chrysostome, J., *Sur l'incompréhensibilite de Dieu*, Sources chrétiennes, Paris 1951.

Emilsson, E. K. (2007), *Plotinus on the Intellect*, Oxford.

Grégoire de Nazianze, *Discours 27–31*, Sources chrétiennes, Paris 1978.

Kopecek, T. A. (1979), *A History of Neo-Arianism*, vol. I–II, The Philadelphia Patristic Foundation, Cambridge MA.

Louth, A. (1996), *Maximus the Confessor*, London.

Mateo-Seco, L. F. and Maspero, G. ed. (2010), *The Brill Dictionary of Gregory of Nyssa*, Leiden.

Meyendorff, J. (1974), *A Study of Gregory Palamas*, St Vladimir's Seminary Press.

Narkevics, E. (2006), "*Skiagraphia*": Outlining the conception of God in Gregory's "*Theological Orations*", in: Børtnes, J. and Hägg, T. ed., *Gregory of Nazianzus, Images and Reflections*, Copenhagen.

Norris, F. W. (1991), Wickham, L., and Williams, F., *Faith gives Fullness to Reasoning*, Leiden.

Rist, J. M. (1967), *Plotinus - The Road to Reality*, Cambridge.

Tollefsen, T. (2008), *The Christocentric Cosmology of St. Maximus the Confessor*, Oxford.

Vaggione, R. P. (1987), *Eunomius, The Extant Works*, Oxford.

Proclus and Christian Neoplatonism: Two Case Studies

Ilaria L. E. Ramelli

The Byzantine Neoplatonist Proclus (412–485 CE), albeit a "pagan," shows impressive thematic and terminological similarities with Christian Neoplatonism. Here I will offer only two case studies, closely related to one another, respectively concerning the doctrine of restoration and the embodiment of souls (and there would be several significant others), not to suggest that Proclus squarely drew his doctrines from Christian Neoplatonists, or to read Proclus through a Christian lens – as interpreters such as fourteenth-century Berthold von Moosburg in his *Exposition on the Elements of Theology of Proclus* did – but to indicate how profound this overlooked cultural osmosis was in the day and in the case of Proclus. I will point out elements that have been entirely missed by scholarship so far and that will hopefully advance research into Byzantine Platonism.

Restoration: Philosophical Trajectories

Proclus speaks quite often of restoration or apokatastasis. The doctrine of apokatastasis – ἀποκατάστασις, restoration or reconstitution – is a remarkable case of a philosophical soteriological doctrine that was elaborated in both "pagan" and Christian philosophy, especially Platonism, not without possible momentous interactions that still need to be investigated. In Stoicism, this doctrine affected the cosmological sphere, and had no soteriological value proper. The term ἀποκατάστασις (from ἀποκαθίστημι, "I restore, I reconstitute") is referred by Eusebius to the Stoics' cosmological conception of the cyclical return of the universe to its original condition at the end of every great year: "The common *logos*, that is, the common nature, becomes more and more abundant, and in the end dries up everything and resolves everything into itself. It returns to the first *logos* and the famous 'resurrection' [ἀνάστασις] that makes the great year, when the universal restoration [ἀποκατάστασις] takes place."[1] The Stoics' use of this term was related to its astronomical meaning, one of the many that this noun bore in antiquity (others were medical, military, political, and so on). It indicated the return of

1. *PE* 15.19.1–3 = SVF 2.599.

a heavenly body to its initial place after a complete revolution, or the return of all stars to their original place after a whole cosmic cycle. The latter is the meaning on which Stoic cosmology drew.

In Stoic cosmology, apokatastasis indicates the periodical repetition of a cosmic cycle (SVF 2.599; 2.625), based on aeons (αἰῶνες) or "great years" that return again and again, identical to one another, in an infinite series. The same persons will exist in each aeon, and these will behave in the same ways, making the same choices, forever. This succession is determined by periodical conflagrations (ἐκπυρώσεις) in which all is reduced to fire/aether/*logos*/*pneuma*, i.e. Zeus, the supreme, immanent divinity. After this, Zeus expands again into a new "whole" or universe (ὅλον): "The Stoics maintain that the planets will return [ἀποκαθισταμένους] into the same constellation [...] Universal restoration [ἀποκατάστασις] takes place not only once, but many times, or better the *same things* will continue to be repeated [ἀποκαθίστασθαι] indefinitely, *without end*."[2]

The Middle/Neoplatonist, Origen of Alexandria, was the main theoriser of the Christian apokatastasis doctrine. He refuted the Stoic doctrine of apokatastasis to further his own, Christian doctrine of universal restoration.[3] There are two main differences between the Stoic theory of apokatastasis and Origen's Christian doctrine: the first is that the Stoics postulated an infinite series of aeons, while Origen posited an end of all aeons precisely at the eventual apokatastasis, which will be one and only one, absolutely eternal, and will put an end to every χρόνος and every αἰών. The second difference is that the Stoics thought that in each aeon everything would happen in the very same way as in all the others, while Origen thought of the aeons as different from one another, in that they are the theatre of the moral and spiritual development of rational creatures, the *logika*.

For example, in *CC* 4.12 and 4.67–68, Origen criticises the Stoic theory in that it denies human free will: "If this is the case, our *freedom of will* is over. For, if during given cycles, out of necessity, the same things have happened, happen, and will happen, [...] it is clear that out of necessity Socrates will always devote himself to philosophy, and will be accused of introducing new divinities and of corrupting the youths; and that Anitus and Meletus will always be his accusers, and that the Areopagus judges will condemn him to death. [...] If one accepts this idea, I do not quite know how *our freedom* will be saved and how *praises and blames* will possibly be justified" (*CC* 4.67–68). In *CC* 5.20 the Stoic doctrine of cyclical worlds is also ascribed to Platonists and Pythagoreans; in *Princ.* 2.3.4 the Stoic notion of apokatastasis is again accused of denying human free will and responsibility:

> If one aeon will be perfectly identical to another, Adam and Eve will do for the second time the same things that they already did [...] Judas will

2. SVF 2.625 = Nemesius, *NH* 38.
3. E.g. in *CC* 4.12; 4.67–68; 5.20; *Princ.* 2.3. See I. Ramelli, *Tempo ed eternità in età antica e patristica. Grecità, Ebraismo e Cristianesimo*, Assisi: Cittadella, 2015, introduction.

> betray the Lord again, and Paul will keep again the mantels of those who were stoning Stephen, and all that has happened in this life will happen again. But this theory can be supported by no argument, since the souls are pushed by their free will, and their progresses and regresses depend on the faculty of their will. Indeed, the souls are not induced to do or wish this or that by the circular movement of the heavenly bodies that after many aeons accomplish the same cycle, but wherever the freedom of their inclination has pushed them, there they orient the course of their actions.

And in *Princ.* 2.3.5 the end of all aeons is explicitly affirmed. It will coincide with apokatastasis itself, "when all will be no more in an aeon, but God will be 'all in all.'" In 3.1 Origen already envisaged "a stage in which there will be no aeon any more," just as in *Comm. in Io.* 13.3.

In Stoicism the restoration had no soteriological implications proper, also given the immanentism and materialism of "orthodox" Stoic doctrine: souls are no less material than bodies, and dissolve at the end of each cosmic cycle if not earlier, and then are reconstituted by necessity in the following aeon (SVF 2.623). In Neoplatonism, both "pagan" and Christian, on the contrary, apokatastasis became the doctrine of the salvation of the soul, with the related crucial question of the *universality* of this salvation. Will all souls be restored and saved, or not all of them? It is meaningful that some late Neoplatonists ascribed the doctrine of universal restoration and salvation back to Plato, in order to dignify their own theory, but in fact Plato did not believe that *all* souls would be liberated from the torments of Tartarus. Origen and other Christian Neoplatonists, on the contrary, did uphold this theory, and their ideas may have been known to "pagan" Neoplatonists who reflected on soteriology.

One possible instance is the Latin Neoplatonist Macrobius. Commenting on the myth of Er at the end of Plato's *Republic*, devoted to the eschatological destiny of such souls, he affirms that, according to Plato, all souls will return to their original place, some sooner and others later, but all of them will eventually return.[4] Even those who have erred most of all, after a very long stay in Tartarus, will return, purified, to their seats. In fact, Plato admitted of some exceptions, for souls who are absolutely irrecoverable. According to him, these will remain in Tartarus forever. For he thought that pains were therapeutic and cured the souls, but that some were incurable (ἀνίατοι) because the crimes they committed were too extreme; therefore, they will never leave Tartarus, where they undergo an eternal punishment.

4. *Saecula infinita dinumerans, quibus nocentium animae, in easdem poenas saepe reuolutae, sero de tartaris permittuntur emergere et ad naturae suae principia, quod est caelum, tandem impetrata purgatione remeare. Necesse est enim omnem animam ad originis suae sedem reuerti, sed quae corpus tamquam peregrinae incolunt cito post corpus uelut ad patriam reuertuntur, quae uero corporum illecebris ut suis sedibus inhaerent, quanto ab illis uiolentius separantur, tanto ad supera serius reuertuntur.* (*In Somn.* 2.17.12–14).

This is stated by Plato in several passages, in particular in *Phaed.* 113E, *Gorg.* 525C, and *Resp.* 10.615C–616A – though in his *Phaedrus* the "law of Adrasteia" (248C2) prescribes that, after migrations and purifications, souls return to their original place, after three thousand years for the souls of philosophers, which become winged again at that time, or after ten thousand years for common souls.[5] This is the only passage – against several others – that might suggest that apokatastasis for Plato was universal. Whereas Plato repeatedly stated that some souls, the "incurable," would not return to their original place, Macrobius, like his contemporary Gregory of Nyssa, the Christian Neoplatonist and follower of the Christian Platonist Origen, thought that all souls, without exception, would return to their "homeland."[6] Those who had erred the most will take a very long time to do so, but nevertheless will return. For Macrobius, apokatastasis would really be universal. All souls will be restored to their original seat, because "necesse est omnem animam ad originis suae sedem reuerti." Universal apokatastasis is grounded in an ontological necessity according to Macrobius.

If Macrobius presents Plato as saying something slightly different from what he actually maintained, this means that Macrobius' conviction concerning universal apokatastasis, the return of absolutely all souls to their original state and place, was truly strong. This conviction was equally strong in roughly contemporary Christian Neoplatonists who supported the doctrine of apokatastasis, such as Gregory of Nyssa or Evagrius, but with the difference that in their view – which is directly based on Origen's view – this was not simply an ontological necessity, but depended on Christ's incarnation, sacrifice, and resurrection, and on the development of human free will.

Macrobius may have had in mind also Porphyry's "universal way for the liberation and salvation of the soul," but it is doubtful that Porphyry wanted to find a way for the restoration of all souls, and at any rate he did not find it. According to Augustine *CD* 10.32, Porphyry concluded the first book of his *De regressu animae* stating that, after examining true philosophy and the doctrines of the Indians and the Chaldaeans, he could not find any philosophy or religion that provided a "universal way" for the liberation of the soul:

> Haec est religio [sc. Christianity], quae universalem continet viam animae liberandae [...] Cum autem dicit Porphyrius in primo iuxta finem de regressu animae libro nondum receptum in unam quandam sectam quod universalem contineat viam animae liberandae, vel a philosophia verissima aliqua vel ab Indorum moribus ac disciplina aut inductione Chaldaeorum aut alia qualibet via, nondumque in suam notitiam eandem viam historiali cognitione perlatam, procul dubio confitetur esse aliquam, sed nondum in suam venisse notitiam.

5. On Plato's doctrine of salvation see S. Menn, "Plato's Soteriology?," in: V. Adluri, ed., *Greek Religion: Philosophy and Salvation*, Berlin: de Gruyter 2013, 191–216.
6. See I. Ramelli, *The Christian Doctrine of Apokatastasis. A Critical Assessment from the New Testament to Eriugena*, Leiden 2013.

Marius Victorinus, who translated many Neoplatonic texts into Latin, also translated Porphyry's *De regressu animae*,[7] making it thereby available to Augustine, who devoted almost one book, the tenth, of *De civitate Dei* to Porphyry. According to Smith,[8] there are three possible interpretations of the *via universalis* allegedly sought by Porphyry, as is clear from other passages in *CD* 10.32: (1) either a way for the liberation of all souls (*qua universae animae liberantur ac per hoc sine illa nulla anima liberatur*), (2) or a way for all peoples (*universis gentibus communis*), (3) or again a way for the liberation of the whole human being (*totum hominem*), or at least for the whole of the soul, both the higher and the lower. Smith thought that Porphyry wished to find a way for the liberation of the higher soul of all human beings, but found that only some people can pursue philosophy, which liberates the higher soul (*De abst.* 1.27–28); Brahmans and Samaneans in India are restricted groups (*ibid.* 4.17), and Chaldean theurgy only purifies the lower soul (Aug. *CD* 10.9).[9] Pierre Hadot[10] thought that Porphyry did not envisage a universal way, because he knew that Platonism was for an élite, and that some non-Greek religious techniques were very limited. Likewise, according to Gillian Clark,[11] that Porphyry was in search of such a universal way for the deliverance of the soul is a notion that is conveyed by Augustine's paraphrase of his *De regressu animae*; the concern for universalism is Augustine's own addition to Porphyry.[12] It is Augustine who opposes Christianity as a religion who instructs everybody ("as though in a lecture room open to both sexes and all ages and ranks": *Ep.* 138.10)[13] to "pagan" philosophy, which was reserved for few people, while

7. And possibly also his *Letter to Anebo* at least according to H. D. Saffrey, *Porphyre : Lettre à Anébon l'égyptien*, Paris : Les Belles Lettres 2012, lxiii.
8. A. Smith, *Porphyry's Place in the Neoplatonic Tradition. A Study in Post-Plotinian Neoplatonism*, The Hague 1974, 136–141.
9. M. B. Simmons, "*Via universalis animae liberandae*: The Pagan-Christian Debate on Universalism in the Later Roman Empire," *Studia Patristica* 42 (2006) 319–324, thinks that the universalistic theme in Eusebius's work is a reaction to Porphyry (see also Idem, "Porphyrian Universalism: A Tripartite Soteriology and Eusebius's Response," *Harvard Theological Review* 102 [2009] 169–192). This is true, but I note there is a strong Origenian basis, and both Porphyry and Eusebius were in dialogue with Origen. Moreover, it is Augustine who presented Christianity, against Porphyry, as the *universalis animae liberandae via* (*CD* 10.32).
10. P. Hadot, "Citations de Porphyre chez Augustin," *Revue des études augustiniennes* 6 (1960) 205–244, esp. 239.
11. G. Clark, "Augustine's Porphyry and the Universal Way of Salvation," in: G. Karamanolis, A. Sheppard, eds., *Studies on Porphyry*, London: University of London 2007, 127–140.
12. Indeed Clark remarks that "where the relevant text [*sc.* cited by Augustine] are extant, as they are in the case of Virgil and some of Augustine's other sources (notably Sallust and Apuleius), we can show just how narrowly Augustine selects his material and how forcefully he interprets it to suit his argument [...] it is much more likely that Porphyry denied any claim that there is a single way of liberating the soul" ("Augustine's Porphyry," 130, 136).
13. Augustine's own concern for universalism should not be confused with a doctrine, or even a hope, that all will be saved, since Augustine was convinced that most will be damned, even though in his anti-Manichaean phase, before his anti-Pelagian phase, he embraced Origen's doctrine of universal restoration – as I have argued in "Origen and Augustine: A Paradoxical Reception," *Numen* 60 (2013) 280–307.

"pagan" religion did not teach moral behaviour to anyone (*CD* 2.6; 2.26). According to Clark, therefore, Porphyry was uninterested in finding a universal way for the liberation and salvation of all souls.

Actually, as Augustine himself reports in *CD* 10.29, in his *De regressu animae* Porphyry repeatedly taught that "every body must be avoided, that the soul may remain with God in blessedness" (*omne corpus esse fugiendum ut anima possit beata permanere cum Deo*). This can be achieved only by an élite of philosophers and ascetics. According to Augustine, Porphyry is "a Platonist who shows how close Platonism is to Christianity": this is why he is so dangerous. Aaron Johnson is now essentially on the same line as Clark.[14]

Porphyry surely knew Origen's doctrine of universal restoration and salvation, but could not share it because it was Christian: it depended on faith in Christ as God and included also the resurrection of the body. Porphyry's *Letter to Anebo* – where he took into consideration philosophy, common notions, Egyptian religion (esp. Chaeremon) and Chaldean religion (the *Chaldean Oracles*) – also makes it clear that he did not consider theurgy and religious rituals to be such a way: these may well be universal, but are not ways to the salvation of the soul. Philosophy alone is. This is also why both Eusebius and Augustine, who knew this letter, highly appreciated it for its criticism of "pagan" religion.[15] The title *De regressu animae* or *The Return of the Soul* actually alludes to the restoration or apokatastasis of the soul (not of the whole human being or rational creature, body and soul, as in Origen's and Gregory Nyssa's thought, where the resurrection of the body is part and parcel of the restoration[16]). It would be interesting to know what Greek term lies behind *regressus*; it is possible that Porphyry had ἀποκατάστασις, or ἐπιστροφή, two terms that in Christian Platonism from Origen onward were virtually synonymic, and will also be closely related in Proclus (see below). In any case, Porphyry did not teach the restoration of all souls, and therefore Macrobius does not seem to have been influenced by him when he maintained that all souls will return to their original condition.

The exact time of composition of Macrobius's works is debated, but it seems to come shortly after two other Latin Christian Neoplatonists who did embrace the doctrine of apokatastasis, Marius Victorinus and Augustine, although the latter did so only during his anti-Manichaean phase, in the 390s.[17] Origen's theory of universal restoration, which Augustine later rejected mainly for the purpose of his polemic against Pelagianism, was espoused

14. A. Johnson, *Religion and Identity in Porphyry of Tyre. The Limits of Hellenism in Late Antiquity*, Cambridge: CUP, 2013.
15. Augustine in *CD* 10.11 praises this letter for claiming that whatever demons do (in pagan cult) is an imposture. Indeed, Augustine described Porphyry as "the most illustrious philosopher among the pagans" and "the most learned of the philosophers, though the most bitter enemy of the Christians" in *CD* 22.3 and 19.22 respectively.
16. See my *The Christian Doctrine*.
17. Demonstration in my "Origen and Augustine," 280–307.

by the "pagan" Neoplatonist Macrobius, whatever the exact relation between Macrobius's apokatastasis doctrine and Origen's may have been. Macrobius might have embraced a Christian doctrine – an Origenian doctrine – but he certainly endeavoured to ascribe it back to Plato: obviously he would have felt uneasy about acknowledging any philosophical debt to Christian Platonism. In Christianity, however, the doctrine of apokatastasis, which entailed universal salvation, was soon banned as "heretical" by the Church of the Empire, in the sixth century, under Justinian – who significantly both condemned Origen as a Christian Platonist and wanted to terminate the "pagan" Neoplatonic school of Athens. These two decisions of his are clearly interrelated.

Proclus too, who lived well before Justinian, seems to have been at least acquainted with, if perhaps not directly influenced by, the Christian theory of apokatastasis.[18] Olympiodorus famously classified Proclus, together with his inspirer Iamblichus of Chalcis (who strongly influenced Proclus), and Syrianus, among the "religious" exponents of Neoplatonism, as opposed to its "philosophical" exponents such as Plotinus and Porphyry: "Some, such as Plotinus, Porphyry, etc., give priority to philosophy; others, such as Iamblichus, Syrianus, Proclus, and the whole priestly school, give priority to the priestly art," ἱερατική (Damasc. *In Phaed.* 1.172, 123.3 Norvin).

Proclus is generally regarded today as the main inspirer – directly or indirectly – of Pseudo Dionysius: some assume that his teacher Hierotheus was in fact Proclus; others have supposed that Hierotheus was a disciple of Proclus.[19] Ps. Dionysius, as I have demonstrated,[20] was also profoundly inspired by Origen. In late antiquity and in Byzantine times, however, Proclus was considered to have been inspired by Dionysius.[21] The theory of apokatastasis, so prominent in Origen and in Ps. Dionysius, is also a major feature of Proclus's thought. Proclus, as I shall show, depicts apokatastasis as ἐπιστροφή, just like Ps. Dionysius.[22] The latter is closer to Proclus than to Origen in respect to an extraordinary importance attached to liturgy; for Proclus, of course, this is theurgy, for Ps. Dionysius, Christian rituals.

In this connection, it is important to note that Proclus knew and cited Origen extensively, and the Platonist Origen he speaks of is likely to be iden-

18. On his thought see now R. Chlup, *Proclus: An Introduction*, Cambridge: CUP 2012; the edition of his *Elements of Theology*, with an extensive commentary, is by E. R. Dodds, *Proclus: The Elements of Theology*, second ed., Oxford: Clarendon 1963.
19. The former hypothesis is common, while the latter has been formulated by Th. Sabo, D. Lioy, and R. Fick, "The Platonic Milieu of Dionysius the Pseudo-Areopagite," *Journal of Early Christian History* 3, 1 (2013) 50–60, who suppose that Hierotheus was Isidore of Alexandria, a disciple of Proclus, and Ps. Dionysius' environment was Egyptian rather than Syrian, with interesting though not compelling arguments.
20. In *The Christian Doctrine of Apokatastasis*, chapter on Ps. Dionysius.
21. Suda, s.v. Διονύσιος ὁ Ἀρεοπαγίτης; Psellus, *De omnifaria doctrina* 74.
22. For apokatastasis as ἐπιστροφή in Ps. Dionysius see my *The Christian Doctrine of Apokatastasis*, chapter on Ps. Dionysius.

tifiable with the Christian Platonist Origen of Alexandria,[23] who was, as I have mentioned, the main theoriser of the Christian doctrine of apokatastasis. In *Theol. Plat.* 2.4 Proclus speaks of Origen's metaphysics. He observes that he cannot explain the reason why Origen, who, as Proclus expressly states, received the same philosophical training as Plotinus from Ammonius Saccas (which is the case also for Origen the Christian philosopher[24]), individuated the supreme principle, not in the One, like Plotinus, but in the Intellect and the first Being. Origen, according to Proclus, stopped short of theorising the Hen (Ἕν, One), which transcends the Intellect, every intellect, and Being itself. Plotinus considered the Hen to transcend the Intellect and Being, but Origen regarded the Intellect as the prime Being and the prime One, and this, in Proclus's view, is definitely not in line with Plato's thinking, but derives from Peripatetic innovations; this is why he cannot agree with Origen. In fact, Origen was well acquainted with Peripatetic teachings, as he shows on a number of occasions, but it is Ex 3:14, in which God says, "I am ὁ ὤν" (LXX), and which Philo sometimes rendered with τὸ ὄν, that was paramount for him. Proclus, like Celsus or Poprhyry, would never have acknowledged the importance of the Bible for a Platonic philosopher, not even as a text to be allegorised. On the basis of Ex 3:14, Origen indeed identified God with the Intellect and Being. In his comment on Ex 3:14 in *Comm. in Io.* 2.13.96 Origen, basing himself on Scripture, identifies God with the supreme Good and with Being, in order to oppose evil to both things and to declare evil to be non-being, non existent (μὴ ὄν); this is one of the metaphysical tenets of Origen's system, which also bears on his apokatastasis doctrine. On the other hand, he also said that God may be considered to be superior to both intellect and being. Thus, for instance, he maintained that the "God of the universe" is either Being itself or "beyond Being" (*Comm. in Io.* 19.6.37; likewise *CC* 7.38

23. The identification is considered to be possible or probable by, e.g., H. Crouzel, "Origène et Plotin élèves d'Ammonios Saccas," *Bulletin de Littérature Ecclésiastique* 57 (1956) 193–214; F. H. Kettler, "Origenes, Ammonios Sakkas und Porphyrius," in: *Kerygma und Logos. Festschrift C. Andresen*, Göttingen: Vandenhoek und Ruprecht 1979, 322–328; Th. Böhm, "Origenes – Theologe und (Neu-)Platoniker? Oder: Wem soll man misstrauen: Eusebius oder Porphyrius?," *Adamantius* 8 (2002) 7–23; P. F. Beatrice, "Porphyry's judgment on Origen," in: *Origeniana V*, ed. by R. J. Daly, Leuven: Peeters 1992, 351–367: 351, and again, on the basis of the sole Numenius, Idem, "Origen in Nemesius' treatise 'On the nature of man'," in: *Origeniana IX*, ed. by G. Heidl, R. Somos, Leuven: Peeters 2009, 505–532: 531: "Origen the Pagan, or the Neoplatonist, has never existed, and the Origen we meet three times in Nemesius' treatise is always the only Christian and Platonist Origen, known to Christian and pagan writers without any distinction"; I. Ramelli, "Origen, Patristic Philosophy, and Christian Platonism: Re-Thinking the Christianisation of Hellenism," *Vigiliae Christianae* 63 (2009) 217–263, and with further arguments "Origen the Christian Middle/Neoplatonist," *Journal of Early Christian History* 1 (2011) 98–130; E. DePalma Digeser, *A Threat to Public Piety: Christian, Platonists, and the Great Persecution*, Ithaca-London: Cornell University Press 2012, 18, 51 and passim (my review is forthcoming in *Adamantius*); A. Johnson, *Religion and Identity*, 153, n. 30, also deems the identification possible. A monograph devoted to Origen (Cambridge University Press) will also address this issue with new arguments.
24. See my "Origen, Patristic Philosophy."

and 6.64). Origen describes God as Intellect, but also as "Monad and Henad" (*Princ.* 1.1.6).

It is well possible that the interpretations of Plato's works that Proclus reports in his *Commentary on the Timaeus*, too, as provided by Origen are ascribable to Origen the Christian philosopher. At his school Origen explained the works of Greek philosophers, among whom Plato had a special prominence (Eus. *HE* 6.17). Likewise here in Proclus we find Origen engaged in the explanation and interpretation of Plato's works. The context of the first relevant passage from Proclus's commentary (1.31) is a debate on the purpose of Plato's *Republic.* In Proclus's account, Longinus and Origen disagreed on what kind of πολιτεία Socrates deals with in that dialogue. According to Longinus, it was the middle πολιτεία, since its guardians were soldiers, but according to Origen it was the first πολιτεία, because its guardians were educated in various disciplines, which eventually would come to be regarded as the liberal arts. These μαθήματα indeed were important, both in Origen's own formation and in his teaching program. It is natural that he stressed their importance also in Plato's *Republic*, which could provide a model. What is more, Proclus himself seems to have not only known Origen's position, but also followed it in his own interpretation of Plato's *Republic.* Here, Proclus does not consider the ideal State delineated by Plato a realistic constitution, but rather a representation of the whole cosmos, where the three classes of citizens symbolise gods, demons, and human beings respectively (*In Remp.* 1.16; 1.47; 1.146; 2.98; 2.325–326). Now this seems to have been also the interpretation of Origen, as reported by Proclus himself in *In Tim.* 1.13. Origen's first πολιτεία is a notion that fits the cosmic πολιτεία, and Proclus seems to be developing Origen's line. Longinus and Origen, the two protagonists of Proclus's report, knew each other well; Longinus himself, in a passage reported by Porphyry in *V. Plot.* 20, mentions Origen together with Ammonius as a philosopher, a Platonist, of extraordinary intelligence, and informs that he had frequented Origen for a long time. The immediate association with Ammonius is surely due to Origen's being a disciple of Ammonius. Longinus, who was probably born in 212 CE, states that he had travelled extensively in his youth for his philosophical studies; he does not say that he frequented Origen's school of philosophy in Alexandria; he may well have frequented it in Caesarea, in the advanced 230s. This, from the historical point of view as well, allows for the identification of this Origen – clearly the same as mentioned in *V. Plot.* 14, since both passages cite his *On Demons* – with the homonymous Christian Platonist.

Another exegetical disagreement between Longinus and Origen is reported by Proclus in *In Tim.* 1.76–77. The focus is again on the interpretation of Plato, and in particular of his myth of Atlantis in his *Timaeus.* This dialogue was indeed very well known to Origen the Christian philosopher, who even read Genesis in its light, as both Philo and Bardaisan had done beforehand. According to Longinus, this myth is an allegorical expression of the order prevalent in the cosmos, with heavenly bodies such as planets and fixed stars, but according to Origen it is an allegory of rational creatures (δαίμονες), some good and some evil. Rational creatures, good and evil, were at the centre of Origen the Christian Platonist's theodicy, protology, philosophy of history, and eschatology. It was natural for him to read Plato's Atlantis myth – concerning an original, happy state of affairs of a whole population, then suddenly destroyed by a catastrophe – in reference to them, and very probably in reference to the original life of the *logika*, before the fall. These rational creatures are called here δαίμονες, just as in the title of one of the two treatises that, according to Porphyry, Origen the Neoplatonist wrote on the basis of Ammonius's teaching.[25] It was also typical of Origen the Christian to allegorise cosmological depictions, such as that of the "upper waters" in Genesis, in reference, not to physical realities, but to rational creatures. Thus, for instance, the "upper waters" are the symbol of good rational creatures (angels), while the inferior waters represent evil rational creatures (demons). This style of allegorisation of the cosmological myth of Scripture, typical of Origen the Christian, is perfectly analogous to that of Origen the Neoplatonist's interpretation of the cosmological myth of the *Timaeus* according to Proclus.

Another philosophical discrepancy between Longinus and Origen the Christian is reported by Proclus in *In Tim.* 1.162. The good condition of body and soul depends, according to Longinus, on earthly physical factors such as a good land and climate, while Origen had it depend on the circular movement of the sky, with an allusion to *Resp.* 8.546A. Proclus pairs the exegeses of Plato's texts offered by these two prominent disciples of Ammonius's.

In addition to those I have analysed so far, the other passages from Proclus's commentary that mention Origen, too, can be very well explained in the light of the Christian Origen's deep interest in both allegoresis and philology, as is clearly testified to by his commentaries, *Hexapla*,[26] and even his homilies; for Origen, allegoresis kept both Scripture's "soul" and its "body," that is, its literal and historical level, without eliminating either of them. Two mentions of Origen's ideas in Proclus's commentary on the *Timaeus* perfectly suit Origen's philological, rhetorical, and literary interests. In *In Tim.* 1.68 Proclus examines Origen's evaluation of the literary style of Plato's dialogues. Origen argued that such phrases as "Heracles' strength" instead of

25. On the attribution of these woks to Origen the Christian philosopher see I. Ramelli, "Origen, Patristic Philosophy."

26. He used his own *Hexapla* not only in his great commentaries, but also in his homilies, including the Greek homilies recently discovered in *Codex Monacensis Graecus* 314: see L. Perrone, "The Find of the Munich Codex: A Collection of 29 Homilies of Origen on the Psalms," in: *Colloquium Origenianum Undecimum*, Aarhus, 26–31 August 2013, ed. Anders-Christian Lund-Jacobsen, Leuven: Peeters 2015. Origen abundantly uses his comparative edition in these homilies, which were delivered in Caesarea perhaps toward the end of his life. Edition: *Origenes: Die neuen Psalmenhomilien. Eine kritische Edition des Codex Monacensis Graecus 314*, ed. L. Perrone, GCS NF 19, Berlin: de Gruyter 2015.

"Heracles" also befit prose, and not only poetry. And in 1.93 Proclus takes into consideration Origen's research into the various meanings of ἐλευθερώτατον in *Tim.* 21C. This research resembles Origen's close investigations into the meanings of terms in his Scriptural commentaries. Also, Proclus in *In Tim.* 1.60 is dealing with the question of the interpretation of Plato's metaphors. This was especially meaningful for an allegorist such as Origen, who was also very appreciative of Plato's myths, both in their form and in their contents, to the point that he interacted with them and used them in his elucidation of Scripture.[27] According to Origen, as Proclus reports, metaphors in Plato's dialogues had cognitive and ethical import; their aim was not to produce pleasure – although Origen admitted that Plato was attentive to stylistic elegance – but to represent passions, i.e. bad emotions, so to eliminate them. Such an interpretation fits both with Origen's ethics, strongly characterised by the pursuit of *apatheia* and the criticism of the Epicurean theory of pleasure, and with his appreciation of Plato's myths and of allegory.

Another interpretive discrepancy is attested to by Proclus in *In Tim.* 1.83.86, again in connection with the exegesis of Plato's works and his myths. Longinus and Origen, again, are said to have entertained different views concerning Plato's myths. Longinus regarded them as ornamental or psychagogical, but Origen as endowed with gnoseological value and not aimed at producing pleasure (again the same motif as in *In Tim.* 1.60). This fits Origen's ethics and his allegorical attitude. Moreover, Proclus remarks in 1.83 that Origen was close to Numenius in his exegesis, in which he refused to see pleasure as the aim of Plato's myths. Numenius, a Middle-Platonist and Neo-Pythagorean, was one of Origen's favourite readings, and also an allegorical interpreter of both Plato and the Bible, like Origen. Even though he does not seem to have been either a Christian or a Jew, he allegorised parts of the Old and New Testament, as Origen testifies. Numenius was also one of the favourite readings of Plotinus, to the point that the latter was even accused of plagiarising Numenius and had to be defended by Amelius.

Proclus speaks again of Origen as an allegorical exegete of Plato in *In Tim.* 1.63–64, in an account of Origen's interpretation of *Tim.* 19DE that is based on Porphyry. The latter knew Origen and may have received this anecdote from Plotinus or Longinus or someone of their circle. The problem debated was whether Plato included Homer among the ancient poets; Origen pained for three days while dealing with this issue. The description of Origen's hard labour in terms of sweating and of a long mental and even physical effort perfectly fits the image of Origen the Christian philosopher as an exceptionally hard worker, which earned him the title of φιλόπονος and φιλοπονώτατος from Athanasius and Eusebius, as well as the byname Adamantius,

27. Full demonstration in I. Ramelli, "The Philosophical Stance of Allegory in Stoicism and its Reception in Platonism, Pagan and Christian: Origen in Dialogue with the Stoics and Plato," *International Journal of the Classical Tradition* 18, 3 (2011) 335–371.

which Origen himself may have elected,[28] and was used by his Christian followers. Origen's extraordinary laboriousness and πόνος are repeatedly emphasised by Eusebius in his biography of Origen.[29] He, like Athanasius, uses φιλοπονώτατος as an epithet for Origen (*Ecl. Proph.* 3.6). Actually, Origen himself emphasised his own hard labour, for instance in his first *Homily on Psalm* 77, 1 (Cod. Monacensis Gr. 314, fol. 215r): "And God knows how much I have laboured [ὅσα ἐκάμομεν], for his sake and thanks to his Grace, examining together both the Hebrew text and the other editions, so to establish the emendation of errors."

Proclus's account of Origen the Neoplatonist's positive attitude toward Homer also corresponds to Origen the Christian's attitude toward this poet, which again suggests that Origen the Neoplatonist and Origen the Christian were one and the same person.[30] Thus, it is perfectly possible – albeit not certain – to identify Origen the Neoplatonist who appears in all these passages of Proclus (and in Porphyry's *Vita Plotini* and in Hierocles of Alexandria's fragments) with Origen the Christian Middle-Neoplatonist.

Restoration and Reversal in Proclus

It is therefore possible, if not probable, that Proclus knew Origen's doctrine of apokatastasis. An investigation into the terminology of ἀποκατάστασις and ἀποκαθίστημι reveals an extraordinary proliferation in Proclus's writings, while the occurrences in earlier "pagan" Platonists are sparse or inexistent: none in Plato, Numenius, or Plotinus, six in Porphyry, five in Iamblichus, two in Hierocles, but 145 in Proclus (mostly in his *Commentaries on Plato's Timaeus* – with the most frequent occurrences – and *Republic*, but also in other works such as *Theologia Platonica* and *Elementa Theologiae*). This dramatic increase – even taking into account the fragmentary state of works such as those of Numenius and Iamblichus – can hardly be accidental. A scholar has to make sense of this in the light of late antique Platonism, "pagan" and Christian alike. Proclus reflected a great deal on restoration, and connected this to the return or reversion movement of ἐπιστροφή. The soul is the main protagonist of the return and restoration, but is by no means alone. The whole cosmos is involved in restoration. In this respect it must be noted that a good deal of occurrences of the terminology of apokatastasis in Proclus – about one fifth of the sum total – are related to the astronomical and cosmological meaning of this term, e.g. the apokatastasis of spheres, planets, or stars[31]

28. See my "Origen, Patristic Philosophy, and Christian Platonism."
29. See the analysis in I. Ramelli, "The Birth of the Rome-Alexandria Connection: The Early Sources on Mark and Philo, and the Petrine Tradition," *The Studia Philonica Annual* 23 (2011) 69–95.
30. Analysis in my "Origen the Christian Middle-Neoplatonist."
31. *In Remp.* 2.23.26: ἐκ τῶν συναποκαταστάσεων τῶν ἑπτὰ σφαιρῶν; 2.30.18: τέλειον ἀριθμὸν χρόνου προσείρηκεν τὸν ἐκ τῶν περιόδων τῶν ὀκτὼ τῆς συναποκαταστάσεως, ὅταν τούτων

(a number of these in the *Hypotyposeis astronomicae*[32]), or the combination of apokatastaseis that keeps the cosmos in order,[33] or the definition of the whole of the time as a period of all the universe, which embraces many restorations of the planets.[34] But Proclus closely connects to this cosmological apokatastasis also the apokatastasis of souls, so that, for instance, as I shall point out soon, the apokatastasis of the universe, comprising those of all planets and making up the whole time, coincides with the apokatastasis of the world soul, which includes those of all souls and extends to the whole time. Consistently, Proclus draws a parallel between cosmic-astronomical restorations and restorations of souls (*In Remp.* 2.267.28).[35] Indeed, he is clear in

πασῶν τὰ τάχη συμπερανθέντα ἔχῃ; 2.45.11: τὴν δὲ ἀποκατάστασιν ὁρίζει τοῦ βασιλέως τῶν ὁρατῶν, ᾗ φησιν Πλάτων (*Resp.* 6.509D); 2.237.12. δεῖ γὰρ τὰ ἀνωτέρω κινεῖσθαι θᾶττον, κἂν δοκῶσιν αἱ ἀποκαταστάσεις εἶναι πολυχρονιώτεραι; *In Tim.* 1.101.1: ὅλας ἀποκαταστάσεις καὶ περιόδους τῶν ἑπτὰ κοσμοκρατόρων; 3.54.29: κατὰ τοῦτο ποιεῖται τὰς ἀποκαταστάσεις· ἄλλο μὲν γὰρ τῆς ἡλιακῆς περιόδου μέτρον, ἄλλο δὲ τῆς σεληνιακῆς; 3.56.11: πλανήτων ταῖς ποικίλαις ἑαυτῶν περιόδοις τὴν ποικιλίαν τῆς γενέσεως διαπλεκόντων· ἕπεται γὰρ ἄλλα ἄλλων ἀποκαταστάσεσι καὶ κατ' ἄλλα μέτρα τὰς ἑαυτῶν συμπεραίνει ζωάς; 3.75.16: Ταῦτα δὲ ὁ Πλάτων πρὸς τὰς ἀποκαταστάσεις ὁρῶν διατάττεται; 3.78.28. πρὸς τὸν χρόνον τῆς ἀποκαταστάσεως; 3.81.4: τὰ μέτρα δείκνυσι τῶν ἀποκαταστάσεων; 3.83.25: ἐκ πόσων ἐστὶν ἐνιαυτῶν ἡ κοινὴ τῶν ὀκτὼ συναποκατάστασις; 3.87.27: τὴν φαινομένην ἀποκατάστασιν ὁ Πλάτων ἔλαβε τῆς ἀπλανοῦς τὴν τὸ νυχθήμερον ποιοῦσαν; 3.87.31: πρὸς τὴν ἀποκατάστασιν τῆς ἀπλανοῦς; 3.88.7: τὴν εἰς τὰ κέντρα φορὰν ἄλλοτε ἄλλην ἔχει καὶ τὴν εἰς τὰ αὐτὰ κατὰ πάντα ἀποκατάστασιν πολυχρονιωτάτην; 3.88.9: τὸ μέτρον τῆς ἀποκαταστάσεως τῆς ταὐτοῦ φορᾶς καλεῖ νύκτα καὶ ἡμέραν; 3.89.1: πόθεν δὲ τὸ διάφορον τῶν ἀποκαταστάσεων ἢ ἀπὸ τῶν διαφερόντων ἀκινήτων αἰτίων; 3.89.15: εἰ γὰρ καὶ διαφέρουσαί εἰσιν αὐτῶν αἱ ἀποκαταστάσεις, ἀλλὰ λόγον ἔχουσι πρὸς ἀλλήλας; 3.90.24: τὴν ἐναρμόνιον κίνησιν καὶ τὴν τάξιν τῶν ἀποκαταστάσεων; 3.91.11: τὰς διαφορὰς τῶν ἀποκαταστάσεων; 3.91.20–25: ἧς σελήνης ἀποκατάστασιν καὶ τὴν ἡλιακὴν ὁμοίως [...] επὶ ταύτας ὅλας καὶ τὴν τῆς ἀπλανοῦς ἐπὶ τὴν μίαν καὶ κοινὴν τῶν πλανωμένων ἀποκατάστασιν; 3.92.4: ἔχουσι τὸν αὐτὸν ὑπ' ἀμφοτέρων τῶν πολλαπλασιασμῶν κοινὸν τῆς ἀμφοτέρων ἀποκαταστάσεως χρόνον; 3.93.2: πάντως ἐστὶ πάντων ἡ παροῦσα τάξις ἀποκατάστασίς τις; 3.93.6: μία τις ἀποκατάστασις; 3.93.12: Καρκίνῳ τῆς ἀποκαταστάσεως γενομένης; 3.146.13: προποδίζοντες μὲν γὰρ προσχωροῦσι ταῖς ἑαυτῶν ἀποκαταστάσεσιν; 3.148.27: τὰς τῶν ποικίλων ἀποκαταστάσεις.

32. 3.53.7: τῶν ἀπλανῶν ἀστέρων ποιουμένους τὴν τήρησιν τῆς ἀποκαταστάσεως; 3.53.9; τὴν ἀποκατάστασιν; 3.54.2: πρὸς τὰ τροπικὰ σημεῖα καὶ τὰ ἰσημερινὰ τὴν ἀποκατάστασιν ὁρᾶν τῆς περιόδου τοῦ τε ἡλίου καὶ τῶν ἄλλων πλανήτων; 3.60.3: τὰς μοίρας τῆς μιᾶς ἀποκαταστάσεως τὰς τξ; 4.83.3: ἄλλην εἶναι κόσμου περιστροφὴν καὶ ἄλλην τοῦ νυχθημέρου ἀποκατάστασιν; 5.23.1: μήκους μὲν ἀποκατάστασις λέγεται, ὅταν ὁ ἐπίκυκλος ἀπὸ τῶν αὐτῶν ἐπὶ τὰ αὐτὰ τοῦ ἐκκέντρου παραγένηται; 5.23.4: ἀνωμαλίας δὲ ἀποκατάστασις, ὅταν ὁ ἀστὴρ ἐπὶ τοῦ ἐπικύκλου φερόμενος ἀπὸ τοῦ αὐτοῦ εἰς τὸ αὐτὸ ποιήσηται τὴν περιδρομήν; 5.24.3: ἐν πόσοις μὲν ἔτεσιν ἕκαστος αὐτῶν πόσας ἀνωμαλίας ἀποκαταστάσεις ποιεῖται; 5.28.1; τὰς διαφόρους αὐτῆς τῶν πρὸς ἥλιον σχηματισμῶν ἀποκαταστάσεις; 5.37.1: ἐν τῷ ἐνιαυτῷ μιᾶς ἀποκαταστάσεως ἑκατέρου γιγνομένης πρὸς τὰ τοῦ ζῳδιακοῦ σημεῖα.
33. *In Remp.* 2.24.14: ἡ συναποκατάστασις, οὐκ οὖσα στάσις ἀλλ' ἀφετηρία τῆς ἑξῆς περιόδου, τηρεῖ τὴν κοσμικὴν τάξιν.
34. *In Tim.* 2.289.12. πολλὰς μὲν Κρονίας ἀποκαταστάσεις, πολλὰς δὲ Ἡλιακάς, πολλὰς δὲ Σεληνιακὰς περιέχουσα, καὶ ἔστιν ὁ πᾶς χρόνος ἐν τῇ μιᾷ περιόδῳ τοῦ παντός.
35. Καθάπερ οὖν *αἱ τῶν κύκλων ἀποκαταστάσεις* ἐν τῇ περιόδῳ συμπεραίνονται πάντων, κατὰ τὰ αὐτὰ δὴ καὶ *αἱ περίοδοι τῶν ψυχῶν* αἱ κατὰ πάντας βίους. And in *In Tim.* 3.19.31 Proclus draws a parallel between the restoration of a human soul and that of heavenly bodies such as the sun and the moon: ἄνθρωπον δὲ τοσόνδε, ἥλιον δὲ ἐν τοσῷδε ἀποκαθίστασθαι καὶ σελήνην.

many passages that apokatastasis involves both corporeal and incorporeal realities.[36] The cycle of restoration (περίοδος καὶ ἀποκατάστασις) involves not only incorruptible realities (ἀδιάφθορα), such as souls, but also all realities subject to generation (πάντα τὰ γενητά, *In Tim.* 3.43.27).

Before analysing Proclus's doctrine of the restoration of the soul, however, it is necessary to remark that Plotinus in fact did receive the *doctrine* of apokatastasis, though, as I have said, he completely lacks the *terminology* of apokatastasis, and developed this theory differently from his fellow disciple Origen. Indeed, in the only two passages in which he refers to this theory (*Enn.* 4.3.12, 5.7.1–3), he adheres to the Stoicising scheme of infinite apokatastatic cycles during which the same events occur and the same individuals live, making the same choices, ad infinitum. This scheme, as I have shown, was criticised by Origen. In 4.3.12 Plotinus presents his closest approximation to the terminology of apokatastasis: κατὰ χρόνους ἀεὶ εἰς τὸ αὐτὸ καθιστάμενα. This periodical reconstitution, Plotinus states, includes the descents and reascents of souls (καθόδοις ψυχῶν καὶ ἀνόδοις). In 5.7.1–3 Plotinus is reasoning within a framework of infinite cosmic cycles (περίοδοι characterised by ἀπειρία) and is asking whether in each of them there exist *logoi* of all the individuals that are generated within a single cosmic cycle. He concludes that "the whole cosmic period includes all *logoi* and therefore the same things happen again and again according to the same *logoi*" (ἡ δὲ πᾶσα περίοδος πάντας ἔχει τοὺς λόγους, αὖθις δὲ τὰ αὐτὰ πάλιν κατὰ τοὺς αὐτοὺς λόγους). Plotinus's adhesion to the Stoic model is clear in 4.7.2: "The same, in every detail, repeats itself from period to period" (τὸ αὐτὸν πάντη ἐν τῇ ἑτέρᾳ περιόδῳ), a point that was not only contested by Origen, but also not taken up by Proclus.[37]

Proclus is closer to Origen than to Plotinus's line when he refuses Plotinus's doctrine of the undescended soul in *Elem. theol.* 211: "Every partial soul, descending into the realm of generation, *descends in its entirety* [ὅλη]: it is not the case that a part of it remains above, and the rest descends." Likewise in *In Parm.* 948: "We ought not to maintain that a part of the soul remains above [...] nor should we point that the soul has the same substance as the gods." Plotinus himself was well aware that his doctrine was still extraneous to the Platonic tradition in his time (*Enn.* 4.8.8: "against the opinion of the others," παρὰ δόξαν τῶν ἄλλων, meaning "of the other Platonists"). Damascius too will reject the doctrine of the undescended soul (*In Parm.* 2.254.3–10), along the lines of Iamblichus and Proclus. Likewise Proclus is closer to

36. E.g. *In Remp.* 2.16.14: καθ' ἕκαστον τῶν ἀεικινήτων ἔστιν τις νοῦς, ὃς καὶ τὴν ζωὴν τὴν ἐν αὐτῷ συμπεραίνει καὶ τὴν ἀποκατάστασιν τὴν *σωματικήν*; 3.28.20: *ψυχάς τε καὶ φύσεις καὶ σώματα* κύκλῳ περιάγει καὶ περιοδικῶς ἀποκαθίστησιν.

37. Plotinus even resumes the terminology of *logoi spermatikoi* – adopted by Justin, Clement, and Origen too – when in 4.7.3 he claims that "we ought not to fear the infinity of seminal reasons (in each cosmic period), since the Soul possesses all," οὐ φοβητέον τὸ ἐν τοῖς σπέρμασιν καὶ τοῖς λόγοις ἄπειρον, ψυχῆς τὰ πάντα ἐχούσης.

Origen than to Plotinus when he rejects the theory that the soul is consubstantial (ὁμοούσιος) with the divine and identifiable with the Intellect and even the One (*In Tim.* 3, 231.5–11 Diehl). Iamblichus's position about the soul, namely that it is changeable and even undergoes changes in its substance, since it descends entirely (differently from what Plotinus thought), does not convince Proclus completely, even if Proclus was heavily influenced by Iamblichus. According to Proclus, the human soul does descend entirely, to be sure, but it does not undergo changes in its substance (*In Tim.* 3.335, 3.338, 3.340). Proclus describes the amphibious nature of the soul as follows: the soul is an eternal substance, but its activities are accomplished in time (*Elem. theol.* 192). Reflecting on Plato's *Timaeus*, where the γένεσις of the soul is described, i.e. the genesis of something ἀγένητον, Proclus takes it to mean that the soul is continually generated, and continually receives the power to exist (*In Tim.* 2.119–132).[38]

Plato in *Tim.* 36B ff. spoke of circles in the soul. For Proclus, the cyclic period of the human soul is "its proper life" (*Elem. theol.* 199, on which see below, and 200). This conception squares perfectly with his restoration-return-reversal scheme. The Neoplatonic use of ἐπιστροφή, which in Proclus sides that of ἀποκατάστασις, must indeed be seen within the triadic movement of μονή, πρόοδος, and ἐπιστροφή. Proclus himself ascribes the theorisation of this movement to Iamblichus in *In Tim.* 2.215.5: the Monad is the principle of identity and the moment of immanence, the Dyad introduces procession, and the Triad is the origin of reversion or return. Procession, according to Proclus, is a movement from better to worse, reversion from worse to better (Procl. *Elem. theol.* 36–37; cf. Plot. *Enn.* 5.8.1, 6.9.9). According to Proclus, only what is incorporeal and without parts, such as the soul itself, can revert or return, i.e. have an ἐπιστροφή (*Elem. theol.* 15). The body does not revert, which also implies that there is no resurrection of bodies. This is in line with "pagan" Platonism, more than with Christian Platonism. In fact, however, Origen, too, ruled out the resurrection of the material ὑποκείμενον of a body, which is permanently in flux, and only admitted of the resurrection of the εἶδος or metaphysical form of the earthly body, transformed into a spiritual body; so also the Christian Neoplatonists Gregory of Nyssa and Evagrius.[39] Indeed, for Origen, Gregory, and Evagrius the resurrection is part and parcel of the restoration process, which involves the soul and the intellect as well as the body (for Evagrius, the body will be elevated to the level of soul and the latter to the level of intellect).[40]

38. Origen applied a similar notion to the generation of the Son: the Son is coeternal with the Father because its generation is eternal, not so much in the sense that the Son continually receives the power to exist, as in the sense that the generation of the Son takes place out of time.

39. See my "Origen's Exegesis of Jeremiah: Resurrection Announced throughout the Bible and its Twofold Conception," *Augustinianum* 48 (2008) 59–78; *Gregorio di Nissa sull'anima e la resurrezione*, Milan: Bompiani, Catholic University of the Sacred Heart 2007.

40. On Evagrius's ideas about the resurrection and about bodies, see my *Evagrius's Kephalaia Gnostika*, Leiden: Brill, Atlanta: SBL 2015.

The connection between reversion (ἐπιστροφή) and restoration (ἀποκατάστασις) is clear especially in the case of souls and is made explicit in *In Tim.* 1.87.30: the decade indicates the reversion (ἐπιστροφή) of all beings in the cosmos toward the One; the ninety indicates the restoration (ἀποκατάστασις) to the monad next to the procession (πρόοδος).[41] Like the reversion, the restoration too is posited next to the procession. Indeed, as I have mentioned, in Ps. Dionysius, who was heavily influenced by Proclus, the restoration is understood as a reversion. In *Elem. theol.* 32 Proclus observes that the reversion or return of the soul, of which Porphyry was speaking in his *De regressu animae* and which parallels Origen's notion of apokatastasis, "is accomplished by virtue of likeness" to the highest principle. And this happens thanks to virtue: for apokatastasis is common to both "souls" and "mortal animals" but with different modalities, because for souls alone it depends on life "according to virtue" (κατ' ἀρετὴν ζωή, *In Crat.* 179.36–37).[42] Interestingly, that apokatastasis is made possible only by the active pursuit of likeness to God, the first principle, in a life of virtue was a major tenet of Origen's apokatastasis doctrine. Origen drew a distinction between being in the image of God, which is an initial datum for every human intellectual soul, and becoming in the likeness of God, which passes through a personal effort and engagement in virtue, and is perfected only in the *telos*, at apokatastasis.[43] Proclus spells out this general principle: "Every return is perfectly achieved by means of the likeness of those who return to the principle to which they return" (πᾶσα ἐπιστροφὴ δι' ὁμοιότητος ἀποτελεῖται τῶν ἐπιστρεφομένων πρὸς ὃ ἐπιστρέφεται, *Elem. theol.* 32). Proclus of course was relying on Plato, *Theaet.* 176B, on the ὁμοίωσις θεῷ, and Origen on both Plato and the Bible (Gen 1:26–27), but neither source includes the specific idea that the *return* or *restoration* will be through likeness. This is rather found in Origen and in Proclus. The latter found in Plotinus that likeness is a fundamental presupposition of all knowledge (*Enn.* 1.8.1, reflected in Proclus *In Tim.* 2.298.27; 3.160.18), and interpreted knowledge as a type of return (*In Tim.* 2.287.1). Salustius relates the idea of likeness to the voluntary adhesion to the divine, like Origen: "When we are good we attach ourselves to the gods through likeness [δι' ὁμοιότητα], but when we become evil we separate ourselves from them through unlikeness [δι' ἀνομοιότητα]." Ps. Dionysius the Areopagite, the Christian Platonist who was very well acquainted with both Origen and Proclus, maintained likewise that likeness is the motor of the return or reversal, which in his view is associated with apokatastasis: "The power of the divine likeness is that which has all beings return [ἐπιστρέφουσα] to their Cause" (*Div. nom.* 9.6).

41. Ἥ τε γὰρ δεκὰς τὴν ἐπιστροφὴν πάντων δηλοῖ τῶν ἐγκοσμίων τὴν ἐπὶ τὸ ἕν, καὶ ἡ ἐνενηκοντὰς τὴν μετὰ τῆς προόδου πρὸς τὴν μονάδα πάλιν ἀποκατάστασιν.
42. Τὰς μὲν ψυχὰς διὰ τῆς κατ' ἀρετὴν ζωῆς τελεσιουργεῖν, τοῖς δὲ θνητοῖς ζῴοις τὴν εἰς τὸ εἶδος ἀποκατάστασιν χορηγεῖν.
43. See my *The Christian Doctrine of Apokatastasis*, section on Origen.

That Proclus had Origen's apokatastasis theory at the back of his mind seems all the more likely if one considers that in the immediately following proposition in the *Elementa theologiae* (33) Proclus enunciates another principle that was also a primary pillar of Origen's doctrine of apokatastasis, namely that the reversion/return/restoration/apokatastasis joins the end (τέλος) to the beginning (ἀρχή): "All that proceeds [προϊόν] from a principle and reverts [ἐπιστρέφον] to it has a cyclic activity. Indeed, if it reverts [ἐπιστρέφει] to the principle from which it proceeds [πρόεισιν], it *joins the end to the beginning* [συνάπτει τῇ ἀρχῇ τὸ τέλος] [...] *all beings* [πάντα] come from the first principle, and all revert to it." The very universality of the reversion/restoration is here enunciated and is certainly in full agreement with Origen's doctrine of universal, and not partial, restoration. The main difference is that Proclus envisages infinite beginnings (ἀρχαί) and infinite ends (τέλη), because infinite are the returns and the apokatastatic cycles in his system, while Origen, although he admits of many aeons, postulates only *one* beginning (ἀρχή) and *one* end (τέλος), which comes after the end of all aeons. Very interestingly, the principle connecting the *telos* to the *arkhē* emerged around the time of Origen also in his fellow disciple Plotinus ("for all beings the beginning is also the end," τέλος ἅπασιν ἡ ἀρχή, *Enn.* 3.8.7; see also 5.8.7). Then it returns in Iamblichus (*De myst.* 31.16) and Syrianus, Proclus's teacher (*In Met.* 38.3).

What is more, one proposition later (*Elem. theol.* 35) yet another tenet of Origen's restoration theory appears: that the reversal/restoration is to *oikeia*, that is, to what is proper and familiar to someone; this principle is reiterated at *In Remp.* 2.162.10: "each being must absolutely be restored [πάντως ἀποκαθίστασθαι] to the wholeness that is proper and familiar to it [εἰς τὴν ὁλότητα τὴν οἰκείαν]."[44] This is also why at *In Tim.* 3.57.3 Proclus speaks of a restoration of the soul "to itself" (ἀποκαθίσταται πρὸς ἑαυτήν). Indeed, another impressive similarity between Proclus and Origen in relation to the notion of the return and apokatastasis concerns precisely the concept of apokatastasis as *oikeiōsis.* Origen, as I have demonstrated elsewhere,[45] was the first who firmly established this link, which was then taken over by Gregory of Nyssa. He claimed that apokatastasis is an *oikeiōsis* because "the restoration is to a condition that is proper and familiar" to the creature who is being restored (ἡ ἀποκατάστασίς ἐστιν εἰς τὰ οἰκεῖα, *Hom. in Ier.* 14.18). No being can be restored to a condition that is alien to it and does not belong to its very nature and primordial state. Likewise Proclus in *Elem. theol.* 35, arguing for the necessity that immanence, procession and return be always present, all of them, excludes that there may ever be a return to a condition that is

44. See also *In Tim.* 3.308.11: ταῖς ψυχαῖς [...] ἡ ἀποκατάστασις εἰς ἓν ᾖ πάσης καὶ μὴ εἰς τὸ σύννομον ἄστρον ἀποκαταστᾶσα διὰ τὴν νομὴν εἰς ἄλλο ἀναγκάζηται ἀποκαθίστασθαι διὰ τὴν εἰς ἐκεῖνο σποράν· οἰκεῖον γὰρ τὸ σπειρόμενόν ἐστι τῷ περὶ ὃ ἔσπαρται κατ' οὐσίαν.

45. "The Stoic Doctrine of 'Oikeiōsis' and its Transformation in Christian Platonism," *Apeiron* 47 (2014) 116–140.

alien to the being that is returning: "If it should return only (without immanence or procession), how could that which has not its essence from that cause *make the return by essence to what is alien to it?*" (τὴν πρὸς τὸ ἀλλότριον ἐπιστροφήν). This is exactly what Origen too maintained, followed also by Gregory of Nyssa.

As Proclus remarks, the steps of the reversion mirror those of the procession: "Every reversion passes through the same terms as the corresponding procession" (*Elem. theol.* 38). In *Elem. theol.* 39, Proclus extends reversion to all beings, but to different degrees: some (inanimate beings) revert only in their being; others (animate but irrational beings) revert in their life too; and intelligent beings, and only these, revert in their knowledge. Indeed, in *Theol. Plat.* 3.6.22.19–23 Proclus explains that Life is participated in by all animate beings, including those which have no share in knowledge, while Intellect is only participated in by beings that are capable of knowledge. Life therefore irradiates its gifts to more beings than Intellect does. Likewise for Origen Christ-Logos is participated in by all rational or intellectual beings (*logika, noes*), the Holy Spirit by the saints – therefore, a more restricted group – and all creatures participate in God the Father and Creator, who is thus participated in by all existing beings.

Proclus's and Origen's similarities and differences in the notion of apokatastasis emerge nicely from *Elem. theol.* 146: in the cycle of procession and reversion "the end is similar to the beginning" (τὰ τέλη πρὸς τὰς ἑαυτῶν ἀρχὰς ὁμοιοῦται), but this process also forms a cycle that "has no beginning and no end" (ἄναρχον καὶ ἀτελεύτητον). Origen precisely maintained that the end will be "similar to the beginning," like Proclus, but unlike him Origen did *not* posit *infinite* cycles of reversion, because he postulated, on the basis of Scripture, both a creation in time and an end of time, so that after apokatastasis there will be no new beginning. He made this clear especially in his above-mentioned polemic against the Stoic theory of apokatastasis.[46]

The same difference can be noted within the following parallel. The supreme deity, to whom the monad belongs, is for Proclus the very cause of every apokatastasis (*In Remp.* 2.21.22; 2.20.5).[47] Origen too considered the supreme divinity, God as "Monad and Henad" (*Princ.* 1.1.6), to be the cause and the ultimate end of universal apokatastasis, but he thought that, once all rational beings have returned to God, there will be no new cycle of distancing from God and return. After all have attained unity with God and in God, this state will be definitive. And again the same difference emerges between Proclus and Origen within another parallel: like Origen,[48] Proclus too relates

46. See my *The Christian Doctrine of Apokatastasis*, ch. 1.

47. 2.21.22: ἡ μὲν μονὰς Διός ἐστι [...] ὁ πατὴρ πάσης ἀποκαταστάσεως αἴτιον; 2.20.5: πᾶσα γὰρ ἡ χρονικὴ σειρὰ τοῦ ἑνὸς ἐκείνου θεοῦ ἀνῆπται, μετροῦσα τῷ πάλιν καὶ πάλιν τὴν ἀποκατάστασιν ἑκάστων καθ' ἕνα καὶ τὸν αὐτὸν ὅρον.

48. He uses both ζωὴ ἀΐδιος, like Proclus, and ζωὴ αἰώνιος, a Biblical expression: see my "Origene ed il lessico dell'eternità," *Adamantius* 14 (2008) 100–129.

apokatastasis to eternal life, after purification (*In Remp.* 2.185.6).[49] However, again, for Origen the attainment of eternal life takes place once and for all for each individual, while Proclus envisages infinite cycles between eternal life and the world of generation. Yet another parallel between Proclus's and Origen's doctrine of apokatastasis concerns the notion that all that which is not already in actuality needs time to reach perfection and restoration by adhering to the Good and collecting all of its own goodness (πᾶν, ὃ μὴ ἀθρόως καὶ ἤδη καὶ ὁμοῦ τὸ πᾶν ἔχει τῆς ἐνεργείας, δεῖται τοῦ χρόνου πρὸς τελείωσιν καὶ ἀποκατάστασιν, δι' οὗ συλλέγει πᾶν τὸ οἰκεῖον ἀγαθόν, *In Tim.* 3.22.6). The very same idea was also found in Origen: apokatastasis can be reached only by adhesion to the Good and by rejecting all evil and collecting all the good that can be present in oneself; now this path toward perfection and restoration takes time (and both Origen and Proclus identify perfection and restoration). This is also why Origen postulated a series of whole aeons before the eventual apokatastasis, to give time to all to reach their perfection. But this is also where the difference between Proclus and Origen emerges again: for Origen there will be one and only one universal restoration at the end of all aeons, whereas for Proclus the restorations are infinite, just as time itself is infinite.

According to Proclus, "The soul measures its own life by circles of restoration" (ἡ ψυχὴ τῷ μὲν ἀποκαταστάσεσι καὶ περιόδοις μετρεῖν τὴν ἑαυτῆς ζωήν, *Theol. Plat.* 3.33.13).[50] He expands on the restoration or apokatastasis of the soul in *Elem. theol.* 199:

> Every soul that is in the cosmos has periods and restorations of her own, proper life (πᾶσα ψυχὴ ἐγκόσμιος περιόδοις χρῆται τῆς οἰκείας ζωῆς καὶ ἀποκαταστάσεσιν). For if it is measured by time and operates in a transitive way,[51] and movement is proper to it,[52] and all that which moves and participates in time, being perpetual [ἀίδιον], has periods and revolves in periods [χρῆται περιόδοις καὶ περιοδικῶς ἀνακυκλεῖται] and *is restored from the same state to the same state each time* [ἀποκαθίσταται ἀπὸ τῶν αὐτῶν ἐπὶ τὰ αὐτά],[53] then it is clear that every soul that is in the cosmos, having movement and operating in time, *will have periods of movements and restorations* [περιόδους τε τῶν κινήσεων ἕξει τε καὶ ἀποκαταστάσεις]. For *every period of perpetual beings involves a restoration* [πᾶσα γὰρ περίοδος τῶν ἀϊδίων ἀποκαταστατική ἐστι].

The association of apokatastasis – of souls and heavenly bodies alike – with cyclical periods is very frequent in Proclus,[54] who also ascribes this concept

49. Καθαιρόντων τὰ περιβλήματα αὐτῶν διὰ θείου φωτὸς καὶ ἀναμιμνησκόντων τῆς ἀϊδίου ζωῆς καὶ τῶν ἀποκαταστάσεων τῶν τελεωτάτων.
50. Cf. ibidem 4.101.17: τὰς περιόδους ἀφορίζουσι τῶν ψυχικῶν ἀποκαταστάσεων.
51. Cf. *Elem. theol.* 191.
52. Cf. *Elem. theol.* 20.
53. Cf. *Elem. theol.* 198.
54. E.g., in *Hypot. astr.* 1.30: τὰς περιοδικὰς ἀποκαταστάσεις; *In Tim.* 2.264.33: αἱ περιοδικαὶ πᾶσαι ἀποκαταστάσεις; 2.290.20: μιμεῖται γὰρ τόδε τὸ πᾶν τὴν ἀφανῆ περίοδον ἐκείνης διὰ

to Egyptians and Chaldaeans.[55] Among the "perpetual beings" of which Proclus speaks in the block quotation as subject to apokatastasis there are surely souls. Origen classified as rational souls (*logika*, more precisely rational beings or rational creatures) or intelligences (*noes*) angels, human beings, and demons. All of these originally enjoyed the same state of beatitude and were not differentiated into these three classes; they became differentiated due to the better or worse choices of their free will.[56] Porphyry, who knew Origen's theory of *logika* very well, in his *Letter to Anebo* asked precisely about the factors that distinguish from one another gods, demons, heroes, and souls (*ap.* Iambl. *De myst.* 61.11; 67.1).[57] Proclus, *In Tim.* 1.142.1, defines demons at large as "souls that are neither divine nor susceptible of transformation," but then in 3.165.11 he further classifies these into angels, demons proper, and heroes (ἄγγελοι, δαίμονες, ἥρωες). This tripartition was already present in the Middle Platonist Celsus and Origen (*C. Cels.* 7.78). The latter also wrote a specific treatise *On demons*.[58]

The cyclical and perpetual nature of the movement of restoration is further expounded upon by Proclus in *Elem. theol.* 198: "All being that participates in time and moves perpetually [ἀεὶ κινούμενον] is measured out by

---

τῆς οἰκείας σωματικῆς ἀνακυκλήσεως καὶ συναποκαθίσταται τοπικῶς τῇ ἀποκαταστάσει τῇ ἐκείνης, ἣν ποιεῖται νοητικῶς, καὶ τοῦτ' ἔστι τὸ ἐξαίρετον τῆς κοσμικῆς ψυχῆς; 2.292.24: πάλιν ἐν τῷ κόσμῳ τὰ αὐτὰ γίνεται, κατὰ δὲ τὰς τῆς ψυχῆς νοήσεις τὰ γιγνόμενα γίγνεται· οὔθ' ὕστερον, ἵνα μὴ ἀναίτιος ἡ ἀποκατάστασις ᾖ· τί γὰρ ἔσται τὸ περιέχον αὐτὴν ὅλην, εἰ μὴ ἡ τῆς ψυχῆς περίοδος; 3.28.29: τὸ εἰς τὸ αὐτὸ ἀποκαθίστασθαι καὶ ἓν διὰ τῆς κατὰ τὸν χρόνον κυκλήσεως; 3.29.20: μετὰ τὴν πᾶσαν ἀνέλιξιν τῆς ἑαυτοῦ δυνάμεως ἀποκαθιστάμενος οὕτω καὶ τὰς τῶν ἄλλων ἀποκαθίστησι περιόδους, ὅλῳ μὲν ἑαυτοῦ τῷ προελθόντι τὴν πρώτως αὐτοῦ μετέχουσαν ψυχὴν περιάγων; 3.57.13: ἡ φυλακὴ τῶν αὐτῶν ἀεὶ περιόδων καὶ ἀποκαταστάσεων; 3.64.3: μιᾶς εὐθείας κινουμένης ἡ ἀποκατάστασις μία, οὕτω καὶ οἱ τούτων ἐπίκυκλοι ποιοῦνται τὴν αὐτὴν ἀποκατάστασιν; 3.89.12: τὸν ἀριθμὸν τῶν ἑκάστου περιοδικῶν ἀποκαταστάσεων; 3.92.27–30: τὰ τάχη τῶν κύκλων τῶν τε οὐρανίων καὶ τῶν ὑπὸ σελήνην: εἰσὶ γὰρ καὶ ἐν τούτοις περίοδοι καὶ ἀποκαταστάσεις [...] καὶ γὰρ αἱ ἀποκαταστάσεις θεωροῦνται πρὸς τὰ αὐτῆς σημεῖα, οἷον ὅτι πάντες ἀποκατέστησαν περὶ τὸ ἰσημερινὸν σημεῖον ἢ περὶ τὸ θερινὸν τροπικόν; 3.127.24: τὰς περιόδους καὶ τὰς ἀποκαταστάσεις; 3.129.26: ἔχοντα καὶ αὐτὰ περιοδικὸν ἀριθμὸν τῆς ἰδίας ἀποκαταστάσεως, καθ' ὃν μετρεῖται ὁ σύμπας χρόνος; 3.138.15: συναποκαθιστὰς αὐτὴν ταῖς ἄλλαις καὶ ποιῶν ἐκ πασῶν μίαν πρὸς τὸν ταὐτοῦ κύκλον ἀποκατάστασιν; 3.150.17: αἵ τε ἀποκαταστάσεις καὶ αἱ ἀρχαὶ τῶν περιόδων; *In Remp.* 2.18.1: χρόνος ὡς χορόνους τις ὤν, τοῦ χορεύειν αἴτιος τῷ κόσμῳ, τῆς κατὰ κύκλον ἀποκαταστάσεως χορείας λεγομένης; 3.33.21: τὴν τάξιν τῶν περιόδων καὶ τὰ μέτρα τῶν ἀποκαταστάσεων; *Theol. Plat.* 4.59.13: περιφέρονται οὖν κύκλῳ καὶ ἀποκαθίστανται, τῆς οὐρανίας περιφορᾶς ἀεὶ τῆς αὐτῆς μενούσης; *Inst. phys.* 2.6: τὸ κύκλῳ κινούμενον ἀποκαθίσταται; *In I Eucl. Elem.* 213.26–214.1: αἱ ψυχαὶ [...] διὰ τῶν ἀποκαταστάσεων καὶ τῶν περιόδων.

55. *In Remp.* 2.236.2: ποῖαι καὶ ὅλων κοσμικῶν περιόδων καὶ ἀποκαταστάσεων ἦσαν ἱστορίαι.
56. Full analysis in my *The Christian Doctrine*, section on Origen.
57. On this work see now the new edition and essays by H. D. Saffrey, A.-Ph. Segonds, *Porphyre : Lettre à Anébon l'Égyptien*, Collection des universités de France. Serie grecque 492, Paris : Les Belles Lettres 2012. Now also Iamblichus's response is available in the same series: H. D. Saffrey, A.-Ph. Segonds, *Jamblique : Réponse à Porphyre (De mysteriis)*, Collection des universités de France. Série grecque 496, Paris: Les Belles Lettres, 2013.
58. Arguments for the attribution of this treatise to Origen the Christian Neoplatonist in: I. Ramelli, "Origen, Patristic Philosophy."

periods [περιόδοις μετρεῖται]. Indeed, since it participates in time, its movement has a share in measure and limit, and it proceeds according to number. And since it moves perpetually [ἀεί], and this perpetuity does not transcend time but is within time [τὸ ἀεὶ τοῦτο οὐκ αἰώνιόν ἐστι, ἀλλὰ χρονικόν],[59] it necessarily has cyclic periods. [...] What moves perpetually *cannot be transformed a limited number of times*. Therefore, *what moves perpetually will return from the same state to the same state, so to form a cyclic period* [ἀπὸ τῶν αὐτῶν ἄρα ἐπὶ τὰ αὐτὰ πάλιν ἥξει τὸ ἀεὶ κινούμενον, ὥστε ποιῆσαι περίοδον]." The perpetuity and infinity of this movement is what distinguishes Proclus's restoration theory from Origen's most of all; it is highlighted by Proclus many times throughout his works, for instance in *In Tim.* 3.18.16 (χρονικῆς *ἀιδιότητος* [...] κυκλικῆς ἀποκαταστάσεως) and also elsewhere.[60]

The apokatastasis of the soul is opposed to the world of generation and becoming. For there are two arrangements: the better, harmonic, tends to the restoration of the soul, the other to the cycles of rebirth (*In Remp.* 2.67.1).[61] Souls have intellectual restorations (αἱ ἀποκαταστάσεις αἱ νοεραί), which cannot be perceived by senses (*In Tim.* 3.149.26; 3.308.22). Each soul has its own periods and restorations, and differences among these are due to partial souls' life in time:

> Every period of the soul is measured by time, but the period of the other souls is measured by a certain time, while the period of the first soul is measured by *the totality of time* [τῷ σύμπαντι χρόνῳ]. For if all movements entail a "first" and an "after," cyclic periods too, then, do. And for this reason they participate in time, and *time is what measures all the cyclic periods of the soul*. Now, if the periods were the same for all souls, and all had the same vicissitudes, the time, too, would be the same for all of them. But if *their restorations are different from one another* [ἄλλαι ἄλλων ἀποκαταστάσεις], *the time of their cyclic periods, too, and their restorations will vary*. [...] All other souls (apart from the world soul) are measured by given measures that are more limited than the whole of time. This is clear from the following consideration. If those souls are more limited than the soul which participates in time primarily, they will not

59. For the meaning of αἰώνιος as "transcending time" in the Platonic tradition and the difference from ἀΐδιος see I. Ramelli, D. Konstan, *Terms for Eternity: Αἰώνιος and ἀΐδιος in Classical and Christian Authors*, Piscataway: Gorgias 2007, new editions 2011 and 2013, and the reviews by C. O'Brien, *The Classical Review* 60, 2 (2010) 390–391 and D. Ghira, *Maia* 61 (2009) 732–734.

60. E.g. *In Tim.* 3.29.7: πάλιν ἀποκαθισταμένη καὶ τοῦτο ποιοῦσα πολλάκις, μᾶλλον δὲ ἀπειράκις; 3.20.29–21.1: ὡς αὐτὸν αἰωνίως προειληφότα καὶ νοοῦντα τὸν σύμπαντα τῶν ἐν τῷ κόσμῳ κινουμένων ἁπάντων ἀριθμόν, καθ' ὃν πάντα τὰ κινούμενα περιάγει καὶ ἀποκαθίστησι περιόδοις θάττοσιν ἢ βραδυτέραις, καὶ πρὸς τούτοις ἀπέραντον διὰ τὴν δύναμιν (τὸ γὰρ πάλιν καὶ πάλιν ἀνακυκλεῖν; *In Parm.* 1218.20: ἔχει τὴν ἴσην ἀποκατάστασιν, αὕτη δὲ κατὰ τὸν αὐτῆς ἀεὶ χρόνον.

61. Διττῆς τῆς ἁρμονίας οὔσης καὶ τῆς ἀμείνονος σαφῶς εἰρημένης εἰς τὴν ἀποκατάστασιν τείνειν τῆς ψυχῆς, ἡ λοιπὴ ἂν εἴη γενέσει φίλη. Proclus speaks of the restoration of souls a number of times, e.g. *In Tim.* 1.54.8: τήνδε τὴν ψυχὴν ἴδῃς ἀποκαταστᾶσαν.

> adapt their periods to the totality of time either, but *their many restorations will be parts of the one great period and restoration* [αἱ πολλαὶ αὐτῶν ἀποκαταστάσεις μέρη ἔσονται μιᾶς περιόδου καὶ ἀποκαταστάσεως], *that in which the soul that primarily participates in time is restored* [ἣν ἡ χρόνου μετέχουσα πρώτως ἀποκαθίσταται]. Indeed, the more limited participation characterises a lesser power, the more universal characterises a greater power. Therefore, the other souls cannot by nature receive the full measure of time during one single life, because they have been assigned a place subordinate to that soul which is measured by time primarily. (*Elem. theol.* 200).

It is clear that each individual soul has its apokatastasis, each one different from those of other partial souls, but the world soul, whose period is measured by the totality of time, has an apokatastasis that coincides with one great period. This notion that the partial restorations of single souls, each involving a fraction of time, make up the universal restoration, which coincides with the totality of time, is hammered home by Proclus in many passages.[62] Thus, Proclus postulates different measures and periods for the restorations of partial souls and bodies, but one single measure and one big period for the universal restoration (*In Tim.* 3.54.21; *In I Eucl. Elem.* 149.1).[63] Partial souls and bodies have different paces, slower or faster, in their periodic restorations,[64] but they are all unified in the cosmic restoration. With its own restoration, the world soul restores the whole universe with itself (τῇ γὰρ αὐτῆς ἀποκαταστάσει συναποκαθίσταται τὸ πᾶν, *In Tim.* 2.292.21).

The totality of time coinciding with a single cyclic period of the world soul, of which Proclus speaks in *Elem. theol.* 200, in turn, cannot be the infinity of time – since a cycle must by definition be finite – but a cosmic cycle, which is concluded by a cosmic apokatastasis, that is, the restoration not of one partial soul, but of all partial souls together. This is the apokatastasis of the world soul, which includes the restoration of all other souls: "Time,

62. *In Tim.* 2.289.29: μόνην ἄρα δεῖ πρὸς τὸν σύμπαντα χρόνον ἐνεργεῖν, αἱ δὲ ἄλλαι πρὸς μόριον τοῦ σύμπαντος χρόνου ἐνεργοῦσι, καθ' ὃ καὶ ἡ ἀποκατάστασις αὐταῖς; 2.290.7: νοοῦσα δ' οὖν καθ' ἓν ἔχει τὴν ἀποκατάστασιν κατὰ τὸν ὅλον χρόνον τὸν περιέχοντα τὴν τοῦ θείου γενητοῦ περίοδον; 2.290.11: πᾶσαι γὰρ ἐν μέρει τοῦ ἑνὸς ἐν τῷ παντὶ χρόνῳ τὰς ἀποκαταστάσεις ἔχουσιν, ἅτε καὶ *μερικώτερα* ἀνελίττουσαι, ἡ δὲ νοερὰ τοῦ ἑνὸς νοητοῦ κόσμου νοοῦσα καὶ ἐκπεριιοῦσα *τῷ ὅλῳ χρόνῳ* συμπεραίνει τὴν ἑαυτῆς περίοδον; 3.306.6: χρόνους, καθ' οὓς ὁ πᾶς μετρεῖται χρόνος τοῦ κοσμικοῦ βίου, καὶ κοινὰς ἔχουσι πρὸς ἐκεῖνον καὶ πρὸς ἀλλήλους ἀποκαταστάσεις.
63. Respectively: Καὶ ταῖς ψυχαῖς αἱ περίοδοι καὶ τοῖς σώμασιν ἐπιτελοῦνται καὶ τὸ ἓν μέτρον τῆς ὅλης ἀποκαταστάσεως, and Ταῖς δὲ ψυχαῖς [...] τὸ ἀποκαθίστασθαι κατὰ τὰς οἰκείας περιόδους. The notion of measure is intrinsic to the periodic movement of apokatastasis: *In Remp.* 2.18.17: ἀποκαθιστὰς πάντα κατὰ τὰ ἑαυτῷ σύμφυτα μέτρα.
64. *In Remp.* 2.20.19: πῶς ἀποκαθίστησι τὸν κόσμον κατὰ τοὺς οἰκείους ὅρους, πάντων οὖσα κινητικὴ τῶν ἐγκοσμίων, τῶν βραχυπόρων καὶ μακροπόρων; 2.226: τοὺς μὲν θᾶττον ἀποκαθίστασθαι, τοὺς δὲ βραδύτερον; *In Tim.* 2.289.18: δεῖ γὰρ ἀποκαταστῆναι πάντως [...] ἡ δὲ ἀποκατά στασις ἄλλη ἄλλαις, ταῖς μὲν βραχυπορωτέρα, ταῖς δὲ μακροπορωτέρα; 3.76.16: ἡ ἀποκατάστασις ἄλλη ἄλλων καὶ τῶν μὲν βραδυτέρα, τῶν δὲ θάττων; 3.87.15: ἡ τῆς ἀπλανοῦς περίοδός ἐστι ταχίστη, τὰ δὲ ἔγγιον αὐτῆς βραδύτερα τῶν πορρωτέρω κατὰ τὴν ἀποκατάστασιν.

revolving upon itself in a circle, *is restored* [ἀποκαθιστάμενος] together with the whole revolving of its own power, and thus it also *restores the cyclic periods of the other souls* [τὰς τῶν ἄλλων ἀποκαθίστησι περιόδους] [...] the same scheme returns again and again, *perpetually*" (*In Tim.* 3.29.18); "the totality of time is the complete number of the restoration of the universe" (ὅλος δέ ἐστι χρόνος ὁ τέλειος ἀριθμὸς τῆς τοῦ παντὸς ἀποκαταστάσεως, *ibidem* 3.95.6). In *In Remp.* 2.11.25 Proclus describes time (ὁ χρόνος) as "the whole measure of the common apokatastasis of all movements, corporeal and incorporeal" (τῆς τῶν ἐν αὐτῷ πάντων ἀσωμάτων κινήσεων καὶ σωματικῶν πασῶν κοινῆς συναποκαταστάσεως μέτρον παντελές):[65] now, this, "continuously recurring [πολλάκις ἀνελισσόμενον], makes up the *infinite time* [ποιεῖ τὸν ἄπειρον χρόνον]." Like Origen, Proclus postulates a universal apokatastasis, but, once again unlike him, Proclus thinks that this apokatastasis does not happen once and for all at the end of time, but repeats itself infinite times, even if on extremely long cycles. For the universe itself is imperishable, it was not created in time and therefore will never perish at a certain point in time: "the entire time embraces the whole life of the apokatastasis of the universe. What does not perish within this time is imperishable. Indeed, nothing perishable can endure for the totality of time" (*In Remp.* 2.12.2).[66]

The doctrine of cosmic cycles, each one concluding with an apokatastasis, seems to have been already present in Middle Platonism, which in turn integrated this element from Stoicism. It is not accidental that Origen, well steeped in Middle Platonism, felt the need to criticise the Stoic doctrine of apokatastasis, as I have mentioned, in order to highlight the main differences between it and his own Christian theory of apokatastasis. The Middle Platonists probably projected the Stoic doctrine of apokatastasis into Plato's *Politicus* myth. Actually I suspect that this myth influenced the Stoic theory of apokatastasis itself.

It seems that, according to Proclus, a cyclic period of a human soul – much shorter than the great, cosmic period – is not to be regarded as one single human life, but as the cycle that begins with the descent of the soul with its incarnation and ends with its restoration to contemplation. This cycle can embrace many human lives. In Plato's *Phaedrus* 248E ff. the minimum interval is said to be 3000 years, encompassing three incarnations of the soul. Plato in *Tim.* 42B seems to admit that the return of a soul to the appropriate star can occur after one incarnation only. Proclus, however, in *In Tim.* 3.291 remarks that this is not a complete ἀποκατάστασις.

65. That universal apokatastasis is both bodily and noetic is made clear in *In Tim.* 2.290.17: ἀνελίττειν καὶ διὰ τοῦτο κατὰ τὸν τέλειον ἀριθμὸν τῆς κοσμικῆς περιόδου ποιεῖσθαι τὴν *νοητικὴν* ἑαυτῆς ἀποκατάστασιν, καθ' ὃν ποιεῖται καὶ τὴν *σωματικὴν* ὅλην περίοδον.

66. Πᾶς ὢν χρόνος τὸν πάντα βίον ἔχει τῆς τοῦ παντὸς ἀποκαταστάσεως, ἐν ᾧ τὸ μὴ φθαρὲν ἄφθαρτόν ἐστιν. οὐδὲν οὖν φθαρτὸν μένει τὸν ἅπαντα χρόνον.

The Embodiment of Souls: Proclus and Christian Neoplatonism

The doctrine of apokatastasis – which concerns primarily souls – is linked in Proclus, just as in Origen, with the theory of the soul-body relation and the vehicles of the soul.[67] Proclus's doctrine of the soul's corporeal vehicle, different from Plotinus's doctrine, will therefore have to be examined as well, at least briefly, and a comparison will have to be drawn with Christian Platonists such as Origen and Gregory Nyssa. According to Proclus, at the beginning of a cyclic apokatastatic period the soul acquires a second vehicle (ὄχημα), after the immaterial and immortal one of which Proclus speaks in *Elem. theol.* 208 and to which I shall return in a moment. This second vehicle is in turn different from the mortal body. At the restoration or apokatastasis, the soul will be purified and liberated from the second vehicle as well as the heavy body (*In Tim.* 3.237). These degrees from an immortal to a mortal and heavy body are also found in Origen from the Christian side of Platonism. Proclus describes the first vehicle of the soul in *Elem. theol.* 208 as follows: "The vehicle [ὄχημα] of every partial soul is immaterial [ἄϋλον], indivisible by essence, and not subject to passions." This corresponds to Origen's description of the spiritual body that all rational creatures had at the very beginning of their creation, an immaterial and impassible body which served as a vehicle of the rational soul. Plotinus, too, spoke of a "luminous vehicle" (αὐγοειδὲς ὄχημα), which souls assume in their descent in *Treatises* 14, 26, and 27. Origen too, Plotinus's fellow disciple at the school of Ammonius Saccas in Alexandria, very probably deemed rational creatures to be endowed, from the very beginning of their existence as substances, with a subtle body, which may or may not become a heavy and mortal body on account of their sin. There is even a verbal resonance between Origen and Plotinus, given that Origen too designated the subtle and spiritual body of rational creatures as both αὐγοειδές and an ὄχημα. The latter notion is clearly conveyed by the sentence, "The soul is said to have first used the luminous body as a vehicle; later this was covered with the skin tunics," that is, mortal corporeality (τῷ δὲ αὐγοειδεῖ τὴν ψυχὴν *ἐποχεῖσθαι* πρώτῳ λέγουσιν, ὅπερ ὕστερον ἐνεδύσατο τοὺς δερματίνους χιτῶνας, *ap.* Procop. *Comm. in Gen.* PG 87.1.221A). Origen's description of the spiritual body as αὐγοειδές is further confirmed by the sixth-century theologian Gobar (*ap.* Phot. *Bibl.* cod. 232.288a).

Exactly like Origen, who rejected the notion of the preexistence of "bare" souls without any corporeal vehicle, Proclus too thinks that every soul always has an immaterial, simple, and impassible vehicle. Origen deems both the rational soul or intellect and its immortal body to be created by God at a

67. On Origen on body/bodies and soul(s), documentation in my "'Preexistence of Souls'? The ἀρχή and τέλος of Rational Creatures in Some Origenian Authors," *Studia Patristica* LVI, 4 (2013) 167–226.

certain point, prior to the existence of the material world, but not coeternal with God. Proclus also speaks of the soul and its immortal vehicle as created (*Elem. theol.* 207: "the vehicle [ὄχημα] of every partial soul has been created [δεδημιούργηται] by an immovable cause") and perpetual in time (ἀίδιον, *ibidem* 208 and 196), though not eternal in the sense of beyond time (the meaning of αἰώνιος in Platonism[68]).

In *Elem. theol.* 196 Proclus makes it clear that the immaterial, invisible, and impassible vehicle of the soul is actually an immortal body, which here he describes as ἀγένετον, not in the sense that it is uncreated, which would contradict *Elem. theol.* 207, but in the sense that it has no beginning in time – otherwise it should also have an end in time, as imposed by the perishability axiom:

> Every participated soul uses at first *a body, which is perpetual and has a constitution without beginning in time and incorruptible* [πᾶσα ψυχὴ μεθεκτὴ σώματι χρῆται πρώτῳ ἀϊδίῳ, καὶ ἀγένετον ἔχοντι τὴν ὑπόστασιν καὶ ἄφθαρτον]. For if every soul is perpetual by essence [κατ' οὐσίαν ἀίδιος] and if by its very being it ensouls primarily one of the bodies, *it will ensoul it always* [ἀεί]; for the being of every soul is unchangeable. If so, the body ensouled by it is *in turn always* [ἀεί] *ensouled and always participates in life*. Now, what lives always much more exists always. But what exists always is perpetual [ἀίδιον]. Therefore, *the body that is at first ensouled and attached to any soul is perpetual* [ἀίδιον]. But every participated soul is at first participated by a body, if it is true that it is participated and not unparticipated, and by its very being ensouls the body that participates in it. Therefore, *every soul that is participated uses at first a body that is perpetual* [ἀϊδίῳ], *not created in time, and incorruptible by essence*. (*Elem. theol.* 196)

The spiritual body, being not created in time, and being not composed, will not decay, nor have an end in time. Unlike Plotinus's or Porphyry's, Proclus's position that a soul perpetually uses a body as a vehicle, from the very beginning and independently of its descent or fall, comes remarkably close to Origen's. Like Origen, also, Proclus thinks that angels have a spiritual body, which per se has no shape – they are ἀμόρφωτοι – but can take on a shape when they condescendingly appear to humans ἐν μορφῇ (Procl. *De sacr. et magia*, *ap.* Psell. *Scripta minora* 1.150.13–14).

As Origen did, then, Proclus too speaks of one single immortal body of each soul, which can be transformed into heavy and earthly by accretion of "tunics" – like Origen's Biblical skin tunics, and Porphyry's skin tunic[69] – upon it:

68. Ramelli-Konstan, *Terms for Eternity*, 22–38.
69. Porphyry, who knew Origen's work, used the same notion of skin tunic in *Abst.* 2.46: "In the Father's temple, i.e. this world, is it not prudent to keep pure our last garment, the skin tunic, and thus, with this tunic made pure, live in the Father's temple?" and 1.31: "We must remove these many garments, both this visible garment of flesh and those inside, which are close to those of skin." Origen maintained that "initially the soul used the luminous

> The vehicle [ὄχημα] of every partial soul descends by way of *addition of tunics that are more and more material* [χιτόνων ἐνυλοτέρων], and ascends together with the soul thanks to the removal of all that is material and to the return to the form that is proper to it, analogously to the soul that uses it. The soul too, indeed, descends by receiving irrational forms of life, while it ascends by dropping off all the powers that activate the process of generation, which the soul had put on during the descent. [...] Since souls, by their very existence, vivify their vehicles, and the latter are *created together* [συμφυῆ] *with their souls*, they change in every respect together with the activities of the souls, and *follow them everywhere*: when the souls experience passions, their vehicles suffer the same with them; *once the souls have been purified, their vehicles are restored together with them* [κεκαθαρμέναις συναποκαθίσταται]; when the souls are lifted up, the vehicles rise with them, desiring their own perfection. For every being attains perfection when it reaches its own wholeness. (*Elem. theol.* 209)

Even Proclus's notion of a common restoration of soul and body after a period of purification, which is clear in this passage, is identical to that of Origen. The same notion that purification must precede apokatastasis to the divine world is reflected in *In Remp.* 1.120.14 in reference to Heracles, who after being purified obtained "the perfect restoration to the deities" (ὁ μὲν γὰρ Ἡρακλῆς διὰ τελεστικῆς καθηράμενος καὶ τῶν ἀχράντων καρπῶν μετασχὼν τελέας ἔτυχεν τῆς εἰς θεοὺς ἀποκαταστάσεως). Restoration is perfect when it crowns a philosophical life. This is why in *In Tim.* 3.291.32–292.2 Proclus, referring to Plato's *Phaedrus*, draws a distinction between non-philosophical souls, who can ascend to their own heavenly body within one period, and philosophical souls, who are restored to the intelligible realm after three periods.[70] If souls attain a restoration without having lived a philosophical life, this restoration is not perfect since they cannot rise to the intelligible realm (*In Remp.* 2.169.8).[71] The perfect restoration of the soul is noetic (*In Tim.* 2.248.20),[72] as Origen, Gregory of Nyssa, and Evagrius also maintained.

[αὐγοειδεῖ] body as a vehicle [ἐποχεῖσθαι], and this body was later clothed in the skin tunics" (*Comm. in Gen.* 3:21, PG 87/1.221A). See also my "Iamblichus, 'De anima' 38 (66.12–15 Finamore-Dillon): A Resolving Conjecture?," *Rheinisches Museum* 157 (2014) 106–111.

70. Τοῦτο ἐν τῷ Φαίδρῳ λέλεκται περὶ τῶν μὴ φιλοσόφων ψυχῶν, ὧν ἄλλη ἡ εἰς τὸ αὐτὸ πάλιν ἀποκατάστασις, ἄλλη ἡ εἰς τὸ σύννομον ἄστρον ἄνοδος· ἣ μὲν γὰρ τριῶν δεῖται περιόδων, ἣ δὲ καὶ διὰ μιᾶς γένοιτο ἄν, καὶ ἣ μὲν εἰς τὸ νοητὸν ἀνάγει τὴν ψυχήν. Likewise *In Tim.* 3.291.22: ὁ τὸν φιλόσοφον βίον ἑλόμενος διὰ τριῶν ἀποκαθίστατο βίων (with reference to *Phaedr.* 249AB). For a soul's restoration to its heavenly body see also *In Tim.* 3.291.18: τῶν μετὰ τὴν πρώτην γένεσιν εἰς τὸ σύννομον ἄστρον ἀποκαθισταμένων [...] αὐτὰς ἀπολειπούσας τὸ σῶμα βίον ἕξειν εὐδαίμονα = *In Remp.* 2.130.24: δηλοῖ δὲ ὁ Τίμαιος τὴν εἰς τὸ σύννομον ἄστρον ἀποκαταστᾶσαν εὐδαίμονα βίον λέγων ἕξειν, both with reference to *Tim.* 42B. Also *Theol. Plat.* 6.34.10: τὰς εἰς τὸ σύννομον ἄστρον ἀποκαταστάσεις; *In Tim.* 3.308.12: μὴ εἰς τὸ σύννομον ἄστρον ἀποκαταστᾶσα διὰ τὴν νομὴν εἰς ἄλλο ἀναγκάζηται ἀποκαθίστασθαι.
71. Ταῖς ἀπὸ γενέσεως στελλομέναις εἰς γένεσιν ψυχαῖς, πρὸ τῆς τελείας, ὡς εἴπομεν πρότερον, ἀποκαταστάσεως;
72. Ἐπειδὴ τὸ ζωτικὸν τῆς ψυχῆς νοερόν ἐστι καὶ ἀποκαταστατικὸν καὶ τὸ νοητὸν πλῆθος ἀνελίττον, ἐπὶ τὸ αὐτὸ πάλιν ἀποκαθίσταται.

Proclus – following Syrianus, as it seems – postulated the existence of two ὀχήματα of the soul, not only in *Elem. theol.* 196 and 207–209, as I have shown, but also in *In Tim.* 3.236 and 3.297–298.[73] The first and higher is, as I have indicated, immaterial, simple, immortal, and not liable to passions, and is called by Proclus αὐγοειδές, ἀστροειδές, and συμφυές. Proclus identifies this vehicle with the vehicle in which the Demiurge places the soul according to Plato, *Tim.* 41E. The inferior, and subsequent, vehicle of the soul is called by Proclus πνευματικόν and is composed by the four elements (on the basis of *Tim.* 42B).[74] It is not the vehicle of the rational soul, as the first, luminous body is, but rather the vehicle of the inferior, irrational soul. As such, even if it survives the death of the mortal, heavy and earthly body, it is doomed to disappear. In *In Tim.* 3.297.21–298.2 Proclus distinguishes the first, immortal vehicle of the soul, the "connate vehicle" (σύμφυτον ὄχημα), from a second one, called "vehicle of irrational life" (ἡ ἄλογος ζωὴ καὶ τὸ ἐκείνης ὄχημα) and "mass" (ὄγκος) derived "from the simple elements" (ἀπὸ τῶν ἁπλῶν στοιχείων), a "compound made of various kinds of tunics" (ἐκ παντοδαπῶν χιτώνων συγκείμενον) which weighs the soul down. This is because a soul could not pass immediately from immaterial pneuma to the earthly body (ἀμέσως ἀπὸ τῶν ἀύλων πνευμάτων εἰς τόδε τὸ σῶμα χωρεῖν). Therefore, "during their descent to earth souls receive, one after the other, different kinds of tunics [χιτῶνας] made of the elements, air, water, and earth, and only afterwards, in the end, enter this thick mass [εἰς τὸν ὄγκον τὸν παχὺν τοῦτον]." The "second vehicle" (τὸ δεύτερον ὄχημα) appears again at *In Tim.* 3.330.20–22, where it is identified once more with "the irrational mass [ὄγκος ἄλογος] drawn from fire, air, water, and earth."[75] Proclus inter-

73. Proclus's doctrine of the two ὀχήματα will be taken over by Philoponus (*De an.* 12–14 Hayduck) and probably also by Macrobius (*In Somn.* 1.12.13), who speaks of a *luminosi corporis amictus*, and who ascribes the doctrine of universal apokatastasis to Plato (see above). Macrobius too was acquainted with the doctrine of apokatastasis of some Christian Platonists. In the passage cited, and in 1.11.12, Macrobius states that the soul, descending through the planetary spheres, acquires a body that is *sidereum* and *luminosum*, which correspond to Greek ἀστροειδές and αὐγοειδές.

74. Proclus, like Origen and most Platonists, rejected the Aristotelian "fifth body" or "element" (*In Tim.* 2.42.9ff.); in *Theol. Plat.* 1.19.51, when he says that they are "immaterial", he uses ἄϋλος in the same relative sense as Origen often uses it, not meaning without matter or body in an absolute sense, but as compared with heavy, earthly bodies. In *CC* 4.56 Origen remarked that Aristotle and the Peripatetics "maintain that aether is immaterial, and is of a fifth substance besides that of the other four elements; against this theory the Platonists and the Stoics adduced noteworthy arguments." Likewise in *Comm. in Io.* 13.266 Origen accepted the four elements. Origen's rejection of the fifth element was in line with that of some Middle Platonists. Atticus, for instance, in fr. 5 Des Places criticised Aristotle for deviating from Plato, who admitted of only four elements. Taurus also seems to have rejected the fifth element (see G. Karamanolis, *Plato and Aristotle in Agreement*, Oxford: OUP 2006, 185). Plotinus certainly did, as is clear from *Enn.* 2.1.2, and Porphyry hammered home that Plato's doctrine contemplated only four elements, and that the doctrine of the fifth element is alien to Plato's teaching (*ap.* Philop. *De aet. mundi* 521–522).

75. For an analysis of these passages see J. Finamore's lecture at the Panel, "Lovers of the Soul, Lovers of the Body: Platonists on the Soul and the Body," ISNS International Conference,

prets the myth of Plato's *Phaedo*, where those who dwell in the high places of the earth are mentioned, as a reference to souls still linked to this inferior, second vehicle, who are awaiting their complete restoration (ἀποκατάστασις, *In Tim.* 3.309.26). This restoration will liberate them from the second vehicle, but not from the first, which is permanently attached to the rational soul. Basically, this is also what Origen assumed. Both at the beginning, at their creation, and at the end, at their restoration, rational souls or intellects are joined with a luminous, immortal, and spiritual vehicle.

The idea that the soul is permanently accompanied by a body, from the very beginning, not only is common to Proclus and Origen – whatever the specific relation between their two theories – but it seems to have been supported by someone else, too, within Platonism: according to Iamblichus (*ap.* Stob. *Anth.* 1.378: 904 Hense), "the followers of Eratosthenes and Ptolemy the Platonist, and others" also thought that the soul is always joined to a body and before having an earthly body had "subtler" bodies (λεπτότερα). What is unclear, however, is whether according to the thinkers mentioned by Iamblichus each soul has one body, which by accretion can become heavier – as Origen and Proclus think – or has different bodies of different kinds. At any rate, Proclus, unlike Plotinus but like Origen and Gregory of Nyssa, seems to refuse to admit that human souls can ever exist without a body, thus denying that souls preexist their bodies and receive a body only as a result of a fault. On the other hand, unlike Iamblichus, but again like Origen and Gregory of Nyssa, Proclus did not admit that the inferior faculties of the soul – the irrational layers of the soul, so to say – are immortal.[76]

Of course Proclus, as a "pagan" Platonist, did not envisage a resurrection of the body together with the restoration of the soul, but the resurrection theorised by Origen and Gregory of Nyssa, a resurrection of the *spiritual* body of the beginning, comes remarkably close to Proclus's idea of the apokatastatic return to the first body, the spiritual body that from the beginning accompanies the rational soul. The real difference between Proclus and those Christian Neoplatonists is not so much the resurrection itself, as – I think – the infinity of the apokatastatic cycles that Proclus maintains in conformity with the theory of the perpetuity of the world. Origen and Gregory of Nyssa, instead, taking for granted that this world was created in time, also thought that it will have an end in time. Their motivation was not only the perishability axiom, well known to all Platonists, but also Scripture, which speaks of the end of the world. As a consequence, both Origen and Gregory thought that there is a cyclical succession of aeons, but this succession is finite, and it will have an end exactly with the eventual apokatastasis. This restoration, at the end

Cardiff University, 12–15 June 2013, forthcoming in: *Lovers of Souls and Lovers of Bodies: Philosophical and Religious Perspectives in Platonism*, eds. I. Ramelli and S. Slaveva Griffin, Cambridge, MA: Harvard University Press.

76. For the immortality of the rational soul but the disappearance of the irrational parts or faculties at apokatastasis according to Gregory Nyssen see my *Gregorio di Nissa sull'anima*.

of all aeons, that is, at the end of time, will occur only once, and not infinite times, as Proclus seems to postulate. This appears to be the main difference between Proclus and these Christian Neoplatonists.

As I have mentioned earlier, Plato in *Phaedr.* 248CE suggested that, if a soul can attain a vision of the Forms, it will be released from incarnation for a cycle of ten thousand years, just as a soul that chooses the life of the philosopher for three subsequent periods of one thousand years. Proclus himself glosses the *Phaedrus* passage as a reference to the apokatastasis of the soul from the realm of generation and becoming[77] to the intelligible world (although the expression was absent from Plato): δηλοῖ δὲ καὶ αὐτὸς ἐν Φαίδρῳ διὰ μυρίων ἐτῶν *ἀποκαθιστὰς τὴν ψυχὴν* ἀπὸ γενέσεως εἰς τὸ νοητόν (*In Remp.* 2.52.19; also *Theol. Plat.* 4.87.14[78]). The perfect restoration is indeed the attainment of "the knowledge of all" or γνῶσις πάντων (*In Remp.* 2.168.16).[79] And again in *In Remp.* 1.175.26 Proclus refers to the same Platonic passage when he states that "souls, after being bridled for nine thousand years on earth, are restored at the tenth thousand" (ἐννέα χιλιάδας ἐτῶν περὶ γῆν αἱ ψυχαὶ καλινδούμεναι κατὰ τὴν δεκάτην ἀποκαθίστανται). Only in one passage does Proclus suggest that the restoration after ten thousand years may be definitive: in *In Remp.* 2.170.27 he says that after such a restoration there is no other biological life, because the myriad is the limit of all generations.[80] This, however, may also mean that there is no other biological life during that myriad, but there can be others in the following myriads. Not all souls, according to Proclus, can attain restoration to the intelligible realm: the less rational among them either are not restored at all to the intelligible realm, or are restored to it only with great difficulty, or as the latest of all (*In Crat.* 117.23).[81]

Among "pagan" Neoplatonists, Plotinus seems to have postulated no release for the soul from the cycles of incarnation, and therefore infinite restorations to the intelligible world at the end of each cycle. Porphyry in *De regressu animae*, at least if one trusts Augustine (*CD* 10.30; 12.27), claimed that the soul of the philosopher alone will finally be released forever. The soul,

77. The passage "from generation to generation before the perfect restoration" is associated by Proclus with the thousand years or chiliad: *In Remp.* 2.161.14: ἔοικεν ἡ χιλιὰς χρόνος εἶναί τις περιοδικὸς ἀπὸ γενέσεως ἐπὶ γένεσιν ἄγων τὰς ψυχάς [...] πρὸ τῆς τελέας ἀποκαταστάσεως. εἰ γὰρ ἄνευ φιλοσοφίας οὐράνιαι γεγόνασιν, οὔπω μὲν ἀνήχθησαν εἰς τὴν νοητὴν φύσιν; 2.328.20: τῆς ἀπὸ γενέσεως ἐπὶ γένεσιν πρὸ ἀποκαταστάσεως τῶν ψυχῶν τελέας χιλιέτους οὔσης πορείας.

78. Ὡς ὁ ἐν τῷ Φαίδρῳ λέγει Σωκράτης, τρισχιλιέτεις καὶ μυριέτεις ἀποκαταστάσεις ἡμῖν παραδιδούς.

79. Δέονται γὰρ *μαθεῖν*, οὐκ ἔχουσαι γνῶσιν πάντων· οὐ γὰρ ἦν ἡ *ἀποκατάστασις* αὐτῶν ἡ *τελεωτάτη* δι' ἔθη βέλτιστα τῆς ἐν οὐρανῷ τυχουσῶν λήξεως.

80. Ἡ παντελὴς διέξοδος ἐτῶν μυρίων μόλις ἀποκαθίστησιν τὴν ψυχήν, καὶ *μετὰ ταύτην ἄλλος οὐκ ἔστι βίος*· πέρας γὰρ ἡ μυριάς, πάντων οὖσα βίων ἀριθμός, πασῶν γενέσεων, πασῶν περιόδων.

81. Τὰ ἀλογωδέστερα τῶν ψυχῶν γένη ἢ οὐδ' ὅλως ἢ δυσχερῶς ἢ ἐπ' ἐλάχιστον εἰς τὸ νοητὸν ἀποκαθίστανται.

"once purified from all evils and established with the Father, will *never again* endure the evils of this world" (*De regr.* fr. 11). Thus, the soul's return or restoration will be definitive and eternal – like that postulated by Origen, albeit in a different way with regard to universality: for Origen, all intellectual creatures will be restored, and there will be no new fall after the definitive apokatastasis – and not temporary in the framework of infinite cycles of restoration always followed by new falls and incarnations. The latter view was supported by Secundus Salustius in *De diis et mundo* 20, on the basis of the natural affinity of the soul for a body and of the limited number of souls, which must necessarily be reincarnated without end, given the eternity of the world.[82] Proclus is on the same line. He argues that, according to the cosmic law, each soul must become incarnate at least once in each cosmic cycle (*In Tim.* 3.278.10), even though in *In Crat.* 117 he envisages the possibility of an exception for souls such as Heracles', who may skip several cosmic cycles. Even in this case, though, the soul must continue to descend at least some times. In these cases, the descent is not a result of sin, but – as already Iamblichus and Origen admitted – is rather the effect of the generosity of a soul that wants to assist lesser souls in the process of salvation: "to do good to less perfect souls, out of providence for those who need salvation" (ἐπ' εὐεργεσίᾳ μὲν τῶν ἀτελεστέρων ψυχῶν, προνοίᾳ δὲ τῶν σωτηρίας δεομένων, *In Alcib.* 328.29).

That the cyclic periods of particular souls are infinite according to Proclus, and therefore their restorations also occur infinite times, is clear from *Elem. theol.* 206 as well, where Proclus also avails himself of the perishability axiom:

> Every particular soul can descend into generation and ascend again from generation to being *infinite times* [ἐπ' ἄπειρον] [...] for what had no beginning in time will have no end either, and what has no end necessarily has no beginning. The consequence is that each soul makes ascents from generation and descents into generation, and *this has no end* [ἄπαυστον] because time is unlimited [διὰ τὸν ἄπειρον χρόνον]. Thus, each particular soul can descend and ascend *infinite times, and this will never stop happening to every soul.*

This infinity of apokatastaseis instead of one single apokatastasis at the end of time appears to be, therefore, the main difference between Proclus's apokatastasis doctrine and that of the Christian Neoplatonists. But the similarities, too, are really remarkable and, given Proclus's knowledge of at least Origen – on whom Gregory depends –, one might not rule out some possible influence.

In this connection, the parallel with Hierocles of Alexandria is striking. In the fifth century, Hierocles too, like Proclus, explicitly mentioned and

82. With regard to the most perfect souls, Salustius says that, separated from the irrational soul and pure, they will dwell with the gods (*ibid.* 21), but not that they will do so forever.

praised Origen the Neoplatonist, who is likely to be the same as Origen the Christian Platonist. According to Hierocles, Origen and Plotinus were Ammonius Saccas' most illustrious disciples (*ap.* Phot. *Bibl.* cod. 214.172b). That Plotinus and Origen were the best of all those who frequented Ammonius's school is even reiterated by Hierocles at cod. 251.461b. This is why Hierocles mentions Origen among the most important Neoplatonists, who followed Plato's "purified" thought, immediately after Plotinus and as a contemporary of his (cod. 214.172b). It is therefore possible, if not probable, that Hierocles knew Origen's doctrine of apokatastasis. Indeed, the two passages in which Hierocles speaks of apokatastasis bear extraordinary similarities to Origen's doctrine of apokatastasis, so that some kind of influence cannot be completely ruled out. First of all, in *In aureum carmen* 20.5, Hierocles identifies the apokatastasis of human beings with their deification, exactly like Origen, and, like him, explains that it can be reached by means of virtue and knowledge of the truth (τυγχάνειν γὰρ τῆς ἀποκαταστάσεως ἡμᾶς – ταὐτὸν δὲ εἰπεῖν τῆς ἀποθεώσεως – διὰ τῆς προασκηθείσης ἀρετῆς καὶ τῆς ἐπὶ ταύτῃ γνωσθείσης ἀληθείας). These elements will be inherited in turn by Evagrius in his own apokatastasis doctrine.[83] The ascetic exercise of the soul in view of virtue, Hierocles adds, is indispensable to this end (τὸ πρὸς τὴν τῆς ἀρετῆς ἄσκησιν ὅλην ἐπιστρέψαι τὴν ψυχήν). Then in 27.2–3 Hierocles links the requirement of virtue in the soul with that of purity in its pneumatic vehicle (ἀρετὴν ἐν ψυχῇ, καθαρότητα δὲ ἐν τῷ πνευματικῷ αὐτῆς ὀχήματι). In this way one can become "entirely healthy" and thus "be restored to the form of one's original condition" (οὕτω γὰρ ὑγιής τις καὶ ὁλόκληρος γενόμενος εἰς τὸ τῆς ἀρχαίας ἕξεως εἶδος ἀποκαθίσταται). Hierocles describes again this restoration as deification, like Origen (τὸ τῆς ἀποθεώσεως ἀπόκειται γέρας); this is the prize for the person who has acquired virtue and the knowledge of the truth in his or her soul and purity in his or her pneumatic vehicle. This in particular entails union with the right Logos (διὰ τῆς πρὸς τὸν ὀρθὸν λόγον ἑνώσεως), the acknowledgment of the divine order in the universe (πάντα τὸν θεῖον κόσμον ἀναγνωρίσας) and of the Creator/Demiurge of the universe itself (τὸν δημιουργὸν τοῦδε τοῦ παντὸς ἐξευρών). After acquiring this knowledge following the due purification (μετὰ τὴν κάθαρσιν), one will be restored to the state that is always enjoyed by those beings who by nature never fall into generation or becoming (ὃ ἀεί εἰσιν οἱ μὴ εἰς γένεσιν πίπτειν πεφυκότες), will be united to the universe thanks to knowledge (ταῖς μὲν γνώσεσιν ἑνοῦται τῷ παντί), and will ascend to God (πρὸς αὐτὸν ἀνάγεται τὸν θεόν). One's body itself will be adapted to one's new state, as both Origen and later Proclus assumed (σῶμα δὲ συμφυὲς ἔχων τόπου δεῖται εἰς κατάταξιν ἀστροειδῆ οἷον θέσιν ζητῶν).

83. On the presence of exactly these traits of apokatastasis in Origen and Evagrius see my *The Christian Doctrine of Apokatastasis*, chapters on Origen and Evagrius.

God's Being All in All: Proclus and Christian Neoplatonism

Another important motif is common to Proclus, Origen, Gregory of Nyssa, Iamblichus, and Ps. Dionysius, and in Origen and Gregory is closely related to the apokatastasis doctrine: the presence of the divinity "all in all" (πάντα ἐν πᾶσιν) but in a manner that suits each recipient and in a given order. The first Neoplatonist in which this principle appears and is deployed throughout is Origen, who grounded it in 1 Cor 15:28, where the perfection of the *telos* is described as the state in which God is "all things in all," or "all in all," τὰ πάντα ἐν πᾶσιν. Origen elaborated a great deal on this notion, making it the cornerstone of his doctrine of apokatastasis and his metaphysics.[84] Gregory of Nyssa followed him and claimed that God will indeed be "all in all" (πάντα ἐν πᾶσιν) according to the capacity of each recipient and in a precise order, depending on the degree of each one's adhesion to the Good: those who are farthest removed from the Good will be the last to be restored and to come to be in God.[85] Plotinus might even have criticised Origen's doctrine – which he knew – when he claimed that the divinity, or the highest principle, far from being "in all," "*is itself in nothing*, but it is the other beings that participate in it, all those which can be present to it and insofar as they can be present to it" (*Enn.* 6.5.3.13–15).

After Origen, this doctrine of the presence of God "all in all" returns in Neoplatonism on the "pagan" side, but in a different form, as the presence of all in all (without focus on God or the highest Principle); it will be only Proclus who will develop the very same formula as Origen, of God being "all in all." Indeed, Porphyry, who, in turn, was well acquainted with Origen's work, in *Sentences Leading to Intelligible Realities* 10 has a different formulation: "Everything is in everything, but in an appropriate way [οἰκείως] according to the essence of each thing: in the intellect in an intellectual way, in the (rational) soul in a rational way, in plants in a seminal way, in bodies in the form of images, and in what is beyond (intellect and being) in a super-intellectual and a super-essential way." Iamblichus, however, says that Porphyry rejected this principle of "all in all" elsewhere (*ap.* Stob. *Ecl.* 1.49.31, 866 Hense). Iamblichus himself used this same principle (cf. Proclus *In Tim.* 1.426.20) and ascribed it to Numenius, a philosopher very well known to Origen (*ap.* Stob. *Ecl.* 1.49.31, 866 Hense). Origen, though, formulated it in reference to God or the supreme ἀρχή, as did Proclus later, who took over both Origen's form and Porphyry's, Numenius's, and Iamblichus's.

Proclus, indeed, develops this principle a number of times, on various occasions, and the very first proposition of *Elementa theologiae* states that

84. Full documentation in my "Christian Soteriology and Christian Platonism. Origen, Gregory of Nyssa, and the Biblical and Philosophical Basis of the Doctrine of Apokatastasis," *Vigiliae Christianae* 61, 3 (2007) 313–356.

85. Thorough analysis in my "Christian Soteriology" and more extensively in *The Christian Doctrine of Apokatastasis*, the section on Gregory Nyssen.

God-the-One is in all, in that all multiplicity participates in the One in some way. In *Elem. theol.* 23 he stresses that the principle is "in all" (ἐν πᾶσίν ἐστι), though at the same time it is not immanent, but transcendent. In *Elem. theol.* 103 he claims that "all things are in all, but in each one in an appropriate manner" (πάντα ἐν πᾶσιν, οἰκείως δὲ ἐν ἑκάστῳ), with the same formulation as in Porphyry's *Sentences*. The Christian Neoplatonist Ps. Dionysius, in turn, took over the principle both in Origen's form and in Proclus's form. The latter case, without reference to God, is evident for instance in *Div. nom.* 4.7: "the community of all in all in a manner appropriate to each one" (αἱ πάντων ἐν πᾶσιν οἰκείως ἑκάστῳ κοινωνίαι). Origen's and Proclus's formula, referring to the first principle, is clear in *Div. nom.* 1.7.596c–597a: "The Cause of All is 'all in all [πάντα ἐν πᾶσι]' according to the saying, and certainly it must be praised in that it is the Giver of existence to all, the Originator of all beings, who brings all to perfection, holding them together and protecting them; their seat, which has them all return to itself [πρὸς ἑαυτὴν ἐπιστρεπτική], and this in a unified, irresistible, absolute, and transcendent way." The formula here – recognised as such by Dionysius and therefore called "saying" – has both Proclus's metaphysical import and Origen's eschatological value, which Dionysius expresses in Proclean terms of reversion or ἐπιστροφή. The formula appears again in *Div. nom.* 11.5 (221 Suchla), in which Dionysius is speaking of the contents of his lost treatise, *Theologikai Hypotyposeis*; here the formula is referred to Jesus qua God and his operations, and has both metaphysical and eschatological overtones: "What could be said of Christ's love for humanity, a love that gives peace in profusion? Jesus who operates all in all [τὰ πάντα ἐν πᾶσι ἐνεργοῦντος] and realises an unspeakable peace established from eternity, and reconciles us to him in spirit, and, through himself and in himself, to the Father. Of these wonderful gifts I have abundantly and sufficiently spoken in the *Theological Outlines*, where to our testimony is joined that of the holy inspiration of Scriptures/of the sages/of the sayings [λογίων]." In *Div. Nom.* 9.5 Dionysius follows Origen's formulation and relates the situation described by 1 Cor 15:28, God's being "all in all," both to "the providence of God" and to "the salvation of all beings." He states that "in his providence, God is close to every being," continually assisting each of them until the end, "and (thus) becomes 'all in all.'" This takes place διὰ τὴν πάντων σωτηρίαν, which is at the same time the preservation of all beings now and their eventual salvation. Gregory of Nyssa already had both Origen's eschatological formulation that God will be all in all, and the non-eschatological formula in *De anima* 132: "The power of the Spirit, which operates all in all/all things/all beings," τὴν τὰ πάντα ἐν πᾶσιν ἐνεργοῦσαν δύναμιν. Obviously he could not be influenced by Proclus, who came after him. Maximus the Confessor, after Proclus and Dionysius, will pick up only Origen's theological and eschatological formulation, once again within the framework of the apokatastasis doctrine: "God will truly come to be 'all in all,' embracing all and giving substance to all in himself, in that no being will have any more a movement independent of God, and no being will be deprived of God's presence. Thanks to this presence, we shall be, and shall be called, gods and children, body and limbs, because we shall be restored to the perfection of God's project" (*Amb.* 7.1092Cff.).

Conclusion: Proclus and Christian Neoplatonism

In this essay I have pointed out that Proclus's theory of reversal and restoration shows striking points of contact with that of Origen. The principal divergence between the two is the infinite number of cycles of restoration according to Proclus, as opposed to the unicity of restoration according to Origen. This does not allow scholars to postulate a direct dependence of Proclus's doctrine of apokatastasis and ἐπιστροφή on Origen's doctrine.

However, the numerous and remarkable elements of contact that I have pointed out, together with Proclus's knowledge and appreciation of Origen – who is probably identifiable with the homonymous Christian Platonist – and together with the extraordinary rate of occurrence of the very terminology of ἀποκατάστασις in Proclus's works – against the scanty or inexistent occurrences and the apparent lack of interest in this doctrine shown by previous "pagan" Platonists – certainly raises at least the suspicion that Proclus worked out his own doctrine of apokatastasis and ἐπιστροφή not without Origen's theory somehow at the back of his mind, or possibly the reformulations of Origen's theory in later Christian Neoplatonism, especially in Gregory of Nyssa and Evagrius Ponticus.

The possible role of these Christian Platonists, though, could not extend so far as to have Proclus embrace the Christian notion of the end of the world. In this respect, Proclus's concept of the infinity of cycles of restoration comes closer to the Stoic theory of apokatastasis than to that of Origen and his followers. But Proclus's Platonic transcendent framework was the same as that of these Christian Neoplatonists who supported the theory of apokatastasis.[86]

86. A substantial part of the research on which the present essay is based has been carried out during a Senior Research Fellowship at Durham University. I am grateful to the colleagues there and the staff of the Library and the Institute of Advanced Studies for great conversations and very kind assistance.

Hierarchies of Beings in the Patristic Thought: Gregory of Nyssa and Dionysius the Areopagite

Dmitry Biriukov

The purpose of this article is to trace how the topic of the hierarchy of natural beings was dealt with in the Patristic thought. This first part of the study will review the doctrine of natural beings in Gregory of Nyssa. Then we will move on to Pseudo-Dionysius the Areopagite whose understanding of hierarchy is substantially different than that of Gregory of Nyssa.

The Strategies of Building Hierarchies in Gregory of Nyssa

Gregory of Nyssa developed the doctrine on the fundamental division (διαίρεσις) of beings into classes. In his earlier works, *On the Making of Man 8*, and *On the Soul and Resurrection* (PG 46, 60AB), Gregory of Nyssa developed the doctrine on the order of beings according to the ascending ladder of vitality and spoke about the division, according to which the existing beings (τὰ ὄντα) were divided into intellectual beings (τὸ νοητόν) and corporeal beings (τὸ σωματικόν). Gregory left the question concerning the division of intellectual beings for another occasion and in these treatises spoke only about the division of corporeal beings.

He stated that *corporeal beings* (σωματικόν) were divided into *living beings* (ζωτικόν) and beings devoid of life; *living beings* were divided into those which possessed sensation, i. e. *sensible* (αἰσθητικόν) (= *animate* (ἔμψυχον)[1]) beings, and those devoid of sensation; beings with *sensation* were divided into *rational* (λογικόν) and irrational beings. According to Gregory, such a division of natural beings was not arbitrary, but corresponded to the order of creation described in Genesis.

Later in his fundamental treatise devoted to the refutation of Eunomius, Gregory of Nyssa also made the distinction within the intelligent realm and

1. At the passage directly describing the hierarchy, Gregory mentions *sensible* beings, but in close proximity he speaks about *animate* beings. It follows from the *De opificio hominis* 8, PG 44, 145.18–23 and 148.17–18 that the level of the *animate* follows the *living* and precedes the *rational*; therefore it is the same as the *sensible*.

spoke about the division of beings into three natures: first, intellectual, uncreated nature (the nature of God), second, intellectual, created nature (angels and human souls) which participated in the first nature in accordance with the goodness of will exposed by the individuals belonging to that nature, and, thirdly, sensible (τὸ αἰσθητόν) created nature.[2]

According to David Balás, "being" (= "the existing") is the summit of the hierarchy of divisions in Gregory of Nyssa.[3] However, I think that we should distinguish between the two strategies of building such a hierarchy which were used by Gregory of Nyssa. According to the first strategy which was built upon the principle of division into genera and species,[4] indeed, "the existing" was the summit – or its basis (depending on the direction from which it is viewed) – in the hierarchy of divisions. "The existing" embraced the intellectual uncreated and the created. According to the alternative strategy which Gregory of Nyssa developed in his *Contra Eunomium* and which he applied along with the first strategy,[5] the uncreated intellectual being, the higher nature (ἡ ὑψηλὴ φύσις),[6] common for the hypostases of the Trinity,[7] was the summit of the hierarchy, giving existence to the created beings.[8] The intellectual created beings long for it as for a source of goodness and participate in it according to the goodness of their will.[9]

It seems that according to the first strategy, inasmuch as existing beings[10] are divided into rational and corporeal, and rational beings are divided into uncreated and created, we should speak only about the epistemological

2. Gregory of Nyssa, *Contra Eunomium* 1.1.270–277, 1.1.295 (ed. Jaeger: *Gregorii Nysseni opera* (1960–1990), ed. W. Jaeger. Vol. 1–10. Leiden: Contra Eunomium Libri: I et II, vol. 1, 1960; III, vol. 2, 1960). In another passage Gregory of Nyssa spoke about the division of beings into the uncreated and created, and about the division of the created beings into the supramundane beings and sensible beings; *Contra Eunomium* 4.100–101 (ed. Jaeger).
3. D. Balás, *Μετουσία Θεοῦ. Man's Participation in God's Perfections according to St. Gregory of Nyssa*, Rome 1966, 34.
4. That is in accordance with the principle according to which the lower level of the hierarchy is related to the higher as a species to genus or as an individual to species.
5. Gregory of Nyssa employed both strategies simultaneously in his *Contra Eunomium* 1.1.270–277. The strategy of the division of beings was also formulated in *De opificio hominis* 8, PG 44, 145.10–11 and in the *Oratio catechetica magna* 6: 9–14 (ed. Srawley: *Gregory of Nyssa, The catechetical oration*, Ed. J. Srawley, Cambridge: Cambridge University Press 1903).
6. Gregory of Nyssa, *Contra Eunomium* 1.1.274.3–4 (ed. Jaeger).
7. Cf. Gregory of Nyssa, *Contra Eunomium* 1.1.274.1–275.1 and 1.1.277.8–13 (ed. Jaeger).
8. Gregory of Nyssa, *Contra Eunomium* 1.1.271.7–272.1 (ed. Jaeger); cf. *Dialogus de anima et resurrectione*, PG 46, 72D–73A.
9. Gregory of Nyssa, *Contra Eunomium* 1.1.274.2–275.1 (ed. Jaeger).
10. That is, being, understood in the sense of "all that exists." In this regard, Gregory shows the influence of Stoic philosophy, where *being-existing* is also on the top or in the basis of the hierarchy of genera-species divisions (see: *Stoicorum veterum fragmenta*, ed. J. von Arnim. Vol. 2. Leipzig: Teubner, 1903 (SVF) II 182) and at the same time it also does not claim any ontological primacy. The link between the concept of "the existing" in Gregory and the Stoic context is confirmed by the usage of the term: in both cases it used the phrase τῶν ὄντων (see in the Stoics: SVF II 182, in Gregory: *De opificio hominis* 8, PG 44, 145.10, *Contra Eunomium* 1.1.270.1, 1.1.295.1 (ed. Jaeger), *Oratio catechetica magna* 6.10 (ed. Srawley)) what is understood in the sense of "[...] out of everything that exists," and in both cases this

nature of the genera-species hierarchy in Gregory (that is, the preceding links of hierarchy in no way, besides for a mind, are higher then the following ones[11]).

Gregory's development of this strategy of genera-species divisions in respect to corporeal beings, which is, in fact, the natural order of beings in his system, implies the ontological, and not just the epistemological nature of the hierarchy of corporeal beings.

The second strategy involved a hierarchy that did not correspond to divisions on the basis of genera and species (that is, the lower hierarchical level did not correspond to the higher level as a species to genus or as an individual to species), but was a hierarchy in the ontological sense with the principal source of being as its hierarchical summit (the uncreated nature) giving existence to other kinds of beings, located in the descending order with respect to the degree of closeness to it and of the capacity to participate in it (created intellectual and created sensible natures).

Thus, we can speak of two versions of hierarchy in Gregory of Nyssa. In one case, the *uncreated intellectual* divine nature is located on the summit of the hierarchy, bestowing existence upon the underlying *intellectual* and *sensible created* natures. In another case, the *existing* forms the basis of hierarchy, and it is divided into the *intellectual* and the *corporeal* levels. In turn, the level of the *corporeal* is divided into *living beings* and beings devoid of life; the level of *living* is divided into *sensible* beings and beings *deprived of senses*; the level of *sensible* is divided into *irrational* beings and *rational* beings which form the summit of this version of hierarchy in the ontological sense. The first version implies the direction of the upward movement along the hierarchy, understood in the ontological sense, from sensible created beings to the divine nature. The second version entails the increase of the hierarchy from the existing to the rational; the criterion of directionality of the increase here is the measure of complexity and ontological superiority (which refers to the levels posterior to the corporeal level, since precedence of levels of the *existing* and the *intellectual* in respect to the following levels, as I have mentioned, cannot claim the ontological status).

As I have shown in another study,[12] the strategy of Gregory of Nyssa, putting "the existing" on the summit (basis) of the hierarchy, traces back to so-called "Tree of Porphyry," combining Stoic, Platonic and Aristotelian

"existing" is divided into corporeal and incorporeal beings (ἀσώματα among the Stoics, and νοητόν in Gregory), although Gregory certainly understood the nature of this incorporeal in a completely different way than the Stoic philosophers.

11. It follows from the general basic principles of Christian theology that nothing can be above the uncreated.
12. D. Biriukov, "'Ascent of Nature from the Lower to the Perfect': Synthesis of Biblical and Logical-Philosophical Descriptions of the Order of Natural Beings in the *De opificio hominis* 8 by Gregory of Nyssa", in: B. Lourié, P. Allen, V. Baranov, eds., *Scrinium: Revue de patrologie, d'hagiographie critique et d'histoire ecclésiastique*, vol. 11: *Patrologia Pacifica Quarta* (2015) [in print].

philosophical lines. I should remind that the Tree of Porphyry is of the hierarchy of genera and species: *substance* (οὐσία) – *body* (σῶμα) – *animate body* (ἔμψυχον σῶμα) – *living being* (ζῷον) (*sensible*[13]) – *rational living being* (ζῷον λογικόν) – *human being* (ἄνθρωπος) – *individual human being.*[14]

In constructing his genera-species hierarchy (if we imagine it linearly) of the *existing* (ὄντα) – *corporeal* (σωματικόν) – *living* (ζωτικόν) – *sensible/animate* (αἰσθητικόν/ἔμψυχον) – *rational* (λογικόν), Gregory generally follows the sequence of levels corresponding to Porphyry's Tree, but introduces certain modifications. In particular, two levels – *living beings* and *animate beings* – in the genera-species structures of Gregory and Porphyry are in the opposite order: in Gregory *living beings* precede *animate beings* (= *sensible*), while in Porphyry *animate* precede *living.*

The context of the *De opificio hominis* 8, where Gregory attempted to synthesize Biblical-cosmological, anthropological, logical, and natural-philosophical conceptual frameworks may help us to reveal the reasons for Gregory's change in the order of genera-species hierarchy as it appears in Porphyry's Tree. The reason why Gregory changed the order of the genera-species hierarchy, present in the Tree of Porphyry, must have been related to Gregory's desire to reconcile the logical and philosophical structure of division, conventional for its time, with the Biblical account, that is, with how the Bible described the order of creating natural beings, and with the logic of this order. Indeed, the Biblical text says that the world of plants was created prior to the world of animals.[15] This determined the structure of division of beings in Gregory, according to which living beings precede animate beings. For this reason Gregory diverged from the order of the hierarchy of beings appearing in the Tree of Porphyry.[16]

Next we should turn to the question of how the hierarchy of beings was understood by Dionysius the Areopagite.

This paradigm is radically different from that of Gregory of Nyssa. The hierarchy, built up by Gregory, does not imply transcendental principles corresponding to the links of hierarchy and participated in by them, while Dionysius, on the basis of the philosophy of Proclus, developed his doctrine of hierarchy involving such principles.

13. See *Isagoge* 10: 3–9, 14–18 (ed. Busse: *Porphyrii isagoge et in Aristotelis categorias commentarium*, ed. A. Busse. Berlin, 1887 (Commentaria in Aristotelem Graeca, 4.1)).
14. *Isagoge* 4: 15–27 (Busse).
15. Cf. Gen. 1:11 and 1:20.
16. In more detail about thus topic see D. Biriukov, "'Ascent of Nature from the Lower to the Perfect'..." .

The Dissimilarity in the Structure of the Hierarchies in Gregory of Nyssa and Dionysius the Areopagite in Connection with the Philosophical Paradigms of Participation in a Substance in Patristic Thought

This difference can be correlated with the rethinking of the concept of participation in a substance, and, in particular, participation in the divine substance in Patristic thought due to the change in the underlying philosophical understanding of the very notion of participation. Below, a short excursion into this subject will be provided.[17]

I will use the expression, "Platonic paradigm of participation" for such a view when the participating entity is understood as being different from the participated entity according to nature (substance), and the expression *by participation* is understood as the opposition to what is *by being* or *by nature* (by possession of nature). For example, a thing, which is not the One, *participates* in It, and therefore is not It as such.[18] In the most general sense, *participation* in this paradigm points to the fact that a certain thing possesses a certain property to a lesser extent than does the embodiment of this property. The "Aristotelian paradigm of participation," opposite to the Platonic, is Aristotle's understanding of participation expressing a logical relationship between the genera-species predicables of varying degrees of generality: less general participates in more general, while the latter does not participate in the former (an individual participates in species and genus; species participates in genus, but not vice versa).[19] Thus *by participation* in the Aristotelian paradigm means the same as *by nature* (substance) or *by being* since in this paradigm the nature of an individual is the species and genus which it belongs to or participates in. Moreover, unlike Platonic language which, when it comes to participation, speaks about a greater or lesser degree of participation, Aristotelian language cannot speak about varying degrees of participation.

The Early Christian authors were inspired to actively use the Platonic paradigm of participation by the well-known passage from the *Second Epistle of Peter*, which stated that Christians would become the partakers of the divine nature (θείας κοινωνοὶ φύσεως) (2 Pet. 1, 3–4). Accordingly, the topic of participation in the divine substance (nature), as implicitly or explicitly

17. Speaking below of the paradigms of participation in Patristics, I am working from the platform of my article: Д. Бирюков, "Тема причастности Богу в святоотеческой традиции и у Никифора Григоры" [D. Biriukov, "The topic of participation in God in the Patristic thought and in Nicephorus Gregoras"], in: Георгий Факрасис, *Диспут свт. Григория Паламы с Григорой философом. Философские и богословские аспекты паламитских споров*. Пер. с древнегреч. Д. А. Поспелова, отв. ред. Д. С. Бирюков (Москва, 2009) [*Georgy Fakrasis, Disputation of St Gregory Palamas with Nicephorus Gregoras, a Philosopher. Philosophical and Theological Aspects of the Palamite controversy*, trans. D. Pospelov, ed. D. Biriukov, Moscow 2009], 113–173.
18. Cf. Plato, *Parmenides* 158a.
19. Aristotle, *Topica* 121a10–15, 122b20–22.

opposite of possessing it,[20] with more or less obvious philosophical connotations and usually with the allusion to 2 Pet. 1, 3–4 was used in the early Byzantine literature by Athanasius of Alexandria,[21] Gregory of Nyssa,[22] Cyril of Alexandria, Macarius the Great[23] and other authors. In Middle Byzantine literature, this topic was dealt with by John of Damascus, who summarized all possible paradigms of participation for his time – Platonic, Aristotelian, and Neoplatonic,[24] as well as by Symeon the New Theologian.[25] This trend of Patristic literature argued that holy people participate in the divine nature (they partake in the divine substance, but do not possess it as hypostases of the Trinity do), while the created world as a whole, according to Gregory of Nyssa,[26] cannot be considered as participating in it.

This paradigm of participation fell into the background in Byzantine Patristic literature in connection with the new philosophical language which appeared in the *Corpus Areopagiticum*. Those notions which earlier Patristic

20. About the opposition *by participation* and *by nature* in Athanasius of Alexandria and the Cappadocians see D. Balás, *Μετουσία Θεοῦ...*, 11–12, 60–62. Cf. Idem, "Participation", *The Brill Dictionary of Gregory of Nyssa*, edited by L. Francisco Mateo-Seco and G. Maspero, Leiden, Boston: Brill 2010, 583.
21. For example, *Epistle 1 to Serapion*, PG 26, 585BC.
22. *Contra Eunomium* 1.1.274.1–4 (ed. Jaeger).
23. The last two authors very often devoted their attention to this subject; each of them has dozens of pertinent passages.
24. For example, see the Platonic paradigm in the *Orationes de imaginibus tres* 3.33 (on partaking in the divine substance by the saints) and the *De fidei orthodoxa* 4 XIII (86): 2–14 (ed. Kotter: *Die Schriften des Johannes von Damaskos (1969–1988)*, hrsg. B. Kotter. 5 Bände. Berlin. (Maßgebliche kritische Gesamtausgabe)); see the Aristotelian paradigm in the *De duabus in Christo voluntatibus* 7; see the Neoplatonic paradigm in *Ibid.*, 11: 9–10 (ed. Kotter) (where John of Damascus, contradicting the *Orationes de imaginibus tres* 3.33, speaks about impossibility of partaking in the divine substance) and in the *De fidei orthodoxa* 7 (51).
25. *Ethical Discourses* 1.3.82–86 (Syméon le Nouveau Théologien, *Traités théologiques et éthiques*, introd., texte crit., trad. fr. et notes par J. Darrouzès. T. 1, Paris 1967, 202); Hymns 7.30–36; 50.153–154, 200–202 (Symeon der Neue Theologe, *Hymnen*, prolegomena und krit. text, besorgt A. von Kambyles, Berlin, 1976, 71; 401; 402–403) etc. See: D. Biriukov, "On the Topic of Participation in the Divine Essence according to St Symeon the New Theologian in the Patristic Context," in: B. Lourié, P. Allen, V. Baranov, eds., *Scrinium: Revue de patrologie, d'hagiographie critique et d'histoire ecclésiastique*, vol. 11: *Patrologia Pacifica Quarta* (2015) [in print]. It is also worth noting that in this version of the theological language, the discourses of participation and knowledge are not similar: the divine substance is participated, however it is unknowable (at least in this life; Gregory of Nazianzus (*Or.* 28.17) admitted the possibility of the comprehension of the divine essence in a future age). In this regard, there is a fundamental discrepancy between the pre-Areopagite paradigm of theological language and the Palamite one, regarding the concept of "essence-energy": i.e. the Cappadocian Fathers opposed knowability of the divine energies to unknowability of the divine substance, although they do not do so in terms of participability and unparticipability as it was in theological language of Gregory Palamas. This discrepancy between the two discourses in the Cappadocian Fathers – the discourse of participation to the divine substance and that of knowledge of the substance – is not often recognized by the scholars. This is the case, for example, of the study by David Bradshaw, *Aristotle East and West: Metaphysics and the Division of Christendom*, Cambridge 2004, 172–178.
26. *Contra Eunomium* 3.3.7.1–8.6 (ed. Jaeger).

authors expressed through the opposition of *by being* (*by nature*) – *by participation*, started to be expressed in the Dionysian philosophical and theological framework by the conceptual triad of *non-participated – participated – participating*[27] (the Neoplatonic paradigm of participation) developed by Proclus and adopted by the author of the *Corpus Areopagiticum*. This paradigm of participation included some aspects of both Platonic and Aristotelian paradigms: the Aristotelian paradigm functioned as a background, in opposition to which the notion of non-participated was elaborated, while the Platonic paradigm manifested itself in relation to the *participated* and the *participating*.

In the process of transferring this triad into Christian theological thought, the Areopagite distinguished in the divinity the *participated* (μετεχόμενον) which he associated with the divine processions and powers, and *non-participated* (ἀμέθεκτος) – the supra-substantial divinity of God.[28] The author of the *scholia* to the *Corpus Areopagiticum* interpreted this in such a way that while divinity could be participated according to its processions and energies, God could not be participated according to His nature.[29] Moreover, this paradigm assumes that He is completely unparticipated for all created beings including saintly people. The topic of the ultimate impossibility of participating in God according to substance (nature) and of the opportunity to participate in God according to energies is exhaustively developed in the writings of Maximus the Confessor (possibly the author of the *scholia* to the *Corpus Areopagiticum* mentioned above).[30] In this way the Aristotelian paradigm became partially borrowed in the understanding that to *participate* in substance meant to possess the substance or to be something according to substance. Thereby, the discourse of the participation of saints (as well as of any created beings) in the divine substance, which was used in the preceding Patristic literature, including Gregory of Nyssa, became forbidden (since in this paradigm the participation of saints in the divine substance would imply for them becoming God according to substance).

After Maximus, the Neoplatonic participation paradigm which implied the complete impossibility of participating in God according to substance, for a time fell out of use, but reemerged among Orthodox theologians after

27. This triad might have been introduced into the philosophical language by Iamblichus; see the testimony of Proclus in his *Commentary on the Timaeus* II, 105.16–28; 313.19–24.
28. *De divinis nominibus* (hereafter *DN*) 2.5; 11.6.
29. PG 4, 221C, 404AB, 404D. It is known that the author of a number of scholia to the Areopagite was John Scythopolis, while the author of some other scholia was Maximus the Confessor. From the index compiled by B. Suchla and quoted in the book Rorem, Lamoreaux 1998, 264–277, it follows that none of these scholia are available in the Syriac translation of the scholia. However it is believed that exactly scholia included into the Syriac translation where written by John Scythopolis. Taking into account that the theme of the impossibility of participating in God according to substance is found in the writings of Maximus the Confessor (see the next notice), we can suppose that the author of the scholia is Maximus.
30. Maximus the Confessor, *Quaestiones et dubia* 173.1–7 (ed. Declerck: Maximi Confessoris Quaestiones et Dubia, ed. J. H. Declerck, Corpus Christianorum, series Graeca 10), Brepols, Turnhout 1982; *Capita theologica et oeconomica*, PG 90, 1180C–1181A.

the rediscovery of the theological heritage of Maximus the Confessor at the end of the lifetime of Nicetas Stethatos, that is, in the last quarter of the eleventh century. Further this paradigm was taken over by Gregory Palamas; eventually in the course of the Palamite controversy the idea of possibility of participation of created beings in the divine substance was rejected in the *Tomos* of the Council of the Church of Constantinople in 1351[31] and anathematized in a special supplement to the *Synodikon of Orthodoxy*.[32]

Gregory of Nyssa used both Platonic and Aristotelian paradigms of participation in his writings. The Aristotelian participation paradigm was used by Gregory when he argued that all people equally partook in the human nature.[33] Gregory used the Platonic participation paradigm in the framework of hierarchy where participation of *intellectual created beings* took place in the *uncreated intellectual being* – or divine substance – according to the goodness of will as participation in the highest level of hierarchy. However, in Dionysius the Areopagite, who borrowed the Neoplatonic paradigm of participation, as well as subsequently in Maximus the Confessor and Gregory Palamas, such a Platonic paradigm of participation became impossible in its application to the divine substance. According to the philosophical paradigm of participation shared by these authors, participation in the divine substance would imply its assimilation, which was prohibited overall in the Patristic theological thought. In fact, the idea of assimilating the divine substance by created beings was "blocked" in this case through the introduction of the concept of non-participation into theological discourse.

Therefore, the authors who adopted the Neoplatonic paradigm of participation in their theological language and whose theological systems implied the utter non-participation in God (non-participation in the divine substance) naturally developed the doctrine of hierarchy entailing participation of created beings, not in the divine substance, but in the higher transcendental principles – processions of God, His qualities, or energies, as it can be found in Dionysius the Areopagite, Maximus the Confessor, and Gregory Palamas, respectively.

Natural and Individual Participation in the Godhead according to Dionysius the Areopagite

The doctrine of the hierarchy of beings which exists in the *Corpus Areopagiticum* is generally associated with the theme of participation in the Godhead. Dionysius speaks about dual participation in God. On the one hand, all beings participate in God *naturally* – by virtue of possessing existence and in accordance with the nature of each being (which will be discussed in more

31. 396–397 (ed. Καρμίρη: Ι. Καρμίρη, *Τὰ δογματικὰ καὶ συμβολικὰ μνημεῖα*, Τ. Ι. Ἀθῆνα 1952).
32. *Synodicon of Orthodoxy* 85.628–633 (J. Gouillard "Le Synodikon de l'Orthodoxie. Édition et commentaire," *Travaux et Mémoires* 2 (1967) 1–316).
33. *Contra Eunomium* 1.1.173.2–175.1 (ed. Jaeger).

detail below). Such a participation is static, and within this paradigm there is no being deprived of participation in the First Cause. On the other hand, Dionysius speaks about the way of individual participation in God (for rational beings), and about the ability to participate in the Divine Goodness for an individual being, which can either be fulfilled or not. In the latter case, Dionysius characterizes a being as not participating in Goodness (*DN* IV, 4: 147.15–148.2 (here and below ed. Suchla[34])). Thus, one of the participation paradigms used by the Areopagite corresponded to natural participation and implied the participation of created beings in God as a given reality. In this paradigm we cannot speak about non-participation of beings in the Godhead in any respect. Another paradigm corresponded to the individual way of participation and implied participation as a condition which may (or may not) become a reality. The latter paradigm presupposed both participation and non-participation of a (rational) individual being in God, if the being chooses to close itself to divine gifts. According to the Areopagite, in both cases beings participate in the divinity in its entirety: God on His part gives Himself entirely, whereas created beings participate in the divinity proportionately to their capacity, both in the ability to receive as defined by their nature, and in terms of individual openness to participating in the divine gifts (for rational beings) (*DN* II, 5: 129.4–6). Later, a similar dual paradigm of the participation of created beings in the divine would be used by Maximus the Confessor and Gregory Palamas.

The Participated and the Participating in Dionysius the Areopagite

Thus, Dionysius the Areopagite developed his theory of processions and principles which are participated in by the created beings in the context of the natural participation of created beings in the divinity. In *On the Divine Names* V, 1 Dionysius speaks about such names of God as *Goodness*, *Being*, *Life*, and *Wisdom* as concerning the order of the divine processions, outspreading on the corresponding realities in the created world and surpassing them.[35] *Goodness* extends on *being* and *non-being*; *Being* extends on *beings*; *Life* on *living beings*, while *Wisdom* extends on *intellectual beings* (angelic powers), *rational beings*, and *sensible beings*. These good processions do not constitute multiple

34. Pseudo-Dionysius Areopagita, *De divinis nominibus*, ed. B. R. Suchla, Patristische Texte und Studien 33, Berlin: De Gruyter 1990.

35. It should be noted that the theological language of Dionysius speaks of divine names in a way that, on the one hand, the names explain the divine processions, while, on the other hand, identifying those names with the processions. Dionysius says in *DN* V, 1 that the names *Goodness*, *Being* and *Life* do not simply apply to non-beings, beings, and living beings, but also *exceed* them (181.1–6). Evidently, the reference that the divine names related to the processions exceed the corresponding realities of the created beings, indicates that Dionysius here identified the divine name and the procession.

principles, but all belong to the One God. At the same time according to Dionysius those beings which are the subjects of the processions and which participate in them, form a hierarchy: *living beings* (τὰ ζῶντα) are above *beings* (τὰ ὄντα); *sensible beings* (τὰ αἰσθητικά) are above *living beings*; *rational beings* (τὰ λογικά) are above *sensible beings*, and *intellects* (τὰ νοερά) are above *rational beings*.[36] Dionysius noted that intellectual beings were the closest to God as having the largest number of natural perfections.[37] This very principle underlying the hierarchy of participating in Dionysius is associated with the concept of conformity or proportionality in the outpouring of divine gifts on the participating beings (see *DN* I, 2–3; IV, 1, 33) both in their natural and individual aspects.

Dionysius speaks of *Goodness*, *Being*, *Life*, and *Wisdom* using not only the terminology of "processions." In relation to these names he also mentions two types of specific realities – *self-supra-substantial* and *self-participating* principles. As a rule, scholars have focused their attention on the Dionysian doctrine of *Goodness*, *Being*, *Life*, and *Wisdom* as the processions of the divine without going into great detail concerning the doctrine of these principles in the *Corpus Dionysiacum*. We should try to understand what Dionysius writes about them.

In *DN* V, 2 Dionysius speaks about self-supra-substantial *Goodness*, *Being*, *Life*, and *Wisdom* pertaining to self-supra-substantial divinity; they are above all goodness, being, life, and wisdom. The principles, as it seems, can be identified with supra-substantial Principle and supra-divine Life which Dionysius mentions in *DN* XI, 6. Yet, in order to standardize our terminological usage, we will refer to these kinds of principles as *self-supra-substantial* principles.

These entities differ from other higher entities established by God. The latter principles, like all beings, constitute the gift and the outpouring of self-supra-substantial *Goodness* (*DN* V, 6) and include the principles (ἀρχαί) with the prefix "self-" (αὐτο-): *Self-Being*, *Self-Life*, *Self-Wisdom*, *Self-Similarity of the*

36. "Yet someone might say, 'Wherefore is Being expands beyond Life and Life beyond Wisdom, when living things are above beings, and sensible things above living ones, and rational things above these, and the intellects are above the rational things and are more around God and closer to him? For, those which participate in God's greater gifts are the higher and surpass the rest. If the intellects are understood that way that they were without being and without life, the saying would be sound. But since the divine intellects are above other beings, and live in a manner surpassing other living things, and think and know in a manner beyond sense and reason, and in a manner beyond all existent things participate in the Beautiful and Good, they are nearer to the Good, participating in it in an eminent way, and receiving from it more and greater gifts; likewise rational things excel sensitive ones, having more by the eminence of reason, and the latter [excel other living things] by sensation, and [living things excel mere beings] by life" (*DN* V, 3: 182.1–14). I have made use the translations of E. Perl, *Theophany: the Neoplatonic Philosophy of Dionysius the Areopagite*, New York 2007, 69–70 and C. E. Rolt, *Dionysius the Areopagite: On the Divine Names and the Mystical Theology*, transl. by C. E. Rolt, Christian Classics Ethereal Library, Grand Rapids, London: SPCK 1920, 133–134. Cf. *DN* II, 7: 131.7–13; IV, 4: 148: 12–18.

37. *DN* V, 3, 182.3–4.

Divinity, *Self-Unity*, *Self-Order* (V, 5, cf. XI, 6), *Self-Goodness* (II, 1; XI, 6), *Self-Eternity* (V, 9), *Self-Equality* (IX, 10; XI, 6), *Self-Peace* (XI, 2; XI, 6), *Self-Divinity* (XI, 6), *Self-Beauty* (XI, 6), and *Self-Holiness* (XII, 1).[38] Dionysius indicates that all existing things, including the principles with the prefix "self-" come from self-supra-substantial *Goodness*, and gives two examples: the first concerns the relation of the number one to other numbers (all numbers are merged in number one, and the more the number is removed from the one, the more it is divided) and the second example deals with a multitude of lines passing through the center of a circle (the farther from the center, the more their divergence is) (V, 6).

Dionysius speaks about the principles with the prefix "self-" as about realities which, being the gift and the outpouring of the non-participated God are participated in by beings, making beings to be and to become called beings, living beings, deified beings, etc. (XI, 6).

Self-Being is the highest principle among the principles with the prefix "self-"; it is participated in by other principles with the prefix "self-," which are called "self-participating" (αὐτομέτοχαι) by Dionysius. These principles are simultaneously participating and participated: they participate in *Self-Being* and are participated in by beings in accordance with qualities corresponding to these names (while some beings may simultaneously participate in several principles (V, 5: 184.11–12, cf. XII, 4: 225.17ff.). The beings, participating in the self-participating principles, through them also participate in *Self-Being* (V, 5).

Although Dionysius the Areopagite called self-participating higher realities *principles* (ἀρχαί) (V, 5), he rejected the possibility of understanding them as creating substances or causes (αἰτίαι) of beings (XI, 6),[39] since the Cause (αἰτία) of beings and their principle is only the supra-substantial divinity in the modes of self-supra-substantiality (self-supra-substantial *Goodness, Substance, Life,* and *Wisdom*) (V, 6; XI, 6). Despite the fact that Dionysius mentions a variety of such modes, the divinity in these modes is one and the same Cause of beings; it is not many causes, and it would be wrong to understand the self-supra-substantial *Goodness, Substance, Life, and Wisdom* as separate causes of beings (V, 2). We may say that according to Dionysius the realities of the self-supra-substantial represent a single Cause and Principle while there is a whole variety of principles with the prefix "self-" (*Self-Being, Self-Life, Self-Wisdom*, etc.) (cf. V, 5–6).

Dionysius says that God can be called both the basis of, for example, *Self-Life* or *Self-Power*, or simply may be called *Self-Life* or *Self-Power* in the proper

38. Speaking of these principles, Dionysius also mentions that *Self-Life* comes from divine *Life* (VI, 1), that God as Power dwells above *Self-Power* (VIII, 2) and is the basis of *Self-Similarity* (IX, 6), *Self-Equality* (IX, 10), and *Self-Peace* (XI, 2).

39. Dionysius probably argues here against Proclus' doctrine of hennads interpreted in the sense of hypostatized principles.

sense of the terms. In the first case, it is said about God as about supra-substantially exceeding all beings and "first beings" (τὰ πρώτως ὄντα) (evidently, under the "first beings" Dionysius here means the principles with the prefix "self-"); in the second case He is named according to the names of beings and first beings[40] as their Cause (XI, 6: 221.13–222.2).

The relationship between the divine processions on the one hand, and the self-supra-substantial realities and principles with the prefix "self-" on the other, are not entirely clear, but it seems that self-supra-substantial realities and principles with the prefix "self-," while differing from each other (the former are the cause and the source of existence for the latter) and not being identical to divine processions, represent different aspects of the processions.[41]

Divine Names in Dionysius the Areopagite and the Neoplatonic Tetrad

Among all divine names as Dionysius describes them we can distinguish the first four: *Goodness*, *Being* (τὸ ὄν) [= τὸ εἶναι = ἡ οὐσία], *Life*, and *Wisdom*. Dionysius writes about these names as related simultaneously to divine procession, to self-supra-substantial realities, and to the principles of beings with the prefix "self-." This sequence of names was borrowed by Dionysius from the Neoplatonic tradition, which elaborated the doctrine of the triad *Being*,

40. It is this language of speaking about the supra-being on the basis of being, which in my opinion may explain the words of Dionysius in the XI, 6: 222.13ff. that *Self-Being*, *Self-Life*, and *Self-Divinity* are spoken about the divine, supra-primary, and supra-substantial Principle and Cause, while earlier (XI, 6: 222.6ff.) Dionysius rejected the notion that *Self-Being* was the divine Cause for all beings, and *Self-Life* was the Cause of all living beings, and said that it was the supra-divine *Life* that was cause of both *Self-Life* and all living beings.

41. It may be noted here that Eric Perl, in fact, identified divine processions in Dionysius with the principles with the prefix "self-" without mentioning it and without posing a question concerning the complexity and originality of the Dionysian doctrine of divine names and their denotations. In my opinion, this position somewhat distorts the doctrine of Dionysius in the form it was presented by Perl. Thus Perl developed the argument about the tetrad of processions *Goodness*, *Being*, *Life*, and *Wisdom* from *DN* V, 1 and went on to *DN* XI, 6. On the basis of the latter passage he pointed out that according to Dionysius divine processions were not mediating creative substances and hypostases (E. Perl, *Theophany...*, 66–67). However, in XI, 6 Dionysius precisely speaks about the principles with the prefix "self-" and not about divine processions in general. Dionysius' purpose, among other things, was to claim that those principles were not the creative causes of beings, whereas the supra-substantial principle and the supra-divine *Life* were the Cause and Principle of all *being* and *life* (XI, 6: 222.3–223.3). It seems that the Dionysian distinction between the concept of "cause" (αἰτία), attributable only to self-supra-substantial (or divine) entities, but not to the entities with the prefix "self-," and the notion of "principle" (ἀρχή), attributable to both of those, is relevant here; see above, the text around note 37). Thus, in my opinion, it is not correct to identify Dionysian divine processions and the principles with the prefix "self-" without specifying details and context, as it was done by Perl, since not everything that Dionysius attributed to the principles with the prefix "self-," he applied to divine processions in general.

Life, and *Mind*.[42] Using this Neoplatonic triad, Dionysius replaced *Mind* with *Wisdom*, wishing, as scholars pointed out, to bring this language closer to the Biblical.[43]

In the Platonic tradition, the triad of *Being*, *Life*, and *Mind* went back at least to Plotinus, who taught about the One as the source of *Being* (τὸ ὄν), *Life*, and *Mind*.[44] Later Neoplatonists, Proclus and Syrianus, also placed *Being*, *Life*, and *Mind* underneath the One, linking the triad to the noetic realm. S. Klitenic Wear and J. Dillon argue that only Porphyry, out of all Neoplatonists, placed the triad at the level of the One, and in this respect we have a crossing point of Porphyry and Dionysius who also considered the triad to correspond to the highest reality.[45]

However it is unlikely that Dionysius built on Porphyry in speaking about the divine names of *Goodness*, *Being*, *Life*, and *Mind*; Proclus was the most likely source. As P. Sherwood noted,[46] in this regard Dionysius relied on the 101st and 102nd theorems of the *Elements of Theology* by Proclus, which referred to the triad of *Being*, *Life*, and *Mind*. One can also notice that in the 8th theorem of this treatise and further on Proclus spoke of *Goodness* as the highest principle. The dependence of Dionysius on Proclus in this respect also follows from the philosophical background of the Dionysian doctrine concerning the tetrad of *Goodness*, *Being*, *Life*, and *Wisdom* in *DN* V, 1–2, analyzed, among other scholars, by E. Perl.[47]

The Hierarchy of Beings in Dionysius the Areopagite

It follows from the above that we may confidently speak about the hierarchy of created beings or hierarchy of participating in Dionysius the Areopagite. This is the following hierarchy (from the lowest level in the ontological sense as well as in relation to the measure of complexity): *being – living being – sensible being – rational being – intellectual being* (V, 3, see the relevant quote in

42. However, P. Rorem indicated that there was also a Biblical background in relation to these divine names; P. Rorem, *Pseudo-Dionysius. A Commentary on the Texts and an Introduction to Their Influence*, Oxford 1993, 153–155; cf. P. Rorem, "The Biblical Allusions and Overlooked Quotations in the Pseudo-Dionysian Corpus," *Studia Patristica* 23 (1989) 64.
43. Cf. S. Klitenic Wear, J. Dillon, *Dionysius the Areopagite and the Neoplatonist tradition: Despoiling the Hellenes*, Ashgate Studies in Philosophy and Theology in Late Antiquity, Aldershot, Burlington: Ashgate 2007, 24, n. 31; 26; E. Perl, *Theophany...*, 129.
44. Plotinus, *Enneades* I 8, 2; see Ch. Schäfer, *The Philosophy of Dionysius the Areopagite. An Introduction to the Structure and the Content of the Treatise On the Divine Names*, Leiden, Boston: Brill 2006, 86. S. Klitenic Wear and J. Dillon mistakenly indicate *Enneades* I 6, 7 in that respect; S. Klitenic Wear, J. Dillon, *Dionysius the Areopagite and the Neoplatonist Tradition...*, 24.
45. S. Klitenic Wear, J. Dillon, *Dionysius the Areopagite and the Neoplatonist Tradition...*, 25–26.
46. P. Sherwood, "Introduction," in: St. Maximus the Confessor, *The Ascetic Life. The Four Centuries on Charity*, Trans. and annot. by P. Sherwood, O.S.B., Ancient Christian Writers, S.T.D. Paulist Press 1955, 40–41.
47. E. Perl, *Theophany...*, 68–69.

note 34). This hierarchy corresponds to the order in the degree of expanding of the processions of God in the triad of *Being*, *Life*, and *Wisdom*, borrowed from the Neoplatonists, where the three levels in the hierarchy of participating – *intellectual, rational,* and *sensible* – correspond to Wisdom. The structure of the hierarchy of participating is such that the more complex species which the being belongs to, the greater amount of transcendent entities the being participates in. This implied the inclusion of each preceding level by the subsequent level, and meant that possession of each subsequent perfection or natural capacity entailed the possession of all preceding capacities, as well as the corresponding participations (although it is still not entirely clear how this worked in the case of angelic powers, corresponding to the level of the intellectual – the highest level of the Dionysian hierarchy, since the nature of angels obviously did not include the preceding perfections in the hierarchy[48]).

Although the order of the participated divine names-processions was borrowed by Dionysius from Proclus, the Dionysian hierarchy of participating is not in fact close to the hierarchy of participating in Proclus, which had the following form: *living beings – vegetative beings – soulless bodies – matter*.[49] Thus, while relying on Proclus in respect to his doctrine of the participated divine names-processions, *Goodness-Being-Life-Wisdom*, Dionysius did not follow Proclus as far as his doctrine on *what* exactly participates in those processions was concerned.

It should be noted that Dionysius does not show a clear correspondence between the stages in the divine processions and the levels in participation hierarchy. As I have mentioned, the whole three levels of hierarchy that participate in Wisdom – *intellectual, rational,* and *sensible* – unexpectedly appear here.

However, is there a correspondence between the participating and the participated in the hierarchical structure? Does the hierarchy of participating beings correspond to a parallel hierarchy of participated beings in terms of participated divine processions? In my opinion, the answer to this question should be negative.

The processions-names *Goodness*, *Being*, *Life*, and *Wisdom* from *DN* V, 1–2, which are participated in by the hierarchically organized created beings do not form a hierarchy, but rather in the words of Eric Perl, "are simply more or less universal modes of the same divine presence,"[50] representing different

48. It should be noted that, unlike Dionysius, Gregory of Nyssa placed the perfection, corresponding to the angelic powers (as well as to the highest ability of the human beings), *intellectual created being*, outside the hierarchy of natural beings. Thus, such a perplexity does not arise in respect to Gregory's doctrine of hierarchies.

49. *Platonic Theology* III, 6. In general see the list in E. R. Dodds, "Commentary," in: *Proclus, The Elements of Theology*. A revised text with transl., introd. and comm. by E. R. Dodds, Oxford 1963, 232–233.

50. E. Perl, *Theophany...*, 70.

limits, upon which the divinity expands itself (ἐκτείνω). That means, as it follows from the V, 3, that *Wisdom* includes *Life*, *Being*, and *Goodness*; *Life* includes *Being* and *Goodness*, etc.[51] Ch. Schäfer called this principle the "Russian-doll-principle."[52] Obviously, the same principle holds true in regard to the entities participating in those processions: *intellectual beings* contain the perfections of *rational*, *sensible*, *living*, and *existing* beings; *rational beings* contain the perfections of *sensible*, *living*, and *existing beings*, etc.

We may speak about the elements referring to a hierarchy of the principles with the prefix "self-," which Dionysius also speaks of as participated entities (see above). Dionysius mentions the deified being, the living being, the unified being, the similar being, and the ordered being as entities participating in those principles (V, 5: 184.8–16; XI, 6: 222.17–223.1), but he assumes that beings with qualities corresponding to the names of the principles participate in each of them. This is why these principles (with the exception of *Self-Being*) are called "self-participating," being both participate (in *Self-Being* and through it in the self-supra-substantial *Goodness*) and are participated in (by the relevant types of participating beings). The element of hierarchical structuring in respect to these principles consists in their participation in *Self-Being* as a "senior principle" (V, 5: 184.8–16). However, Dionysius does not seem to give reason to think that self-participating principles in his system form some kind of hierarchy among themselves apart from the fact that each of them participates in *Self-Being*.

Thus, if we take a closer look at the examples which Dionysius provides in speaking about the origin of all beings, including the principles with the prefix "self-," out of *self-supra-substantial Goodness*, namely, the example of many lines passing through the center of circle and the example of the relationship of one to other numbers (V, 6, supra), we may see that the first example does not imply any hierarchy, while the second example may imply it. However, one example is not sufficient to make any conclusions about the hierarchical structure among the principles with the prefix "self-" in Dionysius, moreover, the first example does not support the hierarchical structure at all. Furthermore, in addition to *Self-Being*, *Self-Life*, and *Self-Wisdom*, such principles include, for example, *Self-Similarity*, *Self-Unity*, *Self-Order*, etc., and the possible structure of hierarchy between them, unlike among the first ones, is unclear.[53]

51. Cf. E. Perl, *Theophany...*, 69–70. It should be noted that Klitenic Wear and Dillon claim that in the Dionysian triad *Being* is above *Wisdom* and *Life*, and that *Life* and *Wisdom* participate in *Being*: "Regarding Being, Dionysius places this name above Life and Wisdom so that Life and Wisdom participate in Being;" S. Klitenic Wear, J. Dillon, *Dionysius the Areopagite and the Neoplatonist Tradition...*, 26. Unfortunately, the authors do not indicate the source for this claim in the text of Dionysius. However, this statement is valid only for the principles with the prefix "self-" (V, 5, see above), but not for all processions as such.
52. Ch. Schäfer, *The Philosophy of Dionysius the Areopagite...*, 87.
53. One might add that even the "Russian-doll-principle," entailing the inclusion of the lesser extended principles by the longer extended principles with certainty refers only to the di-

The Hierarchies in Dionysius the Areopagite and Gregory of Nyssa: Resume

Thus, we can identify four elements concerning the subject of participation in the system of Dionysius, defined by the Neoplatonic paradigm which involved such aspects of participation as the *non-participated*, the *participated*, and the *participating*. The four elements include, firstly, the *non-participated* – the supra-substantial divinity of God; secondly, the *participated* – divine processions and self-supra-substantial principles; thirdly, the *participated* and *participating* – the principles with the prefix "self-," and, fourthly, the *participating* – the created beings in their individual and natural aspects, and, in particular, the hierarchy of beings.

Unlike Gregory of Nyssa, Dionysius did not use either the Aristotelian paradigm of participation according to substance, that is, when the language of participation is used for saying that some individual being belongs to some species, or species to genus, or the Platonic paradigm of participation according to substance, implying the opposition *by participation* (corresponding to the possession of a certain property) and *by being* (corresponding to what this property objectified). Instead of using those paradigms, Dionysius uses the combined Neoplatonic paradigm of participation, which implied a distinction between the *non-participated* and *participated* in the divinity. This fact defines the general concept of the hierarchy of beings in Dionysius in the sense that it is exactly the hierarchy of the *participating*.

Thus, Gregory of Nyssa and Dionysius diverge in the very understanding of the hierarchy of beings, since in Gregory this hierarchy did not imply any transcendental principles with respect to the types of created beings in which these types participate, while in Dionysius the hierarchy entailed the existence of such principles or some universals-prior-to-beings. The triad of the divine processions *Being*, *Life*, and *Wisdom* claims this role in Dionysius. Even though this triad represented a unified Cause of beings, it constituted a sequence of links differing in the degree of the expansion of the divinity. In addition, the principles with the prefix "self-" – *Self-Being*, *Self-Life* and *Self-Wisdom*, representing some aspects of the divine processions – also claim this role, for in the system of Dionysius they also are participated in. Moreover, as far as we may understand Dionysius, these principles are distinct realities, since Dionysius speaks of a multitude of such principles (V, 5).

We may also point to certain common features in the hierarchies of beings by Gregory and Dionysius. There is a definite similarity in the sequence of levels in the hierarchies. Keeping in mind this similarity, we may suggest the dependence of Dionysius on Gregory in some respect.

Thus the Dionysian hierarchy of participating beings is the following: *beings* (τὰ ὄντα) – *living beings* (τὰ ζῶντα) – *sensible beings* (τὰ αἰσθητικά) – *rational*

vine processions (discussed in *DN* V, 1–2), but not to the principles with the prefix "self-," and we cannot make any definitive conclusions concerning their subordination to this principle in Dionysius.

beings (τὰ λογικά) - *intellectual beings* (τὰ νοερά). In Gregory, if we take his hierarchy with the basis/summit as *being* and present the genera-species divisions in a linear way, we will have the following sequence of links: *existing = beings* (τὰ ὄντα) – *corporeal* (σωματικόν) – *living* (ζωτικόν) – *sensible/animate* (αἰσθητικόν/ἔμψυχον) – *rational* (λογικόν).

In Gregory, the hierarchy with *being* at its basis is the hierarchy of genera and species. In Dionysius, the hierarchy of the participating beings (as well as relationship between the divine processions) according to its structure is also similar to the genera-species hierarchy.[54] This follows from the understanding of the hierarchy, in which each successive level contains all the preceding levels, that is, from the "Russian-doll-principle."

Further, the level of the corporeal is missing in the hierarchy of Dionysius compared with Gregory,[55] while the level of intellectual is missing in the hierarchy of Gregory compared to that of Dionysius.[56] At the same time the hierarchies of Gregory and Dionysius show similarity with respect to the sequence of levels *beings - living beings - sensible beings - rational beings.*

Interestingly, the hierarchy of the participating beings according to nature in Dionysius contains the level of *sensible beings.* Its presence, as it was mentioned above, is quite unexpected, because it does not match *Wisdom* - the procession of the divinity in which it participates, and in general it falls out of the Dionysian order of divine processions (*Being, Life, Wisdom*) which are participated in by the levels of hierarchy. This level is missing in Proclus' hierarchy of the participated entities. It should also be noted that in the Dionysian hierarchy the level of the *sensible* is located in the same place where it was in the hierarchy established by Gregory of Nyssa – between *living beings* and *rational beings.* Thus, taking into account the general similarity in terms of the sequence of levels in the hierarchies of Gregory and Dionysius, we may assume that the appearance of such a level in the hierarchy of the naturally participating beings in Dionysius was caused by his reworking of the hierarchy of beings, provided by Gregory of Nyssa. If this is the case, Dionysius might have borrowed the level of the *sensible* from Gregory's hierarchy, installing it in the appropriate place of his own hierarchical structure.

As I have mentioned, the presence of the level of *sensible beings* in the place where it was located in the hierarchy of Gregory of Nyssa, that is, between *living beings* and *rational beings,* is related to the fact that in the course of developing his hierarchy, Gregory had in mind the Biblical and cosmogonic order of natural beings (as it is mentioned in Gen. 1:11 and 20), and

54. The difference from the genera-species structure in this case is only that the hierarchical language in Dionysius does not imply the links representing privative elements, symmetrical to the main links of the hierarchy (non-intellectual, non-rational, non-sensible, etc.), as is the case in Gregory's hierarchical structure.
55. As a matter of fact, this link is present in the hierarchy of participating according to Proclus, who, as we have seen, in many ways influenced the doctrine of Dionysius.
56. Sf. note 48 and the text around it.

on this basis changed the order of levels in the hierarchy compared to the Tree of Porphyry, which he generally followed.

Thus the Biblical trend in terms of the order of natural beings through Gregory of Nyssa penetrated the Dionysian discourse and through it penetrated the corresponding doctrines of the subsequent authors, which I intend to discuss in the second part of this study.[57]

57. D. Biriukov, "Hierarchies of Beings in the Patristic Thought: Maximus the Confessor, John of Damascus and the Palamite literature," in: B. Lourié, N. Seleznyov, eds., *Scrinium: Revue de patrologie, d'hagiographie critique et d'histoire ecclésiastique*, vol. 10: *Syrians and the Others: Cultures of the Christian Orient in the Middle Ages* (2014) 281–304.

Christology After Chalcedon and the Transformation of the Philosophical Tradition

Reflections on a Neglected Topic

Johannes Zachhuber

1. Introduction

The question as to what impact the rise of Christian theology had on the philosophical tradition is not new. Among the various approaches that have been taken to this topic, however, a detailed analysis of Christological debates after Chalcedon has not been a prominent starting point. In fact, this approach has arguably been neglected.[1] There are several reasons for this neglect: Western scholarship has tended to move straight from the Council of Chalcedon to the early Middle Ages, and those theologians who have taken an interest in the later Eastern debates were often less interested in philosophy than in other theological developments. Historians of philosophy, on the other hand, often bypass Greek theological authors from late antiquity altogether.[2]

In addition, anyone who seriously wishes to engage with intellectual developments in this period faces a number of objective challenges: significant texts are transmitted in various languages, including Syriac and Arabic, that are not usually read and understood by students of intellectual history. Many

1. An interesting exception to that rule is Werner Elert's posthumously published study *Der Ausgang der altkirchlichen Christologie: Eine Untersuchung über Theodor von Pharan und seine Zeit als Einführung in die alte Dogmengeschichte*, ed. W. Maurer, E. Bergsträßer, Berlin: Lutherisches Verlagshaus 1957.
2. Among the exceptions to this rule the most significant was arguably Michael Frede. Cf. his: "Der Begriff des Individuums bei den Kirchenvätern," *Jahrbuch für Antike und Christentum* 40 (1997) 38–54; "John of Damascus on Human Action, the Will, and Human Freedom," in: K. Ierodiakonou, ed., *Byzantine Philosophy and its Ancient Sources*, Oxford: OUP 2002, 63–95. See also below at n. 9.

of these texts, moreover, are not well edited. Critical studies are in short supply; those that exist do not usually pay close attention to philosophical problems.[3] At the same time, the sophistication and complexity of the arguments advanced by discussants on all sides of those debates is considerable. Martin Grabmann saw in the theology of those centuries a form of early scholasticism,[4] and there certainly is something to be said for such an assessment.

In this situation, my own reflections can only be provisional and tentative. With this caveat, however, I should suggest that a careful consideration of the philosophical implications of post-Chalcedonian Christological debates will not simply fill a gap in our knowledge of theological and philosophical developments, but has the potential to transform our understanding of the way the rise of Christian theology changed some of the most fundamental patterns of the Greek philosophical tradition.

This is the case I shall make in my chapter, which will begin with some preliminary remarks about the relationship between philosophy and theology during the first millennium before moving on with a historical narrative starting in the late fourth century but focussing on developments between the sixth and the eighth centuries.

2. Theology and philosophy in late antiquity

Any attempt to understand the relationship between theology and philosophy in late antiquity is hampered by the inadequacy of our modern conceptual and terminological categories. We tend to think of "philosophy" and "theology" as two disciplines; but this conceptualisation is altogether misleading when applied to late antiquity. As is well documented, this particular framework only emerged with the foundation of the medieval European university with its "theological" and "philosophical" faculties.[5] If we ask how early Christian authors conceived of their rational reflection about their

3. This is true for the most comprehensive treatment of the last generation, the multi-volume work by A. Grillmeier, *Jesus Christus im Glauben der Kirche*, 5 vols., Freiburg: Herder 1986–, but also for J. Lebon's by now classical study "La christologie du monophysisme syrien," in: *Das Konzil von Chalkedon*, ed. A. Grillmeier, H. Bacht, 3 vols., Würzburg: Echter 1951, 425–580. By contrast, philosophical problems are at the heart of the following publications: U. M. Lang, *John Philoponus and the Controversies over Chalcedon in the Sixth Century*, Leuven: Peeters 2001; R. Cross, "Perichoresis, Deification, and Christological Predication in John of Damascus," *Mediaeval Studies* 57 (2000) 69–124; id., "Individual Natures in the Christology of Leontius of Byzantium," *Journal of Early Christian Studies* 10 (2002) 245–265; Ch. Erismann, "The Trinity, Universals, and Particular Substances : Philoponus and Roscelin," *Traditio* 63 (2008) 277–305; id., "L'individualité expliquée par les accidents. Remarques sur la destinée 'chrétienne' de Porphyre," in : *Compléments de substance : études sur les propriétés accidentielles offertes à Alain de Libera*, eds. C. Erismann, A. Schniewind, Paris: Vrin 2008, 51–66; B. Glede, *The Development of the Term ἐνυπόστατος from Origen to John of Damascus*, Leiden: Brill 2012.
4. M. Grabmann, *Die Geschichte der scholastischen Methode*, 2 vols, Darmstadt: Wissenschaftliche Buchgesellschaft 1956, vol. 1, 92–116.
5. B. Geyer, "Facultas theologica: Eine bedeutungsgeschichtliche Untersuchung," *Zeitschrift für katholische Theologie* 75 (1964) 133–145: 143.

faith, the one answer we can give with some certainty, therefore, is a negative one: they certainly did not think that their work constituted a discipline called "theology." In fact, the term theology *in this sense* is once again a product of the high Middle Ages.[6]

It is much more difficult to give a positive definition of the character of Christian "theology" in late antiquity, but for the purposes of this paper I would propose that we may think of it as a kind of philosophy which, for want of a better word, we may call Christian philosophy. Philosophy in late antiquity existed in a wide variety of schools, including not merely the Neoplatonic schools of Alexandria and Athens, but medical and grammatical schools as well.[7] In some ways, Christian theology can be understood as one such school. The intellectual principles and rules of this philosophy would be determined by the needs and requirements specific to the school and imposed on those wishing to participate in its discourse. In the case of theology, Scripture and a growing body of agreed positions (doctrines) would be relevant, but also a particular institutional structure (the church) that arguably was more rigidly authoritarian than that predominant in other schools. One has to be careful, however, not to simplify a complex web of relationships. While "theological" reflection was curtailed by these factors, which therefore functioned as external limits imposed on "theologians" during the period, it is also the case that all these delimiting factors were themselves conditioned and shaped by theological reflection and thus not merely extraneous with regard to theology. In other words, doctrinal decisions were only made on the basis of previous theological argument, and even the use of Scripture was only practicable once hermeneutical principles of exegesis had been agreed upon and applied.

All ensuing problems cannot be addressed in the present place, but what has been said may be sufficient to evade the clichés that are conventionally applied to the relationship of nascent Christian theology to the intellectual traditions of pagan antiquity. These clichés are the well-known notion of the "Platonism" of the church fathers (or, more rarely but similarly, their Stoicism or Aristotelianism) on the one hand and its opposite, the idea that the fathers were principled anti-Platonists or even anti-philosophers on the other. Both positions, I think, suffer from the way in which they consider Christian theology a derivative phenomenon rather than understand it on its own terms.

It is, then, the fundamental premiss of my own argument that we should look at Christian theology in late antiquity as a form of philosophy. As such, it was first and foremost shaped by its own inherent needs and principles.

6. W. Pannenberg, *Wissenschaftstheorie und Theologie*, Frankfurt/M.: Suhrkamp 1973, 11–12.
7. Cf. D. King, "What is Ancient Philosophy?," *Journal for Late Antique Religion and Culture* 7 (2013) 90–100: 99.

These principles, however, were developed and discussed with the help of intellectual tools provided by traditional philosophical reflection. While such a distinction between "principles" and "tools" may not be entirely clear-cut it is, I believe, helpful in understanding the dynamics of Christian theological debate: once the doctrine of the Trinity, as defined by the Council of Nicaea in 325, had become official Church doctrine, Christian thinkers were not at liberty to adopt a position that was at variance with it; they would not accept a line of reasoning that led to a different conclusion however attractive this might seem from a purely rational point of view. Likewise, a Christian author was not in a position to reject an argument that used a biblical reference by questioning the authority of Scripture. Yet within the limits thus set, Christian authors would argue. They would expose the weaknesses of their opponents' case and seek to bolster the plausibility of their own position with the help of rational arguments or what they thought passed for the latter.

The outcome of this practice, which continued over many centuries, was the emergence of a Christian philosophy which in fundamental ways departed from, and was incompatible with, some of the most basic assumptions of the older Greek tradition. This observation has tempted scholars studying the period to think of Christianity as a major force of irrationality, the great opponent of philosophy. Recently, the philosopher William Matson judged that "the impact of Christianity on the Greek intellectual life was like that of an asteroid hitting the earth."[8] Christianity, Matson suggests, sought to "stamp out philosophy." This perception is not entirely unwarranted insofar as Christian thought did indeed pose a radical challenge to philosophy as it was understood at the time. Where I would beg to differ, however, is in the equation implicit in Matson's formulation of ancient philosophy with "philosophy." The case I seek to argue is, rather, that Christian thought produced a new and different kind of philosophy. It is my contention, furthermore, though I shall not be able to argue this case here in any detail, that the ensuing "Christian" philosophy has remained influential over the centuries and, in some ways, is much closer to later medieval and even modern forms of rationality than we might suspect.

* * *

If we accept the interpretation I have just proposed, the question arises which time period and which authors we ought to consider in establishing this case? Very recently, George Karamanolis has published a book under the title of *The Philosophy of Early Christianity*.[9] In some ways, his argument is similar to my own. Yet the period he chooses for his study begins in the

8. W. Matson, *Grand Theories and Everyday Beliefs: Science, Philosophy, and their Histories*, Oxford: OUP 2011, 66, 134.
9. G. Karamanolis, *The Philosophy of Early Christianity*, Durham: Acumen 2013.

second and ends in the fourth century. Much can be said in favour of such a decision. Notably, to speak of "early" Christian theology suggests a time reasonably close to the historical origin of the religion. And yet, I think there is also a danger in focussing too much on this very early period. For reasons that are not entirely easy to explain, Christianity unlike Islam took a long time to develop a philosophy of its own. In some ways, therefore, the full result of the transformation effected by Christian theology becomes apparent only towards the end of the first millennium. It is for this reason that I shall concentrate instead on the period between the Council of Chalcedon (451) and the eighth century as a crucial but neglected phase on the development of Christian thought.

3. Gregory of Nyssa and the classical theory

While my historical narrative in its essentials covers post-Chalcedonian developments, it must start in the late fourth century. For it is during this time that what I would like to call the "classical theory", was created. This theory, I would argue, is the first properly Christian philosophy in the sense that it contains a notion of what being itself is and how it ought to be understood. It is Christian insofar as it came about as an offshoot of the Trinitarian debate. It owes its existence to the so-called Cappadocian theologians, in particular Basil of Caesarea and Gregory of Nyssa. But while it could not have been conceived of without this particular doctrinal environment, it was not, I would suggest, incompatible with earlier Greek philosophy. Thus far, I would agree with those contemporary theologians who resource the Cappadocians for a broadly Platonic theology[10] and disagree with those, such as John Zizioulas and Colin Gunton, who ascribe to the Cappadocians an ontological revolution.[11]

The latter assessment, as is well known, rests on the notion that the Cappadocians introduced a radically innovative valuation of the human person which, through their emphasis on *hypostasis*, they postulated as the very ontological foundation of all being.[12] In reality, I think, the classical theory is very nearly the precise opposite: it is, for all intents and purposes, a theory of universal being even though it also holds that the latter can only exist as instantiated in individual entities. It is for this reason that, when the theory *became* the classical theory, and was, therefore, assumed to be applicable to Christology, which was the major problem confronting the Christian Church

10. S. Coakley, "Introduction – Gender, Trinitarian Analogies, and the Pedagogy of the 'Song,'" in: *Rethinking Gregory of Nyssa*, ed. S. Coakley, Oxford: Blackwell 2003, 1–13.
11. J. Zizioulas, *Being as Communion: Studies in Personhood and the Church*, Crestwood, N.Y.: St Vladimir's Seminary Press 2002; C. E. Gunton, *The One, the Three and the Many: God, Creation, and the Culture of Modernity*, Cambridge: CUP, 7th ed. 2002.
12. J. Zizioulas, *op. cit.*, 36–49.

from the fifth century onwards, enormous difficulties ensued: and these difficulties could no longer be solved within the intellectual framework provided by ancient metaphysics.

In order to grasp the Cappadocian theory in its essentials, its doctrinal background is of paramount importance. As Rowan Williams has shown in a seminal article, one of the arguments advanced against the Nicene dogma that the Son was *homoousios* with the Father was this: if Father and Son are *homoousios*, there must be a further thing, the *ousia*; in fact, this third item, divine substance, would be ontologically first and the two persons derived from it.[13] This, of course, was meant as a *reductio ad absurdum*: after all, it was universally accepted that the Father was the first ontological principle and the source of the trinitarian Godhead. The Cappadocians, however, developed their own theory partly in response to this Platonising objection,[14] and for what I call the classical theory this insight is crucial. It meant that whatever the common item (τὸ κοινόν), *ousia*, was, it could not be something separate; it could not exist somehow in addition to or on top of the individual hypostases. Somehow, in the Trinity the three Persons *are* also the one God even though at the same time they are irreducibly distinct.

The solution to this conundrum consists in the idea that being is universal but exists only in a finite number of individuals.[15] There is one God who only exists in three hypostases, and there is equally "one man" (as Gregory of Nyssa argues[16]) existing in a finite number of human hypostases whose concrete unity can be compared to a single body.[17] In both cases, there is a dynamic element added to explain the unity-in-diversity: the Godhead has its origin in the Father, who generates the Son and breathes the Spirit. Likewise, the unity of human nature only exists in the temporal progression of the human race.[18]

To this concrete account of being is then added an abstract complement. This is the celebrated Cappadocian doctrine of *idiomata* or properties.[19] We can differentiate universality and particularity by means of shared and individual properties. Taken in itself, this perspective might be seen to cancel out the emphasis on concrete being I sketched above, as it seems to direct our attention not to any individual thing or person, but to properties abstracted

13. R. Williams, "The Logic or Arianism," *Journal of Theological Studies* 34 (1983) 56–81.
14. J. Zachhuber, *Human Nature in Gregory of Nyssa: Philosophical Background and Theological Significance*, Leiden: Brill, 1999, 28–37.
15. I have analysed and discussed this theory in detail in *Human Nature...*, esp. 61–79 and "Once again: Gregory of Nyssa on Universals," *Journal of Theological Studies* 56 (2005) 75–98.
16. Esp. in *Ad Ablabium*, *GNO* III/1, 40, 5–9 and *Ad Graecos*, *GNO* III/1, 23, 21–25, and J. Zachhuber, *Human Nature...*, 108–118.
17. Gregory of Nyssa, *De hominis opificio* 16, PG 44, 185C.
18. J. Zachhuber, "Once again: Gregory of Nyssa on Universals," 91–97.
19. J. Zachhuber, *Human Nature...*, 70–79.

from them. Alternatively, the notion of shared properties might seem to suggest the postulation of an immanent form or essence.[20] It is easy to arrive at such an interpretation on the basis of certain Cappadocian texts, but I am now convinced that such a reading falls short of their intention. The reason is, once again, that their theory was primarily meant to serve trinitarian doctrine, and it is evident that divine *ousia* cannot be an abstract divine essence. I therefore think that the two accounts, which I would call, for the sake of convenience, the concrete and the abstract, are meant to be complementary even though there is no evidence, as far as I am aware, that their precise relationship was ever explained.

Still, for my reconstruction of the Cappadocian theory, the assumption is crucial that they sought to hold together, in an admittedly tensional unity, a vision of universal ontological unity, existing in irreducibly individual instances *and* a logical distinction of universal and particular on the basis of properties. Whereas the former of the two stresses the unity of being, the latter permits conceptual distinction between the level of universality and the level of particularity.

* * *

This theory, then, became classical; by this I mean not so much that there emerged a kind of Cappadocian school comparable to the existence of Origenist theologians, for example, but that this particular way of thinking and the specific elements that made up the Cappadocian account of being turned into something like a universally shared idiom of Greek theologians uniting many different theological schools and even, or so I would argue, the different churches emerging from the post-Chalcedonian schism.

In fact, problems inherent in the classical theory are to some extent to blame for the deep divisions emerging within Christendom from the latter half of the fifth century. As the Cappadocian theory did not have a proper account of the individual nor indeed of individualisation, it became a liability once Christology was the major doctrinal driver of theological debate. I am aware that this claim goes against the received wisdom of Patristic scholarship, which has usually considered the differentiation of *ousia* and *hypostasis* on the analogy of species and individual as the very achievement of Cappadocian theology. While I am not, of course, denying the significance of this conceptual innovation, it seems to me that the way it was formulated by those fourth century thinkers left crucial problems open or even prevented them from being properly addressed.

What I mean is this. It is admittedly accurate to say that we can distinguish in a human person that which this person shares with other human

20. R. Cross, "Universals in Gregory of Nyssa," *Vigiliae Christianae* 56 (2002) 372–410.

beings from that, which marks him or her out as an individual. This in itself, however, does not yet explain what it means that humanity *becomes* individual in this person. In fact, it stands in the way of such an explanation inasmuch as such an account creates the impression that we deal, as it were, with two separate realities, the person's universal humanity and his or her individual identity. The problem of individuation, by contrast, can be put into the proposition that universal humanity becomes individual in the person. If, for example, Socrates is ill, a human being is ill. This does not imply that every single human individual is suddenly ill, but Socrates' sickness does not only affect his "Socratesness" either but his whole humanity.

The lack of such an element in the classical theory was not, I think, an oversight. We know that Gregory of Nyssa rejected the notion of "particular substances" as individualised universals because he felt, rightly, that they threatened the strong realism he needed to defend his trinitarian theology against the charge of tritheism.[21] The needs of trinitarian theology, after all, firmly determined whatever position could be held in the classical theory! The Cappadocian view proved its worth by settling the trinitarian controversy, which had threatened the very existence of the Christian church in the fourth century and therefore stood at the centre of theological attention and concern during that period. When this was no longer the case, its unique adaptation to trinitarian theology precipitated its crisis.

4. Christology and the crisis of the classical theory

Consider now the case of Christology. Assuming that John 1,14 is shorthand for the notion of the Incarnation, it can arguably be restated to mean that "in Jesus Christ God became human." What does "God" stand for in this proposition? According to the classical theory only two interpretations are possible: either "God" denotes divine nature or it stands for the individual property of one trinitarian person.[22] But neither of the two conveys the meaning this statement has in Christian theology. For if "God" signified divine nature, the statement would have to be true for the Trinity as a whole, with the result of Patripassianism; if, on the other hand, it referred to the individual properties of the Son it would exclude divinity proper from the Incarnation. Even though the biblical text says that "the Logos" became flesh, however, it has always been taken for granted that this implies that in and through the second person of the Trinity Godself became human.

This problem, it seems, was not immediately recognised. Otherwise, it would be hard to understand why the Council of Chalcedon included in its

21. Gregory of Nyssa, *Ad Graecos*, *GNO* III/1, 23, 4–13.
22. Cf. Gregory of Nyssa, *Ad Graecos*, GNO III/1, 19, 1–5: "Εἰ τὸ θεὸς ὄνομα προσώπου δηλωτικὸν ὑπῆρχεν, τρία πρόσωπα λέγοντες ἐξ ἀνάγκης τρεῖς ἂν ἐλέγομεν θεούς· εἰ δὲ τὸ θεὸς ὄνομα οὐσίας σημαντικόν ἐστιν, μίαν οὐσίαν ὁμολογοῦντες τῆς ἁγίας τριάδος ἕνα θεὸν εἰκότως δογματίζομεν, ἐπειδὴ μιᾶς οὐσίας ἓν ὄνομα τὸ θεός ἐστιν".

credal formula the statement that Jesus Christ was "of the same substance as God according to his divinity, and of the same substance as we according to his humanity."[23] As we have seen, the classical theory mandated, quite sensibly, that in the case of the Trinity the term *homoousios* implied two tenets: on the one hand the applicability of common generic predicates, such as "eternal," "good," and "almighty;" on the other hand, the exclusive existence of the single nature in three hypostases. Above, I have called the former the "abstract" and the latter the "concrete" component of the Cappadocian theory. It is easy to see that the "double-*homoousion*" committed Chalcedonian theologians to either of two assumptions. If they upheld the classical theory in both its concrete and its abstract aspects, the consequence would be that Christ's two natures had to exist in two hypostases. If, however, they maintained, in line with the teaching of the Council, that there was only one hypostasis in the saviour, they inevitably reduced the classical theory to its abstract dimension. In other words, *homoousios* would merely mean that two or more objects shared the same set of generic predicates. Not surprisingly, the opponents of the Council of Chalcedon chided its supporters for embracing the former, obviously heretical, option, while the Chalcedonians themselves chose the latter without, initially, realising how far this removed them from the classical theory.

The self-perception of the Chalcedonian theologians as stalwarts of the Cappadocian theory has largely been accepted by modern scholarship where the conflict about Chalcedon has often been presented as a controversy between defenders and critics of the Cappadocian heritage.[24] It should be clear by now that I regard such a view as a considerable simplification of a rather more complex picture, as it underestimates the degree to which the Christological problem really was the crux of the classical theory. That it has, nevertheless, gained such wide currency may be due to the fact that Gregory of Nyssa himself, in his polemic against Apollinarius of Laodicea, had rejected his opponent's Christology by reducing the classical theory to its abstract component. In fact, Gregory came close to endorsing the double *homoousion* himself.[25] As has often been pointed out, the Bishop of Nyssa was hardly at his best in this particular controversy,[26] but however this may be,

23. *Acta Conciliorum Oecumenicorum* 2, 1, 2, 129, 26–7: "ὁμοούσιον τῷ πατρὶ κατὰ τὴν θεότητα καὶ ὁμοούσιον ἡμῖν [...] κατὰ τὴν ἀνθρωπότητα."

24. J. Lebon, "La christologie...," 465 ; B. Glede, *Development...*, 50–56.

25. Without ever combining them in a single passage, Gregory in the *Antirrheticus* applied both aspects to Christology. On the one hand, he insisted that Christ's divinity is *homoousios* with the Father without any intermingling of human nature, as otherwise the Father too would be incarnate and have a body (*GNO* III/1, 157, 26–158, 6). On the other hand, he rejected Apollinarius' claim that Christ was not *homoousios* with human beings "according to the most important part" (κατὰ τὸ κυριώτατον) on the grounds that "that which is not *homoousios* is altogether of a different substance (ἑτεροούσιος)" (*GNO* III/1, 165, 8–9).

26. Cf. the criticism in J. Tixeront, *Histoire des dogmes dans l'antiquité chrétienne*, vol. II, Paris : Victor Lecoffre 1912, 128 (English Text: *History of Dogmas*, vol. II, St. Louis: Herder 1914, 127.

his example supplied some Cappadocian authority for a *prima facie* application of the classical theory to Christology as it was later practised by many Chalcedonians.

It will be the purpose of the remainder of my chapter to present a different account of those debates. Concentrating on Chalcedonians and their Miaphysite opponents, I shall aim to show how the classical theory formed the starting point for radical intellectual innovations in both camps. In other words, defenders as well as critics of the Council of Chalcedon retained elements of the classical theory – in fact, this is why I regard it as the "classical" theory in the first place – but both also had to move consciously and decisively beyond its original framework in order to account for the argumentative needs created by the context of the Christological controversy. In this sense, I propose to consider the rival philosophies emerging in the wake of Chalcedon as competing responses to the same fundamental problem.

5. Chalcedonians and Miaphysites in the sixth century

When read through the lens of the classical theory, the Council of Chalcedon had dealt a difficult hand to its theological supporters. Their opponents exploited these difficulties to the best of their abilities. Leontius of Byzantium's adversary in his *Epilyseis* – as indicated by the full title of the work, this was the celebrated Severus of Antioch, the major theologian of the Miaphysite tradition – opened his case against the Chalcedonians with the following question:

> Did the Word assume human nature as seen in the species or in the individual?[27]

Elsewhere, he explained that without such a distinction no orthodox Christology was possible:

> For if you say that in Christ there are two substances (i.e. natures), it must by necessity be said also that both Father and Spirit and, to say it in one word, the Holy Trinity itself is incarnate in the whole of humanity, that is the human race.[28]

The line of argument is clear. If the Chalcedonians maintain that in Christ universal divine nature assumed universal human nature, they are in effect saying that the whole Trinity became incarnate in the whole of humanity. If on the other hand they accept (as Severus evidently thought they should)

27. Leontius of Byzantium, *Epilyseis* I, PG 86, 1916D–1917A: "Φύσιν ὁ Λόγος ἀναλαβῶν ἀθρωπίνην, τὴν ἐν τῷ εἴδει θεωρουμένην, ἢ τὴν ἐν ἀτόμῳ ἀνέλαβεν."
28. Si vero dicitis Christo duas esse substantias, necessario dicendum est et Patrem et Spiritum et, ut summatim dicamus, ipsam sanctam Trinitam toti humanitati incarnatam esse, id est humano generi. Quoted in: John of Caesarea ("the Grammarian"), *Apologia Concilii Chalcedonensis* 14, 8, 72–75, Richard.

that the Incarnation is about individual natures, then the coexistence of two of them in the Incarnate Christ leads to an affirmation of two hypostases as well.

Throughout the sixth century, Chalcedonian authors such as John the Grammarian, Leontius of Byzantium, and Anastasius of Antioch responded to this question by rejecting its alternative.[29] According to Leontius, saying that the universal is nature "seen in many" (ἐν πλήθει θεωρεῖται), while the individual is seen in what is numerically one (ἐν ἑνὶ τῷ ἀριθμῷ),[30] is misleading, precisely because universal nature is the same in all individuals and whole in each of them. This he finds indicated in the univocal predication of the formula of substance or nature:

> The same formula of the nature is given in both many and one: whatever formula you give for nature unqualifiedly, this is given to you for nature considered in one [sc. subject], and neither does the fact that many participate in the nature make the one [nature] many natures, nor does it make the many [individuals] one.[31]

Along the same lines, Anastasius of Antioch, time after time in his writings, denied the conceptual need for individual or particular natures. It is enough to invoke the universal to provide a full explanation of Christological doctrine:

> We call him God, not a God, and we call him man, not a man. For he is God and man, and the [use of the] universal terms indicates that of which he is [composed] – not of particular hypostases but of universal substances.[32]

Both Leontius and Anastasius evidently follow in the wake of Gregory of Nyssa's anti-Apollinarian argument. For them, the mere fact that the Incarnation was said of the universal term was enough to steer clear of the problem of two hypostases. Christ is not a mixture of an "individual" God (i.e. a divine hypostasis) and an individual human person, but one individual partaking of divine and human natures. Opponents of the Chalcedonian position disingenuously insinuate that it leaves the duality of natures unresolved; the opposite is true: precisely by insisting on a duality of universal natures (as distinct from individuals) the problem of "two Christs" is avoided.

We have already seen that in spite of its seeming congruity with Gregory of Nyssa's argument, the position of these Chalcedonians represented a break

29. Cf. also Justinian, *Contra Monophysitas*, PG 86, 1137D–1140B.
30. Leontius of Byzantium, *Epilyseis* I, PG 86, 1917A.
31. Leontius of Byzantium, *Epilyseis* I, PG 86, 1917B. English Text: R. Cross, "Individual Natures...," 255.
32. Anastasius I Antiochenus, *Oratio* III, 54, 15–18, Sakkos. Cf. G. Weiss, *Studia Anastasiana I: Studien zum Leben, zu den Schriten und zur Theologie des Patriarchen Anastasius I von Antiochien (559–598)*, München: Institut für Byzantinistik und neugriechische Philologie der Universität 1965, 200–202.

with the "classical theory" insofar as they elided its concrete aspect and reduced community of being to the sharing of generic properties. I now want to take this argument one step further: not only has traditional scholarship been wrong to assert fundamental continuity between the classical theory and later Chalcedonians; it has also been mistaken, or at least one sided, in positing a stark contrast between the Cappadocian view and the philosophical theology of the later Miaphysites. Rather, both sides were faced with the incompatibility between the classical theory and the technical needs of Christology. Both camps therefore sought to adapt it, but also retained as much of it as they could. For the Chalcedonians this meant giving up on the concrete aspect of the classical theory. What can be said about their Miaphysite opponents?

At the beginning of the second part ("second speech") of his major polemical work against John the Grammarian, Severus of Antioch gives a thorough and differentiated account of how he conceived of the theoretical foundations of their debate.[33] At first sight, this text confirms the suspicion that his thought marks a radical departure from Cappadocian principles because Severus starts from the assertion, supported by the authority of Athanasius, that *ousia* and *hypostasis* ultimately mean the same, namely being. Being, he argues, is one and ultimately grounded in God who, according to Exodus 3, 14, is being itself. Both terms can be traced back to this most fundamental notion and must not, therefore, be separated from each other.[34] Later in the same passage, Severus refers to the distinction between *ousia* and *hypostasis*, but Lebon, in his classical study on the subject, has dismissed this reference as a mere concession to the prevailing orthodoxy of the time.[35] Such an assessment, however, fails to take into account the complexities of the issue. As we have seen, the classical theory only distinguished between the two terms in its "abstract" component. Insofar as it also embraced the principle that universal natures only exist in concrete hypostases, it indeed all but identified *ousia* and *hypostasis*. Prestige therefore was not entirely wrong when, in his sharp criticism of neo-Chalcedonian theology, he essentially took Severus' view, asserting that for the Cappadocians *ousia* and *hypostasis* nearly meant the same thing.[36] For Severus, the basic unity of *ousia* and *hypostasis* is a premise without which their distinction by authors such as Basil and Gregory of Nyssa cannot properly be understood.

Being is one, Severus argues, but it can be looked at in two dimensions – as concretely existing individual being and as the universal that encompasses

33. Severus of Antioch, *Contra impium grammaticum* II, 1–2, 43–55, Lebon.
34. Severus of Antioch, *Contra impium grammaticum* II 1, 44f., Lebon. He refers to Athanasius, *Ep. ad Afros episcopos*, PG 26, 1036; cf. also *Contra impium grammaticum* II 3, 56, Lebon.
35. This seems to be Lebon's view: "La christologie...," 455.
36. G. L. Prestige, *God in Patristic Thought*, London: SPCK 1964, 271: "It is grossly untrue to affirm that theologians had employed ousia in the sense of species. The writer would have been nearer the mark if he had said that ousia and hypostasis were synonymous."

and includes all individuals.[37] If therefore *ousia* and *hypostasis* are to be distinguished, this is not because the individual person is not an *ousia* – Peter evidently is a human being! – but because it makes sense to differentiate between the way being subsists and is seen in its individual instantiations, and the way it is seen in their totality. For this duality of perspective, as it were, Severus adduces scriptural references to "man" (ἄνθρωπος) in the singular indicating humankind in its entirety (e.g. Gen. 9, 6),[38] while on the other hand citing biblical texts in which individual properties are added to the generic name to identify the individual person.

Severus' relationship to the classical theory, then, is no less ambivalent than that of his Chalcedonian opponents. In many ways, the Cappadocian view forms the background of his own argument. While his Chalcedonian opponents reconstruct the classical theory from its conceptual (and thus abstract) side and for this reason emphasise the *distinction* between universal and particular, Severus starts from its concrete side according to which, as we have seen, *physis* is the totality of the individuals, and the latter are the one and only way universal being ever exists.[39]

Judged from this vantage point, the Chalcedonian assumption of two natures in one hypostasis must indeed appear a monstrosity. Severus' extensive references to the etymological and biblical justifications for the use of *ousia*, *physis*, and *hypostasis* in theology would seem to suggest that, according to him, the transformation of the former pair into the notion of an abstract essence would cast the shadow of doubt over the whole project of their adoption by Christian theology. "No nature without a hypostasis" (οὐκ ἔστιν φύσις ἀνυπόστατος) therefore became the rallying cry of Severus' followers.[40] It is important to realise that in this they felt perfectly justified by the classical theory.

Yet if Severus's position is not as alien from the classical theory as many scholars seem to think, this is not, of course, to say that he simply accepted the Cappadocian model. Concerned as he was with the Christological problem, he could not do that. It was all very well to accuse his Chalcedonian opponents of teaching an Incarnation of the whole Trinity in the whole of humanity, but Severus must have been aware that the problem ultimately lay

37. Severus of Antioch, *Contra impium grammaticum* II 1, 45, Lebon: Igitus, quoad hoc quidem communio inter substantiam et hypostasim et existentiam [ὕπαρξις] habetur, quoad aliud autem magna est longinquitas et distantia atque differentia. Nam substantia quidem etiam significativa est generis et notionis comprehendentis multas species; hypostasis autem limitatio quaedam est significativa unius formae, id est personae, cum ad homogenea secundum proprietatem communionem non habet et distinctio charactere subiectum includit. Cf. for the wording [Basil], *Ep.* 38, 2, 11–16, vol. I, 81f., Courtonne.

38. Severus of Antioch, *Contra impium grammaticum* II 1, 45, Lebon.

39. It is therefore true that in a sense for Severus *physis* and *hypostasis* mean the same thing, but this is less mysterious than Lebon and others have thought (cf. Lebon, "La christologie...," 465). After all, the same individual is both "man" and "Peter!"

40. References for this motto in U. M. Lang, *John Philoponus...*, 63.

with the classical theory itself. There is no reason to doubt that he believed his innovative conceptual distinction, the introduction of particular natures, was merely an adaptation of the classical theory to the needs of Christology. After all, it seemed designed to specify what was implicit in Gregory of Nyssa already, that universal nature subsisted only in particulars. To say, then, that nature insofar as it was seen in one particular could be distinguished from nature insofar as it was seen in all particulars might appear as a mere terminological and conceptual clarification. In reality, however, this modification of the classical view was not at all innocent.

The weak point in Severus' argument was perceived already by his direct opponent, John of Caesarea ("the Grammarian"). John responded to the charge that without individual natures the Incarnation could not be conceptualised with the following riposte:

> For they [i.e. the opponents, specifically Severus] mean to subject the substance of the Godhead to division so that one of its parts appears in the Father, another part in the Son and another in the Holy Spirit so that the properties of divinity are seen in each of the hypostases in part rather than [whole] in all of them.[41]

The Grammarian does not make the ultimate consequence of his charge explicit, but it seems evident that what emerges here is the spectre of tritheism. Is not, John insinuates, the mention of individual natures tantamount to denying the actual unity of universal nature? He clearly has a point. Gregory of Nyssa had emphatically rejected the theory of individual or particular natures, arguing they were precisely what he meant by hypostasis.[42] For Gregory, the possibility of maintaining realism rested on his construction according to which particulars are in essence the same; they are nothing but their nature insofar as it subsists. If Severus now insisted there were individual natures as well, he was either introducing a mere terminological innovation or he believed that those individual natures were a third category in addition to, or better in between, universal nature and individual hypostases. Yet if this meant universal nature was itself modified in the process of individuation, this would jettison the very realism that had enabled the classical theory to underwrite the trinitarian settlement of the late fourth century.[43]

41. Putant enim [sc. adversarii, i.e. Severus] divinitatis substantiam divisioni subiacere eiusque partem quidem in Patre, partem autem in Filio, partem autem in Spiritu sancto apparere, ita ut unaquaeque ex hypoastasibus in parte, non autem in omnibus iis, quae divinitatis propria sunt, concipiatur: John of Caesarea (the Grammarian), *Apologia Concilii Chalcedonensis* 14, 8, 76–80, Richard. Cf. A. Grillmeier, *Christ in Christian Tradition*, II/2, 56–63.

42. Gregory of Nyssa, *Ad Graecos*, GNO III/1, 23, 4–13.

43. I leave to one side here the interesting question of whether the fact that Severus tends to refer to the relation between genus and species for *ousia* and *hypostasis* is of any relevance (cf. Severus, *Contra impium grammaticum* II 1, 45, Lebon; the full quotation is given above at n. 37). It was generally acknowledged that the genus *was* modified by the species (cf. A. C. Lloyd, *The Anatomy of Neoplatonism*, Oxford: Clarendon Press 1990, 76–78). Philoponus in his tritheistic fragments seems to emphasise the genus-species relationship as the paradigm for the Trinity (cf. *On theology*, fr. 13).

Severus had indeed not been clear about the relationship he envisaged between individual and universal nature. His followers, however, found it difficult to escape from the vicious alternative his proposal seemed to pose: either they would concede that individual nature was nothing other than a different name for hypostasis, in which case the Miaphysite argument (a single hypostasis requiring a single nature) was tautological; or they had to accept that Severus' use of individual natures implied that the nature once individuated was no longer common. The latter interpretation would be able to explain how in the Incarnation God, "one of the holy Trinity" as a famous slogan had it, became man without this entailing the unwanted consequence that all three Persons became incarnate. Yet it would seem difficult, to say the least, to uphold such a theory without at the same time denying the realistic universal Gregory of Nyssa had stipulated to escape from the charge of tritheism.

Given this unattractive alternative, it is not too surprising that within the Miaphysite community the Trinity once again became a controversial topic of debate. So-called tritheists maintained that it was admissible to speak of "three natures" and "three substances" with regard to God insofar as any of the three members of the Trinity could be called (and had been called by the Fathers) "a substance" and "a nature."[44] For most of them, it is difficult or impossible, due to the dearth of sources, to know how precisely they understood these claims or how they justified them. This is different only, and only to some extent, for the most prominent advocate of tritheism, John Philoponus.

Philoponus, in a way, marks one endpoint of the development this chapter seeks to establish.[45] He certainly exemplifies the notion that Christian thought led to philosophical ideas that were incompatible with the earlier Greek tradition. He is well known for his cosmological arguments deployed against the major representative of pagan Neoplatonism, Proclus, and ultimately against Aristotle himself. Philoponus' ideas, consciously based on a Christian foundation, were eagerly picked up by Islamic as well as early modern thinkers. Most of them, arguably, follow from theistic principles and the specific character of the Christian doctrine of creation. Is there, in addition, evidence that his particular stance in the Christological debate shaped his Christian philosophy?

His theory of the universal, which he defends extensively in his theological works, is largely indistinguishable from the mainstream Neoplatonic theory known to us from commentaries on Aristotle's *Organon*. Philoponus then, one might say, was the first consciously to apply a philosophical theory to arbitrate in a theological controversy, an attitude altogether alien to earlier generations of theologians.[46] Yet even if it is granted that the philo-

44. *Monophysite Texts of the Sixth Century*, ed. A. van Roey, P. Allen, Leuven: Peeters 1994, 127.
45. On Philoponus cf. U. M. Lang, *John Philoponus...*; Ch. Erismann, "The Trinity...".
46. This is why his major Christological treatise is called *Arbiter* – a writing addressed to the Emperor Justinian in the run-up to the council of 553 with the express advertisement that

sophical notions underwriting Philoponus' theological stance can be traced back to the Aristotelian commentaries he authored as a young man, his willingness to use them in doctrinal debates sets him apart from his Neoplatonist peers who consistently upheld Porphyry's principle according to which Aristotle's philosophy – and the logical writings in particular – only applied to sensible reality.[47] By contrast, Christian authors from the time of Basil of Caesarea had found it unexceptionable to use principles culled from the *Organon* for the clarification of doctrine. In this practice they had, of course, been eclectic; in fact, in some ways the "classical theory" can be described as a selective reception of Aristotelian logic in Neoplatonic interpretation.[48] Thus far, Philoponus is in continuity with a time-honoured Christian tradition.

With Severus and his followers, Philoponus considered the central task of Christology that of being able unambiguously to express that it was the Son who had become incarnate; in this sense he accentuated the traditional μία φύσις-formula by speaking of the "one incarnate nature of God the Logos."[49] He rejected the Chalcedonians' insistence on universal natures in the Incarnation with the same arguments we have encountered before. Uwe Michael Lang summarises Philoponus' doctrinal reasoning as follows:

> The common nature of the divinity that is recognised in the Trinity has not become incarnate, otherwise we would predicate the Incarnation also of the Father and the Holy Spirit. Nor has the common intelligible content of human nature been united with God the Logos, otherwise the whole human race before and after the advent of the Logos would have been united to him.[50]

For Philoponus, this problem was identical or at least very similar to a well-known logical difficulty: we can say that a man dies, and yet this does not mean that human nature in its entirety dies. To resolve this, it was convenient to allow particular substances; once instantiated in the particular, human nature is no longer common to all, but modified by individual properties and therefore this or that person's human nature. So if Peter falls ill or gets married, this concerns his humanity, but not Paul's. In fact, this was more or less the standard view among the Aristotelian commentators, and Philoponus certainly subscribes to it in his philosophical works.[51] It is on the basis of this very theory that he subsequently suggested far-reaching and radical solutions to the central doctrinal problems of the Christian faith.

---

using philosophy was key to the solution of the doctrinal impasse. Cf. U. M. Lang, *John Philoponus...*, 42–47.

47. Cf. Ch. Evangeliou, *Aristotle's Categories and Porphyry*, Leiden: Brill 1988, esp. 9–10.
48. J. Zachhuber, *Human Nature...*, esp. 79–93.
49. John Philoponus, *Arbiter* 7 = John of Damascus, *De haeresibus* 83 addit., 52, 86–53, 87, Kotter.
50. U. M. Lang, *John Philoponus...*, 62.
51. John Philoponus, *Arbiter* 7 = John of Damascus, *De haeresibus* 83 addit., 52, 55–65, Kotter.

Philoponus first of all asserts that natures cannot exist apart from individuals.[52] This, as we have seen, is a restatement of Severus' position with perfectly traditional, Cappadocian credentials. John, however, on the basis of his philosophical considerations moves one decisive step further, clearly and unequivocally asserting that the nature is one (and thus truly "universal") only when abstracted from the many because *in* them it is different with each:

> Now, this common nature of man, in which no one differs from any other, when it is realised in any one of the individuals, then is particular to that one and is not common to any other individual [...]. Thus that rational animal that is in me is common to no other animal.[53]

We can see how Philoponus thought this solved the Christological problem and at the same time demonstrated that there could only be one nature in the saviour. In the Logos, *God* truly became human, but this did not imply that the whole Trinity became incarnate because it was, as it were, only Christ's "own" divinity that was the subject of the Incarnation. The same was true on the human side as well, and so Jesus was fully man without the need to predicate the Incarnation of the entire human race.

What, however, did this mean for universal nature? If this was another ontological reality, existing in addition to, and on top of, its particularised instantiations, the explanatory value of Philoponus' theory was once again lost. For if, in this case, the Incarnation, could not be predicated of universal nature, this would mean that *God* had not truly and fully become human. But if the Incarnation *was* predicated of universal divine nature, Philoponus had not achieved anything because it was, once again, unclear how Patripassianism could be avoided. Philoponus therefore opted for an alternative: he denied that universal nature as shared was an ontological reality. It was real as individualised but universal only as abstracted from its individual instantiations.

This is a view frequently found in the Aristotelian commentators and usually justified by Aristotle's famous line in *De anima* I (402^b7) that "the universal animal was either nothing or posterior," a passage Philoponus himself was evidently fond of. Yet nothing in this tradition can explain the radical consequences he drew from this philosophical theory. In order for Christ to be properly individual, Philoponus was willing to jettison the unity of God as resting in the single substance (*mia ousia*) taught by the Nicene Fathers:

> For what should the one nature of the divinity be if not the common intelligible content of the divine nature seen on its own and separated in the conception (τῇ ἐπινοίᾳ) of the property of each hypostasis?[54]

52. John Philoponus, *Arbiter* 7 = John of Damascus, *De haeresibus* 83 addit., 51, 46–48, Kotter.
53. John Philoponus, *Arbiter* 7 = John of Damascus, *de haeresibus* 83 addit., 52, 52–55, Kotter; English Text: Ch. Erismann, "The Trinity...," 289f.
54. John Philoponus, *Arbiter* 7 = John of Damascus, *de haeresibus* 83 addit., 52, 72–73, Kotter; English Text: U. M. Lang, *John Philoponus...*, 62.

This theory has earned Philoponus his reputation of being a tritheist. It is not crucial for the present purpose to assess the fairness of this charge. More important is the recognition that, on this point, the Alexandrine stands in radical antagonism to the classical theory of the Cappadocians. Gregory of Nyssa's undivided *in re* universal is replaced by a conceptual *post rem* universal that abstracts from *in re* forms modified in each individual and thus particular to them. Individuation, therefore, can no longer be understood as the hypostatisation of a universal, which at the same time remains one and whole, but crucially involves individuating properties functioning more or less exactly like specific differences at the level of genera. Individuals, finally, are no longer mere hypostases of one common *ousia*, but become particular substances whose being rests at least partly in themselves.

At the same time, it would be wrong to reduce Philoponus' theory to an alternative model intended to supersede and replace the Cappadocian one. While it is likely that he felt some professional contempt for the amateurish philosophy of fourth century Fathers,[55] he is not simply detached from the earlier Patristic tradition. He accepts their fundamental premiss that logical principles can be applied to doctrine and thus to God, considers nature as immanent, and subscribes to the irreducible complementarity of nature and hypostasis. Even the principle that nature is only known by and through individuals is by no means a departure from the Cappadocians. It is, really, in one regard only that his theory reverses the one Gregory of Nyssa had offered. For the latter, nature is one-in-many, a reality whose unity appears no less distinctly when encountered in its individual instances. On the contrary, it was the empirical study of the physical world, which for Gregory revealed behind its plurality a deeper ontological unity in a way that, perhaps, ultimately even threatened to obliterate the particular.[56]

For Philoponus, on the other hand, the fact that nature appears only in the particular turns the empirical world into a mass of individuals whose unity becomes an abstract postulate sprung from mental activity. What is more, this plurality is no longer grounded in the absolute unity of a single, metaphysical source of being, but persists even at the level of deity. While the fragmentary remains of John's writings makes it difficult to gauge the extent of his metaphysical pluralism, it is evident that the emphasis on true individuality required by Christology opened the door to novel and unprecedented metaphysical options.

55. Cf. his fragments *De resurrectione* as cited in: L. Wickham, "John Philoponus and Gregory of Nyssa's Teaching on Resurrection: A Brief Note," in: *Studien zu Gregor von Nyssa und der christlichen Spätantike*, eds. H. Drobner, C. Klock, Leiden: Brill 1990, 205–210: 206.

56. Cf. Gregory of Nyssa, *De anima et resurrectione*, PG 46, 25A–29B and J. Zachhuber, "Die Seele als Dynamis bei Gregor von Nyssa: Überlegungen zur Schrift 'De Anima et Resurrectione,'" in: *Patristik und Resilienz: Frühchristliche Einsichten in die Seelenkraft*, eds. C. Sedmak, M. Bogaczyk-Vormayr, Berlin: Akadmie Verlag 2012, 211–231.

6. *The Chalcedonian solution: introduction of the concept of an anhypostatic nature*

On the Miaphysite side of the debate, then, Christology led to a new form of radical particularism. It remains to be seen what the philosophical consequences of the same debate were among the Chalcedonian theologians. Throughout the sixth century, as we have seen, the major representatives of this tradition simply refused to accept there was a problem with the classical theory. From the seventh century, however, things begin to change. The result of that change is the view that Christ's single hypostasis is his divine Person *within which* his humanity exists without a hypostasis of its own (*anhypostaton*).[57] Given that the traditional sense of the term *anhypostatos* was that something was non-existent, it is understandable that authors felt somewhat uneasy using this particular term. Evidently, their intention was not to deny that Christ's humanity "was there." What they asserted, however, was in its own way no less radical: that this nature existed without being a separate hypostasis. In a way, of course, this had been the Chalcedonian position right from the beginning insofar as the Council's formulation had to be defended against the charge that alongside the two natures it also mandated two hypostases. Yet something like a viable explanation for this anomalous assumption which, moreover, is incompatible with the classical theory, did not emerge until much later.

In the present context the details of the doctrinal debate are less important than their philosophical underpinnings. I hope to show that, while very different from the principles we found in John Philoponus, they too move decisively beyond not only the classical theory but also, ultimately, the frame provided by ancient metaphysics more generally. Let me begin by considering the relationship between this new view and the classical theory of the Cappadocians. The latter had held in a (tensional) unity two assumptions: (1) that the universal is the concrete whole consisting of hypostatic individuals and (2) that universal and particular can be distinguished by means of shared and individual properties. We have seen, further, that Chalcedonian Christology early on led to an elision of the concrete universal: the so-called "double homoousion" in effect reduced universal nature to an abstract essence in which any number of individuals can participate. The logical next step on this way, then, is the elision also of the concrete individual.

This occurs in the concept of an "individual nature" that becomes increasingly accepted by Chalcedonian authors from the seventh century onwards and is found in classical form in John of Damascus. At first sight, it might appear as if its emergence signifies that these theologians had finally given in to the remorseless hammering of their doctrinal opponents who had for centuries demanded that particular natures had to be recognised in order to

57. For a full account of the emergence of this doctrine see now B. Glede, *The Development....*

make sense of Christology. However, I believe that Richard Cross was right to argue for a difference between the two.[58] To put it briefly, the individual nature to be found in Leontius of Jerusalem and John of Damascus is not so much an individualised universal (as it is found in Peripatetic authors from the time of Alexander of Aphrodisias[59]), but an abstracted notion of a complete individual. In other words, it is the notion of a particular, the sum total of universal and particular properties, but consciously detached from that person's actual existence.

We can see the ingenuity of this, as far as I can see absolutely novel, philosophical concept by considering it relative to the doctrinal need it was meant to serve. Christ, we are to think, was fully human (that is, not merely possessing the properties of human nature but also those of an individual: being Jewish, a carpenter, of a certain age, with facial and other physical features etc.), but there was no human "hypostasis" corresponding to this. Now we may say that this was a rather rare instance; on the principles of Christian doctrine, it was, in fact, a unique case. Yet the philosophical nature of doctrinal debate meant that it could only be defended with the help of a generalised theory, and the participants in this doctrinal debate are fully conscious of this principle. So we find Leontius of Jerusalem appealing to the example of people who are dead or whom we only know from biblical stories to press the point that we can have the full concept of an individual without connecting them with actual, hypostatic existence.[60]

The concept of an individual nature, I believe, provides a real solution for the philosophical problems that had arisen when the "classical theory" had been confronted with Christology. But this solution, much as its sibling on the Miaphysite side, comes at a price. In order to explain how a fully individualised human being could exist without a hypostasis of its own, the Chalcedonian theologians come up with two ontological innovations: first, they introduce the concepts of essence and existence into philosophical thought. This distinction, which later becomes so fundamental in medieval thought, had no place in ancient philosophy nor indeed in the classical theory inaugurated by the Cappadocians. In Basil and Gregory, hypostasis meant the concrete realisation of a universal nature; in John of Damascus it only means existence pure and simple. *Ousia* and *physis*, consequently, which in Gregory of Nyssa could not be conceived independently of their concrete existence in particulars, lose any such necessary attachment to their hypostatic realisation. These two new concepts, secondly, are treated in strict separation from each other. The later Chalcedonians detach being from existence making it thus abstract both on the universal and on the particular level. Their ontology is concerned with essences, we might say, whose actual existence is contingent.

58. R. Cross, "Individual Natures...," 250–253.

59. This is what Simplicius in a famous passage calls the universal "in the many" (ἐν τοῖς πολλοῖς): *In Categorias Commentaria*, 83, 12–14, Kalbfleisch.

60. Leontius of Jerusalem, *Contra Nestorianos* II 19, PG 86, 1580AB.

This is, I think, as complete a break from the Cappadocian "classical theory" as Philoponus' particularism. While Basil and Gregory often speak abstractly of an individual's properties, this for them was just another way of speaking about that individual's concrete, hypostatic existence as one instantiation of an equally concrete species. Being for them was one, even though it could be conceived from different perspectives and, therefore, had to be described in more than one way. Leontius of Jerusalem and John of Damascus, by contrast, operate with a duality of being and existence. While there is no trace yet in them, as far as I have found, of the later idea that in God essence and existence are, uniquely, identical and that, therefore, he exists of necessity, it is now only a small step to this line of argumentation.

Conclusion: the rise of Christian theology and the end of ancient metaphysics

In this chapter, two major theories have been described as emerging in the process of post-Chalcedonian Christological debate. Both theories ultimately have the same starting point: they go back to the Cappadocian theologians of the late fourth century and their uniquely influential Christian philosophy. This "classical theory," however, could not account for the specific doctrinal requirements posed by Christology and was therefore radically modified. While neither of the two views specifically examined in my paper, gave up on all the tenets that had made up the classical theory, they both resulted in philosophies that were fundamentally incompatible with it, albeit in different ways: the Miaphysite tradition, most radically developed in John Philoponus, preserves the notion that being only exists in concrete individuals but gives up on an ontologically real universal and thus creates an extreme form of particularism. The Chalcedonian tradition, on the other hand, unties being (*ousia*) from existence (*hypostasis*) and thus, in a different way, gives up on ontological realism as well.

Yet with this eclipse of realism, the two schools emerging from the Christological controversy not only modified the classical theory of earlier Christian thought, but also took leave of the older Greek ontological tradition. This tradition had been sustained by a vision of universal nature whose reality was never really in doubt. It therefore, in spite of its unique fruitfulness had overall little to say about the individual nor indeed about contingency. From a philosophical point of view, the rise of Christian theology signified the end of this certainty: earthly existence became contingent and ultimately rooted in the creative will and power of God, not the continuity of nature. At the same time, individual existence became a focal point of intellectual engagement. While the need to conceptualise the unique personality of the God-man was not the only context within which this happened – one could also, for example, think of the doctrine of the resurrection – it was not just any context: the Church's decision to turn Christology into formal dogma may have been the direct cause of the unique intensity of these debates, but this decision itself is ultimately rooted in the awareness that faith in Jesus Christ is at the very heart of Christianity and its conceptualisation, therefore, at the centre of Christian theology.

Anthropology of Conversion in Dionysius the Areopagite

José María Nieva

It has been stated that the horizon of Dionysian thought or the axis that organizes his whole intellectual concern is to determine the divine essence, that is to say, "the background of all Dionysius' problems is the possibility and the nature of the knowledge we have of God. Precisely, all the difficulty in understanding his speech actually comes from this attitude, almost exclusively, of his work" (Couloubaritsis 1982: 322).

Approaching his thought thus, one inevitably highlights the purely speculative aspect of his writings. Or, in other words, an exaggerated interest in a cognitive technique and in an epistemology of subjective character arises, which finds its expression in the act of denial.

Consequently, it seems that any possible reference or consideration about the world and men are left outside the scope of Dionysian reflection.

Thus, many scholars have pointed out that "anthropology is the most forgotten aspect of his system" (Sheldon-Williams 1967: 473), while others, on the contrary, have stated that "neither the anthropology nor the moral constitutes in themselves a different subject, in some way autonomous of the dionysian thought" (Roques 1962: 237).

The problem does not seem to have an easy solution if we take into account that in passage 696c, chapter I, of his work *On the Divine Names* Dionysius mentions a writing – lost or fictitious – called *On the soul* that leads us to think about a possible and specific philosophical approach.

No matter what might have happened with this writing, it is possible to find some features of deep consideration in relation to men scattered and inserted throughout key passages of his work that allow building a Dionysian anthropology.

In this sense, the pages that follow have the purpose of building such anthropology.

For that purpose we will focus on chapter IV of *On the divine name,* taking special interest in the idea of conversion, of *epistrophé,* but also taking into account other fundamental passages of the same writing.

In this chapter – as well as all through the Areopagite´s thought – the influx of Neoplatonic philosophy can be appreciated. Dionysius approaches the divine denomination of Good and Beauty and we may find, in effect, clear echoes of the Greek tradition: The sun as image of Good, almost as a transposition of the famous platonic image of *Republic VI*, the close link that is established between beauty (*kalón*) and the act of calling (*kaleîn*), all of which Dionysius employs in usufructing the etimology of passage 416b of Plato's *Cratylus*. This passage also has a clear relevance in Proclus philosophy – a thinker whose influence in the Dionysian works cannot be denied – and a precise allusion to passage 211a–b from the platonic *Symposium* when it says "God is called Beautiful because he is completely beautiful and beyond beautiful and he is always beautiful in the same way, and in this way he is not born nor dies, he does not enlarge nor diminishes, he is neither partly beautiful nor partly ugly, sometimes he is and sometimes he is not; nor beautiful in relation to something and ugly in relation to other, not beautiful here and ugly there, so that he is beautiful for some and ugly for others, but he is always beautiful in himself and because of himself" (*On the divine names* IV, 701d). From this Beautiful and Good, which are beyond being, that is, of this supra essential Good, depend, not only in their being but also in their movement, the intelligible and intellective powers of the sacred intelligences that make up the celestial hierarchies and, after these, both the rational and irrational souls; all the sensitive and the vegetative beings, which in their essential condition depend on him.

To the degree to which it can appreciated, we find here a clearly hierarchical universe, structured in an orderly way according to a dignity of being that reveals the way in which every one of its components is able to receive the abundant luminosity that is manifested from Good. Thus, every being has a certain receptive capacity to hold analogically in itself the luminosity of the First Principle.

The Supra essential Good that is also called the One beyond the essence – according to chapter XIII of *On the Divine Names* –, angelic intelligences that have in themselves the *kósmos noetós* of Greek tradition, and in the end, the rational soul that can be elevated towards them. Then, can it be denied that the architecture of neoplatonic metaphysics underlies Dionysius' thought? This question sets out many other questions that still disturb anyone who tries to understand these complex and difficult works, questions that we could simplify as follows: Is Dionysius the Areopagite a platonizing Christian or a neoplatonic Christian?

Let us answer this question clearly, if possible, emphasizing the notion of conversion and taking into account that Dionysius tells us that:

Ψυχῆς δὲ κίνησίς ἐστι κυκλικὴ μὲν ἡ εἰς εἴσοδος ἀπὸ τὸν ἔξω καὶ τῶν νοερῶν αὐτῆς δυνάμεων ἡ ἑνοειδὴς συνέλιξις ὥσπερ ἔν τινι κύκλῳ τὸ ἀπλανὲς αὐτῇ δωρουμένη καὶ ἀπὸ τῶν πολλῶν

There exists a circular movement of the soul, the entrance into herself from the outer things and the uniform withdrawal of her intellective powers that are given by the inerrant as in a circle and from the multiplicity

τῶν ἔξωθεν αὐτὴν ἐπιστρέφουσα καὶ συνάγουσα πρῶτον εἰς ἑαυτήν, εἶτα ὡς ἑνοειδῆ γενομένην ἑνοῦσα ἡνωμέναις δυνάμεσι καὶ οὕτως ἐπί τὸ καλὸν καὶ ἀγαθὸν χειραγωγοῦσα τὸ ὑπὲρ πάντα τὰ ὄντα καὶ ἓν καὶ ταὐτὸν καὶ ἄναρχον καὶ ἀτελεύτητον (*On the divine names* IV 9, 705a).

of outer things that returns her and gathers in herself and then once she becomes uniform, joining her with the powers united as a whole, and, in that way, leading her to the Beautiful and the Good, towards what is above the beings and remains one and the same, without a beginning and without and end."

Conversion – *epistrophé* – belongs to the genre of movement whose semantic nucleous is present in the verb *strephein* (to turn). In this way it acquires the precise meaning of spinning to something, turning to something, coming back to the beginning. This term, in relation to the prepositions *eis, epí, prós,* points out a certain direction, a certain orientation. This linkage of words specifies the *télos* of movement, its realization, its completion, its perfection, its full *stásis*; in consequence, a precise objective towards which such movement moves.

In the field of philosophy, *epistrophé* will have a cosmological and a non ethical sense, the circle being the symbol of return to itself, typical of intelligence. But as observed by Lloyd (1990:126) the term *epistrophé* is ambiguous because it can mean either to turn to something only as a tendency or to return to the Beginning in its full and precise sense. On the one hand, Beierwaltes (1990:200) points out that this term has three meanings: 1) in the platonic *periagogé* sense, that is, when man distances himself from the sensitive and turns to his soul, to the dimension of the true being or to the truth of the being and thus means the return of men to their true identity and self-awareness; 2) as the self reflection of the Spirit or thinking Intellect that is fulfilled as a being of thought and is experienced when founded in the pre-reflective One and in its preexisting self; 3) as a return of the effect to the cause, which is present in the effect because it maintains the being and gives origin to the movement of conversion. On the other hand, Dodds (1963:218) states that "the history of the words strophé and epistrophé shows a progressive development from a general to a technical meaning: notewhorty are 1) Plato's language about the turning of the eye of the soul (Rep. 519b); 2) the use of epistrophé, epistrephein for a religious turning or conversion (Ev. Luc. 22,32; Act. Apost. 15.3); 3) Albinus, Didasc. 10: (ho prôtos théos) tén psyche toû kósmou epegeíras kaì eis eautón epistrépsas. Comparing the later with the term in which Seneca speaks of the return of the soul to its source, we may fairly conclude that the Neoplatonic concept of reversion has its roots in Middle Platonism".

What we have said so far highlights that it is necessary to focus on the first of these three meanings because if in fact – as we have pointed out – the conversion belongs to the genre of movement, this cannot imply a change of place or a movement for men. In consequence, what does *epistrophé* imply for a being that is able to think? Doesn't it allude to the need of a total change or a complete modification in its way of thinking?

In relation to that conversion towards oneself, it has been pointed out that "Neoplatonism discovered the concept of the self that achieved in its speculations a richness never seen before in the history of philosophy. Neoplatonic philosophy exhorts us to return to ourselves and to find in ourselves everything about reality even the divine principle" (Steel 2006:201).

We could think, then, that it is possible to understand the Dionysian circular movement of the soul in this way?

Dionysius talks not only about a circular movement of the soul but also about a spiral and linear movement. These three movements are also part of the angelic intelligences but it is clear that they strongly differ from human movement, since they are incorporeal and immaterial and thus, they can understand in a hyper cosmic way that is immediate without need of demonstration and thus, in a synoptic way.

The helicoidal movement of the soul reveals her discursive capacity, exactly rational, because it demands complex, combined and successive activities. In other words, this movement is the space of an itinerary, going back and forth, with the aim of reaching certain truth in the divine knowledge. Dionysius alludes to that movement with brevity and concision and it is better understood if one pays attention to chapter VII. In that chapter, the same hierarchical structure found in chapter IV can be perceived. There, when referring to the divine name of Wisdom, he explains that from Her, souls have the rationality that allows them to move discursively around the truth of the beings. This discursive movement distances them from the unitary intelligences, that is, of the angelic powers, due to the partial and multiform variety of their rational, logical and demonstrative operations; however, "because of the withdrawal of many of those activities towards the one, the souls can become worthy of the understanding similar to those of the angelic powers, in as much as it is possible" (τῇ δὲ τῶν πολλῶν εἰς τὸ ἓν συνελίξει καὶ τῶν ἰσαγγέλων νοήσεων, ἐφ' ὅσον ψυχαῖς οἰκεῖον καὶ ἐφικτόν, ἀξιούμεναι) (868c).

The rectilinear movement implies that the soul makes use of outer things that are around her, such as symbols that allow her to ascend to simple and united contemplations.

It is necessary to take into consideration two fundamental aspects of this last movement that will lead us to understand the relevance given by Dionysius to the circular movement.

First, the close link that we can observe between what is rectilinear and the symbols. In chapter I of *On the Divine Names*, precisely in passage 592d, the Areopagite draws a clear distinction between angelic and human intelligences. The latter, have the peculiarity of being subjected to time and transitivity and of achieving their knowledge through a process of effort and of combination. This effort implies discerning what is hidden in the symbols and consequently, understanding what is symbolized. The task of intelligence is to have access to and sense the hidden message transmitted by symbols when unveiling them from their peculiarity and materiality This is clearly expressed by Dionysius when he says "well, as it is accessible to us, we use appropriate symbols in the divine things and from these we elevate ourselves, according to our capacity, towards the simple and unitary truth of the intelligible contemplations" (*On the divine names* I 5, 592d).

The temporal and consequently, successive dimension of human knowledge is also characterized in passage 708, chapter IV, 11 when he says that "it is necessary to know, according to right reason, that we use elements, syllables, letters and words due to our senses."

Even though we could not say that Dionysian anthropology is metaphysical, if understood as a deep reflection about the principles that build the human existence, we do sustain that it is a symbolic and dynamic anthropology – as we will further explain – like the entire Dionysian universe. Thus, in this universe, symbolism in its clear aesthetic current is the equivalent to ontological participation and in that sense, there is a metaphysics of symbol in the thought of Dionysius the Areopagite. We say in its "aesthetic current" because Dionysius enjoys the contemplation of what is real as more than an essential expression of Goodness and Beauty.

Thus, not only does sensitive knowledge reveal the tie of men to their corporeal nature and to their sensitivity, for which there is not an exaggerated rejection of in Dionysius – as far as we appreciate it – but on the contrary, he reveals a positive attitude here, in as much as this opens the way to better, purer, more stable and more meaningful knowledge.

From the symbol to what is symbolized and from the sensitive to the intelligible, the road is straight, the movement is rectilinear with the condition of being able to discern what is hidden in the closest things, the most evident in the clearness of the beings that, paradoxically, can veil it. Nevertheless, this clearness should be overcome by an intelligence that discovers in the anagogic force of denial the force that propels her to transcend the sensitive.

The most important and relevant thing here is that Dionysius sharply points out that when the soul moves with this type of movement, that is, with the rectilinear movement, she does not enter herself and she does not move with an intellective, unique and simple activity which is in accordance with the circle.

In the circular movement a call to conversion is hidden, a turn from the multiple and the exterior towards the one, a return of the soul to herself, a return to what we could call her inner being.

In that sense, in my opinion, it does not seem appropriate to say that in Dionysius the subject of *epistrophé eis heautón* is not present, as it is in Beierwaltes (1990:407).

It is true that if we understand it as an introspection or as an exquisite inner being that deals with all the aspects of the human existence, as the one unfolded by Augustine in *Confessions*, where explores his fears, wishes and hopes, it is necessary to say that the subject is not treated in the Areopagite.

But if introspection means a conversion towards oneself, in the search of finding an identity that is expressed in the clearer and clearer demonstration of an objective to which it is aimed, it should be said that Dionysius has taken that aspect into consideration.

This is made clear in the passage that has called our attention if we take into account two meaningful phrases that allow us to justify our reading.

The circular movement shows the entrance of the soul into herself, that is, the end of the movement is marked precisely by the *eisodos* and reinforced by the preposition *eis*. This entrance of the soul into herself distances her from the multiplicity in order to place her on the road of unification of the greatest simplicity.

It can be noticed here that subject so dear to Neoplatonism of the opposition between the multiple and the one, and at the same time the odyssey of the soul to reach a simpler or unified state that will allow her to be in touch with the supra essential One.

I believe that in a certain way, this is present in Dionysius if we pay attention to the expression *enoeidès synélixis*. This expression clearly states that the circular movement begins with a withdrawal – according to our translation – of the soul towards herself that makes her uniform, i.e, what is aimed at is the unification of the multiple intellective powers in only one end or objective. On the other hand, the idea of withdrawal states very clearly that it is about a movement that the soul has to perform from the exterior, from the outside to the inside, towards the deepest, we could say, with the purpose of conquering her true identity. This movement involves going backwards, contrary to all dispersion towards the exterior that would mean distancing from one self.

Conversion is then, a road towards identity, towards the inner being, towards sameness.

We cannot avoid a disturbing question: what did Dionysius understand by sameness, identity and interiority? Does the aim of this anthropology imply that man has to change his condition with the purpose of acquiring the truest one? In this last case, which would his true identity, his truest self, be?

The conversion of the soul towards herself, the entrance into herself, gives her two main characteristics: first, that uniform withdrawal makes her inerrant, that is, stops her from wandering that also means stopping her from roaming. The soul can know unequivocally when she returns and withdraws and at the same time she obtains certain stability, firmness and perseverance.

The phrase *epistréphousa kaì synágousa eís heautén* is of relevance here. The withdrawal makes her come back to herself, reuniting the soul to achieve only one activity and, in that way, she can reach an unerring state achieved "in a certain circle". Now, why does Dionysius need "in a certain circle" and does not say circularly?

Apparently what is suggested by the Areopagite in this irrelevant expression is that the soul cannot leave, abandon or neglect the sensitive condition in which she is found as the incarnated spirit. In my opinion, this means that what he intends to make clear with the expression "in a certain circle" is that this circular movement is not continuous, permanent and stable as with the angelical intelligences.

The expression *peri heautàs ameptáptoti synelíxeis* is used in paragraph 2, chapter IV to refer to the perseverance that angelic intelligences have with regard to themselves and the knowledge they acquire when they receive the luminosities of the Good, and in the *On the Celestial Hierarchy* 333b in relation to the symbolism of clothing, the chasuble's waist of the high priest means the power that celestial intelligences have of "secluding themselves to join and withdraw (synelissésthai) in a harmonic circle around themselves in an unfailing identity."

The sensitivity and temporality in which the soul finds herself do not give her the continuous perseverance that is enjoyed by the powers unitarily united, the angels.

By means of this subtle differentiation what Areopagite means is that for the soul, the circular movement is an aim to achieve that cannot be considered as already fulfilled, as already obtained. It is able to be conquered as much as it is possible, from its condition and from the temporality in which it is found only if it is capable of returning to itself, to enter itself, thus, to know itself.

Now then, this conversion gives her another characteristic: by means of this uniform withdrawal, by means of this return and self reunion, the soul, can join the powers unitarily united and thus be guided towards Beauty and Good.

Isn't this conversion in essence a true transformation? Is Dionysius telling us that our aim is to acquire the angelic condition? Does this fact mean, beyond the value of the senses, a rejection of the true human condition? In other words, is it possible to think that the platonic subject of the real man as soul and therefore as intellect is present here?

In that sense, the use Dionysius makes of the expression *eis heautèn eisioûsa* to refer to the soul when she moves in circles brings us closer to certain platonic or better, proclean memories.

In effect, in *Platonic Theology* I, 3, when Proclus refers to Plato's *Alcibiades* I, he tells us that Socrates clearly states that the soul obtains the vision not only of the intelligible but also of God when she turns into herself, *eis heautèn eisioûsa*. Proclus points out that the soul, due to her entrance into herself, finds the intellect and beyond that, Good, her divine Foundation, as much she is similar in nature to Good.

For Neoplatonism, the philosophical way starts with this self-knowledge that means, at the same time, the knowledge of its origin. In this sense, Dodds (1963: 203) states that "introversion acquires a deeper significance in Neoplatonism because the self which is thus known is not an isolated individual, but contains in potentia the whole range of reality." When becoming herself, when coming back to herself, the soul can discover everything she is and everything she is not. Thus, when the soul comes back to herself she finds her divine basis, and that takes place when she exceeds the perceptible reality and frees herself from all her multiplicity to make her uniform essence shine. In spite of the differences between Licius and Plotinus it seems that the thought of the former lies upon the echoes of the latter when it is pointed out that each one is a *kósmos noetós* (*Enn.* III 4, 3, 23) and that the intellect returns to itself when it turns towards its Principle (*Enn.* VI 9, 2, 35).

It is true that identity in the way of thinking cannot be derived from the similarity of expressions or language; nevertheless, it is difficult not to admit an impression when it is believed that the Neoplatonic influence in Dionysius is not at a minimum at all. However, it is worth pointing out that in the Areopagite, the soul, when returning to herself, neither finds her divine Grounds nor what by nature bears a similarity with Good. On the contrary, this is fulfilled by means of a cathartic and anagogic process that starts at sensitive realities.

Another turning point in front of pagan Neoplatonism is that, according to Courcelle (1971: 165), the echoes of Plato's *Alcibiades* I imply in Dionysius a preparatory phase to achieve union beyond the intellect through the similarities with unitary powers that Dionysius identifies with the angels of Christianity.

Nevertheless, from my point of view, such impressions can be appreciated in the importance granted to the circular movement as an example of a perfect movement, a movement that characterizes mainly angelic intelligences but also souls. Previously, we also pointed out that in the Dionysian universe they perform the role of *kósmos noetós* of Greek tradition. Besides, we have observed Dionysius' needs for the circular movement to provide an immediate and immaterial unitary way of knowing that, as it is typical or specific of angelic powers, allows a synoptic vision for the indivisibility and immateriality of divine intellects (*On Divine Names* VII 2, 868b; cf. V 2, 816c).

Now, the image of the circle has a deep meaning in Neoplatonism.

Thus, for example, in *Enneads* VI 9, 8, 10 Plotinus says that "if the soul gets to know herself and if she recognizes that her movement is not performed in a straight line but when she experiences a break, but that her movement when it is according to nature is similar to that in a circle, not around something that would be external to her but around a centre where the circle comes from. This soul will move around that centre and she will suspend from it." And, in *Enneads* IV 4, 16, 20 Plotinus states that "if we compare Good with a centre, we would compare Intelligence with an unmoving circle and the soul with a circle in movement but moved by desire. This is because Intelligence possesses and surrounds Good directly whereas the soul wishes what it is beyond Intelligence."

On his behalf, in *Commentary on the Republic* II 46, Proclus asserts that "the circle is the image of the Intellect." Indeed, it remains steady as regards its centre, it acts according to its generative powers and turns to itself (*epistréphei pròs heautón*) according to the knowledge that surrounds it everywhere in the same way.

The echoes of Plato's *Timaeus* 34a, 40a and *Phaedrus* 247a – to which we would add *Laws* X 897c–898c – are evidenced in both thinkers, mainly those of the first dialogue if we consider that according to the realistic speech stated in this dialogue, the soul must correct the errant revolutions of her intellect to make them correspond with those of the world in which there is a predominance of identity and stability. The echoes of Aristotle are also present in both thinkers (*On the heaven* I, 2, 269b; *Phys.* VIII, 9, 265a).

The first dialogue mentioned above also transmits the beautiful image of the man as a celestial plant whose roots are at the top and states that the head, set as a sphere, "is the most divine and the Lord of everything that surrounds us" (*Timaeus* 44c). This image will endure if we think of passage 416 of Aristotle's *De Anima* and passage 1050 of Proclean *Commentary on the Parmenides of Plato*, and more precisely, his *Commentary on the Republic* II 159 when he states that "it is the mind the one that tends to life in heaven."

As regards Dionysus, it is important to notice the way in which this consideration can be present.

In previous pages we have supported that the anthropology is symbolic. Indeed, the Areopagite emphasizes the way in which, through the symbols, a hidden or veiled truth can be known; in other words, they have both a gnosiological and a pedagogical role in educating intelligence in the search of the real sense that lies in them.

In chapter IX of *On the divine names*, he tells us that "if discourse represented the soul in a corporeal way [...] we would name the intelligence head and neck the opinion as situated between reason and irrationality, mood would be the chest, desire the belly, nature would be legs and feet, using the names as symbols of the powers."

In this representation of the soul her outstanding platonic tripartition with her corporeal representations according to *Timaeus* 69d–70a should be noticed.

Then, the fact that the head is represented by the intelligence calls our attention.

As we have seen before, the image of the circle to refer to its constant movement allows us to emphasize in the Areopagite that this anthropology of conversion is meant to clarify the tension or the tendency that exists in men.

Indeed, everything tends to Good, but each being acts according to its own way or analogical capacity.

In the case of the man as an intellective being, his tendency towards Good is performed by means of knowledge, thus, Good is the suitable aim for its way of being (*On divine names* IV). However, for this tendency to be more effective or complete, man must abandon all multiplicity and dispersion in order to get a continuous or progressive unification: to gather around himself his intellectual powers to turn them uniform.

The soul can get closer to Good once she overcomes the rectilinear and helicoidal shaped movement that acts in a discursive way to exercise herself in the circular and unifying movement.

The anthropological *epistrophé* is a gnosiological conversion. It does not mean a change of place or a simple movement, on the contrary, it means a change in the way of thinking and getting to know that it is, at the same time, a transformation in the way of being.

The *epistrophé* is that way of knowing and thinking that sets uniformity, that finds its complete sense realization in Good as an end. Thus, at the same time she carries out its ascent towards Good, towards the One, towards the Principle. In other words, the *epistrophé* has a theoretical role in combining the soul's entrance in herself and assigning her another way of thinking that frees her from temporality and sensitivity.

This fact states the problem we have referred to in previous pages: Does Dionysus urge us to a conversion towards the angelic condition?

The angelic powers or saint intelligences are immaterial and incorporeal beings. These characteristics allow them a constant and incessant circular movement and at the same time a synoptic vision of divine archetypes by the illumination of Good.

This is the aim of the soul's circular movement that she is able to reach when she gathers and becomes herself. Nevertheless, this movement is fragile due to the corporal and temporal situation in which she finds herself.

But Dionysius specifies that this temporal situation is temporary and that the aim to which man aspires will be fully realized in a timeless situation. In *On divine names* I 4, Dionysius tells us that "when we are uncorrupted and immortal and we achieve a Christ like and blessed state, we will always be with the Lord – according to the Oracle –, fulfilled with his divine presence, visible in saintly contemplations that illuminate with blazing lights, as the disciples in that divine transfiguration; taking part in an intelligible donation of God´s light in unemotional and immaterial intelligence, and of the union beyond intelligence in unknown and blessed effusions from very brilliant rays. We will be equal to angels in a more divine imitation of celestial intelligences – as stated by the Oracle truth – and God's sons because we are sons of the resurrection" (cf. X 3, 937d; *On Ecclesiastical Hierarchy* VII 2, 553d–VII 3, 557a).

Thus the imitation of the angelical condition has a far reaching spiritual meaning. Such spiritual meaning is observed when emulating the incessant and unavoidable movement of the essences superior to us as regards Good. This movement is a choral dancing image around Thearchy which reflects the final aim our life expects to reach.

It is worth pointing out here the reception that Neoplatonism may have if it is considered that such image is fundamental in Proclus who believes that the perfect movement of intelligence is present in the circular movement, in the choral movement around the One. This image is restated by Damascius in his *Commentary on the Phaedo* who explains that the perfection of intelligence is present when it tends towards what is intelligible and when it settles in its own action carrying out a truly intellective justice (II, 86).

Dionysius attempts to portray his way of understanding the human condition by means of a Neoplatonic vocabulary and with deep ideas of philosophical meaning. Although the human condition is settled down in what is sensitive, it is not limited within the temporal and successive limits of a way of understanding which is not exempt of certain threats and distortions. Man is called to find himself in a greater and greater unification, in a process that starts with the symbol. Purifying what is sensitive is purifying himself in moving away from every multiplicity. Afterwards, this conversion towards himself and in himself raises him to the intelligible contemplation in a continuous effort to search for the stability and the act of not wandering, which the angelic intelligences enjoy. But this process does not find there its final aim. The union beyond the intellect is the supreme desire of the soul, which can start to be perceived here but which is definitive only in the day of the Glory.

The Neoplatonic philosophers knew nothing of this day, but the one that has come to be known as St Paul's convert, though infused of Greek culture, takes over a message that in its *kérygma* shows the Light the soul desires and throws light to every man that comes to this world.

Bibliography

Armstrong, A. H. (1990), "The Negative Theology of Nous in Later Neoplatonism," in: *Hellenic and Christian Studies*. London: Variorum.

Aubin, P. (1963), *Le problème de la conversion*. Paris : Beauchesne.

Beierwaltes, W. (1990), *Proclo. I fondamenti della sua metafisica*, Milano: Vita e Pensiero.

Beierwaltes, W. (2000), *Platonismo nel Cristianesimo*. Milano: Vita e Pensiero.

Bernard, C. A. (1978), "Les formes de la Théologie chez Denys l'Aréopagite," *Gregorianum* 59, 1.

Couloubaritsis, L. (1982), "Le sens de la notion demostration chez le Pseudo-Denys," *Byzantinische Zeitschrift* 75.

Courcelle, P. (1971), "Le 'Connais-toi toi-même' chez les néoplatoniciennes grecs," in : P. Schuhl, P. Hadot, éd., *Le Néoplatonisme. Colloques Internationaux*. París : CNRS.

Charles-Saget, A., ed. (1998), *Retour, repentir et constitution de soi.* Paris : Vrin.

Dodds, E. (1963), *Proclus. The Elements of Theology. A Revised Text with Translation, Introduction, and Commentary*, Oxford: Clarendon Press.

Gersh, S. (1978), *From Iamblichus to Eriugena. An Investigation of the Prehistory and Evolution of the Pseudo-Dionysian Tradition.* Ledien: Brill.

Gerson, L. (1997), "'Epistrophè pròs heautón': History and Meaning," in: *Documenti e Studi sulla tradizione filosofica medievale*, VIII. Brepols: Turhnout.

Golitzin, A. (1994), *Et Introibo ad Altare Dei. The Mystagogy of Dionysius Areopagita with special reference to its Predecessors in the Eastern Christian Tradition.* Thessaloniki: Analecta Vlatadon.

Hadot, P. (1999), *Plotin, Porphyre. Études Néoplatoniciennes.* Paris : Les Belles Lettres.

Klitenic Wear, S. & Dillon, J. (2007), *Dionysius the Areopagite and the Neoplatonist Tradition. Despoiling the Hellenes.* London: Ashgate.

Lloyd, A. (1990), *The Anatomy of Neoplatonism.* Oxford: Clarendon Press.

Lossky, V. (1930), "La notion des analogies chez Denys le Pseudo-Aréopagite," *Archives d'Histoire Doctrinale et Littéraire du Moyen Age* V.

Nieva, J. M. (2014), "Lêxis in Dionysius the Areopagite," *Journal of Literature and Art Studies*, Vol. 4 N° 2, February, 129–136.

Pépin, J. (1971), *Idées grecques sur l'homme et sur Dieu.* Paris : Les Belles Lettres.

Perl, E. (2007), *Theophany. The Neoplatonic Philosophy of Dionysius Areopagite.* New York: State University of New York.

Remes, P. (2008), *Neoplatonism.* London: Acumen.

Ritter, A., Heil, G, (1991). *Corpus Dionysiacum II.* Berlin: Walter de Gruyter.

Roques, R. (1962), *Structures Théologiques. De la gnose à Richard de Saint-Victor.* Paris : PUF.

Roques, R. (1983), *L'univers dionysien. Structure hiérarchique du monde selon le Pseudo-Denys*, Paris : Cerf.

Rorem, P. (1993), *Pseudo-Dionysius. A Commentary on the Texts and an Introduction to Their Influence.* Oxford: Oxford University Press.

Schäfer, C. (2006), *The Philosophy of Dionysius the Areopagite. An Introduction to the Structure and the Content of the Treatise On the Divine Names.* Leiden: Brill.

Sheldon-Williams, I. (1967), "The Pseudo-Dionysius," in: Armstrong, A., ed., *The Cambridge History of Later Greek and Early Medieval Philosophy.* Cambridge: Cambridge University Press.

Steel, C. (2006), "Is Christian Neoplatonism the true heir of the Ancient Philosophical Tradition?," in: Barbanti, M., Martello, C., eds., *Neoplatonismo Pagano vs Neoplatonismo Cristiano. Identità e intersezioni.* Catania: CUECM.

Suchla, B. R. (1990), *Corpus Dionysiacum I.* Berlin: Walter de Gruyter.

Eros as a Divine Name According to Dionysius the Areopagite

Filip Ivanović

The Dionysian discourse on love develops over three levels, each of which applies to terms, to God, and to humans, respectively. These concern: 1) the terminological determination of love, exemplified in the relationship between ἔρως and ἀγάπη; 2) love as a divine name, as in "God is Love," and 3) human love expressed through hierarchies. The subject of this chapter will be Dionysius' understanding of love as a divine name; however, one cannot neglect the terminological aspect of his erotology, which represents a curiosity in the sense that Dionysius almost always uses the term *eros*, even when referring to what is usually designated by *agape*.

Eros or Agape?

A widespread discussion on the meaning and usage of the terms ἔρως and ἀγάπη has provided a conclusion that the former is used in ancient Greek thought and that it has earthly connotations, a meaning of desire, while the latter represents genuine selfless Christian love. Though it is true that the widespread term for love in ancient philosophy is ἔρως, one cannot truly agree with the exclusive and absolute distinction between the two terms in late antiquity and the medieval period. The thesis of, e. g. Anders Nygren,[1] on the difference between ἔρως and ἀγάπη as a clear demarcation line between paganism and Christianity is by far exaggerated, and, besides the importance of this work, it testifies more to the agenda of the author than to a real and proper understanding of the issue.[2] Although Nygren himself, in the introduction to his book, admits that these terms became so interwoven that it was impossible to speak of either without being drawn to the other, he nevertheless claims that "it is most important to insist on the original absence of any relation between Eros and Agape."[3]

1. A. Nygren, *Agape and Eros*.
2. See J. Rist, "A Note"; C. Osborne, *Eros Unveiled: Plato and the God of Love*, Oxford: Clarendon 1996, throughout the book; C. De Vogel, "Greek Cosmic Love," 61: "Obviously the Swedish theologian had not the faintest idea of what the spirit of Platonism was. But even the 'love of God' among Christians appears to him a rather suspect affair."
3. A. Nygren, *Agape and Eros*, 31.

This conception has led Nygren to explain Dionysius' use of eros in the sense that this term "was the reality he knew, so he naturally preferred to speak of the thing by its right name,"[4] thus implying that Dionysius' reality was the eros of ancient thought, namely Neoplatonism, while the opposite term of Christian agape was unfamiliar to him, i.e., it did not represent his particular reality.

However, if one turns to Dionysius himself and his texts, it becomes clear that he knew both realities very well – he was fully aware of the term agape, and not just that: he knew that equalizing eros and agape could provoke some misunderstandings, and so not only did he provide an answer to the possible opposition of his time, but he also anticipated Nygren's conclusions. Being aware as he was of the relationship between the two terms, Dionysius consciously decides to proclaim them as synonymous:

> So let us not fear this title of "yearning" (ἔρως) nor be upset by what anyone has to say about these two names, for, in my opinion, the sacred writers regard "yearning" and "love" (ἀγάπη) as having one and the same meaning. They added "real" to the use of "yearning" regarding divine things because of the unseemly nature such a word has for men.[5]

Clearly, Dionysius here shows his awareness about the possible confusion that eros might introduce, and therefore he warns his reader that he is talking about the "real" eros, and not the defective, divided one:

> The title "real yearning" is praised by us and by the scriptures themselves as being appropriate to God. Others, however, tended naturally to think of a partial, physical, and divided yearning. This is not true yearning but an empty image or, rather, a lapse from real yearning. The fact is that men are unable to grasp the simplicity of the one divine yearning, and, hence, the term is quite offensive to most of them. So it is left to the divine Wisdom to lift them and to raise them up to a knowledge of what yearning really is, after which they no longer take offense.[6]

But, what exactly is the Areopagite's intention here? Is he just trying to equalize his own reality with a reality not so familiar to him, in Nygren's words, or is he developing a cunning masterful plan to introduce pagan terminology into Christianity, as some have claimed? In fact, it is none of the above. Dionysius, in the first instance, is an enlightener, a revealer, as many later Fathers used to call him, and a teacher. His main intention is to reveal certain truths he holds important, and to pass on a knowledge significant for the proper understanding of Christian doctrines. He reveals that eros and agape

4. *Ibid.*, 589, n. 2.
5. *DN* IV.12, 709B. Unless otherwise specified, all the quotations from the *Corpus* are given in Colm Luibheid's translation, in Pseudo-Dionysius, *The Complete Works*.
6. *DN* IV.12, 709BC.

are one and the same, and that these terms can be used interchangeably and synonymously. But he is also aware of the difficulty this might create, so he clearly distinguishes the true, "real," eros from its divided, partial counterpart. In doing so, he is obviously keen on preserving an ancient terminology, but he does not hesitate either to point to its appropriate and true use. Therefore, besides revealing the unity of eros and agape in God, the Areopagite also acts pedagogically, as a teacher explaining to his pupils the terms and their correct use and meaning. Thus, the true opposition is not between eros and agape, but between "real love" and "divided love,"[7] since Dionysius himself says: "In my opinion it would be unreasonable and silly to look at words rather than at the power of the meanings."[8]

The source of Dionysius' use of eros is most probably ancient philosophical, namely, Neoplatonic thought, but he nonetheless struggles to show that this use is justified even in the Christian sphere. Thus he is delighted to be able to quote scriptural passage "Yearn for her and she shall keep you; exalt her and she will extol you; honor her and she will embrace you,"[9] and a phrase from the deuterocanonical Book of Wisdom "I yearned for her beauty,"[10] as well as Ignatius' proclamation "My Eros is crucified."[11] Dionysius is not the only one who quotes Ignatius for this purpose; before him it was done by Origen, in his *Commentary on the Song of Songs*: "I remember that one of the Saints, I think Ignatius, said about Christ: 'My love is crucified.' In my opinion he is not to be blamed for that."[12] Obviously both Dionysius and Origen interpret this phrase in the same way – Eros here refers to Christ, and so they both use it to justify the possibility of naming God as eros and as agape, i.e., as "amor" and as "caritas."[13]

In justifying his preference for eros, Dionysius points out that "indeed some of our writers on sacred matters have thought the title 'yearning' to be more divine than 'love.'"[14] This stance is taken by Gregory of Nyssa who in his work on the Song of Songs claims that eros is a more intense form

7. See Y. de Andia, *Henosis*, 148.
8. *DN* IV.11, 708BC.
9. Prv 4:6–8.
10. Wis of Sol 8:2.
11. *Ep. ad Rom.* 7, 2, although this quotation could compromise Dionysius' pseudonym since Ignatius died around 107.
12. Origen, *Comm. In Cant. Cant.*, Prologus 71.
13. Some scholars claim that Origen's (and Dionysius') understanding of Ignatius' phrase is not correct, as he does not refer to Christ when speaking of eros, but eros in his words means a desire for earthly things. So "My Eros is crucified" would mean that his desire for earthly things is destroyed (See A. Nygren, *Agape and Eros*, 390; C. De Vogel, "Greek Cosmic Love," 72–73). However, as Rist has argued, the phrase (ζῶν γὰρ γράφω ὑμῖν, ἐρῶν τοῦ ἀποθανεῖν. ὁ ἐμὸς ἔρως ἐσταύρωται, καὶ οὐκ ἔστιν ἐν ἐμοὶ πῦρ φιλόυλον) rather means that he desires death because Christ has been crucified and therefore true love is to be found through death, i.e., he desires the same fate that Christ has accepted (J. Rist, "A Note," 243, n. 22).
14. *DN* IV.12, 709B.

of agape,[15] although he usually uses both concepts interchangeably, which in fact prompted Nygren to conclude that "Agape in Gregory is but another name for what is otherwise called Eros."[16]

What Origen, Gregory, and Dionysius did is in fact build their ideas about love upon the previously constructed basis, provided by Biblical-Christian and ancient philosophical traditions. The thinkers' cultural and religious background made it possible for them to use words, experiment with their meaning and construct new ideas. Their insistence on the synonymy of eros and agape, together with their elaborations on the issue, testify that they knew both terms very well, not just their meaning, but also their intellectual history. Thus, one cannot conclude with Nygren that Dionysius did not know what agape was, since it was not his reality, nor can one agree with Horn that agape lost its force and became irrelevant by the sixth century.[17]

The ancient sources of the Areopagite's concept of love are more evident. Some brief remarks could be useful at this point. Eros played an extremely important role in ancient Greek mythology and philosophy. As the son of Poverty and Plenty, he is a *daimon*, half way between god and man, and he always searches for something he lacks.[18] However, the concept of eros goes much beyond that, starting with Plato and continuing through Neoplatonic philosophy.

In *Symposium,* Plato goes beyond the usual concept of eros as an acquisitive desire in order to arrive at an eros which is not a desire for any desirable object, but a desire for an object that is good, which refers to the standard of absolute and eternal good. Furthermore, it is not just a desire for good, but a desire for *perpetual* desire of good; thus this desire stops being an acquisitive eros and becomes a creative one instead.[19] In *Phaedrus,* this eros leads the lover towards working on and adorning the beloved as if he was an image of the patron god, and thus both the lover and the beloved become more like the god himself.[20] Therefore, this love is not just a selfish need, but a desire for absolute good and beautiful. A similar image is present in Plotinus, who, however, directs the lover to work on his own statue in order to make himself perfect. In addition, he attributes eros to the Good: "He is at once lovable and love and love of himself."[21] In later Neoplatonism, Proclus is more lim-

15. PG 44, 1048C. Gregory prefers the term φιλανθρωπία for expressing the idea of agape.
16. A. Nygren, *Agape and Eros*, 440.
17. G. Horn, "Amour et extase," 279. In "Greek Cosmic Love," 60–61, C. De Vogel writes: "The history of the classical word φιλεῖν, so frequently found in the Socratic dialogues, is that in the connotation of 'loving' it went more and more out of use from the fourth century B.C. onward, while ἀγαπᾶν was more and more used instead of it. That as early as the second century B. C. ἀγαπᾶν was the common word for 'loving', both in the spoken and in the written language of everybody, is a verifiable fact. There is nothing 'sacred' about it, and the New Testament use of the term is by no means an almost isolated fact."
18. See F. Ivanovic, "Ancient Eros and Medieval Agape," 93–114.
19. A. H. Armstrong, "Platonic Eros and Christian Agape," 107.
20. Plato, *Phdr.*, 252d–253a.
21. Plotinus, *Enn.*, VI.8.15.

ited than Plotinus; he ascribes love to certain kinds of gods, but not to the One, which is unparticipated.[22] As god, Eros is given a place in Proclus' system within the Pistis-Aletheia-Eros triad, springing from the "Paternal Nous" (πατρικὸς Νοῦς), but it is not the First and ultimate Principle.[23]

Given these brief considerations, it comes as no surprise that Dionysius felt it possible to combine both his philosophical and Christian backgrounds, even in his erotology. However, he does not appropriate the ancient philosophical inheritance without any modification; on the contrary, he reshapes it to a certain extent and incorporates it in his own Christian worldview. In his equal use of eros and agape, the Areopagite does not apply these terms only to God, but he also uses them side by side when speaking about the creation's love for God: "And so it is that all things must desire, must yearn for, must love ἐφετὸν καὶ ἐραστὸν καὶ ἀγαπητὸν the Beautiful and the Good."[24] It is not just that the Good is an object of desire, yearning, and love, but also the Cause of everything is the divine love, understood as eros and agape.

Divine Love and Different Forms of Love

As already mentioned, Dionysius takes up the theme of the divine love in the fourth chapter of his *Divine Names.* He discusses it together with good and beautiful, which already implies a tight connection between the three, expressed in a previously quoted phrase by which Dionysius finishes the discourse on good and beautiful and proceeds to the discourse on love: "And so it is that all things must desire, must yearn for, must love, the Beautiful and the Good." He proceeds:

> Because of it and for its sake, subordinate is returned to superior (ἐπιστρεπτικῶς), equal keeps company with equal (κοινωνικῶς), superior turns providentially to subordinate (προνοητικῶς), each bestirs itself (συνεκτικῶς) and all are stirred to do and to will whatever it is they do and will because of the yearning for the Beautiful and the Good. And we may be so bold as to claim also that the Cause of all things loves all things in the superabundance of his goodness, that because of this goodness he makes all things brings all things to perfection, holds all things together, returns all things. The divine longing (ὁ θεῖος ἔρως) is Good seeking good for the sake of the Good.[25]

It is possible to identify in this passage four types of love or, to be more precise, of erotic movement:

1) ἔρως ἐπιστρεπτικός, which goes from inferiors to superiors, by way of return (conversion),

22. E. Perl, *Theophany*, 45.
23. See C. De Vogel, "Greek Cosmic Love," 67–69.
24. *DN* IV.10, 708A.
25. *DN* IV.10, 708AB.

2) ἔρως κοινωνικός, which represents the relationship between equals, by way of communion,
3) ἔρως προνοητικός, which goes from superiors to inferiors, by way of providence,
4) ἔρως συνεκτικός, which is the love of each being for itself, by way of conservation.

It is possible to trace this scheme to its ancient origins, which Cornelia De Vogel reassumes as follows:

> The first of these four kinds is Plato's ἔρως extended to everything in nature. As to the second, this recalls Boethius' *foedus perpetuum* and *socia fides*. The words κοινωνία, ὁμόνοια and φιλία for the interrelations of the elements and things on earth are of Pythagorean origin [...] Evidently it is the late form of Pythagoreanism, fused with Plato's later doctrine, in which both Stoic and Aristotelian elements have been incorporated [...] The third kind [...] is the love of a higher, divine being towards those of a lower level. It is certainly not the notion of providence which is surprising: Divine providence was a very important dogma both for Plato and in the Stoa, and for Plotinus and the Neoplatonists as well [...] It is Dionysius' fourth kind of love which in particular brings us back to the Stoa: the ἔρως συνεκτικός of natural objects for themselves appears as an extension of the οἰκείωσις which by the Stoics was attributed to all living beings.[26]

Although providence and love do play a role in Plotinus' system, they are however never combined. While the One does provide for what he creates, it cannot be argued that the One actually loves his creation. In the *Enneads* it is said that "we breathe and hold our ground because the Supreme does not give and pass but gives [provides] on for ever, so long as it remains what it is,"[27] but besides the fact that Plotinus here does not use the term eros, he does not describe the One as a subject, but only as an object of love, whereas love is a property of soul: "Love [is] an act of a Soul seeking good [and] this Love [is] leader of the particular Souls to The Good."[28] So it happens that "all that exists desires and aspires towards the Supreme by a compulsion of nature, as if all had received the oracle that without it they cannot be,"[29] while the One "remains, then, poised in wisdom within itself; it could not enter into any other; those others look to it and in their longing find it where it is."[30] It is clear how eros constitutes an important part of Plotinus' philosophy, but it nevertheless seems that the idea of a providential love ascribed to the One has to be dismissed:

26. C. De Vogel, "Amor quo caelum regitur," 15–16.
27. Plotinus, *Enn.*, VI.9.9.
28. *Ibid.*, III.5.4.
29. *Ibid.*, V.5.12.
30. *Ibid.*, VI.5.10.

> Plotin enseigne aussi que "la vie est une puissance universelle", car la vie est ici synonyme d'amour et de désir, et ce désir de l'Origine, cet amour qui a pour objet le Principe suprême, est universel : "Tout être engendré désire et aime celui qui l'a engendré". Mais la réciproque n'est pas vraie : l'Un n'est en rien comparable à un dieu généreux qui créerait le monde par bonté ou amour, car alors l'amour signifierait un attachement de l'Un à l'inférieur, à autre chose qu'à lui-même. S'il y a, certes, un dynamisme érotique à la source de la procession, dynamisme dont le principe est l'Un Amour de soi, dans l'inférieur, ce dynamisme se renverse en amour pour le générateur. En effet, l'amour infini qui a l'Un pour objet est identique à la puissance immense et à la force infinie qui proviennent de l'Origine, identique à "la vie qui est une puissance illimitée et universelle."[31]

The source of Dionysius' terminology in the first and third kind of erotic movement seems to be Proclus, by whom our author is greatly influenced – in his *Commentary on the First Alcibidiades*, Proclus says: "And gods then love gods, the superior ones the inferior ones, but providentially (προνοητικῶς), and the inferior ones love the superior ones, but revertively (ἐπιστρεπτικῶς)."[32] However, it has to be noted that the Neoplatonic philosopher does not ascribe providential love to the One itself, but only to gods inferior to the One. In his *Elements of Theology*, he speaks of the providence of gods:

> For all other things which are posterior to the Gods, act providentially through the participation of them: but providence is connascent with the Gods. For if to impart good to the subjects of providential activity is the prerogative of the providential peculiarity, but all the Gods are goodnesses, either they do not impart themselves to anything, and thus nothing will be good in secondary natures. And whence will that be derived which subsists according to participation, except from those natures which primarily possess peculiarities? Or, if they do impart themselves they impart good, and because of this providentially attend to all things. Providence, therefore, subsists primarily in the Gods. For where is the activity which is prior to intellect, except in superessential natures? But providence (πρόνοια), as the name signifies, is an energy or activity prior to intellect (ἐνέργειά ἐστι πρὸ νοῦ). The Gods, therefore, by reason of their essence, and because they are goodnesses, provide for all things, filling all things with the goodness which is prior to intellect.[33]

In *The Theology of Plato*, Proclus expresses an idea that could be related to Dionysius' second movement of love, ἔρως κοινωνικός:

> Such therefore, in short, is divine beauty, the supplier of divine hilarity, familiarity and friendship. For through this the Gods are united to and

31. A. Pigler, *Plotin*, 87.
32. Procl., *In Alc.*, 55–56.
33. Procl., *El. Th.*, prop. 120.

> rejoice in each other, admire, and are delighted in communicating with each other, and in their mutual replenishings, and do not desert the order which they are always allotted in the distributions of themselves.[34]

Through beauty, therefore, gods are united and communicate with each other. In addition, beauty is strictly connected with love since it "converts and moves all things to itself, causes them to energize enthusiastically, and recalls them through love," and so "it is the object of love, being the leader of the whole amatory series, walking on the extremities of its feet, and exciting all things to itself through desire and astonishment."[35] It is possible, then, to conclude that in Proclus' view those gods inferior to the One are linked through a kind of reciprocal love, although this is not defined in terms of ἔρως κοινωνικός which is Dionysius' innovation.[36] It should be mentioned, however, that, as De Vogel notes, "the term ἔρως [...] is absent from the *Elementa Theologiae* and hardly occurs in the *Theologia Platonica*, and this while the whole apparatus of such terms, as προνοητικός, ἀγαθοιδής, σωστικός, τελειωτικός and συνεκτικός is fully present in those works."[37] From this, De Vogel concludes that eros was not essential to Proclus' theology. On the contrary, Perl argues that this does not make Dionysius essentially different, since it would mean to concentrate on expression, instead of meaning, because "everything Dionysius *means* by ἔρως is centrally present in Proclus."[38]

While this might be a valid argument, especially if one considers the Areopagite's own opinion that "it would be unreasonable and silly to look at words rather than at the power of the meanings," a certain "suspicion" has to emerge – is it not curious that Proclus does not use the notion of ἔρως in his theological works, particularly if he already gave an important place to those terms that Dionysius would later pair with his concept of love? It would be quite unfair to assume that Proclus simply avoids this theme for no specific reason, or that he did not consider it important, since the discourse on love definitely appears in his other works. The reason stands in his metaphysical system which makes a distinction between participated and unparticipated terms, between the One and the henads. It was therefore quite difficult for Proclus to ascribe a providential love to the One. On the other hand, he ascribes it to inferior gods, and in his commentary on *Timaeus* he criticizes Christians for not believing in gods proceeding from the First Principle, namely gods who act providentially: "Thus, all religions and sects acknowledge that there is a first principle of things, and all men invoke God as their helper; but all do not believe that there are Gods posterior to this

34. Procl., *Theol. Plat.*, I.24.
35. *Ibid.*
36. Cf. P. Podolak, "L'amore divino," 320.
37. C. De Vogel, "Greek Cosmic Love," 71.
38. E. Perl, *Theophany*, 126, n. 35.

principle, and that a providential energy proceeds from them into the universe."[39] Proclus obviously felt a certain aversion towards the Christian attitude of ascribing providence to the First Principle, i.e., God, and this could help in reflecting upon the reasons why the Athenian scholarch talks about providential love only on the level of inferior gods.[40]

The idea of different kinds of love, together with love's relationship to the Good and the Beautiful, is underlined by Dionysius, not just in previously quoted passage, but also in a successive one:

> What is signified [by "love" and yearning"] is a capacity to effect a unity, an alliance, and a particular commingling in the Beautiful and the Good. It is a capacity which preexists through the Beautiful and the Good. It is dealt out from the Beautiful and the Good through the Beautiful and the Good. It binds the things of the same order in a mutually regarding union. It moves superior to provide for subordinate, and it stirs the subordinate in a return towards the superior.[41]

The idea of Good as Love was not strange to Plotinus, as he also identified Good as Eros. Nonetheless, the free and unselfish giving of goodness is attributed to the Good, rather than to the Good as Eros. Eros is not productive of good, or procreative, so "the Good as Eros creates, but the power of creating *per se* is not attributed to Eros."[42]

The love of God who cares and provides for his creation is expressed by Dionysius as ἔρως ἐκστατικός:

> This divine yearning brings ecstasy so that the lover belongs not to self but to the beloved. This is shown in the providence lavished by the superior on the subordinate. It is shown in the regard for one another demonstrated by those of equal status. And it is shown by the subordinate in their divine return toward what is higher.[43]

Again ἔρως ἐπιστρεπτικός, ἔρως συνεκτικός, and ἔρως κοινωνικός along with ἔρως προνοητικός appear together in the same image of love. This time, however, they are all characterized as ecstasy, as ἔρως ἐκστατικός, which is a genuinely Dionysian innovation, and "it would seem merely perverse to deny that Dionysius' Christianity is the direct cause of this adaptation."[44] The ecstatic power of love makes beings go out of themselves as providence (πρόνοια) of the superior, cohesion (συνοχή) of the equals, and return (ἐπιστροφή) of inferiors to superiors. Dionysius finds the basis of this ecstatic love in the Scripture, in St Paul's words "It is no longer I who live, but Christ

39. Procl., *In Tim.*, 286DE. See H.-D. Saffrey, "Allusions anti-chrétiennes chez Proclus," 558–559.
40. Cf. P. Podolak, "L'amore divino," 321.
41. *DN* IV.12, 709D.
42. E. Buckley, "Ecstatic and Emanating," 44–45.
43. *DN* IV.13, 712A.
44. J. Rist, "A Note," 239. Cf. Podolak, "Il divino amore," 323–325.

who lives in me."[45] Paul, "swept along by his yearning for God and seized of its ecstatic power," was, for Dionysius, "truly a lover [...] possessing not his own life but the life of the One for whom he yearned, as exceptionally beloved."[46] So Paul becomes the example of love, in his case of the ἔρως ἐπιστρεπτικός, since he goes out of himself to reach God and to be possessed by him, to belong not to himself but to the beloved.[47] However, this is not the only movement of love – as man goes out of himself for God, so God goes out of himself for man, seeking the other.[48] As every relationship of love, so too this love has a twofold character – for one to be able to give, the other must be able to receive love. This is why God also goes out of himself in the direction of man, just as man goes out of himself in the direction of God, until the two finally meet and touch, so that one lives in the other. And therefore the Areopagite continues:

> And, in truth, it must be said too that the very cause of the universe in the beautiful, good superabundance of his benign yearning for all is also carried outside of himself in the loving care he has for everything. He is, as it were, beguiled by goodness, by love, and by yearning and is enticed away from his transcendent dwelling place and comes to abide within all things, and he does so by virtue of his supernatural and ecstatic capacity to remain, nevertheless, within himself.[49]

In this passage Dionysius employs a characteristically erotic vocabulary, as if he were talking about two lovers, who are beguiled by love and desire, and enticed away from their dwelling, in an attempt to satisfy their burning love for each other. However, these words applied to God do not have the same connotation, or at least not completely the same. If one interprets this passage in an analogy to human love, then the ancient notion of eros as need or lack would come to light. But God cannot in any way be in need of something, and he lacks nothing. The Areopagite is fully aware of this, which is why he safeguards the completeness of God by saying that he goes out of his dwelling place and abides within all things, but "he does so by virtue of his supernatural and ecstatic capacity" which allows him "to remain, nevertheless, within himself," and to be "intrinsically ecstatic."[50] Consequently God goes out of himself, but at the same time he remains within himself. This is a secret of divine love, a mystery by which God goes out of himself by remaining within himself, and by which he loves his creation but is not in need of anything. This is possible because of his superessential capacity (power, δύναμις) and because of the fact that he is not a thing, not a being, but he is always "all in all." He still proves a sort of jealousy:

45. Gal 2:20.
46. *DN* IV.13, 712A.
47. See Y. de Andia, *Henosis*, 151.
48. See C. De Vogel, "Greek Cosmic Love," 70.
49. *DN* IV.13, 712AB.
50. Cf. E. Perl, *Theophany*, 46.

> That is why those possessed of spiritual insight describe him as "zealous" because his good yearning for all things is so great and because he stirs in men a deep yearning desire for zeal. In this way he proves himself to be zealous because zeal is always felt for what is desired and because he is zealous for the creatures for whom he provides. In short, both the yearning and the object of that yearning belong to the Beautiful and the Good. They preexist in it, and because of it they exist and come to be.[51]

This jealousy is not, however, a jealousy for something that he lacks or needs. God's eros, as already said, is not a result of a need; on the contrary, he is jealous because of his providential love, because of his care for his creation, which he draws to himself.[52] In addition, both love and the object of love are found in the Beautiful and the Good, and so the being's love for God coincides with God's love for the being, meaning that the being's return to God coincides with God's drawing of the being to himself, while God's giving to the being coincides with the being's self-giving to God. That is how not only Paul, but also every being, can and should claim that it is no longer them who live, but it is God who lives in them.[53] Dionysius does not miss the chance to develop this concurrence further:

> Why is it, however, that theologians sometimes refer to God as Yearning and Love and sometimes as the yearned-for and the Beloved? On the one hand he causes, produces, and generates what is being referred to, and, on the other hand, he is the thing itself. He is stirred by it and he stirs it. He is moved to it and he moves it. So they call him the beloved and the yearned-for since he is beautiful and good, and, again, they call him yearning and love because he is the power (δύναμις) moving and lifting all things up to himself, for in the end what is he if not Beauty and Goodness, the One who of himself reveals (ἔκφανσις) himself, the good procession (πρόοδος) of his own transcendent unity? He is yearning on the move (ἐρωτική κίνησις), simple, self-moved, self-acting, preexistent in the Good, flowing out from the Good onto all that is and returning once again to the Good.[54]

God is therefore described here not just as the object of love and yearning, but also as "the thing itself," as power (δύναμις), manifestation (ἔκφανσις), and procession (πρόοδος). He is also a movement, which constitutes the eternal endless circle of love:

51. *DN* IV.13, 712B.
52. Cf. C. Osborne, *Eros Unveiled*, 194.
53. See E. Perl, *Theophany*, 48. It should be noted that this, however, does not mean that the soul has an innate eros for the Good, as it is the case in Plotinus, but since the soul is created in image and likeness of God, it does not automatically follow that the soul's return to God is ontologically ensured (see E. Buckley, "Ecstatic and Emanating," 58).
54. *DN* IV.14, 712C.

> In this divine yearning shows especially its unbeginning and unending nature traveling in an endless circle through the Good, from the Good, in the Good and to the Good, unerringly turning, ever on the same center, ever in the same direction, always proceeding, always remaining, always being restored to itself.[55]

The eternal circle is, then, love as both procession and return, it is God who is present in all things and who gives them their goodness, beauty, power, and being. Love is thus identified as power, manifestation, procession and erotic movement which preexists in the Good, goes out of the Good, and circularly moves therefrom towards beings, and then, in reversion, returns to the Good. As Dionysius claims, all this has been set out by his great teacher, Hierotheus, in his *Hymns of Eros*. Hierotheus, according to the Areopagite, describes love as follows:

> When we talk of yearning, whether this be in God or an angel, in the mind or in the spirit or in nature, we should think of a unifying and co-mingling power which moves the superior to provide for the subordinate, peer to be in communion with peer, and subordinate to return to the superior and the outstanding.[56]

Hierotheus here distinguishes between five appearances of love: divine (εἴτε θεῖον), angelic (εἴτε ἀγγελικὸν), intellectual (εἴτε νοερὸν), spiritual (εἴτε ψυχικὸν), and physical (εἴτε φυσικὸν). These five appearances of love are articulated through the three movements mentioned already: the providential movement of superior towards the subordinate, the movement of communion between equals, and the movement of return of the subordinate towards the superior. In the following passages, Hirotheus orders multiple yearnings according to procession from the One to the concentration of all the yearnings into the single yearning. As the movement of love is circular, so it begins and it ends in singular:

> I have set out in due order the many yearnings springing from the One and I have explained the nature of the knowledge and power appropriate to the yearnings within the world and beyond. These are surpassed, according to the clear intention of the argument, by the orders and ranks of the intelligent and intelligible yearnings. After them are found the most truly beautiful yearnings which are self-intelligible and divine and which quite rightly are praised by us. But now, once more, let me take all of these yearnings and concentrate them into the single yearning which is the father of all yearnings. First let me divide in two their general powers as yearnings. The irrepressible cause of all yearning has command and primacy over them and is the cause beyond them all and

55. *DN* IV.14, 712D–713A.
56. *DN* IV.15, 713AB.

> indeed is the goal toward which everything everywhere strives upward, each as best it can.[57]

Consequently, different types of love are divided as follows: 1) those coming from the world; 2) those which are superior to the world; 3) intelligent and intelligible loves, and finally 4) the most truly beautiful loves. Ysabel de Andia[58] identified the source of such disposition in the hierarchy of henads in Proclus' *Elements of Theology*: 1) Τὸ Ἕν; 2) ἑνάδες νοηταί; 3) ἑνάδες νοεραί; 4) ἑνάδες ὑπερκόσμιοι (ψυχή); 5) ἑνάδες ἐγκόσμιοι.[59] All these types of love are concentrated into the single love which is their father, but this single love, again, should be distinguished from the total love (ὁ ὁλικὸς ἔρως) which proceeds from all beings, precisely, as de Andia warns, because of the origin of their procession – the divine love proceeds "through the Good, from the Good, in the Good, and to the Good"[60] in a circular movement, while total love proceeds from all the beings towards the absolute Cause of all love.[61] However, Hierotheus' goal is to gather these into a unity, in order to conclude

> [...] that there is a simple self-moving power directing all things to mingle as one, that it starts out from the Good, reaches down to the lowliest creation, returns then in due order through all stages back to the Good, and thus turns from itself and through itself and upon itself and toward itself in an everlasting circle.[62]

So at the end of his treatment of eros, Dionysius defines it as a simple self-moving power, which moves in an endless circle, thus expressing again the concept of procession and return, acting in order to put all things into union: through the love of superior for inferiors, of inferiors for superiors, and of equals among themselves, one simple power of eros comes to light, and as it unifies different types of love, so it brings all things into union.

It is clear that Dionysius' concept of eros has a creative, productive character. This in combination with the frequent use of terms such as "excess," "overflow," or "superabundance" (ὑπερβολή) raises the question of the very character of creating, in the sense of freedom or necessity. Since God loves all and is love, and since this love moves to the giving of itself, the question is if this affects God's own will, i.e., does the superabundance of love, which must give itself, somehow limit God's freedom? Although this distinction between freedom (or will) and necessity is often over-simplified and misconceived,[63] some thought should be given to the issue.

57. *DN* IV.16, 713BC.
58. Y. de Andia, *Henosis*, 154.
59. Procl., *El. Th.*, prop. 162–165.
60. Cf. Rom 11:36: "All things are from him and through Him and for him."
61. Y. de Andia, *Henosis*, 155.
62. *DN* IV.17, 713D.
63. Cf. I. Trethowan, "Irrationality in Theology," 21; E. Perl, *Theophany*, 49; A. Golitzin, *Et Introibo*, 82–83.

Generally, the misconception of freedom or necessity, when it comes to creation, often comes from the too anthropomorphic understanding of God, in the sense of putting alternatives before God, one of which he has to choose: "God's plan for creation is what it is because he is who he is. This is freedom in the fullest, most positive sense where it coincides with necessity in the fullest, most positive sense."[64] This is fairly true, since Dionysius himself would be contrary to our application of human distinctions to God, but it can hardly suffice for our need to understand certain issues, one of which is determining whether there can be something by which God is limited or forced to do one thing rather than another. Perl argues that the misconception goes back to the Neoplatonists, and some unreliable interpretations of emanations, i.e., of creation by the One. Although Plotinus does indeed talk about necessity in terms of creation, this does not however mean that there is some higher universal law to which all beings, including the One, are subject. This is simply because the One is not a being, not even the highest being, and so it cannot be subordinate to a "law of emanation," but rather "as Giving or Production, is itself the law or paradigm to which all things, in producing, conform," and so the One would be the power of all things, and as such absolutely unconditioned.[65] As a result, Perl concludes, tension between "Neoplatonic necessary procession" and "Christian free creation" is a misconception, and so it would be wrong to put Dionysius in either of these two categories.[66] It this sense God would be nothing but the making of all things, and so God cannot not create: "That yearning which creates all the goodness of the world preexisted superabundantly within the Good and did not allow it to remain without issue."[67] From the utterance "did not allow," Perl concludes that there can be no alternatives, and that God "cannot not produce," although this "cannot" is within himself.[68] However, one could argue that precisely this "did not allow" is precisely a testimony of certain choice, since if something is allowed or not allowed, than there has to be an alternative – if something is not allowed to be done, than it follows that it *could* be done, but it is not allowed; otherwise, there would be no sense in speaking of permitting or not permitting something. If something is the only possible thing, than it simply must happen, it must be done, and so allowing it or forbidding it would be absurd:

> In Christian belief we understand the world as that which might not have been, and correlatively we understand God as capable of existing, in undiminished goodness and greatness, even if the world had not been. We know that there is a world, so we appreciate the world as in fact created, but we acknowledge that it is meaningful to say that God

64. I. Trethowan, "Irrationality in Theology," 21.
65. E. Perl, *Theophany*, 50.
66. *Ibid.*, 51.
67. *DN* IV.10, 708B.
68. E. Perl, *Theophany*, 52.

> could have been all that there is. Such a "solitary" existence of God is a counter factual, but it is meaningful, whereas it would not be meaningful for the pagan sense of the divine.[69]

On the other hand, it would not be correct to speak about alternatives before (or in) God, since there is nothing higher than (or equal to) God, which could present alternatives before him, from amongst which he would have to choose. There is nothing that can compel God to do or not to do something, and nor can there be some sort of internal struggle within God. The "did not allow" sentence is, therefore, not be understood in the sense of alternatives (whether their presence or their absence), but in the sense, so to say, of the rhetorical,[70] which means that God acts in accordance with his nature, he bounds himself (freely) by goodness, love, justice, etc., because he wants it so. But it would be wrong to say that God cannot do otherwise: "House of Israel, can't I deal with you like this potter, declares the Lord? Like clay in the potter's hand, so are you in mine, house of Israel!"[71] He obviously could do harm, and could destroy just as he created, but he wills good, and therefore acts good.

The question at stake also implies the issue of God's omnipotence – if God is omnipotent, than he can do anything, but he can also do nothing; he can create, but he can also not create: "He can do whatever he wants."[72] If one relies only on the superabundance in God, which implies that the creation happens out of excess or overflow, then one could be led to another misunderstanding. God does not create simply because he is superabundant (of love, or of essence – it does not matter), as if he were unable to contain all that excess, so he outpours it through creation, but he creates out of love, which is the keyword in the entire question. He is not some transcendent image of Nietzsche's nobleman who gives because of the overflow of his richness, and from an impulse of the superabundant power.[73] On the contrary, he creates and gives himself out of love, and is it not that every act of love is an act of freedom, just as every act of giving is free, as otherwise it would not be love and it would not be a gift? For freedom does not always include love, but love always presupposes freedom. Besides, as Golitzin has pointed out, Dionysius does make certain distinction between will and nature, between

69. R. Sokolowski, *The God of Faith and Reason*, 19.
70. Cf. for example *DN* X.1, 937A: "He generates everything from out of himself as from some omnipotent root and he returns all things back to himself as though to some omnipotent storehouse. Being their omnipotent foundation, he holds them all together. He keeps them thus in a transcendent bond and he *does not permit* them either to fall away from him or to be destroyed by being moved from their perfect home."
71. Jer 18:6.
72. Ps 115:3.
73. F. Nietzsche, *Beyond God and Evil*, frg. 260: "There is the feeling of plenitude, of power, which seeks to overflow, the happiness of high tension, the consciousness of a wealth which would give and bestow: the noble man also helps the unfortunate, but not out of pity, but rather from an impulse generated by the super-abundance of power."

God's essence and "powers," and he places creation exactly in the latter, as God in relation is God in his πρόοδοι.[74] Golitzin also shows how in the *Corpus*, "God's will or willing is in every case clearly associated with his goodness, that is, his love acting on and for his creation."[75] So the point regarding God's omnipotence, his goodness and his love is that God can do everything, but he does what he wills – and he wills only good.

This however does not mean, as pointed out above, that God stands before two (or more) possible alternatives, from amongst which he has to choose one. He is good, and he provides for things capable of partaking of his goodness; he is loving, and so he loves all his creatures. But this does not happen because God *must* act like that, or that he is forced to do one thing and not the other – it simply means that he *need not* deliberate or choose over an activity that is fully in accordance with his nature and will.[76] It is in this sense that the exaggeration of tension between freedom and necessity should be understood. Or, by applying the Dionysian method of apophatic and cataphatic theologies, by which every name is applied to God but yet he is none of them, one could say that God is Freedom, but then also that God is not Freedom, therefore God is *beyond* Freedom; or that God is Necessity, but again that God is not necessity, so God is *beyond* Necessity.[77] The point is that the discourse

74. A. Golitzin, *Et Itroibo*, 83.
75. *Ibid.*
76. C. Osborne, *Eros Unveiled*, 196.
77. I am not prepared to agree with Torstein Tollefsen's view that Dionysius did not adopt or develop the Christian doctrine on divine freedom (T. Tollefsen, *Activity and Participation*, 111–113). In his philosophical consistency and academic honesty, Tollefsen himself presents three possible objections to his own conclusions, although he does not see them as sufficient to undermine his views. These objections refer to the fact that Dionysius explicitly states human freedom (*CH* IX.3, 260CD), which would imply also freedom of God; secondly, in one place Dionysius claims that "without the One there is no multiplicity, but there can still be the One where there is no multiplicity" (*DN* XIII.2, 980A); finally, the fact that Maximus the Confessor, great Orthodox thinker and careful follower of Dionysius, does not express any critique towards the Areopagite, could serve as "proof" of his Orthodoxy. In my opinion, the first two objections are already sufficient to "justify" Dionysius: the fact that he does not develop a discussion on this issue does not mean his refusal to accept the doctrine on God's freedom, and I do not think that *argumentum ex silentio* could be valid here. Dionysius wrote his works with a clear idea on the topics of discussion, on each work's disposition, as well as on the intention of his writings and their audience. It is not, therefore, acceptable to expect him to write any more or any less of what he did actually write. If one cannot find a developed and detailed treatment of a certain controversial issue, that does not justify classifying Dionysius in the heterodox or heretic party, but simply implies that a certain topic is not of his interest, whether in the overall plan of the work, or perhaps in the attempt to safeguard his pseudonym. Furthermore, the *Corpus* contains many places where the author affirms the freedom of both God and creation. Besides the passages cited by Tollefsen, it might be useful to cite a locus where the Areopagite says that God is "free of every limitation, beyond every limitation" (*MT* V, 1048B), or where he claims that the names Time, Days, Season, Eternity "refer to someone totally free of change or movement [...], someone who is the cause of eternity, of time and the days" (*DN* X.2, 937B). The Areopagite also says that "intelligent beings, because of their free will, can fall away from the light of the mind" (*EH* II.3.3, 400A), while speaking of hierarchs he writes that the hierarch

on freedom, necessity, choice, deliberation, etc., is based on our human conceptions, and is not applicable to God in absolute and definite terms; simply, he is beyond such discourse.[78]

While I am aware that my argument could also bear an accusation of being anthropomorphic, which I denounced earlier as improper when speaking of God, I still however think that these considerations could help to clear up our own human understanding of the issues that interest us, since these are the questions posed by our reason, by our own rational nature, which provoke rational thought and discourse, though they might not be appropriate for a genuine theological discourse on God, who is ineffable and rationally incomprehensible. In this regards, it seems advisable to open the floor to Dionysius once again:

> This is something which was marvelously grasped by that truly divine man, my teacher and yours and the light of our common instructor. For this is what he said: "The foolishness of God is wiser than men." Those words are true not only because all human thinking is a sort of error when compared with the solid permanence of the perfect divine thoughts but also because it is customary for theologians to apply negative terms to God, but contrary to the usual sense of a deprivation. Scripture, for example, calls the all-apparent light "invisible." It says regarding the One of many praises and many names that he is ineffable and nameless. It says of the One who is present in all things and who may be discovered from all things that he is ungraspable and "inscrutable." And here the divine apostle is said to be praising God for his "foolishness," which in itself seems absurd and strange, but uplifts [us] to the ineffable truth which is there before all reasoning.[79]

In the end, Dionysius' erotology represents a magnificent example of the reception of ancient philosophical thought and of its amalgamation with Christian doctrines. Theories of love (and not only love) present in Plato, Plotinus, and Proclus clearly did not lose their significance with the appearance of the monotheistic Christian religion, but, on the contrary, they were taken over and adapted, and thus became a part, not only of pagan, but also of Christian intellectual and religious heritage. The Areopagite's treatment of love is significant not only as a testimony of the synergy between antiquity and Christianity, but also because it shows the author's courage to use an ancient

---

prays to God "only for what is suitable to the divine promises, for what pleases God, and for what God will freely give" (*EH* VII.3.7, 564B). All this indicates that Dionysius did accept freedom as characteristic to both God and humans, and in this he does not fall away from the Christian doctrine, although in his works this doctrine is found in a quite incomplete and fragmentary form.

78. See an interesting discussion on different forms of divine freedom, and attribution of "freedom of indifference" to God in K. A. Rogers, "Anselm on God's Perfect Freedom," 1–8, and K. M. Staley, "God's Personal Freedom," 9–16.

79. *DN* VII.1, 865BC.

term, with mainly physical and earthly associations at that time, and to restore its previous meaning by applying it to God himself, and not just to one of the multiplicity of pagan gods, but to one and only God of Christianity. On the other hand, Dionysius the Areopagite is proof that a strict demarcation of concepts and thoughts, in terms of their affiliation to paganism or to Christianity, is not scholarly justified or meaningful. Finally, the sense and form of his considerations on love show that Dionysius' work does only not possess historico-philological, but also timeless, actual significance.

Bibliography

Primary sources

Dionysius Areopagita, *Corpus Dionysiacum*, 2 vols, ed. B. R. Suchla, G. Heil and A. M. Ritter, Berlin: De Gruyter 1990-1991. (Tranlastion in: Pseudo-Dionysius, *The Complete Works*, transl. C. Luibheid, New York: Paulist Press 1987)

Gregorius Nyssenus, *Opera omnia*, in: *Patrologiae cursus completus.* Series graeca, ed. J-P. Migne, 162 vols, Paris: Migne 1857-1886, vol. 44.

Ignatius, *Epistle to the Romans*, transl. A. Roberts and J. Donaldson, Ante-Nicene Fathers, vol. 1, Buffalo, NY: Christian Literature 1886.

Nietzsche, F., *Beyond Good and Evil: Prelude to a Philosophy of the Future*, transl. W. Kaufmann, New York: Random House 1966.

Origen, *Commentarius in Canticum canticorum*, ed. L. Brésard, H. Crouzel and M. Borret, Sources chrétiennes, vol. 375, Paris: Cerf 1991-1992.

Plato, *Platonis Opera*, ed. J. Burnet, Oxford: Oxford University Press 1903.

Plotin, *Ennéades*, Texte établi et traduit par E. Bréhier, Paris: Collection Budé 1924-1938.

Plotinus, *The Six Enneads*, transl. S. MacKenna, Chicago: Encyclopædia Britannica 1952.

Proclus, *Commentary on the first Alcibiades of Plato*, ed. L. G. Westerink, Amsterdam: North-Holland 1954.

Proclus, *Commentary on the first Alcibiades of Plato*, ed. L. G. Westerink, Amsterdam: North-Holland 1954.

Proclus, *Théologie platonicienne.* Texte établi et traduit par H.-D. Saffrey et L. G. Westerink, 6 vols, Paris: Les Belles lettres 1968-1997.

Proclus, *In Platonis Timaeum commentaria*, ed. E. Diehl, 3 vols, Leipzig: Teubner 1903-1906.

Secondary sources

Armstrong, A. H. "Platonic Eros and Christian Agape," *Downside Review* 79 (1961) 105–121.

De Andia, Y. *Henosis : L'union à Dieu chez Denys l'Aréopagite*, Leiden : Brill, 1996.

De Vogel, C. "Amor quo caelum regitur," *Vivarium* 1:1 (1963) 2–34.

De Vogel, C. "Greek Cosmic Love and the Christian Love of God: Boethius, Dionysius the Areopagite and the Author of the Fourth Gospel," *Vigiliae Christianae* 35:1 (1981) 57–81.

Esposito-Buckley, L. M. "Ecstatic and Emanating, Providential and Unifying: A Study of the Pseudo-Dionysian and Plotinian Concepts of Eros," *The Journal of Neoplatonic Studies* 1:1 (1992) 31–61.

Golitzin, A. *Et Introibo ad Altare Dei: The Mystagogy of Dionysius Areopagita with Special Reference to its Predecessors in the Eastern Christian Tradition*, Thessaloniki: PIPM 1994.

Horn, G. "Amour et extase d'après Denys l'Aréopagite," *Revue d'ascétique et de mystique* 3 (1925) 278–289.

Ivanovic, F. "Ancient Eros and Medieval Agape: The Concept of Love in Plato and Maximus the Confessor," in: K. Boudouris & M. Adam, eds., *Greek Philosophy and the Issues of Our Age II*, Athens: Ionia 2009, 93–114.

Nygren, A. *Agape and Eros*, London: SPCK 1953.

Osborne, C. *Eros Unveiled: Plato and the God of Love*, Oxford: Oxford University Press 1996.

Perl, E. D. *Theophany: The Neoplatonic Philosophy of Dionysius the Areopagite*, New York: SUNY Press 2007.

Podolak, P. "L'amore divino nella tradizione platonica e nello ps. Dionigi l'Areopagita," *Adamantius* 14 (2008) 311–328.

Rist, J. M. "A Note on Eros and Agape in Pseudo-Dionysius," *Vigiliae Christianae* 20:4 (1966) 235–243.

Rogers, K. A. "Anselm on God's Perfection," *The Saint Anselm Journal* 1:1 (2003) 1–8.

Saffrey, H.-D. "Allusions anti-chrétiennes chez Proclus, le diadoque platonicien," *Revue des sciences philosophiques et théologiques* 59 (1975) 553–563.

Sokolowski, R. *The God of Faith and Reason: Foundations of Christian Theology*, Washington, DC: Catholic University of America 1995.

Staley, K. M. "God's Personal Freedom: A Response to Katherin Rogers," *The Saint Anselm Journal* 1:1 (2003) 9–16.

Tollefsen, T. *Activity and Participation in Late Antique and Early Christian Thought*, Oxford: Oxford University Press 2012.

Trethowan, I. "Irrationality in Theology and the Palamite Distinction," *Eastern Churches Review* 9 (1977) 19–26.

Leontius of Byzantium and His "Theory of Graphs" Against John Philoponus

Basil Lourié

1. Introduction

Who[1] was the prototype of the Acephalus in the *Solutio argumentorum a Severo objectorum* (*CPG* 6815) [thereafter *Solutio*] by Leontius of Byzantium?[2]

Some early scholars believed that it was Severus of Antioch in person.[3] Even Aloys Grillmeier continued – probably after Brian E. Daley[4] – to say that

1. The article was written with the support of the Russian Foundation for Basic Research, project Nr 13-33-01026 "The Function of Concept of Force/Possibility in Aristotle's Natural Philosophy." I would like to express my gratitude to Dmitry Birjukov for his continuous help and fruitful discussion of related topics and to Dirk Krausmüller – for both discussions on Leontius of Byzantium and improving my translations into English from Greek.
2. The works of Leontius will be quoted according to the unpublished PhD thesis by Brian E. Daley, *Leontius of Byzantium: A Critical Edition of His Works, with Prolegomena*, Oxford University 1978 [thereafter B. Daley, *Leontius*] (with page numbers only) but providing as well the references to the columns of PG 86.
3. Friedrich Loofs evaluated Severus' authorship of a hypothetical polemical work answered by Leontius in the *Solutio* as only "wahrscheinlich;" F. Loofs, *Leontius von Byzanz und die gleichnamigen Schriftsteller der griechischen Kirche*, 1. Buch: *Das Leben und die polemischen Werke des Leontius von Byzanz*, TU III, 1–2, Leipzig: J. C. Hinrichs'sche Buchhandlung 1887, 35. However, Johannes Peter Junglas, without further argumentation, was going as far as considering the Leontius' work as the only remaining source of the text of the lost Severus' polemical work whose existence, to Junglas, was no longer hypothetical but quite certain: "Demnach hatte Leontius eine polemische Schrift Severs als Vorlage seiner Arbeit. Die von Leontius in der *Epilysis* vorgebrachten *ἀπορίαι* Severs sind bez. ihrer Richtigkeit kontrollierbar an uns noch erhaltenen Fragmenten Severs;" J. P. Junglas, *Leontius von Byzanz. Studien zu seinen Schriften, Quellen und Anschauungen*, Forschungen zur Christlichen Literatur- und Dogmengeschichte, Bd. 7, H. 3, Paderborn: F. Schöningh 1908, 3–4, here 3).
4. Brian E. Daley, without mentioning Richard's criticisms (see below, n. 6), continued to insist on the existence of a lost Severus' work behind Leontius' polemics: "Although there is no mention of Severus in the body of the text, the title identifies him as the source of objections; if this is true, the most likely date for the work's composition would be the time when both Severus and Leontius were in Constantinople, between the winter of 535 and March, 536;" B. Daley, *Leontius*, xxxiii. Thus, Daley tried to treat the title *Ἐπιλύσεις τῶν ὑπὸ Σευήρου προβεβλημένων συλλογισμῶν* in the most literalistic way, even though he himself was realising that this is not the unique option. Even Richard Cross calls the Acephalus "a placeholder for Severus, as the full title of the work suggests"; R. Cross, "Individual Natures in the Christology of Leontius of Byzantium," *Journal of Early Christian Studies* 10 (2002) 245–

"the headless one" of the *Solutio* "really speaks for Severus."[5] It is not the case, however. As Marcel Richard has shown, the Acephalus is a collective image of Severianist critics of Leontius' previous work *Contra Nestorianos et Eutychianos* (*CPG* 6813) [= *CNE*].[6] Marcel Richard believed that Leontius' audience was here neo-Chalcedonian rather than properly Severianist: "Léonce ne nous dit pas, en effet, qu'il a été repris par les monophysites ; mais que beaucoup de gens ont trouvé son système peu efficace contre le monophysisme et lui ont reproché d'avoir négligé certaines objections de ces hérétiques ;" then, Richard concluded that Leontius' interlocutor is "un néo-chalcédonien."[7]

I, for one, once proposed to identify the Acephalus with John Philoponus (regardless of whether Philoponus did criticize *CNE* or not) – however, with no proper explanation of historical circumstances and without appropriate reservations.[8] I was then sharing Michel van Esbroeck's conviction that the *De Sectis* (*CPG* 6823) with its polemics against Philoponus is a work by Leontius of Byzantium and is to be dated to the period from 543 to 551.[9] However, now I am convinced by Uwe Lang's criticism of van Esbroeck's analysis and reestablishment of the traditional, for the twentieth-century scholarship, date of the *De Sectis*, between 580 and 608, which precludes its attribution to Leontius of Byzantium.[10] Therefore, after having excluded the *De Sectis* from

---

365, here 254. This remark in Cross' mouth is especially odd, because Cross himself provides a long note (255, n. 29) dealing with difference between Acephalus' and Severus' positions and, then, calls Acephalus "the [fictitious?] Severan opponent of Leontius" (259; square brackets by Cross).

5. A. Grillmeier with Th. Hainthaler, *Christ in Christian Tradition*, vol. 2/2: *The Church of Constantinople in the Sixth Century*, tr. P. Allen, J. Cawte, London: Mowbray, Louisville, KY: Westminster John Knox Press 1995 [original publ. 1989], 193.
6. Thus Marcel Richard in his decisive criticisms of Loofs' argumentation: "Contre cette hypothèse nous pouvons alléguer le fait que Léonce s'adresse toujours à ses adversaires au pluriel (col. 1916C, 1937A)"; moreover, Richard put forward chronological reasons against the very possibility of a direct polemic against Severus by Leontius; M. Richard, "Léonce de Byzance était-il origéniste ?", *Revue des études byzantines* 5 (1947) 31–66 (repr. *idem*, *Opera minora*, t. 2, Turnhout : Brepols 1976, Nr 57), here 58, esp. n. 2.
7. M. Richard, "Léonce...", 58–59, here 58.
8. В. М. Лурье, при участии В. А. Баранова, *История византийской философии. Формативный период* [B. Lourié, with a participation of V. Baranov, *The History of the Byzantine Philosophy. The Formative Period*], St Petersburg: Axioma, 2006 [thereafter IVF], 334–348; a Serbian translation available: В. Лурје уз сарадњу В. А. Баранова, *Историја византијске философије. Формативни период.* Превела с руског Јелена Капустина. Сремски Карловци, Нови Сад: Издавачка књижарница Зорана Стојановића 2010.
9. M. van Esbroeck, "Le 'De Sectis' attribué à Léonce de Byzance (CPG 6823) dans la version géorgienne d'Arsène Iqaltoeli", *Bedi Kartlisa* 42 (1984) 35–42, and *idem*, "La date et l'auteur du 'De Sectis' attribué à Léonce de Byzance," in: C. Laga, J. A. Munitiz, L. Van Rompay, eds., *After Chalcedon. Studies in Theology and Church History offered to Professor Albert Van Roey for His Seventieth Birthday*, Orientalia Lovaniensia Analecta 18, Leuven: Peeters 1985, 415–424.
10. U. M. Lang, "The Date of the Treatise 'De Sectis' Revisited," *Orientalia Lovaniensia Periodica* 29 (1998) 89–98. The most convincing part of Lang's argumentation is, to my opinion, chronology of publication of Philoponus' "tritheistic" works criticized in the *De Sectis*. I am unaware of van Esbroeck's reaction to this paper.

consideration, we have no direct evidence for any discussion between Leontius of Byzantium and John Philoponus. This is not to say, however, that such a discussion did not take place. Moreover, we still have a witness preserved by Germanos of Constantinople (early eighth century) that it was Leontius who answered Philoponus in defence of the Council of Chalcedon; Germanos, however, means the whole work of Leontius rather than any specific treatise.[11] Germanos' source is unknown.

Thus, the question about possible direct polemics between Philoponus and Leontius could be reopened. I have nothing to object against Richard's conclusion that Leontius aimed at a (neo-)Chalcedonian audience, but my point is that this audience was especially alarmed by John Philoponus' unifying idea which has been proposed on the eve of the Constantinopolitan Council of 553. In this sense, the prototype of the Acephalus is John Philoponus as the author of the *Arbiter*.

2. The *Solutio*: Problems of Dating

From the text of the *Solutio*, we know that it is a continuation of a previous work by Leontius,' *CNE* (p. 77.3–15; 1916C). However, the general chronology of Leontius' works – and his life as well – is not very precise. It heavily depends on our presuppositions concerning his identity with other personalities bearing the same name. I will try to avoid here using any suppositions going beyond the texts. Thus, we can follow the "common opinion" that *CNE* is datable to either the 530s[12] or early 540s (not later than 543), that is, before the Justinian's decree against the "Three Chapters" (543 or early 544).[13] This

11. Germanos of Constantinople in the *De haeresibus et synodis* (*CPG* 8020), ch. 33, says that Philoponus, μᾶλλον δὲ Ματαιόπονος, "struggled against the Council" (κατὰ τῆς συνόδου ἠγωνίζετο) and "almost agreed with Origen in his teaching about resurrection" (μικροῦ καὶ τῷ Ὠριγένει συμπνέων εἰς τοὺς περὶ ἀναστάσεως λόγους); Leontius, however, "[...] composed a very appropriable book defending this Council and has written down in it many witnesses of the notion of duality [*sc.* of the natures in Christ], and this is why this book is called the *Leontia*" (Λεόντιος δὲ ὁ τῆς ἐρήμου μόναχος βιβλίον συνέθηκεν εὐαπόδεκτον, ὑπὲρ τῆς τοιαύτης συνόδου ἐνιστάμενος· πολλὰς δὲ μαρτυρίας ἐν αὐτῷ καταγράψας περὶ τῆς δϊϊκῆς φωνῆς, ὅθεν καὶ *Λεόντια* τὸ βιβλίον ἐκ τούτου ἐκλήθη) (PG 98, 69C–72A). I proposed a reconstruction of Philoponus' teaching on the resurrection in B. Lourié, "John Philoponus on the Bodily Resurrection," *Scrinium* 9 (2013) 91–100; an enlarged Russian translation: В. М. Лурье, "Идентичность человеческой личности по Иоанну Филопону: физическое тело в пространстве и человеческое тело по воскресении [The Identity of the Human Personality according to John Philoponus: the Physical Body in the Space and the Human Body after the Resurrection]," *Εἶναι. Проблемы Философии и Теологии* 1, 1 (2012) 307–339; the relevant pages of IVF (243–248) contain my earlier erroneous views.
12. Thus Daley and almost the whole previous scholarship, although with important exceptions (see the next note): "[...] its [*CNE*'s] content seems to belong best in the heated theological atmosphere of the 530s;" B. Daley, *Leontius*, xxxii–xxxiii, here xxxiii.
13. Marcel Richard opts for the exact date just before the decree against the "Three Chapters," 543; M. Richard, "Léonce...," 50–53 *et passim*, whereas David Evans accepts the interval from 540 to 543; D. B. Evans, *Leontius of Byzantium: An Origenist Christology*, Dumbarton Oaks Studies 13, Washington, D.C.: Dumbarton Oaks Center for Byzantine studies 1970, 2–3.

dating, "prior to 544," seems to me results from the text of *CNE* without any particular assumption concerning the identity of Leontius. However, dealing with the *Solutio*, we have nothing except this *terminus post quem. A priori*, it is unclear whether Leontius wrote his *Solutio* soon after publication of *CNE* or that he revisited his polemics after having several years spent.

Thus, for the *Solutio*, our main *terminus ante quem* is the date of the death of Leontius – which is, unfortunately, unknown. Anyway, it is within the limits of probability that he was still alive and active, at least, for about one decade beyond the early 540s, that is, up to the time of the Second Council of Constantinople (553). This decade is to be defined as the most probable time of composition of the *Solutio*.

3. *The Polemical Context*

The author of the *Solutio* needs to explain, throughout the whole of his treatise, why the "one composite hypostasis" of the Chalcedonians does not mean the same as the "one composite nature" of the anti-Chalcedonians. This eternal polemical motive between the partisans and the adversaries of the Council of Chalcedon is interpreted, in *this* work of Leontius – not in *CNE* – quite unusually: Leontius tries to explain the difference between the notions of hypostasis and *particular* nature, because he does admit, from the very beginning, that the humanity of Christ is not a general nature but a particular one. This is neither the common opinion of the Chalcedonian authors nor Leontius' own attitude in *CNE*. This feature of the *Solutio* passed scarcely noticed by the patristic scholars, with a unique and important exception of Richard Cross.[14] At least, nobody realised here the fact of a radical deviation from the Chalcedonian tradition, already established in the epoch of Leontius and being perpetuated by Maximus the Confessor and the Christological doctrines of the defenders of the holy icons in the ninth century.

From the early sixth century, and then again, from the early ninth century onwards we see Chalcedonian Orthodoxy insisting that the Logos became incarnated in the common nature of humankind. This was certainly taken to be the *consensus patrum* already in the eighth century, because, in

14. See R. Cross, "Individual Natures...," Before him, this fact had been first noticed – but left without any substantial analysis – by M. Richard, "Léonce de Jérusalem et Léonce de Byzance," *Mélanges de science rêligieuse* 1 (1944) 35–88, here 60–61; repr. in *idem*, *Opera minora*, t. 3, Turnhout: Brepols 1977, Nr 59], and, then, was briefly analysed by A. Grillmeier, *Christ in Christian Tradition*, vol. 2/2, 189–193, but see Cross' criticism of the latter (R. Cross, "Individual Natures...", 246–247), which I consider quite justified (not to say that the whole context of this later Leontius' Christology needs to be studied in the context of Philoponus and Eutychius of Constantinople, see below). Brian Daley has tried to show that even in *CNE* Leontius held the same opinion about the nature of Christ as in the *Solutio* (B. Daley, "'A Richer Union:' Leontius of Byzantium and the Relationship of Human and Divine in Christ," *Studia Patristica* 24 (1993) 239–265, here 248–252), but his argumentation is convincingly criticised by R. Cross, "Individual Natures...," 248–250; cf. also my analysis in the next section.

the early ninth century, we see this postulate as the common ground of both iconoclastic and anti-iconoclastic theologies. Moreover, we see the same idea already in Maximus the Confessor in the seventh century. However, in general, the situation in the sixth and seventh centuries was different, and not without the participation of Leontius of Byzantium.[15]

Near 519, we see Severus of Antioch writing against a Chalcedonian, Sergius the Grammarian (*Contra impium Grammaticum*).[16] Sergius, in his polemical work in defence of the Council of Chalcedon (written in the 510s, now available through Severus' quotation only) mentioned that the Logos was incarnated into the common nature of humankind. This point becomes a subject of a long refutation on the part of Severus – although still somewhere on the margin of the polemic. Severus' point was a *reductio ad absurdum*: if the humanity of the Christ is the common nature of the whole humankind, then, the Logos is incarnated not into a particular human, Jesus, but into everybody.[17]

Unfortunately, we don't know whether this refutation by Severus was, in turn, addressed by somebody from the Chalcedonian camp. In the middle of the same (sixth) century, we see, however, that the contrary opinion is shared by such Chalcedonians as our Leontius and patriarch Eutychius of Constantinople (552–565, 577–582, one of the key theological figures of this epoch).[18]

There was an established tradition, going back to the understanding of "particular nature" in the *Isagoge* of Porphyry, of equating this term with the Christian notion of hypostasis.[19] Richard Cross, in his very valuable article on Leontius, argues that there was as well another tradition, represented at

15. For an outline of the relevant doctrines, see IVF.
16. P. Allen, C. T. R. Hayward, *Severus of Antioch*, London, New York: Routledge 2004, 44–46.
17. I. Lebon, *Severi Antiocheni Liber contra impium Grammaticum, Oratio prima et secunda*, CSCO, vols. 111–112; Scr. Syri, tt. 58–59 (Ser. IV, t. IV), Paris: E typographeo republicae 1938, 166–172/130–134 (txt/tr.). The title of the corresponding chapter II, 18: "Investigatio confutationis clare significans hanc assertionem: 'Christus est in duabus substantiis secundum commune substantiae significationem (ܕܐܘܣܝܐ ܓܘܢܝܐ ܒܫܘܘܕܥܐ)' ad stultissimam ducere blasphemiam, *scilicet* ad id, quod sancta Trinitas toti humanitatis generi incarnata censeatur" (166/130). The next two chapters (II, 19–20) are dedicated to the same topic (*ibid.*, 172–179/134–139). Insisting that, in Christ, there is neither human nature nor hypostasis, Severus avoids any precising of his own understanding of the notion of particular nature.
18. For Eutychus of Constantinople in his historical context, especially his dependency on theological views of Philopon, see B. Lourié, "Un autre monothélisme : le cas de Constantin d'Apamée au VIe Concile Œcuménique," *Studia Patristica* 29 (1997) 290–303 ; *idem*, "Le second iconoclasme en recherche de la vraie doctrine," *Studia Patristica* 34 (2000) 145–169, and IVF, *passim*, but esp. 261–267.
19. Cf. IVF, *passim*, but esp. 524–525, where I mention the recent discussion between J.-Cl. Larchet and D. Bathrellos, which seems to me now finished with the review of Bathrellos' monograph *The Byzantine Christ. Person, Nature, and Will in the Christology of Saint Maxim the Confessor*, Oxford 2004 by Larchet, *Revue d'histoire ecclésiastique* 101/102 (2006) 182–185, 359; see here the further bibliography. Bathrellos' idea that, according to Maximus the Confessor, the human nature of Christ is allegedly a particular one, is disproved by Larchet as well as by the evidence referred to in IVF.

least, by John of Damascus and Leontius in the *Solutio*, assuming the existence of "individual natures." Cross coined the latter term himself referring to John of Damascus' and Leontius' definitions of the natures ἐν ἀτόμῳ.[20]

Cross proposes a distinction between the "particular natures" (φύσεις μερικαί) – which, indeed, do not exist, according to the Chalcedonians, including both John of Damascus and Leontius – and "individual natures," which are not the same thing as the hypostases and which do really exist – at least, according to John and Leontius in the *Solutio*. The "particular natures" are produced as an abstraction from the hypostases when their individual characteristics are taken off, whereas the "individual natures" preserve their individual characteristics without being identical to the hypostases.

I have to note that Cross' explanation is hardly acceptable even for John of Damascus: it is normally held that John's "individual natures" are another term for the hypostases and so far there is hardly one other scholar who would follow Cross' understanding. Moreover, Cross' interpretation of this term in John of Damascus remained unknown to the later generations of Chalcedonian theologians, including Nicephorus of Constantinople and Theodore the Studite, who were dealing with the problem of the humanity of Christ. And a further question remains, namely why it is not a hypostasis if it contains hypostatic characteristics of a human person, Jesus?[21] This is a powerful argument to assume that Cross' interpretation was unknown to John of Damascus himself as well.

Anyway, in the interpretation of Leontius' *Solutio*, Cross (and those before him) overlooked the very key moment. In my opinion, Leontius in the *Solutio* conceded to his Severianist adversary in the acknowledgement of the "particular natures," but gave this notion a very specific interpretation.

4. A New Understanding of "(Particular) Nature"

From the very beginning of the dialogue, Leontius' *alter ego*, the Orthodox, acknowledges that the human nature in Christ is a particular nature. The dialogue starts with the following "objection of the Acephalus:" "The human nature which the Logos received, was it that which is considered in the species or in an individual?" (ch. 1; p. 77.16–17; 1916D–1917A: Ἀντίθεσις Ἀκεφάλου: Φύσιν ὁ Λόγος ἀναλαβὼν ἀνθρωπίνην, τὴν ἐν τῷ εἴδει θεωρουμένην ἢ τὴν ἐν ἀτόμῳ ἀνέλαβεν;).

The Orthodox, at first, asks whether there is a difference between these two kinds of natures (77.18–19; 1917A). The Acephalus answers that, indeed, there is a difference: one is considered in a plurality, whereas another in the

20. R. Cross, "Individual Natures...," 251–265; cf. his earlier paper, *idem*, "Perichoresis, Deification, and Christological Predication in John of Damascus," *Mediaeval Studies* 62 (2000) 69–124.

21. For a detailed review of these ninth-century doctrines on hypostasis, as well as their sixth-century forerunner, Eulogius of Alexandria, see B. Lourié, "Le second iconoclasme..."

unique number" (77.20; 1917A: [...] ἡ μὲν ἐν πλήθει θεωρεῖται, ἡ δὲ ἐν ἑνὶ τῷ ἀριθμῷ). The Orthodox tries to explain that, in both cases, the nature is the same, regardless of whether it is considered in a unique individual or in a plurality (77.11–78.5; 1917AB) – in the same manner as the same white colour (ἡ λευκότης) could be considered in either a unique instance or in a plurality of objects (εἴτε ἓν εἴτε πλείονα) (77.21–27; 1917A).

The Acephalus, however, needs to obtain an unequivocal answer: "Thus, [Christ] received a particular nature? (Τὴν τινὰ οὖν ἀνέλαβε φύσιν;)" – "Yes, but one that is the same as the species (Ναί· ἀλλὰ τὴν αὐτὴν οὖσαν τῷ εἴδει)," answers the Orthodox. This answer allows to the Acephalus to pose his main question: "But what is the difference between this and the hypostasis? (Τί δὲ παρὰ ταύτην ἡ ὑπόστασις;)" (78.6–8; 1917B). The whole treatise then turns out to be the answer of the Orthodox.

Let us recall what we would have been prepared to hear from the Leontius known to us from *CNE*: "there could be no nature, that is, essence, without a hypostasis;" a hypostasis is a nature, but not *vice versa*: a nature is not a hypostasis; "the nature has meaning of being, whereas the hypostasis has also that of separate being; the former has the meaning of species, whereas the latter reveals the particular [...] The definition of the hypostasis is either what is the same according to nature but different according to number, or what is composed of different natures but has the communion of being together and in each other."[22]

Briefly, we could expect from Leontius the answer that the hypostasis produces a difference in number, that is, the difference of physical objects, whereas the nature does not produce such a difference. The real answer of Leontius is somewhat strange: "[The hypostasis differs from the particular nature in that] the participation in it produces a different [object], and not a difference (Ὅτι τὸ μετέχειν αὐτῆς ἄλλον ποιεῖ, οὐκ ἀλλοῖον)" (78.9; 1917B). Acephalus' first reaction is to check whether the Orthodox changed the traditional definition of the hypostasis – but he did not. Instead, the Orthodox basically confirmed Acephalus' understanding of the hypostasis applied to the humanity of Christ (in Acephalus' wording, that "the humanity of Christ is separated from the common [humanity] with the differentiating characteristics"[23]).

If the traditional understanding of hypostasis as a particular being remains unchallenged, then, according to the Acephalus, his opponent has to

22. Ἀνυπόστατος μὲν οὖν φύσις, τουτέστιν οὐσία, οὐκ ἂν εἴη ποτέ· οὐ μὴν ἡ φύσις ὑπόστασις, ὅτι μηδὲ ἀντιστρέφει. Ἡ μὲν γὰρ ὑπόστασις καὶ φύσις, ἡ δὲ φύσις οὐκέτι καὶ ὑπόστασις· ἡ μὲν γὰρ φύσις τὸν τοῦ εἶναι λόγον ἐπιδέχεται· ἡ δὲ ὑπόστασις, καὶ τὸν τοῦ καθ' ἑαυτὸ εἶναι· καὶ ἡ μὲν εἴδους λόγον ἐπέχει, ἡ δὲ τοῦ τινός ἐστι δηλωτική· [...] ὑποστάσεως δὲ ὅρος ἢ τὰ κατὰ τὴν φύσιν μὲν ταὐτὰ, ἀριθμῷ δὲ διαφέροντα, ἢ τὰ ἐκ διαφόρων φύσεων συνεστῶτα, τὴν δὲ τοῦ εἶναι κοινωνίαν ἅμα τε καὶ ἐν ἀλλήλοις κεκτημένα [...] (*CNE* I, 1; 9.3–14; 1280AB).

23. Οὐκ ἦν οὖν τοῖς ἀφοριστικοῖς ἰδιώμασιν ἡ τοῦ Χριστοῦ ἀνθρωπότης τοῦ κοινοῦ τὸ ἴδιον αὐτοῦ χωρίζουσα; (78.13–14; 1917C); cf. 78.15–26; 1917CD.

acknowledge that the particular nature shares with the hypostasis its most obvious feature, namely, the producing of numerical difference. Thus, he asks (this question opens ch. 2 of the *Solutio*): "But do you really say that, although the hypostasis reveals the divided and self-standing, the number, and especially the number two, means something different from that? Because any number (consists) in the quantity, and only the one is non-quantitative. However, even if to the one (belongs) the non-quantitativity and because of this it is individual, to the two and any other number (belong) the quantity and the divisibility."[24]

Leontius as we know him from *CNE* would have nothing to object. Indeed, in *CNE*, I.4, he said:

> One can discover that things of different species join in relationships with things of the same species in varying ways: for in respects in which things of like species are joined with things of different species, they differ towards each other; and in the respects in which they differ from things of different species, they are joined to each other. For they are distinguished from each other but joined to things of other species by *number*, and they are joined to each other but distinguished from things of other species by *definition* (τῷ μὲν γὰρ ἀριθμῷ πρὸς ἑαυτὰ διακρινόμενα, τοῖς ἑτεροειδέσι συνάπτεται· τῷ δὲ ὅρῳ πρὸς ἑαυτὰ συναπτόμενα, τῶν ἑτεροειδῶν διακέκριται) (14.25–15.4; 1285D–1288A).[25]

Thus, Leontius ("the Orthodox") would have to choose between only two kinds of distinction: "by number" and "by definition." The former is applicable to the hypostases, the latter to the natures. If the human individuality of Jesus was different "by number" from other human hypostases, then, his humanity is a separate hypostasis, and this regardless of the Chalcedonians' efforts to cover their crypto-Nestorianism. If it is different only "by definition," then one has to acknowledge that the humanity of Christ is a separate particular nature – which further would be easy to present as a constitutive component of the composite μία φύσις τοῦ Θεοῦ Λόγου σεσαρκομένη in a Severianist sense. Both Leontius and his opponent would not allow any φύσις ἀνυπόστατος ("a nature without hypostasis:") the particular nature of Jesus' humanity would be confined, together with the nature of divinity, within the hypostasis of the Logos.

The real amplitude of problem could be realised from the further Christological discussions in Byzantium, starting from the Christological contents

24. Ἀλλ' ἐκεῖνο οὐκ ἂν εἴποις, ὡς ἡ μὲν ὑπόστασις τὸ διῃρημένον καὶ καθ' ἑαυτὸ ὑπάρχον δηλοῖ, ὁ δὲ ἀριθμὸς, καὶ μάλιστα τῆς δυάδος, ἄλλο τι παρὰ τοῦτο σημαίνει; Πᾶς γὰρ ἀριθμὸς ἐν ποσότητι, μονὰς δὲ μόνη ἄποσον· εἰ δὲ τῆς μονάδος τὸ ἄποσον καὶ διὰ τοῦτο ἄτομον, δυάδος ἄρα καὶ παντὸς ἀριθμοῦ τὸ ποσὸν καὶ διῃρημένον (78.27–31; 1917D–1920A).
25. B. Daley's tr.: "'A Richer Union'...," 251. Italics by Daley.

of the second quarrel on the holy icons in the ninth century onwards.[26] The simultaneous application of the two conditions – the presence of the hypostatic characteristics of Jesus in the humanity of Christ together with the absence of any human hypostasis in this humanity – turned out to be logically paraconsistent, as Eulogius of Alexandria (late sixth century) warned in advance at the beginning of the discussion, when it was only one hundred years old. This is one of the key problems of the Orthodox dogmatics where the Fathers had recourse to the paraconsistent logic (as it had been called since the 1970s: a logic which does not avoid the contradictions but relies on them).[27] Leontius of Byzantium remained outside of this non-classical mainstream of patristic logical thought in Christology. His personal contribution, although unaccepted by further tradition and never going beyond classical logic, is nevertheless most interesting from the viewpoint of the history of both mathematics and cognitive science.

Leontius ("the Orthodox") surprises his opponent with an idea that has never been heard before or after him,[28] namely, there is a third kind of distinction or, more precisely, the second kind of distinction "by number."

5. The Second Kind of Numerical Distinction: "by Relation" (ἐν σχέσει)

Now we arrived to the moment when we have to read carefully the part of Leontius' text (*Solutio*, 2) which is mostly overlooked by the scholars. And I must apologize for such a long quotation from a monologue of the Orthodox (79.1–23; 1920BC).

Οὐκοῦν ἐπειδὴ ἀριθμοῦ καὶ τῶν περὶ αὐτὸν ἰδιωμάτων ἐμνήσθης, ἀναγκαῖον ἐκεῖνο εἰπεῖν, ὡς ἀριθμὸς διττὸς λέγεται, ὁ μέν τις ἁπλῶς καὶ καθ' ἑαυτὸν, ὁ δὲ ἐν σχέσει καὶ πράγμασι θε-	Surely then, if you have recalled the number and its features, it is necessary to say that "number" could be said in two meanings. One meaning is somewhat simple and *per se*, whereas another is considered in relationship

26. See, e.g., B. Lourié, "Le second iconoclasme..." ; *idem*, "Une dispute sans justes : Léon de Chalcédoine, Eustrate de Nicée et la troisième querelle sur les images sacrées," *Studia Patristica* 42 (2006) 321–339 ; *idem*, "Michel Psellos contre Maxime le Confesseur : l'origine de l' 'hérésie des physéthésites'", *Scrinium* 4 (2008) 201–227.
27. There is, so far, no comprehensive introduction to the paraconsistent logics in the Fathers. As a first sketch, one can see B. Lourié, "The Philosophy of Dionysius the Areopagite: An Approach to Intensional Semantics," in: T. Nutsubidze, C. B. Horn, B. Lourié, with the Collaboration of A. Ostrovsky, *Georgian Christian Thought and Its Cultural Context. Memorial Volume for the 125th Anniversary of Shalva Nutsubidze (1888–1969)*, Texts and Studies in Eastern Christianity 2, Leiden, Boston: Brill 2014, 81–127. The paraconsistent logical constructions were formed from the classical "blocks" in the same manner as, in the Quantum physics, the nonclassical phenomena are described in classical terms used according to Niels Bohr's "correspondence principle." Thus, even a correct study of these "blocks" taken alone, that is, regardless of the theological intuition they serve to express, would not allow one to grasp the paraconsistent way of thinking.
28. It could be likely that the same idea was implied by Eutychius of Constantinople, but our data are too scarce to judge; cf. B. Lourié, "Un autre monothélisme..."

ωρούμενος, ὥσπερ λευκὸν ἥ τε λευκότης καὶ τὸ λευκασμένον. Αὐτὴ τοίνυν ἡ φύσις τοῦ ἀριθμοῦ καθ' ἑαυτὴν οὔτε συνάπτει οὔτε διαιρεῖ, οὐδὲ γὰρ ἔχει ὑποκείμενα πράγματα· ἀλλ' ὥσπερ τὸ ἄνω καὶ τὸ κάτω πρὸς τὴν σχέσιν λέγεται τοῦ ἀναβαίνοντος ἢ καταβαίνοντος, αὐτὸ δὲ ἀπολύτως λεγόμενον οὐδ' ὁπότερόν ἐστιν ὅτι καὶ ἀμφότερα δέχεται, καὶ ἄνω μὲν ὡς πρὸς κάτω, κάτω δὲ ὡς πρὸς τὸ ἄνω λέγεται, ἀφορίζεται δὲ τῇ τοῦ ἀνιόντος καὶ κατερχομένου σχέσει, οὕτως καὶ ὁ ἀριθμὸς αὐτὸς καθ' ἑαυτὸν οὔτε διαιρεῖ οὔτε συναπτεῖ, ἀλλ' ἀμφότερα δέχεται τῇ ποιᾷ σχέσει, οἷον ἡ δυὰς, ἡ τετρὰς, καὶ ἑξῆς. Εἰ μὲν γὰρ τὰς μονάδας αὐτὰς θεωρεῖς ἐξ ὧν συνέστηκεν, εἰς ταύτας διαιρεῖται· εἰ δὲ τὴν ὁμάδα τούτων σκοπεῖς, ἐκ τούτων συνάπτεται. Δύο γὰρ καὶ δύο, εἰ τύχοι, εἰς τέσσαρα συντίθεται, τὰ δὲ τέσσαρα εἰς δύο καὶ δύο διαιρεῖται· ὥστε παντὸς ἀληθέστερον τὴν φύσιν τοῦ ἀριθμοῦ μηδὲν ἀφωρισμένον ἔχειν, μήτε τὸ διῃρημένον μήτε τὸ ἡνωμένον, ἐν δὲ τῇ τῶν πραγμάτων ἐπιπλοκῇ καὶ συνθέσει τοῦτο ὑφίστασθαι.

and in things – in the same manner as "white" is said about either the white paint or a thing painted white. Thus, the nature of number itself is *per se* neither joining nor dividing, because it does not contain real things as subjects. However, in the same manner as "up" and "down" are defined in relationship to the ascending or the descending, but when they are said unconditionally, they are nothing of the two, because they can be understood in both senses, and "up" is defined in relation to "down," whereas "down" in relation to "up," and they are to be discerned in relationship to the ascending and descending, – in the same manner the number, too, is itself and *per se* neither dividing nor joining but contain both in a certain relationship, such as the two, the four, etc. Because if you consider the units they are composed from, they are divided into them, whereas if you see them as a whole, they are collected from them. Thus, two and two, taken together, result into four, whereas four could be divided into two and two. It is thus the most true to take the nature of number as defined in no way, neither as divided nor as united, but existing in one or another way depending on its combination and composition with the real things.

Ἀπαίδευτον οὖν τὸ τῇ φύσει τοῦ ἀριθμοῦ ἀναγκαίως τὴν διαίρεσιν τῶν πραγμάτων ἕπεσθαι νομοθετεῖν, ἀλλὰ μὴ τῇ τῶν πραγμάτων ἡνομένων τε ἢ διῃρημένων φύσει τὸν ἀριθμὸν σημεῖον ποιεῖσθαι δηλωτικὸν τοῦ πόσου τῶν ὑποκειμένων, ἄλλου λόγου καὶ οὐ τοῦ ἀριθμοῦ ταῦτα διαιροῦντός τε καὶ συνάπτοντος [...]

Thus, it would be uneducated to take as a law that the nature of number is necessarily followed by a division in the real things, instead of making the number a sign of real things either united or divided by nature, revealing the quantity of subjects which are able to be divided or joined together because of a different reason than the number [...]

Here we can take a break to evaluate what has been said so far. The numbers and their corresponding subjects (τὰ ὑποκείμενα) can correspond to two different kinds of reality: not only to the number of mutually divided real things but also to the number of different *positions* within a unique real thing, such as "up" and "down" ("top" and "bottom"). In the latter case, the different positions can be defined only through each other, according to their mutual relationships.

In the following part of the same monologue, Leontius (the Orthodox) continues to explain his idea with different examples, e.g., a ten-cubit piece of wood, whose unity did not undergo any division into ten different pieces (79.26–28; 1920C). A horse, a human, and a bull represent three different natures, but they are not divided according to quantity (κατὰ τὸ ποσόν) but are different according to species (τὸ παρηλλαγμένον κατὰ τὸ εἶδος). He goes on to say, however, that "[...] concerning three different men, such as Peter, Paul, and John, we would imply that they are divided and, moreover, that such is their amount (τρεῖς δὲ ἀνθρώπους, εἰ τύχοι, Πέτρον καὶ Παῦλον καὶ Ἰωάννην, τὸ διῃρημένον αὐτῶν μᾶλλον καὶ ὅτι τοσοῦτοι οὗτοι οἴδε παριστῶμεν)" (79.31–80.4; 1920D).

Oddly enough, Leontius' distinction between the two kinds of numbers and numerical difference passed unnoticed by the scholars who analysed the *Solutio* – despite the obvious fact that this is the central point of Leontius' explanation of his understanding of the particular nature.

6. Triadological Implications

Then, Leontius reaches the most delicate domain of "theology," that is, Trinitarian doctrine (θεολογία, in contrast with οἰκονομία/"œconomy" as the doctrine of incarnation). The Acephalus will answer with an attendant argument of the anti-Chalcedonians that the meaning of such terms as "hypostasis," "nature," and "essence" must not be the same in the "œconomy" as in the "theology" (80.22–26; 1921B). This part of the discussion focused on the patristic *testimonia* is not especially original, and so, will be out of our scope.[29] We need to read, however, in the light of the above explanation, the Trinitarian idea of Leontius (80.4–10; 1920D–1921A):

Ὥσπερ ἐπὶ τῆς ἁγίας Τριάδος τρεῖς μὲν ὑποστάσεις ὁμολογοῦμεν, μίαν δὲ τούτων φύσιν καὶ οὐσίαν καταγγέλομεν, οὐδ' ὁποτέραν μὲν τούτων ἀνούσιον γινώσκοντες, οὐ μὲν καὶ ἀριθμὸν ἀφοριστικὸν ποσότητος οὐσιῶν ἐπιφημίζοντες, εὖ εἰδότες τὸ ἑτερούσιον ταύτῃ συνάγεσθαι· ὃ δὴ καὶ οἱ Ἀρειανοὶ συναισθόμενοι, ταῖς ὑποστάσεσιν, ἐνουσί-

Thus, concerning the Holy Trinity, we confess three hypostases, but we profess as unique their nature and essence, without, however, acknowledging any of them as having no being, because we do not define the number as a delimitation of quantity of essences, knowing well that, together with the latter, the (idea of the) different essence is to be introduced – as, indeed, the Arians effectuated, when they, dealing with the hypostases that have their essence, introduced the (notion of) essence into the definition of hypostasis

29. It occupies the whole ch. 3 of the *Solutio* (80.22–83.16; 1921B–1925B). This topic continued to be discussed in ch. 6 (85.9–86.14; 1928D–1929D).

οις οὔσαις, τὰς οὐσίας ἐπεφή-μιζον, ταύτῃ τὸ ἑτεροούσιον συμπλέκοντες.	and, in this way, introduced [*sc.*, into the Trinity] a complication with the (idea of the) different essence.

At the end of the quotation, my translation becomes more verbose and explicative, but I hope to grasp Leontius' idea adequately. Leontius says that the three hypostases are, indeed, existing and real, but they are different from each other in the same "numerical" but "relational" sense just as "up" differs from "down." This difference between the divine hypostases is opposed to the example of three really divided men, Peter, Paul, and John, which has just been referred to. Thus, Leontius would be certainly opposed to the future "Tritheism" of John Philoponus.

It is implied – in Leontius unlike Philoponus – that there is some real object, the common nature, that is divided into particular natures differentiated by their "position." This kind of difference implies that the different objects (particular natures within the unique common nature) differ exclusively in relation to each other. Applied to the Trinity, this approach leads to a certain kind of Modalism rather than "Tritheism."[30]

It is in such a "Modalist" sense that, I think, one has to understand Leontius' earlier triadological formulation:

For the nature of the Father, the Son, and the Holy Spirit is not fulfilling [or: completing – οὐ γὰρ συμπληρωτική], so that it would be more in the one than in the three. In fact, by nature, the Trinity is the same as any one of those which are seen in the Trinity ([...] ὡς οὖν μᾶλλον ἐν τῷ ἑνὶ ἢ ἐν τοῖς τρισί· καὶ τοῦτο τῇ φύσει ἡ Τριάς, ὅπερ ἂν ἕν τι τῶν ἐν Τριάδι θεωρουμένων τυγχάνοι) [...][31]

30. Therefore, Loofs was not right in his claim that "[u]nser Verfasser selbst würde bei tritheistischen Consequenzen ankommen, wenn er der Anwendung seiner philosophischen Gedanken auf die Trinitätslehre noch genauer nachgienge" (F. Loofs, *Leontius von Byzanz...*, 63), which has been pointed out by R. Cross, "Individual Natures...," 260, n. 44. However, Cross' own understanding of Leontius ("[...] Leontius never abandons his belief that natures are universals; his point about Christ's human nature is that it has the universal human nature as a part;" *ibid.*) is not quite correct, because to be numerically differentiated "by relation" within a unity is not the same thing as to be a part of this unity. In the field of "Theology," Cross summarises the passage of the *Solutio* quoted above in a not quite correct way: "The Arian worry is circumvented by claiming that, although the three divine persons are not natures or essences, none is *anousios* – each divine person has the one divine nature," and continues in a footnote: "This is, of course, precisely the move made by Philoponus a few years later" (*ibid.*, 259, n. 42); the mention of Philoponus refers to his "Tritheism." Unlike Philoponus, however, Leontius does not allow any individualisation of the hypostases of the Trinity other than their relations to each other. This idea has something in common with the Scholasticism but is alien to the Byzantine patristic tradition; cf. a discussion of a "relational" understanding of the notion of hypostasis at the Council of Florence in 1439; B. Lourié, "L'attitude de S. Marc d'Ephèse aux débats sur la procession du Saint-Esprit à Florence. Ses fondements dans la théologie post-palamite," *Annuarium Historiae Conciliorum* 21 (1989) 317–333.

31. *CNE* I, 4; 15.14–17; 1288B; tr. by István Perczel, "Once Again on Dionysius the Areopagite and Leontius of Byzantium," in: T. Boiadjiev, G. Kapriev, A. Speer, eds., *Die Dionysius-Rezeption im*

Here, the identity of any one hypostasis with the whole Trinity remains unexplained,[32] but the new idea of the numerical difference "by relation" provides a strong rational foundation to it. If I dare to call such a decision modalistic, I have in mind a "Modalism" in a very specific sense: it recognises a specific but true reality of the objects whose numerical distinction is only "relational."[33] Nevertheless, Leontius' "Modalism," too, avoids the patristic paraconsistent logic with its famous equation "1 = 3" and the corresponding mathematical ideas with whom the modern thought became accustomed only after Richard Dedekind's and Georg Kantor's theory of infinite sets.[34]

7. *Leontius' Theory of Graphs*

The "numbers" defined through relation to each other are known in the modern mathematics as graphs. The very idea of the modern theory of graphs goes back directly to Leibniz's *geometria situs*, although Leibniz himself saw its roots in some "Veteres" (scholars of Greek antiquity, especially Euclid) and even Descartes.[35] According to the earliest of Leibniz's formulations, there are two different approaches in the mathematical analysis: "[...] je croy qu'il nous faut encor une autre analyse proprement geometrique ou lineaire, qui nous exprime directement *situm*, comme l'Algebre exprime *magnitudinem*."[36] In Leibniz's *geometria situs*, both modern theory of graphs and

Mittelalter: Internationales Kolloquium in Sofia vom 8. bis 11. April 1999 unter der Schirmherrschaft der Société internationale pour l'étude de la philosophie médiévale, Rencontres de Philosophie Médiévale 9, Turnhout: Brepols 2000, 41–85, here 54.

32. For the whole context and especially the following quotation from Dionysius, in Leontius, which is posed by him in a different context to distort its meaning, see Perczel, "Once Again..." Perczel's interpretation of Leontius seems to me very plausible, regardless of my sceptical attitude toward his interpretation of Dionysius.
33. Both historical and modern recensions of the Modalist Triadology operate with the unique – classical – kind of numerical distinction. See esp. the logical analysis by Daniele Bertini, "Una difesa della trattazione modalista della Trinità," in: D. Bertini, G. Salmeri, P. Trianni, eds., *La Trinità*, Roma: Edizione Nuova Cultura (forthcoming), and a larger article published on-line as preprint: "Che cosa non va nel modalismo?", in: *Elaborare l'esperienza di Dio*, Atti del Convegno "La Trinità", Roma 26–28 maggio 2009; http://mondodomani.org/teologia/bertini2011.htm (accessed on 25. 07. 2015).
34. There is no, so far, a comprehensive study of the paraconsistent logic in the patristic Triadology, but I have touched several related points in B. Lourié, "The Philosophy of Dionysius the Areopagite: An Approach...".
35. These references are given in Leibniz's programme article *De analysi situs* (*ca* 1693): G. H. Pertz, ed., *Leibnizens gesammelte Werke aus den Handschriften der Königlichen Bibliothek zu Hanover*, III. Folge, 5. Bd.: G. I. Gerhardt, *Leibnizens Mathematische Schriften*, II. Abt., Bd. 1. Halle: H. W. Schmidt 1858, 178–185. For a detailed analysis of Leibniz's historical context, see V. De Risi, *Geometry and Monadology. Leibniz's "Analysis Situs" and Philosophy of Space*, Science Networks. Historical Studies 33, Basel, Boston, Berlin: Birkhäuser 2007.
36. Letter to Christian Huygens, 8 September 1679: G. H. Pertz, ed., *Leibnizens gesammelte Werke...*, III. Folge, 2. Bd.: G. I. Gerhardt, *Leibnizens Mathematische Schriften*, I. Abt., Bd. 2., Berlin: A. Asher & Comp. 1850, 17–27, here 19. This is the first document marking the idea of the *geometria situs* as already presented in Leibniz's mind. As it has been shown only recently,

topology were still united.[37]

The next and decisive step toward the theory of graphs was performed by Leonhard Euler in 1735, who kept in mind Leibniz's idea (and called it "etiamnum admodum ignotae" – "almost unknown, however").[38] Nevertheless, until Oswald Veblen in the 1930s, the theory of graphs has never been separated from the topology as a self-standing mathematical discipline.

In Leontius' example, the "top" (or "up") and "bottom" (or "down") are clearly two vertices of a graph acting as two different positions in the space. Even his example of a ten-cubit piece of wood is a demonstration of the possibility of an arbitrary spatial organization introduced into a given spatial zone.

A graph is, by definition, a representation of a set of objects, where some pairs of objects are connected by links (called edges) and the interconnected objects are represented by mathematical abstractions called vertices. Thus, the graphs are pure representations of mutual relations, and are thus identical with the numbers in Leontius' second meaning.

However, neither three men nor the three persons of the Holy Trinity and the two natures in Christ are related to a space in the ordinary sense of the word, that is, to a physical space. And yet, they too are vertices of graphs drawn in what we call now, after Peter Gärdenfors, "conceptual spaces."[39] This is a late twentieth-century idea also preconceived by Leontius that a spatial representation of information is inherent to the humanity. As Gärdenfors wrote, "I will advocate a third form of representing information that is based on using geometrical structures rather than symbols or connections between neurons. Using these structures *similarity* relations can be modelled in a natural way. The notion of similarity is crucial for the understanding of many cognitive phenomena. I shall call my way of representing information

Leibniz did not stop developing his new mathematical discipline until his death in 1716: cf. V. De Risi, *Geometry...*

37. One can additionally quote Leibniz from a recently published fragmentary text dated to 1682: "Geometria tractat de rerum magnitudine et figura. Itaque duabus scientiis subordinata est, uni de magnitudine in genere et magnitudinum comparatione sive aequalitate et ratione ; alteri de rerum formis in genere sive de rerum similitudine et dissimilitudine" ; V. De Risi, *Geometry...*, 623.

38. L. Euler, "Solutio problematis ad geometriam situs pertinentis", *Commentarii Academiae scientarum Petropolitanae* 8 (1735) [published in 1741] 128–140; republished by L. G. du Pasquier, *Leonhard Euleri Opera omnia:* Ser. I, vol. 7: *Commentationes algebraicae ad theoriam combinariorum et probabilitatum pertinentes*, Leipzig: Teubner 1923, 1–10. Cf. reprint of du Pasquier's publication, English translation, and a discussion in the context of the modern theory of graphs in H. Fleischner, *Eulerian Graphs and Related Topics*, part 1, vol. 1, Annals of Discrete Mathematics 45, Amsterdam: Elsevier 1990.

39. See esp. his seminal monograph: P. Gärdenfors, *Conceptual Spaces: the Geometry of Thought*, Cambridge MA: MIT Press 2000, where the graphs in the conceptual spaces are discussed as well.

the *conceptual* form since I believe that the essential aspects of concept formation are best described using this kind of representation."[40] Here the very wording, such as "geometrical structures" and "similarity relations," sounds very Leibnizian [...]

Gärdenfors shows that the conceptual spaces should be dealt with using mathematical methods, including the theory of graphs. And the latter is the case with Leontius: his main innovation was not, of course, a spatial representation of the problems discussed, but in introducing a new and "relational" notion of number, which is nothing other than what we call now graphs – or, as Leibniz would say, not *magnitudo* but *situs*.

So far, historians of mathematics have not known of any precedent of the *geometria situs* before Leibniz. However, I would prefer to leave open the question whether Leontius himself discovered this new kind of mathematical object or borrowed this idea from somebody else. There are reasons to think that we are still far from a complete understanding of the progress in philosophy and scholarship achieved in the sixth-century Byzantium. Nevertheless, Leontius' mathematical innovation in the theological discussion was produced out of the fear of logical inconsistency and, more precisely, in an attempt to avoid the recourse to the paraconsistent logic. Thus, in this general logical and theological inspiration, Leontius was in accord with his anti-Chalcedonian and Nestorian or crypto-Nestorian opponents, and therefore in disagreement with mainstream Byzantine patristic thought, both Cappadocian and Dionysian.

8. An Intermezzo: Forbidding the Singletons

The primary purpose of the following discussion in the *Solutio* is to explain why the humanity of Christ does not form a separate subject beside the Logos. There was no explanation *prêt-à-porter*. After having explained his own logical presuppositions (ch. 1–2) and having discussed the inevitable hermeneutical issues on some patristic sayings (ch. 3 and 6), Leontius, at first, completes an initial outline of his doctrine with an explination – rather obvious in such context – of why "the unique composite nature" of the anti-Chalcedonians is, in fact, not a nature but a hypostasis (ch. 4; 83.17–84.15; 1925B–1928A). Then (ch. 5; 84.16–85.8; 1928B–D) follows a curious exchange – especially with respect to the history of science – about the possibility for the "unique nature of Christ" to be simply the unique instantiation of a species (the sun being another such example). Leontius answers that such a thing has to be properly called "hypostasis" and not "nature," whereas the natures in Christ are different from each other. This question by the Acephalus and the

40. P. Gärdenfors, "Conceptual Spaces as a Framework for Knowledge Representation", *Mind and Matter* 2 (2004) 9–27, here 10.

resulting part of the Orthodox's answer is a *locus communis* of the polemics around the Chalcedon.

The peculiarities of the species represented in unique objects had already been discussed by Aristotle (*Metaphysics* Z.15, where the sun is mentioned among such objects) but had never ceased to be under discussion. Only the "old-fashion" Neoplatonic tradition – those who were faithful to the Platonic view *universalia ante res* – accepted them without problems. All others confronted difficulties,[41] especially dealing with the cases when more than one instantiation was thought to be theoretically impossible.[42]

Leontius certainly surprises his readers – not only his direct opponent(s) – with the claim that, in a sharp contrast with the common opinion, such things as the sun or heaven are not single in their species: "Whether you do not know, oh my dear friend, that the nature of the sun is the same as that of the stars? And that the heaven is the same as the others heavens?"[43]

Leontius had to be strongly motivated to make such a deviation from both normative cosmology[44] and the standard logical textbooks of his epoch. Such a radical claim – that there is no uniquely instantiated natures at all – looks too excessive for a habitual philosophical ping-pong game on the margins of the theological discussion with the anti-Chalcedonians. At first glance, this was not an advantageous position to take within the discussion. Thus, one has to conclude that Leontius needed such a claim for the logical consistency of his system as a whole.

In the philosophical traditions available to Leontius, the claim that there are no such things as species represented with unique individuals is a rather rare thing. Such a claim would be equivalent to the statement that even a

41. Cf. P. Adamson, "One of a Kind: Plotinus and Porphyry on Unique Instantiation," in: R. Chiaradonna, G. Galluzzo, eds., *Universals in Ancient Philosophy*, Seminari e convegni 33, Pisa: Edizioni della Normale 2013, 329–351, where the ancient authors discussed are not only those mentioned in the title.
42. Cf. R. W. Sharples, "Alexander of Aphrodisias on Universals: Two Problematic Texts," *Phronesis* 50 (2005) 43–55. Sharples discusses two kinds of universals in Alexander: those that are, in fact, exemplified in many instances and those that only *could* to be exemplified in many instances.
43. Ἀλλ' ἠγνόησας, ὦ βέλτιστε, ὅτι ἡ τοῦ ἡλίου φύσις ἡ αὐτή ἐστι τῇ τῶν ἄστρων; Καὶ ὁ οὐρανὸς ὁ αὐτὸς τοῖς λοιποῖς οὐρανοῖς; (84.19–20; 1928B). The idea of plurality of heavens seems to me rather Jewish-Christian than Greek.
44. In the normative (geocentric) cosmologies of antiquity the sun with its rotation around the earth was sharply divided from the fixed stars. However, the sun as one of the stars could be conceived in the heliocentric system of Aristarchus of Samos (*ca* 310–*ca* 230 BC), whose ideas are available to us (as, most probably, already to Leontius) through Archimedes, *Psammites* (*Arenarius et dimensio circuli*); another and especially probable source of Leontius' view would be Anaxagoras (5th cent. BC) with his idea that "the sun and the moon and all the stars are fiery stones [...]" (*apud* Hippolytus, *Refutation of All Heresies*, 1.8.1.6; P. Curd, *Anaxagoras of Clazomenae, Fragments and Testimonia. A Text and Translation with Notes and Essays*, Phoenix pre-Socratics 6, Phoenix. Supplementary vol. 64, Toronto: University of Toronto Press 2007, 95); cf. Plato, *Phaedo* 97b8–98c2 (*ibid.*, 101).

unique instantiation of a nature is impossible if this nature would be taken-off. There is only instance, a saying ascribed to Alexander of Aphrodisias (2nd– early 3rd century), whose literal sense is like that.[45] However, Alexander was much more known by his apparently opposite statements, namely, that the unique objects such as the sun do not need to have anything common above them.[46] We have neither the need nor the possibility of going deeper into understanding the views of Alexander or those ascribed to him. We have to retain from this survey that Leontius' rejection of natures with unique individuals was, indeed, a radical move away from the backdrop of sixth-century Aristotelism, although this was probably not entirely unique.

Now we know, especially thanks to David Lewis that the assumption of the classes having only one element (so-called singletons) leads to the paradox within any consistent logic. So far, there is no way to either define the class or the set without referring to the idea of the plurality of its elements or to provide a good logical foundation for the prohibition of singletons. Leontius, had he lived in our epoch, would face the same problem as David Lewis: the existence of modern mathematics which is based on the modern set theories. The latter, all without exception (including the NF theory by Quine, although Quine himself thought otherwise), do allow the existence of singletons, but, in this way, the mathematics reveals its problems with the logical consistency. Lewis has joked that it is certainly somebody else, not he, who would bring to the mathematicians this news. He personally was convinced that the paradox would be resolved in the future: "Singletons, and therefore all classes, are profoundly mysterious. Mysteries are an onerous

45. *Quaestio* XIa: διὸ ἀναιρουμένῳ μὲν ἑνὶ τῶν ὑπὸ τὸ κοινὸν οὐ συναναιρεῖται τὸ κοινόν, διότι ἐστὶν ἐν πλείοσιν· εἰ δ'ἀναιρεθείη τὸ κοινόν, οὐδ' ἂν τῶν ὑπὸ τὸ κοινὸν εἴη τι, οἷς τὸ εἶναι ἐν τῷ ἐκεῖνο ἔχειν ἐν αὐτοῖς ("Therefore, doing away with one of the items under the common item does not do away with the common item as well, because it exists in many. But if the common item should be done away with, there would not exist any of the items under the common item, since their being lies in having that [common item] in them"); I. Bruns, *Alexandri Aphrodisiensis Praeter commentaria, Scripta minora: Qaestiones, De Fato, De Mixtione*, Supplementum Aristotelicum, vol. II, pars II, Berlin: G. Reimer 1892, 21.17–20; tr. M. M. Tweedale, "Alexander of Aphrodisias' Views on Universals", *Phronesis* 29 (1984) 279–303, here 289. This Martin M. Tweedale's article was considered until now as the most exhaustive collection of the data relevant to its title.

46. See esp. but not uniquely Simplicius (early 6th century), *Commentary on the* Categories, 85.13 Kalbfleisch: ἀλλὰ κοινόν, φησίν, οὐδὲν εἶναι δύναται χωρὶς ἀτόμου, ἄτομον δὲ ἔστιν χωρὶς κοινοῦ, οἷον ἥλιος καὶ σελήνη καὶ κόσμος ("But he [Alexander] says that the common item can be nothing apart from the individual, but the individual exists apart from the common item, for example, the sun, the moon, and the universe"); quoted and translated by Tweedale, "Alexander of Aphrodisias'...," 283. As to the interpretation of the apparent contradictions within the works attributed to Alexander, it continues to be in the focus of a discussion. Cf., first of all, the same paper by Tweedale, and, then, among others, Sharples, "Alexander of Aphrodisias on Universals...," and Ch. Helmig, *Forms and Concepts. Concept Formation in the Platonic Tradition*, Commentaria in Aristotelem Graeca et Byzantina. Quellen und Studien 5, Berlin, Boston: De Gruyter 2012, 161–164.

burden [...] And so I have to say, gritting my teeth, that somehow, I know not how, we do understand what it means to speak of singletons."[47]

The mathematics Leontius knew was still working without the set theories. Thus, Leontius' condition was easier than that of Lewis: he could simply reject the singletons, as he did. What remained after this procedure is a consistent theory of universals, albeit a bit overloaded with the necessity of seeking for an appropriate common to any apparently unique individual of a species.

It is interesting to note that, although Leontius' theory which belongs to the domains of philosophy and logic was obviously inspired by his theological thought, Lewis' research led to the same point – acknowledgement of, at least, an apparent incompatibility of the singletons with logical consistency – out of his repulsion for what he has called "theology."[48] In fact, both of them were acting out of their common repulsion for what we call now "intensional entities."[49] In the case of Lewis, as well as with his direct predecessors Quine and Leśniewski, the intensional entities were rejected out of philosophical nominalism. The attitude of Leontius was somewhat similar but different, and it could be easily – but unjustly – confused with nominalism, and so needs to be approached after some preliminary explanations.

9. *Moderate Realism and Its Problems of Consistency*

As is well known,[50] the mainstream in the understanding of the universals throughout the whole "Byzantine Millennium" was the so-called moderate realism: *universalia in rebus* – and, thus, neither *ante res* nor *post res*. This

47. D. Lewis, *Parts of Classes*, Oxford: Blackwell 1991, 29–59, quoted 57, 59. The corresponding ideas of this book were rewritten in a more succinct way and with further elaboration in his 1993 paper, reprinted, with some corrections once more, as: D. Lewis, "Mathematics is megethology," in: *idem*, *Papers in philosophical logic*, Cambridge studies in philosophy, Cambridge: Cambridge University Press 1998, 203–229. Lewis criticizes, among others, Quine's attempt of excluding singletons from his own theory of sets, which is, according to Lewis, incomplete and, therefore, unsuccessful. Cf. esp. W. V. O. Quine, *Set Theory and Its Logic*. Rev. ed., Cambridge, MA, London: The Belknap Press 1969, 31–34. The complete and consecutive exclusion of the singletons (as something different from their elements) is a feature of an alternative to the modern set theory, the mereology of Stanisław Leśniewski, first proposed by him in 1916; cf. R. Urbaniak, *Leśniewski's Systems of Logic and Foundations of Mathematics*, Trends in Logic 37, Cham etc.: Springer 2014, 113–114.

48. Cf. "Must set theory rest on theology? – Cantor thought so!" (Lewis, "Mathematics is megethology," 215).

49. For this notion and its value in patristics, cf. B. Lourié, "The Philosophy of Dionysius...," 89–92.

50. Especially after a series of studies by Linos Benakis. See his summarising article Λ. Γ. Μπενάκης, "Τὸ πρόβλημα τῶν γενικῶν ἐννοιῶν καὶ ὁ ἐννοιολογικὸς ρεαλισμὸς τῶν Βυζαντινῶν [1978–1979]," in: *idem*, *Βυζαντινὴ Φιλοσοφία. Κείμενα καὶ Μελέτες*, Athens: Παρουσία, 2002, 107–136, as well as several others reprinted in the same volume.

attitude, however, is the most difficult from a logical point of view. The classical logic does allow without problems both the strong realism of the Platonics (*ante res*) and nominalism, and the latter was not by chance so dear to the hearts of Leśniewski, Quine, David Lewis, as well as many other modern philosophers. Moderate realism leads to problems with the logical consistency, which either need to be accepted as such or taken as the impetus to look for a workaround. This is why, I suppose, concepts of this sort are so unpopular among modern philosophers, who prefer either Platonism or nominalism.

Basically, the problem is the following: what is an individual together with its universal, given that the latter exists, in some way, within this individual? If we consider a species as having a plurality of instantiations, then, there is a chance to evade the question with respect to a connection (but of what sort?[51]) between this given individual and all others within the species. If we discuss a singleton, even this loophole is closed.

We are dealing with a paraconsistent statement having the same type as that of the Russell set ("set of all sets"), namely, of the lack of self-identity, $X \neq X$. The Russell set includes all sets, and so, includes itself and, therefore, is not identical to itself:

$$(1) \qquad \exists x((x \in x)f \wedge (x \notin x))$$

The same is true about the singleton of a species which exists *in rebus*.[52] Such an individual contains nothing but itself (because there is no Platonic idea accompanying it but having existence of its own) but, moreover, it contains its species (although we do not discuss in what way it is contained). Extensionally, it possesses self-identity but, intensionally, it does not. One can write for an individual x, which is the unique member of the singleton set $\{x\}$:

$$(2) \ \forall x((x = \{x\}) \wedge (x \neq \{x\}))$$

One can see from this that paraconsistency follows from the acknowledgement of intensional entities without allowing to them separate (*ante res*) existence.

The left part of the conjunction (2) represents the nominalist attitude, whereas its right part the strong realist (Platonic) attitude, and only their

51. Cf. Lewis' discussion of the "Lasso hypothesis" invented – and rejected – by himself: Lewis, *Parts of Classes*, 42–45.

52. Here and below I omit the reservations for excluding the ontological commitment, because they are rather self-evident (we can easily substitute for "existence" something like "existence in some possible/impossible world(s)" etc.) and, although necessary for an exhaustive logical discussion, are excessive in the case of the problems discussed within the framework of the "applied philosophy" of Byzantine dogmatics. All these problems were considered in relation to our unique real world, although this world itself was somewhat different from the world where the most of modern philosophers live...

paraconsistent conjunction results in the moderate realism of the *universalia in rebus*.

If we do not accept nominalism, this intensional "addition" to its self-identity has some ontological weight – it is an existing intensional entity. Therefore, ontologically, the individual of a singleton contains itself as a class containing an individual but, at the same time, it is contained itself and therefore differs from itself as the containing one. The above statement, first written for the Russell set, is applicable to any singleton, *given that the* universalia *do exist* in rebus.

The "mystery" of the singleton, as David Lewis coined it, consists in its paraconsistency – tolerated in the "naïve" set theory by Cantor,[53] passed undiscussed by Zermelo and Fraenkel, and unsuccessfully attacked by Quine. The singleton is equal to itself but is also more than itself; it contains itself but is also contained by itself. The singleton is a member of itself and is not a member of itself – precisely in the same manner as the Russell set. This understanding of the singleton the naïve and ZF set theories share with the mainstream of Byzantine ontology[54] – but not with Leontius of Byzantium.

Leontius does not allow the paraconsistent conjunction (2) but he does not subscribe to the nominalist formula $\{x\} \equiv x$, either. He does not allow singletons at all. For him, the species exist if and only if they are instantiated in plurality of individuals. Thus, he avoids both paraconsistency and nominalism. He managed to find out a workaround. We have already seen that Leontius' original idea was lying in the field of mathematics: he invented graphs to become able to construct a consistent and original ontology.

10. Unreality of the Division between the Two Natures in Christ

Leontius explains his original Christological ideas only in the last two chapters of the *Solutio* (chs. 7 and 8). Before this, he was mostly concerned with his original ideas in logic, numerology, and ontology. In the last chapters he shows what purpose this newly created philosophical doctrine serves.

At first, the Acephalus formulates the main argument known from the *Arbiter* of Philoponus (esp. its ch. 7 preserved in Greek). It is very friendly toward the Chalcedonians and was, indeed, elaborated in the perspective of

53. On some of Cantor's paraconsistent intuitions, as well as recent proposals of paraconsistent set theories, see W. Carnielli, M. E. Coniglio, "Paraconsistent set theory by predicating on consistency," *Journal of Logic and Computation*, advanced access published 09. 07. 2013; doi:10.1093/logcom/ext020. For different ways open to "rehabilitation" of the "naïve" set theory, see A. Weir, "Naïve Set Theory Is Innocent!," *Mind* 107 (1998) 763–798, esp. 792–793.

54. See above, section 4, on Eulogius of Alexandria and, after him, the Christology of the defenders of icons in the ninth century.

the union (which failed at the Council of 553):[55] your unique but composite hypostasis is the same thing as our unique but composite nature (86.15–25; 1929D–1932A). Some phrases here are of special interest, however. "We too, consider the (two) natures only in thought (Τὰς φύσεις μόνῃ τῇ ἐπινοίᾳ καὶ ἡμεῖς θεωροῦμεν)," given that the concrete and the real one is one resulting from the two nature of Christ; "in the same manner, you understand the (two) hypostases in thought and unify them into the unique hypostasis [...] (Ὧι γὰρ λόγῳ ὑμεῖς τὰς ὑποστάσεις τῇ ἐπινοίᾳ λαμβάνοντες, καὶ ταύτας ἑνώσαντες εἰς μίαν ὑπόστασιν αὐτὰς συντίθετε [...])" (89.15–18; 1929D).

One can see that, so far, the Acephalus still does not grasp the difference between the particular nature in its Leontian understanding and the hypostasis. Thus, he understands "from two natures" (a common slogan of the two sides of the conflict over the Chalcedon) in the Chalcedonian terminology as equivalent to "from two hypostases." Moreover, he accepts that the two natures of Christ before the union existed "only in thought." This can be understood in either a traditional (for both anti-Chalcedonians and neo-Chalcedonians) way, that the two natures of Christ before union could be discussed only in a speculative manner, or in a properly Philoponian way, that these natures are *per se* abstractions without any self-standing existence. We will see that Leontius ("the Orthodox") will perceive the term τῇ ἐπινοίᾳ in the latter sense.[56]

In his response, Leontius defines two different kinds of ἐπίνοια (86.26–87.10, quoted below 86.26–87.6; 1932AB):

Τὴν ἐπίνοιαν οἱ Πατέρες καὶ ὁ ἀληθὴς λόγος διττὴν ἀπεφήναντο εἶναι. Ἡ μὲν γὰρ οἷον ἐπέννοιά τίς ἐστι καὶ ἐπενθύμησις, τὴν ὁλοσχερῆ καὶ ἀδιάρθρωτον τῶν πραγμάτων ἐξαπλοῦσά τε καὶ διασαφοῦσα θεωρίαν καὶ γνῶσιν, ὡς τὸ τῇ αἰσθήσει δόξαν εἶναι ἁπλοῦν, τῇ πολυπραγμοσύνῃ τοῦ νοῦ πολυμερές τε καὶ ποικίλον ἀναφαίνεσθαι·

The Fathers and the true reasoning defined two different kinds of *epinoia*. According to the first one, it is something like (analytical) reflection,[57] which unfolds and clarifies for contemplation and knowledge the wholeness and non-compositeness of real things, whose being seems to the sensual apperception to be simple but, with (the help of) the inquisitiveness of the intellect, is revealed to be manifold and diversified.

ἡ δὲ ἀνάπλασμα διανοίας τυγχάνει,

According to the second meaning, it is the ima-

55. See for all details, U. M. Lang, *John Philoponus and the Controversies over Chalcedon in the Sixth Century. A Study and Translation of the "Arbiter,"* Spicilegium Sacrum Lovaniense. Études et documents, fasc. 47, Leuven: Peeters 2001.

56. Unfortunately, I had no access to the complete text of the monograph by Antonio Orbe, *La epinoia. Algunos preliminares históricos de la distinción κατ' ἐπίνοιαν. (En torno a la Filosofía de Leoncio Bizantino)*, Roma: Pontificia Universitas Gregoriana 1955.

57. On the pair of synonymic words ἐπέννοια and ἐπενθύμησις precisely in our text, see G. W. H. Lampe, *A Patristic Greek Lexicon*, Oxford: Clarendon Press 1961, 514, *s.vv.* The first of the two is lacking from the Liddell–Scott dictionary.

κατὰ συμπλοκὴν αἰσθήσεώς τε καὶ φαντασίας ἐκ τῶν ὄντων τὰ μηδαμῶς ὄντα συντιθεῖσα καὶ εἶναι δοξάζουσα· τοιαύτη δέ ἐστιν ἡ τῶν ἱπποκενταύρων καὶ Σειρήνων καὶ τῶν τοιούτων μυθοπλαστία [...]	gination[58] which, combining the (data of) sensual (apperception) and the fantasy, constructs from the existing things what can never exist but believes them to be existing: such are the mythical creatures like hippocentaurs or Sirens [...]

The *epinoia* of the second kind takes some parts of the really existing things and composes, albeit only in the mind and the words (ἐν τῇ διανοίᾳ καὶ τοῖς λόγοις), something new which has neither hypostasis nor essence (τὰ μηδαμῶς ἐν ὑποστάσει καὶ οὐσίᾳ θεωρούμενα).

Then, the Orthodox becomes able to proceed to the salient question: "Thus, which one of these two kinds of *epinoia* do you mean, oh excellent one, when you consider the two natures?" (87.11–12; 1932B: Κατὰ ποίαν τοίνυν, ὦ θαυμάσιε, τῶν ἐπινοιῶν τούτων θεωρίαν τὰς δύο φύσεις λαμβάνεις;). Of course, the second alternative would lead to an arbitrary fantasy, if not directly to the idolatry (87.14–17; 1932BC). But the first one is not much better: "If (you mean) the first kind (of *epinoia*), you would define the Christ as being a gathering of objects of contemplation but not as coming together of the (two) natures, because such is the nature of the things that are contemplated only by *epinoia*" (87.11–14; 1932BC: Εἰ μὲν οὖν κατὰ τὴν πρώτην, θεωρημάτων ἄθροισμα ἀλλ' οὐ φύσεων σύνοδον τὸν Χριστὸν εἶναι ὁρίσῃ· τοιαύτη γὰρ ἡ φύσις τῶν ἐπινοίᾳ μόνῃ θεωρητῶν).

We have to retain from there this clear definition of *epinoia*, in whatever meaning, as something that is related to mental constructs outside the reality.

What follows is a critic of Monophysitism, but not only for "mixing" the two natures into one but also for denying their existence whatsoever: "Because, from the very fact of understanding the natures only with *epinoia*, it follows for them to be nonexistent and non-being, or demolished and disappeared" (88.5–7; 1932D: Αὐτὸ μὲν οὖν τὸ τῇ ἐπινοίᾳ μόνῃ τὰς φύσεις γνωρίζειν τὸ ἀνύπαρκτον αὐτῶν καὶ ἀνούσιον, ἢ τὸ συγκεχυμένον καὶ ἠφανισμένον κατασκευάζει).

Leontius' own teaching – that he, of course, ascribes to "our Fathers" – is that not the natures themselves but only their division in Christ is to be apprehended by the *epinoia* in the first meaning of the term.[59] Thus, he considers the division of the natures in Christ as not only understandable through an analytical procedure but also existing only in our mind.

58. The meaning of the idiom ἀνάπλασμα διανοίας is precisely that, "imagination".
59. 87.17–19; 1932C: ὅπότε οἱ θεσπέσιοι ἡμῶν Πατέρες οὐ τὰς φύσεις τῇ ἐπινοίᾳ εἶναι ὡρίσαντο, ἀλλὰ τὴν διαίρεσιν τούτων κατὰ τὴν πρώτην ἐπίνοιαν ἐξειλήφασιν.

11. Unreality of "Three" in the Holy Trinity?

The most revealing of Leontius' triadological passages is found in a long explanation about two kinds of difference: the purely mental one, by *epinoia*, and the real one which he calls "by energy" (ch. 7, *passim*, with repetitions in ch. 8). There is no need to collect all the relevant formulations by Leontius because all of them repeat the same idea.

The natures themselves exist not "by *epinoia*," as said the Acephalus, but "by energy" (in reality), however, the difference between them is only "by *epinoia*:" the Fathers "[...] demonstrated the natures as being and called according to the energy, whereas the division between them they understood by *epinoia* (87.22–23; 1932C: [...] τῇ μὲν ἐνεργείᾳ τὰς φύσεις εἶναί τε καὶ καλεῖσθαι ἀπεφήναντο, τὴν δὲ τούτων διαίρεσιν κατ' ἐπίνοιαν ἔλαβον).

The division "by energy" would produce difference between the hypostases, and this is why – Leontius here continues to answer the initial question of the Acephalus – we do not say that Christ is produced from the two hypostases (88.10–21; 1933AB): "[...] the division by energy implies and establishes hypostases, whereas the division by *epinoia* does not entail the number of hypostases" (88.19–21; 1933B: [...] τῆς κατ' ἐνέργειαν διαιρέσεως τὰς ὑποστάσεις ἐχούσης τε καὶ τιθεμένης, ἡ κατ' ἐπίνοιαν διαίρεσις τὸν τῶν ὑποστάσεων ἀριθμὸν οὐ παραδέχεται).[60] – Let us notice the mention of number here. Leontius demonstrates that Christ is not divisible into two hypostases, and so, the notion of number here is the ordinary one.

Immediately after the sentence just quoted Leontius continues, taking an example from the Holy Trinity (88.21–24; 1933B):

Ὡς γὰρ τὸ κατ' ἐπίνοιαν μεῖζον ἐπί τε Πατρὸς καὶ Υἱοῦ, τῇ τοῦ αἰτίου λεγόμενον φύσει, τὸ τῇ φύσει μεῖζον οὐ συνεισάγει, οὕτω τὸ κατ' ἐπίνοιαν διαιρετὸν τὸ κατ' ἐνέργειαν οὐ συνεισάξει ποτὲ, καὶ διὰ τοῦτο οὐδὲ τὰς ὑποστάσεις.	When it is said by *epinoia* "greater" concerning the Father and the Son [John 14:28] because of being the cause by nature,[61] nothing greater is co-introduced to the nature. In the same manner, the division by *epinoia* would never co-introduce the division by energy, and, therefore, (never co-introduce) the hypostases.

One question would be in order here: in what manner then do the hypostases of the Holy Trinity differ from each other, by *epinoia* or by energy – or even somehow else? Leontius does not give us any explicit answer, neither does he provide any third kind of division. The division could be either real, by energy, like that between three men, or by *epinoia*, as between the two

60. Leontius elaborates further on the topic, but either repeats himself or repeats the standard anti-Nestorian argumentation of his epoch. Cf. in the same ch. 7, 89.13–90.8; 1933D–1936C; ch. 8, 95.30–96.13; 1944D–1945A.

61. Leontius alludes to the common patristic understanding of John 14:28 as pointing out that the Father is the "cause" within the divine nature, that is, the principle of the μοναρχία in the Holy Trinity.

natures of Christ, but also – let us recall what was said by Leontius in ch. 2 – between ten cubits within a ten cubit piece of wood[62] and, as we now are forced to acknowledge, between the three hypostases of the divine nature.

I admit that now I am trying to carry through what Leontius himself left unarticulated. Indeed, had he said that the three hypostases of the Holy Trinity differ only by *epinoia*, he would face charge of Sabellianism. He would also have had a hard time explaining his original theory of graphs.

Leontius defends the unity of the conceptual apparatus used in both "theology" and "œconomy," and so we would expect from him an explanation of why he describes the three divine hypostases in conformity with his own definition of particular natures but still calls them hypostases. In his language where the particular natures differ from each other as the vertices of a graph, whereas the hypostases differ from each other as enumerable things divided "by energy," the notion of hypostasis was tacitly changing its meaning when applied to the Holy Trinity. Leontius' escaping from the paraconsistency of patristic thought cost him inconsistency in his own usage of a key term, hypostasis.

Leontius left too many loose ends after having changed his mind from the Christology of *CNE* to that of the *Solutio*. The building of his dogmatics was left with no chance to be completed.

12. Christology

We still have not quoted the famous Christological passage of ch. 8 but our analysis of Leontius' philosophy and logic is accomplished. We still need, however, to learn more about his theology. This is why ch. 8 will be especially important to us. Mostly, this final chapter contains various repetitions of earlier statements or the *trivia* of such polemics, but among them there are important theological applications of the logical and ontological principles formulated earlier.

Leontius revisits his initial problem with which he had started the whole discussion in the very beginning of his treatise: how to understand the human individuality of Christ. Now, it has already been explained that, in logical categories, it is a particular nature, in Leontius' specific understanding of this notion. Thus, it is time to explain it in a more theological way.

The larger context is as follows. Leontius needs to explain why his understanding of the human individuality in Christ does not lead him to acknowledge Jesus as a human hypostasis (as the Nestorians do). However, he turns

62. This example must be understood in the context of Leontius' "geometrical" approach. Thus, the cubits here are geometrically different (within a graph), and the whole example is not to be confounded with the unity of money in the bank account (the famous comparison explaining the indiscernibility of quantum objects invented by Erwin Schrödinger in the 1950s); cf. S. French, D. Krause, *Identity in Physics: A Historical, Philosophical, and Formal Analysis*, Oxford: Clarendon Press 2006, 142–143, 159, 220, 370–371.

out to be unable to exclude the pre-existence of Christ's humanity on a purely theoretical level, albeit he, of course, excludes it as a fact. Marcel Richard was still too moderate when saying, about this statement of Leontius, that "[c']était jouer avec le feu."[63]

Probably, Leontius did not explicitly contradict any authoritative text of his epoch but he did certainly contradict the mainstream (among the neo-Chalcedonians) theological intuition which, in the 580s, resulted in Eulogius of Alexandria's (paraconsistent) statement that the conjunction of a nature with the individual characteristics of an individual still does not form a hypostasis. There would be no Jesus without the divine Logos, who accepted the individual characteristics of Jesus and thus became – but only the Logos himself now called Jesus – one of the individuals of the *human* common nature. Jesus is simply the name of the Logos as a hypostasis of the human nature, in the same manner as the Son is the name of the same Logos as a hypostasis of the divine nature. The one and unique hypostasis of the Logos thus became common to the two natures at once and acquired the individual characteristics (idioms) as an individual of each of the two natures. I recalled these explanations of Nicephorus of Constantinople and Theodore the Studite to facilitate our tracing of Leontius' attempts to avoid these (paraconsistent) Christological conclusions.

Leontius approaches the problem of the pre-existence of Christ's humanity from the analogy of the resurrection of the dead (94.24–95.18; 1941D–1944B). This example allows him to conclude that "from this it is shown that it is acceptable for a hypostasis to be produced out of the previously existing things without (their) change, even if it is not completely applicable to Christ because he is not created beforehand."[64] It is worth noting that Leontius considers the resurrected bodies as being materially identical to the dead ones, and so, he is following the line of Gregory of Nyssa rather than the Origenistic line of Philoponus or Eutychius of Constantinople.[65]

Then, Leontius proceeds to the issue that turns out to be the touchstone of his Christology (95.19–30; 1944CD)[66]:

Τὸ δέ τινας λέγειν, διὰ τὸ μὴ προδιαπεπλάσθαι μηδὲ προϋφεστᾶναι τὴν τοῦ Κυρίου ἀνθρωπότητα μηδὲ τελείαν προσειλῆφθαι, ἀλλ' ἐν τῷ Λόγῳ	As to the fact that some say: because the Lord's humanity was not formed or did not exist beforehand, and because it was not assumed already complete, but has its being in

63. M. Richard, "Léonce...", 60.
64. 94.32–34; 1944A: Ἐξ ὧν δείκνυται ὅτι καὶ ἐκ προϋφεστώτων πραγμάτων ὑπόστασιν γενέσθαι ἀτρέπτως ἐνδέχεται, εἰ καὶ ὅλως ἐπὶ Χριστοῦ τοῦτο οὐ δίδοται, ὅτι οὐ προδιαπέπλασθαι.
65. Cf. B. Lourié, "John Philoponus on the Bodily Resurrection"; В. М. Лурье, "Идентичность человеческой личности по Иоанну Филопону...".
66. I mostly owe my English translation below to Brian Daley, "The Origenism of Leontius of Byzantium," *Journal of Theological Studies*, N. S. 27 (1976) 333–369, here 338.

ὑποστῆναι, διὰ τοῦτο μίαν ὑπόστασιν ἀμφοτέρων ποιεῖν, τὸ μέν τι ἀληθὲς, τὸ δὲ οὐκ ἀληθὲς ὂν τυγχανει. Τὸ μὲν γὰρ μὴ προϋφεστᾶναι μηδὲ προδιαπεπλάσθαι καὶ ἡμεῖς δώσομεν, τὸ δὲ διὰ τοῦτο μίαν ὑπόστασιν ποιεῖν, ὡς οὐκ ἐγχωροῦν ἄλλως οὐδὲ δυνατὸν Θεῷ καὶ τελείῳ ἀνθρώπῳ οὕτως ἑνωθῆναι, οὐκέτι δώσομεν. Τί γάρ; Οὕτως ἢ ἐκείνως ἔχον τι πλέον ἔσται Θεῷ εἰς ἕνωσιν; Οὔτε γὰρ ὁ χρόνος τῆς ἑνώσεως ἢ ὁ τόπος ἢ τὸ ἀτελὲς τοῦ σώματος, ἀλλ' αὐτὸς ὁ τῆς ἑνώσεως τρόπος τὸν ἕνα Χριστὸν πεποίηκεν. Οὐ τοίνυν διὰ τὸ ἀδύνατον, ἀλλὰ διὰ τὸ μὴ πρέπειν ψιλήν ποτε καὶ ἄνευ θεότητος εἶναι τὴν τοῦ Κυρίου ἀνθρωπότητα, τὴν προδιάπλασιν ἐκβάλλομεν.

the Logos therefore they make one hypostasis of both – part of this is true and part is not. We, too, grant that (his humanity) did not preexist, was not formed first; but we do not at all grant that one therefore makes one hypostasis of both, as if it were not permitted for things to be otherwise, or as if it were impossible for God to be united even with a complete man in this way. But why? Is there any importance for God whether the union would be in this way or another? In fact, the unique Christ is made not by the time or the place of the union or by the imperfection of the body[67] but by the very mode (*tropos*) of union. We reject the prior formation [i.e. of Christ's humanity] not because it was impossible, but because it was not fitting that the humanity of the Lord should once have been alone and without his divinity.

Thus, the particular human nature of Jesus, according Leontius, existed independently of the fact of the incarnation, even though its creation was synchronised with the moment of incarnation.

Of course, even in the case of the "prior formation" of Christ's humanity, the principle forbidding any φύσις ἀνυπόστατος[68] would not be broken. This particular nature of Jesus would use, for its temporary being without divinity, some other hypostasis than that of the Logos, that is, a human hypostasis – for instance, of some Mr X, let us say. In Leontius' approach, this would not cause a problem with the identity of the humanity of the further Jesus with that of Mr X: the unity of subject would be guaranteed by the human particular nature that was at first ἐνυπόστατος in Mr X, then in the Logos viz. Jesus. It is needless to say that such a thought experiment would render quite a different result in the classical perspective of the Byzantine (neo-Chalcedonian) patristics: here, the humanity of Mr X would be inseparable from the hypostasis of Mr X, because no such things as particular natures which are different from the hypostases exist.

Leontius' treatment of the humanity of Christ makes it a separate subject within the unique Christ, and so, is really crypto-Nestorian from any "neo-Chalcedonian" point of view.

67. "Imperfection" in the sense that the incarnation took place at the very moment of conception, unlike the alternative scenario – considered by Leontius as theoretically acceptable – as if it took place when Jesus grew up, that is, when his body became "perfect." Cf. discussion above in ch. 8 and the standard mode of speaking about growing of the human body.

68. *CNE* I, 1, quoted in footnote 22 above.

Now we are in position to summarise the Christological doctrine of Leontius. For this purpose, we have to recall Leontius' "theory of graphs" as was used by him to create an original understanding of the notion of particular nature.

The doctrine of Leontius could be summarised in these three points:

1) The humanity of Jesus does not exist and never existed as a numerically distinct separate entity. This is why both open Nestorianism and Theodore of Mopsuestia's Christology are unacceptable.
2) It does exist since the incarnation – and *could* exist before incarnation but actually did not – as a numerically distinct *position* within the common nature of the humankind, which is a particular human nature. This is an original idea of Leontius himself and exists in his *Solutio* only.
3) The humanity of Jesus is not the common nature of the humankind – *pace* the whole *consensus* of the Chalcedonian theologians including Leontius himself in *CNE*.

It is tempting to suppose that Leontius' "theory of graphs" was designed to supply a rational model for the Origenistic *Henas*. At least, its Christological and Triadological applications would fit the theology of the *Protoctist* Origenism, and I sympathise with István Perczel's idea that Leontius belonged to that group.[69]

13. John Philoponus behind the Scenes

It was only Richard Cross who asked himself what happened to Leontius between *CNE* and the *Solutio*, but his answer was "It is not clear why LB changed his mind [...]"[70] Given that the time span when the *Solutio* could have been written is to be expanded up to the epoch of the Council of 553, and especially with reference to the preceeding Christological discussions, we can take a fresh look at the already known polemical parallels between the *Arbiter* by Philoponus (esp. its ch. 7) and Leontius of Byzantium.

Philoponus was trying to present "the unique nature" of the Severians as the same thing as "the unique hypostasis" of the (neo-)Chalcedonians. The idea of the humanity of Christ as a particular nature was in the core of his argumentation. There are some other polemical parallels with the *Solutio*, one of them being already reviewed by Uwe Lang.[71] This is Philoponus' argumentation against those Chalcedonians who deduce their "unique hypostasis" from the fact that the humanity of Christ did not exist prior to the incarnation. To the contrary, Philoponus himself deduces from the same fact

69. I. Perczel, "Once Again...".
70. R. Cross, "Individual Natures...", 250.
71. U. M. Lang, *John Philoponus...*, 70–72.

Christ's "unique nature." Leontius, as we have just seen, denies the argumentation of both sides, because he does not allow as a derivative of this fact anything featuring the mode of the union (ὁ τῆς ἑνώσεως τρόπος) in Christ. It appears then that it was Leontius who wrote after Philoponus, and not *vice versa* (*pace* Lang). But, anyway, this is a secondary detail.

The main project of Philoponus on the eve of 553 was a reinterpretation of the Chalcedonian "unique hypostasis" as a particular nature, which would open the way to allow the official Church under Justinian to adopt the basic assumptions of Severian Christology. We see the Chalcedonian position that there is no such thing as a particular nature which is not identical to the hypostasis staggered precisely in the middle of the sixth century. This is the historical context in which Leontius' change of mind would seem most natural – especially if he did really keep his Origenistic skeleton in the closet.

This is why I would consider the *Solutio* to be a response provoked by a challenge of John Philoponus.

The Transformation of Neoplatonic Philosophical Notions of Procession (proodos) and Conversion (epistrophe) in the Thought of St. Maximus the Confessor

Vladimir Cvetković

I. Introduction

Since S. L. Epiphanovich's claim, in his classical study *Преподобный Максим Исповедник и византийское богословие* published in 1915, that the purpose of the Incarnation is the original plan of the Great Council (Isaiah 9:6),[1] and not a response to the fall of Adam,[2] there is hardly any serious scholar of Maximus who did not stress this feature of the Confessor's thought. There is a long list of both eastern (Justin Popović,[3] Dumitru Staniloae,[4] Georges Florovsky,[5] Artemije Radosavljević,[6] Vasilios Karayiannis,[7] Atanasije

1. For the idea of the Great Council in Maximus see A. Jevtić, "Veliki Savet Božiji kod Svetog Maksima Ispovednika (The Great Council of God According to St Maximus the Confessor)", in: *Sveti Maksim Ispovednik. Život i izbor iz dela*, Vrnjci: Bratstvo Svetog Simeona Mirotočivog, Trebinje: Manastir Tvrdoš, Los Anđeles: Eparhija Zapadnoamerička 2012, 320–349.
2. С. Л. Епифанович, *Преподобный Максим Исповедник и византийское богословие*, Москва: Мартис 1996, 87–88.
3. Prepodobni otac Justin (Popović), *Pravoslavna filosofija istine*, tom 2, *Sabrana dela Oca Justina Novog*, knjiga 18, Beograd: Zadužbina Sveti Jovan Zlatousti Svetog Justina Novog i Manastir Ćelije kod Valjeva ²2004 (1st edition 1935), 9.
4. D. Stăniloae, *Filocalia sfintelor nevoințe ale desăvrșirii*, vol. 3, Bucharest 1948, 496.
5. G. Florovsky, " 'Cur Deus Homo?' The Motive of the Incarnation," in: *Evharisterion. Festal Volume of the 45 Anniversary of Prof. Hamilcar Alivisatos*, Athens 1957, 70–79. Reprinted in Chapter VI, "Dimensions of Redemption" of the *Collected Works of Georges Florovsky. Vol. III: Creation and Redemption*, Nordland Publishing Company: Belmont, Mass. 1976, 163–170: 168.
6. Hieromonk Artemije (Radosavljević), *Τὸ Μυστήριον τῆς Σωτηρίας κατὰ τὸν Ἅγιον Μάξιμον τὸν Ὁμολογητήν*, dissertation, Athens 1975, 180–196. The text is also available in English translation at the following web-address: http://www.synodinresistance.org/pdfs/2009/03/26/20090326aGiatiEnsB7%20Folder/20090326aGiatiEnsB7.pdf. See also his "Le problème du 'présupposé' ou du 'non-présupposé' de l'Incarnation de Dieu le Verbe," in: F. Heinzer, C. Schönborn, éd., *Maximus Confessor. Actes du Symposium sur Maxime le Confesseur, Fribourg, 2-5 septembre 1980*, Paradosis 27, Fribourg (Suisse) 1982, 193–206.
7. V. Karayiannis, *Maxime le Confesseur. Essence et énergies de Dieu*, Théologie historique 93, Paris : Beauchesne 1993, 485.

Jevtić[8]) and western (Hans Urs von Balthasar,[9] Polycarp Sherwood,[10] Irénée-Henri Dalmais,[11] Lars Thunberg[12]) theologians, who embraced the position that Christ's Incarnation is neither a corrective of the original Divine plan and nor a response to the human fall.

The Incarnation of Logos is central to Maximus' thought and it should be treated accordingly. If Maximus' cosmology is Christocentric as Torstein Tollefsen claims in the title of his recent study,[13] then the Neoplatonic conceptual framework employed by Maximus should underline the role of Christ in the divine design. However, if the whole divine design, from creation to deification, is pursued on the principles of the Neoplatonic concepts of remaining–procession–return, then the Incarnation of Logos seems to be something auxiliary. The Neoplatonic or Proclean remaining refers to the state of the preexistence of the creation in the form of *logoi*, as divine wills and thoughts about the future world. The procession (πρόοδος) may be further identified with the creation of both, universals and particulars. Finally, the conversion seen as the return of the creatures to their source would refer to the future state of deified creation.[14] This scheme can hardly pertain to the purpose of Incarnation as something more than a corrective of the Adam's fall.

The aim of this paper is to explore the way in which St. Maximus the Confessor adapted the Neoplatonic philosophical concepts of "procession" (πρόοδος) and "conversion" (ἐπιστροφή), in order to articulate the central theme of his thought, namely the Incarnation of God in human form.

In his portrayal of the unity between God and the creation in terms of the relationship between Logos and *logoi*, Maximus employs the revised form of the Neoplatonic dialectical pair of procession and reversion (πρόοδος–ἐπιστροφή):

> Because the One goes forth out of goodness into individual being, creating and preserving them, the One is many. Moreover the many are directed toward the One and are providentially guided in that direction.[15]

8. A. Jevtić, art. cit., 320–349.
9. H.-U. von Balthasar, *Kosmische Liturgie. Das Weltbild Maximus des Bekenners*, Einsiedeln: Verlag 1961, 270. See also H.-U. von Balthasar, *Cosmic Liturgy. The Universe According to Maximus the Confessor*, San Francisco: Ignatius Press 2003, 134.
10. P. Sherwood, "Introduction to St Maximus the Confessor," in: *The Ascetic Life. The Fourth Centuries on Charity*, New York: Newman Press 1955, 71–72; 232–3, n. 292.
11. I.-H. Dalmais, "Texte choisi. Le mystère du Christ (Question à Thalassius 60)," *Connaissance des Pères de l'Église* 17 (1985) 19–21.
12. L. Thunberg, *Microcosm and Mediator. The Theological Anthropology of St Maximus the Confessor*, Chicago and La Salle, IL.: Open Court 1995, 456.
13. T. Tollefsen, *The Christocentric Cosmology of St Maximus the Confessor*, Oxford: OUP 2008.
14. T. Tollefsen, *The Christocentric Cosmology of St Maximus the Confessor*, doctoral thesis, Oslo 2000, 271.
15. *Ambigua ad Joannem (= Amb.)* 7, PG 91, 1081C: κατὰ μὲν τὴν ἀγαθοπρεπῆ εἰς τὰ ὄντα τοῦ ἑνὸς ποιητικήν τε καὶ συνεκτικὴν πρόοδον πολλοὶ ὁ εἷς, κατὰ δὲ τὴν εἰς τὸν ἕνα τῶν πολλῶν ἐπιστρεπτικήν τε καὶ χειραγωγικὴν ἀναφοράν τε καὶ πρόνοιαν. The English translation in: P.

To put it differently Maximus claims that the one Logos are many *logoi* on the basis of the creative and preservative procession (ποιητική καί συνεκτική πρόοδος), while many *logoi* are the Logos due to the converting and hand-leading transference and providence (ἐπιστρεπτικὴ καὶ χειραγωγικὴ ἀναφορά τε καὶ πρόνοια).

II. Creative and Preservative procession (ποιητικὴ καὶ συνεκτικὴ πρόοδος)

The procession, according Maximus, consists of two elements: one creative and another preservative (ποιητικὴ καὶ συνεκτικὴ πρόοδος).[16] The creative procession can be identified with the creation of the world in accordance with the divine wills about created beings. Maximus explains the divine creative power in the following words:

> Because he held together in himself the *logoi* before they come to be, by his gracious will he created all things visible and invisible out of nothing. *By his Word and by his Wisdom* he made all things and is making all things, universals as well as particulars.[17]

It is possible to distinguish here two kinds of *logoi* or divine wills about the world, the *logoi* of universals and *logoi* of individuals. There is also a difference between what God has already created and what He is creating.

The structure of the *logoi* may be graphically presented as arranged in the Porphyrian tree beginning from the most general *logoi* of being and nature and subsequent *logoi* of highest genus (γενικώτατον γένος), intermediate *genera* (γενικώτερα γένη), species (εἴδη), and specific species (εἰδικώτατα εἴδη),[18] to the *logoi* of individuals (ἄτομα) and accidents (συμβεβηκότα). All the *logoi* are undivided by their participations in the higher *logos* of being: the accidents are undivided due to the unity in substance, the individuals due to the unity in specific species, specific species due to the unity in species, species due to the unity in intermediate *genera*, intermediate *genera* due to the unity in the highest *genus*, and the highest *genus* in the most general *logos* of being. The most general *logos* of being is also undivided from the Logos of God, because it has its cause and the source in him.

The *logos* of each particular being maintains the beings undivided in the general order but it also maintains the beings so as to remain unconfused, one with another. Maximus elaborates this fixedness of every being in the general order in its own *logos* of being in *Ambiguum* 15:

M. Blowers, R. L. Wilken, *On the Cosmic Mystery of Jesus Christ. Selected Writings from St Maximus the Confessor*, Crestwood, NY: St. Vladimir's Seminary Press 2003, 57.

16. *Amb.* 7, 1081C.
17. *Amb.* 7, 1080A; Blowers & Willken, 55.
18. *Amb.* 10, 1177C. The English translation in: A. Louth, *Maximus the Confessor*, London: Routledge 1996, 138.

> [Things] are motionless in their nature, their capabilities, and their effects; in their place in the general order of things; in their stability of being, they never leave their peculiar natural place, never turning into other things or confusing themselves.[19]

The natural logos of every being is defined and circumscribed not only by the *logoi* of essence, nature or species but also by the *logoi* of relationship, mixture, position, power, activity, passion, quantity and quality that preserve the particular being unconfused with the other beings.[20]

In the process of creative procession God predetermines every being by its *logos*. The term predetermination should be taken in a loose sense, because the level of resemblance of the created beings with their *logoi* depends either on the character of the *logoi* or on the inclination of created beings. The level of binding authority of *logoi* is again within divine power. Maximus claims that the particular beings are immutable by their *logos* of nature, while they are movable in their properties and accidents.[21] Therefore, the *logoi* of the universals such as the most general *logoi* of being and nature and subsequent *logoi* of highest genus (γενικώτατον γένος), intermediate genera (γενικώτερα γένη), species (εἴδη), and probably specific species (εἰδικώτατα εἴδη),[22] as well as the *logoi* of time and the *logoi* of providence and judgment determine the immutability of created nature and the inclination of the particular being cannot affect the established order. The binding authority of the *logoi* of individual rational beings is weak, not because the Creator was not able to impose his power over the particulars, but mainly because he has left the freedom to them to attentively (διὰ προσοχῆς) fulfill the purpose for which they were created. The freedom is given to the rational beings that are angels and humans, while the sensible creation merely defined by the general *logoi* or genera and species is changeable on the level of properties and accidents due to their participations in the different *logoi* such as *logoi* of mixture, position, quantity and quality.

Maximus explains the difference between what God has already created and what he is still creating in the following way:

> The *logoi* of all things known by God before their creation are securely fixed in God. They are in him who is truth of all things. Yet all this things, things present and things to come, have not been brought into

19. *Amb.* 15, 1217AB: Ἀκινήτως δὲ κινεῖσθαί τε καὶ φέρεσθαι τὰ ὁρώμενα εἴρηται τῷ διδασκάλῳ τῷ μὲν λόγῳ, ᾧ γέγονε ταῦτα, κατά τε φύσιν καὶ δύναμιν καὶ ἐνέργειαν, τάξιν τε καὶ διαμονὴν ἀμεταστάτως ἔχειν, καὶ μὴ ἐξίστασθαι καθ' ὁτιοῦν τῆς φυσικῆς ἰδιότητος καὶ μεταβάλλειν εἰς ἄλλο καὶ φύρεσθαι. The English translation of this passage is from H.-U von Balthasar, *Cosmic Liturgy*, 154.
20. *Amb.* 15, 1228AC. See also on this point J.-Cl. Larchet, "La conception maximienne des énergies divines et des logoi et la théorie platonicienne des Idées," *Philotheos* 4 (2004) 276–283, especially 281.
21. *Amb.* 15, 1217B.
22. *Amb.* 10, 1177C.

> being contemporaneously with their being known by God; rather each was created in appropriate way according to its *logos* at the proper time according the wisdom of the maker, and each acquired the concrete actual existence in itself.[23]

Due to the different place of each individual being in the course of time God is constantly repeating his creative act. The creative processions happen in accordance with the original divine design, which is in fact a very refined structure of the *logoi* of beings. The difference between the original creative act and every subsequent creative act of the divine power is in the creation of universals and individuals. While God was originally creating according to *logoi* of universals and to those *logoi* of individuals whose proper time was then, he is subsequently creating not any more universals but concrete beings in accordance with their individual *logos* and the *logoi* of time and position.

Maximus' understanding of the preservative procession is best presented in a passage from his *Mystagogia* 1:

> For God who made and brought into existence all things by his infinite power contains, gathers, and limits them and in his Providence binds both intelligible and sensible beings to himself and to one another. Maintaining himself as cause, beginning and end all beings which are by nature distant from one another, he makes them converge towards each other by the singular force of their relationship to him as origin. Through this force he leads all beings to a common and unconfused identity of movement and existence [...][24]

God preserves created beings by containing, gathering and limiting them, as well as leading them to a common and unconfused identity of movement and existence. While the created beings are contended, gathered and limited by their *logoi*, the movement of the being is "a way of establishing itself as a particular and distinguishing itself from every other nature" as Balthasar rightly pointed out.[25] Every created being is endowed with movement, which is intrinsic to the nature of being. However, every movement is directed toward an end and we can define every movement in accordance with the goal of the movement. Maximus claims that God endows us with movement at the beginning, but he also endows us with the mode in which we should move toward him as an end.[26] Interpreted in accordance with the previous passage

23. *Amb.* 7, 1081A; Blowers & Wilken 56–57.
24. *Mystagogia* (= *Myst.*) 1, 2; in: Ch. Boudignon, ed., *Maximi Confessoris Mystagogia*, Corpus Christianorum. Series Graeca 69, Turnhout: Brepols 2011, 10–11, 132–139: Ὥσπερ γὰρ ὁ Θεὸς πάντα τῇ ἀπείρῳ δυνάμει ποιήσας καὶ εἰς τὸ εἶναι παραγαγὼν συνέχει καὶ συνάγει καὶ περιγράφει, καὶ ἀλλήλοις καὶ ἑαυτῷ προνοητικῶς ἐνδιασφίγγει τά τε νοητὰ καὶ τὰ αἰσθητά, καὶ περὶ ἑαυτὸν ὡς αἰτίαν καὶ ἀρχὴν καὶ τέλος πάντα περικρατῶν τὰ κατὰ τὴν φύσιν ἀλλήλων διεστηκότα, κατὰ μίαν τὴν πρὸς αὐτὸν ὡς ἀρχὴν σχέσεως δύναμιν ἀλλήλοις συννενευκότα ποιεῖ, καθ' ἣν εἰς ταυτότητα κινήσεώς τε καὶ ὑπάρξεως ἀδιάφθορον καὶ ἀσύγχυτον ἄγει τὰ πάντα. For the English translation see G. C. Berthold, ed., *Maximus the Confessor, Selected Writings*, London: SPCK 1985, 186.
25. H.-U. von Balthasar, *Cosmic Liturgy*, 155.
26. *Amb.* 7, 1073C.

from *Mystagogia* that God in his preservative role maintains himself as cause, beginning and end of all beings, it means that there are only two proper directions of movement for rational beings. One direction of the rational beings is to move forward toward God as the end (τέλος) of movement, while the other is the movement toward their own beginning and cause. According to Maximus whatever direction the rational being takes it will reach God because "the end of movement of those who are moved is 'eternal well-being' itself [God], just as its beginning is being itself which is the giver of being as well as well being."[27] However, Maximus classifies movements according to nature and to will. The movement toward the proper end is the movement according to nature and it is performed by mind out of love; the movement toward the beginning and cause of beings is movement in accordance to will that is performed by reason (*logos*) for the purpose of gaining knowledge.[28] Maximus acknowledges the abilities of reason to know God by claiming that even if the rational being moves toward its beginning, it does not flow away from God, but it reaches God as its proper beginning and cause.[29] Maximus describes the movement in accordance to nature as ecstasy over what is loved that intensifies movement of being until it is embraced wholly by the object of its love and desire.[30] The movement driven by a creature's desire and will to understand its own purpose and the source of existence is a proper movement only if a) there is no end toward which it can be moved and b) it is moved in no other way than toward its beginning.[31] This explains to a certain degree that the movement of mind as natural movement and the movement of reason as movement of will are not alternative one to another, but rather complementary, because they both end in the Logos of God.

The movement of reason or will, as different from natural movement, is not directed out of the rational being, but it remains within the borders of the definition imposed by its own *logos*. By striving to understand its own *logos*, the human being experiences certain delimitations, because it[32] initiates processes of establishing its existence not only on its particular *logos*, but also on the higher *logoi* of species and genera. By attaining the most general *logos* of being, the human being realizes that its beginning is nowhere else than in the Logos of God. Therefore, Maximus states that the human being should not move toward any other end than its beginning.[33] However, by ascending

27. *Amb.* 7, 1073C.
28. *Amb.* 7, 1073C.
29. *Amb.* 7, 1080C.
30. *Amb.* 7, 1073D.
31. *Amb.* 7, 1080C; Blowers & Wilken, 56.
32. My usage of the third person singular pronoun "it" for the "human being," is actually in compliance with Maximus' theology. Maximus himself uses pronoun τό in order to stress that a human person after transcending sexual differentiation is neither "he" nor "she;" *Amb.* 41, 1304D. See A. Louth, 155, 211, n. 8.
33. *Amb.* 7, 1080C; Blowers & Wilken, 56.

the hierarchical structure of *logoi* that ends in attaining union with the Logos of God, the rational being does not enter in the highest union with God. Maximus points out that the *logos* of being and the mode of existence of each rational being acquire their purpose only in the light of the Incarnation of the Logos:

> As earlier, neither by the mode [of existence], nor by the logos of essence nor by the hypostasis, according to which all the beings are considered in general, the nature had found the unity of God, now it is hypostatically one with God through the ineffable union, while by maintaining unchanged its proper logos, which is different from the divine essence, it has a union based on hypostatical unity and difference. So by the logos of being, in which it became and in which it is, it continues to be itself properly and without diminishing, and also, by the logos of how it is, it takes hold of its divine foundation, without inclining toward anything else that it may know or may be attracted to. Thus, the Logos has accomplished a more paradoxical communion with human nature from the earlier one, by essentially uniting this nature with Him in one hypostasis.[34]

Not only the movement of rational being toward its cause, but also the natural movement toward God as its goal is understandable only through the Incarnation. By natural movement the rational being *moves out of itself* (this is the literal meaning of *exstasis*) and it enters the union with its objects of love, which is God. This movement is natural, because it constitutes the ontological structure of human being, which bears the icon and likeness of God. Maximus' claim that "God and the human being are paradigms one of another" and "that as much as God is humanized to human being through love for humankind, so much is the human being able to be deified to God through love,"[35] actually explains that the human being is created to establish its own existence not on itself, but on God. Therefore, the Incarnation of God is prerequisite for establishing humanity as deified:

> He who, by the sheer inclination of his will, established the beginning of all creation, seen and unseen, before all the ages and before that beginning of created beings, had an ineffably good plan for those creatures.

34. *Amb.* 36, 1289CD: Πρότερον μὲν γὰρ κατ᾽ οὐδὲν τρόπον ἢ λόγον οὐσίας ἢ ὑποστάσεως, τῶν ἐν οἷς τὰ ὄντα πάντα καθολικῶς θεωρεῖται, τὸ ἕν πρὸς τὸν Θεὸν ἡ φύσις εἰλήφει, νῦν δὲ τὸ καθ᾽ ὑπόστασιν ἕν πρὸς αὐτὸν διὰ τῆς ἀφράστου ἑνώσεως ἔλαβε, τὸν οἰκεῖον δηλαδὴ κατὰ τὴν οὐσίαν ἀναλλοιώτως πρὸς τὴν θείαν οὐσίαν διάφορον διαφυλάττουσαν λόγον, πρὸς ἣν ἔχει διὰ τῆς ἑνώσεως τὸ καθ᾽ ὑπόστασιν ἕν καὶ διάφορον, ἵνα τῷ μὲν τοῦ εἶναι λόγῳ, καθ᾽ ὃν γεγένηται καὶ ἔστι, διαμένοι τὸ ἑαυτῆς ὂν κυρίως ἔχουσα κατὰ πάντα τρόπον ἀμείωτον, τῷ δὲ τοῦ πῶς εἶναι λόγῳ τὸ ὑφεστάναι θεϊκῶς λαβοῦσα τῆς περὶ τι ἄλλο κινήσεως τὴν ῥοπὴν παντελῶς μήτε γινώσκῃ, μήτε προσίηται. Ταύτῃ γοῦν πολὺ τῆς προτέρας παραδοξοτέραν τὴν πρὸς τὴν φύσιν τῶν ἀνθρώπων ὁ λόγος ἐποιήσατο κοινωνίαν, αὐτὴν τὴν φύσιν οὐσιωδῶς ἑαυτῷ καθ᾽ ὑπόστασιν ἑνώσας.
35. *Amb.* 10, 1113B; A. Louth, 98.

> The plan was for him to mingle, without change on his part, with human nature by true hypostatic union, to unite human nature to himself while remaining immutable, so that he might become a man, as he alone knew how, and so that he might deify humanity in union with himself.[36]

The union established between divine and human nature by the Incarnation of Logos is a union much higher than the union that the human being had with God in paradise. Moreover, the second union has been already established in the person of Christ and it should be accomplished by the whole humanity. Therefore, the goal of humanity is not given by creation, but rather by the Logos' incarnation, because the hypostatic union between the two natures in Christ models the nature of the future union between God and human being.

III. Incarnation of Logos as creative and preservative procession

As we have seen above the Incarnation of Logos can be perceived both as creative and preservative procession (ποιητικὴ καὶ συνεκτικὴ πρόοδος).[37] However, it is difficult to distinguish between the preservative and creative elements in Christ's procession, because sometimes he preserved what he did not create in order to glorify human nature, and sometimes he recreated what became so characteristic of creation. Generally speaking, the preserving procession consists in Christ's preservation of the human nature in its original state, but since Christ paradoxically took the nature, which he did not create, the nature of fallen Adam,[38] this is not the nature he wanted to preserve intact. Similarly, the creative procession reveals Christ's creative activity in endowing the human nature with something new, which it has lacked previously, but which was a part of the ontological structure of humanity. In order to improve human nature Christ had to preserve it first by returning it to its original state. The preservation of human nature means its restoration to the previous state of incorruptibility. However, this restoration into previous state happened by various methods, some of them applicable to the original plan, and some of them not. For example, Christ is conceived without intercourse[39] and born by a virgin without corruption.[40] By alluding to Gregory the Theologian's *Sermon* 39.13 Maximus describes the preservation of the ontological structure of humanity as "instituting nature

36. *Quaestiones ad Thalassium (= Ad Thal.)* 22, in: C. Laga, C. Steel, eds., *Maximi Confessoris Quaestiones ad Thalassium*, Corpus Christianorum. Series Graeca 7, Turnhout: Brepols 1980, 137; Blowers & Wilken, 115.
37. *Amb.* 7, 1081C.
38. *Ad Thal.* 54, CCSG 7, 459.
39. *Amb.* 10, 1141D; A. Louth, 115.
40. *Amb.* 41, 1313C; A. Louth, 160.

afresh."[41] The "new" way of human generation rather pertains to the preservation of human nature, than to its recreation, because it does not change the *logoi* of nature, but only the modes (*tropoi*) of its existence.

According to Maximus, by being born in sinless way, Christ avoids the sin itself, but not the liability to passions:

> Taking on the original condition of Adam as he was in the very beginning, he was sinless but not incorruptible, and he assumed, from the procreative process introduced into human nature as a consequence of sin, only the liability to passions, not the sin itself.[42]

Therefore, Christ assumed the corrupted and mortal nature of Adam, but he did not assume the sin that is associated with it. Thus, by being liable to passions he was able to heal the consequences of sin, without being sinful. For Maximus, Christ broke the link between liability to passions and unnatural passions. He defeated the passions connected to pleasure while being tempted in the desert, and the passions connected to pain, by experiencing death on the cross.[43] Therefore, Christ's triumphant victory over evil passion is connected with his death on the cross, because when his soul departed the evil powers could not find anything sinful in the passibility proper to human nature.[44] Christ restored all original human powers by saving the image of God in the human being, by making human flesh immortal and by cleaning the human nature from evil.[45] The victory on the cross is the climax in the process of procession,[46] but it is also the beginning of the process of proper conversion, because by freeing human nature from the evil he instituted the possibility for immortality of the human flesh.

IV. Converting and Hand-leading Transference (ἐπιστρεπτικὴ καὶ χειραγωγικὴ ἀναφορά)

The process of the converting transference (ἐπιστρεπτικὴ ἀναφορά) begins with the decision made by the rational being to move toward its cause

41. *Opuscula Theologica et Polemica* (= *Opusc.*) 3, PG 91, 48C; *Amb.* 5, 1049B–1052B; *Amb.* 31, 1273D–1276D; *Amb.* 41, 1313CD. See also A. Louth, 50–53.
42. *Ad Thal.* 21, CCSG 7; 129: ἐκ μὲν τῆς κατὰ τὴν γένεσιν τοῦ Ἀδὰμ πρώτης συστάσεως λαβὼν εἶχε δίχα τῆς ἀφθαρσίας τὸ ἀναμάρτητον, ἐκ δὲ τῆς ὕστερον διὰ τὴν ἁμαρτίαν ἐπεισαχθείσης τῇ φύσει γεννήσεως μόνον εἴληφε δίχα τῆς ἁμαρτίας τὸ παθητόν; Blowers & Wilken, 111.
43. *Ad Thal.* 21, CCSG 7; 131.
44. *Ad Thal.* 21, CCSG 7; 131.
45. *Ad Thal.* 54, CCSG 7; 459: ἵνα καὶ τὴν εἰκόνα σώσῃ καὶ τὴν σάρκα ἀθανατίσῃ καί, τὸν ἐνηχηθέντα τῇ φύσει λόγον τοῦ ὄφεως παντελῶς ἐξαφανίσας, ὡς ἐξ ἀρχῆς καθαρὰν κακίας πάλιν παραστήσῃ τὴν φύσιν.
46. The symbolical significance of the cross is often underlined in the Orthodox iconography by the iconographer's replacement of biblically more accurate form of the inscription nailed on the cross above Christ's head "Jesus the Nazarean, King of the Jews" with the form "The Jesus the Nazarean, King of Glory." The iconographer releases himself from the historical necessity, not only by showing that the theological significance of the cross lies in the resurrection, but also that the human nature is already restored to its glory at the cross.

and beginning or its proper end. In both cases the final destination of this movement will be God. While by returning to its cause and beginning the rational being will find the purpose of its existence or its own *logos*, by moving toward its proper end or the final union with God, apart from knowing the purpose of its creation, the rational being will also know the way how to fulfill this purpose. By his incarnation, the redemptive work of the preservation of human nature in its original state and the deification of human nature, Christ has shown the way, which every human being should take in order to become deified. Therefore, the process of conversion of creation toward God has already started in Christ, who has reoriented humanity toward God. Christ has reoriented humanity toward God, because previously Adam had oriented human nature toward creation expecting to find in nature the purpose of his being and the proper end of his movement. Christ not only converted (ἐπιστροφήν) human nature toward God, but he also led it step by step until he finally offered it to the Father. Therefore Maximus instead of using the Neoplatonic term (ἐπιστροφή), opts for more precise terms such as "the converting and hand-leading transference or offering" (ἐπιστρεπτικὴ καὶ χειραγωγικὴ ἀναφορά). In order to achieve this final union with God, preconceived before the ages, every human being should follow Christ's path:

> For whoever does not violate the *logos* of his own existence that pre-existed in God *is* in God through diligence; and he *moves* in God according to the *logos* of his well-being that pre-existed in God when he lives virtuously; and he *lives* in God according to the *logos* of his eternal being that pre-existed in God. On the one hand, insofar as he is already irrevocably one with himself in his disposition, he is free of unruly passions. But in the future age when graced with divinization, he will affectionately love and cleave to the *logoi* already mentioned that pre-existed in God, or rather, he will love God himself, in whom the *logoi* of beautiful things are securely grounded. In this way he becomes a "portion of God," insofar as he exists through the *logos* of his being which is in God and insofar as he is good through the *logos* of his well-being which is in God; and insofar as he is God through the *logos* of his eternal being which is in God, he prizes the *logoi* and acts according to them. Through them he places himself wholly in God alone, wholly imprinting and forming God alone in himself, so that by grace he himself "is God and is called God." By his gracious condescension God became man and is called man for the sake of man and by exchanging his condition for ours revealed the power that elevates man to God through his love for God and brings God down to man because of his love for man. By this blessed inversion, man is made God by divinization and God is made man by hominization. For the Word of God and God wills always and in all things to accomplish the mystery of his embodiment.[47]

47. *Amb.* 7, 1084BD; Blowers & Wilken, 59–60.

Maximus identifies a few steps on the human being's path to achieve the final union with God. The first step for every human being is to acknowledge its *logos* of being and not to go against it. The next step consists in a virtuous life and it represents acting in accordance with the *logoi* of well being that preexist in God for every human being. The final step of every human being is the realization of its *logos* of eternal being or achieving eternal life. All three steps of the human progression toward the final union with God resemble the whole divine design with the Incarnation of the Logos as the central point.

The process of the descent of the Divine into human beings that is considered as the procession has not begun with the Incarnation, but it has begun with the creation and it reached its peak in the Incarnation. Similarly, the process of the deification of human nature that can be identified with the conversion did not end when Christ, with his redeemed (= preserved) human nature, became seated "at right side of the Father." The process of conversion should be the process of the deification of whole human kind and it has not yet come to an end. Therefore Maximus claims that God divided the whole history into two periods, one intended for God to become human, and another intended for humanity to become divine.[48] The event that divides, but also unites these two periods, by giving meaning to the whole history at the same time, is the Incarnation of Logos in the person of Jesus Christ and His salvific work that culminated in his Crucifixion, death and Resurrection. For Maximus these historical events symbolize the ontological structure of the entire creation:

> The one who knows the mystery of the cross and the tomb knows the principles of these creatures. And the one who has been initiated into the ineffable power of the Resurrection knows the purpose for which God originally made all things.[49]

Maximus actually states that the mystery of the cross hides the *logoi* of the sensible nature, while the mystery of the tomb hides the *logoi* of intelligible nature. The cross signifies the separation of everything perceived by senses and the tomb represents the withdrawal of mind from everything conceived by mind. Only by a total denial of everything perceived by senses and mind can the soul recognize the *logoi* of creation, which are beyond everything created. As the Resurrection links the cross and the tomb by explaining their purpose, the final unity of the Logos and *logoi* as preconceived by God from eternity explains the coexistence of the sensible nature together with the intelligible nature. Maximus' parallel between the cross, the tomb and the Resurrection and the *logoi* of sensible nature, *logoi* of intelligible nature and the providence regarding the final union between the Logos and the *logoi* demonstrates that Christ's conversion is also the conversion of the entire creation toward the final union with God.

48. *Ad Thal.* 22, CCSG 7; 137; Blowers & Wilken, 115.
49. *Capita Theologica et Oeconomica* (= *Cap. Gnost.*) I, 66, PG 90, 1108; G. C. Berthold, 140.

Although Christ's Resurrection is the summit of the historical *Triduum* – Good Friday, Holy Saturday, and Easter Sunday, as well as the highest of the three stages of the Christian life, ascetic struggle, natural contemplation, and mystical theology[50] – Maximus stresses that the resurrection is a *re-formation* of nature that surpasses creation in paradise, generally, due to the unchangeability of all, and specifically, due to the inexpressible deification of the saints by grace.[51]

Moreover, Maximus distinguishes between the resurrection of Christ and the resurrection of all or to be precise between Christ's salvific deeds and their appropriation by all:

> It is also said that the first Sunday (= Pascha) is the symbol of the future physical resurrection and incorruptibility, while the second Sunday (= Antipascha) conveys the icon of the future deification by grace. If, therefore attaining of the goods is preferred than the moral purification from the evils, and possessing the perfection of true knowledge than healthy and virtuous inclination, and regeneration by the deification and grace than the incorruptibility of nature, of which the first Sunday conveys the type, and the second Sunday is symbol, then the teacher [Gregory the Theologian], guided by the Spirit, rightly called the Sunday of renewal higher than the sublime one.[52]

It is valuable to notice another terminological invention employed by Maximus. He does not use the term ἐπιστροφή but he replaces it with the more precise term ἀντιστροφή. While the term "conversion" (ἐπιστροφή) describes just the process of the human being's return to God, the process of "reversion" (ἀντιστροφή) refers to the process of God's hominization as well as to that of the human being's deification. The term "reversion" (ἀντιστροφή) deals also with the final result of these corresponding processes.

The "reversion" (ἀντιστροφή) is not only a term that expresses the reciprocity or correspondence between two periods, one from the creation of the world to Christ's death on the cross, and another from Christ's Resurrection to the final deification of all creation, but it also describes the final result of these two processes. As the final result of the process of the hominization

50. *Cap. Gnost.* I, 55. Cf. also A. Louth, "Ecclesiology of St Maximos the Confessor," *International Journal for the Study of the Christian Church* 4, 2 (2004) 109–120: 114.

51. *Ad Thal.* 54, CCSG 7, 475: Ἡ ἀνάστασις ἀνάπλασίς ἐστι τῆς φύσεως, πλεονεκτοῦσα τὴν τῆς φύσεως ἐν τῷ παραδείσῳ διάπλασιν· γενικῶς μέν, τῇ καθ̓ ὅλου τῶν ὅλων ἀντρεψίᾳ· ἰδικῶς δέ, τῇ κατὰ χάριν ἀῤῥήτῳ θεώσει τῶν ἁγίων.

52. *Amb.* 63 PG 91, 1388–1389B: Καὶ αὖθις τὴν μὲν πρώτην Κυριακήν τῆς μελλούσης φυσικῆς ἀναστάσεως καὶ ἀφθαρσίας εἶναι σύμβολον, τὴν δὲ δευτέραν τῆς κατὰ χάριν μελλούσης θεώσεως φέρειν εἰκόνα. Εἰ τοίνυν τῆς μὰν καθαρευούσης κακῶν ἕξεως ἡ τῶν ἀγαθῶν ἀπόλαυσίς ἐστι τιμιωτέρα, τῆς δὲ κατ' ἀρετὴν ὑγιοῦς προαιρέσεως ἕξις τῆς κατὰ τὴν ἀληθῆ γνῶσιν τελειότητος, καὶ τῆς φυσικῆς ἀφθαρσίας ἡ ἐν χάριτι πρὸς τὸν Θεόν κατὰ τὴν θέωσιν μεταποίησις, ὧν ἡ μὲν πρώτη Κυριακὴ φέρει τύπον, ἡ δὲ δευτέρα τυγχάνει σύμβολον, εἰκότως ὑψηλῆς ὑψηλοτέραν ἀγόμενος πνεύματι, τὴν καινὴν ὁ διδάσκαλος ἔφη Κυριακήν. The same text occurs in *Amb.* 10, PG 91, 1176A.

of God was the hypostatic union between divine and human nature in Jesus Christ, thus the final result of the process of the deification of human being should be also the hypostatic union between divine and human nature in every human being. Here it is important to stress that the process of deification is the common work of God and the human being, like the process of the Incarnation of Logos was the common work of God and human beings, or in the last instance the work of the Holy Spirit and Mary, the Mother of God. In both, the Incarnation of Logos and the deification of humanity, God takes a leading or hand-leading (χειραγωγική) role.

> For He accepted to be unchangeably created in the form like us and through his immeasurable love for humankind to become type and symbol of Himself, and from Himself symbolically to represent Himself, and through the manifestation of Himself to lead to Himself in His complete and secret hiddenness the whole creation.[53]

The human being is led by God to the final union with him and on this course it "becomes God, being made God by God."[54] Maximus describes this process of deification as the transference (ἀναφορᾷ) of all created beings in the union with God, in which beings become united without confusion (ἀσυγχύτως) among themselves and with God.[55] Maximus prefers more the term "transference" (ἀναφορᾷ) than the term "conversion," for at least two reasons. Firstly, the "transference" (ἀναφορά) or the whole phrase "converting and hand-leading transference" (ἐπιστρεπτικὴ καὶ χειραγωγικὴ ἀναφορά) refers not to one, but rather to two agents in this process. It is obvious that the conversion takes place in the created rational beings (humans and angels), but the guidance of the transference belongs to God. Secondly, the term ἀναφορά apart from "transference" means "offering" and in this context is exclusively employed in the liturgy. This term again refers to certain cooperation between God and rational beings, because if there is offering it should be also a reception of this offering. Thus, rational beings offer themselves and the whole of creation back to God who receives them and bestows deification upon them.

In conclusion, Maximus randomly employs the Neoplatonic philosophical notions of "procession" and "conversion," but even then it is obvious that these terms are used in a strictly Christian context and with different meanings. In many cases the adaptation of the Neoplatonic notions was followed by the invention of additional terms or synonyms meant to capture

53. *Amb.* 10, 1165D: Εἴδει γὰρ αὐτὸν καθ ἡμᾶς ἀτρέπτως κτισθῆναι δι' ἄμετρον φιλανθρωπίαν καταδεξάμενον ἑαυτοῦ γενέσθαι τύπον καὶ σύμβολον, καὶ παραδεῖξαι ἐξ ἑαυτοῦ συμβολικῶς ἑαυτόν, καὶ δι' ἑαυτοῦ φαινομένου πρὸς ἑαυτὸν ἀφανῶς πάντη κρυπτόμενον χειραγωγῆσαι τὴν ἅπασαν κτίσιν καὶ τῆς ἀφανοῦς [...]; A. Louth, 132. The idea of God as χειραγωγός can be also found in Dionysios the Areopagite. See *De divinibus nominibus* 3, 11, PG 3, 694D.
54. *Amb*, 7, 1084A: [...] ὅν γίνεται Θεός, ἐκ τοῦ Θεοῦ τὸ Θεός εἶναι λαμβάνων [...].
55. *Amb*, 7, 1077C: [...] τῇ πρὸς αὐτὸν τῶν πάντων ἀναφορᾷ δι' ἑαυτὸν ἀσυγχύτως ὑπάρχοντα.

the complexity of the Christian message. Maximus supplements the Neoplatonic notion of procession with the attributes "creative" and "preservative" in order to underline the permanence of the divine presence in the world. By replacing the term "conversion" with the term "reversion," Maximus shows how the incarnated God concluded the process of procession and initiated the process of conversion. Finally, Maximus expresses the process of the return in terms of offering (ἀναφορά) clearly showing that God and creation equally contribute to this process. These are the major transformations that these Neoplatonic terms underwent on the ontological level in the work of St. Maximus the Confessor.

Mystagogy - Today

Gorazd Kocijančič

In a recently published volume of conversations with Dan Arbib, the well-known French phenomenologist, Jean-Luc Marion, stressed the philosophical significance of exploring the patristic heritage, inasmuch as it differs from the discourse that has established itself in the later part of European thought, and specifically in its onto-theological structure, the structure of "metaphysics" (in Martin Heidegger's sense of the word).

> [...] the Fathers find themselves in a pre-metaphysical position, and so not yet in the metaphysical position that we undoubtedly are no longer really in. In the era of the Fathers, metaphysics had not yet constituted itself as a system; today one might reasonably say that, historically, this constitution is accomplished with Duns Scotus and extends until Nietzsche. The Fathers, essentially, are evidently thinking before this system of metaphysics, and even without knowledge of its medieval foundation, with the corpus of Aristotle as it was variously, successively introduced. We ourselves are beginning to enter into a post-metaphysical condition. It is not that we are already freed from metaphysics, nor that we have truly surpassed it; rather, it is at least because we can no longer confine ourselves to it and survive on the repetition of the system and language of metaphysics. So we could perhaps enter into a privileged rapport with the Fathers, on the condition that the Fathers of the Church do not remain devalued.[1]

A certain part of the Byzantine philosophical heritage was surely not immune to the temptation of onto-theological metaphysics, in which God is conceived as Supreme Being, and the logos as the capacity for universal argumentation, with which man is endowed even when intelligible reality is concerned, without regard to his life and concrete experiences. In particular, I have in mind the part of this philosophical heritage that was under the predominant influence of Aristotelianism and that defined a certain Byzantine scholasticism.[2]

1. J.-L. Marion, *La rigueur des choses, entretiens avec Dan Arbib*, Paris : Flammarion 2012, 213.
2. Although even in this regard, scholars have recently been uncovering profound creative breaks with Aristotle within Byzantine Aristotelianism, cf. especially D. Bradshaw, *Aristotle East and West: Metaphysics and the Division of Christendom*, Cambridge, New York: Cambridge University Press 2004. On the importance of commentators of Aristotle for Maximus, see A. Louth, "Recent Research on St Maximus the Confessor: A Survey," *St Vladimir's Theological Quarterly* 42, 1 (1998) 73–74.

Still, we find in the most important thinkers of Byzantium an entirely different kind of thought that transcends the system of metaphysics as onto-theology. The key to this kind of thought is the *concept of symbol.* In its wider usage, symbol – not the expression, but the concept, which is at once a practice and a way of thinking expressed in the whole spectrum of words – not only defines an important part of Byzantine philosophy, it also shapes the basic mould of meaning in Byzantine exegesis, iconography and architecture, perhaps in Byzantine culture generally.

The decisive question that poses itself to the modern philosophical reader who is "beginning to enter into a post-metaphysical condition" is whether this concept is only a Byzantine transformation of (a vulgar understanding of) Platonist onto-theology, which sees in the sensible reality of images, words, and metaphors the reflection of intelligible, existing realities, of beings (*tà ónta*). Is Byzantine thought, in its understanding of symbol, simply a Christianized Platonism? Or is there, at least at times, something radically different at play?

For the answer to this fundamental hermeneutical question of our day, which will define our global understanding of Byzantine philosophical thought and our fundamental horizon for reading its texts, it is worth turning to the *Mystagogy* of St. Maximus the Confessor.

* * *

The *Mystagogy*, the "initiation into the mystery," is the most condensed presentation of the basic thoughts of Maximus the Confessor apart from his *Short Commentary on the Lord's Prayer*, and hence "a good introduction to the Confessor's central concern."[3] This short writing namely contains "the entire anthropological and cosmological theory of St. Maximus, sketched in its

3. "[...] *das zentrale Anliegen des Bekenners*;" H.-U. von Balthasar, *Kosmische Liturgie. Das Weltbild Maximus des Bekenners*, Einsiedeln: Johannes-Verlag ²1961, 345. For a bibliography of publications, translations and discussions of the *Mystagogy*, see J.-Cl. Larchet, *Saint Maxime le Confesseur (580–662)*, Paris : Cerf 2003, 68–69; M. Knežević, *Maximus the Confessor (580–662): Bibliography*, Belgrade: Institute for Theological Research 2012, 108–110. On our topic, see especially L. Thunberg, "Symbol and Mystery in St. Maximus the Confessor," in: *Maximus Confessor. Actes du Symposium sur Maxime le Confesseur, Fribourg, 2-5 septembre 1980*, édités par F. Heinzer et Chr. Schönborn, Paradosis. Études de littérature et de théologie ancienne 27, Fribourg, Suisse : Éditions Universitaires 1982, 285–308, especially 287–288; J.-C. Larchet, *La divinisation de l'homme selon Saint Maxime le Confesseur*, Paris : Cerf 1996, 426– 430 ; M.-L. Charpin-Ploix, *Union et différence. Une lecture de la "Mystagogie" de Maxime le Confesseur*, 2 vol., diss., Paris : Institut catholique et Université de Paris IV 2000 ; Ch. Boudignon, *La "Mystagogie" ou traité sur les symboles de la liturgie de Maxime le Confesseur (580-662). Édition, traduction, commentaire*, diss., Université de Provence (Aix-Marseille I, France) 2000 ; P. Mueller-Jourdan, *Typologie spatio-temporelle de l'"Ecclesia" byzantine. La Mystagogie de Maxime le Confesseur dans la culture philosophique de l'Antiquité tardive*, Vigiliae Christianae. Supplementum. Texts and Studies of Early Christian Life and Language 74, Leiden, Boston: Brill 2005; E. Ayroulet, "Maxime le Confesseur : Une compréhension symboliste et réaliste de l'eucharistie," *Théophilyon* XVI–2 (2011) 381–401 ; D. Haynes, *Grace and Metaphysics in Maximus the Confessor*, diss., Nottingham 2011, especially 265–270.

most condensed form,"[4] and thus also his ecclesiology in the most profound philosophical sense, since Maximus understands the human being and the cosmos on the ground of their "ecclesiality." By its very form - the text does not seek to be an expression of "original" thoughts, but a commemorative rehearsal of the spiritual contemplations of an unnamed "holy old man," a guardian of the Tradition,[5] a bearer of spiritual insights into the hidden life of the Church - the *Mystagogy* exhibits Maximus's super-individual, communal situatedness in the life of the Christian congregation (although for us, this only underlines the originality of his text).

The *Mystagogy*, along with the *Short Commentary on the Lord's Prayer* and *Ambigua*, was written in the 7th century, around 630 or a little earlier.[6] The interpretation of the liturgy presented in it is indebted to St. Dionysius the Areopagite's work *On the Ecclesiastical Hierarchy*, but in his own work Maximus concentrates more on the *symbolism* of the church *building* and the community gathered therein, and only then goes on to give an allegorical interpretation of some central places in the Eucharistic liturgy. In this, the Confessor's interpretation of the liturgy follows the tradition, but his anthropological and ascetic thoughts are a novelty in the mystagogical genre, as they are not as much an initiation into the mystery of the liturgy as they are an initiation into mystery *based on* the liturgy.[7] We can therefore recognize in it the basic structure of the Byzantine line of thought that sees a "forest of symbols" in nature as well as in history.[8]

4. D. Stăniloae, "Eisagogé," in: *Mystagogía toû hagíou Maxímou toű Homologetoû. Eisagogé, schólia... protopresbyteros Demétrios Stanilóe*, Athens 1973, 74.
5. This mysterious figure also appears in other works of Maximus, especially in *Ambigua* 1044AB, 1269D, 1272BD, 1288D, 1301B, 1349B, 1393B; in *Opusculum* 16; 91, 185D he is named "the venerable monk." I.-H. Dalmais, "Théologie de l'Église et mystère liturgique dans la Mystagogie de S. Maxime le Confesseur," in: *Papers Presented to the Sixth International Conference on Patristic Studies Held in Oxford, 1971, Part II, Classica et Hellenica, Theologica, Liturgica, Ascetica*, edited by E. A. Livingstone (*Studia Patristica*, vol. XIII = "Texte und Untersuchungen zur Geschichte der altchristlichen Literatur," Band CXVI), Berlin 1975, 145–153, suggests, that the mysterious old man might have been Sophronius of Jerusalem; a similar view was held by A. Sidorov, "Nekotorie zamečania k biografii Maksima Ispovednika", *Vizantiiskii vremennik* 47 (1986) 116–118. In his notes for the translation of the *Mystagogy*, however, Sidorov considers, in the light of the Syrian biography, that the old man might be Pantoleon, the abbot of the Lavra. Th. Nikolaou suggests that he has in mind some monk at the monastery of Chrysopolis or in the community of St. George at Cyzicus; cf. Th. Nikolaou, "Zur Identität des makários géron in der Mystagogia von Maximus dem Bekenner," *Orientalia Christiana Periodica* 49 (1983) 407–418.
6. D. Stăniloae, op. cit., 37.
7. Cf. I.-H. Dalmais, "Place de la 'Mystagogie' de saint Maxime le Confesseur dans la théologie liturgique Byzantine," in: *Papers Presented to the Third International Conference on Patristic Studies Held at Christ Church, Oxford 1959, Part III, Liturgica, Monastica et Ascetica, Philosophica*, edited by F. L. Cross (Studia Patristica, vol. V = "Texte und Untersuchungen zur Geschichte der altchristlichen Literatur," Band XC), Berlin 1962, 277–283.
8. A. Nichols uses this expression of Baudelaire's (though misattributed to Mallarmé) to characterize the thought of Maximus in *Byzantine gospel: Maximus the Confessor in Modern Scholarship*, Edinburgh: T&T Clark 1993, 191.

That forest is not hidden in the mist of the indefinite. Maximus is concerned with setting out the basic structure of the events of the history of salvation and of the Christian ascetic life. The cosmos is already in itself unified in its mysterious Meaning, the Logos, but in the drama of freedom that began with the creation of spiritual beings, particularly humans, and that ended mystically with the Divine Incarnation, it opened up the possibility of the most profound unification of created with Creator, of deification. In the Church – as the truth of all sociality – the general movement of the cosmos is at its most transparent; the seeds of Truth are everywhere, and yet it is only in Christ and in the Church of His saints that God as Unifier is most manifestly present. "The Church dwells at the bosom of the world, yet the world is also in the Church" – and as the former applies in the actual moment, whereas the latter is only as yet unrealized potentiality, we may say that "the world and the human beings participate in the Church only when they convert to the state of the true world and the true human being."[9]

* * *

If we wish to approach the *Mystagogy* philosophically, if we want to understand the "how" of Maximus's symbolical thinking,[10] which defies onto-theological metaphysics, two things in particular must be kept in mind:

1) the content of the prologue, in which he – with unsurpassable radicalism of expression – sets out *the content and structure of Christian apophaticism*, that is, the thought of God's radical ineffability and His incomparability with any created thing whatsoever;
2) the *Sitz im Leben of the Mystagogy in liturgy and prayer*, which defines the very state of the logos, the pre-reflexive "encodedness" of thought.

Maximus's conception of symbol rests entirely on these two points, but to us they are largely incomprehensible to the extent that we still remain trapped in the patterns of metaphysical thinking.

* * *

The Greek word *sýmbolon* is derived from the verb *symbállein*, which means "to cast (throw, put, place) together."[11] In antiquity, the symbol as

9. D. Stăniloae, ibidem.
10. Cf. J. G. Lollar, *"To See Into the Life of Things." The Contemplation of Nature in Maximus the Confessor's "Ambigua to John,"* ProQuest, UMI Dissertation Publishing 2012, 17: "what remains to be done... is to get 'inside' Maximus' way of thinking about the world in order to identify not simply what he thought, as that may be determined in the words he wrote, but how he thought."
11. For a more detailed philosophical analysis, compare P. Crome, *Symbol und Unzulänglichkeit der Sprache. Jamblichos-Plotin-Porphyrios-Proklos*, München 1970, 201–211 (Anhang: Zur Etymologie des Wortes Symbol); A. Riou, *Le monde et l'église selon Maxime le Confesseur*. Préface par M.-J. Le Guillou, Théologie historique 22, Paris : Beauchesne 1973, 108–110.

a sign of connection originally meant a wooden, stone or earthenware object that was broken when an agreement, a contract, or a ceremonial promise of friendship was made. If the friends or their children happened to meet after long years, they would put the broken object together again in order to "identify" themselves. This original meaning of the word, which denotes a conventionally defined sign connected with the act of or the wish for a communion, with a bare link between the absent and the present, or in general with "two becoming one,"[12] underwent many transformations in the history of Western thought, to the point that "the semantic dispersion of the symbol is such that we must despair of fully forming a conception of it."[13]

And yet it is more or less clear how such a conception is formed by our Zeitgeist.

Contemporary post-structuralist and analytic thought (as an expression and speculative condensation of the contemporary mentality of the Westerner) understands symbol in general as an entirely arbitrary connection, although it can be defined by a social or anthropological necessity. Symbol is the site where "the world" emerges as the common, intersubjective world, and yet its connection with an extra-linguistic reality remains completely insecure (at best). Following the Cartesian understanding of world, the *cogito* and its (ultimately quite irrational) transformations are understood as the final symbol of being, which on the metaphysical level gives grounds for varieties of the later iconoclastic reductionisms (including the Freudian-Lacanian one, which remains faithful to the mentality of the secularist Enlightenment). The symbol, as a possible "mirroring" of the Other in the human unconscious and conscious inwardness, may be acknowledged in its functionality, but never in its (meta)ontological referentiality.

* * *

The difficulties a modern philosophical reader has with understanding the *Mystagogy* begin on such an abstract level, even though it may seem to him that he is only struggling with the linguistic complexity or with the different ecclesial and cultural environment reflected in the text. In Maximus' text we are dealing with "symbols" in the wide-ranging semantics of different expressions,[14] yet they are surpassed by the fundamental *aporia*.

What, then, is that fundamental prejudice of ours that prevents us from getting close to the *Mystagogy*? In our instinctive conviction the *linguistic* symbol, which due to the universality of linguistic structures is key to all other symbols, comes into being with the duplication of the "reference"

12. "ein Einswerden-von-zwei;" P. Crome, *op. cit.*, 204.
13. G. Lardreau, s. v. "Symbole <gen.>", in : *Les notions philosophiques. Dictionnaire. Encyclopédie philosophique universelle*, Paris 1990, 2512.
14. These expressions, the nouns *eikón* and *sýmbolon* and the verbs *eikonízo* and *semaíno* as they are distributed through the text of the *Mystagogy* are analyzed in B. Bošković's "Ikoničnost u 'Mistagogiji' sv. Maksima Ispovednika," *Otačnik* IV, 1–2 (2010) 231–259 (tabulated on 238).

in language. The symbol arises with the mental or intuitive distinction by which we begin to distinguish the "figurative" sense of the word (or the image, the gesture, the act) from the "real," "literal" communicative reference, the reference of words to things in "everyday usage." And yet the referentiality of the symbol in all this remains questionable. Do all our symbolic words, images and gestures ultimately refer to themselves? Does the mystery of the *Mystagogy*, then, as an "initiation into mystery," the mystagogical understanding of symbol, ultimately lie in its self-referentiality, a kind of infinite *semeiosis* of an autism that does not know the shock of otherness?

In principle, the question of the relation of the "fictitious" meaning to "reality" has two possible answers, which we may express in a more or less sophisticated way. According to the first view, which expresses the everyday mentality, the modern *dóxa*, language is essentially one-dimensional: the "real" meaning must functionally correspond to objective reality; its criterion is the formal language of science. The figurative meaning is secondary, fictive, "poetic." According to the second conception, which traces its roots to mythical antiquity and finds its first speculative expression in Neo-Platonism, in medieval symbolic theology, and in modern times in the metaphysics of the Romantic era and its heirs, all the way to Heidegger and the hermeneutical school, it is just this poetic meaning that expresses the deeper truth of the world. "Poetry," which in the formal sense is a language of symbols, of "metaphors" (in the broad sense of the word), does not have a secondary status, as it recognizes that metaphors are not deficient or wrong namings; rather, it uses them to express the deep structure of reality, intuitive insights into the similarity of the different, and hence, by extrapolation, insight into the Logos of all things: creative, "poetic" thinking articulates the Being of being. Thought can creatively (re)create the (meta)ontological connection, can catch sight of "something" as something "other," despite their apparent difference.

But is this "other" in Maximus once again only the existing reality? A being among beings? Does the sight of something as something other remain trapped in metaphysics-as-Platonism?

* * *

The fundamental characteristic of Maximus's thought in the *Mystagogy* is that it embraces a conception of symbol that not only prepares the ground for the (meta)poetic experience of reality, but also transcends, in advance, the above-mentioned alternative (the post-structuralist rejection of the reality of symbol *versus* the hermeneutics of metaphor), without being surpassed by the insights of (post)modernity. With his understanding of symbol, Maximus also *ante litteram* transcends the contradiction between the (post)structuralist and linguistic/analytic movements that see nothing but text in the "world," and those approaches that continue to insist on a more or less sharp distinction between the word and the world ("reality") and seek to level this distinction with the analysis of various modes of meaning and signification.

As the prologue of his *Mystagogy* goes to show, Maximus the Confessor is well aware of the ontological aposteriority of symbols, their secondarity; but he nevertheless clearly understands symbols as actual *signs* of reality – "the signs of the elements that are never representable in themselves."[15] To him, therefore, the (liturgical) symbol is not merely a convention; yet it is also not something unconventional, it is not an ontological revelation, an onto-logical disclosure of beings. Maximus does not conceive of symbol as a language essentially inscribed into the cosmic order, and yet it is for him an epiphany of the transcendent Meaning in the world.[16]

Maximus thus precludes in advance any understanding of his symbolic thought within the framework of any ontotheology.

"God," the absolute Signified, can offer himself in His otherness, according to Maximus, only in such "signification" that cancels its own meaning in the sign of the Unknown. The radicalism of *apophasis*, in which he follows our and his great teacher Dionysius the Areopagite, transcends all meanings:

> Let my words and thoughts be guided by God, the only Mind/Meaning (*noûs*) of the intelligent and intelligible realities, the Word/Sense (*lógos*) of the speaking and the spoken realities and the Life of the living realities and those brought to life, who is and becomes everything to everyone because of the very existing and becoming things, but who for Himself is never and in no way nothing, and does not become anything of that which pertains to any of the existing and becoming things, as by His nature He does not have anything in common with any of the existing things. He therefore rather allows Non-Being (*tò mè eînai*) to be said of Him, on account of His Super-Being, as this designates him better (than Being). If we are to really get to know the difference between God and things, we have to understand that to posit the Super-Being is to remove the existing things, and to posit the existing things is to eliminate the Super-Being; we have to see that we indeed contemplate both names on Him, and yet neither is right; I speak, of course, of the names being and non-being. They are both truly right, since "being" posits God as the cause of all existing things; the other name ("non-being") entirely removes the transcendental Cause of being (*toû eînai*) from all existing things. And then again, neither one of them is truly right, as neither really presents what the Sought is in his very being (*ousía*) and nature (*phýsis*). It is appropriate that no existing or uttered or non-existing and non-uttered thing is close to the One who is united with none of the existing and uttered things as their natural cause, neither with the existing nor the non-existing things.

15. F. Schlegel, Frg. 1197; *Kritische Friedrich-Schlegel-Ausgabe, Paderborn 1959*, vol. XVIII.
16. The words of R. Bornert are therefore true, of course, on the one hand, but fundamentally mistaken on the other: "Avec toute la tradition platonicienne, Maxime voit dans l'image non pas tant le signe d'une réalité absente que cette réalité elle-même, rendue en quelque manière présente par le signe ;" R. Bornert, *Les commentaires byzantins de la divine liturgie du VIIe au XVe siècle*, Archives de l'Orient chrétien 9, Paris: Institut Français d'Etudes Byzantines 1966, 113–114.

Such apophatic radicalism transcends every modern idea of deconstruction. In this prologue (which is also a *prayer*) the Confessor clearly sets out what Otherness/Difference means to the ecclesial consciousness. The reality expressed by the metaphors of the logos is not only "unsuitably" signified on account of the problematic linguistic ideals of the doxic mentality and "scientific" philosophy. The unsuitability of signification is inscribed in the heart of the believing understanding of the linguistic symbol: it is annihilated by the intellectually unfathomable unsignifiability of God Himself, which is reflected also in the apophatic essence of every finite being.[17]

Symbolism, glimpsed in liturgy and observed in contemplation, cancels all the usual schemes of descriptive and/or metaphorical significations. The delimitation of the signifier and the signified, the distinction that enables the juxtaposition, "two becoming one,"[18] changes in the signification of the Unsignifiable into a series of signifieds *that discover the Signified in the foundation of the signifier*, in the fathomless, pre-ontological *a priori* of the subject of signification.

The *sym-bállein* of such a subject is fundamentally a *prayer*: devotion to the fathomless Signified on which it is founded and at the same time love, *agápe*, openness to the Christic closeness to others, as only that Christian who is fully a member of the Community "who by imitating God out of love for people (*philanthropía*) heals the suffering of those who suffer as is befitting for God, and who, by the saving Providence that is proportionate to Him, proves to be a human being who with regard to his internal state (*diáthesis*) has the same power as God."

The language of the *Mystagogy* "poetically" *traces* the meaning of the Whole, which due to its being founded in the Divine mystery becomes detached from every "object," but it still understands the symbol with an element of devotion, which differs from the pure play of imagination. The site where symbol can emerge as symbol is for Maximus therefore the *metapoetical* apophatic absence of the Beginning and the End, the lack of transparency, which does not exclude the *self-mediation of the Other* as Meaning in the reality of the praying and contemplating subject. The absence of a Beginning and an End, the opaqueness of Nothingness, and the absence of pure Being are changed through grace into the nearness of realised eschatology, into *liturgy*.

* * *

17. Cf. *Ambigua* 17, 1225C2–3: "What a thing is essentially therefore remains ineffable, for anything one might give as an answer to the question 'What is this?' could only be a certain attribute or collection of attributes that could just as well be attributed of an ox, a horse, or anything else."
18. Cf. P. Crome, *op. cit.*, 204.

This brings us to the second point: to the rootedness of Maximus's conception of the symbol in pre-reflexive experience, where the logos attains its incomparable tonality.

The liturgy of Orthodox Church begins with the words: "Blessed is the kingdom of the Father and of the Son and of the Holy Spirit," that is, with a greeting of the coming kingdom as well as with a doxology of the rule of God, which has already set in. The sym-bol thus radicalized enables the unfolding of re-lativity, a repeated re-lation: the phenomenon that shows itself to the heart is the heart of the Non-Phenomenal, the self-giving God-Man himself, "his flesh and blood:"

> On this blessed and all-holy bed is celebrated that thrilling mystery of unification in which God becomes one with the Church/soul and the soul becomes one flesh and one spirit with God. How can I marvel enough at You, O Christ, for Your Goodness (I dare not say "How can I glorify You?" for I have not enough strength even to marvel)?! "The two will become one flesh. This is a profound mystery – but I am talking about Christ and the Church,"[19] says the Apostle, and elsewhere: "Whoever is united with the Lord is one with him in spirit."[20]

With this understanding of symbol, the thought of Maximus – and this holds for symbolical Byzantine thought as a whole – is the guardian of the *ecclesial eucharistic experience* and its grateful and thankful speech. This is also the *Sitz im Leben* of the transformed philosophical logos. The depth of the ecclesial subject is for the Christian eucharistic experience the transparency of the Spirit itself, of the God who reveals Himself: the Holy, wholly Other, transcendent "God," the absolute principle of all beings, who is not only *Deus absconditus*, the hidden God, apophatic Nothingness, but also *Deus revelatus*, the revealed God, the God of splendor, the God that works in the history of revelation...

The ultimate unity that by offering itself "gives grounds" for the identity of the subject eludes us, as does the "ipseity" of the phenomena: we can only grasp the ungraspable relationality in its relation towards us and the phenomenality as our phenomenality.

For Maximus the very writing and reading of the disclosure of the world in the Christ event, that communion without mixing of the phenomenal and the Absolute, of the Unity itself and the manifold, has its sole authoritative exegesis, which is fulfilled in the repetition of the expected eschatological Event:

> The spiritual kiss that all greet with a shout is the advance image and description of the like-mindedness, the harmony and the identity of meaning of all with all in faith and love: this will come true with the revelation of the future ineffable goods, in faith and love – and for this reason

19. Eph. 5, 32.
20. *Mystagogy* 5; Cor. 6, 17.

> those who are worthy receive closeness/relatedness with the Word (*Lógos*) of God. For the mouth is *the symbol of the Word, by which all who partake of the Word as creatures sensitive to meaning/thought/the word, grow together with the first and the one Word, that is the cause of every word/thought.*

* * *

Thus in *Mystagogy* the wholeness of the natural, the historical and the linguistic in their "inspired" significations becomes the ineffable and unexplainable sým-bolon of the transcendent theandric Communion. The radical otherness of God is not petrified in its difference from the words/meanings; it is the very power over the logos – and the meaning (*logos*) itself:

> The soul strides onward and gathers in the one and only summit that uniformly embraces these meanings, namely, in the world of the Gospel, in which all meanings (*lógoi*) of providence and existing things pre-exist in harmony with one encompassing Power. Then the untroubled eyes of the mind that are beloved of God may come to see, based on divine perception, the Word (*Lógos*) of God coming to it from the heavens.

The horizon of symbolic thought in Maximus's perspective is not the discovered meaning of all beings or the absence of this meaning, but the disclosure of the apophatic Darkness into the light "that gives light to everyone" (John 1:9). In his interpretation of liturgical, cosmic and anthropic symbolism, therefore, Maximus can use methods quite similar to those of his biblical exegesis.[21]

The relevance of this symbolic thought can therefore only be understood within the horizon of a particular conception of truth: *Truth has a liturgical dimension*, as it finally discloses itself only in the church prayer, where ecclesiality prevents the error of individual self-will, but it is still aware that the "symbol" is a reflection of its syn-ergetic creativity with God.

Strict apophaticism is therefore only the first precondition for understanding Maximus's conception of symbol.

The second precondition is the shared "form of life," participation in the same liturgical movement, the discovery of the meaning of existence that is given by faith in Jesus as true God and true human being, and the joy that the Spirit gives to all who hold that belief: the joy over

> Jesus, my God and Savior, eternally absolutely full, who (though He cannot ever go out of Himself) wondrously brings me, a human being, back to Himself when I come to partake in salvation, or to put it better, who

21. R. Bornert, "Explication de la liturgie et interprétation de l'Écriture chez Maxime le Confesseur," in: *Papers Presented to the Fifth International Conference on Patristic Studies held in Oxford, 1967, Part I, Editiones, Critica, Philologica, Biblica, Historica, Liturgica et Ascetica*, edited by F. L. Cross (Studia Patristica, vol. X = "Texte und Untersuchungen zur Geschichte der altchristlichen Literatur," Band CVII), Berlin 1970, 323–327.

> brings me back to God, from whom I have received being (*tò eînai*) and toward whom I stretch myself, because I long to receive well-being as well. Whosoever may come to know this from his own experience/suffering of what has been said, will surely come to know from experience his own worth: namely, how that which (is created) according to the image is returned to the image (*eikón*) of God, what honor has been shown to the archetype of the image, how powerful is the mystery of our salvation and for whom Christ has died, how we may again remain in Him and He in us. (70–85)

Elsewhere – and even more radically – Maximus notes in a striking sentence that Christ is the absolute truth of the symbol because he is the symbol of himself:

> Christ, who is identical to us in his appearance (he accepted this being without changing it because of his infinite love for humanity), became *the image and the symbol of himself. He revealed himself as a symbol.* He took by the hand the entire creation through himself, who was revealed, because of himself, who remained completely hidden as if he had not revealed himself. And as an index of the infinity that does not reveal itself, that remains hidden beyond everything and that cannot be understood or expressed in any way or manner understandable to beings, he offered to man, because of his love towards man, the works of deification (*theourgíai*) by revealing himself in flesh. (*Ambigua* 1165D)

Liturgical-theurgical communion is thus for Maximus the site where the mystical "reference" of mystagogical discourse is uncovered. The Mystagogy, then, articulates its own peculiar *meta-ontology of symbolic reflection* with which it points us to the vanishing and self-giving, absently ever-present Reference of this reflection, to Christ, who as true God, true Man and head of the mystical Body enables a "correspondence" between God, the Church and the world:

> When someday we pass from the grace in faith to the grace of vision [...] God and our Savior Jesus Christ will change us into Himself, as he removes all the marks of our perishability and mercifully gives to us those archetypal mysteries that have only been shown to us by our sensible symbols here.[22]

This is not mere theology. Nor is it philosophy under the aegis of metaphysical ontotheology. Thanks to this bold and original conception of symbolism, the text of the *Mystagogy* is able, with timeless relevance, to disclose to us the

22. *Mystagogy* 20.

Christic character of Being itself:[23] *Being as such is a symbol*: ever more transparent in its giving and glorifying movement toward its eternal, apophatic Source.

Post-modern thinking can only close itself to this understanding of symbol because it *wants* to be closed, not because it has any kind of an argument.

Maximus's mystagogy remains as alive today as it was when it was written.

Translated by Christian Moe and Nike K. Pokorn

23. Cf. *Capita Gnostica* 1, 66, PG 90, 1108AB: "Therefore the mystery of the incarnation of the Word contains in itself the whole meaning of the riddles and symbols of Scripture, the whole significance of visible and invisible creatures. Whoever knows the mystery of the cross and the tomb knows the meaning of things. Whoever is initiated into the hidden meaning of the resurrection know the purpose for which God created everything in the beginning;" cf. also *Quaestiones ad Thalassium* 60, Corpus Christianorum. Series Graeca, 22, 73, 75, 79.

Transcendental Byzantine Body. Reading Dionysius the Pseudo-Areopagite, Gregory of Nyssa and Plotinus in the Unfolded Marble Panels of Hagia Sophia

Uroš T. Todorović

In an attempt to contribute to the understanding of the often elusive theological influences in the Byzantine art of the Pre-Iconoclastic period,[1] I shall focus in this study on the unfolded marble panels inside the interior of Hagia Sophia of Constantinople and particularly on the way in which their selection and the conception of their installation may have been influenced by the mystical teachings of Dionysius the Pseudo-Areopagite and possibly by those of Gregory of Nyssa. The likelihood of other, philosophical influences will also be considered, such as the teachings of Plotinus. In addition to the Proconnesian variegated marble, quarried on the island of Proconnesus, present-day Marmara in Turkey, a variety of stones in varied colours and from dif-

1. In the field of Byzantine art, especially in consideration of artworks from the early Byzantine period, one of the biggest challenges for art historians has been to detect and interpret the visual outcome of those influences which are mainly theological and differentiate them from influences which, although in part also theological, are primarily morphological and structural. Accordingly, in respect to the period from the emergence of early Christian art until the period preceding the Iconoclastic controversy, the demanding task of comprehensively relating particular theological ideas and trends to particular examples of art has yet to be accomplished. On the other hand, comparatively speaking, in this particular regard the period of Iconoclasm and the succeeding periods of Byzantine art have been examined more studiously. Among more recent publications which relate to Iconoclasm are the following: Brubaker 2012, Ivanovic 2010. There are numerous publications which discuss Byzantine art as it developed after the iconoclastic controversy. We indicatively note the following: L. Brubaker, *Vision and Meaning in Ninth Century Byzantium: Image as Exegesis in the Homilies of Gregory of Nazianzus*, Cambridge: Cambridge University Press 1999; R. Cormack, "Interpreting the mosaics of St Sophia at Istanbul," *Art History* 4, 2 (1981); A. Cutler, *The Hand of the Master: Craftsmanship, Ivory, and Society in Byzantium (9th–11th centuries).* Princeton: Princeton University Press 1994; O. Demus, *Byzantine Mosaic Decoration: Aspects of Monumental Art in Byzantium.* London: Routlidge and Kegan Paul 1948, [r]1976; H. C. Evans, W. D. Wixon, eds., *The Glory of Byzantium: Art and Culture of the Middle Byzantine Era, A.D 843–1261*, New York: The Metropolitan Museum of Art 1997; H. Maguire, *Rhetoric, Nature and Magic in Byzantine Art*, Ashgate: Variorum 1998.

ferent regions, such as Africa, Thessaly and Asia, have been selected for the abstractly designed sixth-century interior-decoration of Hagia Sophia.

The concept of book-matching or cutting the veined marble and unfolding it in order to create visual patterns seems to have originated in Hellenistic architecture and was applied in certain Late Roman buildings.[2] It is a process of splitting and unfolding a block of veined marble once, or multiple times, in order to create an extended repetition of the natural pattern of the marble. In Christian architecture, this ancient technique was employed from the period of Constantine the Great[3] until the late Byzantine period. For example, besides Hagia Sophia, it can be encountered in San Vitale of Ravenna (6th century), in Saint Demetrius of Salonica (reconstructed in 7th century), in Hosios Loukas near the town of Distomo in Greece (11th century), in Nea Moni on the Greek island of Chios (11th century) and in the church of Chora of Constantinople (rebuilt in the 11th century and renovated in 14th century).

The numerous sixth-century examples of the unfolded marble panels inside Hagia Sophia have been approached and interpreted by researchers in various ways. For example, they have been compared to the Rorschach test[4] and to the concept of Gestalt groupings,[5] and in her study entitled *The aesthetics of marble and coloured stone*, Bente Kiilerich argues that besides their beauty, these stones from three different continents (from Africa, from Thessaly and from Asia) "present a 'territorial' display of imperial power and might, suggesting the extent of Justinian's empire.[6]" The possible influence of the culture of ekphrasis and *encomium* (praise) on the way marbles in Hagia Sophia were perceived by the late antique viewer, has been discussed by John Onians, who argued that the development of imagistic capabilities which allowed viewers to observe naturalistic and anthropomorphic forms in the ab-

2. Pentcheva 2011: http://iconsofsound.stanford.edu/aesthetics.html
3. Kleinert 1979: 45–93.
4. Kiilerich 2006: 21–26. Explanation: The Rorschach test, named after its creator, Swiss Freudian psychiatrist and psychoanalyst Herman Rorschach (1884–1922), is a psychological test in which the subject observes inkblots while their perceptions are recorded and then analysed as part of a personality assessment. Given that these inkblots are made by symmetrical folding and pressing of the paper which is previously stained with ink, they are characteristic for their symmetry.
5. Halper 2001: http://www.perceptionweb.com/ecvp/ecvp01.pdf Explanation: Gestalt laws of grouping are a set of principles in psychology, organised into six categories: Proximity, Similarity, Closure, Good Continuation, Common Fate, and Good Form. They were first proposed in the 20th century by Gestalt psychologists who argued that the human mind is naturally predisposed to perceive patterns in the stimulus based on certain rules, and that humans naturally perceive objects as organised patterns and shapes. Irvin Rock (1922–1995) and Stephen E. Palmer have built upon the work of Max Wertheimer (1880–1943) and others and have identified additional grouping principles.
6. B. Kiilerich, "The Aesthetic Viewing of Marble in Byzantium: From Global Impression to Focal Attention," in: *Proceedings of the 21st International Congress of Byzantine Studies, London, 21-26 August 2006*, v. 1, 238. Note: Only a short abstract of Kiilerich's study was available before the publication of the present text.

stract features of veined marble, is owed to the increased role of ekphrasis.[7] Ekphrasis, or description, is an exercise of late antique rhetoric incorporated by the Byzantines as part of their primary education, even as late as the 15th century.[8] Ekphrasis could be employed to describe not just examples of art but also persons, deeds, times, places and many other things. Hence, Bissera Pentcheva has insightfully discussed the appearance of marble and gold in the sixth-century interior of Hagia Sophia while exploring also their psychological effect on the spectator as recorded in Byzantine ekphrasis and liturgical texts.[9]

Bearing in mind the variety of previous approaches to this topic, in this study I will attempt to demonstrate that there is a previously unexplored, distinct and indicative aesthetic connection between the concept of unfolded marble panels in Hagia Sophia of Constantinople and certain core aspects of transcendental teachings of Dionysius the Pseudo-Areopagite, such as the symmetric double semantics of apophatic terms in his writings, his idea of the infiltrating transcendental vision and the related concept of "divine darkness." Having said this, in this study I shall simultaneously discuss the relevant influence of both the writings of Plotinus and those of Gregory of Nyssa on Dionysius the Pseudo-Areopagite. This hypothesised connection may serve as an indicator that the sixth-century unfolded marble panels in Hagia Sophia embody entirely abstract and deliberately cryptic visual representations of theological meanings, as well as abstract representations of human presence and of God's presence, as phenomena which are owed to the influence of a centuries long development in theological discourse, which began in Neo-Platonism and matured in the writings of Dionysius the Pseudo-Areopagite.

As seen in *plate 1*, not just their size but also the treatment of many of these unfolded marble panels as a kind of natural ready-made icons, which is observed in their elaborate framing, undoubtedly indicates the iconic importance that their creators observed in them, as does the fact that they are installed in the entire ground floor and in sections of the gallery (*plates 14, 15, 16* and *17*).

Such immense emphasis on this creative enterprise could certainly not have been realised without the approval from Emperor Justinian and his qualified advisers, who were making their decisions regarding the interior of Hagia Sophia at a time when the teachings of Dionysius the Pseudo-Areopagite were exerting a rising influence on the meaning and function of the icon.

7. Onians 1980: 1–23. See also: J. Trilling, "The Image Not Made by Hands and the Byzantine Way of Seeing," in: *The Holy Face and the Paradox of Representation*, Villa Spelman Colloquia, 6, ed. H. Kessler and G. Wolf, Bologna 1998, 109–128.
8. See: R. J. H. Jenkins, "The Hellenistic Origins of Byzantine Literature," *Dumbarton Oaks Papers* 17 (1963) 39 ff., esp. 43, and M. Baxandall, *Giotto and the Orators*, Oxford 1971, 85.
9. Pentcheva 2011: 93–111.

Having said this, in the present study I shall try to accomplish the following two tasks that to the best of my knowledge have not previously been realised.

Firstly, I shall attempt to examine the possible ways in which the writings of Dionysius the Pseudo-Areopagite, as well as certain pre-existing ideas that he crystallised, could have exercised an aesthetic kind of influence on the concept and process of the cutting, selection and installation of unfolded panels of colourful veined marble that decorate the interior of Hagia Sophia. Given that there are no known Byzantine texts that record the actual aesthetic intentions behind the design of Hagia Sophia, rather than claiming the undoubted existence of such an influence, I primarily aim at pointing out the previously unexamined indicative parallels between the mystical teachings of Dionysius the Pseudo-Areopagite, Gregory of Nyssa as well as those of Plotinus and the unfolded marble panels in the interior of Hagia Sophia.

Secondly, by discussing these parallels, I shall aspire to explain the existence of a phenomenon that should best be understood as an entirely abstract Byzantine icon, one which is not essentially related to the iconoclastic ideas. Due to the theological influences that underpin it, which shall shortly be discussed, I have named this phenomenon *Transcendental Byzantine Body*.

The methodology of this study will entail comparing certain of Dionysius' ideas which regard notions of vision, transcendence and enlightenment and which can also be encountered in the writings of Gregory of Nyssa and to an extent in those of Plotinus, to the aesthetic characteristics observed in the sixth-century concept of unfolded marble panels in Hagia Sophia. The comparisons which shall be made are accompanied by visual demonstrations by which I aim to explain how in particular, in a practical sense, these theological ideas might have influenced the concept of unfolded marble panels in Hagia Sophia.

As is very well known, Hagia Sophia was built between 532 and 537 while the first known reference to the writings of Dionysius the Pseudo-Areopagite is found in the work of Severus of Antioch entitled *Adversus apologiam Juliani,* which scholars tend to date to 519 and which was translated into Syriac in 528. Although there is some disagreement regarding their dating,[10] it is not accidental that the writings of Dionysius the Pseudo-Areopagite historically emerged undoubtedly about a decade before the construction of Hagia Sophia and thereafter assumed a significant influence in the thought of the

10. For example, in her book entitled *Pseudo-Dionysius as Polemicist: The Development and Purpose of the Angelic Hierarchy in Sixth Century Syria*, Rosemary A. Arthur says: "Given that they are so sparse and localized, it is possible that the so-called references to Dionysius the Areopagite in the writings of Severus may be later interpolations by editors, or others who wished to prove that Dionysius was prior to Severus rather than contemporary with him. Similar attempts, by Liberatus of Carthage and others, to prove his 'antiquity' have been revealed." (105)

Church as well as in the realm of ecclesiastical arts. Of course, as was mentioned earlier, the basic concept of installing unfolded marble panels in order to create visual patterns is much older than both the writings of Dionysius and the church of Hagia Sophia.

However, as noted by Ernst Kitzinger in his study entitled *The Cult of Images in the Age Before Iconoclasm*, the adaptation of Neoplatonic philosophy to Christian needs, which is realised in the writings of Pseudo-Dionysius, provided a theoretical basis on which to build up a defence of Christian image worship[11] – and this could have easily influenced both the emerging and the already existing art techniques. For the present topic, this means that in Hagia Sophia, which was built about a decade after the appearance of Dionysius' writings, the connections to Dionysius' teachings and to the pre-existing ideas which his teachings entail, should be sought not so much in the basic concept and technique of unfolded marble panels but rather in the aesthetic particularities of the choices made in the selection and installation of these panels. Given that the topic is vast, I shall mainly discuss the type of the unfolded marble panels which consists of two rectangular pieces cut from the same block of marble and splayed in order to form antithetical patterns of veins (*plate 1*), while other types of combined marble panels in the interior of Hagia Sophia will be given more attention in the extended version of this study.

* * *

One of the simpler ways in which we could conceive of the concealed theoretical influence of apophatic theology on the conception of these unfolded panels of marble relates to the twofold meaning of apophatic terms used by Dionysius the Pseudo-Areopagite. For example, in his writings the apophatic or negative meanings which refer to God can and should also be understood as cataphatic or affirmative, that is, they can and should be understood as an affirmation of the state of lacking, which is stressed by the negative letter *a* in the beginning of such words, such as: *aoratos* (ἀόρατος), meaning invisible.[12]

Thus, although it is a negative name, *aoratos* simultaneously expresses an affirmation of the state of lacking visibility. In fact, in Orthodox tradition generally, regardless of whether one adheres to the apophatic or cataphatic method of theology, in each case, one symmetrically implies the other. This means that there are two equally important implications within adjectives such as "invisible," i.e. the first denoting the lack of visibility and the second confirming the invisibility. In order to translate this into a visual paradigm,

11. Kitzinger 1976: 120. In particular, Kitzinger states: "So far as clergy was concerned, the adaptation of Neoplatonic philosophy to Christian needs, which had been effected towards the end of the fifth century in the writings of Pseudo-Dionysius, provided a theoretical basis on which to build up a defence of Christian image worship."
12. The word ἀοράτῳ is used in the first chapter of the *Mystical Theology* by Dionysius the Pseudo-Areopagite.

we could imagine these two implications as two visual panels which complete one another simply by being joined together and thus showing that they in fact stem from and reflect the same experience and meaning (*plate 2*).

As seen in the comparison between *plate 2* and *plate 3*, this symmetric twofold meaning of Dionysius' apophatic terms could have possibly provided the creators of Hagia Sophia, Isidorus and Anthemius, or their assistants, with a particular inspiration in the process of cutting, selecting and installing the double marble panels, where in each individual case, the exhibited surface comprising a symmetrical pattern vividly presents the viewer with an open insight into a careful incision which was made in the single solid stone – being understood as a selected piece of matter that belongs to the sphere of God's Creation. As seen in *plate 3*, similarly to the twofold meaning of Dionysius' apophatic terms, the two sides of the split marble, although seemingly standing as antithetical to one another, exhibit the inside of a content of a single piece of matter, thus making a reference not so much to division or contradiction but rather to a sense of harmonious wholeness that can not be denied. This analogy can take us even further. According to Dionysius, God is not adequately approached simply by the earlier mentioned twofold meanings of apophatic terms, but is considered, as expressed in the last words of *Mystical Theology*,[13] to be beyond every denial, free from any limitation and beyond them all. In a manner which is to an extent comparable, at the first level of the concept of unfolded marble panels, the viewer is invited to literally enter the solid mass of the stone and thereby to also exercise vision of the otherwise closed and concealed content of matter which is created by God. In a sense, this can be understood as an attempt to look inside the concealed levels of Creation in order to learn about both its Creator and its numerous implications for Man himself.

Inside the Creation, that is inside the otherwise closed mass of the stone, as seen in *plate 4*, by exercising a bilateral, bird-kind of vision of the two sides, the viewer encounters abstract colourful veins which, as we shall see, can be interpreted in various ways. But before any interpretation takes place, the first level of this concept of seeing the inside of the stone offers the bare phenomenon itself – which speaks of nothing else but of its own self. A noteworthy parallel with Dionysius' writings can be detected. In particular, as insightfully noted by Moshe Barasch, in Dionysius' writings, "the symbolon, while never negating the difference between symbol and symbolised, represents mainly what they have in common. Symbolon, in his view, is not only a sign, but is actually the thing itself.[14]"

As can be observed in *plate 3*, when two marble panels are placed next to each other so that their colourful grains together form a symmetric pattern, that which is immediately achieved is a sense of order in the vision of the

13. Διονυσίου Ἀεροπαγίτου, *Περὶ μυστικῆς θεολογίας*, V, 150 (PG 3, 1048B).
14. Barasch 1992: 167.

otherwise apparently random-flowing content of Creation. Thus, while this is an exhibition of the concealed content of Creation, or of the thing itself, roughly speaking, there are two main points of minimal human intervention which took place before its installation within the interior of Hagia Sophia: (a) the cutting of the stone, or more precisely, the incision in the closed matter, and (b) placing of the two halves next to one another and exhibiting their so far unseen surface so that the act of incision can be perceived as an infiltrating, in-depth kind of vision. As shall be discussed in the following, this idea of the infiltrating vision is vividly reminiscent of Dionysius' teachings regarding the infiltrating, transcendental vision and divine *darkness*.

* * *

As noted by Lossky, even before specifically Christian exegesis, Philo of Alexandria, a Hellenised Jewish philosopher who lived in the 1st century BC and 1st century AD,[15] interpreted the darkness of Exodus as a condition of the knowledge of God.[16] As in regards to the Christian tradition, already in the writings of Clement of Alexandria (ca. 150–ca. 222/231), the darkness into which Moses entered according to the Book of Exodus,[17] represented the ultimate inaccessibility of God, and later, regarding this issue, the Cappadocians followed Clement instead of Origen.[18] However, unlike in Cappadocian thought which was developed in the 4th century, in Clement's writings which date to the late 2nd and early 3rd century, the idea of darkness is not so much representative of the incomprehensibility of the transcendent God as it is of the ignorance of the human reason about God. It was in fact Gregory of Nyssa, who in the 4th century employed the notions of ignorance and darkness as a means of experiencing the transcendent God.[19] After Gregory's contribution, in late 5th and early 6th century (three centuries after Clement) when Dionysius the Pseudo-Areopagite speaks of the divine *darkness,* he does not speak of ignorance, something that would place an emphasis on the necessity of intellectual kind of learning about God, but he understands this *darkness* as the Light which cannot be seen because it transcends human logic.[20] Thus, the "*darkness* of God" implies that man's logic is limited, which is why the term *gnofos* (γνόφος), which Dionysius uses for *darkness* in this context and which was used before him in a like manner by Gregory of Nyssa, is an antithetic

15. Born 15–10 BC, Alexandria – died AD 45–50, Alexandria.
16. http://www.apostoliki-diakonia.gr/en_main/catehism/theologia_zoi/themata.asp?cat=patr&NF=1&contents=contents_Texts.asp&main=texts&file=2.htm
17. "And the people stood afar off, and Moses drew near unto the thick darkness where God was" (Exodus 20:21).
18. Brooks 1958:108.
19. http://www.apostoliki-diakonia.gr/en_main/catehism/theologia_zoi/themata.asp?cat=patr&NF=1&contents=contents_Texts.asp&main=texts&file=2.htm
20. Διονυσίου Ἀεροπαγίτου, *Ἐπιστολαί*, V, 162[1–3] (PG 3, 1073A): "Ὁ θεῖος γνόφος ἐστὶ τὸ 'ἀπρόσιτον φῶς', ἐν ᾧ κατοικεῖν ὁ θεὸς λέγεται, καὶ ἀοράτῳ γε ὄντι διὰ τὴν ὑπερέχουσαν φανότητα καὶ ἀπροσίτῳ τῷ αὐτῷ δι' ὑπερβολὴν ὑπερουσίου φωτοχυσίας."

term that actually means *darkness of the light* (γνόφος τοῦ φωτός). More particularly, according to Dionysius, it is only by transcending the realm of logic that one can begin to experience God as Light – otherwise He is experienced as *darkness.* Also, he teaches that this transcendental process of experiencing God as Light is itself endless.

In chapter 2 of *Mystical Theology*, Dionysius instructs that through not seeing (δι' ἀβλεψίας) and through not knowing (καὶ ἀγνωσίας) we may arrive at the darkness which is beyond light (ὑπέρφωτον γνόφον). In the continuation of that text he uses an interesting metaphor by referring to the process of carving a marble statue, where the real emphasis is not so much on the statue but rather on the process of removal of the excess material which hinders the path of one's "clear vision." In fact, as we shall see, when the text is read analytically, it becomes clear that the metaphor implies that the "clear vision of the hidden" (τῇ καθαρᾷ τοῦ κρυφίου θέᾳ) is in fact synonymous with the deducting process of carving or chiselling. The metaphor of carving is of course much older than Dionysius. For example, there is the following similar passage by the Neoplatonist philosopher Plotinus, who lived in the 3rd century: "Withdraw into yourself and look; and if you do not find yourself beautiful as yet, do as does the sculptor of a statue [...] cut away all that is excessive, straighten all that is crooked, bring light to all that is shadowed [...] do not cease until there shall shine out on you the Godlike Splendour of Beauty; until you see temperance surely established in the stainless shrine."[21]

The analogous segment incorporating the carving metaphor from Dionysius' 2nd chapter of *Mystical Theology,* reads as follows:

> We pray that we may come unto this *gnofos* (darkness) which is beyond light, and that, through unseeing and through unknowing, we come to see and to know that which is above vision and knowledge, precisely through not-seeing and through not-knowing – because this in fact is the truthful seeing and knowing – and thus praise, superessentially, Him who is superessential, by the abstraction of all things, like those who, making a self-existent statue, deduct all the surrounding material that hinders the vision of the concealed, and simply by that abstraction, show the hidden beauty.[22]

21. *Ennead*, I. 6. 9. The original excerpt in Greek reads as follows: "ἄναγε ἐπὶ σαυτὸν καὶ ἴδε· κἂν μήπω σαυτὸν ἴδῃς καλόν, οἷα ποιητὴς ἀγάλματος, ὃ δεῖ καλὸν γενέσθαι, τὸ μὲν ἀφαιρεῖ, τὸ δὲ ἀπέξεσε, τὸ δὲ λεῖον, τὸ δὲ καθαρὸν ἐποίησεν, ἕως ἔδειξε καλὸν ἐπὶ τῷ ἀγάλματι πρόσωπον, οὕτω καὶ σὺ ἀφαίρει ὅσα περιττὰ καὶ ἀπεύθυνε ὅσα σκολιά, ὅσα σκοτεινὰ καθαίρων ἐργάζου εἶναι λαμπρὰ καὶ μὴ παύσῃ 'τεκταίνων' τὸ σὸν 'ἄγαλμα', ἕως ἂν ἐκλάμψειέ σοι τῆς ἀρετῆς ἡ θεοειδὴς ἀγλαΐα, ἕως ἂν ἴδῃς σωφροσύνην ἐν ἁγνῷ βεβῶσαν βάθρῳ."
22. Διονυσίου Ἀεροπαγίτου, *Περὶ μυστικῆς θεολογίας*, II, 145^{1-7} (PG 3, 1025AB): "Κατὰ τοῦτον ἡμεῖς γενέσθαι τὸν ὑπέρφωτον εὐχόμεθα γνόφον καὶ δι' ἀβλεψίας καὶ ἀγνωσίας ἰδεῖν καὶ γνῶναι τὸν ὑπὲρ θέαν καὶ γνῶσιν αὐτῷ τῷ μὴ ἰδεῖν μηδὲ γνῶναι – τοῦτο γάρ ἐστι τὸ ὄντως ἰδεῖν καὶ γνῶναι – καὶ τὸν ὑπερούσιον ὑπερουσίως ὑμνῆσαι διὰ τῆς πάντων τῶν ὄντων ἀφαιρέσεως, ὥσπερ οἱ αὐτοφυὲς ἄγαλμα ποιοῦντες ἐξαιροῦντες πάντα τὰ ἐπιπροσθοῦντα

Despite the fact that it was Plotinus who was first to understand not simply the activity but also the existence of the sensible world as dependent upon the One,[23] as can be observed through the comparison of the above citations, Plotinus understood matter as intrinsically evil, and through that understanding his philosophy noticeably reflects the old Platonic and Aristotelian dualism of two eternal principles that exist independently. Therefore, it is noteworthy that it is mainly from Plotinus and thereafter that the dividing gap between the sensible and noetic (intelligible) worlds is bridged,[24] and Dionysius in a sense concludes that process – and thus says in the 2nd chapter of *Celestial Hierarchy*, that it is lawful to portray Celestial Beings "in forms drawn from even the lowest of material things."[25] Having said this, it should also be noted that theological symbolism is very important in Dionysius' writings because within it, the symbol functions as a mediating experience through which meanings can be passed from the realm of the incomprehensible God to earth and through which man can anagogically ascend towards the incomprehensible God.

Therefore, Dionysius' originality is not to be detected in the metaphor of carving itself but in the particularity of the transcendental meaning that he ascribes to it, that is, in the idea of the anagogical, infiltrating and transcendental vision which implies seeing and experiencing *that* which is beyond vision and knowledge. The main quality of such a transcendental vision is seeing through things and seeing within things – or seeing the content of things which is otherwise unapproachable and then arriving at a new state of unknowing or not-seeing as at another level of ceaseless evergrowing enlightenment. Accordingly, in the 2nd chapter of *Mystical Theology*, the adjective *apokekrymmenon* (ἀποκεκρυμμένον = hidden) which refers to the beauty of the metaphorical statue, and the adjective *apokryptomenon* (ἀποκρυπτόμενον = hidden/concealed) which refers to super-essential Darkness (ὑπερούσιον γνόφον) that, in Dionysius' words, "is hidden by all the light that is in sensible things" (τὸν ὑπὸ παντὸς τοῦ ἐν τοῖς οὖσι φωτὸς ἀποκρυπτόμενον), both allude to the vision of that which is otherwise unapproachable by ordinary sight and understanding.

τῇ καθαρᾷ τοῦ κρυφίου θέᾳ κωλύματα καὶ αὐτὸ ἐφ' ἑαυτοῦ τῇ ἀφαιρέσει μόνῃ τὸ ἀποκεκρυμμένον ἀναφαίνοντες κάλλος."

23. O'Brian 1971: 28.

24. See K. I. Κορναράκης, *Κριτικές Παρατηρήσεις στις Εικονολογικές Θέσεις του Υπατίου Εφέσου*, Αθήνα 1998, 55.

25. Διονυσίου Ἀεροπαγίτου, *Περὶ τῆς οὐρανίας ἱεραρχίας*, II, 4, 15$^{1-7}$ (PG 3, 144BC): "Ἔστι τοιγαροῦν οὐκ ἀπᾳδούσας ἀναπλάσαι τοῖς οὐρανίοις μορφὰς κἀκ τῶν ἀτιμωτάτων τῆς ὕλης μερῶν, ἐπεὶ καὶ αὐτὴ πρὸς τοῦ ὄντως καλοῦ τὴν ὕπαρξιν ἐσχηκυῖα κατὰ πᾶσαν αὐτῆς τὴν ὑλαίαν διακόσμησιν ἀπηχήματά τινα τῆς νοερᾶς εὐπρεπείας ἔχει καὶ δυνατόν ἐστι δι' αὐτῶν ἀνάγεσθαι πρὸς τὰς ἀΰλους ἀρχετυπίας, ἀνομοίως ὡς εἴρηται τῶν ὁμοιοτήτων ἐκλαμβανομένων καὶ τῶν αὐτῶν οὐ ταὐτῶς, ἐναρμονίως δὲ καὶ οἰκείως ἐπὶ τῶν νοερῶν τε καὶ αἰσθητῶν ἰδιοτήτων ὁριζομένων."

As used by Dionysius, these adjectives also allude to something which is not a product of one's fantasy or imagination, but which exists regardless and independently of one's vision and understanding of it. This is explicitly implied in the carving metaphor mentioned above, where Dionysius says "like those who, making a self-existent statue [...]." More particularly, Dionysius uses the Ancient Greek adjective αὐτοφυές (*aytofyes*) which is composed of two words, αὐτο + φύομαι (*ayto* + *fyomai*). The first word in this context means "that" – denoting a thing, a fact or other phenomenon, and the second means "(I am) begetting." Hence, the adjective *aytofyes* (αὐτοφυές) does not simply mean "natural" but also bears the implication of "self-existent" and "non-artificial."

Of course, Dionysius' conception of vision and understanding constitutes a product of a centuries-long maturing of philosophical and theological discourse. As was mentioned earlier, Dionysius' early sixth-century idea of divine transcendental darkness is quite different to Clement's early third-century idea of darkness as ultimate inaccessibility of God, because Clement's idea is not so much representative of the incomprehensibility of the transcendent God as it is of the ignorance of the human reason about God. Comparatively speaking, Clement of Alexandria was more of a philosopher. Of course, in Dionysius' writings the Platonic influence can be detected in the differentiation between the sensible and the noetic (intelligible), but his idea that transcendental vision should in fact infiltrate through things or rather, embody things which are unapproachable to ordinary sight, is presented in his text in a rather authentic manner. In particular, by relating the transcendental vision to the idea of darkness which is beyond all the light that is in sensible things, Dionysius ascribes to the process of seeing one paradoxical attribute. Despite the nuances of philosophical influences, this attribute which Dionysius ascribes to vision is distinctly original when compared to the earlier traditions of ancient Greek optics, which can roughly be divided into three broad categories: (a) medical tradition, (b) physical or philosophical tradition and (c) mathematical tradition.[26] In particular, Dionysius ascribes to the experience of vision a bodily quality, where in a certain sense vision is understood as an experience of the entire body. In the following pages I shall elaborate on this understanding of vision and on how its influence could be perceived in the unfolded marble panels in Hagia Sophia.

* * *

Firstly, Dionysius' understanding of infiltrating vision is most probably significantly inspired by the writings of St. Gregory of Nyssa and more particularly by his understanding of the earlier mentioned term *gnofos*, meaning

26. In his book entitled *Theories of Vision from Al-kindi to Kepler*, D. C. Lindberg states: "Despite some overlapping, three broad traditions appear to contain the great bulk of Greek optics: a medical tradition, concerned primarily with the anatomy and physiology of the eye and the treatment of eye disease; a physical or philosophical tradition, devoted to questions of epistemology, psychology, and physical causation; and a mathematical tradition, directed principally toward a geometrical explanation of the perception of space." (1)

divine darkness, stipulated in his work entitled *The Life of Moses*. The common understanding and usage of the term *gnofos* and the usage of the verbs *diadyi* (διαδύῃ)[27] and *eisdynei* (εἰσδύνει),[28] which both mean "infiltrates" and which are implemented in Gregory's and Dionysius' work respectively, are among the aspects that leave little doubt that Dionysius borrowed from Gregory's understanding of the vision of God. In the following, I shall cite a small segment of the aforementioned work by Gregory of Nyssa in which he addresses the question of what it means that Moses, when stepping in front of the burning bush on Mount Horeb, actually entered the *gnofos* and there saw God:

> What does it mean that Moses entered the darkness (gnofos) and then saw God in it? [...] Therefore what is perceived to be contrary to religion is darkness, and the escape from darkness comes about when one participates in light. But as the mind progresses and, through an ever greater and more perfect diligence, comes to apprehend reality, as it approaches more nearly to contemplation, it sees more clearly what of the divine nature is uncontemplated. For leaving behind everything that is observed, not only what sense comprehends but also what the intelligence thinks it sees, it keeps on penetrating deeper until by the intelligence's yearning for understanding it gains access to the invisible and the incomprehensible, and there it sees God. This is the true knowledge of what is sought; this is the seeing that consists in not seeing, because that which is sought transcends all knowledge, being separated on all sides by incomprehensibility as by a kind of darkness. Wherefore John the sublime, who penetrated into the luminous darkness, says, no one has ever seen God,[29] thus asserting that knowledge of the divine essence is unattainable not only by men but also by every intelligent creature.[30]

27. Γρηγορίου Νύσσης, *Εἰς τὸν βίον Μωυσέως*, II, 87^{1-6} (PG 44, 376D–377A): "Καταλιπὼν γὰρ πᾶν τὸ φαινόμενον, οὐ μόνον ὅσα καταλαμβάνει ἡ αἴσθησις, ἀλλὰ καὶ ὅσα ἡ διάνοια δοκεῖ βλέπειν, ἀεὶ πρὸς τὸ ἐνδότερον ἵεται, ἕως ἂν διαδύῃ τῇ πολυπραγμοσύνῃ τῆς διανοίας πρὸς τὸ ἀθεάτόν τε καὶ ἀκατάληπτον κἀκεῖ τὸν θεὸν ἴδῃ."
28. Διονυσίου Ἀεροπαγίτου, *Περὶ μυστικῆς θεολογίας*, I, 144^{9-15} (PG 3, 1001A): "Καὶ τότε καὶ αὐτῶν ἀπολύεται τῶν ὁρωμένων καὶ τῶν ὁρώντων καὶ εἰς τὸν γνόφον τῆς ἀγνωσίας εἰσδύνει τὸν ὄντως μυστικόν, καθ' ὃν ἀπομύει πάσας τὰς γνωστικὰς ἀντιλήψεις, καὶ ἐν τῷ πάμπαν ἀναφεῖ καὶ ἀοράτῳ γίγνεται, πᾶς ὢν τοῦ πάντων ἐπέκεινα καὶ οὐδενός, οὔτε ἑαυτοῦ οὔτε ἑτέρου, τῷ παντελῶς δὲ ἀγνώστῳ τῇ πάσης γνώσεως ἀνενεργησίᾳ κατὰ τὸ κρεῖττον ἑνούμενος καὶ τῷ μηδὲν γινώσκειν ὑπὲρ νοῦν γινώσκων."
29. Gospel according to St John, 1:18.
30. Γρηγορίου Νύσσης, *Εἰς τὸν βίον Μωυσέως*, II, 86^{11}–87^{13} (PG 44, 376C–377A). The original excerpt in Greek reads as follows: "Τί δὲ δὴ βούλεται τὸ ἐντὸς γενέσθαι τοῦ γνόφου τὸν Μωϋσέα καὶ οὕτως ἐν αὐτῷ τὸν Θεὸν ἰδεῖν; [...] Διότι τὸ ἐξ ἐναντίου τῇ εὐσεβείᾳ νοούμενον σκότος ἐστίν· ἡ δὲ ἀποστροφὴ τοῦ σκότους τῇ μετουσίᾳ τοῦ φωτὸς γίνεται. Προϊὼν δὲ ὁ νοῦς καὶ διὰ μείζονος ἀεὶ καὶ τελειοτέρας προσοχῆς ἐν περινοίᾳ γινόμενος τῆς τῶν ὄντων κατανοήσεως, ὅσῳ προσεγγίζει μᾶλλον τῇ θεωρίᾳ, τοσούτῳ πλέον ὁρᾷ τὸ τῆς θείας φύσεως ἀθεώρητον. Καταλιπὼν γὰρ πᾶν τὸ φαινόμενον, οὐ μόνον ὅσα καταλαμβάνει ἡ αἴσθησις, ἀλλὰ καὶ ὅσα ἡ διάνοια δοκεῖ βλέπειν, ἀεὶ πρὸς τὸ ἐνδότερον ἵεται, ἕως ἂν διαδύῃ τῇ πολυπραγμοσύνῃ τῆς διανοίας πρὸς τὸ ἀθεάτόν τε καὶ ἀκατάληπτον κἀκεῖ τὸν Θεὸν ἴδῃ. Ἐν τούτῳ γὰρ ἡ ἀληθής ἐστιν εἴδησις τοῦ ζητουμένου καὶ ἐν τούτῳ τὸ ἰδεῖν ἐν τῷ μὴ ἰδεῖν, ὅτι ὑπέρκειται πάσης εἰδήσεως τὸ ζητούμενον, οἷόν τινι γνόφῳ τῇ ἀκαταληψίᾳ πανταχόθεν διειλημμένον.

It is instructive that, just like in the above citation of Gregory's text, who in explaining what it means when it is said that Moses actually entered the *gnofos*, used the verb *diadyi* (διαδύῃ), which means "infiltrates," the related verb *eisdynei* (εἰσδύνει) which also means "infiltrates," is used in relation to Moses in the following characteristic way by Dionysius, in the 1st chapter of *Mystical Theology*:

> And then he (Moses) becomes also set free from that which is seen and from that which sees, and he infiltrates into the *gnofos* (darkness) of unknowing, into the truly mysterious, where he renounces all perception that stems from knowledge, and he arrives at that which is altogether intangible and invisible, surrendering his entire self to Him who is beyond all, and belonging neither to his own self nor to someone else; and through the deactivating of all knowledge, being united at a higher level with the entirely unknown, by not knowing anything, knows beyond all knowledge.[31]

Given that in many available English translations of the above excerpt from Dionysius' *Mystical Theology*, the verb *eisdynei* (εἰσδύνει), meaning "infiltrates," is insufficiently translated as "plunges," in order to clarify the significance of the correct understanding of its implications, I shall briefly explain the etymology of the related verb *diadyi* (διαδύῃ) which is used in the third person by Gregory of Nyssa, as well as the etymology of the verb *eisdynei* (εἰσδύνει) which is used in the third person by Dionysius the Pseudo-Areopagite. The verb *diadyo* (διαδύω), as it is written in first person, consists of two following parts:

δι(α) + δύω

through + setting/sinking/diving in.

The verb *eisdyo/eisdyno* (εἰσδύω/εἰσδύνω), as it is written in first person, consists of two following parts:

εἰς + δύω

in + setting/sinking/diving in.

In the particular context in which these verbs are used by Gregory of Nyssa and Dionysius the Pseudo-Areopagite, they imply that not simply Moses' vision, but rather, in a bodily sense, Moses himself: (a) goes through the unknown, (b) enters into the unknown and (c) finally sinks deep within

---

Διό φησι καὶ ὁ ὑψηλὸς Ἰωάννης, ὁ ἐν τῷ λαμπρῷ γνόφῳ τούτῳ γενόμενος, ὅτι· Θεὸν οὐδεὶς ἑώρακε πώποτε, οὐ μόνον τοῖς ἀνθρώποις, ἀλλὰ καὶ πάσῃ νοητῇ φύσει τῆς θείας οὐσίας τὴν γνῶσιν ἀνέφικτον εἶναι τῇ ἀποφάσει ταύτῃ διοριζόμενος."

31. Διονυσίου Ἀεροπαγίτου, *Περὶ μυστικῆς θεολογίας*, I, 144$^{9-15}$ (PG 3, 1001A). My translation. The original excerpt in Greek reads as follows: "Καὶ τότε καὶ αὐτῶν ἀπολύεται τῶν ὁρωμένων καὶ τῶν ὁρώντων καὶ εἰς τὸν γνόφον τῆς ἀγνωσίας εἰσδύνει τὸν ὄντως μυστικόν, καθ' ὃν ἀπομύει πάσας τὰς γνωστικὰς ἀντιλήψεις, καὶ ἐν τῷ πάμπαν ἀναφεῖ καὶ ἀοράτῳ γίγνεται, πᾶς ὢν τοῦ πάντων ἐπέκεινα καὶ οὐδενός, οὔτε ἑαυτοῦ οὔτε ἑτέρου, τῷ παντελῶς δὲ ἀγνώστῳ τῇ πάσης γνώσεως ἀνενεργησίᾳ κατὰ τὸ κρεῖττον ἑνούμενος καὶ τῷ μηδὲν γινώσκειν ὑπὲρ νοῦν γινώσκων."

the unknown. This can also be observed in Gregory's formulation ἐντὸς γενέσθαι τοῦ γνόφου,[32] meaning that Moses, before seeing God, literally "entered into the gnofos" - being the divine darkness. As was already cited, Dionysius says that Moses *εἰς τὸν γνόφον τῆς ἀγνωσίας εἰσδύνει*, that is "infiltrates into the *gnofos* of unknowing."[33]

This concept of a bodily kind of infiltration into a sphere which is normally off limits, could have inspired those who were in charge of cutting and selecting marble blocks and installing them thereafter as panels within Hagia Sophia. They could have reinvented this concept for it to be applicable to the cutting of solid marble blocks in a rather immediate way. The visual explanation of how the reinvention of Dionysius' and Gregory's concept of the infiltrating transcendental vision could have occurred in the process of producing unfolded marble panels, is offered in plates *7, 8,* and *9.* These three images attempt to reconstruct a scene at one of the Proconnesian marble quarries. They depict a sixth-century Byzantine viewer responsible for selecting marble slabs to be used, who in his contemplation of the unfolded stone: (a) goes through the stone, (b) enters the stone, and finally (c) infiltrates deep into the stone - which is the analogical stage at which the actual act of the transcendental vision commences and where, metaphorically speaking, the viewer himself becomes identified with the *self-existent, non-artificial* statue (aytofyes agalma/αὐτοφυὲς ἄγαλμα) mentioned in Dionysius' carving-metaphor, and thus becomes immersed in the divine darkness which then is experienced by him as Light. Within that Light the body becomes vision itself and exercises a new kind of seeing.

Thus, in *plates 7* and *24* we are presented with an image which aims at explaining how Dionysius' concept of vision that – to use his terms – can "carve" or "infiltrate" its way through stone in order to embody its content and reach its hidden beauty, could have practically influenced those who were responsible for the entire process from cutting and selecting to installing the marble panels in Hagia Sophia. More particularly, in *plate 8* we discern a human figure which stands between two freshly cut marble blocks, as if trying to envisage how it would be to see within the closed mass of the marble before it was cut. Accordingly, in *plate 9*, we see how the same human figure becomes absorbed into the colourful veins of the marble and thus becomes one with its own vision. More precisely, *plate 9* shows how the body of the sixth-century Byzantine viewer transcends into vision itself and thus can hardly be differentiated from it. Through the act of infiltrating, transcendental vision, the body is absorbed by the beauty of the absolute Other. This experience could also be formulated in the following way: *contemplating the uncreated and in his*

32. Γρηγορίου Νύσσης, *Εἰς τὸν βίον Μωυσέως*, II, 86^{11}–87^{13} (PG 44, 376C–377A): "Τί δὲ δὴ βούλεται τὸ ἐντὸς γενέσθαι τοῦ γνόφου τὸν Μωϋσέα καὶ οὕτως ἐν αὐτῷ τὸν Θεὸν ἰδεῖν;"
33. Διονυσίου Ἀεροπαγίτου, *Περὶ μυστικῆς θεολογίας*, I, 144^{9-15} (PG 3, 1001A): "Καὶ τότε καὶ αὐτῶν ἀπολύεται τῶν ὁρωμένων καὶ τῶν ὁρώντων καὶ εἰς τὸν γνόφον τῆς ἀγνωσίας εἰσδύνει τὸν ὄντως μυστικόν [...]"

essence incomprehensible Creator in view of the beauty of Creation means truthful being and truthful seeing of the oneness and unity of everything. It should be noted that this experience of the viewer becoming vision itself, observed in the unfolded marble panels of Hagia Sophia, is reminiscent not only of Dionysius' and Gregory's teachings but also, to an extent, of Plotinus' idea as expressed in his own words: "If you see that this has happened to yourself, since you will become vision itself, having trust in your own self, without needing someone to show you, since you would have already ascended, focus your gaze and see, because only such an eye sees the great Beauty."[34]

But despite the obvious similarities between Plotinus' and Dionysius' concepts of transcendental vision, once again, their differences become obvious when they elaborate on their ideas by relying on examples from the realm of art practices and this is understandably of particular importance for the present topic. For example, in his text entitled *Regarding the Noetic Beauty* (Περὶ τοῦ νοητοῦ κάλλους), when Plotinus compares the two hypothetical adjacent stone masses, one untouched by the human hand and amorphous and the other a statue of a god or of a man, he argues that: "It is apparent that the stone in which the art has begotten a form is beautiful not because it is a stone, because in such a case any stone-mass would be equally beautiful, but because of the kind of form or idea which was given to it by art."[35] This stipulation by Plotinus allows us to understand that he does not speak of a kind of *self-existent, non-artificial* statue or beauty (aytofyes agalma/αὐτοφυὲς ἄγαλμα) of which Dionysius speaks three centuries later. In contrast to Plotinus' concept of beauty, which is rather dependent on the practical execution of an idea, Dionysius' notion of the *non-artificial* beauty which exists in matter even without human intervention corresponds much more to the unfolded marble panels inside Hagia Sophia, for he says in the 2nd chapter of *Celestial Hierarchy*:

> It is, then, permissible to depict forms, which are not discordant, to the celestial beings, even from portions of matter which are the least honourable, since matter also, having been granted its existence from the truly Beautiful, has throughout the whole range of its material composure some echoes of the noetic reverence; and it is possible through

---

34. *Ennead*, I. 6. 9. My translation. The original excerpt in Greek reads as follows: "εἰ τοῦτο γενόμενον σαυτὸν ἴδοις, ὄψις ἤδη γενόμενος θαρσήσας περὶ σαυτῷ καὶ ἐνταῦθα ἤδη ἀναβεβηκὼς μηκέτι τοῦ δεικνύντος δεηθεὶς ἀτενίσας ἴδε· οὗτος γὰρ μόνος ὁ ὀφθαλμὸς τὸ μέγα κάλλος βλέπει."

35. *Ennead*, V. 8. 1. My translation. The original excerpt in Greek reads as follows: "Κειμένων τοίνυν ἀλλήλων ἐγγύς, ἔστω δέ, εἰ βούλει, [δύο] λίθων ἐν ὄγκωι, τοῦ μὲν ἀρρυθμίστου καὶ τέχνης ἀμοίρου, τοῦ δὲ ἤδη τέχνηι κεκρατημένου εἰς ἄγαλμα θεοῦ ἢ καί τινος ἀνθρώπου, θεοῦ μὲν Χάριτος ἤ τινος Μούσης, ἀνθρώπου δὲ μή τινος, ἀλλ' ὃν ἐκ πάντων καλῶν πεποίηκεν ἡ τέχνη, *φανείη μὲν ἂν ὁ ὑπὸ τῆς τέχνης γεγενημένος εἰς εἴδους κάλλος καλὸς οὐ παρὰ τὸ εἶναι λίθος–ἦν γὰρ ἂν καὶ ὁ ἕτερος ὁμοίως καλός – ἀλλὰ παρὰ τοῦ εἴδους, ὃ ἐνῆκεν ἡ τέχνη. Τοῦτο μὲν τοίνυν τὸ εἶδος οὐκ εἶχεν ἡ ὕλη, ἀλλ' ἦν ἐν τῶι ἐννοήσαντι καὶ πρὶν ἐλθεῖν εἰς τὸν λίθον·* ἦν δ' ἐν τῶι δημιουργῶι οὐ καθόσον ὀφθαλμοὶ ἢ χεῖρες ἦσαν αὐτῶι, ἀλλ' ὅτι μετεῖχε τῆς τέχνης. Ἦν ἄρα ἐν τῆι τέχνηι τὸ κάλλος τοῦτο ἄμεινον πολλῶι." (Emphasis added)

> these echoes to be anagogically led to the immaterial archetypes, under the condition that, as was said, similarities are understood dissimilarly and are not defined as identical – thus the qualities should be understood in the harmonious and appropriate way concerning on the one hand the noetic and on the other the sensible beings.[36]

In view of the possible influence of Dionysius' appreciation of raw matter, the unfolded marble panels in Hagia Sophia could be understood as examples of the exhibited beauty of raw matter, which of course is not *self-existent* (aytofyes/αὐτοφυὲς) in a "self-created" sense, but self-existent in a sense that it is created by God as beautiful even without further intervention. Thus, Dionysius gives us reasons to observe these marble panels as paradoxical natural icons created by God and revealed by man.

On the other hand, Plotinus' opinion that beauty is not caused by symmetry and also his general discussion of symmetry (in his text entitled *On Beauty*[37]), could have exercised a certain kind of dialectical influence in the obvious preference for symmetrical patterns created by the joining of the two panels of marble cut from the same block. Of course, the opposite perception that the principles of beauty are harmony, symmetry and symphony among separate elements is much older and can be found in Plato's thought. For example, In Plato's dialogue entitled *Philebus*, Socrates refers to Protarchus and says: "So now the power of the good has taken refuge in the nature of the beautiful; the measure and symmetry are turned into beauty and virtue."[38]

In the centre of the lower section of *plate 16*, we discern a framed composition of unfolded marble panels whose veins collectively produce a symmetrical pattern, while on each side of this composition there are two single marble panels whose patterns do not produce symmetry but nevertheless are directed towards the piece in the middle. As we look upwards in the same image we discern a narrower horizontal stripe of marble panels whose veins do not form any kind of symmetry. Then above this horizontal stripe we have three framed compositions of marble panels. The two which are bigger on each side consist of unfolded panels and produce particularly symmetrical patterns, while the middle one, which is of a different colour, is a single one-piece panel. As can be seen more clearly in *plate 17*, this rhythmical repetition

36. Διονυσίου Ἀεροπαγίτου, *Περὶ τῆς οὐρανίας ἱεραρχίας*, II, 4, 15$^{1-7}$ (PG 3, 144BC). My translation. The original excerpt in Greek reads as follows: ""Εστι τοιγαροῦν οὐκ ἀπᾳδούσας ἀναπλάσαι τοῖς οὐρανίοις μορφὰς κἀκ τῶν ἀτιμωτάτων τῆς ὕλης μερῶν, ἐπεὶ καὶ αὐτὴ πρὸς τοῦ ὄντως καλοῦ τὴν ὕπαρξιν ἐσχηκυῖα κατὰ πᾶσαν αὐτῆς τὴν ὑλαίαν διακόσμησιν ἀπηχήματά τινα τῆς νοερᾶς εὐπρεπείας ἔχει καὶ δυνατόν ἐστι δι' αὐτῶν ἀνάγεσθαι πρὸς τὰς ἀΰλους ἀρχετυπίας, ἀνομοίως ὡς εἴρηται τῶν ὁμοιοτήτων ἐκλαμβανομένων καὶ τῶν αὐτῶν οὐ ταὐτῶς, ἐναρμονίως δὲ καὶ οἰκείως ἐπὶ τῶν νοερῶν τε καὶ αἰσθητῶν ἰδιοτήτων ὁριζομένων."
37. *Ennead*, I. 6.1.
38. My translation. The original excerpt in Greek reads as follows: "Σωκράτης: νῦν δὴ καταπέφευγεν ἡμῖν ἡ τοῦ ἀγαθοῦ δύναμις εἰς τὴν τοῦ καλοῦ φύσιν: μετριότης γὰρ καὶ συμμετρία κάλλος δήπου καὶ ἀρετὴ πανταχοῦ συμβαίνει γίγνεσθαι." *Philebus*, 64e, 6.

which exploits the antithesis between the symmetrical and the amorphous, continues upwards all the way until the gallery level in Hagia Sophia. It is possible that the choice of these motifs and the way they are organised owes to an extent to the theories mentioned above regarding beauty and symmetry by Plato and Plotinus respectively. However, while the possible influences of the philosophical-aesthetic discourse of the Ancient Greek world can indeed be detected in the unfolded marble panels of Hagia Sophia, they seem to be less pronounced than the possible influence of the experience of the infiltrating, transcendental vision of Dionysius the Pseudo-Areopagite, according to which the archetypal beauty of the matter can be discovered within its content and without additional human intervention.

Therefore, with multiple layers of their likely theoretical influences from the history of philosophy and theology, the framed icon-like marble panels in Hagia Sophia, such as that shown in *plate 1*, could be understood as Pre-Iconoclastic, abstract Orthodox icons which simultaneously depict the following: God, through His creative act; Creation, through the inside of a stone; and Man, through his minimal intervention to the stone and his free interpretations of the abstract patterns. These examples of abstract Orthodox icons, do not owe their abstraction to iconoclastic ideas but to iconophile theories of Dionysius the Pseudo-Areopagite, to the teachings of Gregory of Nyssa and possibly to those of Plotinus. We know that Dionysius' theories could have easily influenced the concept of the unfolded marble panels in Hagia Sophia not simply because these theories exercised a rising influence on the perception of icons at the time, but also because such importance was given to the island of Proconnesus generally in this period where such a significant amount of marble was quarried for Hagia Sophia, that emperor Justinian I (483–565) erected a large convent on the island. As noted by Alexandra Karagianni, this convent eventually had active libraries established by educated monks, who worked as scribes of religious books, psalms and Greco-Roman philosophical texts.[39] This convent also attracted a significant number of pilgrims[40]. Having in mind this intellectual activity on the island of Proconnesus whose marble quarries were exploited in the same period for the construction of Hagia Sophia, it appears as plausible that Dionysius' and Gregory's theories, but also Plotinus' teachings, besides being well known in intellectual circles, where the interest in theory prevailed, also became creatively understood as applicable, in a practical sense, to the artistic conceptualisation of unfolded marble panels. In addition, as noted by Professor Pavlos Kalligas, an interesting link could also be observed in the fact that one of the architects of Hagia Sophia, Anthemius of Tralles (ca. 474–ca. 534), was most likely a student of Proclus (412–485) whose school exercised an influence on Dionysius the Pseudo-Areopagite. This assists us in understanding how philo-

39. Karagianni (year?): 4.
40. Ibid., 4.

sophical and theological ideas of that period were able to unassumingly find their way to practical application in the realm of art and architecture.[41]

The previously described idea of standing within that which is normally unapproachable, bears instructive resemblance to later Byzantine depictions of Moses taking off his sandals upon God's request in front of the burning bush. One characteristic example of such depictions is an early 13th century icon from Mount Sinai shown in *plate 6*, where Moses is shown taking his sandals off after hearing God saying: "[...] Take off your sandals, for the place where you are standing is holy ground" (Exodus, 3:5).

The symmetrical patterns, such as those in *plates 1*, *3*, and *13*, must have been selected according to certain agreed-upon criteria, since most of them are quite impressive and remind of letter-like or arabesque-like symbols rather than merely accidental shapes. A possible inspiration for the actual selection of these patterns is not detectable only in Dionysius' *Mystical Theology* but also in his other writings, such as the second chapter of his text entitled *Celestial Hierarchy*, which bears the subtitle: *That Divine and Celestial things are appropriately revealed, even through dissimilar symbols.* For example, in one characteristic section of that chapter Dionysius gives an instructive explanation of how one could be led to immaterial archetypes even through portions of matter which, as he puts it, are "the least honourable."[42] Having in mind that the descriptions of Moses' encounter of the burning bush by Gregory of Nyssa involve the motif of thorns,[43] perhaps Dionysius, by using the phrase "portions of matter which are the least honourable," though admittedly not speaking of Moses in that section, was nevertheless inspired by the fact that the Hebrew word "seneh" (סנה), used for the bush which was burning in front of Moses, refers in particular to a thorn-bush or bramble.

In case Dionysius' phrase "portions of matter which are the least honourable" (τῶν ἀτιμωτάτων τῆς ὕλης μερῶν) is indeed inspired by the thorn-bush which was burning in front of Moses, this would imply that the notion of Moses standing at a transcendental place where he was asked by God to take off his sandals, permeates much more of Dionysius' thinking than what

41. http://www.sgt.gr/players/athensdialogues/20131115/en/

42. Διονυσίου Ἀεροπαγίτου, *Περὶ τῆς οὐρανίας ἱεραρχίας*, II, 4, 15^{1-7} (PG 3,144BC): "Ἔστι τοιγαροῦν οὐκ ἀπᾳδούσας ἀναπλάσαι τοῖς οὐρανίοις μορφὰς κἀκ τῶν ἀτιμωτάτων τῆς ὕλης μερῶν [...]"

43. Γρηγορίου Νύσσης, *Εἰς τὸν βίον Μωυσέως*, II, 41^{2-16} (PG 44, 333C): "Ἐν τούτῳ τοίνυν γενόμενος τότε μὲν ἐκεῖνος, νυνὶ δὲ πᾶς ὁ κατ' ἐκεῖνον τῆς γηΐνης ἑαυτὸν ἐκλύων περιβολῆς καὶ τὸ ἐκ τῆς βάτου φῶς βλέπων, τουτέστι πρὸς τὴν διὰ σαρκὸς τῆς ἀκανθώδους ταύτης ἐπιλάμψασαν ἡμῖν ἀκτῖνα ἥτις ἐστί, καθὼς τὸ εὐαγγέλιόν φησι, τὸ φῶς τὸ ἀληθινὸν καὶ ἡ ἀλήθεια, τότε τοιοῦτος γίνεται οἷος καὶ ἑτέροις εἰς σωτηρίαν ἀρκέσαι καὶ καθελεῖν μὲν τὴν ἐπικρατοῦσαν κακῶς τυραννίδα, ἐξελέσθαι δὲ πρὸς ἐλευθερίαν πᾶν τὸ τῇ πονηρᾷ δουλείᾳ κατακρατούμενον, τῆς ἀλλοιωθείσης οὖν δεξιᾶς καὶ τῆς εἰς ὄφιν μεταβληθείσης βακτηρίας τῶν θαυμάτων καθηγουμένης. Ὧι μοι δοκεῖ δι' αἰνίγματος τὸ διὰ σαρκὸς τοῦ κυρίου παραδηλοῦσθαι μυστήριον τῆς φανείσης τοῖς ἀνθρώποις θεότητος, δι' ἧς γίνεται ἥ τε τοῦ τυράννου καθαίρεσις καὶ ἡ τῶν ὑπ' αὐτοῦ κρατουμένων ἐλευθερία."

has so far been anticipated. Also, due to Dionysius' influence, those responsible for the cutting, selecting and installing the marble panels in Hagia Sophia might have approached the abstract features created by veined marble as the lowest of material things that nevertheless may portray Celestial Beings.

After selecting the pieces to be cut into even panels and after bringing them from the quarry, the hidden beauty (ἀποκεκρυμμένον κάλλος) observed in the inner world of the veined marble was then not only installed within the interior of the church, but was also superbly and vividly framed. The argument which I would like to put forth here is that in each individual case, the paired panels of marble were envisaged by their installers as a ready-made kind of an icon, or more precisely, as an icon which through its aspect of minimal human intervention, becomes a natural icon which simultaneously refers to the mysteries of God, Creation and Man – without necessarily depicting any of them formally. As seen in *plates 1, 3, 13, 14, 15, 16* and *17*, perhaps the most obvious indication that these pairs of marble panels were indeed envisaged as icons, is the fact that most of them are deliberately and tastefully framed either by narrow decorative frames or broader frames carved with vegetal ornament. The abstract effect of the patterns of the veined marble is of course intended and desired. It is well known that the original sixth-century decoration of the interior of Hagia Sophia is entirely abstract – the only exception is observed in the section of the sixth-century mosaic decoration depicting the leafy rinceau, in the soffits of the gallery colonnade, which constitutes a small part of the entire decorated area.[44]

Of course, the Byzantines were not using the term "abstract" to describe any of the aspects of their art and we can indeed conceive of how they were quite able to read into symmetrical abstract features of unfolded veined marble and employ some of those features as parallel inspiration in rendering the monumental cherubs in the pendentives of Hagia Sophia. One of those cherubs is shown in *plate 20*, where, for example, we might also compare the cherub's head immersed in massive wings (*plate 21*) to the central feature in the middle of the unfolded marble panel shown in *plate 22*. The dense curvy flow and the almost impressionistic effect of the features created by marble veins are reminiscent of volcanic lava and are present in a number of examples in Hagia Sophia, such as those shown in *plates 15* and *22*. These are aesthetic characteristics which can to a significant extent be detected in the way the cherub's wings are rendered and in the way they tightly and dynamically surround the portrait of the cherub (*plate 21*). The drawing and colours of the cherub echo a kind of immediacy that can be compared to Van Gogh's portraits (*plate 23*). The overall rendering of the cherub, especially its flame-like wings (*plate 20*), bespeaks the notable Persian influence and reminds us that the influence of the Eastern artistic traditions, including that of Persia, played a significant role in the formative centuries of Byzantine art.

44. Mango 1977: XLII.

As shown in *plate 23*, the austere and monumental expression of the cherub and his emphasised widely open eyes can be interpreted to bespeak a pressing importance of the kind of infiltrating vision conceived by Dionysius the Pseudo-Areopagite and Gregory of Nyssa. As is very well known, Dionysius discusses cherubs in his *Celestial Hierarchy*, where he says that "the most Holy Thrones, and the many-eyed and many-winged hosts, named in the Hebrew tongue Cherubim and Seraphim, are established immediately around God, with a nearness superior to all."[45]

The hypothesis that the symmetrical patterns in unfolded marble panels may have influenced the rendering of the cherubs in Hagia Sophia is also conceivable for the following reason: The selected marble panels were installed in their place after the structural walls of the church were raised. This means that by the time the construction of the church reached the level of the pendentives and then later the level of the dome, these marble panels were already visible for a considerable amount of time. There would have been enough time for a subconscious kind of influence from the symmetrical patterns in unfolded marble panels to set in the minds of those who were eventually assigned to render the voluminous cherubs. A comparison between *plates 21* and *22* is only one of many that may serve to indicate to the probability of this hypothesis. In *plate 15* we observe other examples of unfolded marble panels in Hagia Sophia that just as well may have inspired the rendering of the cherubs. Also, perhaps the similarity of the cherub's wings (*plate 20*) to abstract shapes in marble panels (*plates 15* and *22*) may provide part of an explanation as to why even well after the construction of Hagia Sophia, the symmetric patterns of unfolded marble panels were mimicked in church decoration by adhering to the technique of painting.

In the unfolded marble panels of St. Demetrius in Thessaloniki, which date back to the 7th century (one of them shown in *plates 10, 11* and *12*) we observe a tendency to select those slabs of marble whose unfolding may produce a pattern reminiscent to an extent of human contours. Thus, in *plate 11*, we can almost discern the basic contours of human features. Because of their reminiscence of human form, the patterns in these marble panels in St. Demetrius may indicate to a continuation of the concept of "infiltrating" of the human figure into the stone, which was begun so authentically in Hagia Sophia and which was then lost in later centuries. For example, the marble panels in the 11th century church of Nea Moni (*plate 26*) on the island of Chios, and the marble panels of the 11th century church of Hosios Loukas near Distomo (*plate 25*), while demonstrating the same methodology, do not insist on the symmetrical pattern achieved through the joining of two panels which are cut from a single slab of marble; fewer of the marble panels

45. Διονυσίου Ἀεροπαγίτου, *Περὶ τῆς οὐρανίας ἱεραρχίας*, VI, 26$^{15-18}$ (PG 3, 200D–201A): "Τούς τε γὰρ ἁγιωτάτους θρόνους καὶ τὰ πολυόμματα καὶ πολύπτερα τάγματα Χερουβὶμ Ἑβραίων φωνῇ καὶ Σεραφὶμ ὠνομασμένα κατὰ τὴν πάντων ὑπερκειμένην ἐγγύτητα περὶ θεὸν ἀμέσως ἱδρῦσθαί φησι παραδιδόναι τὴν τῶν ἱερῶν λογίων ἐκφαντορίαν."

in these two churches adhere to this concept and when they are collectively compared to marble panels in Hagia Sophia of Constantinople and to those in St. Demetrius of Thessaloniki, the fading away of the concept of *infiltrating of the human figure into the stone*, becomes evident. Also, in the church of Chora of Constantinople, which was rebuilt in the 11th century and renovated in the 14th century, this concept is clearly preserved (*plate 18*).

Conclusion

Before the conclusion of this study is made, it should be noted that due to reasons which are not directly related to the abstract appearance of the sixth-century marble panels in Hagia Sophia, the succeeding period of Iconoclasm had brought with it the contempt of representational and anthropomorphic art and thus created a polarised iconological quarrel which eventually permanently influenced the way in which both the Byzantines and later art historians viewed non-anthropomorphic Byzantine art. Because of this, until now, the unfolded marble panels in Hagia Sophia, as well as many other abstract aspects of its sixth-century interior-decoration, have at times been regarded as examples of art that allude to the early iconoclastic tendency.

Contrary to this understanding, the present study has approached the unfolded marble panels in Hagia Sophia as art which is not necessarily non-representational and which is possibly profoundly inspired by the developments of the theology between the 3rd and early 6th century. Thus, because of the aesthetic characteristics discussed above and given the likely theological influences which were explained in this study, in the sixth-century unfolded marble panels in Hagia Sophia we can discern the previously unobserved characteristic process of the notion of vision becoming body-like, in a sense that rather than being understood as the function of simply seeing an object, vision becomes an experience of embodying an object from within and thereby of identifying itself with it. Simultaneously, in the same process, the notion of the human body becomes more vision-like, in a sense that it becomes closely identified with the objects that the vision embodies.

As I tried to demonstrate in this study, especially through the argumentation involving *plates 7, 8* and *9*, this characteristically transcendental experience of vision observed in unfolded marble panels of Hagia Sophia, is best understood as an entirely abstract and yet not necessarily non-representational Byzantine *icon* which entails the cryptic and anagogical experience of the *transcendental byzantine body* and which is likely inspired by the writings of Dionysius the Pseudo-Areopagite, Gregory of Nyssa, as well as possibly by those of Plotinus. As was already said, this experience of the *transcendental byzantine body* is not related to iconoclastic ideas. Of course, the stipulated aims of this study are realised only to an extent. There are other types of multiple unfolded marble panels in Hagia Sophia that have not been discussed in relation to the teachings of Dionysius the Pseudo-Areopagite, Gregory of

Nyssa and Plotinus. Also, there are other aspects of the discussed theological and philosophical teachings that could be related to the concept of unfolded marble panels in Hagia Sophia. It is hoped that this study may serve as an indication of the possible new directions of future research exploring connections between the theology of the Pre-Iconoclastic period and Byzantine art.

Epilogue

The influence of these sixth-century unfolded marble panels on later examples of Byzantine art could be traced in a separate study. We can perhaps perceive such an influence when we look at the 14th century depiction of *Transfiguration* (*plate 19*) where the symmetrical rendering of the mountainous landscape as well as the repetition of the stripe-like rays of light which emanate from Christ, remind us of some of the symmetrical abstract patterns of unfolded marble panels in Hagia Sophia.

Lastly, there are several ways in which we can observe an aesthetic connection between the discussed sixth-century unfolded marble panels and the experience of modern art. For example, as is very well known, the central thought in Dionysius' teaching is that the transcendental path to deification is not through acquiring the supposed knowledge of God but through the rejection of all knowledge for the sake of enlightenment which exceeds human understanding itself. In the context of art-making, this idea of the rejection of all knowledge is to an extent comparable to the 20th century artistic concept of a found or ready-made object, an object which has undergone minimal or no human intervention. The concept of a "found object" was developed by a 20th century, French-American artist Marcel Duchamp (1887–1968). Found objects or "Readymades" were simply found objects which Duchamp chose and then presented as art. His idea was to question the notion as well as the adoration of art – which he found redundant. Duchamp sought new methods of expression because he was not interested in art that was only visual or as he called it, retinal art. Around 1915, he began creating "readymades" as an antidote to "retinal art." However, before Duchamp, in his piece entitled *Still Life with Chair Caning* (1912), as part of the actual work, Picasso used a found object, the actual chair caning. Thus, it could be argued that the concept has its early beginnings in Picasso's work.

It appears that in the transhistorical context of art-making, the ancient theological concept of "rejecting all knowledge" for the sake of enlightenment which characterises Dionysius' thought, can be creatively translated to "rejecting to intervene in a material" but rather simply exercising various new perceptions of it. The analogy in the interior of Hagia Sophia is that the found *object* is observed in the unfolded marble panels, where, roughly speaking, the only human intervention is the splitting of the solid stone and displaying its two halves over a vertical axis as a single symmetrical pattern.

In this sense, similarly to the 20th century concept of a found object, the unfolded marble panels in Hagia Sophia could be understood as revelations of Creation as it becomes experienced when it is seen from within. For different reasons but with comparable artistic needs, the sixth-century Byzantine creators and the 20th century creators sought for ways in which they could bring their perception alone to an experience of enlightenment.

Bibliography

Primary Sources:

Διονυσίου (Ψευδο)'Αρεοπαγίτου

Ἐπιστολαί : *Corpus Dionysiacum*, II. *Epistulae*, hrsg. von G. Heil und A. M. Ritter, Patristische Texte und Studien 36, Berlin: Walter de Gruyter 1991, 151–210 (= PG 3, 1065–1122).

Περὶ μυστικῆς θεολογίας : *Corpus Dionysiacum*, II. *De mystica thelogia*, hrsg. von G. Heil und A. M. Ritter, Patristische Texte und Studien 36, Berlin: Walter de Gruyter 1991, 139–150 (= PG 3, 997–1064).

Περὶ τῆς οὐρανίας ἱεραρχίας : *Corpus Dionysiacum*, II. *De coelesti hierarchia*, hrsg. von G. Heil und A. M. Ritter, Patristische Texte und Studien 36, Berlin: Walter de Gruyter 1991, 7–59 (= PG 3, 119–369).

Γρηγορίου Νύσσης

Περὶ ἀρετῆς, ἤτοι εἰς τὸν βίον Μωυσέως, H. Murusillo, Gregorii Nysseni Opera VII.1, *De Vita Moysis*, Leiden 1964, 1–145 (= PG 44, 297–430).

Secondary Sources:

Arthur R. A. 2008. *Pseudo-Dionysius as Polemicist: The Development and Purpose of the Angelic Hierarchy in Sixth Century Syria*, Ashgate Publishing Limited.

Asgari N. 1978. "Roman and early byzantine marble quarries of Proconnesus," in: *The Proceedings of the Xth International Congress of Classical Archaeology*, 467–480. Ankara: Turk Tarih Kuruma.

Asgari N., 1988. "The stages of workmanship of the Corinthian capital in Proconnesus and its export form," in: N. Herz, M. Waelkens, eds., *Classical Marble: Geochemistry, Technology, Trade*, 115–125. The Netherlands: Kluwer Academic Publishers.

Asgari N. & Drew-Bear T. 1998. "The quarry inscriptions of Prokonnesos," in: J. Herrmann, N. Herz, R. Newman, eds., *Interdisciplinary Studies on Ancient Stone*, 1–7. Boston: Archetype Publications.

Baggley, J. 1988. *Doors of Perception: Icons and their Spiritual Significance*, Crestwood: St. Vladimir's Seminary Press.

Bahrim D. 2008. "The Anthropic Cosmology of St Maximus the Confessor," *Journal for Interdisciplinary Research on Religion and Science* 3 (2008) 11–37.

Balthasar, H. U. von, 2003. *The Cosmic Liturgy: The Universe According to Maximus the Confessor,* Ignatius Press.

Barasch, M. 1985. *Theories of Art: From Plato to Winckelmann*, New York: New York University Press.

Barasch, M. 1992. *Icon: studies in the history of an idea*, New York: New York University Press.

Barasch, M. 1997. *The language of art: Studies in interpretation*, New York: New York University Press.

Barasch, M. 2001. *Blindness: The History of a Mental Image of Western Thought*, New York: Routledge.

Barber, C. 2002. *Figure and Likeness. On the Limits of Representation in Byzantine Iconoclasm*, Princeton: Princeton Univ. Press.

Baxandall, M. 1971. *Giotto and the Orators*, Oxford.

Beardsley M. C. 1975. *Aesthetics from Classical Greece to the Present: A Short History*. University of Alabama Press.

Beckwith, J. 1968. *The Art of Constantinople*, London, New York.

Bergmann, S. 2005. *Creation Set Free: The Spirit as Liberator of Nature.* Sacra Doctrina. Grand Rapids: Eerdmans.

Betsch, W. 1977. *The history, production and distribution of the late antique capital in Constantinople*, Philadelphia: University of Pennsylvania.

Beykan M. 1988. "The Marble Architectural Elements in Export-form from the Sile Shipwreck," in: N. Herz, M. Waelkens, eds., *Classical Marble: Geochemistry, Technology, Trade*, 127–131. The Netherlands: Kluwer Academic Publishers.

Bluemel, C. 1955. *Greek Sculptors at Work*, The Phaidon Press.

Brooks O. 1958. "Cappadocian Thought as a Coherent System," *Dumbarton Oaks Papers* 12.

Brubaker, L. 1999. *Vision and Meaning in Ninth Century Byzantium: Image as Exegesis in the Homilies of Gregory of Nazianzus*, Cambridge: Cambridge University Press.

Brubaker, L. 2012. *Inventing Byzantine Iconoclasm*, London: Bristol Classical Press.

Bychkov, V. 1999. *Βυζαντινή Αισθητική: Θεωρητικά Προβλήματα* (Μετάφραση: Κ. Π. Χαραλαμπίδης), Εκδόσεις Ε. Τζαφέρη. (Original title: *Vizantijskaja estetika. Teoretičeskie problemy*, Moskva: Isskustvo 1977)

Connor, C. L. 1991. *Art and Miracle in Medieval Byzantium: The Crypt at Osios Loukas and its Frescoes*, Princeton, N.J.

Cooper, A. G. 2005. *The Body in St Maximus the Confessor: Holy Flesh, Wholly Deified*, Oxford: Oxford University Press.

Costache, D. 2006. "Going Upwards with Everything You Are: The Unifying Ladder of St Maximus the Confessor," in: B. Nicolescu, M. Stavinschi, eds., *Science and Orthodoxy: A Necessary Dialogue*. Bucharest: Curtea Veche 2006: 135–144.

Damian, Th. 2011. "The Doctrine of Creation in Pseudo-Dionysius Areopagite's Theology," *Annals of the Academy of Romanian Scientists Series on Philosophy, Psychology, Theology and Journalism* 3, 1–2.

Elsner, J. 1995. *Art and the Roman Viewer. The Transformation of Art from the Pagan World to Christianity*, Cambridge.

Evans, H. C. & Wixon, W. D., eds., 1997. *The Glory of Byzantium: Art and Culture of the Middle Byzantine Era, A.D. 843–1261*, New York: The Metropolitan Museum of Art.

Fisher, J. 2001. "The Theology of Dis/similarity: Negation in Pseudo-Dionysius", Chicago, Illinois.

Forsyth, C. H., Weitzmann, K. 1971. *The Monastery of St Catherine at Mount Sinai: The Church and Fortress of Justinian*, Ann Arbor Uni.

Freely J., Çakmak, A. 2010. *Byzantine Monuments of Istanbul*, New York: Cambridge University Press.

Gavrilyuk, P. L. 2008. *The Reception of Dionysius in Twentieth-Century Eastern Orthodoxy*.

Gera, D. L. 2003. *Ancient Greek Ideas on Speech, Language and Civilization*, Oxford: Oxford University Press.

Grabar, A. 1966. *Byzantium. From the Death of Theodosius to the Rise of Islam*, France.

Grabar, A. 1968. *Christian Iconography. A Study of Its Origins*. Princeton.

Halper, F. 2001. "Visual symmetry and subjective contour in the Ayasofya of Istanbul," *Perception* 30 ECVP Abstract Supplement. URL: http://www.perceptionweb.com/ecvp/ecvp01.pdf

Hathaway, R. F. 1969. *Hierarchy and the Definition of Order in the "Letters" of Pseudo-Dionysius. A Study in the Form and Meaning of the Pseudo-Dionysian Writings*. The Hague: Nijhoff.

Haynes, D. 2009. "The Church Mystagogy and its Cosmic Mediation: Ecclesiology and Theurgy in the Thought of Maximus Confessor," A Paper Presented at the Conference *Returning to the Church: Catholicity, Ecclesiology, and the Mission of the Church of England St. Stephen's House, Oxford, January 5th, 2009*.

Hemenway, K., & Palmer, S. E. 1978. "Organizational factors in perceived dimensionality," *Journal of Experimental Psychology: Human Perception and Performance* 4, 388–396.

Holum, K. 1982. *Theodosian empresses: women and imperial dominion in late antiquity*, Berkeley: University of California Press.

Ivanovic, F. 2010. *Symbol & Icon: Dionysius the Areopagite and the Iconoclastic Crisis*, Pickwick Publications.

James, L. 2004. "Senses and Sensibility in Byzantium," *Art History* 27, 4.

James, L. 1996. *Light and Colour in Byzantine Art*, Oxford: Clarendon Press.

Jenkins, R. J. H. "The Hellenistic Origins of Byzantine Literature," *Dumbarton Oaks Papers* 17 (1963).

Kähler, H. 1967. *Hagia Sophia*, translated by E. Childs, Frederick A. Praeger Inc Publishers.

Karagianni, A. *The Harbour of Proconnesus in Greco-Roman and Early Byzantine Times: The Marble Trade, a Source of Financial and Cultural Development.* Department of Byzantine Archaeology, Faculty of Philosophy, Aristotle University of Thessaloniki, Greece.

Kapitan, G. 1969. "The Church Wreck off Marzamemi," *Archaeology 22*, 122–133.

Kharlamov, V. 2009. *The Beauty of the Unity and Harmony of the Whole: The Concept of Theosis in the Theology of Pseudo-Dionysius the Areopagite.* Eugene, OR: Wipf & Stock.

Kidd, I. 2011. *Feyerabend, Pseudo-Dionysius, and the Ineffability of Reality.*

Kiilerich, B. 2006. "The aesthetics of marble and coloured stone," in: *Proceedings of the 21st International Congress of Byzantine Studies, London, 21–26 August 2006, Volume II, Abstracts of Panel Papers*, Ashgate Publishing.

Kiilerich, B. 2006. "The Aesthetic Viewing of Marble in Byzantium: From Global Impression to Focal Attention," in: *Proceedings of the 21st International Congress of Byzantine Studies, London, 21–26 August 2006*, v. 1.

Kitzinger, E. 1976. *The Art of Byzantium and the Medieval West: Selected Studies.* Edited by W. Eugene Kleinbauer. Bloomington, London: Indiana University Press.

Kitzinger, E. 1958. "Byzantine Art in the Period between Justinian and Iconoclasm," in: *Berichte zum XI Internationalen Byzantinisten-Kongress*, Selected Studies, Number VI, München 1958.

Kitzinger, E. 1954. "The Cult of Images in the Age before Iconoclasm," *Dumbarton Oaks Papers* 8.

Kitzinger, E. 1976. *Selected Studies*, Bloomington-London.

Kitzinger, E. 1977. *Byzantine Art in the Making. Main lines of Development in Mediterranean Art, 3rd–7th Century*, London.

Kitzinger, E. 2002. *Studies in Late Antique, Byzantine and Medieval Western Art*, London.

Kleinert, A. 1979. *Die Inkrustation der Hagia Sophia: Zur Entwicklung der Inkrustationschemata im römischen Kaiserreich*, Münster.

Krautheimer, R. & Ćurčić, S. 1985. *Early Christian Byzantine Architecture*, 4th ed. Harmondsworth: Penguin Books.

Ladner, G. B. 1954. "The Concept of The Image in the Greek Fathers and the Byzantine Iconoclastic Controversy." *Dumbarton Oaks Papers* 7, 1–34.

Lindberg, D. C. 1976. *Theories of Vision from Al-kindi to Kepler*, The University of Chicago Press.

Lossky, V. 1976. *The Mystical Theology of the Eastern Church.* Crestwood, NY: St. Vladimir's Seminary Press.

Louth, A. 1997. "St Denys the Areopagite and the Iconoclast Controversy," in: *Denys l'Aréopagite et sa posterité en Orient et en Occident*, edited by Y. de Andia, Paris Institut d'Études Augustiniennes, 329–339.

Louth, A. 1981. *The Origins of the Christian Mystical Tradition: From Plato to Denys*, Oxford: Clarendon Press.

Louth, A. 2002. *St John Damascene: Tradition and Originality in Byzantine Theology*. Oxford Early Christian Studies. Oxford: Oxford University Press.

Louth, A. 2005. "'Truly Visible Things are Manifest Images of Invisible Things:' Dionysius the Areopagite on Knowing the Invisible," in: *Seeing the Invisible in Late Antiquity and the Early Middle Ages*, ed. by G. de Nie, K. F. Morrison and M. Mostert, 15–24. Utrecht Studies in Medieval Literacy 14. Turnhout: Brepols 2005.

Lowden, J. 1997. *Early Christian Art*, London: Phaidon.

Lowden, J. 2008. *Early Christian and Byzantine Art*. Art and Ideas. London: Phaidon.

Maguire, H. 1974. "Truth and Convention in Byzantine Descriptions of Works of Art," *Dumbarton Oaks Papers* 28.

Maguire, H. 1981. *Art and Eloquence in Byzantium*, Princeton: Princeton University Press.

Maguire, H. 1987. *Earth and Ocean. The Terrestrial World in Early Byzantine Art*, Pennsylvania Uni. Park, London.

Maguire, H. 1996. *Image and Imagination: The Byzantine Epigram as Evidence for Viewer Response*, Toronto.

Maguire, H. 1996. *The Icons of Their Bodies: Saints and their Images in Byzantium*, Princeton University Press.

Maguire, H. 1998. *Heaven on Earth*, Pennsylvania State University Press.

Maguire, H. 1998. *Rhetoric, Nature and Magic in Byzantine Art*, Ashgate.

Maguire, H. 1999. "The Profane Aesthetic in Byzantine Art and Literature," *Dumbarton Oaks Papers* 53.

Mainstone, R. J., Rowland J., 1988. *Hagia Sophia: architecture, structure, and liturgy of Justinian's great church*, Thames and Hudson.

Mango, C. 1977. *Hagia Sophia, a vision for Empires.* Essay by Cyril Mango principal photography Ahmet Ertug.

Mango, C. 1963. *Antique Statuary and the Byzantine Beholder*, Washington, DC: Dumbarton Oaks Papers XVII.

Mango, C. 1980. *Byzantium: The Empire of New Rome*, London: Weidenfeld and Nicholson.

Mango, C. 1984. *Byzantium and its Image: History and Culture of the Byzantine Empire and its Heritage*, London: Variorum Reprints.

Mango, C. 1986. *The Art of the Byzantine Empire 312–1453: Sources and Documents*, Toronto: University of Toronto Press.

Marion, J.-L. 1991. *God Without Being: Hors-texte*. Religion and Postmodernism. Chicago: Chicago University Press.

Mathew, G. A. 1963. *Byzantine Aesthetics*, London: John Murray.

Mathews, T. F. 1998. *The Art of Byzantium*, Calmann & King Ltd.

Mathews, T. F. 1971. *The Early Churches of Constantinople: Architecture and Liturgy*, University Park: Pennsylvania State University Press.

Mathews, T. F. 1990. "The Transformation Symbolism in Byzantine Architecture and the Meaning of the Pantocrator in the Dome," in: Morris, R., ed. 1990. *Church and People in Byzantium,* Centre for Byzantine Studies, University of Birmingham.

Meyendorff, J. 1982. *The Byzantine Legacy in the Orthodox Church.* New York: St. Vladimir's Seminary Press.

Meyendorff, J. 1979. *Byzantine Theology: Historical Trends and Doctrinal Themes.* New York: Fordham University Press.

Nelson, R. S. (et al) 2000. *Visuality Before and Beyond the Renaissance*, Cambridge University Press.

O'Brian, D. 1971. "Plotinus on evil. A Study of Matter and the Soul in Plotinus' Conception of human evil," in: *Le Neoplatonisme, Royaumont, 9–13 Juin 1969,* Paris: Éditions du Centre National de la Recherche Scientifique.

Onians, J. "Abstraction and Imagination in Late Antiquity," *Art History* 3, 1 (1980) 1–23.

Palmer, S. E. 1975. "The effects of contextual scenes on the identification of objects," *Memory and Cognition* 3, 519–526.

Palmer, S. E. 1975. "The nature of perceptual representation: An examination of the analog/propositional controversy," in: R. Schank, B. L. Nash-Webber, eds., *Theoretical issues in natural language processing.* Arlington, Va.: Tinlap Press.

Palmer, S. E. 1976. "Cognitive science: An auspicious beginning. Review of D. Bobrow & A. Collins, eds., *Representation and understanding: Studies in cognitive science,*" *Contemporary Psychology* 21, 522–523.

Palmer, S. E. 1977. "Hierarchical structure in perceptual representation," *Cognitive Psychology* 9, 441–474.

Palmer, S. E. 1978. "Structural aspects of perceptual similarity," *Memory and Cognition* 6, 91–97.

Palmer, S. E. 1978. "Fundamental aspects of cognitive representation," in: E. Rosch, B. L. Lloyd, eds., *Cognition and categorization.* Hillsdale, N.J.: Erlbaum, 259–302.

Palmer, S. E., Hemenway, K. 1978. "Orientation and symmetry: Effects of multiple, rotational, and near symmetries," *Journal of Experimental Psychology: Human Perception and Performance* 4, 691–702.

Pensabene, P. 1998. "Inscribed architectural elements from the Prokonnesos in Durazzo, Tartous, Cilician Aphrodisias and Caesarea," *Asmosia 5. Interdisciplinary studies on ancient stone.* Boston: Archetype Publications, 328–334.

Pentcheva, B, V. 2011. "Hagia Sophia and Multisensory Aesthetics," *Gesta* 50, 2, 93–111.

Pentcheva, B. V. 2006. "The Performative Icon," *The Art Bulletin* 88.
Riordan, W. K. 2008. *Divine Light: The Theology of Denys the Areopagite*. San Francisco: Ignatius.
Rorem, P. 1984. *Biblical and Liturgical Symbols within the Pseudo-Dionysian Synthesis*. Studies and Texts 71. Toronto: Pontifical Institute of Mediaeval Studies.
Rosemary, A. A. 1988. *Pseudo-Dionysius as Polemicist: The Development and Purpose of the Angelic Hierarchy in Sixth Century Syria*, Ashgate Publishing Limited.
Runciman, S. 1975. *Byzantine Style and Civilisation*, Baltimore Md: Penguin.
Strezova, A. 2008. "Relation of Image to its Prototype in Byzantine Iconophile Theology," *Byzantinoslavica* 66, 87–106.
Talbot-Rice, D. 1958. *The Great Palace of the Byzantine Emperors: Second Report*, Edinburgh.
Talbot-Rice, D. 1972. *The Appreciation of Byzantine Art*, London: Oxford University Press.
Thunberg, L. 1985. *Man and the Cosmos: The Vision of St. Maximus the Confessor*, St. Vladimir's Seminary Press.
Tollefsen, T. 2008. *The Christocentric Cosmology of St Maximus the Confessor*, Oxford Early Christian Studies.
Trilling, J. 1998. "The Image Not Made by Hands and the Byzantine Way of Seeing," in: *The Holy Face and the Paradox of Representation*, Villa Spelman Colloquia, 6, ed. H. Kessler and G. Wolf, Bologna, 109–128.
Underwood, P. A. 1975. *The Kariye Djami*, vols. 1–3 (New York, 1966), vol. 4 (ed. by P. A. Underwood) Princeton: Princeton University Press.
Ward-Perkins, J. B. 1951. "Tripolitania and the Marble Trade," *Journal of Roman Studies* 41, 89–104.
Ward-Perkins, J. B. 1980. "Nicomedia and the Marble Trade," in: H. Dodge, J. B. Ward-Perkins, eds. *Marble in Antiquity, Collected Paper, Archaeological Monographs of the British School of Rome*, 61–105. London.
Ward-Perkins, J. B. 1992. "Materials, Quarries and Transportation," in: H. Dodge, J. B. Ward-Perkins, eds. *Marble in Antiquity, Collected Paper, Archaeological Monographs of the British School of Rome*, 13–17. London.
Worringer, W. 1980. *Abstraction and Empathy: A Contribution to the Psychology of Style*, New York: International Universities Press Inc.
Γκιολές, N. 2007. *Παλαιοχριστιανική Μνημειακή Ζωγραφική (π. 300–726)*. Αθήνα.
Γαρίτση, Κ. 2002. *Όρασις αοράτου. Η διδασκαλία του ωραίου στον Διονύσιο Αρεοπαγίτη*, Θήρα: Θεσβίτης.
Κοκκορού-Αλευρά, Γ. 1990. *Η Τέχνη της Αρχαίας Ελλάδας: Σύντομη Ιστορία (1050–50 π.Χ.)*, Τρίτη βελτιωμένη έκδοση, Εκδόσεις Καρδαμίτσα.
Κορναράκη, Κ. 1998. *Η Θεολογία των ιερών εικόνων κατά τον όσιο Θεόδωρο το Στουδίτη*, Κατερίνη: Επέκταση.

Κορναράκης, Κ. Ι. 1998. *Κριτικές Παρατηρήσεις στις Εικονολογικές Θέσεις του Υπατίου Εφέσου*, Αθήνα.

Αρχιμ. Κύρρης Αναστάσιος-Σάββας, 1998. *Θεωρία και πράξη κατά τον Άγιο Μάξιμο τον Ομολογητή*, Λευκωσία (Διδακτορική Διατριβή).

Λουδοβίκος, Ν. 1989. *Η ευχαριστιακή οντολογία στη Θεολογική σκέψη του Αγίου Μάξιμου του Ομολογητή*, Θεσσαλονίκη (Διδακτορική Διατριβή).

Λόσκι, Β. 2004. *Η Θέα του Θεού*, Πρέβεζα: Εκδόσις Ιεράς Μητροπόλεως Νικοπόλεως.

Ματσούκα, Ν. 1980. *Κόσμος, άνθρωπος, κοινωνία κατά τον Μάξιμο Ομολογητή*, Αθήνα: Γρηγόρη.

Ματσούκα, Ν. 2007. *Δογματική και Συμβολική Θεολογία Α': Εισαγωγή στη θεολογική γνωσιολογία*, Θεσσαλονίκη: Πουρναρά.

Ματσούκα, Ν. 2010. *Δογματική και Συμβολική Θεολογία Β΄: Έκθεση της ορθόδοξης πίστης σε αντιπαράθεση με τη δυτική χριστιανοσύνη*, Θεσσαλονίκη: Πουρναρά.

Ματσούκα, Ν. 2009. *Ιστορία της Φιλοσοφίας. Αρχαίας Ελληνικής - Βυζαντινής - Δυτικοευρωπαϊκής, Με σύντομη εισαγωγή στη φιλοσοφία*, Θεσσαλονίκη: Πουρναρά.

Μελλή, Μ. 2001. *Ανθρωπολογία και πορεία προς τη θέωση κατά τον άγιο Μάξιμο τον Ομολογητή*, Θεσσαλονίκη (Διδακτορική Διατριβή).

Μιχελής, Π. 2002. *Η Αρχιτεκτονική ως Τέχνη*, Ίδρυμα Παναγιώτη και Έφης Μιχελή.

Μιχελής, Π. 2006. *Αἰσθητικὴ Θεώρηση τῆς Βυζαντινῆς Τέχνης*, Ίδρυμα Παναγιώτη και Έφης Μιχελή.

Μπετσάκου, Β. 2006. *Στάσις αεικίνητος. Η ανακαίνιση της αριστοτελικής κινήσεως στη θεολογία Μαξίμου Ομολογητού*, Θεσσαλονίκη: Αρμός.

Μπήλιου, Κ. 2000. *Η φιλοσοφία του Μαξίμου του Ομολογητή*, Θεσσαλονίκη (Διδακτορική Διατριβή).

Σκουτέρη, Κ. Β. 1998. *Ιστορία Δογμάτων. Τόμος 1ος. Η Ορθόδοξη δογματική παράδοση και οι παραχαράξεις της κατά τους τρεις πρώτους αιώνες*. Αθήνα: Διήγηση.

Σκουτέρη, Κ. Β. 2004. *Ιστορία Δογμάτων. Τόμος 2ος. Η Ορθόδοξη δογματική διδασκαλία και οι νοθεύσεις της από τις αρχές του τέταρτου αιώνα μέχρι και την Τρίτη Οικουμενική Σύνοδο*. Αθήνα.

Φειδάς, Β. 2002. *Εκκλησιαστική Ιστορία Α': Απ' αρχής μέχρι την Εικονομαχία*, Τρίτη Έκδοση, Αθήνα: Διήγηση.

Φειδάς, Β. 2002. *Εκκλησιαστική Ιστορία Β΄: Από την Εικονομαχία μέχρι τη Μεταρρύθμιση*, Τρίτη Έκδοση, Αθήνα: Διήγηση.

1. One of the unfolded marble panels inside Hagia Sophia of Constantinople; 6th century.

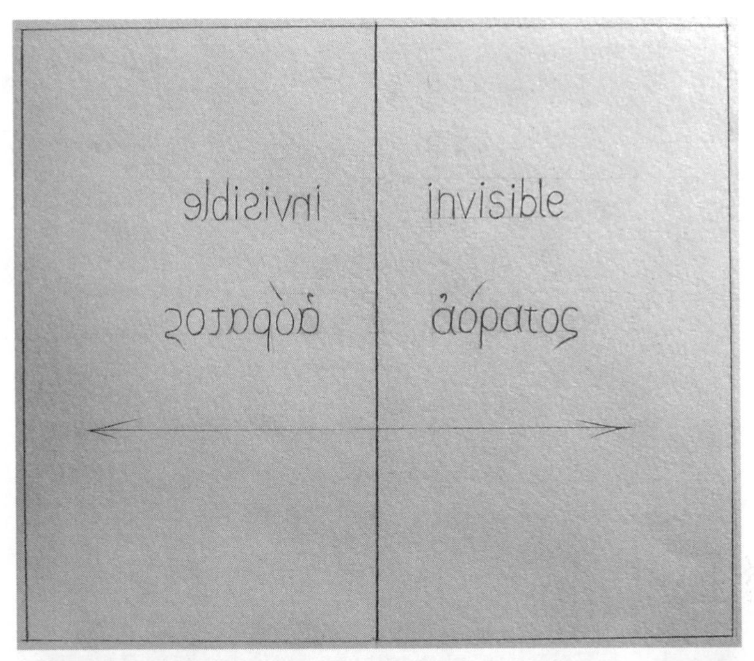

2. Explanation drawing.

3. One of the unfolded marble panels
inside Hagia Sophia of Constantinople; 6th century.

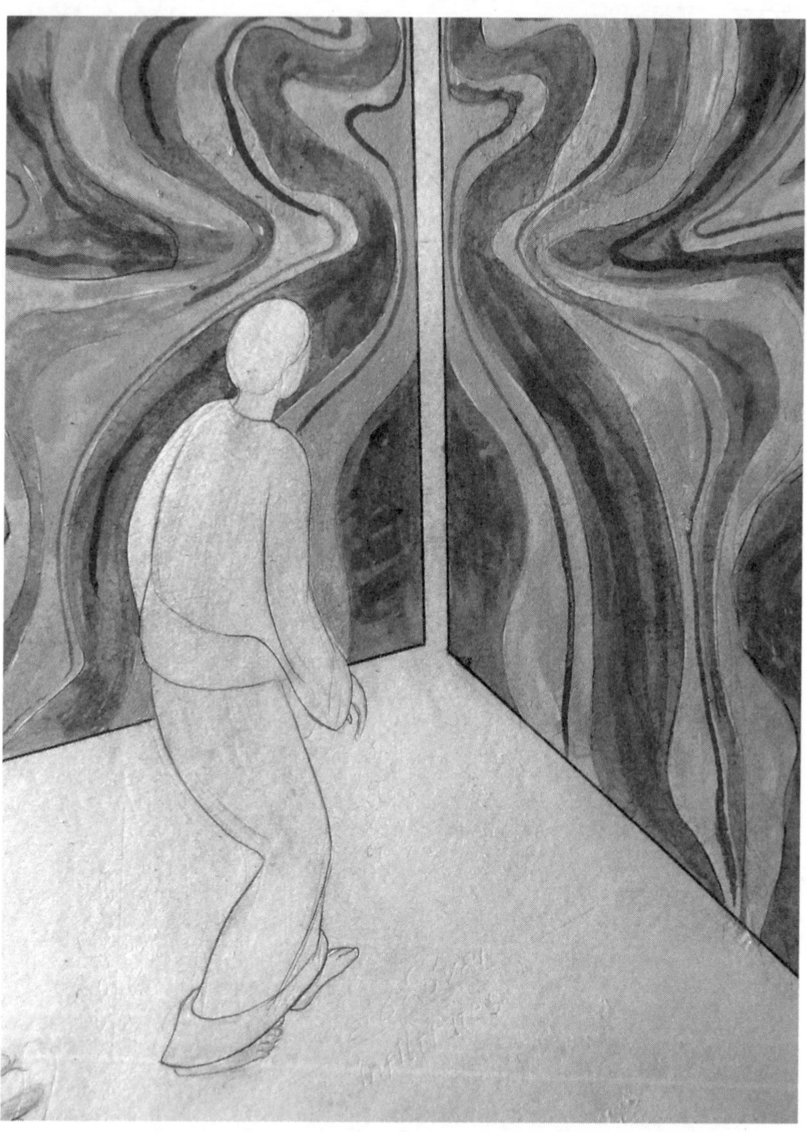

4. Detail of visual demonstration II (plate 8), showing the human figure standing between two freshly cut marble blocks, as if trying to envisage how it would be to see within the closed mass of the marble before it was cut.

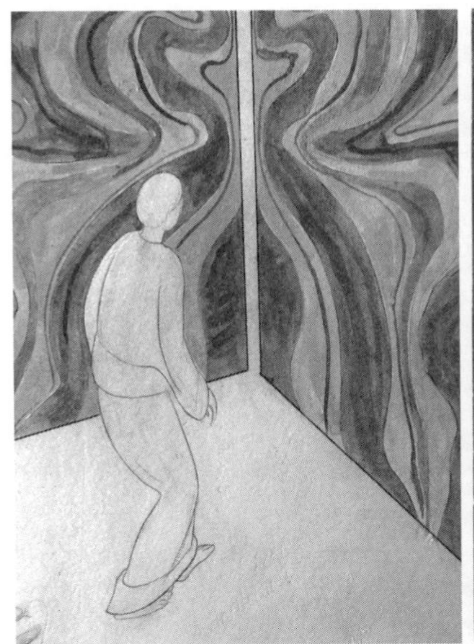

5. Left: Detail of visual demonstration II (plate 8), showing the human figure standing between two freshly cut marble blocks, as if trying to envisage how it would be to see within the closed mass of the marble before it was cut.

6. Right: Byzantine icon depicting Moses in front of the burning bush; early 13th century, St Catharine's Monastery on Mount Sinai.

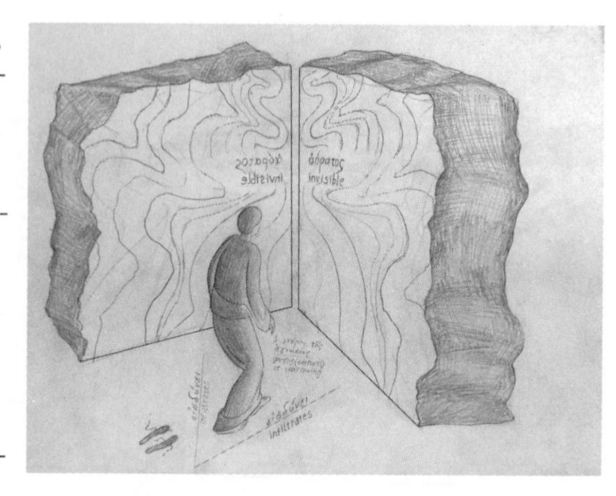

7. *Visual demonstration I*, showing a sixth-century Byzantine viewer and explaining schematically how, not simply the viewer's vision of the inside of the stone, but rather like Moses, the viewer himself, in a bodily sense: (a) goes through the unknown, (b) enters into the unknown, and finally (c) infiltrates deep into the unknown.

8. *Visual demonstration II*, showing the human figure standing between two freshly cut marble blocks, as if trying to envisage how it would be to see within the closed mass of the marble before it was cut.

9. *Visual demonstration III*, showing how, through the process of observing the inside of the marble, the human figure becomes absorbed into the colourful veins of the marble and thus becomes one with its own vision.

10. One of the unfolded marble panels inside the church of St Demetrius in Thessaloniki; 7th century.

11. One of the unfolded marble panels inside the church of St Demetrius in Thessaloniki; 7th century.

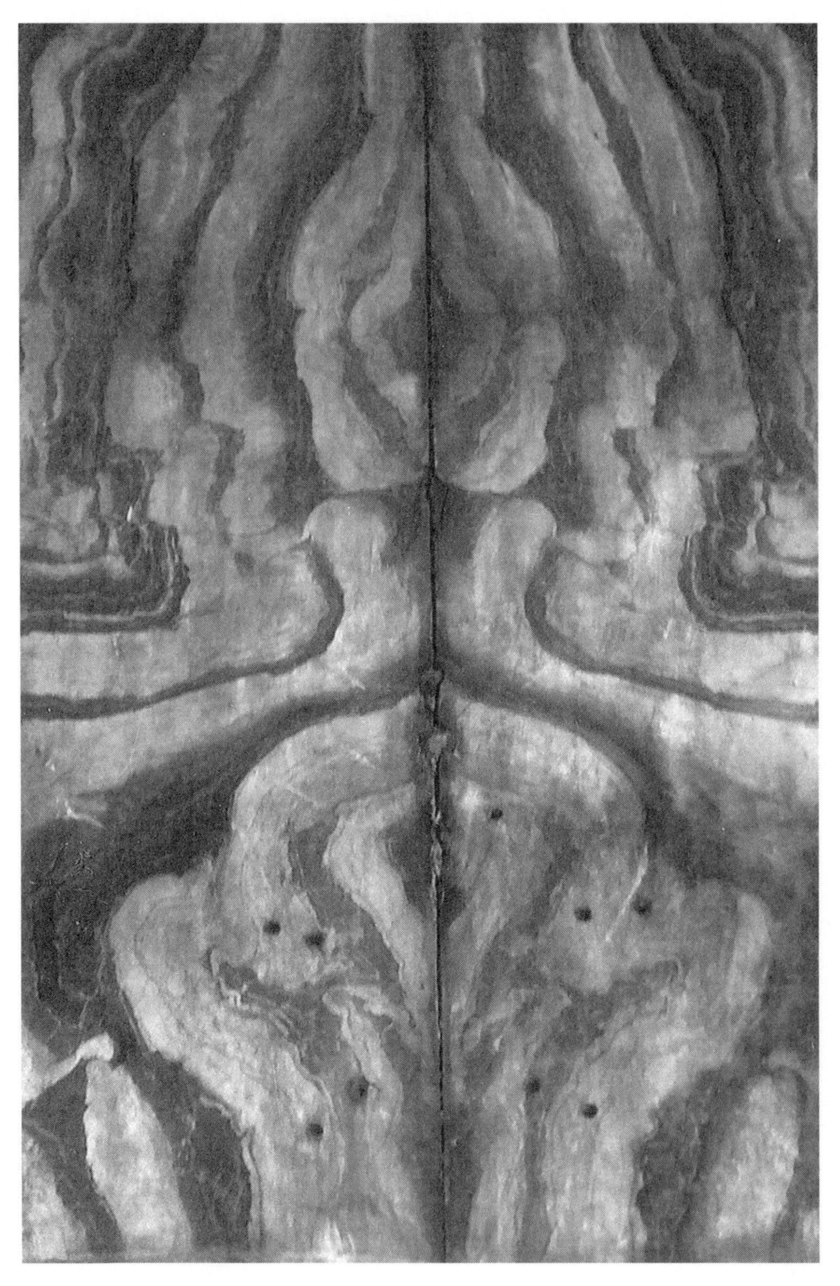

12. One of the unfolded marble panels inside the church of St Demetrius in Thessaloniki (detail); 7th century.

13. One of the unfolded marble panels inside Hagia Sophia in Constantinople; 6th century.

14. Unfolded marble panels inside Hagia Sophia of Constantinople; 6th century.

15. Unfolded marble panels inside Hagia Sophia of Constantinople; 6th century.

16. Unfolded marble panels inside Hagia Sophia of Constantinople; 6th century.

17. Unfolded marble panels inside Hagia Sophia of Constantinople; 6th century.

18. Unfolded marble panels inside the church of Chora in Constantinople; rebuilt in the 11th century and renovated in the 14th century.

19. The Transfiguration of Christ, Byzantine manuscript, 1347-1355, National Library, Paris.

20. One of the four cherubs which are rendered in the pendentives of Hagia Sophia in Constantinople.

21. Detail of one of the four cherubs which are rendered in the pendentives of Hagia Sophia in Constantinople.

22. One of the unfolded marble panels inside Hagia Sophia of Constantinople; 6th century.

23. Detail of one of the four cherubs which are rendered in the pendentives of Hagia Sophia in Constantinople.

24. Detail of *Visual demonstration I* (plate 7), showing a sixth-century Byzantine viewer and explaining schematically how, not simply the viewer's vision of the inside of the stone, but rather like Moses, the viewer himself, in a bodily sense: (a) goes through the unknown, (b) enters into the unknown, and finally (c) infiltrates deep into the unknown.

25. Detail of the interior of the 11th century church of Hosios Loukas near Distomo in Greece.

26. Detail of the interior of the 11th century church of Nea Moni on the island of Chios in Greece.

John Damascene's "Dialectic" as a Bond Between Philosophical Tradition and Theology

Slobodan Žunjić

I

It is perfectly hopeless to seek some kind of wholly original and entirely philosophical work in Byzantine spiritual life at the end of the 7th and beginning of the 8th centuries. If we are to judge according to that which has reached us, in those times philosophy was the work of ecclesiastical people only, and exclusively so within their theological studies. The bond with theology in fact represents the only form of philosophical life in those times, and this doubtlessly represents a serious fall for philosophy considering its previous position of queen of all sciences, whereas for theology – despite some previous cases in which certain Fathers and apologists opened up towards philosophical tradition – it represents a new phase in relation to Hellenic educatedness. It is precisely within this symbiosis of philosophy and theology that Damascene's *Fountain of Knowledge* emerges as a work of great synthesis which, within itself, unifies the Hellenic philosophical legacy with Christian theological thought. However, this synthesis is not entirely unified within itself since, in fact, it is comprised of three particular tracts. Within manuscripts the first of these bears no title, or, it is named with a neutral phrase only, i.e., as the "Philosophical Chapters" (Κεφάλαια φιλοσοφικά). This means that in subsequent tradition and in contemporary literature the common title *Dialectic* cannot be considered as original.[1] The second of these offers a historical overview of various heresies according to Epiphanius of Cyprus, Theodoret and Timotheus and it is most commonly cited under its Latin title *De haeresibus*[2] (Περὶ

1. The history of this title and its relation towards the content of the book itself are discussed in the author's monograph *Logic and Theology* (in Serbian).
2. The first eighty chapters of this overview bring forth only a slightly edited text Ἀνακεφαλέωσις from the so called *Panarion* of Epiphanius of Cyprus (PG 62), while the next 20 chapters represent an excerpt out of Theodoret of Cyrus, Leontius of Byzantium and other authors, but not out of Timotheus and Sophronius, as is sometimes (K. Krumbacher) wrongly cited due to mere coincidence of the manuscripts. Only the last three heresies,

αἱρέσεων), while the third of these, the most voluminous one, brings forth *An Exact Exposition* (or edition) *of the Orthodox Faith* (Ἔκδοσις /ἔκθεσις/ ἀκριβὴς τῆς ὀρθοδόξου πίστεως), that is to say dogmatics in the real sense of the word.[3]

As is already apparent from this differentiation itself, the first part of the *Fountain*, the so called *Dialectic*, is conceived as some sort of introduction to Orthodox theology, both of its wings included: the negative (refutation of heresies) and the positive (exposition of true doctrine). This conception – also announced in the short introductory epistle to Cosmas of Maiuma (524C–525A) – was initially supported by a short introductory tract of fifty chapters, out of which were to follow much more developed historical and systematic expositions containing a hundred chapters each (that is, *Heresiology* and *Dogmatology*). However, through time and by developing the introductory part further, Damascene himself disordered and brought into question his ideal plan for a comprehensive compendium of faith, and, he did so to such an extent that he brought into question both the mutual connection and original sequence of individual parts of the trilogy which, in the meantime, were further modified and developed. All parts of the *Fountain of Knowledge* finally received new extended or reordered versions which, regarded in mutual relation, offered new combinations. For this reason among others, in the manuscript tradition the *Dialectic* and *Dogmatic* started to gain independence, and the tract on heresies was either entirely omitted or placed at third position within this infirm trilogy. Indeed, this was completely contrary to the previous order.[4]

---

marked by numbers 101, 102 and 103 (autoproscoptic, iconoclastic and aposchitic) are perhaps described in an author's fashion by Damascene himself, although F. Diekamp holds that they have been inscribed later since they are not contained in the collection of writings known as *Doctrina patrum* – the one that was in this case used by Damascene as the referential text (*Doctrina patrum de Incarnatione verbi*, ed. F. Diekamp, Aschendorf [2] 1981, LXX–LXXI). H.-G. Beck joins the opinion of Diekamp. He states that the part on heresies is only an expanded excerpt from *Doctrina patrum* (*Kirche und theologische Literatur im byzantinischen Reich*, München 1959, 479). However, this opinion is brought into question by B. Kotter who indicates that this relation could be rather the reverse. That is to say, the tract on heresies from the *Fountain of Knowledge* made its way into the *Doctrina patrum* (*Die Überlieferung der Pege gnoseos des hl. Johannes von Damaskos*, Ettal 1959, 211–213). But, neither does he question the fact that the heresies after number one hundred have been added later, either by John Damascene himself (after 726) or by subsequent transcribers and translators.

3. In literature we find both versions of the title cited: ἔκδοσις and ἔκθεσις.
4. Since the Greek manuscripts mostly do not bring the part on heresies, or they merely add it at the end of the *Dogmatic* (but with the adage that this is the exposition by "blessed Epiphanius" and that it hence stems from the *Doctrina patrum*) the doubt appears whether the text which we today know under that name is a work of Damascene at all. The disharmony between Damascene's plan of the trilogy and the place which, presently, the tract on heresies occupies in Greek transcriptions can be explained only by help of the hypothesis about the chronological evolution of the pre-original intention, which was obviously revised in accordance with the gradual increase of independence of the *Dialectic* (cf. the research of G. Richter, *Dialektik des Johannes von Damaskus*, Ettal 1964, 14). Roughly speaking, the outcome of this revision may be formulated as follows: the *Dialectic* drew closer to a real encyclo-

The most significant changes, nevertheless, affected the introductory part of the trilogy. The re-working of the introductory part in fact triggered the abandonment of the earlier conception of a tightly structured whole comprised of three interrelated parts. Ultimately, from the pre-original fifty chapters (a number, it seems, which was posited in proportion to the hundred chapters of the *Dogmatic* and pre-original hundred chapters on heresies) the *Dialectic* grew to 68 chapters. This led to a confusing coexistence of two different versions of this tract, both in terms of length and content. In critical literature their mutual relation has been discussed for an entire century. Still, an accord between experts is gradually being forged in the sense that the shorter version of the *Dialectic* is deemed the earlier one, and that the longer version came forth as the consequence of the aspiration to allow more space and right to philosophical contents in relation to the pre-original purpose, according to which they were to have only an auxiliary (introductory) role.[5]

Obviously, the primordial intention of the composer of the *Fountain of Knowledge* was primarily dogmatic: that is, to gather and expound the basic propositions of the Orthodox faith. In other words, Damascene wanted to create a reference book of basic dogmas which would, in a synoptic and clear way, determine all the key theological concepts necessary for the understanding of the Eastern-Christian *confessio fidei*. Although the need for such a dogmatic was considerable, it, nevertheless, represented almost an absolute novelty. And this was so because the prior Byzantine tradition was almost completely unacquainted with such a genre. The only possible prototypes for this, which could have been accessible to Damascene, were Origen's

pedia of philosophical-logical knowledge, however, it did so at the price of destroying the ambitiously conceived trilogy, so that the title *Fountain of Knowledge* relates only to its bond with the *Dogmatic*.

5. The two versions differ particularly with regard to the first part of the *Dialectic*. The shorter version commences with chapters 4 and 10, whereas the longer version has entirely new chapters at its beginning – i.e. chapters 1, 2, 3 and 5 – furthermore, in the middle, it contains a short unknown group of chapters – i.e. chapters 18–28 – and, on top of that, chapters 6, 7, 8 are converted into chapters 14, 15 and 16, while 12, 13 and 14 become chapters 6, 7, and 8. Although we can still find authors who argue in favor of the primacy of the longer version (Studer, Gordillo), it seems that the reasons laid out by the second camp (Kotter and Richter) – who argue in favor of the primacy of the shorter version – are becoming increasingly convincing (for example, chapter 4 is indeed adequate for a beginning of a treatise as regards the shorter version, but it is no longer suitable as regards the longer version; genus and species are discussed together in the shorter version, as well as in the small introduction to the dogmas, whereas in the longer version this discussion is distributed into two particular chapters). The general explanation of the relation between the two versions is also more logical if one starts from the premise that the shorter version is the older one. In that case, the longer version emerges from Damascene's aspiration to take the initially compressed collection of definitions from the short *Introduction to the Dogmas* (which, in the meantime, was expanded in the shorter version of the *Dialectic* to the level of a propedeutical handbook for logic) and develop them even more, thus bringing them closer to the philosophical tradition of commentary (G. Richter, *op. cit.*, 60–62).

treatise *On First Principles* (Περὶ ἀρχῶν) and the fifth book of Theodoret's treatise *Compendium of Heretical Accounts* (Αἱρετικῆς κακομυθίας ἐπιτομή). This treatise by Theodoret of Cyrus expounds an outline of an orthodox dogmatic which, in turn, is taken as a conclusion to the foregoing overview of heresies. That Damascene significantly followed Theodoret's treatise is noticeable not only from the pre-original plan of the *Fountain of Knowledge*, which did envisage the positing of the book on heresies before the one on dogmatics, but also from the concordance of the inner articulation of the dogmatic exposition, which does reflect Theodoret's sequence: the Trinity, creation, man, free will, the fall, salvation and resurrection.[6] However, Damascene gradually started to abandon this initial combination of dogmatics and heresiology, for he begun to increasingly accentuate the philosophical support for propositions of faith. The consequences of that were reflected in a twofold manner: in the exclusion of the part on heresies from the trilogy and in the expansion of the part dedicated to logical and philosophical concepts.

II

Although the scope of the *Dialectic* did change over time, the basic idea, which inspired the inception of this treatise, did not change significantly. The main goal in the *Dialectic*, taken as a sort of philosophical prolegomena, was and continued to be the introduction and clarification of all the concepts of classical Hellenic discursive culture which were thereafter utilised or presupposed in an exact exposition of the dogmas of the Christian faith. Before anything else, these are the concepts of *essence*, *nature* and *hypostasis* (οὐσία, φύσις, ὑπόστασις) and then a whole series of eminently logical concepts, such as *genus*, *species*, *difference*, *property* and *accident* (γένος, εἶδος, διαφορά, ἴδιον, συμβεβηκός), which descend from the elaboration of Aristotle's logic in late antiquity or, more precisely, from neo-Platonic commentaries on Aristotle's *Categories*.[7]

All the other concepts of Aristotle's logic, the ten categories, the so called antepredicaments and postpredicaments, as well as the other following concepts (definition, concept, name, sign, etc) were invested with an auxiliary role in the establishment of the Byzantine theological armature. Damascene took them over from their classical definitions without major changes, which makes this fact even more significant. Moreover, not for a single moment did he try to conceal the circumstance that in his preparation for the dogmatic

6. The correspondence of Book 5 of Theodoret's treatise with the systematization realized in the *Fountain of Knowledge* and especially in the *Exact Exposition of the Orthodox Faith* has been noted by both B. Tatakis, *La philosophie byzantine*, Paris 1959, 113 and H.-G. Beck, *op. cit.*, 479.
7. The Byzantines received the texts of Aristotle's *Organon* mostly through the neo-Platonic commentaries, primarily through the Alexandrian ones, but also through Simplicius' Athenian works in which one senses that same spirit of a solid exegetical school (In terms of education Simplicius, too, was the fruit of the Alexandrian school).

exposition he relied directly upon the conceptual legacies of pagan Hellenic thought. On the contrary, already in the prologue of the *Dialectic* he emphasizes that "he shall first expound what is best from the Hellenic wise men, knowing that if something is good it is given to men from above, from God" (Kotter 52, 43–45). Hence, one should not refrain from drawing profit even from the "enemy" (52, 50).

To us as contemporary members of the Western European philosophical areal such openness towards classical philosophy, certainly, comes across as a self-evident presupposition. But in the 7th and 8th centuries it could still have been a very debatable thing. Hence, Damascene had to justify it in advance. That is, one should not forget that in Byzantine culture there always existed a certain distaste towards Hellenic tradition, especially towards Aristotle's philosophy, although, as many examples demonstrate – from Gregory of Nazianzus all the way to the hesychasts of the 14th century – it was expressed precisely in terms of classical conceptual culture.[8] Therefore, we should not be overly surprised to see how Damascene, in the first chapter of the *Dialectic*, immediately deals with a possible objection stating promptly that his reference to pagan philosophy is not appropriate to "the enhypostatized wisdom of Christ."[9] His justification of such an act is twofold. Damascene first emphasizes that "nothing is more valuable than knowledge, for knowledge is the light of the rational soul" (53, 1–2). But, sensing that an apology of knowledge in principle does not mean much to those who are already distrustful towards knowledge, he strengthens his standpoint by recurring to the apostolic authority of Apostle Paul, whose reserve towards the "outer wisdom" of Greek philosophers was doubtlessly sufficiently well known to Byzantine readers: "Since the divine Apostle says: 'But test everything; hold fast that which is good' (1 Thess. 5, 21), let us also test the teachings of outer wise men. Perhaps we shall find something useful and reap something that will be of profit for the soul. For every craftsman has need, also, of certain things for the completion of his work. And it is also fitting for the queen to be waited upon by certain handmaidens" (PG 94, 532B; Kotter 54, 52–58).

The defence of "outer wisdom," which at the time was the usual name for Greek pagan philosophy, therefore, is here founded in the need to preserve what is "useful for the soul" (ψυχωφελές), namely, that which at the same

8. The aversion to Aristotle was part and parcel of the general reserve towards classical philosophy. In relation to this we find good testimony preserved in the well known saying of Gregory of Nazianzus: ἁλιευτικῶς, ἀλλ' οὐκ ἀριστοτελικῶς (*Or.*, 23, 12, PG 35, 1164C). "In the manner of the fishermen, not in that of Aristotle!" How difficult it is to remain on that "fishermen" level is nicely shown by the case of Gregory Palamas. His main distinction, that between essence and energy, in virtue of which he was triumphant in the dispute with the syllogists of the Aristotelian kind (Barlaam, Akindynos), rests in fact on Aristotle's concepts οὐσία and ἐνέργεια.
9. "Enhypostasized" (ἐνυπόστατος) is in fact a term from neo-Platonic psychology which entered the *Dialectic* from the treatise of Leontius of Byzantium, precisely within the process of accepting Aristotelian concepts (see below).

time may serve as an instrument of "inner" (the queen's) wisdom. In that sense philosophy in this citation is compared with a "means" of the craftsman or with the queen's "handmaiden." The very parable about "queen" and "handmaiden" is quite old – let us remember how much effort Plato and Aristotle invest in order to demonstrate that philosophy, in the sense of principle, is the mistress in relation to all other sciences (*Met.* 982b 4). Therefore, Damascene, too, accepts this thesis about the necessary hierarchy of knowledge in which the lower sciences have the task to "serve" the higher sciences. However, he totally inverts the meaning of this figure. It is entirely clear who, in an order thus rearranged, now needs to be "queen" and who "handmaiden." But it is also no less clear that Damascene does not bring into question the justifiedness of knowing and using (Greek) philosophy. On the contrary, Hellenic philosophy procures something proper and useful, therefore it should be studied. Hence, the metaphor about the "queen" and "handmaiden" in fact suggests a considerably more pacificatory relation between philosophy and theology in the Byzantine system of knowledge than the one which Tertullian (*de praescriptione haereticorum*, c. 7) and Tatian (*or. ad Graecos* 2, 25) have pleaded for – following in the steps of the famous warning of Apostle Paul ("See to it that no one makes a prey of you by philosophy and empty deceit, according to human tradition, according to the elemental spirits of the world, and not according to Christ" Col. 2, 8). Tertullian labelled Aristotle as miserable due to his wrangling with dialectical craft (*miserum Aristotelem qui illis dialecticam instituit artificem*) and Gregory of Nazianzus without hesitation named this skill an evil craft (*Orat.* 6). Not very different are the statements given by Epiphanius and Theodoret – statements which Damascene does use in composing the handbook on heresies. Still, the stance of univocal condemnation was gradually transformed into a stance of conditional acceptance. In a word, philosophy now subsists because it can be useful, and it is useful as *ancilla theologiae* (an expression which was first deployed in wider usage by Clement of Alexandria, but which was in fact introduced by Philo of Alexandria).[10]

From a relation thus posited – which, fortuitously, not even Damascene abides by altogether literally and consistently – one should understand why in his work he does not journey into any kind of theoretical deliberation on

10. Using the biblical narrative about the two wives of Abraham (Sarah and Hagar) Philo interprets pagan philosophy allegorically as a handmaiden (*De congressu eruditione gratia*, 71–80) and Clement takes up this figure in *Strom.*, I, 5; 29, 10–32, 4 (cf. H. Hunger, *Die hochsprachiche profane Literatur der Byzantiner*, München 1978, 42; also from the same author *Reich der neuen Mitte. Der christliche Geist der byzantinischen Kultur*, Graz 1965, 356). However, it is important to stress that in the East this formula was never institutionalized in an educational and ideological sense, since the living tradition of non-theological education in the sciences and philosophy persisted there till the very end (in fact, theology was taught privately and independently, through the practice of reading, and not at university). It is therefore a true assertion that the strict application of this formula is more an act of the West than that of the East.

the criterion of true cognition. The cognition of truth is in the possession of God: it is laid out in the *Holy Scripture* and, therefore, it is not necessary to give a special explanation of the position of philosophy in relation to theology. Hence, for Damascene the relation of philosophy and theology does not represent some systematic problem which would, also, require a thorough systematic resolution. He simply commences from the fact that theology for a very long time has been using philosophical concepts while formulating key statements about the nature of Christ and the nature of the Trinity. He wishes only to expound and articulate this practice in clear terms, and not to re-examine it, let alone to put it under the question mark. As we shall see, this intention, in essence innocent as it is, during the process of its fruitful development, faces a series of difficulties and unforeseen situations.

III

As was noted a long time ago, the encounter of religion and the logical-mathematical spirit always was and ever remained potentially possible on the basis of their common authoritarian nature. In historical experience you shall find a sufficient number of examples which confirm the truth that faith often turned towards philosophical logic from which it expected, by virtue of its stringency and consistency, in the domain of mind to demonstrate the same power of coercion which in the domain of emotions was demanded by the religious legalist.[11] Damascene's *Dialectic* is just one case of this regularity. Taking Hellenic concepts into the service of Christian faith, in fact, is no peculiarity of Damascene's, but, rather, one of the characteristic traits of the whole of Byzantine philosophy, from its inception to its very end. This early Byzantine opening-up towards Aristotelian logic may come us a surprise only to those who are totally non-initiated. However, it was a natural consequence of Christianity turning into a universal religion. And, in regard to its past, it had already traversed the path of a long pre-history of the Hellenization of its (Christian) theology. The first important step in the theological reception of Aristotle was achieved in the first half of the 6th century when Leontius of Byzantium transported the statements of faith in their entirety into the language of Aristotelian concepts. Through an appropriate defining of the terms *essence* and *nature* (οὐσία, φύσις) he succeeded in demonstrating that the three hypostases of the Holy Trinity have only one nature, while the two natures of Christ comprise only one hypostasis.[12] According to Leontius,

11. Cf. S. S. Averincev, "Evolucija vizantijske filosofije do VII veka," *Istočnik* 7–8 (1993) 45. On the other hand, mathematical formalism and pure empirism are no strangers to mysticism, as is evident in many examples from Kepler to Whitehead; cf. M. Horkheimer, *Kritička teorija*, II, Zagreb s. a., 883.
12. Therefore, contrary to Philoponus, who equalized nature with hypostasis, Leontius brought together the concepts of nature (φύσις) and essence (οὐσία), and then he opposed them together against the concept of hypostasis (ὑπόστασις). Although, on one hand, for him essence (in wholly Aristotelian manner) is a particular "thing" – which thence by defini-

Christ was essentially a noetic being which, through its will, assumed human nature. In order to explain this duality of Christ, Leontius used the comparison between body and soul in the human being, claiming that in Christ as well one finds such a union of natures: that is to say, that there is a proportion between the hypostasis of the human being and the hypostasis of the Logos. The former hypostasis is the carrier of the soul and bodily essence at the same time. Likewise, the latter hypostasis is the carrier of human and divine nature.

But, in difference to the monophysites, Leontius kept adding that the union of two natures in Christ does not produce the physical union of one nature, since the proportion is valid in the inverse sense as well, so that both soul and body exist as independent essences also before the union. That would mean that both the divinity and humanity of Christ, which in him join in union, exist independently before that union. Such a conclusion is also confirmed by the fact that for Leontius the main characteristic of the hypostasis is that it subsists "in itself" (καθ' ἑαυτὸ ὑφεστῶς; *Epilys.*, PG 86, 1933A). However, Leontius avoided this heretical conclusion by declaring that in the case of Christ it is a logical possibility only, but not simultaneously a real possibility (*Epilys.*, PG 86, 1944C). He named the union of divinity and humanity in Christ as the "essential union" (ἕνωσις οὐσιώδες) or as the "union according to essence" (ἕνωσις κατ' οὐσίαν), which are basically Aristotelian terms by means of which, in a convenient way, one avoids the stating of physical union of that which is in fact incompatible (*Contra Nest. et Eut.*, 1297D, 1300AB; *Epilys.*, 1941AB).

tion is opposed to that which is "accidental" (PG 86, 1277D) – he, on the other hand, defines it as mere existence (ὕπαρξις) which is totally undetermined and says "neither what nor how" about a given being (*Epilys.*, 1921C). In that case essence signifies the universal (PG 86, 2, 1927AB), existence in general, in difference to hypostasis which represents existence in the individual, particular form (1280A). In signifying only the essence of some being with regard to what makes it different to other kinds of being, essence becomes synonymous with nature (*physis*), in which the number of things that participate in it is not definitorially determined. It should be said that the "second" substance (or better: essence) is equal to "nature" only if it relates to the hypostases, which contain it as a common element, that is to say, it is not an universal common element of all beings. The hypostazing of nature makes it into some determined thing of that nature, which gathers into itself the proper accidents. Therefrom every hypostasis is a nature, but not every nature is necessarily a hypostasis (Leontius, PG 89, 1, 1280A). The relation between hypostasis and nature, therefore, is not symmetrical and reciprocal. Such a differentiation could have been made only by someone well acquainted with Aristotelian logic and its elaboration in Porphyry's *Isagoge* and other neo-Platonic commentaries; and this is admitted by Sheldon-Williams as well, who otherwise highlights the Platonic aspects of the teaching of Leontius of Byzantium (cf. *The Cambridge History of Later Greek and Early Medieval Philosophy*, ed. A. H. Armstrong, Cambridge 1967, 488). In counter-distinction to this reference to Leontius' part in the spreading of Byzantine Aristotelism, G. Podskalsky is very skeptical both in regard to the ambit and in regard to the quality of this "Aristotelism" (*Theologie und Philosophie in Byzanz*, München 1977, 97), for he does not acknowledge the fact that Leontius' ἀπορία καὶ λύσεις are a fully fledged derived form of primordial Aristotelian aporetics.

In order to explain the possibility of this communion of two natures in one hypostasis, Leontius at a given locus also introduces the term "enhypostatic union" (1300A; *contra Nest. et Eut.*, 1277CD),[13] the reflection of which one encounters in John Damascene as well.[14] By means of this expression the linear equation either one nature - one hypostasis, or two natures - two hypostases, is completely avoided and it is clearly affirmed that the hypostasis does not signify a numerical parted being (in any case, it can have the same nature as some other), and, moreover, that it can also signify the union of different natures in the sense of "existing within something." The fact that not every nature is a hypostasis does not mean that a certain nature can exist independently of a certain hypostasis. On the contrary, natures which are not hypostases exist in hypostases, that is to say, as "enhypostatic" natures. According to Leontius, "enhypostatic" nature is a nature which itself is not a hypostasis, but which exists only in a hypostasis thus making up its essence. While the hypostasis (ὑπόστασις) is that which subsists in itself (τὸ καθ' ἑαυτὸ ὑπάρχειν; PG 86, 1945A), the "enhypostatic" (ἐνυπόστατον) is defined as that which signifies essence, but such which only comprises a part of something, or, even better, of someone (PG 86, 1277CD). It could be said that the hypostasis signifies someone in the immediate sense, while "enhypostatic" indicates that what is at hand is not an accidentality which exists within another, but, rather, an essential union.

After Leontius it is Maximus the Confessor who takes over many Aristotelian formulations into his Christology,[15] although he was much closer in spirit to the mystical (neo-Platonic) tradition of Pseudo-Dionysius the Areopagite, to whose opus he added elaborate scholia.[16] In fact, he mutually combined the Platonic and Aristotelian viewpoints as two perspectives of things from which the entirety of the created needs to be understood. The first perspective is determined by the concept of essence (λόγος τῆς οὐσίας), while the other one stems forth from the transient way of existence of a given being (τρόπος τῆς ὑπάρξεως). Beings strive to unify both perspectives,

13. J. Meyendorff, *Hristos u istočno-hrišćanskoj misli*, Hilandar 1994, 154; Sheldon-Williams, *op. cit.*, 491.

14. In the *Dialectic* two meanings of this term are ascertained: on one hand, ἐνυπόστατον is simple being (ἁπλῶς ὄν, ἁπλῶς ὕπαρξις) and, on the other hand, it is that which is indivisible, that is, the individual, the hypostasis in itself (Kotter 93, 4–7). A further locus from the same chapter 45 (Kotter 109, 1), which has its full parallels in the Oxford manuscript (Kotter 165, 9–11) and *Doctrina patrum* (137, 4), states that ἐνυπόστατον can also be accidental, but it is immediately added that in that case it is in fact ἑτεροϋπόστατον and not the hypostasis in the real sense. Cf. G. Podskalsky, "Untersuchungen zu einigen Zentralbegriffen der patristischen Personenspekulation in der vom Exarchen Johannes geschaffenen slavischen Erstübersetzung der Ἔκθεσις ἀκριβὴς τῆς ὀρθοδόξου πίστεως des Johannes von Damaskus," *Die Welt der Slaven* 2 (1970) 151.

15. Cf. K. Oehler, "Aristoteles in Byzanz," in: *Aristoteles in der neueren Forschung*, hrsg. P. Moraux, Darmstadt 1968, 393sq.

16. Still, it seems that the major part of those scholia are the work of John of Scythopolis; G. Podskalsky, *op. cit.*, 30, 102.

that is, to take the other one, Aristotelian nature, and subsume it under the first one, the Platonic idea or Christian salvation. This way leads from becoming (γένεσις), via movement (κίνησις), to non-movement (στάσις), which signifies the stadium of eternal being (ἀεὶ εἶναι). In relation to this developmental process, Maximus supplements Aristotle's ontological conceptual pair possibility-necessity (δύναμις-ἐνέργεια) with a third, final instance of unperturbed non-activity (ἀργία). The extent of Maximus' knowledge of Aristotle's logical works may be discerned from his lesser works in which we find explanations of the concepts of quality, property, difference, essence, nature, hypostasis and person (PG 91, 245–257; 260–264).[17]

All of the said convinced even the diehard sceptics that Aristotle's philosophy, of course, with certain precautionary measures, was very exploitable for expressing the most important theological statements and distinctions. The Byzantine theologians thus finally grasped that the very same concepts which led many into heresy can be used for the defence of Orthodox doctrine from erroneous interpretations.[18] Through the works of Leontius of

17. Cf. H. Hunger, *Die hochsprachliche profane Literatur der Byzantiner*, Bd. I, Munchen 1978, 47. In the manuscripts two shorter texts from the 7th century with definitions (*Cod. Vat. gr.* 504, f. 147 and *Cod. Athos Vatop. gr.* 57, ff. 257–261) – which, as the title states, thematize Porphyry's *Introduction* and Aristotle's *Categories* – are ascribed to Maximus, with whose various definitions (PG 91, 149sq) and with the definitions of unity (PG 91, 213sq) they do show certain similarities (M. Roueché, "Byzantine Philosophical Texts of the Seventh Century," *Jahrbuch der Österreichischen Byzantinistik* 23 (1973) 63). Even if they are not his authentic work, the fact that they are found exclusively in the manuscripts of his writings seems to indicate that, perhaps, they were originally discovered as part of his legacy, which would additionally confirm his interest for Aristotelian definitions. In the manuscripts Maximus also introduces the Aristotelian passages of Theodore of Raithu (Προπαρασκευή), which were translated into Church Slavonic as early as the 10th century.

18. At the same time, naturally, negative reactions were manifested as well. For Aristotle's philosophy was at first suspected as the source of all possible heresies (cf. Clement of Alexandria, *Protr.* V, 66, 4). Besides, this was not without reason, if one knows that among Christians it was firstly utilized by Syrian Nestorians and by Alexandrian monophysites. Both of these sects, that were soon to evolve into particular Churches (the Syrian one and the Coptic-Egyptian one), reached their key points of view – about two, that is about one nature of Christ – through Aristotle's concepts of essence (οὐσία) and nature (φύσις), and in some other points, too, they manifest coincidences and bonds with Aristotelism. The Nestorian rejection of the birth of God, that is, the assertion that Christ is only a man who, through exceptional moral life and cognitive effort, earned the subsistence of the divine Logos within him – were motivated by the Aristotelian understanding of human nature as something which is directed towards perfection and which strives towards immortality. That is to say, in Aristotelian tradition the divine is not something absolutely other and otherworldly, but something which does subsist in the perfect human being (*EN*, 1177b 28, 33; 1145a 19). It is therefore no coincidence that Ibas of Edessa (the centre of Nestoriansim) translated Aristotle's pragmatia into Syrian, together with the works of Theodore of Mopsuestia (in which the influence of Aristotle can already be detected). Monophysitism drew more from Alexandrian neo-Platonism and generally from Platonic understanding that human existence is some sort of falleness from a higher spiritual state – which meant, in the given case, that Christ can only be an epiphany of God in man – than from Aristotelism; but, the usage of Aristotelian concepts potentialized the difference, issuing therefrom, of divine natures. Philoponus, seduced by the logic of the concepts of essence and nature, became a

Byzantium, and then also Maximus the Confessor, including a series of other anonymous ecclesial writers of that era as well, Aristotle's concepts gained the right of citizenship in Byzantine theology, as early as the second half of the 6th century.[19] John Damascene's *Dialectic* represents precisely this, conditionally speaking, "logical" current of Byzantine patristics, which definitely opens the doors to concepts of Aristotle's philosophy, but not as much to those of his metaphysics as much as, primarily, to those of his logic. Therefore, it stands not at the beginning but at the end of Byzantine philosophical articulation of the dogmas, which was rightly named as the "Christianisation of Aristotle's logic."[20]

IV

What is more, this turning towards the Greek rationalistic philosophy of concepts occurred earlier in the East in comparison to the West, although the presence of Aristotle's metaphysical concepts later became more prominent in Western European theology.[21] Better said, if Hellenic philosophy is taken to mean the late-classical school philosophy and its conceptual apparatus, built by means of the fusion of Aristotle's logic and Plato's metaphysics, then, in Byzantium there never was any real break with the language of Greek

monophysite. Witness to this is given by fragments of his treatise *Διαιτησίας ἢ περὶ ἑνώσεως*; and, when he applied these concepts to the doctrine on the Trinity he was accused of tritheism (cf. *Doctrina patrum de incarnatione verbi*, 272, 20cq). It could be said that tritheism, too, has an Aristotelian origin, for it treats the relation of divine persons towards divine nature as the relation of individual examples towards species. Even the Arian rejection of the equality of the Son with God the Father in eternity and in essence (such as derived in Eunomius, who deduces the Son and the world from the enactedness of the highest essence) betrays the background action of Aristotelian conceptual apparatus (comp. E. Ivanka, *Hellenisches und Christliches im frübyzantinischen Geistesleben*, Wien 1948, 18, 21, 85, 95).

19. This is displayed in a whole series of neglected manuscripts dispersed throughout European libraries. One group of these anonymous texts, which were created as excerpts or as paraphrases of parts of the Alexandrian commentaries, was presented by M. Roueché, "Byzantine Philosophical Texts of the Seventh Century," *Jahrbuch der Österreichischen Byzantinistik* 23 (1974) 61–76. Various collections of definitions are based upon them, such as the one by Theodore of Raithu. In the middle ages this particular one was known amongst us as well, in translation (the collections of the Svyatoslavian type in Chilandari and in the Romanian Academy of Sciences), or, the one by Pseudo-Athanasius, which was transcribed into Greek by Nikon of Jerusalem in the monastery of Gorica, on the Skadar lake (on matters relating to that transcription see M. Marković, "Novi rukopis ps. Atanasijevog traktata *de definitionibus* i Eusebijeve sinopse Jevanđelja," *Živa antika* 1–2 (1952) 159–167; Greek text PG 28, 534–554.
20. H. Schaeder, "Die Christianisierung der aristotelischen Logik in der byzantinischen Theologie, repräsentiert durch Johannes von Damaskos und Gregorios Palamas," *Θεολογία* 33 (1962) 1–21 (also in: *Kerygma und Dogma* 8 (1962) 293–309). Schaeder proves this process on the basis of the reception of the concept ἐνέργεια. However, such a choice of example is not most fortuitous because ἐνέργεια is not a concept of logic and plays no role in the *Dialectic*.
21. The merit for this in great measure belongs to John Damascene, for his opus, as is admitted by F. Copleston, *A History of Philosophy*, vol 2, part I, New York 1962, 52, did help in preparing for the reception of Aristotle in the West.

philosophy. The prohibition against the pagan Academy in 529 was more a legal expression of an ideological standpoint than a description of the real state of affairs. For, Justinian's edict did not terminate the activity of philosophers in Athens (Simplicius' famous commentaries were written precisely on Greek soil after 533, that is, after the Sassanid exile of the neo-Platonics), let alone the work of schools in other centres such as Alexandria or Antioch.[22] And much later, when the old Stoic, Epicurean and neo-Platonic sects completely stopped working, the educational contents of philosophy did not change much in relation to what was offered by the late-classical (pagan) educational system, regardless of the fact that the very powerful monastic movement, which had its own independent educational institutions, came forward ceaselessly against an unrestrained assimilation of Hellenic tradition.[23]

The fact that in Byzantium education retained all of the most important elements of the late-classical philosophical programme had extraordinary significance for the transmission of Aristotle's concepts into the confession of Christian doctrine. In all the great schools of that time the study of philosophy was founded on logical manuals which contained determinations of the basic philosophical concepts in the spirit of Aristotle's philosophy, that is, more precisely stated, in the spirit of Aristotle's logic. This holds as true not only for the public schools and universities, but also relates to the main

22. In a very instigative article, "La Fin de l'Academie," published in the collection of works *Le Neoplatonisme*, Rouaumont 1969, Paris 1971, A. Cameron tried to totally revise the in-rooted historical image according to which the development of Greek philosophy was definitely severed in 529. However, he was only partly successful in this endeavor (cf. especially 283, 288). Cameron demonstrated that the pagan philosophers continued their work, although their efforts were followed by ceaseless harassment by the authorities, which in 532 provoked the intervention of Persia on behalf of the protection of the "human rights" of philosophers (these were specially fixed in terms of the peace treaty). However, that is not sufficient to turn Justinian's prohibition of teaching – binding upon all those "sick from the sacrilegious disease of the Hellenes" (*Cod. Just.*, 1, 11, 10) – into a mere myth, and to claim that philosophizing in Athens was much more endangered in 579 due to the destructive raid conducted by the Slavs (a match to the annihilation of Rome by Alarich) than by the confiscation of the goods of the Academia by imperial governance. That is, it must be admitted that in the long run the constant administrative persecution of philosophers, not only in psychological terms, was more lethal for philosophy than the passing external (barbaric) threats, despite the fact that some philosophers for years on did find protection within the imperial court itself. The other extreme is the viewpoint of P. Lemerle who gives his undivided trust to not altogether trustworthy reports by the chroniclers Malala (XVIII, 451) and Agapius (II, 23–31, 70). Taking reference in them, he thenceforth claims that Justinian's prostaxis, as an act of state intolerance, referred to the banishment of paganism as a whole and that it, therefore, affected all pagan teachers of philosophy; *Le premier Humanisme Byzantin*, Paris 1971, 71.

23. This is a situation which is entirely different to the one in the West were the educational centers soon became closely tied to the episcopal and monastic schools. On the organization of teaching of philosophy and on programmes in Byzantium cf. L. Brehier, "L'Enseignement classique et l'enseignement religieux a Byzance," *Revue d'Histoire et de Philosophie religieuse* 21 (1941) 34–69; idem, *Vizantijska civilizacija*, Beograd 1976, 407sq; K. Fuchs, *Die höheren Schulen von Konstantinopel im Mittelalter*, Amsterdam [12]1954; V. Janićijević, "Dijalektička logika u periodu Vizantije," *Filozofske studije* XXIV (1992) 16–19.

fortresses of neo-Platonism (the Academy and the Mouseion) in which Aristotle's logic was understood as the best introduction to "real" philosophy, that is, to Plato's initiation (μυσταγωγία) into the great "mysteries of philosophy." The "small mysteries" of philosophy were contained in Aristotle's logic, which had the task to prepare students for that "mystagogical" ascent towards Plato. This is the formulation used by Proclus' disciple Marinus (*Vita Procli*, XIII) and it expresses very well the spirit of that movement, very prone to religiosity and mystical feelings, but without neglecting the classical conceptual culture and philosophical technique, which attained its highest stadium of development precisely in Aristotle's philosophy.[24] The founding support for this discursive side in this synthesis were the notes from Aristotle's numerous lectures (especially those in logic), the so called *pragmatia*, which precisely at that time, at the expense of the previously much more esteemed Stagirite's dialogues, enter into the forefront of interest. It was thought that these works, which came forth from a long standing member of the Academy, were an expedient and valid replacement to the unwritten school lectures of Plato, in the light of which the most important dialogues of Plato are to be interpreted (the so called Canon of 10 dialogues).[25]

This endorsement of Aristotle from the side of neo-Platonic schools, at first glance, represents a very unusual amalgam. For Plato's speculative philosophy was traditionally understood as a striking opposite to Aristotle's "sober" science. However, it should be known that the later neo-Platonics accepted Aristotle as the finest pupil of Plato, and also as one who did not betray the thought of his teacher in anything, but succeeded in further developing and systematizing it in the categorial sense.[26] The Platonic school commenced the reception of Aristotle's concepts as early as the so-called Middle Platonic (Albinus, Atticus, Apuleius), and the borrowing of the Stagirite's logic intensified in Plotinus's school of neo-Platonism, although Plotinus himself, as is well known, was very critical towards Aristotle's logic.

Plotinus' pupil Porphyry (232/3–301/305), however, endeavoured to prove that there is no essential disharmony between Plato's and Aristotle's philosophy, but only a difference in the domain of validity: Aristotle's logic

24. In this sense the thought of Aristotle recommended itself in pedagogic terms as a suitable point of departure for the exploration of Plato. After ascertaining that Aristotle does not contradict Plato, Elias in his *Introduction to Aristotle's Categories* states openly that an interpreter of Aristotle needs to understand his writings as an introduction to the writings of Plato: *τὰ Ἀριστοτέλους τῶν Πλάτωνος εἰσαγωγὴν ποιούμενος* (*Eliae in Aristotelis Categorias Commentarium*, CAG XVIII 1, 123, 1–11).
25. The 10 canonical dialogues (according to Iamblichus) included these, in the following order: *Alcibiades, Gorgias, Phaedo, Cratylus, Theaetetus, The Sophist, The Statesman, Phaedrus, Symposion, Philebus*, and after these, as the crown, came two "perfect" dialogues, *Timaeus* and *Parmenides*; cf. L. G. Westerink, *Anonimous Prolegomena to Platonic Philosophy*, Amsterdam 1962, XXXVIII.
26. That is, Aristotle was more committed to logic, which prepares us for the understanding of Plato's ontology – this separation of logic from ontology represents the basic strategy of almost all subsequent tendencies of harmonizing the thought of Plato and Aristotle.

refers to this world, while Plato's ontology is valid for the world of noetic essences. This means that these two philosophies are complementary and that, therefore, the study of Aristotle is not only useful but also necessary. In order to show this Porphyry wrote two commentaries on Aristotle's *Categories* and, on top of that, the renowned *Introduction* to this treatise (Εἰσαγωγή εἰς τὰς Κατηγορίας),[27] in which the status of the categories is determined, definitions of the so called five voices (πέντε φωναί) are given, and their mutual relations are thoroughly clarified within the framework of the tripartite division of Aristotle's works into antepredicaments, predicaments (categories) and postpredicaments.[28] Porphyry's work on Aristotle's logical works had a huge influence on the further development of philosophy in the Middle ages, both in the West (through Boethius' translation), which is common knowledge, and also in the East, in Byzantium, which, sadly, is not sufficiently known, let alone understood. Namely, Porphyry's commentaries and the mentioned *Introduction* instigated a series of further commentaries both on Aristotle's categories themselves and on Porphyry's commentaries as such and on his *Introduction.*[29]

27. As is rightfully underlined by Christos Evangeliou, it was Porphyry who opened a new page in the relation of the Academy towards the Peripatetic (*Aristotle's Categories and Porphyry*, Leiden 1988, XI, 5), and he did so against the previously prevalent repulsive standpoint of the neo-Platonics towards Aristotle (cf. Plotinus' critique in *Enn.*, VI, 1). Of the two of Porphyry's commentaries on the *Categories* only the smaller one is preserved (and incompletely): it was composed in pseudo-dialogical form (in fact, these are *erotapokriseis*, questions and answers of pupil and teacher), while the other, written in exegetical form, much more systematical and elaborated (it had 7 books), was sadly lost. However, its content was taken over in large by later neo-Platonic commentaries on the *Categories*, especially those of Simplicius, Philoponus, Olimpiodorus and Elias. In view of these two commentaries the question is raised with regard to the purpose of the only fully preserved text by Porphyry (and in addition to that, the most influential one), which is usually called the *Introduction to the Categories* (cf. *Porphyrii Isagoge in Aristotelis Categorias*, CAG IV, 1, ed. A. Busse, Berlin 1887). It seems that this was an introduction to Aristotle's logical writings as a whole rather than to the *Categories* themselves (this follows from a Syrian collection of writings about Porphyry's *Introduction*, saved in the Vatican codex *Vat. Syr.* 158, and also from the remark by Amonius that *Isagoge* is the path for all of philosophy; 20, 24).
28. The "five voices" are comprised of the following concepts: genus, species, difference, accident and property (γένος, εἶδος, διαφορά, συμβεβηκός, ἴδιον). These concepts are widely used in Aristotle's logical writings, but they find their full and explicit elaboration only with Porphyry's deliberation on the status of Aristotle's categories. In order to make a difference in relation to Aristotle's categories, which in Latin are named *praedicamenta*, Porphyry's five voices were signified by the term *praedicabilia*. The division into antepredicaments, predicaments and postpredicaments reflects the common division of Aristotle's treatise into three parts: where in the first part are discussed the concepts which come before the categories, in the second the categories, and in the third concepts which come after the categories.
29. Today, the structure of these introductions to Aristotle's *Categories* may be discerned by comparison of the preserved commentaries (cf. L. G. Westerink, *op. cit.*, XXV–XXXII), and such a reconstruction is of great value for an appropriate understanding of the inner structure of Damascene's *Dialectic.* Within the framework of the series of commentaries *Commentaria in Aristotelem Graeca* (*CAG*) *edita consilio et auctoritate Academiae litterarum Regiae Borussicae* (Berlin 1882sq) the following commentaries of the *Categories* and of Porphyry's *Introduction to the Categories* were published: IV 2 *Dexippi in Aristotelis Categorias Commentarium*, ed. A.

This nearly paroxistic flowering of commentary activity, which in the end led to the commentaries themselves being commented, transpired within the process of the shaping of the philosophical educational programme, which from the end of the 3rd century, within the circle of neo-Platonics, would commence with Aristotle's logical works and the interpretation of Aristotle's *Categories*. However, it was soon realised that in philosophical schooling it is not sufficient to start with the immediate interpretation of the *Categories*, for it is necessary beforehand to prepare a prior introduction to the whole of Aristotle's thought. It seems that it was Proclus (410–485) who was the first to inaugurate such a practice. Before going onto the interpretation of the *Categories*, in his Athenian lectures he would give a short introduction to Aristotle, within which, in ten sections, he would explain to his listeners the origin of the different philosophical schools, the division of Aristotle's works, the point of departure of tuition, the goal of reflecting upon those works (the cognition of God as first cause), the study plan of the disciplines, the necessary preparation for pupils and interpreters, the style of the writings, the nature of Aristotle's unclarities and, in the end, the properties of each and every of Aristotle's works in particular.[30]

All of these points are transported further into subsequent commentaries of the *Categories* as their foregoing part, onto which the interpretation of this logical tract is then adjoined naturally. However, since the neo-Platonics regarded Aristotle's philosophy only as an antechamber of philosophy, but not as philosophy proper, it was felt that this introduction and the introduction to the categories needs to be headed by another even more general introduction to philosophy in which the nature of philosophy would be determined and the division of its disciplines expounded. This step was executed by Amonius Hermias (435/7–517/526), who listened to Proclus in Athens and then became the rector of the school in Alexandria, where he developed an exceptionally fruitful activity which was successful in completely marking the philosophy of the sixth century.[31] Before the explanation of Aristotle's *Categories* Amonius introduced into the schooling programme the interpretation

Busse 1888; IV 3 *Ammonius in Porphyrii Isagogen sive quinque voces*, ed. A. Busse 1891; IV 4 *Ammonius in Aristotelis Categorias Commentarius*, ed. A. Busse 1895; VIII *Simplicius in Aristotelis Categorias Commentarius*, ed. C. Kalbfleisch 1907; XII 1 *Olympiodori Prolegomena et in Categorias Commentarium*, ed. A. Busse 1902; XIII 1 *Joannes Philoponus in Aristotelis Categorias Commentarius*, ed. A. Busse 1898; XVIII 1 *Elias in Porphyrii Isagogen et Aristotelis Categorias Commentaria*, ed. A. Busse 1900; XVIII 2 *Davidis Prolegomena et in Porphyrii Isagogen Commentarium*, ed. A. Busse 1904.

30. It is David who refers to Proclus as the founder of such an approach; cf. A. Baumstark, *Syrische Kommentare zur Eisagoge des Porphyrios*, Leipzig 1900, 157.
31. Amonius did not write much. But, he had a very ramified teaching activity out of which, on the basis of his students' notes (that is, in the final count ἀπὸ φωνῆς), came forth various commentaries, either under his name (in that form we have as preserved the commentaries on the *Isagoge*, *Categories*, *Prior Analytics*), or under the names of his successors (Asclepius' commentary on the *Metaphysics* is a contamination of Amonius' lectures with segments of Alexander, while Philoponus' commentaries on the *Categories*, *Prior and Posterior Analytics*,

of Porphyry's *Introduction*, whereby the previous deliberation on ten questions about Aristotle's philosophy ceased to serve as a general introduction to the exposition of the categories and to the teaching of philosophy. In terms of an outcome, this opened up a space for a new more general introduction to Porphyry's *Introduction*, and thus into philosophy itself as well. Amonius met this need. He did so in the following way: before going on to the interpretation of Porphyry's *Introduction* (understood almost as an integral part of Aristotle's logical works) he would expound a more general part in which he elaborated on 6 classical definitions of philosophy and deduced the division of philosophy, explaining beforehand the very concept of definition, division and subdivision.[32]

Thus the structure of the basic philosophical manual was procured. It was comprised of three parts: the general introduction to philosophy, the general introduction to Porphyry's *Introduction* and the interpretation of the *Introduction* or *Categories* (προλεγόμενα τῆς φιλοσοφίας, προλεγόμενα τῆς εἰσαγωγῆς, ἐξήγησις τῆς εἰσαγωγῆς / κατηγορίων). This nucleus of the philosophical encyclopaedia was further developed – both in ambit and in thematic – by the pupils of Amonius. But, the basic structure remained the same. Some components of a manual conceptualised in suchlike manner are recognizable in Damascene's *Dialectic* as well.

V

Comparative research demonstrates clearly that the promotion of Aristotle's logic into a philosophical introduction to Plato's philosophy anticipated a certain position of Damascene's *Dialectic* in relation to true knowledge offered by Christian revelation. That is to say, Damascene's *Dialectic* stems from the neo-Platonic incorporation of Aristotle's *Categories*, instigated by Porphyry's commentaries and the *Introduction to the Categories*. At the same time Porphyry's work had a decisive role in forming the content and language of Damascene's manual. But, it did so only as a point of departure and as a remote basis of the conceptual apparatus of this dogmatic and its philosophical propedeutic. The structure of the *Dialectic*, its way of exposition and its formulations, albeit as refracted through the prism of ecclesial refurnishing, is far more influenced by later Byzantine commentaries of Porphyry's *Introduction* and of Aristotle's *Categories*. These were previously conduced through a

---

Physics, *On Generation and Corruption*, *On the Soul*, *On the Generation of Animals* were produced by the reception of Amonius' lectures and then adding some remarks of his own).

32. Before Amonius, including Porphyry, no one has this introduction, while all the commentaries of Porphyry's *Introduction*, which came out of his school, have this prolegomena, so the unavoidable conclusion is that it was introduced by Amonius as a valid novelty. While Amonius' general introduction is still relatively short, subsequent texts are constantly increasing, and this finally led the prolegomena to be quadrupled in size, in David. The comparative overview of the initial and final stadium of this development is given in L. G. Westerink, *op. cit.*, XXVIII–XXXI.

series of restructurings, shortenings and adaptations, and they were in fact the sources which gave Damascene the basic conceptual presuppositions and logical knowledge needed for his exposition of the dogmas of Christian faith.

The main transmitter of this conceptual influence of Aristotelian-directed neo-Platonism into the Byzantine spiritual world was the Alexandrian school, which continued its work unimpeded even after the official victory of Christianity. In the Alexandrian school Plato's and Aristotle's works were intensively commented on – even as early as the 4th century, with the belief that the whole truth is expounded within them, and that philosophizing can henceforth only have an exegetical character.[33] This purely exegetical directedness in which, in the school sense, the most important place was occupied precisely by commentaries of the *Categories* and by Porphyry's interpretations of that work, allowed for the relaxation of that sharp confrontation between pagan philosophy and Christian spirituality, which in Athens had led to the prohibition of 529, the victim of which was the local successor of Proclus, Damascius, the last scholarch of the Academy. In contrast to the Athenian and Syrian schools of neo-Platonism which constantly attracted the suspicion of the new state ideology, due to their religious-speculative proclivities, the Alexandrian school constructed a neutral scientific attitude. This allowed it not only to survive, but to break-through into the Christian world.[34]

33. This spirit of exegesis, which allowed for novelty only in the form of commentary of the old, of "any classical text," is qualified by Sergej Averincev as "cognitive traditionalism" and as the "current way of conducting philosophy" (*op. cit.*, 43). But, he was sufficiently cautious to add that all of that "does not foreclose the pathways of originality, for it only places it within specific conditions" (*ibid.*). That originality is entirely possible in such conditions is shown by the commentary activity of Proclus or Amonius or, in our times, by Alexandre Kojeve, who expressed a similar feeling of impossibility of philosophizing in terms of authorship in relation to Hegel.
34. The highest educational teaching of philosophy was not affected by Justinian's edict: namely, not in the sense that it thenceforth became religious in spirit (cf. H. I. Marrou, *op. cit.*, t. II, 163) and that after the edict certain different Christian schools of philosophy were founded, as opposed to pagan schools; P. Lemerle, *Le Premier Humanisme Byzantine*, 47. For this reason it is prudent to avoid referencing the year 529 as a mark of the end of Greek philosophy. And, if it is to be used as a technical date, it should be viewed as a difficult breaking-point after which the second millennium of development of Greek spirituality issues forth. These next thousand years represent a direct extension of Greek philosophy, at least in the linguistic and conceptual sense, if not in terms of ideas. Bearing that in mind, it is perhaps not inappropriate to speak about Greek philosophy in its second, Byzantine phase. Although it should never be forgotten that the price of the transformation thus realized was truly high in the philosophical sense. Damascius, who in Athens heroically held onto the principles of pagan philosophy, wrote with bitterness about Amonius' pragmatic (or conformist) attitude in relation to the violence of the new state religion. The Alexandrian scholarch accepted all of that massive pressure as a higher force. Therefore, without resistance, he even signed one humiliating agreement with the Alexandrian bishop with regard to the mode of allowed teaching about Plato and Aristotle (*Vita Isidori*, fr. 316). But, in virtue of this malleable stance Amonius was able to educate generations of new students, who transported a lot of things into the new faith as well (In this spirit the Alexandrian school continued its work after the fall under Arabic rule, in 647, moving out firstly into An-

It is in this light that one needs to consider the naming of Stephanus of Alexandria as official teacher of Plato's and Aristotle's philosophy at the Constantinopolitan Pandidakterion, that is, at the university, sometime in 612. It is obvious that Stephanus, upon whom the emperor Heraclius bestowed the title of "ecumenical teacher" (οἰκουμενικὸς διδάσκαλος), had the task to pass onto students of philosophy in the capital, not only knowledge from the classical *quadrivium* (arithmetic, geometry, astronomy and music), but also the conceptual apparatus of Aristotle's logic, such as it was elaborated in Alexandria. Although his commentary of the *Categories* was probably composed earlier, in Alexandria, he was certainly active in the new environment. This is corroborated by numerous traces which it had left in other Byzantine writers.[35]

The Alexandrian school, primarily in the terrain of logic, thus succeeded in accomplishing that which in other centres was unimaginable. Namely, in the medium of the Hellenistic language of Aristotelian concepts it brought together the pagans, Christians and heretics. Already starting with Amonius among its listeners one would find a growing numbers of Christians who, in the end, from Olympiodorus (c. 495–c. 570) onward, became its main lecturers. The comparison of neo-Platonic commentaries written by pagan scholars of the Alexandrian school and, for instance, those written by Christian professors from the same centre, demonstrates how imperceptible in fact was the transition from neo-Platonic exegesis to Christian theological exegesis. For example, the difference between Amonius,' Asclepius' and Olympiodorus' commentaries, on one hand, and those of John Philoponus, Elias (first half of the 6th century) and David (the second half of the 6th century), on the other hand, is entirely neglectable. That these persons were Christians we know in virtue of their names, but not due to the content of their interpretations of the *Categories* and *Isagoge*, which, to the very last thread, follow Amonius' model of the school introduction to philosophy.[36]

tioch and subsequently into Baghdad). Therefore, the changes at the boundary of the two eras of Greek philosophy, no matter how big and significant, were not as abrupt and sharp so as to be able to nullify all continuity between Hellenic and Byzantine philosophy; cf. K. Oehler, "Die Kontinuität in der Philosophie der Griechen bis zum Untergang des Byzantinischen Reiches," in: *Antike Philosophie und Byzantinisches Mittelalter*, München 1969, 19.

35. For example, Stephanus' conceptual determinations are cited in a section on definitions of a collection known under the editor's title *Doctrina patrum de incarnatione verbi*, ed. F. Diekamp, Münster 1907, [2]1981.

36. The Christian scholars in Alexandria adopted the philosophical teachings of their predecessors to such an extent that they uncritically took over even those suppositions (for example, the eternality of the world and divine nature of the celestial bodies), which were otherwise the subject of fierce disputes with the pagans. These were refuted already by John Philoponus in his polemic with Proclus and Simplicius (cf. H. Hunger, *Die hochsprachiche profane Literatur der Byzantiner*, München 1978, 29). But, his disciple Stephanus of Alexandria, nevertheless, did not think that it was consequentially necessary to intervene in the commentaries themselves in terms of consistently cleansing the adopted texts (*de Anima*, 448, 6–7; 540, 27; 541, 20–542, 5; 595, 33–598, 7). Elias acts in a similar way (120, 16–17; 187, 6–7).

This model, taken as a criterion-positing norm, is apparent in Damascene's *Dialectic*. Namely, the *Dialectic* of John Damascene is dependent on Alexandrian commentaries of the *Introduction to the Categories* and on the *Categories* themselves – not only with regard to its thematic (choice and elaboration of concepts), but also in relation to the accepted order of material, as well as many individual formulations. However, the definitions of concepts and their elaboration in examples are much shorter in the *Dialectic* than is the case in neo-Platonic commentaries (although not as short as in some related and somewhat older Byzantine manuscripts). But, the inner structure of the whole is the same one which is, also, seen in Alexandrian interpretations of Porphyry's *Introduction* and of Aristotle's *Categories*. Roughly considered, in all of these works the exposition is divided into five big parts which in turn are articulated into smaller wholes. In the case of the *Dialectic* (that is, its longer version) this division, schematically represented,[37] would look like this:

I. Introductory part: general questions and the announcement of the main theme (chapters 1–8)

II. Porphyry's predicabilia (chapters 9–14)

Similarities and differences, the so-called 35 voices (chapters 18–28)

III. Antepredicaments: terms before the categories: synonymy, homonymy, paronymy (chapters 31–38)

IV. Aristotle's predicaments: categories (chapters 46–56)

V. Postpredicaments; terms after the categories: opposition, prior, posterior, simultaneous (chapters 57–62).

As can be seen, in this scheme a whole series of chapters has been omitted, for instance chapters 15–17, 29–30, 39–45, 63–68. This is no pure coincidence. Our overview of the structure of the *Dialectic* mirrors the state of things from the general introductions to philosophy, yet these chapters have an entirely different origin. They have entered the *Dialectic* from the theological manuals of subsequent ecclesial authors. And, furthermore, due to their predominantly theological content, they do not belong to the basic structure of the exegetical introductions to philosophy. This is obligatory even for the final chapters 62–68. According to Damascene's opinion, these bring forth everything that in theology one should additionally know from philosophy, and

37. In his scheme of the structure of the *Dialectic* Richter selects only three main parts of the *Dialectic*. But, this difference (although important in itself) is virtual for he, too, groups the individual chapters in the same way (cf. *op. cit.*, 55). It should be noted that chapters 11, 33, 34, 48 and 58, although they are introduced into this structure for the sake of continuity, do not belong to it without reserve: this is so because at the same time they contain conceptual clarifications which fall out of the framework of a general introduction to philosophy and introduction to the categories. On the other hand, some chapters (for example 63 and 68) have fallen out of the scheme. Yet, these chapters do contain propositions from the *Categories* (statement, affirmation, negation, dialectical methods, etc.): that is, they are merely added at the end of the *Dialectic*, hence they fall out of bounds of the main wholes.

even from the natural sciences.[38] Since they forge no firm systematic bond with the basic skeleton of the *Dialectic*, these chapters, with no greater loss, may be omitted from our exposition. Damascene simply added them alongside the main part, without much worry about the coherence of the whole of the text. Genetically they probably represent the final (third) level of the material out of which the *Dialectic* was produced. Although the composing of it (the *Dialectic*), as is demonstrated by research conducted by G. Richter, seems to have commenced precisely from these chapters, which represented the initial philosophical-theological nucleus, to which the mentioned corpus of Alexandrian introductions to philosophy was then gradually added.[39] We shall briefly overview several of the opening parts of this corpus. We do so in order to better illumine the content of the *Dialectic* as well as the mutual relations of its constituent parts in the light of the general relation of philosophy and theology.

VI

If we put aside the epistle to Cosmas of Maiuma, the bishop at whose request Damascene allegedly composed his *Fountain of Knowledge*, the introductory part of the *Dialectic* has eight chapters, which bear the following titles: 1) on knowledge, 2) what is the purpose, 3) on philosophy, 4) on being, essence and accident, 5) on voice, 6) on division, 7) on that which is by nature prior and 8) on definition. This introductory content, basically, issued forth from the later neo-Platonic tradition of commentary. It is for this reason that we shall seek for it in vain in Porphyry who, otherwise, initiated the consideration of voices and categories. Both in his *Introduction* and in his commentaries on the *Categories* he strictly holds onto the tripartite division of Aristotle's work. This means that he is acquainted only with the III, IV and V part of the previously quoted scheme, but not with the special introduction to general philosophical questions and principal concepts. The real paradigms for Damascene's introduction should be sought for in Amonius' school of commentaries on Porphyry's *Introduction* and Aristotle's *Categories*, with the caveat that not even there can we expect to find a perfect overlap, because of the mediation of ecclesial literature.

As regards Damascene, it is immediately evident that, in relation to the introductions to the *Isagoge*, the general introduction to Aristotle's philosophy is missing, while in relation to the special introductions to the *Categories*

38. Damascene believed that the knowing of nature gives a reasoned account of theology as well. His excerpts often seem enlightening if compared to folk superstitions about thunder, lightning and other; S. Averincev, *op. cit.*, 81.

39. Cf. G. Richter, *op. cit.*, 55, 222. The (as yet unpublished) anonymous treatise from the monastery Vatopedi (*Cod. Athos Vatoped. gr.* 57, ff. 257–261), at least judging by the content given by M. Roueché, *op. cit.*, 74–75, mirrors the most rudimentary framework out of which the *Dialectic*, too, was constructed: I Porphyry's voices, II antepredicaments and III Aristotle's categories.

we observe the understandable omitting of the consideration of titles, subjects, authenticity and other moments tied exclusively to the interpretation of this work. Damascene's introduction is in fact some sort of combination of elements from both types of introduction. From the latter he adopts the custom of giving account of the purpose and expected benefit from his enterprise (although he does not select this exposition in terms of particular points), while from the former (the so-called general introduction) he adopts the determinations of philosophy, its division, the refutation of the sceptical objection against the possibility of philosophy (chapter 3), the consideration on division (chapter 6) and definitions (chapter 8). Having in mind this span of borrowings it could be said that Damascene's introduction is much more similar to the introductions to Porphyry's *Isagoge*, that is, to the general prolegomenon to philosophy as it was established from Amonius onwards in Alexandria, than to the interpretations of the *Categories*, with which it establishes only a subsidiary overlap. The basic similarity lies in the twofold division of the introduction: namely, into the part which deals with the general questions of philosophy and the part which introduces the teaching on "voices" and categories.

Still, even in relation to the general prolegomena to philosophy we do observe important differences. While the introductions of the neo-Platonic commentators of the *Isagoge* sometimes, however, themselves have eight sections, their principal standpoint – despite the formal correspondence – is essentially different. This is so because, in the beginning, they do not appeal to the "illuminating grace" of the Spirit which is expected to "open their mouth," as Damascene does (Kotter 52, 34–35), for they immediately expound the definitions of philosophy and its division, and then go on to the consideration of Porphyry's *Introduction*, its subject matter, usefulness, titles, authenticity, position, mutual relations of the "five voices," methods of exposition and the domain of philosophy to which this exposition belongs.[40] The similarity with Alexandrian introductions to philosophy, therefore, is more of a thematic kind. But, even in this regard it is restricted in terms of content to several chapters only, while the other contents of Damascene's introduction don't have a match in the philosophical introductions of the Alexandrian commentators.

Since the analysis of the definition of philosophy and of its division, as the most important theme of a given introduction to philosophy, due to its generality transcends the deliberation of particular logical concepts, and since the text of chapter 3 appears again towards the end of the *Dialectic* (chapter 67), Damascene's determinations of philosophy are to be tackled in an ensuing

40. Differently in regard to Amonius (who, after a short determination of definition, immediately expounds the six definitions) David first tackles the skeptical objections to philosophy (2, 31–10, 37), and then in nine points amply discusses the problems of defining (11, 1–26, 28). The phrase "with the help of God," which sometimes appears at the end of certain chapters (lectures) in Elias and David, most likely derives from later scribe glosses.

particular section.[41] Presently, we shall direct our attention towards chapters 4, 5, 6, 7 and 8. In the mentioned chapters Aristotle's ontological-logical concepts are taken over through an intertwining of perspectives of Porphyrian, Alexandrian and theological interpretation of philosophical categories. This intertwining of different perspectives is most conspicuous in chapters 4 and 5. That is so since in their text, within the *Dialectic*, different conceptual layers of the long history of transmission of Aristotle's logical apparatus congregate but also part. And it is these which interest us in this reconstruction of the Byzantine symbiosis of philosophy and theology.

The main theme of chapter 4 is the determination of *essence* (οὐσία). This determination is derived through a constant opposition to the determination of *accident* (συμβεβηκός), whereby it is clearly declared that these are correlative concepts and that their relation has fundamental importance for the understanding of other logical concepts. Due to this concentration primarily on the relation of essence and accident this chapter entirely falls away from the tradition founded by Porphyry. For the mentioned tradition contemplates all logical concepts as "voices," turning principally to the analysis of the so-called predicabilia. Therefore, within it there are no parallels with the Alexandrian commentaries which, through Amonius, hold onto Porphyry's approach. The earlier, shorter version of the *Dialectic* opens precisely with this chapter. And this was possible due to the fact that in this version we don't find the ten chapters on similarities and differences of the "five voices" and, generally, in it the Porphyrian tendency is less prominent than in the longer version.

However, despite the acknowledged fundamentality of the relation essence–accident, the exposition does not take its point of departure from there, for it is not primordial. Hence, it must be derived from a preceding concept, the concept of *being* (τὸ ὄν) or *a being*. Namely, according to Damascene, being is "a general concept (common name)" of all that is (a being) which is then, subsequently, ontologically and logically dislayered into essence and accident. In chapter 4 of the *Dialectic* four basic differences between essence and accident are posited. First, essence is that which has existence in itself, and not in another, as is the case with accident; second, essence is some(thing) underlying, like matter, while accident is that which is observed in essence as that which is the underlying something: for example, copper and wax are essence, whereas shape, image and colour are accidents, or, soul is essence, and science is accident; third, essence remains whereas the accidental changes; and fourth, essence is one in relation to the multitude of accidental (subsidiary) properties which come to it as added (Kotter 57–59, 1–47).

41. Cf. S. Žunjić, "The definitions of philosophy in the 'Dialectica' of John Damascene: Their ancient sources and their Byzantine meanings," in: K. I. Boudouris, ed., *Philosophy and Orthodoxy*, Athens: International Center for Greek Philosophy and Culture & K. B. 1994, 294–323.

The listed determinations of essence, although they do omit the moment of essential and fundamental being, sound very Aristotelian. This impression is correct in many ways, starting with the general approach all the way to individual examples. Namely, Aristotle, too, reaches essence through being, claiming in the *Metaphysics* (1028b 2–3) that the question what is being (τί τὸ ὄν) as of old and now refers us to the question what is essence (τί ἐστι οὐσία). For him, too, essence is that which is underlaying and matter in relation to the accidental, whether we grasp this accidental as some real quality or as the designation of some property in terms of predication. Furthermore, the cited illustrations as well, of the relation of essence and accident (soul-science, wax-shape) may be found in Aristotle's opus. However, in Damascene we find a total lack of the connection between essence and form, which together with shape and image is tacitly transported into the sphere of the accidental.[42] This is the reason why he allows the forefront to be taken only by the characteristic of independent existence, which, in the conclusion, gives the following definition of essence: "Essence is a self-existent thing not in need of another for its existence" (Kotter 59, 62–64).[43]

This definition has no match in the commentaries which are totally ignorant of the expression "self-existent" (αὐθύπαρκτον). However, the same determination is to be found in the collection of sayings of the holy Fathers known under the name *Doctrina patrum*, in the section which carries the heading "on the difference of essence, nature, hypostasis and person according to outer philosophers."[44] In this book it is not stated who these "outer philoso-

42. In the text σχῆμα is equalized with μορφή, while Porphyry understands their relation as the relation of genus and species (*Eisag.*, 4, 4). This also confirms the non-Porphyrian origin of this text.

43. Out of the three criteria which in the *Metaphysics* Aristotle establishes as conditions for something to be essence: a) not to be said of another but to be that about which another is said, b) to be a separate being (χωριστόν) and c) to be something concrete (1017b 23–5; 1029a 8–27), this definition affirms only the second criterion – with the replacement of "separate" existence with "self-existence." With regard to separatedness as a criterion of essence, in the metaphysical writings Aristotle gives advantage to the undividedness of its form. The shifting of the meaning of Aristotle's teaching on essence as expressed in this definition and in its subsequent translations into our language is extensively discussed in the final part of our article "Razvoj srpske filozofske terminologije," *Zbornik Filozofskog fakulteta u Beogradu* XIII–2 (1983) 238–241 (the mentioned part has the following heading: "five stages in the development of one example").

44. F. Diekamp, ed., *Doctrina patrum de incarnatione verbi*, Aschendorff, Münster [2]1981, 40, 25–26. This is in fact an excerpt from Athanasius the Sinaite (*Quest.* 54, PG 1401A), who still regards this determination as a teaching of "outer philosophers," while John Damascene adopts it already as a conception of the fathers, which is then continued in Theodore of Raithu as well (*An. Patr.*, 201, 14). In Diekamp's collection there is a parallel, as well, for the formulation according to which accidents are said as that which is observed in essence as the underlying thing (45, 5). At the same time, this determination is cited as a commentary of Aristotle's view from the *Categories*: οὐσία ἐστι ἡ κυριώτατα καὶ πρώτως καὶ μάλιστα λεγόμενη (*Cat.*, 2a 11). This moment of principality and primariness of essence, however, is completely dropped in the *Dialectic*, which also tells us that *Doctrina patrum* reflects a state of affairs which preceded Damascene's treatise.

phers" are, but it is clear these are neither Porphyry nor the Alexandrian commentators. This whole chapter was written according to a different, non-Porphyrian model of introduction to Aristotle in which the leading thread was the interpretation of the relation of nature, essence and accident. Today, to this type of *Isagoge* witness is given only by fragments of a Syrian translation by Athanasius of Balad,[45] and by fragments of a lost introduction to Aristotle's *Categories* written by Pseudo-Archita.[46]

We don't know how Damascene obtained this non-Porphyrian text, and we also don't know why he retained it in the longer version of the *Dialectic* in which it now stands out quite conspicuously, for the subsequent chapters do not build upon it. He was probably keen to also have in place, at the beginning, determinations of the most general concepts of being and essence, and these run throughout the whole subsequent exposition. And precisely this is enabled by the text of chapter 4. Aside from that, one may presuppose that this chapter was taken over together with the whole template which Damascene used for the entire *Dialectic*. And this template, surely, was already subjected to ecclesial and theological re-workings.[47] Testimony to this is borne by the fact that particular propositions from this chapter are to be found in the mentioned holy Fathers' collection. And, the circumstance that after the quoted definition Damascene cites examples of essence which are understood accordingly, where God is placed in first position, indeed, is a contribution proving the theological re-working of it as well. However, since in that case God (although the status of first essence is attributed to him) would be equalised with his creatures – which can be essences as well, under the condition that they have independent existence – Damascene immediately interpolates a correction into this Aristotelian discourse. Namely, in the style of

45. Sometime around 645 Athanasius of Balad translated into Syrian one Greek *Isagoge* whose author is not known to us by name; but, it was in use both in Syria (fragment in *Cod. Vat. Syr.* 158) and in Byzantium, for its influence, apart from chapter 4 of the *Dialectic*, is felt in chapter 16 of the *Logical Epitome* by Nikephoros Blemmydes (PG 142, 797–804); cf. A. Baumstark, *Syrische Kommentare zur Eisagoge des Porphyrios*, 214.

46. In fragment 35a of Ps.-Archita we read the following variation of our definition: ἡ οὐσία πρᾶγμα ἀυθύπαρκτον καὶ ὑφεστώς, μὴ δεόμενον ἑτέρου πρός σύστασιν (J. Nolle, *Ps.-Architae Fragmenta*, Diss. Münster. Tüb. 1914, 34, 27. (In the shorter version of the *Dialectic*, too, we find πρός σύστασιν instead of πρός ὑπάρχειν). Ps.-Archita does not belong to the Alexandrian school and in his commentary he applies a different method of interpretation, which in the intellectual sense abides more with the letter of Aristotle's text, although it does make it quite shorter. That would explain the strong Aristotelian tones in chapter 4, but also certain omissions.

47. This however does not help us solve the question why Damascene even in the allegedly longer version of the *Dialectic* did not retain the formulations from the earlier, shorter version which, according to general opinion, are more concise, more precise and more successful in terms of composition, but, instead, gave himself to its redaction so as to finally introduce into the text the stylistically poorer version. Richter attempts (not very convincingly) to explain this illogicality by means of the hypothesis about a subsequent literal adoption of an unknown source in its entirety, which Damascene previously abbreviated successfully (*op. cit.*, 83).

Pseudo-Dionysius Areopagite and the Cappadocian Fathers he adds that God is in fact "super-essential" (ὑπερούσιος). Such theological interpolations are strewn across the whole text of the Dialectic.[48]

VII

In the fifth chapter, which exists only in the longer version of the *Dialectic*, Damascene undertakes the consideration of "every voice of the philosopher (if it is expressed) simply" (περὶ πάσης ἁπλῶς φιλοσόφου φωνῆς). And for this reason he wishes first to explain "what kind of voice does philosophy thematize" (Kotter 60, 1–4). To this question, however, he does not give a direct answer, but, instead, conducts a comprehensive division of that which is called "voice." According to Damascene, the voice is firstly divided into the "non-signifying" (ἄσημος), that is, the one which signifies nothing, and the "signifying" (σημαντικός), that is, the one which signifies something. Both of these kinds of voice, furthermore, are divided into the "inarticulate" and "articulate" voice, where the first type of non-signifying sound – taken as inarticulate noise, say, of some stone or barking dog – cannot be written, while the other, taken as articulate, can be written, even if it represents the sound of an invented word which signifies nothing (Damascene's example is σκίνδαψος = the play of strings). However, of far greater importance is the division of the "signifying" sound into "inarticulate" and "articulate." And this is so because through the latter one reaches the sound which can be particular (for example, Peter or Paul) or universal (for example, man).

This whole division is in fact deduced so as to extricate that conceptual area of the voice, which lies at the last branch of the division, since it represents the proper subject of philosophy. Therefore, bearing in mind all the cited parts of this division, Damascene now concludes that the subject of philosophy is neither the non-signifying voice, nor the signifying yet non-writable, nor the signifying writable yet particular voice, but only the signifying, articulate and universal voice, which is common to many things and which is expressed in relation to them (Kotter 60, 25–28). But the "philosophical voice" appears as twofold as well. Namely, on one hand, it can be essential (οὐσιώδης), if it indicates the essence and "nature of things" (for example, such a one is produced when we say that man is a "rational mortal being"), and it can also be non-essential (ἐπουσιώδης), if it shows only that which is "accidental" on something (for example, when we say that a man is "white").

The "essential voice" expresses either the very essence or the essential quality of things. When it indicates the "whatness" of things it signifies either several species, in which case it comprises genus (γένος), or it covers

48. This difficulty appears if essence is applied in a generalized sense – as mere existence (as Leontius begun to do). The expression ὑπερούσιος is also found in the small *Introduction to the Dogmas*.

many individual examples (hypostases), in which case it comprises species (εἶδος). The "essential voice" which indicates the quality of something is difference (διαφορά), wherewith Damascene chiefly underlines the special (specific) difference, which the philosophers call the "most proper" (Kotter 63, 113–118). The other two voices issue forth from non-essential attributions. When the oncoming voice belongs to one species only it is called proper (ἴδιον), and when it is attributed to a greater number of species it represents the accidental (συμβεβηκός) in the proper meaning of the word. The accidental, which is not expressed definitorially as proper, but in virtue of possibility, can be separable from that to which it is attributed (for example, that someone is sitting or laying) or inseparable (for example, snub, which is inseparable from nose),[49] although this does not mean that it is constitutive for the given species.

Summing up these deducements about genus, species, difference, property and accident, Damascene says "these are the five voices to which every philosophical term may be reduced" (Kotter 62, 94–95). If we now carefully survey this entire exposition we shall notice that the main expression of the whole chapter – voice – is not thematized as such at all, and that it is used, rather, as a starting term which needs no further defining. Obviously, this is so due to the fact that it is adopted from the Porphyrian tradition of commentaries, that is, as a completed and explained matter. However, in Damascene's times it was just as poorly clarified as it is today. Hence, one needs to answer a whole series of questions which are related to it. Firstly, what does "voice" mean here at all and, secondly, why does Damascene's exposition commence with it? The answer to the first question is that "voice," evidently, is taken in the widest meaning of sound, which is then further differentiated so as to finally reach the signifying words in philosophical discourse. The answer to the second question is that the plane of semantics is here, obviously, regarded as more fundamental than that of ontology, for it is tacitly believed that commencing with sounds, words and concepts one reaches things, and not conversely: that is, commencing with individual things and then reaching philosophical concepts. Moreover, the consideration of philosophical voices is of immediate benefit for the understanding of categories (46–56) and four dialectical methods which are discussed at the end of the *Dialectic* (68).[50]

49. "Snub" (σιμότης), too, is an example from Aristotle's *Metaphysics*, by means of which he signifies that which belongs in itself and not by accident. Namely, snubness cannot exist apart from the nose, but, nevertheless, it is not the carrier of the existence of nose (*Met.*, 1030b 20).

50. This justifies the introduction of this chapter into the prefatory part of the *Dialectic*, although this does not eliminate the possible suspicion with regard to its purposefulness at this place, since this connection is not explicitly highlighted in the text itself. Starting with such a consideration G. Richter notes critically that it was not necessary to go all the way to the level of voice and inarticulate sound in order to introduce certain logical concepts necessary for theological deductions, the more so since the chapter on voice "neither according to content nor according to form does not belong to any other section of the *Dialectic*" (*op.*

This "linguistic" shift of the pre-original ontological-logical discussion about universal concepts was not executed by Damascene himself, who rather inherits this whole discussion from preceding introductions to philosophy.[51] It is the result of a lively and prolonged debate among Greek philosophers which was conducted from 3rd to 5th century in relation to the status of Aristotle's *Categories.* Describing the momentum and range of this debate the Platonist Dexippus (3rd century) in his commentary of the *Categories* wrote down that "there was neither more contradicting nor were more disputes instigated concerning a given postulation, not only among the Stoics and Platonists, who aspire to unsettle Aristotle's categories, but among the Peripateticians themselves as well [...]" (5, 19–22). The debates caught fire due to the matter of "simple words" (αἱ ἁπλαῖ λέξεις) and "that which is signified by them" (τὰ ὑπο τούτων σημαινόμενα), that is, due to that which Aristotle had in mind when he spoke about the "being said" (τὸ λεγόμενον). Namely, already at the earliest phase of interpretation of the *Categories* the commentators posed the question of what in fact this "being said" is – a word (voice), a thing or a concept (Dexip., 6, 31). According to the answer given to this question, the commentators parted along three paths: the first claimed that Aristotle spoke of words or articulated voices (λέξεις, φωναί), others held that by "being said" Aristotle refers to things and beings (πράγματα, ὄντα), while the third believed that "being said" stands for concepts (νοήματα). The first conception we could name as grammatical, the second as ontological and the third as logical.

In giving the biggest possible importance to the term "voice" in chapter 5 Damascene is obviously starting from the grammatical interpretation of philosophical discourse. The subjects of consideration, such as implied in this chapter, are not existent things in their basic aspects (as in chapter 4), but that by which these things are expressed, that is, articulated and signifying signs produced by the human voice. That was Porphyry's starting point

cit., 86, 92). Looking from the viewpoint of a thus conceptualized economy of exposition this truly is a proper objection. But, if we view things within the whole of the intellectual legacy from which the *Dialectic* issues forth, then the fifth chapter does not appear as a foreign body in the text of Damascene's work, because it originally belongs to the framework of what follows suit.

51. Although it does not directly connect to any other subchapter, this chapter does have its place in introductions, as can be seen from the parallel part in the Syrian compendium, included in Severus bar Shakko's *Dialogue* which explicitly raises the question (question 18) of what use is knowledge about the "five voices." The answer to this question is that the voices are presupposed in the consideration of categories, division, analysis, definition and demonstration (cf. segment in A. Baumstark, *op. cit.*, 209, 35–210, 16). In his *Introduction to Porphyry's Introduction* Elias, too, refers to four dialectical methods and their four questions (whether [something] is, what is, how [something] is and why [something] is) as the proper *skopos* (purpose) of the discussion on voices (37, 9cq). Somewhere in the preceding re-workings this clarification fell out of the template of the *Dialectic.* But, nevertheless, in it itself (i.e. the *Dialectic*) the discussion about the categories and four dialectical methods is retained.

as well in his understanding of the main generalities (categories and genera).[52] However, this point of departure, which may serve as a preliminary basis for the understanding of the theme, is too simplified and one-dimensional to be brought into full harmony with the whole of Aristotle's analysis of the categories. Hence, Porphyry expanded his interpretation by understanding the voice as a mediate reference to things, claiming that Aristotle's work, too, speaks "about simple signifying voices inasmuch as they signify in regard to things which do not differ mutually by number but by genus" (58, 5–7).

This last clarification helps us to comprehend the real nature of "simple signifying voices" which, in the *Categories*, are taken to be the main subject of philosophical reflection. The categories, which the philosophers discuss, therefore, are neither beings which differ mutually by number (for example, Socrates, Plato), nor beings which differ mutually by species (for example, man, horse), but things (beings) which differ mutually by genus. These are entirely special voices which, in difference to species, signify the most abstract genera of things, or, conversely said, these are the most general genera which are mutually distinguished like Aristotle's ten categories.[53] Therefore, the categories are not mere grammatical kinds of words – Porphyry labels these as "names of the second postulation" (58, 3) – but the most general genera which encompass everything that is.

Such a "middle" or comprehensive interpretation of philosophical categories as voices which signify the genera (genuses) of things was initiated by Alexander of Aphrodisias, Hermias and Boetius of Sydonia, and Porphyry in fact takes it over from them.[54] After him it is endorsed as the standard interpretation of the categories and, as such, it also enters into the commentaries of the Alexandrian neo-Platonics who, all without exception, hold the position according to which the purpose of Aristotle's work is the consideration of signifying voices which, in fact, signify concepts (Amm., 12–15; Olimp., 22–25; Elias, 132–134; Simpl. 13–20). Elias expresses this understanding as follows: "The purpose of the treatise on categories is to reflect on the

52. The terminology "simple signifying voices" (ἁπλαῖ φωναί σημαντικαί), which is used by Damascene, too, for genera and categories, was introduced by Porphyry (*Porphyrii in Categorias proemium*, 58, 5). The adjective "simple" (or adverb "simple" in Damascene) herewith signifies that the most general aspects of things, expressed by the cited voices, differ neither by number nor by species. Porphyry also calls the "simple voices" the "first postulation of the name" (58, 1–2).

53. This refers to the philosophical categories, which are ten in number. In chapter 48 Damascene says the following about these: "One must know that in all there are ten categories, or most general genera, to which is referred every expressed voice in the simple sense" (*Dial.*, Kotter 113, 5–6; similarly Porphyry, 58, 9–14). Of course, there is also the category in the general sense of species; but this is a philosophically non-specific concept, one which Porphyry determines as "every simply signifying word when it is named and expressed according to the signified thing" (56, 8–9). On the other meanings of *eidos* see more comprehensively in the *Dialogues* by Severus bar Shakko (203, 19–204, 2).

54. Porphyry does not mention Alexander as his predecessor, but Simplicius does refer to him (10, 11–19); cf. Chr. Evangeliou, *Aristotle's Categories and Porphyry*, Leiden 1988, 26.

first postulation of ordinary voices which signify simple things through the mediation of simple concepts" (131, 23–24).

How does Damascene's exposition of voices relate to the comprehensive interpretation of that which is predicated by the categories? We did say that his point of departure – in regard to the fundamental role of the voice – is grammatical. But now we need to make this evaluation more precise. Although in chapter 5 Damascene does de-ontologize the philosophical concepts, one could not say that his position, regarded as a whole, is purely grammatical. Despite the fact that the theological reception of Aristotle always inclined towards a nominalist emptying of concepts, Damascene did not show special interest for such radicalism: partly because – to start with – he was not conscious of all implications of the debate on voices, and partly because it had already entered the texts of ecclesial manuals, in the form of a comprehensive interpretation. That is why his interpretation, too, at least unconsciously, was close to this balanced line of interpretation. However, the definite position of the commentators, according to which Aristotle speaking about categories in fact speaks equally about words and about things and about concepts, is not reflected in the chapter about voice. But, it is to be found already in the announcement for that chapter, with which the third chapter of the prefatory part ends. This announcement states the following: "Therefore, we shall discuss simple voices which through simple concepts clarify simple things" (Kotter 57, 62–64).

This proposition repeats almost verbatim Elias' conception, which in fact came from Alexander of Aphrodisias (Simpl. 10, 11–19). However, that this is not merely a literal harmonization is seen from the next chapter of the *Dialectic*. In that chapter voice is used synonymously with concept (also in ch. 64). And this may be seen in chapter 11 of the *Dialectic* as well in which it is underlined that names reveal things. Nothing more is needed to confirm that in Damascene the Porphyrian voices are not any kind of *flatus vocis*. Hence, all that is left to do is to explain why Damascene expressly reduces the number of voices to five, although there are ten categories, and they are regarded as philosophical voices as well.

This inconsistency or ambivalence originates from Porphyry, that is, from his *Isagoge*. Namely, admitting in his commentaries that ten categories comprise the philosophical voices which are applied in the sensual world, in his *Introduction* (which is something more than an introduction to *Categories* for it relates to the *Topics* as well) Porphyry gives special attention to the five voices or predicabilia (κατηγορούμενα), which encompass all the meaningful (signifying) predicates except personal names. At the same time he does not follow the external motif, in the sense of trailing after his master Plotinus who reduced Aristotle's ten categories to five (adding to Aristotle's first four categories Plato's category of movement). But, rather, he is intent on viewing the whole thing from another angle and from a meta-level. Namely, while Aristotle reduced all beings to ten categories, Porphyry reduced all the philosophical voices – by means of which determinations of being are said – to five (David 83, 27–9).[55]

According to Porphyry, every predicate which is said of several things (namely, more than one) must be either genus or species or difference or property or accident (*Eisag.*, 1, 1–9). All these concepts were used by Aristotle as well, but he did not elaborate them systematically, nor did he allocate special status to them.[56] He simply uses them as operative concepts in the exposition of the teaching on definition, whereas Porphyry – furthermore – thematizes them outside this narrow methodical framework. In this sense, it can be said that he introduced them next to the ten categories, although he himself in his *Introduction* refers to what other philosophers have established about them (2, 15). Moreover, Porphyry gave explicit definitions only of the first three voices (γένος, εἶδος, διαφορά) while the remaining two (ἴδιον, συμβεβηκός), the meaning of which clearly issues forth from his interpretation, were formed only in the subsequent commentary work (Amm. 109, 10; Elias 89, 26cq; David 201, 8).[57] In any case, after Porphyry the reflection on five voices, in distinction to the special introduction to the categories, becomes integral part of the general introduction to philosophy. In time it succeeds in spreading through the Alexandrian commentaries. And, finally, this general introduction completely merges with the introduction to Porphyry's *Introduction.*

The semantical deliberation on Porphyry's five concepts, with all of its polysemy and layering, enters Damascene's *Dialectic* from this *Introduction.* However, it doesn't do so directly. Naturally, Damascene was not familiar – and he could not have been – with all the phases of this discussion on the status of the categories and five voices. All he did was take over its particular

55. That is why David's analogies – with grammar which thematizes eight parts of speech and with rhetoric which thematizes thirteen forms of speech – cannot stand (83, 27–29).

56. This does not mean that Aristotle merely "used five voices," as is written down by Amonius (62, 3, 7), that is to say, that he did not determine these concepts at all. Quite the contrary, he provided the nucleus of Porphyry's determinations and thereby of the whole subsequent tradition, which extends from the Alexandrian commentaries to Damascene's *Dialectic*. For example, in the second book of the *Topics* (c. 5) he determines *property* as that which, admittedly, does not express the essence of some particular thing, but which nevertheless belongs exclusively to it (102a 18–19). Furtherstill, *genus* is defined as that which according to whatness is said about many things which mutually differ according to species (102a 31–33), while he clarifies *accident* as that which may and may not belong to one same thing (*Top.*, 102b 6–7). And all of these are elements which, in one form or another, are transmitted all the way to the literature of the holy Fathers. Most of the examples originate from Aristotle as well. For instance, white as that which is accidental to man is taken from the Delta book of *Metaphysics* (1025a 14), etc.

57. There is a beginning for συμβεβηκός in Porphyry (11, 7), but in the *Introduction* it is used for the determination of difference. The definition of ἴδιον is elaborated via Aristotle as well, according to meaning. The definitions of γένος, εἶδος and διαφορά in this form are found in Porphyry wherefrom they move into the commentaries and theological debates. For γένος see *Doctrina patrum*, 254, 13; for εἶδος see *Doctrina patrum*, 258, 2; Leontius of Byzantium, PG 86, 1193A; for διαφορά see *Doctrina patrum*, 255, 10.

parts and results, which were not always mutually correspondent. Nevertheless, the *Dialectic* brings forth the elements of the most developed (final) stage of the discussion about philosophical voices. This may easily be ascertained by comparing Damascene's division of voices with the one which is found in the Alexandrian commentators. Moreover, in particular segments – especially as regards the elaboration of division and determinations of difference, property and accident – Damascene's material overarches the content of the commentaries. For instance, Amonius divides the voice into non-signifying and signifying. He then differentiates the latter type according to expression "according to one" (Plato or Socrates) or "according to many," and finally ending the division by differentiating voices "according to many" into those which are predicated essentially and those which are expressed non-essentially (59, 1–4) – and this term subsequently appears in the *Dialectic* as well. Out of this division Amonius derives the calculation according to which there are seven voices in total. But, since philosophy does not deal with non-signifying voices and proper names he, too, establishes the number of five philosophical voices (59, 13–16).

While Amonius still expounds his succinct consideration of signifying voices in the commentary on Porphyry's *Introduction*, and not in the general prologue to that introduction, Elias places the division thereof into a special short introduction to the interpretation of Porphyry's *Introduction* (35, 18–36, 20). Instead of Amonius' expressions "according to one" and "about one" for two kinds of signifying voice, he introduces the terms "general" and "particular" (καθόλου – μερικαί; 35, 26), and these appear in the *Dialectic* as well. He connects the thematizing of non-signifying and special signifying voice to poetry and grammar, and since the same limitation is taken over by Damascene we thereby procure another argument against the reduction of his interpretation to a grammatical one. David offers a very articulate division of voice (83, 31–84, 24cq). In terms of articulateness it in fact comes very close to the *Dialectic*. But, neither with him do we find all of that which can be read in the fifth chapter of Damascene's treatise.[58] That is, David commences his discussion with the division into the articulate and non-articulate voice (83, 32) and not with the division into the signifying and non-signifying, which is introduced only after that (84, 2). David divides the non-essential and essential voice according to whether they harmonize with one or more natures (84, 26). The non-essential voice, which is connected to more natures, gives the common accident, which in turn is divided into separate (for example, movement) and non-separate (for example, whiteness for swan or blackness for

58. Compare G. Richter, *op. cit.*, 88. According to Richter, Elias and David develop the semantic division in relation to the second chapter of Aristotle's treatise "on interpretation" (86) in which Aristotle determines name as a voice which signifies something according to convention, and distinguishes non-articulate voices of animals from names, even when the former signify something. Nevertheless, his discussion is obviously developed entirely aside from the general division of names.

raven). The essential signifying voice is twofold as well: if it is accepted by many natures, and is predicated in whatness, then it gives genus, and if allocated to one nature only it gives species (85, 10–24). Although David often uses the same examples, which also appear in the *Dialectic*, it is conspicuous that he does not determine species through numerical difference of individual specimens as does Damascene, and markedly so.

Generally, Damascene's text in chapter 5 is much more loaded and the definitions are more systematic and better formed than in the Alexandrian commentaries. It is therefore evident that between David's commentary, on one hand, and the *Dialectic*, on the other hand, there also exist some intermediate grades. These were probably introduced by Stephen in whose commentary on Aristotle's treatise "on interpretation" we also find some phrases which are to be found in chapter 5 of the *Dialectic* (6cq).[59] All things considered, in the next phase the fusion of the lost Stephen's introduction with parts of Aristotle's logical works came to pass.[60] And, after Elias and David the extraction of the discussion on five voices (together with respective definitions and examples) was accomplished. These were placed into a particular section which, in terms of length and development, surpassed not only Porphyry's original discussion but all subsequent commentary interpretations as well. From this last but one phase of formation we have as preserved one Oxford manuscript under the title of the "Philosopher" (*Cod. Oxon. Bodl. Auct.* T. 1. 6).[61] It was erroneously ascribed to John Damascene, the reason being

59. In his commentary on Aristotle's treatise *On Interpretation* Stephen uses the term "signifying voice" (φωνή σημαντική), at the same time determining the voice itself as the highest genus of name and, in that sense, as matter (*Stephani on liber de interpretatione*, CAG XVIII–3, 7, 7, 9).

60. In the *Dialogues* by Severus bar Shakko (13th century), aside from translations of Arabic scientific texts, we encounter the Syrian reworking of the general introduction to philosophy which itself rests upon an earlier Syrian compendium of logic from the end of the 7th or beginning of 8th century (therefore, this manual originates from the time of Damascene and, according to content, in many places – especially those regarding the discussion of five voices, their definitions and examples – indicates significant similarities with Damascene's *Dialectic*). The mentioned compendium is not an original work of Syrian philosophy, for it was created according to the lost Stephen's commentary on Porphyry's *Introduction*. Moreover, Stephen's commentary is derived from Philoponus' commentary of Porphyry's *Introduction* (this commentary also being lost). Hence, it could be said that Stephen in relation to his master is that which Elias is in relation to Olympiodorus. This branch of commentaries that issued forth from the school of Amonius, which is preserved in Syrian fragments only, also represents one of the sources of Damascene's *Dialectic*. Compare A. Baumstark, *op. cit.*, 185.

61. This anonymous manuscript, preserved in a transcription on pergament: dating from the end of the 12th and beginning of the 13th century, contains a series of parts which – almost to a hair's length – converge with Damascene's work (the *Dialectic* and the *Exposition of Faith*). Precisely this relates to the chapter on "voice" which otherwise is not found in the shorter version of the *Dialectic*. This then – in this point – excludes the Oxford manuscript as a term of comparison for the mutual dating of the two versions of Damascene's introduction. Apart from several sentences, the Oxford manuscript in fact brings forth an identical text of that chapter. This tells us that it was already an established part of the manual even before Damascene decided to compose the longer version of his *Dialectic*. In other words, this allows us

that in it – with insignificant discrepancies: in several sentences or words – whole chapters of the *Dialectic* are to be found, and among them, in the first introductory part, precisely the chapter "on voice" (Kotter 151, 1–153, 82). Since after this chapter follow sections in which Aristotle's categories are thematized, and after them Porphyry's voices as well (which is the logical order of things), the following conclusion asserts itself: namely, that precisely this manuscript brings forth the basic text, which preceded the *Dialectic*, and which (or one of its versions) the Damascene then subjected to final refurnishing, however, this time it was executed in a much more expressed theological spirit.

This subsequent refurnishing is evident in virtue of the fact that pagan school examples such as Socrates, Plato are transformed into regular Christian names Peter and Paul,[62] but even more so due to the referencing of the holy Fathers amidst the positing of definitions of species, as well as the concluding determination of the indivisible (individual) in the sense of hypostasis, which is mentioned in the Oxford manuscript but only superficially (152, 50–51). That is to say, Damascene inserts two small theological sections: the first in which he states that members of species do not differ in terms of beingness (nature) but only according to number – to which he adds the remark that that which differs by number, that which is apart and individual, is named as person and hypostasis (Kotter 61, 66–67); and the second in which the non-separable accident, which appears in some hypostasis, is named as the "characteristic particularity" (χαρακτηριστικόν ἰδίωμα). This twofold mention of hypostasis (61, 67; 63, 128) in decisive places switches again the logical consideration of concepts into the theological domain, thus preparing the terrain for dogmatic inferences which are to follow suit in chapter 11 and then again in chapter 30. That is, the fifth chapter concludes with the equalization of hypostasis with the indivisible, that is, the individual (ἄτομον), which is determined as that which subsists in itself out of essence and accident, and which at the same time indicates not something but someone (Kotter 64, 136–138).

to grasp that it is also older than the shorter version. Although the *Dialectic* totally covered this manuscript in terms of breadth, it, nevertheless, withstood because the transcribers regarded it as a work of John Damascene, under whose name it was incorporated into the codex of other similar works (*Doctrina patrum* and collections of various philosophical definitions). The philosophical parts from the beginning of that Oxford collection (*Cod. Oxon. Bodl. Auct.* T I 6, Misc. 184) were published by B. Kotter – as a supplement to his critical edition of the *Dialectic* (151–173, Berlin 1969). M. Rouché thinks that the Oxford manuscript is dependent on the *Dialectic* (and not conversely, i.e. that the latter is dependent on the former). However, he lists no arguments in support of his claim (*op. cit.*, 67). That is all the more odd since on the basis of the obvious rudimentary form of the Oxford text one can only draw a conclusion backing the claim of its precedence. And Rouché in fact does draw such a conclusion in regard to other texts of similar character.

62. The Christian transformation of pagan names is already noticeable in the Oxford manuscript (Kotter, 152, 47, 48). Aristotle offers the example of man for the general, and for the particular he cites his regular name Kalias (*On Interpretation*, p. 7). The pagan names Socrates and Plato still stand in the Syrian fragments.

However, the equalization of the individual (*atomon*) in the sense of the individual member of species – separate and different by number – with hypostasis in the theological sense of person, is not all that appears as a novel theological nuance – one which is still not sufficiently discernible in the Oxford manuscript.[63] In the first insertion, without any immanent conceptual motivation, Damascene conducts the equalization of species, nature and essence. And, to this chain of equality, he adds both image and genus: "And the holy Fathers named both species and genus (as that which is general) as nature, image and essence" (Kotter 62, 79–81). That this equalization of species and genus is too wide and imprecise in the philosophical sense may be seen from the subsequent consideration in which it is clearly shown that from essence in the sense of genus are born different species and natures (62, 81–84). However, Damascene doesn't think that this is a sufficient reason to correct the holy Fathers' usage of these concepts. The similar thing also holds true for the determination of indivisible as hypostasis. It is given as some sort of sixth voice. Yet, such a one cannot exist according to Porphyry's postulations.[64] The motif for its introduction is obviously Christological. And the same also holds true for the term "characteristic property," which appears in later chapters as well (30 and 66).

VIII

After the introduction to "voices" (chapter 5) – taken as the second main part of the beginning of the *Dialectic* (the first being the determination of philosophy and the distinguishing of being, essence and accident) – the preparation for understanding the teaching of the categories follows, as the third main part of this introduction. It spans from the 6th to 8th chapter. Hence, it needs to be viewed as a small whole.

In the sixth chapter the concepts of *division* (διαίρεσις), *redivision* (ἐπιδιαίρεσις) and *subdivision* (ὑποδιαίρεσις) are explained. Division is defined as the first section of a thing, redivision is defined as the second sec-

63. The Oxford text does not contain even nearly all that the *Dialectic* brings forth in regard to ἄτομον, and this is so because it follows the Porphyrian model much more closely. This means that this manuscript contains the more original text of tradition and thus in no way represents an excerpt from the *Dialectic*.

64. Already Porphyry had defined ἄτομον as that which is individual (the individual) within the most proper whose totality in another would never give the same (7, 21–23). In the sense of individual (indivisible) Aristotle, too, who otherwise uses the term ἕκαστον, introduces the concept ἄτομον in the second chapter of *Categories* as the sign for first essences. This originally atomistic phrase thereby begins to denote the limit of division of the general which cannot be meaningfully breached any further (the individual cannot be further divided). By comparing Severus' *Dialogues* it can be seen that within the framework of the considerations on voice there truly was space enough for the determination ἄτομον – if in the sense of the individual it appeared from the relation towards species and genus (209, 32; similarly Elias also, 36, 13). But, through time, it became reinterpreted into hypostasis in the theological sense. It was already said that Porphyry uses ὑπόστασις (57, 4), but in an entirely different sense – that of existence. Therefore, here by means of hypostasis a long path has been traversed: from the logical concept of the individual to the existential concept of person.

tion of the same thing, but according to some other principle, while subdivision is determined as a further section of that which is already sub-divided (Kotter 64, 1–15).[65] Further on it is said that everything which may be divided is divided either according to itself, that is according to essence, or according to accident, with the provision that the division (of) according to itself can be twofold. That is, one where the division of thing is conducted, or one where division of voice is conducted. In regard to the said it is established that, consequently, there are all together eight modes of division: 1) as genus into species, 2) as species into individuals, 3) as whole into parts, with the provision that parts may be equal or unequal, 4) as equivocal concepts into different signifieds, which refer either to the whole concept or only to some part of it, 5) as essences into different accidents, 6) as accidents into different essences, 7) as accidents into accidents and 8) as things which are derived from one or which relate to one (Kotter 65, 45–67, 115).

This chapter offers testimony to the fact that Damascene, at least occasionally and as much as it was possible in his time, took into account the results of philosophical debates on particular open questions of philosophical logic. In this case he showed nerve for certain subtle nuances in the understanding of the problematic of logical division, which was initiated as early as Plato's Academy, and which – in particular points – was treated differently in the neo-Platonic commentaries on Aristotle. In favour of this spirit of discernment, which proves that the text of the *Dialectic* does not remain on the level of one-dimensional simplified and dogmatic exposition, speaks the warning which states that division and redivision do not exist in every domain (Kotter 65, 27–29), as well as the reference to "some" (philosophers) who dispute the division of species into individuals, for they regard it more as enumeration rather than division, since, in difference to proper division, it has an unlimited number of members (Kotter 67, 125–130; also in c. 10: 79, 167–168).

It would be an exaggeration to say that Damascene knew and understood first hand all these nuances and preceding grades of the debate, which he summarized in chapter 6. In fact, he utilized finished templates in which this work was already mostly done, and his contribution consisted in combining and supplementing those sources. That this was precisely the method that Damascene used is demonstrated through comparison with the respective

65. In the shorter version of the *Dialectic* the determinations are given in a more logical order: first the divisions and subdivisions, and only after that the redivisions (64, 1–20). This order is accepted in the Oxford manuscript as well. As an example of redivision the sectioning of people into men and women is proposed. This is cited by Elias in order to illustrate the sectioning of essences into accidents (68, 9–10). While all texts of this tradition mostly hold onto the same examples when referring to division and subdivision, an almost total parting of ways is discernible in the case of examples for redivision. It could be said that, in terms of choice and systematicity of examples, the longer version of the *Dialectic* has achieved the greatest possible scope of overview and uniqueness, since everything in it is concentrated towards the division of the concept of living being.

piece of the Oxford manuscript (Kotter 159, 1–160, 45), the first part of which very much resembles the longer, and the second part of which resembles the shorter version of the sixth chapter of the *Dialectic*. The longer version, however, in many things deviates from the initial model, especially in terms of new material. This means that it was composed by adding material from some wider template – since the additions which widen the text both in relation to the shorter version of the *Dialectic* as well as the Oxford manuscript occasionally display a certain similarity with the content of the Alexandrian commentaries.[66] Furthermore, this means that the final formatting of the text was influenced by the school philosophy which made its way to Damascene despite the ecclesial filtration of sources.

Nevertheless, the differences in regard to the commentaries are too great to allow us to also include the direct usage of these. Before all else, we need to emphasize that this chapter – both in articulation and in wealth of examples – surpasses the respective parts of the commentaries. Amonius explains the concept of division, subdivision and redivision very succinctly (9, 29–10, 10) and after that considers three tropes of division: genus into species, whole into parts (with subdivision into equal parts and non-equal parts) and the division of equivocal concepts into different signifieds (81, 17sq). It is Elias who already knows of six modes of division, although he rejects the division of genera (genuses) into species (67, 26–69, 18), while the derivation of one and in relation to one is mentioned only conditionally as the seventh way of division (70, 21).

It is only with David that we find all eight types of division (65, 16–68, 19). However, despite the accordance of initial propositions about division, as well as particular examples in the further exposition (for instance, the example for the division of univocal voice into different signifieds is the same as in the *Dialectic* – sea-dog, land-dog and dog-star; with David as well man as essence is divided according to accident into white and black; and, the division of accidents into essences is same as well), the general tone of David's consideration is much more neutral and indeterminate. Hence, David lends the same weight both to (Amonius') understanding according to which only

66. Richter thinks that the shorter and longer version of the sixth chapter are independent from one another. That is to say, he holds the opinion that the longer one did not develop from the shorter one by simple expansion of the text, nor did the shorter one develop from the longer one by making it shorter – rather, both of them derive from different textual templates (*op. cit.*, 95). Therefore, while writing the longer version of the *Dialectic* Damascene did not commence from the shorter version, because he took an altogether new textual template in which all that material was already worked over in a different (albeit in a basically similar) way (*op. cit.*, 97). The conclusion about the existence of two separate templates, one for the shorter version and one which served for the longer version, is further supported by the repetition of the exposition on eight types of division in the longer text – and this is a repetition which was possibly already realized in that second template, for two different sources may be sensed in the Oxford manuscript as well.

three ways of division exist: genus into species, whole into parts and univocal concept into different signifieds (66, 24; 67, 32), and to the mentioned inventory of eight tropes, which differs essentially in relation to Damascene's viewpoint which gives clear advantage to the thesis of eight tropes of division. Finally, while David lists Socrates, Plato and Alcibiades as individual members of humankind, Damascene takes Christian names Peter and Paul to signify particular individuals, and only for the unpleasant (non-Christian) division into non-equal parts does he use the example of division of Socrates into head, arms and legs.[67] For all these reasons, especially because of the total lack of warning that division and sub-division are not possible ubiquitously, it is not justified to think of Alexandrian commentaries as the immediate source for the expanded version of the sixth chapter of the *Dialectic.*

The real referential point is here represented by Severus bar Shakko's *Dialogues:* not because the names Peter and Paul appear within them,[68] but because they reveal the philosophical background of the cited warnings, distinctions and cautions given by Damascene. Although Severus speaks only about six ways of division, his formulations are mostly concordant with Damascene's. Since the *Dialogues*, too, give the same explanation of why division of species into individual members cannot be regarded as sub-division,[69] it is justified to presuppose that this proposition in both texts originates from the same source – this being the Philoponean branch of neo-Platonic tradition. Through the lost commentary by Stephen of Alexandria, via one Syrian compendium of logic, it was transported to Severus bar Shakko, on one hand, and, also in mediatory fashion, to Damascene's template (unknown to us), on the other hand.[70] Towards this common connection point a series of other concordances, most of all the identical principal introduction to eight types of division, then the common limitation of the universality of division as an analytical method, as well as the baffling interchange of the phrase concept (ὅρος) with the phrase definition (ὁρισμός).[71] There are too many concordances in a small space to regard them as the result of mere coincidence.

Therefore, it is evident that the sixth chapter issued forth from the preceding very diversified textual tradition in which all of the cited determinations were formed and in which were noted many of the dilemmas from earlier disputes on division. Still, reliance on sources does not diminish the

67. As an example of division of the whole into non-equal parts the commentators take the face (Amm., 83, 12; Elias, 68, 6).
68. Compare A. Baumstark, *op. cit.*, 206.
69. *Ibid.*, 195.
70. In Severus' *Dialogues* direct reference to "philosopher Stephen of Alexandria" has been preserved (196, 36–37).
71. In the *Dialectic* (Kotter 66, 68; 74); in Severus (Baumstark 196, 3, 8). Confusion exists in the reverse order as well: ὅρος is used where it would be appropriate to say ὁρισμός (Baumstark 193, 12; 195, 25; 196, 1, 5). This (inter)change is a common weakness of Christian texts and is discernible in Leontius, David and in the Oxford manuscript. (However, Elias posits correctly: 68, 4).

value of the transported content. Since, in many elements, it surpasses the framework of a purely logical-technical debate. This holds true especially for the eight type of division: that of derivative "from one" (ἀφ' ἑνός) and that of "relative to one" (πρός ἕν), which is introduced with an enviable capacity for differentiation. That is, at the end of the enumeration of different types of division it is added with the words "there is still another way" of division – which is an entirely appropriate separation, for this mode of division does not belong to the same rung and level as do the preceding seven. In fact, this is an Aristotelian structuring of those things which cannot be grouped within some genus yet still remain interconnected in a certain way. From such a form of connectedness, an ontologically weaker one, Aristotle derives his articulation of the existent into ten categories, with the focal point in essence.[72] It is not odd, therefore, that the examples, too, for both of these relations are taken from Aristotle: the example for derivation from one is the paronymic connecting of medical instrument and medical manual with the craft of the medic, while the relation of relative to one is illustrated by the relation of healthy beverage and food towards health.[73]

The concluding remark of the chapter – that not one of the cited divisions, apart from the last one mentioned, allow gradation according to prior and posterior, that is, according to more and less – also reflects the historical framework of the genesis of Aristotle's specific ontological-logical position, which was developed through the acceptance of this rule of priority forged by the Academy.[74] In the longer version of this chapter Damascene

72. David says that the relation *derivative from one* or *relative to one* was the middle way between (Platonic) co-vocity (division within genus which thus connects different species) and mere (sophistic) univocity which creates only an illusion of connectedness (159, 6). As is said at the very beginning of David's prolegomena, concrete being (a being) is not univocal but "from one" (3, 12). Compare elaborate explanations given in the book S. Žunjić, *Aristotel i henologija*, Beograd 1988, 265sq.

73. Aristotle, too, speaks about the relation of that which protects health (healthy food), that which creates health (walking), that which signifies health (healthy cheek) or that which receives health (healthy body) towards health itself (*Met.*, 1003a 34–35). But, nowhere does he use the pleonastic phrase "healthing medicine." Also, neither does he speak of "medical manual" when he directs various phrases of the medical towards the focal point of medical craft (1003b 1). In fact, in the *Metaphysics* both groups of examples (those of the medical and of those of health) are given within the frame of the focal relation of "relative to one" which, in Aristotle, completely displaces the paronymic relation of "from one." Therefore, Aristotle's examples are somewhat changed here. However, this may be interpreted not only as the spoiling of his original preciseness, but also as a further developing of his thought. The majority of these changes can be noticed already in connection to the commentators: Elias speaks about the medic's manual and healthy urine (70, 24; 71, 2), and David, too, speaks about the medic's manual (159, 12), but he also mentions the "health manual" (159, 15–16), and, the division into two forms of relation towards one is found everywhere.

74. The layering into prior and posterior is a characteristic Academy method of gradation by means of which ontical primacy is established. According to Aristotle, the Academicians refrained from introducing any kind of superior generality (universal) in such areas (*EN*, 1096a 17; cf. *Met.*, 999a 6; 1079a 14, 1087b 23). By positing essence into a relation of prior towards other categories, Aristotle endorsed this limitation as well: a limitation placed by

(or his source) does not use a single word in order to mention that the layering into prior and posterior in the relation from one and relative to one was established primarily in order to thereby enable the institution of categorical division as the ontological principle of all that is. However, that he was acquainted with this application, aside from the bygone context, is discernible from chapter 46. Namely, in that chapter it is explicitly cited that the relation from one and relative to one (or the division of equivocal voice) is the principle of division of being (a being) into essence and accident (Kotter 110, 27–28). This means that here, too, exists the distinction between that which is by nature prior and posterior.[75]

The mention of layering into prior and posterior indicates towards the thematic of the following seventh chapter. But, in terms of content, it belongs within the consideration of post-predicaments.[76] The prior by nature (beingness) is determined as that which is included (in something else) while in itself it does not include (this other), that is, as that which annihilates something else when it itself is annihilated, but is not necessarily "co-destroyed" when this other is destroyed (Kotter 68, 2–3).[77] For example, man includes living being, but living being does not necessarily include man, for without man other living beings remain in existence, while without living beings there cannot be man either. This means that genus is by nature prior to species. Alongside this it is added that no species is more beingful than any other, nor is something individual more (beingful) than some other individual.

---

the Academy. This means that there is no sort of generality (universal) above the categories. Since in the *Categories* and in the *Dialectic* (69, 19) it is claimed that essence is genus, it is obvious that this rule is here suspended and that the Platonic genus-frame is in fact rehabilitated again (in regard to which the relation "relative to one" had managed to emancipate itself); compare H. Krämer, "Zur geschichtlichen Stellung der aristotelischen Metaphysik," *Kant-Studien* 58 (1967) 342. It is beyond doubt that such a return to the genus-structure was suitable for the theological usage of the concept of *essence*.

75. The same is said at the end of the shorter version of chapter six whereby, in clearer fashion than in the longer version, the connection with chapter 4 is established – a connection that indicates towards some unknown *Isagoge* in the background of this part of the *Dialectic*. That in the case of essence and accident there is layering into prior and posterior is well known to the Alexandrian commentators. Already Amonius ascertained that in the case of categories there is a prior and posterior for they are not species of one genus (Amm., 82, 10–14), and subsequently this explanation only varies. For example, Elias says that in the case of species there is no prior and posterior (68, 22). Severus develops this explanation further, noticing that in the case of essence we do not necessarily think of accident while the contrary is not the case, which tells us that essence is prior by nature (A. Baumstark, 193).
76. That is why a doubling of this text is noticeable in the second section of chapter 59. The relation of prior and posterior is explored in some other chapters as well, without limitation to the relation of genus-species.
77. The translation offered by F. Dölger, i.e. "By nature the property is co-brought and not the concept which introduces it, and, conversely, the concept which excludes the property, and not the property which is therewith excluded" – which is referenced by G. Richter, *op. cit.*, 100, is neither clear nor precise. The verb "co-destroy" (συναναίρεσθαι) appeared in the Academy – specifically in debates concerning that which has ontical primacy.

This primacy of genus over species does reflect the Platonic standpoint endorsed by the commentators, although in the *Categories* Aristotle himself explains that genus is prior to species, with the argumentation that the existence of genus does not necessarily presuppose the existence of all of its species, while the opposite always is the case (*Cat.*, 14a 26). However, in the ontological sense, in the *Metaphysics* Aristotle clearly gives primacy to species over genus.[78] Contrary to that, the neo-Platonic commentators, beginning from Porphyry (*Eisag.*, 15, 16–20) all the way to Elias (*Eliae in Porphyrii Isagogen* 95, 7) and David (155, 28), give precedence to genus over species. The argumentation for this precedence was given by Amonius who, while doing so, used a twofold rule: prior by nature is that which "co-destroys" when it itself is not "co-destroyed," as well as that which is included (implied) when it itself does not include (imply) (*In Porphyrii Isagogen* 120, 15 – 23).[79] Since almost

78. According to a fragment preserved in the Arabic translation of the treatise by Alexander of Aphrodisias, Xenocrates reaches the conclusion "that species is prior to genus and by nature superior to it" (A. Badawi, *La transmission de la philosophie grecque au monde arabe*, Paris 1968, 143–144). Xenocrates understood the relation of species and genus according to the model of the whole and its parts, and since the part has natural primacy over the whole he concluded that consequentially the species, too, has primacy in relation to genus. Aristotle accepted this point of view and developed it further in the central books of the *Metaphysics* (Zeta, Eta), in which it is species (εἶδος) which is proclaimed to be the first essence. This conclusion contradicts the Platonic standpoint according to which the more general comes before the particular and part, and, inasmuch, it is genuinely Aristotelian. However, at least at first glance, it is not in accord with the standpoint that he endorses in the *Categories* according to which first essence is that which is individual, while the other essences are give as genera (genuses) and species. In view of this, already in classical times the authenticity of the *Categories* was brought into question. However, as was shown by H. Krämer, this contradiction is illusory and is explainable historically. In the *Categories*, taken as Aristotle's early work, great proximity to Plato is mixed with a radical departure from his position. The sign of the first is the non-selective proclaiming of genera and species for second essences, and the sign of the second is the transference of ontological brunt onto that which is individual, which is a turn already made by Speusippus who ascribed independent existence to individual beings only (H. Krämer, "Aristoteles und die akademische Eidoslehre," *Archiv fur Geschichte der Philosophie* 55 (1973) 161). However, Aristotle corrects this radicalism in the *Metaphysics* where he parts species from genus for the latter represents mere generality. At the same time he does not abandon the position taken in the *Categories* but only more consequentially and more precisely applies the same methodological principle accepted in the *Categories* as well – that ontological primacy is possessed by that which is more particular and unique. The individual from the *Categories* now becomes the "composite" (σύνολον) of the *Metaphysics*, in which the generality of species is manifested in the individual form of shape (μορφή). While in the *Categories* individuals are contained in the species, in the *Metaphysics* the species is incarnated in the individuals. The crossing to species as first essences and thus to these as the ontological ground of reality as well, was already prepared in the *Categories*, because there Aristotle claimed that first essences (therefore, the individual) relate to other essences and accidents like species relate to genus (*Cat.*, 2b 17–19). Therefore, the path from the *Categories* to the *Metaphysics* is a path of continuity in which the same criteria of primacy are acknowledged. However, the theological reception of Aristotle returns totally to the position of the *Categories*, thereby reducing essence to Platonic generality.

79. In the mentioned treatise Alexander of Aphrodisias refuted Xenocrates' comparison, demonstrating that the termination of the part does not terminate the whole, while the

identical formulations, together with the example of relation of man and living being, do appear in the *Dialectic*, the inevitable conclusion follows suit. Namely, that chapter 7 came out of commentary material in which, at the beginning, there was no special treatment of the post-predicaments, while the chapters in which the relations between prior and posterior are considered Damascene took over from some other source.[80]

In chapter 8 definition (ὁρισμός), concept (ὅρος) and description (ὑπογραφή) are determined. "A definition is a concise sentence which sets forth the nature of the underlying thing" (Kotter 69, 2–3), while a concept is the "complete name" (69, 15) of a thing: such which signifies it in a more general way (71, 83–84).[81] The essential function of definition is derived from its etymology (ὁρίζειν = to partition, to limit), that is, to distinguish the nature defined from every other nature (70, 39–40). In regard to definition it is said that it is structurally comprised from genus and "constituent differences" which are to be understood as "essential differences" (69, 16). Such a definition is perfect for it leaves out nothing of the thing defined nor does it add anything else. In fact, it is totally exchangeable with it, wherewith genus corresponds to the thing and differences to the form of the thing defined (Kotter 70, 23). Those definitions which are taken both from the goal (purpose) and from the thing (subject) are perfect as well (71, 74). In any case, definitions are given only for essence and its species, while individual things and accidents are subject only to description. In its turn, description is comprised from non-essentialities, that is, from accidents and particularities (72, 90–94).

The chapter on definitions marks the entry into one of the most important areas of late-classical and Byzantine introductions to philosophy. Namely, the teaching on definitions appears within the framework tied to the problematic of division, precisely at the crucial point of the introduction – and this is the case as early as Amonius' treatise and remains so till David's prolegomena which, in terms of its formulations, resembles Damascene's chapter most.[82] The fact that Damascene first considers division

termination of a species does not have that effect upon the genus (only the termination of all species but one), and that neither the termination of the whole terminates its parts, while the termination of the genus terminates its species. However, by means of this refutation Alexander managed to demonstrate only the following: namely, that there is no full adequation between part and whole and species and genus, but not that the species has no ontological *prius*. In fact – it does. For what is more simple, in the act of its own termination, terminates what is more complex, and not the other way around; H. Krämer, "Aristoteles und die akademische Eidoslehre," 141.

80. The same in G. Richter, *op. cit.*, 101.

81. The concept is determined through the name, while the name (term) is determined as "concept according to seeing" (I read σύνουις according to David's commentary, 12, 2, instead of σύναυις, as it stands in Migne).

82. Richter offers a comparative overview of concordances with David's introduction to Porphyry's *Eisagoge* (*op. cit.*, 104–105). Of these doubtlessly the most important is the identical definition of definition (11, 17) as well as the instance of the exemplary definition of man:

and only then moves on to the debate about definition (which the Alexandrians by rule take as the point of departure for the whole exposition[83]) is doubtlessly an unusual difference in regard to the commentators. This difference, however, compliments Damascene, for his order of things is the consequence of the insight that that which cannot be defined is nevertheless subject to division and, in this sense, it is prior to definition in terms of generality. This insight, which issued forth from the refutation of the skeptics' questioning of philosophy as science of being (τὸ ὄν), was not explicitly formulated by Damascene, but, that it stood in the basis of his new and correct order of things can be seen from Severus' *Dialogues* in which it is stated that if being does not allow concept (*n.* it should say definition) it, nevertheless, is subject to division and thus, through division, enables defining (193, 12–15).

Therefore, we can conclude that the text of the eighth chapter is the fruit of a longer path of development, through which the teaching on definition passed previously. The same conclusion is confirmed by the canonical position of the definition from most proximate genus and adequate differences. This form of definition, which (under the name *per genus proximum et differentiam specificam*) later acquired the value of a model in technical manuals of logic, was not particularly emphasized – and was the case not only in Aristotle, but in the first commentators as well. What is more, it was still disputed in the time of Elias (56, 30–57, 3), who unambiguously opts for definitions from subject, purpose and both (6, 24–25). Damascene, however, gives this status to exemplary form, while definitions from subject and purpose (in certain circumstances) are allowed as possibilities of second order (71, 75–79).

Damascene's examples (70, 24–27) of definitions from subject (medical craft is concerned with human bodies) and from purpose (medical craft is a skill productive of health) are identical with examples from David's commentary (17, 33–18, 3). But, this doesn't mean that they have been taken over directly from there. The same can be said for the explication of the structure of the model form of definition taken as the combination of matter and form. Still, this pre-original Aristotelian comparison of genus with matter and difference with form is mentioned by David in two places (91, 4–5; 213, 3).[84] But, he doesn't make it the basis of definition, whereas Damascene does. The concluding warning that the accidental is not to be taken

a sentient mortal being capable of rationality and science – an example which is also found in Philoponus, Anastasius and Sextus Empiricus (*Pyrrh. hypot.*, II, 5).

83. Regardless of the fact that he first expounds the division into equal parts and non-equal parts (10, 8–18) David states that concept (that is, definition) precedes division (10, 30), adding the argument that definition signifies monad, while division presupposes plurality (10, 28). On the other hand, he himself cites the Platonic standpoint according to which nothing can escape division (9, 30), and later on, reflecting upon the relation between diaretic and choristic, he even says that division precedes definition (89, 25).

84. Elias makes no analogy at all of genus and difference with matter and form.

into definition has its pendant in David as well,[85] who demonstrates that non-essential determinations of man – such as "erect walking being," "being with even nails," "laughing being" – are not necessary (12, 26; 12, 33). But, since such propositions represent a commonplace in the manuals of that era, it is not possible to draw reliable conclusions from these about the direct dependency of the *Dialectic* on the commentaries. It is obvious that its basic content derives from school philosophy (which is particularly true as regards the additions which characterize the longer version), but it is likewise clear that the formulations, despite significant similarity, are not taken over directly from the commentaries for they (i.e. the formulations) have passed through one or more inter-redactions.[86]

Considering that almost all of Damascene's philosophical propositions have been taken over from preceding philosophical manuals, it is clear that one can speak of his philosophical originality only with regard to his work as selector and compilator. Nevertheless, in virtue of a subsequent positing of the *Dialectic* within its philosophical background – from Aristotle's *Categories* and Porphyry's *Eisagoge* to Alexandrian commentaries and ecclesial logical manuals – a perspective is opened for a more adequate understanding of the ambit and depth of Damascene's personal philosophical educatedness. Lamentably, evaluations of Damascene's educatedness, the intellectual quality of his work and of his ability for understanding philosophical matters differ considerably in contemporary literature. This is partly due to mistaken understandings of his effects, and partly due to different understandings of his own programme. On one side stand researchers who unhiddenly underestimate Damascene's intellectual capacities and his understanding of the

85. Therefore, David here represents the rule *neque accidentia definiri posse*. But, as was noticed already by Lequien, in chapter 37 he allows for *accident* to procure the definition from purpose and thing (PG 94, 557B, note 13).

86. Roueché believes that – in one short section which is ascribed to Maximus the Confessor (*Cod. Vat. gr.* 504; M. Roueché, "Byzantine Philosophical Texts of the Seventh Century," *Jahrbuch der Österreichischen Byzantinistik* 23 [1973]) – he has discovered the text mediating between David's commentary and Damascene's chapter on definition (*op. cit.*, 66). However, the comparative inspection of this text, which he published together with David's commentary and Damascene's *Dialectic*, does not confirm such a conclusion at all. Damascene could have had immediate access to Roueché's text, but he did not rely on it as the underlaying support for his own exposition; and this is confirmed by a whole series of essential additions, expansions and differences. Damascene's chapter is much richer than Roueché's sparse anonymous text in which no mention is made of the distinction between definition and name, of the statement that essence is genus, nor is any comparison made between genus with matter and difference with form. Aside from that, Damascene's exposition is not only wider but it is more precise as well in distinguishing ὅρος from ὁρισμός (comp. 70, 6, Roueché and 69, 16, Kotter). On top of all that, if the unknown author of the cited short text truly did derive his fragment from David's commentary – and this seems to be indicated by the final selection of four questions (whether it is, what it is, of what sort it is and why it is, Roueché, 71, 51) – then the following question is raised: why did Damascene totally neglect that part, if, to start with, he followed that text as template?

philosophical heritage. Among such, one also finds those who explore Damascene's opus with in-depth thoroughness. Hence, we cannot accuse them of not being knowledgeable with regard to the true state of affairs. The most characteristic example of a negative viewpoint is given by Gerhard Richter himself, who nevertheless remains meritorious. Without hesitation he states that Damascene does not possess philosophical knowledge, that he is a "non-philosophical head" which has no understanding of what it cites, that is, of what it copies. On the other side stand those who evaluate Damascene's opus within the historical framework of his epoch and in relation to Damascene's own programme. Among those a prominent figure is Basil Tatakis who claims that Damascene did receive a sufficiently good general education and that he, in addition to that, had a solid knowledge of the Greek philosophers and science. There is no doubt that already in his youth Damascene passed through general rhetorical education and that, later on, he did have the opportunity to acquaint himself with philosophical literature, both in Greek and Syrian language. Therefore, it seems that a more positive approach to the *Dialectic* is not only more just but also more adequate with regard to the understanding of Damascene's accomplishments, which are not meager. Moreover, together with Klaus Oehler it can be claimed that Damascene understood much more of philosophy than seems to be the case at first glance, that he did have both the necessary philosophical education and knowledge, and that he was, therefore, capable of developing a subtle philosophical argumentation within those philosophical frames that he placed before himself.

Translation from Serbian to English by Bogdan Lubardić

John of Damascus on Genus and Species

Scott Ables

Introduction

There[1] seems to be growing academic interest in John of Damascus, no doubt do in part to the continued publication of his works in modern critical editions.[2] Further, there has been growing interest in the philosophic aspects of John's work.[3] John's works on logic, however, are not commentaries,[4] although Christian philosophers were engaged in such in Alexandria a century prior to John, and some activity continued among John's Syro-Palestinian contemporaries.[5] Compendia were popular in John's milieu, whether florilegia, catenae or lists of technical terms, and G. Richter notes John had a preference for florilegia.[6] John's philosophic works, however, in-

1. I acknowledge the generous support of the Oxford Centre for Christianity and Culture of Regent's Park College, the University of Oxford, as well as the wise counsel of Richard Sorabji, Mossman Roueché, Phil Booth, and Johannes Zachhuber.

2. B. Kotter , R. Volk, eds., *Die Schriften des Johannes von Damaskos*, Patristische Texte und Studien, 7, 12, 17, 22, 29, 60/1, 61/2, 68, Berlin, New York: De Gruyter 1969, 1973, 1975, 1981, 1988, 2008, 2009, 2013.

3. See, for example recent essays on John of Damascus by C. Erismann, A. Zhyrkova, M. Frede, and R. Cross.

4. Per Kotter the background to the *Dialectica* is primarily Aristotle's *Categories* and the commentaries on it without there being direct dependence. Kotter, i, 45. G. Richter notes that B. Studer doubted that John knew the Alexandrian commentaries directly, G. Richter, *Die Dialektik Des Johannes Von Damaskos: Eine Untersuchung Des Textes Nach Seinen Quellen Und Seiner Bedeutung*, Studia Patristica Et Byzantina, 10; Ettal: Buch-Kunstverlag 1964, 11.

5. At least the following philosophers of the sixth and seventh centuries in Alexandria were Christians: John Philoponus, Elias, David, Ps. Elias and Stephanus, in: R. Sorabji, ed., *Aristotle Transformed: The Ancient Commentators and Their Influence*, London: Duckworth1990, 10-15, especially 14. S. Brock surveys Syriac activity, including translations and commentaries by contemporaries of John of Damascus, examples include Jacob of Edessa (d. 708) translated and commented on Aristotle's *Categories* as did George, bishop of the Arabs (d. 724) on *Categories, De interpretatione* and *Prior Analytics*. S. Brock, "The Syriac Commentary Tradition," in: Ch. Burnett ed., *Glosses and Commentaries on Aristotelian Logical Texts: The Syriac, Arabic and Medieval Latin Traditions*, Warburg Institute Surveys and Texts; London: The Warburg Institute, University of London 1993, 3–18.

6. John appended florilegia to *Orationes de imaginibus tres* (Kotter, I, oration.section=1.28–65, 2.24–68, 3.43–116), *Contra Jacobitas* (Kotter, IV, 102, 109–153), *Epistola de hymno trisagio* (Kotter, IV, 294, 304–332), *De sacris jejuniis* (PG 95, 64). G. Richter, *Johannes Von Damaskos: Philosophische Kapitel*, Bibliotek Der Griechischen Literatur, Stuttgart: Anton Hiersemann 1982, 67.

clude no florilegia, and they greatly exceed extant lists of terms to which he may have had access.[7] There are several lists of logic terms attributed to Maximus the Confessor, but no clear reference to these by John.[8] In light of the late collection of Maximus' works, this raises the question just how dependent was John on Maximus for his philosophic thought?[9] Rather, John's editor points to the *Doctrina Patrum* (*DP*, c. 700) and the Alexandrian commentators or compendia based on them as potential sources. Consequently, John appears to be engaged in a somewhat different project than either recapitulating philosophic aspects of Christian tradition or providing rudimentary editing of philosophic compendia.

Whatever the case, John's philosophic acumen has not escaped notice, as M. Roueché suggests, "If we exclude Maximus, who was a theologian well versed in Aristotle but not an Aristotelian in the sense that the Alexandrian lecturers were, we discover that after Stephanus, the next certain Aristotelian appears over a century later in the person of John Damascene."[10] John's philosophic works are more than lists or compendia but less than commentary, so what did John intend? Such questions are stifled by detractors who take John's statement to say nothing new quite literally, e. g. following G. Richter without demur, A. Louth, regarding John's principle philosophic work, writes, "John seems to have been neither the author nor even, save in a very minor way, the compiler of the *Dialectica*."[11] Further, G. Richter himself claims that the *Dialectica* stands alone with the *Expositio* making no use of it.[12] This negative assessment is not, however, universal. K. Oehler finds contra Richter that John is both a scholar and a thinker, lamenting that Richter made nothing of the one contribution in John he recognized, bringing philosophy and theology together in a new way, thus K. Oehler argues dramatically that John "broke the mold of the Church's tradition" that kept theology and philosophy separate.[13]

---

7. On compendia and lists of definitions, see M. Roueché, "Byzantine Philosophical Texts of the Seventh Century," *Jahrbuch der Österreichischen Byzantinistik* 23 (1974) 61–76: 66–67. And, recently C. Furrer-Pilliod, *Ὅροι Καὶ Ὑπόγραφα: Collections Alphabétiques De Définitions Profanes Et Sacrées*, Studi E Testi, Città del Vaticano: Biblioteca Apostolica Vaticana 2000.
8. For examples of lists attributed to Maximus the Confessor see PG 91, 149B–153B (*Opusc. 14*), 213A–16A (*Opusc. 18*), 260D–268A (*Opusc. 23*), and 276B–280B (*Opusc.* 26b), which fall within the *Theological and Polemical Opuscula*. A quick perusal of Kotter's apparatus for the *Dialectica* did not turn up any reference to these texts. Further, following Bram Roosen, Jankowiak and Booth, reject *Opusculum 23* and *26b* as spurious. Marek Jankowiak and Phil Booth, "A New Date-List of the Works of Maximus the Confessor," in: *The Oxford Handbook of Maximus the Confessor*, edited by P. Allen, B. Neil, Oxford: Oxford University Press, forthcoming.
9. An early witness to the transmission of Maximus' works is the ninth century *Bibliotecha* (codices 192A–195) of Photius. M. Jankowiak, Ph. Booth, "A New Date-List," forthcoming.
10. Roueché, 65.
11. A. Louth, *St. John Damascene: Tradition and Originality in Byzantine Theology*, Oxford: Oxford University Press 2002, 45–46.
12. G. Richter, *Johannes Von Damaskos: Philosophische Kapitel*, 82.
13. K. Oehler, *Antike Philosophie Und Byzantinisches Mittelalter*, Munich: C.H. Beck 1969, 295–296.

Tradition

The seventh century saw an end to the institutional Aristotelian commentary tradition in Alexandria, whether the result of Persian or Arab conquest is uncertain.[14] Subsequently, compendia were compiled of the extant commentaries in order to extract the minimum needed, and Christians followed suite compiling terms needed for theological debate, for example Maximus the Confessor or his circle seems to have compiled several lists of definitions and even compendia.[15] After perhaps a century of this, John of Damascus edited the *Dialectica*, which was much more than just a list of terms or a compendia, but a complete if minimal handbook of logic.

Philosophy and theology in late antiquity were closely related enterprises.[16] Not only did philosophers, whether Christian or pagan, write commentaries on the works of Plato and Aristotle, but both saw their work as religious and in competition.[17] In his philosophic works, John is compiling the thoughts of both the Fathers and the philosophers. C. Erismann suggests Christians initially rejected Aristotelian logic but gradually came to accept it, as epitomized in John.[18] The evidence suggests an uneven process of sporadic grudging acceptance tempered by polemical *ad hominem*. The *DP* still displays the trope of disparaging Aristotelian logic.[19] Further, even the irenic borrowing of aphorisms and the cherry picking of definitions from classic and philosophic authors by the circle of Maximus the Confessor is recognized but

14. R. Sorabji, ed., *Aristotle Transformed: The Ancient Commentators and Their Influence*, London: Duckworth 1990, 19. For an overview of late antique Aristotelianism and its revival in 9th century Bahgdad see G. Fowden, *Before and after Muhammad: The First Millenium Refocused*, Princeton: Princeton University Press 2014, 127–163.
15. Following Bram Roosen, Jankowiak and Booth, although excluding as spurious *Opuscula 23* and *26b* as noted above, attribute to Maximus or his circle the compendia *Additamentum 34*, which "is a collection of excerpts from lectures on the *Isagoge* of Porphyry and Aristotle's *Categories*," Marek Jankowiak and Phil Booth, "A New Date-List," (forthcoming).
16. An informative survey of the relationship between philosophy and religion from antiquity to late antiquity can be found in P. Merlan, "Religion and Philosophy from Plato's 'Phaedo' to the Chaldaean Oracles," *Journal of the History of Philosophy* 1/2 (1963) 163–176. For an example of philosophy as the handmaid of theology see H. R. Drobner, "Gregory of Nyssa as Philosopher: 'De Anima Et Resurrectione' and 'De Hominis Opificio,'" *Dionysius*, New Series 18/December (2000) 69–101.
17. See Kotter, i, 56f, 3.1–65 = γ′ Περὶ φιλοσοφίας, 136f. For John "The love of God, therefore, is the true philosophy," (ἡ οὖν ἀγάπη ἡ πρὸς τὸν θεὸν αὔτη ἐστὶν ἡ ἀληθὴς φιλοσοφία) (Kotter, i, 56, 3.26–27). See also, C. G. Conticello and V. Kontouma-Conticello, "Philosophie Et Théologie À Byzance," in: Ph. Capelle-Dumont, O. Boulnois, eds., *Philosophie Et Théologie Au Moyen-Âge. Anthologie-Tome II*, Paris: Éditions du Cerf 2009, 43–61. On the religious texts of pagan philosophers, see *et al.* Syrianus, *Pythagoras and Plato with the Chaldean Oracles*, Proclus, *Platonic Theology*, and *Commentary on the Chaldean Oracles*, Porphyry, *Against the Christians*, and Iamblichus, *On the Mysteries of the Egyptians* or *Theurgy*. Finally, Aristotle's *Metaphysics* was read in late antiquity as a religious text.
18. C. Erismann, "A World of Hypostases: John of Damascus' Rethinking of Aristotle's Categorical Ontology," *Studia Patristica* 50 (2011) 269–287: 271.
19. F. Diekamp, ed., *Doctrina Patrum De Incarnatione Verbi*, Münster 1907, 217 II.

eclipsed by John's adaptation of the introductory logic curriculum in the *Dialectica*, baptizing Aristotelian logic into a handbook. John is selective, however, taking from the compendia only that part corresponding to Porphyry's *Isagoge* and Aristotle's *Categories*.[20]

Definitions had been collected from antiquity and by Christians as early as Clement of Alexandria. From the circle of Maximus are preserved some fifty definitions, while John ended the tradition with some two hundred.[21] This tradition may have shaped the late antique genre of logical compendia, even limited it to some degree, and may have waned in certain circles given the wide circulation of the *Dialectica*. Nevertheless, John is clearly in the Maximian trajectory: he equated *ousia* with *physis*, *hypostasis* with *prosopon*, and defined *enhypostatin*, *diaphora*, and *idion* among other terms,[22] so too, the *DP*, gave definitions including genus and species, which are not unlike statements in John.

If John subverted the modesty *topos*, as A. Alexakis claims, his commitment to say nothing new is merely polite.[23] He must therefore be taken seriously, contra those who take him literally, when he commits to "set forth the best contributions of the philosophers of the Greeks," preserving for Christianity what compendia apparently could not.[24] In John references to Aristotle are devoid of the polemic common to other late antique theologians. Further, John refers to Socrates some thirty-two times, whereas mention of Socrates is very rare in theologians after Chalcedon.[25] C. Stead suggested that rising Aristotelianism left Nicaea incoherent by providing two definitions of *ousia*, "which distinguished between the individual and the species."[26]

20. A. Louth, *St. John Damascene: Tradition and Originality in Byzantine Theology*, 40, G. Richter, *Johannes Von Damaskos: Philosophische Kapitel*, 75–76. For Maximus on aphorisms see PG 91, 817–28, and on definitions see PG 91, 149–53, 213–16, 260–8.
21. This is based on Furrer-Pilliod, 34–35, 38–40. However, this may need to be revised in light of recent work on Maximus, see the forthcoming Marek Jankowiak and Phil Booth, "A New Date-List," *forthcoming*.
22. Respectively οὐσία, φύσις, ὑπόστασις, πρόσωπον, ἐνυπόστατον, διάφορος, ἴδιος, for which see PG 91, 149–152.
23. A. Alexakis, "The Modesty 'Topos' and John of Damascus as a Not-So-Modest Author," *Byzantinische Zeitschrift* 97, 2 (2004) 521–530.
24. τῶν παρ' Ἕλλησι σοφῶν τὰ κάλλιστα παραθήσομαι εἰδώς (Kotter, i, 52 <Προοίμιον>, 43–44). The translation is Chase's: S. John of Damascus, *Saint John of Damascus: Writings*, trans. Frederic H. Chase, New York: Fathers of the Church, Inc 1958, 5. This is not to say that commentaries were not available, but whether John used a commentary or a compendia in his work on the *Dialectica* remains an open question for me. I am not convinced by B. Studer's thesis that John did not know the commentaries directly noted above.
25. M. Frede, "The Early Christian Reception of Socrates," in: L. Judson, V. Karasmanes, eds., *Remembering Socrates: Philosophical Essays*, Oxford: Clarendon 2006, 188–202: 195, 201. John may be responding to a Syro-Palestinian impulse that viewed Aristotle and philosophy, and thus Socrates, in a more favorable light. I am looking into this further.
26. C. Stead, *Philosophy in Christian Antiquity*, Cambridge: Cambridge University Press 1994, 161. Stead summarizes the problem: "if *homoousios* is understood as implying 'same individual,' the [Nicene] Creed seems to be declaring the Father, Son and Spirit are one Person, not three. But if it implies only 'same species,' it gives no sufficient expression of divine unity."

And, a near contemporary of John, Anastasius of Sinai, continues the anti-philosophy trope, being more interested in exposing Aristotle's *Categories* as the root of Monophysite error.[27] John, however, seems to ignore this trope, selectively accepting Aristotelian logic.[28]

In the *DP* John finds a florilegium that stands as a ready witness to the chalcedonian ecclesial mind;[29] consequently, it makes a good proxy for the tradition in which he situates himself. For example, one of John's references to the *DP* appears to be the definitions of genus and species, which I give below:

Genus in the *DP* and the parallel in the *Dialectica*:[30]

Doct Patr	*Dialectica*
1. Γένος ἐστὶ τὸ κατὰ πλειόνων καὶ διαφερόντων τῷ εἴδει ἐν τῷ τί ἐστι κατηγορούμενον. σημαίνει δέ τὸ γένος καὶ τὴν πατρίδα, ὡς ὅταν λέγωμεν τὸν Πέτρον Γαλιλαῖον τῷ γένει. σημαίνει δέ καὶ τὴν ἀρχὴν τῆς τινων γενέσεως, ὡς ὅταν λέγωμεν τούς ἐξ Ἰσραὴλ Ἰσραηλίτας τῷ γένει. 2. Γένος ἐστὶ τὸ καθ' ἑαυτὸ θεωρούμενον πρᾶγμα.	Γένος οὖν ἐστι τὸ κατὰ πλειόνων καὶ διαφερόντων τῷ εἴδει ἐν τῷ τί ἐστι κατηγορούμενον, ὥσπερ τὸ ζῷον γένος ὂν κατηγορεῖται ἀνθρώπου καὶ ἵππου καὶ βοὸς καὶ ἄλλων πλειόνων ἐν τῷ τί ἐστιν, ἅτινα τῷ εἴδει διαφέρουσιν ἀλλήλων· ἕτερον γὰρ εἶδος ἀνθρώπου καὶ ἄλλο ἵππου καὶ ἄλλο βοός. Ἐν τῷ τί δέ ἐστι κατηγορεῖται. Ἐρωτώμενοι γὰρ "τί ἐστιν ἄνθρωπος," φαμὲν "ζῷον." Ὁμοίως καὶ ἵππος· ἐρωτώμενοι "τί ἐστιν," λέγομεν "ζῷον." Ὥστε γένος ἐστίν, ᾧ ὑπόκειται τὸ εἶδος. Τὸ γὰρ γένος εἰς εἴδη διαιρεῖται καὶ καθολικώτερον τοῦ εἴδους ἐστὶ καὶ περιέχει τὰ εἴδη καὶ ἐπάνω αὐτῶν ἐστιν.
1. A genus is that predicated in respect of the essence of many things which differ in species. The word genus also indicates one's fatherland, as when we say Peter is [by	A genus, therefore, is that predicated in respect of the essence of many things which differ in species, as for instance the genus, animal, which is predicated in respect of the essence of man and horse and ox and many other things,

27. *Viae dux*, 6.2.1–17. K.-H. Uthemann, ed., *Anastasii Sinaïtae, Viae dux.*, CCSG 8, Turnhout 1981. Prior to this the *De sectis* insisted on quoting Gregory of Nazianzus to correct Aristotle, which is repeated in the *DP*, Diekamp, 217–218, II.
28. John slips into old patterns once in his polemic in the *Contra Jacobitus* (Kotter, iv, 113, 10.13). He disparages his opponents as posing Aristotle the thirteenth apostle.
29. The *DP* is a florilegia that seeks "to present the doctrine of the faith systematically through patristic citations." A. D. Berardino, ed., *Patrology: The Eastern Fathers from the Council of Chalcedon (451) to John of Damascus (750)*, trans. Adrian Walford, Institutum Patristicum Augustinianum, James Clarke 2000, 167.
30. Diekamp, 254, 13–18, 21 \|\| Kotter, i, 73, 9.24–35. In Diekamp the first definition is anonymous (τὰ τοιαῦτα ἀνεπίγραφα εὗρον), the second from an anonymous pagan philosopher (τῶν ἔξω φιλοσόφων). The translations are mine.

race] from Galilea. It also indicates the origin of a certain race, as when we speak of those from Israel as Israelites [by race].
2. Genus is that which is contemplated in each [concrete real] thing.

which differ from one another in species. For the species of man is one thing and of horse another, and of ox another. It [genus] is predicated of the essence [what something is]. For when asked, "what is Man?" We say, "Animal." So also horse; when asked, "what is it?" We say, "Animal." Therefore, genus is that to which the species is subject. For the genus divides into species, is more universal than the species, contains the species, and is above them.

Species in the *DP* and the parallel in the *Dialectica:*[31]

Doct Patr

Εἶδος κατὰ δύο σημαινομένων φέρεται. λέγεται γὰρ εἶδος καὶ ἡ μορφή, οἷον „πρῶτον μὲν εἶδος ἄξιον τυραννίδος".[32] λέγεται εἶδος καὶ τὸ ἀπὸ τοῦ γένους διαιρούμενον, ὡς ὅταν τὸν ἄνθρωπον εἶδος λέγωμεν τοῦ ζῴου. εἶδός ἐστι τὸ ὑπὸ τὸ γένος ταττόμενον. καὶ πάλιν εἶδός ἐστιν, οὗ τὸ γένος ἐν τῷ τί ἐστι κατηγορεῖται. καὶ πάλιν εἶδός ἐστι τὸ κατὰ πλειόνων καὶ διαφερόντων τῷ ἀριθμῷ ἐν τῷ τί ἐστι κατηγορούμενον.

Dialectica

Καὶ τὸ εἶδος δὲ τῶν ὁμωνύμων ἐστίν, διςσῶς λεγόμενον· λέγεται γὰρ εἶδος καὶ ἡ ἑκάστου μορφή, καθ' ὃ εἴρηται· "Πρῶτον μὲν εἶδος ἄξιον τυραννίδος." Ἔστι πάλιν εἶδος τὸ οὐσιῶδες τὸ τασσόμενον ὑπὸ τὸ γένος. Καὶ πάλιν εἶδός ἐστιν, οὗ κατηγορεῖται τὸ γένος ἐν τῷ τί ἐστι. Καὶ πάλιν εἶδός ἐστι τὸ κατὰ πλειόνων καὶ διαφερόντων τῷ ἀριθμῷ ἐν τῷ τί ἐστι κατηγορούμενον.

The word species bears two significations. For it is also called form, as for instance, "A first species worthy of sovereignty." Species is also called that which divides the genus, as when we say man from animal. Species is that classed under the

Καὶ τὸ εἶδος δὲ τῶν ὁμωνύμων ἐστίν, διςσῶς λεγόμενον· λέγεται γὰρ εἶδος καὶ ἡ ἑκάστου μορφή, καθ' ὃ εἴρηται· »Πρῶτον μὲν εἶδος ἄξιον τυραννίδος«. Ἔστι πάλιν εἶδος τὸ οὐσιῶδες τὸ τασσόμενον ὑπὸ τὸ γένος. Καὶ πάλιν εἶδός ἐστιν, οὗ κατηγορε-

31. Diekamp, 258, 15–23 || Kotter, i, 74, 2/10.4–10. In Diekamp the definition is from an anonymous pagan philosopher (τῶν ἔξω φιλοσόφων). The translations are mine.
32. Eurip. *Aeolus* 15, 2. As noted in Diekamp, 258. Per Barnes, "shape there means 'surface lineament,'" and not "substantial shape" nor is it synonymous with genus. J. Barnes, *Porphyry: Introduction*, trans. Jonathan Barnes, Clarendon Later Ancient Philosophers, Oxford: Oxford University Press 2003, 93–94. Aeolus is a lost play; the fragment is of four lines only in F. Jouan, H. V. Looy, eds., *Euripide: Fragments 1re Partie Aigeus-Autolykos*, 8, Paris: Les Belles Lettres 1998, 30. John following the *DP* takes *eidos* here to mean *morphe* or form. In my view, pace Barnes, who speaks of Porphyry's intent not John's, this is meant to elicit that appearance is indicative of nature, i.e. the beautiful appearance of the child indicates its destined life of nobility.

genus. And again, species is that of which the genus is predicated in respect to essence.

ῖται τὸ γένος ἐν τῷ τί ἐστι. Καὶ πάλιν εἶδός ἐστι τὸ κατὰ πλειόνων καὶ διαφερόντων τῷ ἀριθμῷ ἐν τῷ τί ἐστι κατηγορούμενον.

Institutio elementaris (IE)

Maximus or his circle collects only those definitions needed as technical terms in Christological debate.[33] With these parallels from the *DP*, however, John has virtually exhausted the post-Chalcedonian dyophysite tradition on genus and species. These definitions, however, are just the tip of the iceberg in John; He adds additional discussion of both genus and species. John realizes that something more than defining terms is needed, for confessional interlocutors continue to fail to come to terms with each other.

Perusing the chapter titles of John's philosophic works suggest how far he went in coopting the philosophic tradition. Further, Kotter indicates parallels for genus and species among John's works: section seven of the *IE*: "On Genus and Species" parallels section two in the *Dial brev*: "On Genus and Species: of the Most General, Specific and Subordinate," and sections nine and ten in *Dial fus*: "On Genus" and "On Species."[34] Searching for *lemmata* of the terms genus and species within one line of each other in John's corpus, further verified that these are the right places to look for genus and species in John.[35] The tables in the appendix outline the results. The search included all of John's texts, but only philosophic texts met the criteria, thus it seems safe to conclude that John's notion of genus and species is largely delineated in his philosophic works, and primarily in the passages indicated above.[36]

33. M. Törönen outlines logical tools in Maximus, including genus and species, but acknowledges that Maximus is not engaging Aristotelianism per se but theological questions, never for example speaking of first and secondary substance. M. Törönen, *Union and Distinction in the Thought of St Maximus the Confessor*, Oxford Early Christian Studies, Oxford: Oxford University Press 2007, 19–26, 138–142.
34. There are two recensions of the *Dialectica* going back to John that Kotter edits in parallel, *recensio fusior* (longer recension, *Dial fus*) and *recensio brevior* (shorter, *Dial brev*) in Kotter, i, 47–146.
35. The TLG search criteria were for "γενος, ειδος (lemma, picked nominative, acc, gen and dat single and plural dominant spellings only w/in one line of each other)." "Thesaurus Linguae Graecae: A Digital Library of Greek Literature," University of California, Irvine: University of California 2009. The lemma γενος occurs 562 times in John and that of ειδος 797, thus I narrowed the field by focusing on places where they converged. The preponderance of these are indeed in the philosophic works, but they are also found independent of each other in John's dogmatica, polemica and hagiographica, thus conclusions regarding their convergence are tentative. This also suggests that any denial of dependence of John's other works on his philosophic needs further clarification.
36. Of course he may elicit nuance in either term where they do not occur within one line of each other, but given the concentration of terms, it seems likely that the appropriate places have been identified.

These texts are from two works. The *IE* stands apart as the earliest, shortest, and an independent work.[37] The other texts are related to the *Dialectica* (hereafter *Dial*), including the *Dial fus* and the *Dial brev*, next is the *Ἕτερον κεφάλαιον/Other Chapter* (hereafter *OC*), a highly edited short chapter of the *Dial*,[38] and finally the *Fragmenta philosophica* (from *Cod. Oxon. Bodl. Auct.* T. 1. 6, hereafter *FP*), which John's editor includes, but following Richter, believes it an independent tradition, not a source of John.[39] Consequently, it is the *IE* and the *Dial* that are in scope.

Because it is brief, independent of the *Dial*, and according to Kotter earlier, the *IE* will be our focus.[40] Further, *IE* section seven, "About Genus and Species," is also unique. It is the longest passage in the letter and also the longest on genus and species in John.[41] Finally, it parallels the corresponding sections in *Dial* as noted above (also apparent from Table 2). First, however, Section seven must be placed in the context of John's programmatic statement at the beginning of the *IE*:[42]

Οὐσία καὶ φύσις καὶ μορφὴ κατὰ τοὺς ἁγίους πατέρας ταὐτόν ἐστιν. Καὶ πάλιν ὑπόστασις καὶ πρόσωπον καὶ ἄτομον ταὐτόν ἐστιν. Καὶ διαφορὰ καὶ ποιότης καὶ ἰδίωμα ταὐτόν ἐστιν. Περὶ τούτων οὖν καὶ τῶν τοιούτων σκοπὸς ἡμῖν ἐστιν εἰπεῖν, περὶ ὧν καὶ ἡ ὑμετέρα συγκαταβατικῶς ἠρώτησεν ὁσιότης.	Essence and nature and form, according to the holy Fathers, are the same thing. And again *hypostasis* and *prosopon* and individual are the same thing. And, difference, quality and property are the same thing. Regarding these things then and things like them, our purpose is to say something, about which also your holiness has humbly asked.

Thus, John intends this letter and section seven to speak to the question he was asked. He starts with three groups of three words, words central to Christological controversy, suggesting he is systematizing what is scattered

37. Kotter, ii, 20–26. Kotter holds that the *IE* was written prior to the *Dialectica*, Kotter, ii, 3.
38. The *Ἕτερον κεφάλαιον/Other Chapter* is given at Kotter, i, 142–146.
39. *Fragmenta philosophica* from *Cod. Oxon. Bodl. Auct.* T. 1. 6. (CPG 8042) for the text see, Kotter, ii, 151–73; for the introduction see Kotter, ii, 149–150. Kotter following Richter dates *FP* prior to the *Dial*, although he sees them as independent of each other. Kotter quotes Richter as recognizing "how far the entire design of the Damascene was already prepared" by the milieu of this text, *FP*. See Richter, *Die Dialektik*, 39. Louth follows this position. Louth, *St. John Damascene: Tradition and Originality in Byzantine Theology*, 32, n. 38. But, *FP* is found in only one ms. from the 12th or 13th centuries, and Roueché argues it could be based on the *Dial*, contra Richter. Finally, if the *FP* is anonymous, parallel too, but not a source of John, and known in only one late mss., perhaps it is a late compilation based on John.
40. Hoeck indicates it is authentic and that "its content is a first draft of the *Dialectica*." J. M. Hoeck, "Stand Und Aufgaben Der Damaskenos-Forschung," *Orientalia Christiana Periodica* 17 (1951) 5–60: 18. Following Richter, Kotter indicates *IE* is earlier. Kotter, i, 3.
41. By "most central" I mean section 7 is the climax of John's presentation in the *IE*, followed by three short unrelated sections (8–10). On this see Richter, *Die Dialektik*, 43.
42. Kotter, i, 20, 1.1–6.

among the Fathers.[43] Section seven provides an extended introduction to genus and species, but to what end?

In order to let John speak for himself, first I provide a translation of the chapter headings and all of section seven since it is not otherwise available in a modern language.

Institutio elementaris/Introduction to Basic Dogma

<Preface>

1. About essence, nature, and form
2. About *hypostasis*, *prosopon*, and individual
3. About difference, quality and property
4. About essential and non-essential difference, or rather natural difference and attribute
5. About separable and inseparable attribute
6. About *homoousios* and *heterousios*
7. About genus and species
8. About energy
9. About passion
10. About will

7. About Genus and Species

The genus is divided into species such as the animal [into] either rational or irrational. See, the animal is a genus of the rational and the irrational, but the rational and the irrational are species of the animal. Again, the rational is divided into the mortal (5) (man) and the immortal (angel). The rational is genus of the mortal and the immortal, but the mortal and the immortal are species of the rational.

So that, therefore, the point would be clearer, let us make it from the beginning.

The first genus is the highest [most general] genus (γένος γενικώτατον), which although a genus is not a species (10) because that genus has no other above it, but the last and subordinate species is the lowest [most specific] species (εἰδικώτατον εἶδος), which in turn although a species is not a genus because there is no other species divided from it. Between the highest [most general] genus and lowest [most specific] species, there are both genera and species, genera of those below and species of those above, whatever subordinate ones are called. For example (15) the essence is a highest [most general]

43. I could find no parallel in the TLG. It is common, however, to see two of the three equated, usually *ousia=physis* and *hypostasis=prosopon*, but only rarely are terms for philosophic difference brought together, but there is one parallel: Ποιότης καὶ ἰδιότης καὶ διαφορὰ καὶ ἰδίωμα ἓν καὶ τὸ αὐτὸ σημαίνει. Anastasii Sinaïtae, *Viae dux*, 2.7.50–51. Interestingly the lemma ἰδιότης/*idiotes* does not occur in *IE* and only twice in *Dialectica*, 21/38.9 and 32/49.25, although it occurs elsewhere in John.

genus. For it has no other genus above it, on which account neither is it a species. It is divided into corporeal and incorporeal, the corporeal is split into animate and inanimate, the animate is split into sentient and non-sentient, the sentient into rational and irrational, the rational into mortal and immortal. There is then, on the one hand, the incorporeal, rational and immortal. (20) Here I mean incorporeal essence, such as soul, angel and demon. Each of these is a lowest [most specific] species. On the other hand, the animal is corporeal, animate, sentient, and man is a mortal rational animal, which is a lowest [most specific] species, and a dog is a barking irrational animal, which is a lowest [most specific] species. Furthermore, the plant is a non-sentient animate corporeal thing. Earth, air, water, or fire, is an absolutely inanimate body (25) of which each is a lowest [most specific] species.

In this way we mean to be more lucid: The essence, which super-essentially contains the uncreated Divinity, and both intellectually and comprehensively all creation, is the highest [most general] genus. This [essence] is either incorporeal, intellectual and immortal, as God, angel, soul, demon, – or an (30) inanimate body, like fire, air, water, earth, – or a plant body, like a grapevine, date-palm or olive tree and so forth, – or a sentient animate body, i.e. an animal, as a horse, dog, elephant and so forth, – or a composite (σύνθετος) out of corporeal [body] and incorporeal soul, as man. Of these the essence, as first, more universal, and containing everything, is the highest [most general] genus. The (35) incorporeal, the corporeal inanimate thing, the corporeal plant [body], and the corporeal, animate and sentient [body], i.e. the animal, are species of this highest [most general] genus. These are called subordinate species and genera. For species are of the essence because they are divided from it. Each of them is divided into other species, and each contains them and is more universal than them. For the (40) incorporeal essence contains God, angel, soul, demon, and the corporeal inanimate thing [contains] earth, water, air, fire, and the corporeal plant [body contains] grape-vine, olive tree, date-palm, and things like these, and the animate and sentient [body] or the animal [contains] horse, ox, dog and things like these, as well as man, who is composed out of incorporeal soul and a body.

(45) Thus, Father, Son and the Holy Spirit are *hypostasis*, individual and *prosopon*. The super-essential and incomprehensible divinity is a species containing them. Further, Michael, Gabriel and the rest of the particular angels are *hypostases*. The angelic nature is a species containing them. Further, Peter, Paul, John and the (50) rest of the particular men are *hypostases*. Further, humanity is a species containing them. Again, this, that or the other horse are *hypostases*; and the simple horse is a species containing them. Again, this or that kind of olive[44] are *hypostases*. And, the simple olive tree is a species containing them.

44. τόδε καὶ τόδε τὸ φυτὸν/*this or that kind*. In Aristotle τόδε τι is a *this*, i.e. a fully specified particular (s.v. LSJ).

One must know, therefore, that only those containing the individuals are called (55) lowest [most specific] species, such as angel, man, horse, dog, olive tree, date palm, and things like these, but only those containing the lowest [most specific] species are called subordinate species and genera, such as the incorporeal, corporeal, inanimate, non-sentient, plant, animate, sentient, animal, rational, irrational, mortal, immortal, two footed, four footed, (60) things that crawl, things that fly, and all such things, which contain the lowest [most specific] species and are genera of them and constituent differentia of them,[45] and which are contained by the highest [most general] genus, which is the essence.[46]

But, above all one must form a judgment about them. All things, however many came to be by one command of God, are of one genus, as for example God commanded that (65) there be fish, and there came into being many different [kinds of] fish. All fish are of one genus, but each of the different fishes is a species. Again, God commanded the waters to bring forth birds, and there came into being many different birds. All the birds are of one genus, but each of the different birds is a species of that genus of birds. And, likewise (70) with respect to reptiles, domesticated animals, wild animals, herbs, vegetables, and trees. It is also said that there is one genus of all living things, and one genus of all plants, and one genus of the absolutely inanimate, also wholly without the capacity to grow or feed, and again one genus of the incorporeal and one genus of the corporeal. And, it is also said that every created thing is one genus, and (75) the differences of created things are many species under the genus of the created thing, and every essence is one genus.[47]

Analysis

In sum, this section appears to provide the fullest discussion of genus and species available in the patristic Fathers up to this time, exceeded only by the *Dial.*[48] However, the brief nature of this essay will not allow us to analyze John's interaction with the tradition of adoption of Aristotelianism by the

45. See LSJ s.v. διαφορά: in Logic, the differentia of a species, "ἐκ τοῦ γένους καὶ τῶν διαφορῶν τὰ εἴδη" Arist. *Metaph.*1057b7, cf. *Top.* 139a29: hence in pl. of species or kinds, Id. *Pol.* 1285a1, 1289a20, *Thphr. HP* 6.4.5; "εἴδη καὶ δ." *Plu.* 2.719e; also "κατὰ διαφορὰν ποιός" *Stoic.* 2.128,al.
46. John may be alluding to technical terms in Logic: see LSJ s.v. περιέχω, in Logic, τὸ περιέχον universal, opp. τὰ περιεχόμενα, the individuals or particulars, Arist. *Metaph.* 1023b27, cf. *APr.* 43b23; ὀνόματα περιέχοντα generic terms.
47. Kotter, i, 23–25, 7.1–76. The translation is mine. There is no modern language translation (Kotter, i, 9).
48. Generally the *IE* presents all that the *Dialectica* does, excepting certain minor details: 1) Species divide up to two or three times, rarely four, five and beyond are impossible (Kotter, i, 79, 2/10.164–165), 2) lowest species do not divide, but enumerate (ἀπαρίθμησιν) individuals (Kotter, i, 79, 2/10.168), and 3) in the *IE* John uses a short form of the Adam-Seth (father-son) analogy when discussing difference (Kotter, i, 21, 3.9f), but in the *Dialectica* he uses only a longer form (Kotter, i, 75, 2/10.56–60).

patristic Fathers; our focus must be more modest, centered on the *IE* itself and its relation to the *Dial*.

The collocation of the terms genus and species, whether indicated by the headings or the corroborative search, are found only in the philosophic works of John (Table 1). Further, genus and species cluster in highly correlative parallels in *IE* section seven, *Dial brev* two, *Dial fus* ten, *Oth Ch* and *FP* (Table 2). This highlights genus and species as among the most highly edited portions of John's philosophic works, strongly suggesting he continually fine-tuned them as central to his program. Further, it should be noted that occurrences of either genus or species are distributed throughout John's works, suggesting their collocation in only the philosophic works may not be evidence that the philosophic works and John's other works are independent as Richter suggests above. Further, following Richter it appears John took only that part of the *Isagoge* and *Categories* that he needed.[49] Rather than blaming Aristotelianism for heresy, John was much more neutral; he co-opted introductory logic into a handbook exceeding his predecessor's penchant for collecting lists of definitions. John of Damascus seems to introduce a rapprochement between the patristic tradition and a select aspect of the philosophic tradition, that of introductory logic.

But here in section seven of the *IE*, Genus and species are devoid of the language of dialectic. The term for predication (κατηγορέω) comes up frequently in the *Dial*, and genus and species are treated as predicates, but this term does not even occur in the *IE*. This may be one example of the development of John's thought from *IE* to *Dial*, although it seems equally plausible that as a letter responding to a basic inquiry, John may have edited the *IE* to strip it of such terminology.

Lines 1–3 (Section 1) rehearse and programmatically equate the three sets of three terms as noted above, while confining the scope of the letter to the inquiry. John starts by indicating everything begins with theology: "On the one hand, the incomprehensible Divinity is superessential essence and nature and form, but on the other, Father, Son and all Holy Spirit are *hypostases* and *prosopa* of the Divinity."[50] Divinity is beyond essence, but every created thing is an essence, and "to put it simply there are many species among created things. Thus, each species is one nature, such as all men are one nature."[51] John clearly maintains the division between created and uncreated, but nevertheless reality mirrors theology; in fact, just as the Godhead submits of both genus and species, being both Divinity and Father, Son and Holy Spirit, so too every created thing submits of the ontology of genus and species. Thus, John introduces species in section one as that which accounts for both what is common and what is different between all created things as a function of divine being.

49. Richter, *Johannes Von Damaskos: Philosophische Kapitel*, 75–76.
50. Kotter, i, 20, 1.9–11.
51. Kotter, i, 21, 1.16–17.

Next (Section 2), John quickly moves to the second set of terms, indicating that "as a result nature and form and essence are what is common and encompass the *hypostases* of the same essence, but *hypostasis*, individual and *prosopon* are what is particular."[52] With (Section 3) the third set of terms, John begins to consolidate his argument: "Thus, each essence differs from another essence and each *hypostasis* from another *hypostasis*. That 'thing' (πρᾶγμα), therefore, in which an essence differs from an essence and species from species or *hypostasis* from *hypostasis*, is called difference, quality and property (ἰδίωμα)."[53] Essential differences (Section 4) distinguish species and essences, and are called "essential, natural, constituent, quality, natural property and a property of nature."[54] But, individuals of the same essence and species are distinguished from each other by "non-essential difference, quality, hypostatic property (ἰδίωμα), and characteristic property (ἰδίωμα), i.e. an accident (τὸ συμβεβηκός)."[55] Next (Section 5), John distinguishes two types of accidents, separable and inseparable, and finally (Section 6), there is a straightforward distinction between *homoousios* and *heteroousios*.

Then John concludes (Section 7) with genus and species, in four successive subsections, finishing with an exegesis of the Creation account, tying God's creative command to his doctrine of genus and species, thus finishing where he began. First, he repeats prior statements as summarizing a sermon: "The essence, which super-essentially encompasses the uncreated divinity, and both intellectually and comprehensively all creation, is the highest [most general] genus."[56] And, then, "Father, Son and the Holy Spirit are *hypostasis*, individual and *prosopon*. And, containing them, a species, is the super-essential and incomprehensible divinity."[57] And, then he ties it back together with his explanation of Genesis: "All things, however many came to be by one command of God, are of one genus, for example God commanded there be fish, and there came into being many different fish. All fish are of one genus, but each of the different fish is a species."[58] Thus, John finishes by reiterating that the created stands over against the uncreated, because creation mirrors the Creator, and thus reality, God, just as the Divinity is one in three, so reality is comprised of the common and particular. Here John appears to differ from Maximus as presented by Törönen, who sees in Maximus a distinction between uncreated being and created being such that God cannot be a genus.[59] Neither does this analogy show up in the *Dial*; consequently, here John's intent may be to present logic in terms of doctrine, i.e. in terms of an appropriate biblical ontology.

52. Kotter, i, 21, 2.7–9.
53. Kotter, i, 21, 3.2–7.
54. Kotter, i, 22, 4.4–5.
55. Kotter, i, 22, 4.14–15.
56. Kotter, i, 24, 7.26–28.
57. Kotter, i, 24, 7.45–47.
58. Kotter, i, 25, 7.63–66.
59. Kotter suggests no parallel in the *Dial* to this assertion, nor could I find one. Törönen, *Union and Distinction in the Thought of St. Maximus the Confessor*, 140–141.

Conclusion

John of Damascus appears to be engaged in more than mere compilation, because in some of his most highly edited material, that on genus and species, there are differences between texts suggesting an editorial plan, i.e. programmatic intent. John crafted a new tradition by incorporating the philosophic into the patristic, offering a rapprochement contra the anti-philosophy trope common in patristic heresiology. Whether he "broke the mold" of the Church's tradition of keeping theology distinct from philosophy may be an overstatement, but if he did not then John is clearly selecting a minority position and harmonizing the two to a new level. John specifically introduces genus and species as part of a process to canonize a logic that distinguished and preserved the patristic separation between the created and uncreated, not exclusive of biblical claims, but rather in terms of them. John was an author who nuanced the presentation of genus and species beyond any concern of the Aristotelian commentary tradition. He showed how creation mirrored the Creator, how genus and species explained Genesis. Later, John would leverage these notions, arguing that the fabric of reality, as mirroring the divine, denies composite natures, if that means the coalescence of incompatible essential differences. This takes us beyond the translation of John's longest passage on genus and species and into his theological deployment of these basic philosophic terms, which will have to wait for further research.

Appendix

Table 1 – Summary

Genus and Species in John Damascene

Work	Hits
Dialectica fusior	116
Dialectica brevior	69
Institutio elementaris	27
Ἕτερον κεφάλαιον/Other chapter	27
De haeresibus	3
Orationes de imaginibus tres	2
Oratio in occursum Domini	1
*Cod. Oxon. Bodl. Auct. T. 1. 6.**	51
*Doctrina Patrum**	15
Total	311

* not a work of John, but given for comparison

Table 1 shows the search results of a TLG proximity search: Looking in the works of John of Damascus for occurrences of the lemmas "γένος" and "εἶδος" within one line of each other.

Table 2 – Detail

<table>
<tr><th colspan="2">Dialectica fusior Section & Title</th><th>Df</th><th>Db</th><th>OC</th><th>IE</th><th>Ox</th><th>DP</th><th>Other</th><th>Total</th></tr>
<tr><td>5</td><td>On Terms</td><td>6</td><td>--</td><td></td><td></td><td>5</td><td></td><td></td><td>11</td></tr>
<tr><td>9</td><td>On Genus</td><td>10</td><td rowspan="2">38</td><td rowspan="2">21</td><td rowspan="2">27</td><td rowspan="2">30</td><td>2</td><td></td><td>128</td></tr>
<tr><td>10</td><td>On Species</td><td>42</td><td>1</td><td></td><td>43</td></tr>
<tr><td>21
22</td><td>Common and Difference of Genus and Species</td><td>8</td><td>--</td><td></td><td></td><td></td><td></td><td></td><td>8</td></tr>
<tr><td>22</td><td>Common and Difference of Genus and Property</td><td>6</td><td>-</td><td></td><td></td><td></td><td></td><td></td><td>6</td></tr>
<tr><td>23</td><td>Common and Difference of Genus and Attribute</td><td>6</td><td>--</td><td></td><td></td><td></td><td></td><td></td><td>6</td></tr>
<tr><td>38</td><td>On Both the Same and Different Genus and Species and Things Differing in Number</td><td>9</td><td>9</td><td></td><td></td><td>3</td><td></td><td></td><td>21</td></tr>
<tr><td>47</td><td>The Difference Between Being and Essence</td><td>6</td><td>1</td><td></td><td></td><td></td><td></td><td></td><td>7</td></tr>
<tr><td>51</td><td>On Relation</td><td>6</td><td>6</td><td></td><td></td><td>3</td><td></td><td></td><td>15</td></tr>
<tr><td></td><td>Other</td><td>17</td><td>15</td><td>6</td><td></td><td>10</td><td>12</td><td>6</td><td>66</td></tr>
<tr><td></td><td>Total</td><td>116</td><td>69</td><td>27</td><td>27</td><td>51</td><td>15</td><td>6</td><td>311</td></tr>
</table>

The search occurrences of Table 1 correlated to *Dialectica fusior*

Column titles in full: *Df=Dialectica fusior, Db=Dialectica brevior, OC=Ἕτερον κεφάλαιον/Other chapter, IE=Institutio elementaris, Ox=Cod. Oxon. Bodl. Auct. T. 1. 6., DP=Doctrina Patrum, Other=De haeresibus, Orationes de imaginibus tres,* and *Oratio in occursum Domini.*

NB: All occurrences in the Other row are outliers and thus not relevant to the analysis, since in no case do they correlate, having in only one case five occurrences in the same section (*Cod. Oxon. Bodl. Auct. T. 1. 6.* section 10 with no correlation to *Dialectica fusior*), and none had four.

NB: The symbol "–" means that in *Dialectica brevior* there is no parallel passage.

NB: Normalizing the *Cod. Oxon. Bodl. Auct. T. 1. 6.* and the *Doctrina Patrum* to the *Dialectica fusior* is not meant to indicate a formal parallel only an approximate one for comparison purposes.

Bibliography

Alexakis, A., "The Modesty *Topos* and John of Damascus as a Not-So-Modest Author," *Byzantinische Zeitschrift* 97/2 (2004) 521–530.

Barnes, J., *Porphyry: Introduction*, trans. J. Barnes, Clarendon Later Ancient Philosophers, Oxford: Oxford University Press 2003.

Berardino, A. D., ed., *Patrology: The Eastern Fathers from the Council of Chalcedon (451) to John of Damascus (750)*, trans. A. Walford, Institutum Patristicum Augustinianum, James Clarke 2000.

Brock, S., "The Syriac Commentary Tradition," in: C. Burnett, ed., *Glosses and Commentaries on Aristotelian Logical Texts: The Syriac, Arabic and Medieval Latin Traditions*, Warburg Institute Surveys and Texts, London: The Warburg Institute, University of London 1993, 3–18.

Conticello, C. G., Kontouma-Conticello, V., "Philosophie Et Théologie À Byzance," in : Ph. Capelle-Dumont, O. Boulnois, eds., *Philosophie Et Théologie Au Moyen-Âge. Anthologie-Tome II*, Paris: Éditions du Cerf 2009, 43–61.

Diekamp, F., ed., *Doctrina Patrum De Incarnatione Verbi*, Münster 1907.

Drobner, H. R., "Gregory of Nyssa as Philosopher: *De Anima Et Resurrectione* and *De Hominis Opificio*," *Dionysius*, New Series 18/December (2000) 69–101.

Erismann, C., "A World of Hypostases: John of Damascus' Rethinking of Aristotle's Categorical Ontology," *Studia Patristica* 50 (2011) 269–287.

Jouan, F., Looy, H. V., eds., *Euripide : Fragments 1re Partie Aigeus-Autolykos*, 8, Paris: Les Belles Lettres 1998.

Fowden, G., *Before and After Muhammad: The First Millenium Refocused*, Princeton: Princeton University Press 2014.

Frede, M., "The Early Christian Reception of Socrates," in: L. Judson, V. Karasmanes, eds., *Remembering Socrates: Philosophical Essays*, Oxford: Clarendon 2006, 188–202.

Furrer-Pilliod, C., *Ὅροι Καὶ Ὑπόγραφα : Collections Alphabétiques De Définitions Profanes Et Sacrées*, Studi E Testi, Città del Vaticano: Biblioteca Apostolica Vaticana 2000.

Hoeck , J. M., "Stand Und Aufgaben Der Damaskenos-Forschung," *Orientalia Christiana Periodica* 17 (1951) 5–60.

Jankowiak, M., Booth, P., "A New Date-List of the Works of Maximus the Confessor," in: *The Oxford Handbook of Maximus the Confessor*, edited by P. Allen, B. Neil, Oxford: Oxford University Press 2015.

John of Damascus, *Saint John of Damascus: Writings*, trans. F. H. Chase, Fathers of the Church, New York: Catholic University of America 1958.

Kotter, B., Volk, R., eds., *Die Schriften des Johannes von Damaskos*, Patristische Texte und Studien, 7, 12, 17, 22, 29, 60/1, 61/2, 68, Berlin, New York 1969, 1973, 1975, 1981, 1988, 2009, 2008, 2013.

Liddell, H. G., Scott, R., *A Greek-English Lexicon*, Clarendon 1996.

Louth, A., *St. John Damascene: Tradition and Originality in Byzantine Theology*, Oxford: Oxford University Press 2002.
Merlan, P., "Religion and Philosophy from Plato's 'Phaedo' to the Chaldaean Oracles," *Journal of the History of Philosophy* 1/2 (1963) 163–176.
Oehler, K., *Antike Philosophie Und Byzantinisches Mittelalter*, Munich: C.H. Beck 1969.
Richter, G., *Die Dialektik Des Johannes Von Damaskos: Eine Untersuchung Des Textes Nach Seinen Quellen Und Seiner Bedeutung*, Studia Patristica Et Byzantina 10, Ettal: Buch-Kunstverlag 1964.
Richter, G., *Johannes von Damaskos: Philosophische Kapitel*, Bibliotek der Griechischen Literatur, Stuttgart: Anton Hiersemann 1982.
Roueché, M., "Byzantine Philosophical Texts of the Seventh Century," *Jahrbuch der Österreichischen Byzantinistik* 23 (1974) 61–76.
Sorabji, R., ed., *Aristotle Transformed: the Ancient Commentators and Their Influence*, London: Duckworth 1990.
Stead, C., *Philosophy in Christian Antiquity*, Cambridge: Cambridge University Press 1994.
"Thesaurus Linguae Graecae: A Digital Library of Greek Literature," University of California, Irvine: University of California 2009.
Törönen, M., *Union and Distinction in the Thought of St Maximus the Confessor*, Oxford Early Christian Studies, Oxford: Oxford University Press 2007.
Uthemann, K.-H., ed., *Anastasii Sinaïtae: Viae dux*, CCSG 8, Turnhout 1981.

Neoplatonic Elements in the Writings of Patriarch Photius

Ivan Christov

Patriarch[1] Photius has a special place in the century-long history of Byzantine culture. He combines in his person the cleric and the erudite authority on *Hellenic* science. Secular and sacred held sway in different periods of his life but the interest in the cultural heritage did not wane with his election to the patriarchal throne. This explains the diversity of centers of conceptual interest in his writings. His philosophical reflections do not always chime with his position as patriarch. The most paradoxical example is perhaps the Christianized Aristotelian concept of God as *actus purus*, a tenet likewise influenced by Neoplatonic philosophy. It might appear that the patriarch, who had initiated the schism of the Churches, was expressing a typical Catholic view, which was to be formulated centuries later by Thomas Aquinas and to meet with the implacable opposition of Byzantine theologians. This is the reason why we should take a closer look at the philosophical and, more particularly, Neoplatonic elements of his writings. The complexity of such an undertaking stems from the controversial nature of the relationship between Neoplatonism and Christianity, the diversity and depth of this philosophy, as well as the scarcity of studies on the subject. So far, the only publications discussing more or less thoroughly the influence of pagan Neoplatonism on Photius's philosophy are those of J. Schamp.[2] In this essay I shall attempt to make a general survey of the presentation of Neoplatonic authors in the *Bibliotheca*, bringing out the main aspects of Photius's interest in the subject, then dwell briefly on the commentary on the *Categories*, with a view to analyzing his doctrine of God as *actus purus* and its dependence on Aristotelian philosophy and Neoplatonism in the *Amphilochia*.

---

1. The research work for this paper was supported by the Scientific Research Fund in 2002/2003. The text presented here is an edited version of the paper published in Bulgarian in: И. Христов, ed., *Неоплатонизъм и християнство*, част II. *Византийската традиция*, София, 2004, 79–108.
2. See: J. Schamp, "La 'localisation' chez Photios : traduction commentée de Questions à Amphilochios, 145," in: *Aristotelica Secunda. Mélanges offerts à Christian Rutten*, C.I.P.L., Liège 1996, 265–279; "Photios aristotélisant ? Remarques critiques," in: *Kainotomia. Die Erneuerung der griechishen Tradition*, Freiburg 1995, 1–17.

Philosophy in the Bibliotheca

The *Bibliotheca* is perhaps the most widely known work of Photius. Twenty five manuscripts have come down to us, comprising the complete text, the most authoritative of which are *Marcianus graecus 450 [A]* of the 10th century and *Marcianus graecus 451 [M]* of the 12th c., as well as many others containing excerpts from it.[3] For the European tradition of modern times, the text was re-discovered by Italian humanists in the second half of the 16th century thanks to Bessarion of Byzantium who had brought it to Italy with his personal library. In April 1597, M. Margunio who had seen and was intrigued by this copy of the *Bibliotheca*, owned by Bessarion, brought it to David Hoeschel's notice who published it in 1601.[4] In the early 17th century alone the work was published three times,[5] testifying to the great interest in it. At present the two best editions are those by Immanuel Bekker[6] and René Henry.[7]

The exact time of the composition of the *Bibliotheca* is still a matter of scholarly debate. According to the traditional viewpoint maintained by J. Hergenröther,[8] K. Ziegler,[9] H.-G. Beck,[10] E. Orth,[11] and A. Severyns[12] it is to be dated to 855. According to F. Halkin, however, the work dates from after Photius's election as patriarch (858), possibly even as late as 875.[13] Earlier datings have also been put forward. Thus, H. Ahrweiler and, with certain reservations, P. Lemerle assign the work to 838.[14] C. Mango takes a more guarded position assuming that at this time Photius wrote the first version of the *Bibliotheca*,[15] but continued working on the text throughout his life. W. Treadgold adduces arguments that it was written in 845.[16] As can be seen,

3. On the manuscript tradition, see: E. Martini, *Textgeschichte der Bibliotheke des Patriarchen Photios von Konstantinopel*, Leipzig 1911, and A. Diller, "Photios 'Bibliotheca' in Byzantine Literature," *Dumbarton Oaks Papers* 16 (1962) 389–396.
4. On the early editions, see E. Martini, *op. cit.* and L. Canfora, *La biblioteca del patriarca: Fozio censurato nella Francia di Mazzarino*, Roma 1998.
5. I. Canfora, *op. cit.*, 198.
6. It was reprinted from *Patrologia graeca*, vols 103–104, Paris, 1824–1825.
7. Photius, *Bibliothèque*, ed. R. Henry, 8 vols., Paris : Les Belles Lettres, 1959–1977. This edition reproduces the page-numbering of I. Bekker, which has remained the standard one to this day. The same edition is included in *Thesaurus linguae graecae* (TLG 4040 001).
8. J. Hergenröther, *Photius, Patriarch von Konstantinopel: Sein Leben, seine Schriften und das griechische Schisma*, vol. III, Regensburg 1869, 341–343.
9. K. Ziegler, "Photios 13," *Realencyclopädie der Classischen Altertumswissenschaft* 20 (1941) col. 685–691.
10. H.-G. Beck, *Kirche und theologische Literatur im byzantinischen Reich*, Münich 1956, 526.
11. E. Orth, *Photiana*, Leipzig 1928, 6–10.
12. Severyns, *Recherches sur la Chrestomathie de Proclos*, vol. I, Liège-Paris 1938, 1–4.
13. F. Halkin, "La Date de composition de la Bibliothèque remise in question," *Analecta Bollandiana* 81 (1963) 414–417.
14. H. Ahrweiler, "Sur la carrière de Photius avant son patriarcat," *Byzantinische Zeitschrift* 58 (1965) 356–361. P. Lemerle, *Le Premier humanisme byzantin*, Paris 1971, 42.
15. C. Mango, "The Availability of Books in the Byzantine Empire AD 750–850," in: *Byzantine Books and Bookmen*, Washington 1975, 37–43.
16. W. T. Treadgold, *The Nature of the Bibliotheca of Photius*, DOS 18, Washington 1980, 31.

in most cases the scholars lean towards dating the work to the years of intensive intellectual pursuits before his election as patriarch. Even his opponents are compelled to acknowledge his exceptional erudition and love for books. Nicetas the Paphlagonian, in his *Life of Patriarch Ignatius*, writes about Photius's versatile learnedness, which encompassed philosophy, medicine, rhetoric, poetry, and almost all knowledge of the "external." "Thanks to his wealth," he comments maliciously, "any book can end up in his pernicious hands."[17] Photius did indeed possess a library which was enormous for its time, amounting to about 150 titles.[18] His devotion to scholarly work implicated him in all sorts of malevolent intrigues. Thus Pseudo-Simeon claims that to reach the heights of *Hellenic* learning, Photius consorted with a Judean magus who made him renounce the sign of the Cross and even receive help from a demon.[19]

Photius wrote his *Bibliotheca* animated by the desire to share his encyclopedic knowledge. The pretext was a request by his brother Tarasius to partake of this learning. Tradition has it that the vast opus was actually a letter to his brother. Indeed, the greater part of the text is addressed to Tarasius, but about one-sixth of it has no specific addressee. Photius could hardly have been motivated solely by the desire to oblige his brother. He must have rather felt an urgent need to share his learning acquired with so much labor and perseverance, and to instruct the Christian readers studying Hellenic culture.

The *Bibliotheca* represents a collection of syllabi and paraphrases of the books Photius had read, accompanied by biographical notes and brief observations mainly of stylistic and historical purport. In the manuscript tradition it bears the title: *Register and enumeration of the books read by us, 279 in number, of which our beloved brother Tarasius desired to have a summary.* In the earliest reference to it from the early Byzantine period it was named "Letter of Photius to Tarasius."[20] In late Byzantine times the work was entitled *Myriobiblon,* while the title *Bibliotheca* was given to it in the 17th century.

The *Bibliotheca* contains 280 numbered descriptions of books by various authors, which scholars and publishers have incorrectly designated as "codices." In fact, in many of them more than one title is discussed. Treadgold's research has shown that there are 386 and not 280 analyses of books read by Photios.[21] Only three of them are "old" and are not written in the minuscule script brought into use in the preceding century. Quite likely the

17. *Vita Ignatii*, PG 105, 509B. The reader will find a penetrating analysis of the sources on Photius's early years and an intellectual portrait of him in a book by L. Symeonova, *Diplomacy of the Letter and the Cross*, Amsterdam 1998, 11–47.
18. See W.T. Treadgold, *op. cit.*, 93–94; C. Mango, *op .cit.*, 39.
19. *Pseudo-Symeon, Annales*, in: *Theophanes Continuatus*, ed. I. Bekker, CSHB, Bonn 1838, 670, 7–22 = PG 109, col. 732B–C.
20. See A. Diller, "Photius' 'Bibliotheca' in Byzantine Literature," *Dumbarton Oaks Papers* 16 (1962) 389–396.
21. W. T. Treadgold, *op cit.*, 5.

greater part of the books were copied specially for Photius on his order.[22] Of them 239 are Christian and Judean, and 147 secular and pagan, that is, the numerical proportion of religious to secular books is 62 to 38%.[23] As far as the size of the texts is concerned, however, things are very much the other way round. According to T. Hägg the proportion here is 58 to 42% in favor of secular titles.[24] W. Treadgold makes an insignificant correction: according to him the relevant ratio is 57 to 43.[25] However we might judge Photius's attitudes as a reader and the analytical side of his compilation, we have to acknowledge the immense importance of the *Bibliotheca* for our knowledge of ancient literature. To put it in the language of numbers: 211 of the works reviewed by him have not come down to us in the form known to Photius, and 110 are irrevocably lost. In a number of cases his testimonies are unique.

Theology is central to the composition of the *Bibliotheca*. Photius shows a pronounced interest in Christology, the subject of cod. 225–230, which make up some 20% of the entire text.[26] He displays conspicuous familiarity with the heretical writings of the Arians, the Nestorians, and the Monophysites. He has read the acts of all seven ecumenical councils.[27] Photius evinced particular interest in Monophysitism, chronologically the last Christian heresy and the only one, which exercised an appreciable influence in the Caliphate and Armenia in the 9th century.[28]

Extensive also was his knowledge in the field of Medicine. The *Bibliotheca* contains conspectuses of 18 texts on medicine. Photius has a flair for technical detail and values highly the usefulness of knowledge for practical purposes. He himself had practiced medicine. Four of his letters contain specific medical prescriptions.[29]

Rhetoric is also well represented. Photius is familiar with the works of nine of the ten Attic orators and of several exponents of the second sophistics. His preference is for Hellenistic orators.[30]

He is less interested in mathematics and natural history, to which he has devoted cod. 180, 187, and 279.

In the domain of history, Photius shows a predilection for the uncommon and the exotic. This also stirred up his interest in Olympiodorus of Thebes.[31] As will be seen, the same taste prevails in the presentation of the philosopher Damascius.

22. *Ibid.*, 98
23. *Ibid.*, 7.
24. T. Hägg, *Photios als Vermittler antiker Literatur: Untersuchungen zur Technik des Referierens und Exzerpierens in der Bibliotheke*, Upsala 1975, 8, n. 2.
25. W. T. Treadgold, *op. cit.*, 8.
26. *Ibid.*, 105.
27. *Ibid.*, 104.
28. *Ibid.*, 105.
29. *Ibid.*, 103.
30. *Ibid.* 103.
31. W. T. Treadgold, *op. cit.*, 100–101.

As to the place accorded to philosophy in the *Bibliotheca*, one can easily be led to the extremes of utter refutation or inordinate praise. The problem lies in the absence of any information on the doctrines of Aristotle and Plato, two figures fundamental to the philosophical studies of that time, while the text abounds in fragmentary references to Hellenistic and especially Neoplatonic philosophy. From this fact one can draw diametrically opposed inferences. The first, and predominant one, is that Photius had no really serious interest in philosophy. In the *Bibliotheca* it is present for the sake of comprehensiveness. Various pieces of information on the subject are drawn from late-antique doxography and all kinds of school anthologies. This would hardly testify to systematic philosophical studies and solid knowledge of philosophy. It is possible, however, to take another approach and see evidence of Photius's and his contemporaries' high standard of knowledge in that he did not deem it necessary to handle universally familiar school texts. His *Bibliotheca* is seen against such a rich intellectual background that its author could allow himself to consider and discuss certain less popular works. "No doubt," writes Treadgold, "the interest, which he shows in the life of philosophers and poets, reflects an interest in philosophy and poetry, concealed by the leaving-out of familiar school texts in the *Bibliotheca*, which however are mentioned by Nicetas Paphlagon."[32] Photius himself has given the reason for such observations, saying in his *Postscript* that he had excluded those texts "the study of and occupation with which is proper to the instruction in the arts and sciences."[33] This seems to be corroborated by his interest in Plato's lexicography. The *Bibliotheca* contains excerpts from the writings of Timaeos (1st/2nd centuries) and Boethus (2nd century) who were explicitly studying Plato's language.[34] Doesn't this show that Photius has left the introduction to the *Dialogues* to schoolish learning, and helped it by incorporating excerpts from the less popular works of the lexicographers? He has certainly read Plato and Aristotle. Evidence of this is letter 208 to Amphilochius of Kyzikos dating from after the composition of the *Bibliotheca*, in which Photius gives a list of the texts he has read, including the dialogues and letters of Plato and the letters and treatises of Aristotle.[35]

Treadgold finds grounds for his high esteem of Photius's philosophical interests in the very selection of the books he had read and reviewed. "Photius's lack of interest in poetry and philosophy," he writes, "is significantly exaggerated by some modern researchers. Although he had to leave

32. *Ibid.* 102. See above, 291.
33. See cod. 280, 545, 2–3. Treadgold draws attention to the connection of these words of Photius to the language of the *Republic*, VII 522 c.
34. In cod. 151 we find excerpts from the *Lexicon to Plato* by Timaeus, and in cod. 154 and 155, *List of Platonic Words* (of which Photius has proved to be the sole source) and *On the Words of Doubtful Meaning in Plato* by Boethius.
35. See also the notes in cod. 37, 8a7; 155,100a21–4; 209, 165b20–23. Photius is familiar with all four orations of Aelius Aristides against Plato and in defence of oratory, directed against the *Gorgias* dialogue (see cod. 248).

aside the poets and philosophers who were considered familiar school authors, Photius has reviewed nine works in verse and two anthologies with numerous poetical sections, as well as three works of pagan philosophy, three biographies of philosophers, several scientific works, and certain writings of Christian philosophers such as Clement of Alexandria and Methodius of Olympus."[36] Whether this is so should become apparent from a survey of the entries on ancient philosophers in the *Bibliotheca*. It does not meet the case to simply mark off the range of names and the number of works reviewed. What is needed is to evaluate the character of the presentation and the selectivity of the approach. In this respect, the statistical data of Treadgold is of no particular use.

The first impression is really overwhelming: Photius rivets the attention of the Christian reader to the names of more than thirty pagan philosophers. The majority, more than two thirds, are exponents of Neoplatonic philosophy. As to Plato and Aristotle, it was already pointed out that the *Bibliotheca* does not offer any information about their works. Their names are mentioned only in connection with the teachings of other philosophers. The reader can obtain some indirect information about their philosophy, in a context that Photius was interested in, from his syllabus of the treatise *On Providence and Destiny* by Hierocles of Alexandria.[37] Similarly, on specific occasions, he mentions the names of Socrates, Democritus and Theophrastus. He shows a somewhat keener interest in the skeptic Aenesidemus of Cnossos (1st century BC), erroneously naming him Aenesidemus "of Aegis."[38] Photius included in the *Bibliotheca* a valuable conspectus of his lost work, *Pyrrhonian Discourses* (*Phyrroneia*).[39] Of the Neopythagoreans, he is familiar with the names of Nikomachos of Gerasa (1st century) and Apollonius of Tyana (1st century). In the *Bibliotheca* are to be found excerpts from Apollonius's biography written by Philostratus of Tyre,[40] as well as a conspectus of a work by Nikomachos, *Theology of Arithmetic* (*Theologumena*), a *sui generis* theology of the numbers in two books.[41] Given that the mythologized figure of the thaumaturge (miracle worker) Apollonius was seen as an alternative to Christ, it becomes clear that Photius's interest in Neopythagoreanism was dominated by the lure of the exotic but, above all, by the need to put up a resistance against paganism. It is not so much to philosophical than to educational considerations that he paid much attention to Plutarch of Chaeronea (c. 46–c. 127), exponent of Middle Platonism. Besides mentioning his name,[42] the *Bibliotheca* contains an appraisal of Plutarch's legacy, which has exercised a profound impact on the

36. W. T. Treadgold, *op. cit.*, 8.
37. See cod. 214, 171b19–173b2 (=251, 460b22–466b24).
38. See cod. 212, 170a41.
39. See cod. 212, 169b18–171a4.
40. See cod. 44, 9b20 sqq (= cod. 241, 323b33 sqq).
41. See cod. 187, 145a31–b7.
42. See cod. 167, 114b14, cod. 242, 340a13.

education of generations after him.[43] Included are excerpts from 19 *Lives*[44] and even Plutarch's texts in the anthology by Sopater of Apamea are identified.[45] The name of Longinus (1st century) is referred to by misunderstanding, owing to an error in the manuscript tradition.[46] Due attention is also paid to Themistius, noted commentator on Plato and Aristotle in the 4th century. Besides mentioning him in the list of philosophers in the anthology of Joannes Stobaeus,[47] Photius includes an extract from the *Epitome* of Hesychius in which his paraphrases of Aristotle's *Analytics*, *On the Soul*, and *Physics* are mentioned, while Themistius himself is presented as a connoisseur and zealous student of philosophy.[48]

The most extensive extracts are undoubtedly those from the works of Neoplatonic authors. These include the above mentioned treatise *On Providence and Destiny* by Hierocles of Alexandria and above all, *On the Life of Isidore*, by Damascius, a valuable source on the history of Neoplatonism. We shall now make a brief survey of the accounts of Neoplatonic authors in the *Bibliotheca*. It is important for us to find out what focal points can be established in their presentation by Photius. This will enable us to make some assumptions as to what has motivated him in his quests. It might also provide us with a key to some of his specific doctrines in *Amphilochia*.

As far Roman Neoplatonism is concerned, the presentation is less than scanty. Plotinus (205–270) is mentioned only by name; there is no analytical discussion of his doctrine. His name appears only in the list of philosophers in the anthology of Joannes Stobaeus (5th century).[49] It also occurs in the list compiled by Hierocles of the followers of Plato and the founder of Neoplatonism, Ammonius Saccas.[50] There is hardly any difference in the case of Porphyrius (234–305). We come upon his name in the lists of the anthology of Joannes Stobaeus[51] and in Hierocles,[52] it being also mentioned among those esteemed by Isidore.[53] He is also said to have been a teacher of Theodore of Asina.[54]

43. See cod. 243, 365a41, 366a40.
44. See cod. 245, 393b7–400b4.
45. See cod. 161, 104a24 sqq.
46. See M. Heat, "Caecilius, Longinus and Photius," *Greek, Roman and Byzantine Studies* 39 (1998) 275; Cf. R. Smith, "Two Fragments of 'Longinus' in Photius," *The Classical Quarterly* 44 (1994) 527–529.
47. See cod. 168, 114b1.
48. See cod. 74, 52a2–21.
49. See cod. 167, 114b17. The anthology by Joannes Stobaeus (5th cent.) is considered one of the most important sources of antique doxography. It continues the tradition started by Theophrastus whose work *Physical Opinions* was amended by Aetius (1st cent.) and again revised by Pseudo-Plutarch in the 2nd century. The anthologies of Aetius and Pseudo-Plutarch have served as the basis of Joannes Stobaeus's work.
50. See cod. 214, 173a21, 173a34 (= cod.251, 461d39).
51. See cod. 167, 114b15.
52. See cod. 214, 173a35.
53. See cod. 242, 337b24.
54. Ibid. 346b21.

The account of Syrian Neoplatonism does not differ appreciably from the preceding one. The most prominent figure of this school, that of Iamblichus (c. 280–c. 330), appears in the list of philosophers in the anthology by Joannes Stobaeus,[55] while in the excerpts from the *Life of Isidore* one finds laudatory appraisals without any analysis of his doctrine whatsoever.[56] Photius was obviously intrigued by his views on theurgy, but his interests do not go beyond the general statement that Iamblichus was one of those who led men down the road to idolatry.[57] Photius cites an excerpt of the critical analysis made by John Philoponus of his (Iamblichus's) work *On Statues*.[58] Theodore of Asina who belonged to the Syrian school of Neoplatonism and was a pupil of Iamblichus is referred to in the above passage merely as a pupil of Porphyrius. More valuable is the information on Sopater of Apamea from whose anthology, now lost, Photius has included extracts in the *Bibliotheca*.[59]

The account of the Neoplatonism of Pergamon is extremely meager. As in the preceding cases, there is no analysis or at least an exposition of the principal ideas of its exponents; not even their affiliation with this particular school is mentioned. The only names the reader will come upon are those of Maximus of Ephesus and Julian the Apostate (331/2–363), but nothing is said about their association with the Neoplatonic tradition.

More fully, or at least in greater historical detail, the Athenian school is presented. The relevant information is drawn from Damascius's work, *On the Life of Isidore*, of which Photius has included large excerpts in his *Bibliotheca*.[60] We learn about Plutarch of Athens (c.350–c.433), that he was praised highly by Proclus who, judging him on his merits, placed him in the golden rank of Plato's followers in Athens.[61] A curious piece of gossip has crept in about his pupil Hierius,[62] testifying to the impiousness and frivolity of Damascius's testimony,[63] but again no word is said about Plutarch's teaching itself. Syrianus of Alexandria (c. 450) is presented as the teacher of Hermias;[64] it is mentioned that he was urged by Isidore to retain the waning philosophy[65] and was ranked by the results of his work among the most esteemed "elated" souls.[66] The information on Proclus (412–485), probably the most noteworthy figure of Athenian Neoplatonism, is purely historical in nature. We learn from the *Bibliotheca* that his *diadochi* (successors) were Marinus[67]

55. See cod. 167, 114b3.
56. See cod. 242, 337b5–11, 337b25, 346a12.
57. See cod. 181, 126a3.
58. See cod. 215, 173b4–31.
59. See cod. 161, 103a198 sqq.
60. See cod. 181, 242.
61. See cod. 242, 346a12.
62. Ibid., 342, 18.
63. Ibid., 342a26 sq.
64. See cod. 242, 341a10.
65. Ibid., 349b11.
66. Ibid., 337b25.
67. See cod. 181, 127a2, cf. cod. 242, 345b18.

and Zenodotus.[68] Also mentioned as his personal disciples are Hermias,[69] Asclepiodotus,[70] and Isidore in whom Proclus saw the true face of philosophy.[71] It is not surprising that the biography of Isidore included in the *Bibliotheca* contains many enthusiastic comments by Proclus on him. Proclus had early estimated the merits of Isidore and his diligence, and planted the roots of the sacred philosophic word in his soul.[72] He is said to have marveled at his face – godlike and animated with philosophical life.[73] The two were so close to each other that Proclus gave a name to Isidore's child.[74] He likewise showed solicitude for Marinus on whom he also set great hopes.[75] There is only scanty information on Proclus himself. It is reported that while he was ill he was advised to abstain from eating cabbage and to take mallow instead, but he held on to Pythagorian's ban on mallow.[76] One comes across reports on his personal modesty as when he admitted that Heraiskos was more knowledgeable than he was.[77] The only reference to his numerous works is that Proclus had written an exceptional commentary on Plato's *Parmenides*, which even Marinus was unable to comprehend.[78] The *Bibliotheca* contains also valuable extracts from Books 1 and 2 of the *Chrestomathia Grammatica*, a basic source for the Cyclic Poems,[79] but it is to be doubted whether their author was the Neoplatonist Proclus.[80] The narrative about his disciple Asclepiodotus (5th century) is rich in fantasies and utterly devoid of philosophical content. It is said that, in contrast to Isidore, he was given all the good things of life,[81] but otherwise was not distinguished by particular intellectual prowess,[82] as he was best suited to music[83] and medicine.[84] On the other hand, he possessed divine power and it is recounted how he came to it.[85] The *Bibliotheca* contains various stories of miracles in which he played a part.[86] More instructive in content though also purely historical in char-

68. Ibid., 127a4.
69. See cod. 242, 341a10.
70. Ibid., 345b6.
71. Ibid., 350b17, 19.
72. Ibid., 351b2.
73. Ibid., 341b19.
74. Ibid., 352b8.
75. Ibid., 346a1, 10, 17, 24, 37.
76. Ibid. 344a32–36.
77. Ibid., 343b2–4.
78. Ibid., 351a31.
79. See cod. 239, 318b22–322a40.
80. According to Treadgold, true to his optimistic view of Photius's scholarly and philosophical interests, their author is nonetheless Proclus, the evidence for which they discovered in "Suda." See W. T. Treadgold, *op. cit.*, 50, n. 53.
81. See cod. 242, 346b2.
82. Ibid., 344a36.
83. Ibid., 344b12.
84. Ibid., 343b23 sqq.
85. Ibid., 343b24 sqq.
86. Ibid., 344b35 sqq, cod. 242, 351a22, sqq.

acter are the reports on Marinus of Flavia Neapolis (5 BC). He is presented as diadochos to Proclus and teacher of Damascius in arithmetic, geometry, and the other mathematical disciplines.[87] It is reported that he instructed Isidore in Aristotle's philosophy and wrote a commentary on Plato's *Philebus*, which however he destroyed himself.[88] Thanks to Damascius we find in the *Bibliotheca* a rather downbeat appraisal of him. Immersed in assiduous and incessant studies, Marinus often used to pass off older teachings as his own.[89] His discourses and the few writings show that he did not leave a deep trace in philosophy.[90] Of Proclus's high opinion of Isidore of Alexandria (5th century) mention was made above.[91] It is also said of him that he was very cautious about giving an opinion when asked what he thought of Marinus's commentary on Plato's *Philebus*, but even so was rightly understood, and his teacher destroyed his work.[92] The name of Hegias is brought up in connection with Isidore's urging him and Syrianus to retain the waning philosophy.[93] The name of another exponent of Athenian Neoplatonism, Zenodotus, diadochos of Proclus, second after Marinus, is barely referred to.[94] Most extensively presented in the *Bibliotheca* is Damascius (c.480–c.550), if not by an analytical review of his teaching, at least by the inclusion of excerpts and syllabi of his works. Particularly precious is the extensive extract from *On the Life of Isidore*, an important source on the history of Neoplatonism that has survived thanks to the efforts of Photius.[95] The *Bibliotheca* contains conspectuses of several more works by Damascius, of which we would never have known without Photius's opus: *On Wonderful Things*; *Wonderful Stories about the Gods*; *Wonderful Stories about the Souls Appearing after Death* and *On Wonderful Animals*.[96] The value of these testimonies should not mislead us. Photius is attracted not so much by the philosophical depth of Damascius than by the exotic and sensational elements in his writings. Even the excerpt from *On the Life of Isidore* does not contain any analytical discussion of Athenian Neoplatonism. Moreover, as T. Hägg justly observes, these texts consist of simple extracts from ancient books, lacking all coherence with Photius's own text.[97] This is about all that is to be found on Athenian Neoplatonism in the *Bibliotheca.*

In contrast to Athenian Neoplatonism, the Alexandrian variant is presented in terms of substance rather than historically. The relatively more

87. See cod. 181, 127a1 sqq.
88. See cod. 242, Ibid., 338a20.
89. Ibid., 345b28–30.
90. Ibid., 345b32.
91. See p. 000.
92. Ibid., 338a19–27.
93. Ibid., 349b11.
94. See cod. 181, 127a4.
95. See cod. 181 and 242.
96. See cod. 130.
97. T. Hägg, *Photios als Vermittler antiker Literatur: Untersuchungen zur Technik des Referierens und Exzerpierens in der Bibliotheke*, Upsala 1975, 192–194.

analytical philosophic texts in the *Bibliotheca* are associated with the names of philosophers belonging to that school. Above all, I have in mind the work of Hierocles of Alexandria, *On Providence and Destiny*,[98] and the critical text of John Philoponus against Iamblichus's treatise on the statues.[99] Here is an overview of the presentation of the philosophers of that school.

Of particular value is Photius's account of its founder, Ammonius Saccas, who was active in the early 3rd century. The *Bibliotheca* is the most important source on the teaching of Ammonius, which reconciles Plato and Aristotle,[100] although this is merely stated without any arguments being put forward for it. In the second place, Photius claims that a pupil of Ammonius was the great Christian theologian Origen. This testimony is unusual, being concordant with the version of Porphyrius,[101] whereas the Christian tradition, beginning with Eusebius of Caesarea, rejects any affiliation of Origen with the school of Ammonius Saccas. The activity of Synesius of Cyrene (c.370–c.430) is likewise briefly mentioned in the *Bibliotheca.* Photius cites from among the works he has read by him, *On Providence* and *On the Kingdom* as well as various letters of his. His assessment comes down to praise of Synesius's lofty style and the force and weightiness of his reasoning.[102] We learn, in passing, a little something about the celebrated *Hypatia* (d. 415). She is compared with Isidore, who was different from her not only in terms of gender but also just like a genuine philosopher is different from a geometrician.[103] Of Hermias, besides the indication that he was the father of Ammonius Hermias, the renowned commentator of Aristotle,[104] we find in the *Bibliotheca* only brief biographical notes and an appraisal of his person.[105] We learn that he was a pupil of Syrianus and Proclus. His human qualities are lauded, but there are some rather skeptical observations on his merits as a philosopher. His son, Ammonius Hermias (6th century), is more fully presented. It is attested of him that he was a pupil of Damascius, his mathematical skills are noted and he is declared the most prolific of commentators distinguished especially by his interpretations of Aristotle.[106] Most comprehensive is the account of John Philoponus (c.490–c.570), and not just as a philosopher, but also as an ecclesiastical author. Photius has read his account of the *Hexaemeron* and includes in the *Bibliotheca* a conspectus of the text.[107] He also adduces quotations from his commentary on the Gospel of John, which are the only ones that have

98. See cod. 214, 171b19–173b2 (= cod. 241, 460b22–466b24).
99. See cod. 215, 173b4–31.
100. See cod. 214, 172a3 sqq; 173a25 sqq, cod. 251, 461a24 sqq.
101. See the translation of the fragments according to Weber in: *Неоплатонизъм и християнство.* Part I. *Гръцката традиция III-VI в.* София: ЛИК 2002, 175–177.
102. See cod. 26, 5b28–6a4.
103. Ibid. 346b13–15.
104. See cod. 187, 145a38.
105. See cod. 242, 341a8.
106. Ibid., 341b22 sqq.
107. See cod. 38, 8a22–25; cod. 43, 9b11–18 and particularly cod. 240, 322b2–323b31.

come down to us.[108] Photius has also read his treatise *On the Resurrection*.[109] The Monophysite views of Philoponus are befittingly judged.[110] Of his philosophical works the *Bibliotheca* contains merely a syllabus of his critique of Iamblichus's treatise *On Statues*.[111] This is moreover one of the most interesting texts from a philosophical viewpoint. Unquestionably, however, the work carrying the greatest weight is the treatise of Hierocles of Alexandria, *On Providence and Destiny*, of which Photius offers a detailed conspectus of the text.[112] In Langerbeck's opinion,[113] Hierocles's treatise represents a *sui generis* summary of philosophy as a whole. The historical part culminates in two high points (173a5–40): 1) Plato (ch. 2) in harmony with whom is Aristotle (ch. 6); 2) Ammonius Saccas who restores the unity of philosophy (end of ch. 6). Book 7 sets forth the doctrine of Ammonius and concludes with a history of Neoplatonism. High praise is given to the person and life-work of Hierocles who, distinguished by superior intellect and power of speech,[114] constantly elaborated on his lectures and did not repeat them from year to year.[115]

It is now time to draw a general overview of the foregoing and put forward an evaluation of the character of Photius's account of Neoplatonism. The first thing to be noted is the feeble presence of analytical texts. With the exception of the above-mentioned works by Hierocles and John Philoponus, the *Bibliotheca* contains predominantly excerpts of texts and syllabi of books of historical rather than theoretical interest. Photius certainly feels more attracted to the exotic and hence the easily refutable. This reveals the attitude of a Christian educator seeking to expand the range of knowledge of his pupils, though without immersing them in the depths of philosophy and putting at risk their Christian awareness. He deems it sufficient to name the principal figures of the tradition, citing a few facts from their lives and lifework. Secondly, Photius's primary sources are not so much the writings of the philosophers as the available anthologies – that of John Stobaeus and the *Epitome* of Hesychius.[116] He has expressly summarized the former and we are much indebted to him for what we know of a lost version of this text.[117] He has also turned to the precious exposition of the history of Athenian Neoplatonism by Damascius. This does not argue, however, for intense philosoph-

108. See cod. 75, 52a25–b16.
109. See cod. 21, 5a25–29.
110. See cod. 55, 15a30–43, 15b1–5.
111. See cod. 215, 173b4–31.
112. See cod. 214, 171b19–173b2 (= cod. 251, 460b22–466b24).
113. See H. Langerbeck, "The Philosophy of Ammonius Saccas," *The Journal of Hellenic Studies* LXXVII (1957) 73.
114. See cod. 242, 338b28.
115. See cod. 242, 338b35.
116. The work represents a biographical reference book written by Ignatius Deacon shortly before 845. See W. T. Treadgold, *op. cit.*, 31.
117. See L. Symeonova, *op. cit.*, 44, n. 85.

ical interests. It was mentioned above that Treadgold sees the evidence of such interests in the exclusion of familiar school texts from the *Bibliotheca*, on the one hand, and the wide range of reports about ancient philosophers, on the other. As can be seen, neither argument can be accepted without reservations. Photius expressly summarizes one anthology and also uses another one – both of them infinitely more "schoolish" than the works of Plato and Aristotle. The wide range of his interests hardly disguises the absence of philosophical analytical propensity. Therefore I subscribe to the opinion of L. Symeonova and the traditional view, which is skeptical toward the claim of any intense interest in philosophy evinced in the *Bibliotheca*.[118] That it has become an invaluable source for certain doctrines is rather due to the loss of the texts, which Photius has drawn on, than to the merits of his compilation. In the third place, we should point out his relatively livelier interest in Alexandrian Neoplatonism. Insofar as one can speak (if at all) of any analytical philosophical texts in the *Bibliotheca*, they are associated with the names of exponents of that school: Philoponus and Hierocles. Four reasons can be adduced to explain this: 1) The Alexandrian school determined the curriculum of philosophical studies in Constantinople;[119] 2) This school elaborated chiefly the more neutral, "technical" aspects of philosophy, commenting the works of Plato and Aristotle in laying particular stress on logic; 3) Alexandrian Neoplatonism adopted an attitude of compromise toward Christianity, and some of its exponents even converted to it, which made it possible for this school to survive all others;[120] 4) It is precisely Alexandrian Neoplatonism that made possible the integration of Aristotelian philosophy into Christian theology.[121] To this interest we can attribute the unusual teaching about God as *actus purus* in *Amphilochia*. Before proceeding, however, it is in order to say a few words about the commentary on Aristotle's teaching of the *Categories*.

The commentary on Aristotle's teaching of the Categories

In contrast to the *Bibliotheca*, which, though composed for the benefit of Photius's brother Tarasius, was obviously intended for a larger audience,[122] the letters and the *Amphilochia* have a specific addressee. Perhaps this would

118. Ibid., 40–41.
119. See G. Lloyd, *The Anatomy of Neoplatonism*, Oxford: Clarendon Press 1990, 5.
120. See L. G. Westerink, "The Alexandrian commentators and the introductions to their commentaries," in: *Aristotle Transformed: the Ancient Commentators and their Influence*, ed. R. Sorabji, Duckworth 1990, 327.
121. See R. M. Jones, "The Ideas as the Thoughts of God," *Classical Philology* 21, 4 (1926) 326; J. Dillon, "Origen and Plotinus: The Platonic Influence on Early Christianity," *The relationship between Neoplatonism and Christianity*, ed. Th. Finan, V. Twomey, Dublin: Four Courts Press 1992, 1019; H. Langerbeck, "The Philosophy of Ammonius Saccas," *The Journal of Hellenic Studies* LXXVII (1957) 67–74.
122. See above, 291–292.

account for their pronounced theological and philosophical content. Such is the case of the commentary on Aristotle's teaching of the categories.[123] This commentary considers the ten categories in obvious dependence on the Neoplatonic tradition. However, it keeps clear of the Christianized commentaries on Aristotle known to us.[124] This has given some scholars ground to assume that the text is a simple compilation or, indeed, plagiarism from a pagan author copied, on Photius's order, by his secretary.[125] Given the present state of our knowledge concerning the Byzantine commentaries on Plato and Aristotle, we ought to be very careful in our pronouncements about this text. Such is the approach taken by J. Schamp in analyzing the claims of originality to be found in it.[126]

We shall therefore confine ourselves to pointing out the elements of Neoplatonic influence in a text the greatest merit of which probably is that it has introduced, with the Patriarch's authority, a Neoplatonic commentary on Aristotle into the Byzantine tradition. As we cannot enter here into extensive analyses we shall restrict ourselves to identifying the elements of textual dependence on Neoplatonic authors, and first and foremost on the commentary of Simplicius on the *Categories.*[127] Much after the time of Photius, in the 11th to 13th centuries, the influence of Simplicius in Byzantium became particularly appreciable.[128] The textual dependence is most conspicuous in the section on homonyms, synonyms, and paronyms.

The first thing that strikes the reader is the absence of the introduction typical for Neoplatonic commentaries, which designates the teaching of the categories as the beginning of the Aristotelian system. The reader is directly introduced to the interpretation of the relationship: thing – thought – word. For the commentators this is a question of principle setting as a prerequisite the discussion of the categories as the articulated unity of these three aspects. Here the peculiar "intentionality" of Aristotelian thinking is manifested. Without going into detail, I would like to refer the reader to my introductory essay to the Bulgarian edition of *The Categories* by Aristotle.[129] It is im-

123. All quotations below are taken from the publication: *Photii patriarche Constantinopolitani Epistole et Amphilociana*, ed. B. Laourdas, L.-G. Westerink, vol. V, Amphilochianorum pars altera, Leipzig 1986, 140–165. The section on Substance has been translated into Bulgarian by G. Kapriev; see *Архив за средновековна философия и култура* VIII (2002) 218–226.

124. See J. Schamp, "La 'localisation' chez Photios : traduction commentée de Questions à Amphilochios," 145," in: *Aristotelica Secunda. Mélanges offerts à Christan Rutten*, C.I.P.L., Liège 1996, 278.

125. W. T. Treadgold, *op. cit.*, 38.

126. J. Schamp, *op. cit.*, 265, 278–279.

127. The best edition of the Greek text for the present is still that of K. Kalbfleisch in the series Commentaria in Aristotelem graeca, vol. VIII, Berlin 1907. The commentary was written after 538, after the unfortunate journey of the six philosophers to Persia (see I. Hadot, "The life and work of Simplicius in Greek and Arabic sources," in: *Aristotle transformed: the Ancient Commentators and their Influence*, ed. R. Sorabji, Duckworth 1990, 290).

128. See I. Hadot, *op. cit.*, 300.

129. See Аристотел, *Категории*, София: Наука и изкуство 1992, 9–31.

portant to point out that in contrast to modern usage, synonyms, homonyms, paronyms, polynyms, and heteronyms are not the words but the concepts. The teaching about the categories, according to the Neoplatonic commentators, is a teaching not of the language but of the being given in the language and mediated by the concept. In the *Categories* the discussion of synonymy, homonymy, etc. lays relative emphasis on one aspect of the triune being (triunity) of the categories: the linguistic, in its relative detachment and, at the same time, dependence on the concept and the thing.[130] Similarly as in the Neoplatonic commentary, in Photius then follows the establishment of the place of polynyms and heteronyms in relation to synonyms and homonyms. "The polynyms," we read in *Amphilochia*, "are opposed in a certain manner to the homonyms, and the heteronyms to the synonyms."[131] This accounts for their exclusion from the span of the discussion since with respect to opposites the science is one.[132] Homonymy and synonymy are of primary importance because behind them stand fundamental ontological structures: the relationship ἀφ' ἑνὸς καὶ πρὸς ἕν behind homonymy, and καθ' ἕν behind synonymy.[133] It is these structures, not the division of names that matter to Aristotle and the Neoplatonic commentators.[134]

"Homonyms," we read further in Photius, "are those things the commonality of which is in the name, and the difference in the word formula (τῷ λόγῳ), whether defining (ὁριστικός) or describing (ὑπογραφικός)."[135] The closeness to Simplicius's commentary is quite obvious: "Synonymy has something in common with homonymy because in synonyms as in homonyms the name is common to both, but they differ in that with synonyms not only the name is common but the word formula (λόγος) referring to this name, whether defining (ὁριστικός) or describing (ὑπογραφικός), is also common to both."[136]

In Photius now follows an important explanation of the terms. "By 'name' (ὄνομα)," we read in his commentary, "one must understand here speech (λέξις) generally, and by 'substance' (οὐσία) – the subsistence underlying the individual object (τὴν ἑκάστου ὑποστατικὴν ὕπαρξιν) whether it be the substance, properly speaking (οὐσία κυρίως), or what is concomitant of it (συμβεβηκός)."[137] By "name" is meant the verbal designation in the broadest sense, regardless of any logical or ontological structure – and it is precisely this looseness of the language, which is the source of the delusion. To

130. See Simpl. *In Cat.* 19, 9 sqq. [CAG 8]. Olymp. *In Cat.*, 38–40; 57 [CAG 12.1].
131. Qu. 137, 4–6.
132. See Simpl. *In Cat.* 23, 7 sqq. [CAG 8]. Olymp. *In Cat.*, 27–25 [CAG 12.1]. Cf. Arist. *Met.* Γ2, 1004a8, K3, 1061a18.
133. See Аристотел, *Категории*, София 1992, 69.
134. See Simpl. *In Cat.* 19,7 sq. [CAG 8].
135. Qu. 137, 7 sq.
136. Simpl. *In Cat.* 33, 27–31 [CAG 8].
137. See Qu. 137, 18–20.

the Greeks, in contrast to us, ὄνομα (name) signified any semantically distinguishable part of speech (form class), including verbs and conjunctions. So it is in Aristotle and in his Neoplatonic commentators.[138]

As to the distinction between the two kinds of "substance," here too is followed the Aristotelian conception that the determinateness of the thing, that which subsists it, can be the substance (i.e. the self-subsistent essence) or what is concomitant of her "in itself" (συμβεβηκὸς καθ' αὑτό). The former is revealed in the definition, the latter in the description.

Further on in Photius's text, homonymy as a subject of the doctrine of categories – a doctrine with a predominant ontological purport, is distinguished from the theory of language: "These words, however," we read in *Amphilochia*, "befit only the homonymous objects, but do not suit the term of homonym the description of which is the following: homonym is a term, which expresses a multitude of different objects with a view to different concepts."[139]

In their turn, "synonyms are those things in which the name and the relevant definition of the substance referred to it (i.e. the subsistence underlying it) is one and the same."[140] Here again a distinction is made between ontological and linguistic sense. "Synonym is the term, which expresses a multitude of different things with a view to one and the same concept."[141]

The paronyms, polynyms, and heteronyms are discussed in a similar manner. We shall not go into the detail of this discussion because they play a part of minor importance in the Neoplatonic commentary, while the significant aspects bearing on them were already stated above. In principle, it was sufficient for the purpose of this study to show the direct link between Photius's text with those of Simplicius and the other commentators. In essence and almost in its entirety, Photius's discussion of the categories is not original. We have already pointed out its importance in that it has legitimized the Neoplatonic interpretations in the Christian tradition. After the Christian Neoplatonists of the Alexandrian school – Olympiodorus, David, and Philoponus – Photius was the first to reproduce this model of Aristotelian commentary. For the tradition this text was consecrated by the patriarch's authority, and thereby the Neoplatonic speculation on Aristotle was legitimized in Byzantium.

A purely Christian feature should be brought to attention here, which has so far eluded researchers. Coming to the issue of God's substance, Photius (or possibly the Christianized commentary he was drawing on) takes it out of the doctrine of categories. It is not a category "because it is much higher

138. See Arist. *De Int.*, 16b9, Porph. *In Cat.* 61.31 [CAG 4.1], Simpl. *In Cat.* 25.20–26.2 [CAG 8], Olymp. *In Cat.* 30.9 [CAG 12.1].

139. Qu. 137, 21–24.

140. Qu. 137, 28–30.

141. Qu. 137, 33–35.

than all these words and concepts, or rather because of its inexpressible superiority it is separated and exalted above them."[142] At this point, however, there follows something unexpected: instead of raising it above the limits of reason and declaring it inaccessible to knowledge, Photius specifies it as a subject of the first philosophy. "In an entirely different manner," he writes, "we name *substance* (what is) the supersubstantial and producing the existing substance, the discussion of which is a task not of the present but of the first philosophy [the study of being *qua* being]."[143] This sounds as odd from a Christian thinker as it does from the philosopher commentator. In Aristotle, there is no opposition between the teaching of the categories and the subject of the first philosophy. What's more, this very doctrine is the first philosophy.[144] No such opposition is to be found in the Neoplatonic commentary either. There the doctrine of God is opposed not to the teaching of the categories but to the teaching of nature.[145] In the present case we cannot but see a succumbing to the inertia of philosophical schemata. A Christian commentator was bound to make a distinction between the substance of God and the category of substance. The contrary would have amounted to equating the Creator with the created. On the other hand, however, he leaves it within the confines of reason as higher (first) philosophy. We could assume that such a doctrine was not characteristic of Photius but had crept in unnoticed into the commentary compiled by his secretary. Things seem to be more complicated. We come upon the same again in a text, which is undoubtedly by him. I have in mind his response to the question by Amphilochius in what way is God present in the world.

The doctrine of God as actus purus

The *Amphilochia* 75 is devoted to the answer to this question. Photius develops here a rather unusual doctrine according to which God is present by his substance in the world. In this manner it becomes possible to reason about Him. He is pure energy (*actus purus*). If this is so and His substance is immanent to the world, then God can be the subject of the first philosophy. Let us follow through the reasoning of Photius.

The problem is that "if God were *in the Universe*, he would not be *beyond it*."[146]

In that case, "the One surpassing all things would be one of them, and the Originator and Creator of the Universe would manifest Himself as something

142. Qu. 138, 18–20.

143. Qu. 138, 5–7.

144. See И. Христов, "Метафизиката в Аристотеловата 'Метафизика,'" in: Аристотел, *Метафизика*, София: Соим 2000, lviii–lxxii.

145. See *Amm. in Int.* 131,4–6, CAG [4.5]; *Amm. in APo.* 8,34–36, CAG [4.6]; Olymp. *In Met.* 4,6–8, CAG [12.2]; Philop. In GC 50,5–10, CAG [14.2]; Philop. *In An.* 25,13–16, CAG [15]; Philop. *In Ph.* 882,11–13, CAG [15]; Simpl *In Ph.* 1,17–21, CAG [9]; Asclep. *In Met.* 56, 23–25, CAG [6.2].

146. Qu. 75, 37 sq.

of what He had created [...]"[147] Thus would be lost the difference between the Creator and the created – the fundamental opposition underlying the Christian world outlook. Entirely in the spirit of the teaching of the Church, Photius responds that the relationship of God to the world is unique and has no analog in anything else. "The Divinity," he writes, "does not connect and does not accord with His creatures like any of the existing things, but his connection with the existing is established in a peculiar and proper only to Him relationship and economy."[148] Photius describes the ambivalent relationship of God to the world as simultaneously transcendent and immanent in it on the lines of Pseudo-Dionysius's theology. Insofar as He is immanent, He may be referred to in predicates, and in so far as He is transcendent, he should be thought of in an apophatic way [in terms of what He is not] by way of denial through superabundance. "Therefore, just as (we say that) the Divinity is at the same time superwise, true God and super-God, actually substance and super-substance, as well as good-in-itself and super-good [highest good], so we also state that It is at the same time present in the Universe and above it."[149] Further down Photius would specify that super-wise, super-God, super-substance and super-good are negative predicates. This is so because they express such fullness of the respective positive attributes as does not match with any positive attribute. Paradoxically, the extremeness of the superlative in the statement turns it into a denial. This way of thinking is characteristic of the mystical theology of Pseudo-Dionysius the Areopagite and through him gained acceptance in the Christian tradition.[150] It is applicable solely to God. "Solely in the inexpressible, many-named and supernatural nature," Photius writes, "the cataphatic type of name has a meaning supplementing (the meaning of those), which reveal (His) will (τὸ βούλημα) by way of apophasis and privation."[151] But what has Divine will to do with all this?

In my opinion, its introduction into this discourse reveals the conceptual connection of the text with the Alexandrian tradition.[152] This would

147. Qu. 75, 19–21.

148. Qu. 75, 24–27.

149. Qu. 75, 27–30.

150. It is not possible to enter into detail here. The reader is referred to other publications of the author, where he will also find bibliographical information. See И. Христов, "Християнският неоплатонизъм в корпуса на 'Ареопагитиките,'" in: *Неоплатонизъм и християнство*, ч. I. *Гръцката традиция III–VI в.*, София: ЛИК 2002, 129–172. Св. Дионисий Ареопагит, *За небесната йерархия. За църковната йерархия*, София: ЛИК 2001.

151. Qu. 75, 30–33.

152. One could only formally find it similar to the theological aporhetics in the "sic" and "non" treatise by certain Stephanus Gobarus (see A. von Harnack, "The 'Sic et Non' of Stephanus Gobarus," *Harvard Theological Review* 16 (1923) 205–234). The latter tended to confuse the issue of the presence of Divine Substance in the body of Christ with its presence in the body of Universe – i.e. in the material cosmos. This means identity of the incarnation and natural revelation that implies identity of the Christian and the philosophical wisdom. This could only provoke Photius to pass his statement on the topic but in no way coincided with his own position.

also account for Photius's particular interest in Hierocles's treatise *On Providence and Destiny*. It was in Alexandria that the need arose of finding an acceptable philosophical formulation of the Christian position against the pantheism of pagan philosophers and against the Gnostic theory, which accepted God's transcendence but gave it such a turn as to declare salvation accessible only to the chosen. I shall quote the opinion given by H. Langerbeck: "with Pantaenus and the catechetic School of Alexandria, the ἐπέκεινα τῆς οὐσίας common to Plato and the Gnostics takes shape as the will of God. Consequently the wholly transcendent God of the Gnostics can be retained, and the creation of the world transferred to him. The connection with Christian doctrine is effected, not, as with the Western opponents of Gnosticism through the Old Testament but through the God of the New Testament (especially of Paul and John), who knows only 'his own' and is known solely by 'his own.'"[153] In Pantaenus, the founder of the Catechetical School of Alexandria, θέλημα θεοῦ (God's will) is raised to an ontological principle. He distinguished the pre-eternal ideas in God's mind, the energies of the Divine substance, from the nature of things without leaving an unbridgeable gap between them. Through it is being thought the ambivalent relationship of God to the world.

The following will cast more light on Photius's connection with Alexandrian theology and philosophy: "But in what way is [God] in the Universe? We have already said that it is in none of the modes of existing things but if we have to say it in an even more abstract way to those who like us anxiously seek to elevate their thinking and do not fear the heights of the subtler theological dogmata, God is in the Universe at once *by energy* (κατ' ἐνέργειαν) and *by substance* (κατ' οὐσίαν). Don't ask me how! We have already indicated that it is in none of the modes of existing things. And in what way is He *by substance*? – In the same way as you think Him as energy. Since everything else is sometimes in potency and sometimes actual (ἐνεργείᾳ), whereas the Divinity, as it is thought by the discerning mind, is always in reality (It never passes from imperfection to perfection, but the Self-substantial (αὐτοούσιον) is none other than self-energy (αὐτοενέργεια), it is clear that where It is *by energy*, there It is also *by substance*, since, on one hand, it realizes (ἐνεργεῖ) the union and steadiness of the existing, and on the other, gives substance to (οὐσιοῖ) and governs the nature of what was created by Him."[154] This is an astounding passage, which raises a number of questions. We see here the identification of substance and energy in God and His being presented as *actus purus*. The same was done in the West by Thomas Aquinas with whose

153. H. Langerbeck, "The Philosophy of Ammonius Saccas," *The Journal of Hellenic Studies* LXXVII (1957) 71.
154. Qu. 75, 41–42.

name this doctrine is associated.[155] In his teaching Thomas followed the very same concept of perfection[156] like Photius.[157]

Wasn't then Photius a Thomist before Thomas? A historical paradox might be fittingly inserted here. When in the late 14th century part of the works of Thomas Aquinas, the Latin theologian, was translated in Byzantium, the reaction that followed went beyond the scope of ordinary theological debate. In confronting him, the Byzantine theologians stood up for their cultural and religious identity. To them this doctrine was in flagrant contradiction to Orthodox tradition, which did not identify God's substance and the energies of God. They argued that it consisted of both the energies and the power (δύναμις). It is precisely the boundless power of God that placed Him beyond all being. This was one of the fundamental objections of Callistos Angelicoudis against Thomas Aquinas.[158] It is not possible here to consider in depth the question of the crucial differences in context in which Photius and Thomas were reasoning. We only note the formal similarity – the similarity in the modes of thinking. It is obvious and, in my opinion, as far as *Amphilochia* is concerned, that it is due to Photius's penchant for philosophy. Photius expresses here a private opinion. This doctrine of his does not belong to the tradition of the Church.

But what is its origin? To which philosophic tradition does it pertain? On the face of it, all seems clear. The philosophical concept of God as pure reality was introduced by Aristotle in the twelfth book of the *Metaphysics*. There, however, the reality (energy) of the Prime Mover comes down to an act of thinking, which is not concerned with the world. The Aristotelian god is unconcerned about what happens in the sub-lunar part of the universe. He thinks of his own self and has no interest in nature and man. Insofar as he exerts any influence on the world, it is by the mechanism of teleological causality. Being a perfect model of imitation, God arouses a yearning in the

155. A typical example is *Contra Gentiles*, lib. 2 cap. 6 n. 7: But the *pure actuality*, which is God, is more perfect than actuality mingled with potentiality [...] (*Actus autem purus, qui Deus est, perfectior est quam actus potentiae permixtus* [...]).

156. One separated substance is like another with respect to their immateriality, but they differ one from another with respect to their grade of perfection according to how far each recedes from potentiality and approaches pure act (*On Being and Essence*, cap. 5, 106–110, tr. R. T. Miller).

157. This common teaching is demonstrated by the following diagram:

(a) imperfection → (b) lower grades of perfection	→ (c) the highest perfection = God
– in (a) and (b) there is *change*	– *no change* from imperfection to perfection
– this means *potentiality* in substance	– *no potentiality* in Divine substance = *pure actuality* Photius: τὸ αὐτοούσιον = αὐτοενέργεια Aquinas: Deus = *actus purus*

158. See *Callistos Angelicoudis contre Thomas d'Aquin*, ed. St. Papadopoulos, Athènes 1970, 330, 162, 20–24.

existing to partake of his perfection. He is not a creative and is not a providential cause for the world. Quite different is what we read in Photius, who examines the issue about God's substance and energies in relation to His attitude to existing things. This emphasis is so strong that no distinction is made between the pre-eternal Divine energies and His economical actions within the existing. It turns out that this very energy, which is identical with God's substance, comes down to the actions of the Creator in the created. One can discern here the influence of Neoplatonism, which, on one hand, links the Aristotelian concept of *energy* with the mechanism of the action of the First Cause in the ranks of being and, on the other, finds no room for internal productive action of the energies – to engender the secondary things they emanate outwards. Therefore, in the context of the reasoning about the energies, the question about His providence acquires particular significance. This also accounts for Photius's special interest in Hierocles's work *On Providence and Destiny*, the more so as this treatise holds a place apart in the Alexandrian tradition. In the context of Neoplatonic philosophy it embodies tendencies by which it also manifests itself in the theology of Pantaenus and Origen.[159] It might be appropriate to recall at this point Photius's categorical stance in support of the claim that Origen belonged to the Neoplatonic school of Ammonius Saccas.

All these observations give us grounds to assume that in the period of intense intellectual activity prior to 858 and during his first exile in 867–868, when he wrote the *Amphilochia*, Photius took a lively interest in the Alexandrian tradition. The specific intellectual atmosphere in this cosmopolitan city prepared the ground for a genuine cultural synthesis in which Christian theology absorbed elements of Hellenic philosophy. To this fact we might also ascribe the philosophical interests of Photius. It was not seldom, however, as can be seen in the example of Clement of Alexandria and Origen, that the inertia of the schemata of thinking led to the emergence of unbalanced doctrines. It is a similar teaching that we detect in the doctrine of Photius, the Patriarch. To conceive God as *actus purus* is a philosophic doctrine deeply alien to the Eastern tradition. It implied the integration of Aristotle's philosophy and its teaching about substance and energies with Neoplatonism, which had given a systematic interpretation of energies as the mechanism of action of the First Cause in the hierarchy of being. This has remained a private opinion of Photius's influenced by the scholarly quests from before his election as Patriarch and by his work during the first exile in 867–868 (*Amphilochia*). Thus, although the Patriarch's acquaintance with Neoplatonic philosophy did not correspond to the wide scope given it in the *Bibliotheca*, this philosophy did influence him and its influence might help us to explain a conception so alien to Eastern Orthodox tradition as is the notion of God as *actus purus*.

159. Cf. H. Langerbeck, *op. cit.*, 73.

"Relation" as Marker of Historicity in Byzantine Philosophy

Smilen Markov

Introduction

In Byzantium history is conceptualized mostly by rejecting the neo-Platonic cosmology of Origen (2nd–3rd c.). Origen is convinced that divine intellect contains the eternal archetypes of all creatures. Their appearance as self-dependent essences in time is merely a modification of the archetypes. The world is a concrete expression of the difference between the eternal intellects and God himself.[1] The view formulated in the 4th century as a counterpoint to this Christian neo-Platonic cosmology, maintains *creatio ex nihilo*: the world is created out of nothing and God refers it not by necessity, but voluntarily. According to this view, the cycle of self-referred expression of God in creation is replaced by the dynamic encounter of the world with God. Divine presence, which maintains the created world, is realized within the borders, traced by God. In the 5th century the anonymous author of *Corpus Dionysiacum* integrates this idea for the first time in a coherent mental system. In the ontological hierarchy of Dionysios the divine monad is perfectly reproduced in all creatures, whereas its activity is manifested according to the ontological potential of each of them. Completing the ontological potential of each created being, God conveys His image to all things, with different clarity. Thus the hierarchy of the cosmos takes part in divine being and the created images of God step in relations, corresponding to the hierarchical order.[2]

Concerning the relations among its human members, the hierarchy of Dionysios is certainly dynamic, because the fullness of divine activity is manifested in rational creatures depending on their existential capacity and voluntary disposition. These two vary in men.[3] Within the frame-

1. Origenes , *De Principiis*, I, 2, 2; I, 4, 3–5. Cf. Ch. Köckert, *Christliche Kosmologie und kaiserzeitliche Philosophie*, Tübingen 2009, 299–302.
2. Dionysios Areopagita, *De divinis nominibus* II, 5 ; II, 7 ; PG 3, 583D, 596D–597A.
3. Cf. Г. Каприев, "Историчността и темпоралността – основни елементи на византийската философия," *Философия - електронно списание за философия и култура* 1 (2012), http://philosophy-e.com/philosophia-e-journal-of-philosophy-and-culture-12012/14.04.2014.

work of this illumination divine eternity becomes operative in the sphere of the contingent. The exposed model of theophany can be defined as "positivism of revelation." History is neither a reflection, nor an unfolding of a transcendent plot, improving the status of creation according predetermined principles, designed by God. Not created essences, but their modes of existence change. In the philosophical and theological speculation concerning this transforming deification the Aristotelian concept of categories, and the category "relation" in particular, acquire special gnoseological and metaphysical importance.

1. *The category "relation"*

In Aristotle's work *Categories* the first four (essence, quality, quantity and relation) are discussed in detail, whereas the rest are merely sketched. Aristotle defines relation (πρὸς τι) as a characteristic of beings, predicated in respect of something else. This term always denotes a comparison, for instance, when one thing is bigger than another. Aristotle would not apply the category in respect of the first or the second essence, as both exist independently and are not defined in relation to other things. Every single man, as well as the general essence of men, are self-dependent and are not relatives.[4] In a "secondary sense" Aristotle associates "habitus" (ἕξις), "disposition" (διάθεσις), "sense perception" (αἴσθησις), "knowledge" (ἐπιστήμη) and "position" (θέσις) with the category "relation."[5]

From the first century onwards the peripatetic school insists that the last six categories are dependent on the first four. This thesis is also popular in neo-Platonism. Olympiodoros (495–570) for instance, draws a scheme of the derivation of all categories. The categories "time" and "place" result from the combination of "essence" and "quantity," the combination of "essence" and "relation" produces "position" and "possessing." These genealogical connections correspond to the neo-Platonic ontological hierarchy: the last six categories are predicated of the corporeal beings, which are subordinate to the intelligible ones.

Porphyry (3rd century) and Plotinus (3rd century) also confirm that the category "relation" is pivotal. For Porphyry the reciprocity of relations indicates perfection. He searches linguistic formulae, which reveal the reciprocity of the category even in those cases, in which it is not distinctly noticeable.[6] Still, Porphyry admits that even the relatives of reciprocal relations do not partake of them simultaneously.[7] Plotinus, in his turn, insists

4. Arist. *Cat.*, 8a 12–25.
5. Arist. *Cat.*, 6b 2–3.
6. He repeats the examples, given by Aristotle. The relation "wing of a bird" for instance is not reciprocal, as it cannot be given in the form: "bird of a wing." Reciprocal is only the relation "wing of a winged;" Ch. Evangeliou, *Aristotle's Categories and Porphyry*, Leiden: Brill 1988, 83.
7. *Ibid.*, 84.

that all relations are mutual, regardless of the moment when the members meet with each other. Notwithstanding a beginning in time, the ontological basis of relation transcends the categories "time" and "space." For Plotinus relations are polyadic: according to contemporary terminology, a relation is polyadic, when it is really present in each of its members. He makes clear that polyadicity of relations should not be ascribed to their belonging to one and the same genus. More plausible for him is the explanation, according to which the reciprocity manifests the energetic character of a relation: for Plotinus the ontological base of relations is essential activity (ἐνέργεια).

Extending his analysis, Plotinus notes that, at first, all relations are only in potency: they are ultimately determined, but are actualized only after a [causal] action. The members of a potential relations are beings that participate in the εἶδος or the λόγος of the relation. In the actual relations the existence of one relative depends on that of the other, as is the relation "cause-caused."[8] In any case, there is no need for an intermediary to guarantee the relation. Participating in a common εἶδος of a relation, as well as partaking of an actual relation, is realized through *ad extra* activity of the essence, which for Plotinus is constitutive for essential being.

2. The concept of relation in Byzantine philosophy

2.1. St. John Damascene

One of the earliest systematic expositions of the category "relation" in Byzantine philosophy is that of John Damascene (650–749) in the work *Dialectica*, in which the author specifies the terminological base of his metaphysical synthesis.[9] When examining the rest of the categories, John reproduces the Aristotelian concept, according to which they are not predicated of the first and second essences. The categories merely reveal the essence, without directly expressing its ontological content. The first essence, i.e. the individual, is characterized through a specific constellation of accidents, which do not define its selfhood. However, the category "relation" is an exception from this rule.

Indeed, the Palestinian monk agrees that the single man, as well as human nature in general, cannot be conceptualized in relation to other beings.[10] Still, he is ready to consider the essence as a relative category, inasmuch as it partakes of a common genus, together with other beings (individuals, species etc.), thus entering a relation (σχέσις). Damascene supports this

8. Plotin, *Enneaden*, VI, 1, 6 (42); *Enneads*, ed. P. Henry, H. R. Schwyzer, III, Oxford 1964.
9. Leontios uses this category in order to clarify in what way Christ's two natures are united (*Contra Sever.*, PG 86 (2), 1904B). In *Contra Nestorianos et Eutychianos* with the category "relation" he describes the connection between soul and body, as well as between Christ's two natures and between father and son.
10. Johannes Damascenus, *Dialectica* (*Dial.*) 51, 2–3; *Die Schriften des Johannes von Damaskos*, ed. B. Kotter, I, Berlin 1969. Cf. Arist., *Cat.*, 8a 12–25.

thesis, by observing that the essence is the ontological foundation of "genus," "species" and "individual." Consequently, essence has a relative aspect, due to which it is able to enter into relations.

One could suggest that, in order to demonstrate the relative character of "essence," John would give Aristotle's examples for relations in the "secondary sense." At stake are the relations, resulting from the possession of a quality. Instead, he lists examples of interhypostatic relations, i.e. relations among self-established (αὐθέδραστος) things.[11] The interhypostatic relation is a mode of personal existence, in which the essential differences are manifested as hypostatic peculiarities. It is an expression of the communion among the relatives – a non-causal, even when resulting from a causal influence. The interhypostatic relations can be natural (φυσικὴ σχέσις), for instance "father-son," and non-natural, for instance "master-slave." Of special interest are the natural hypostatic relations. John has in mind a relation, which activates nature and is not reducible to generation of one hypostasis from another. At stake is a dynamic togetherness between "bearing" and "born."

Being the base of interhypostatic relations, nature is not a *fundamentum*, present in the relatives as in a subject, according to the concept of relation in scholastic philosophy. Nature is enhypostasized in the relatives and the ontological foundation of the relation is comprised of the selfhood of each of the hypostases. The paradigm of hypostatic generation, referred by John, is the eternal Birth of the Son from the Father: the selfhood of the Son is defined through His eternal Birth from the Father. In this context the term αὐθέδραστος, introduced by John, indicates the complexity of convergence of the *natural* and the *hypostatic* order. As the interhypostatic relations have an existential core, they do not simply exemplify a static configuration, produced by the essence and guaranteed by the hypostasis; they construct an intersubjective reality.

Plotinus differentiates between "potential" and "actual" relation in respect of the two modes of natural activity *ad extra*, namely, existential and causal. However, he does not offer a solution for linking the two types of relation in one coherent system. John integrates relation in the coherent ontological model, developed in Byzantine philosophy. Specific for this metaphysical system is the axiom that the external causal action of an essence manifests the immanent essential act. And the pillar of essential energetic manifestation is the single hypostasis.

2.2. St. Patriarch Photios of Constantinople the Great

The view according to which relations are based on the dynamic character of essential being, is further developed by Photios (810–893). He defines relations as the identity between the being of a subject and the way

11. *Dial.*, 51, 46; 47; 51.

this subject refers to something else.[12] Unlike Aristotle, Photios associates "participation" (μέθεξις) with the category "relation," same as "production" and "passion." Obviously, "relation" for Photios is one of the expressions of essential activity.

The last six categories from Aristotle's list, which receive quite a vague treatment in Photios' text, are, according to the author's insistence, of no lesser value, although not directly resulting from the first four. Notwithstanding the fact that all categories, except for the essence, denote accidents, "relation," "quantity" and "quality" stay closer to the essential core than all other variable properties. At the same time, Photios underlines that the characteristics of the four primary categories enable the rest. After a detailed analysis, he demonstrates that all six resulting categories contain a facet of relativity.[13] The latter is an attribute of the act of essence (ἐνέργεια), which is more fundamental than the particular causal alterations and determines them. For instance, the category "action" depends on two determinants, namely: "more" (excess) and "less" (lack). These two denominators belong to the domain of relation.

The fact that the concept of a certain individual property contains in itself a relative element, suggests that "relation" is a characteristic of the communion of *self-dependent*, and not of relatively determined hypostases. In his *Amphilochia* Photios insists that a differentiation be made between the hypostasis itself and that, which is around it.[14] The accidents denote not the hypostatic selfhood, but the peculiarities borne by the hypostasis, through which it manifests its uniqueness. Specific for the category "relation" is that it denotes the interaction between these individualizing peculiarities and the peculiarities of other hypostases. Relation denotes the matching of the existential movements of a number of hypostases. As this matching produces certain accidents, each accidental property possesses a relative determinant.

The most telling example for compatibility between existential interaction and hypostatic peculiarity is an act of will, directed towards a certain object: πρὸς τὶ πρᾶγμα βούλησις.[15] This particular wish initiates a series of discursive considerations, legitimizing certain disposition of the will, i.e. a special mode (τρόπος) of realizing the act of will. In that sense relation is a prerequisite for volitional confirmation and manifestation of hypostatic selfhood. In *Mystagogia* Photios explains why it is correct to apply the category "relation" to the Trinity. Curiously enough, he does not refer to the production of selfhood within the Trinity, but to the co-existence of the hypostases,

12. Photios, *Amphilochia* (*Amph.*) 141, 2–3; *Photii Patriarchiae Constantinopolitani Epistulae et Amphilochia*, ed. L. Westerink, Leipzig 1986.
13. The second property of "place" is "spatial relation." "Being-in-a-position" is a combination of "state" and the subject of the state. The category "when" results from the combination of the stream of time (χρόνος) with that, which is in time. This combining includes necessarily the conception of relation.
14. *Amph.*, 229, 43–48.
15. *Amph.*, 80.

generated by the Father. Photios justifies the position that the Holy Spirit does proceed only from the Father and not from the Son as well, by emphasizing the capacity of the relation "Father-Spirit" to assert the divine primacy and the divine nature of the Spirit.[16] Relation is apparently a characteristic of the existential exchange, which is not to be reduced to a singular causal effect. Hypostatic selfhood itself is non-relative.

The non-causal existential core of "relation" is the implicit justification of the somewhat provocative thesis of Photios, that in His relation to the world, God is present not only by energy (κατ' ἐνέργειαν), but also by essence (κατ' οὐσίαν). Photios explains that in the created world relations are realized on two levels: by mere potency (δύναμις) and by energy (ἐνέργεια), the latter being the complete form. For the presence of divine grace in the world such scale is not relevant, because God's act is perfect and there is no room for optimization. Photios underlines that creation has no access to divine being itself, but to an intentionally revealed reality of divine life. Although this reality is not created, it is adjusted by God to the boundaries of creation. The content of the encounter of the world and divine energy is that of a relation, although divine essential energy is not reducible to relations, being perfect and united. God is non-relative but self-acting (αὐτοενέργητος) and self-essential (αὐτοουσίος).[17] Therefore, He is present in creation also by essence.

One can conclude that for Photios relation is a concept, explaining the essential manifestation within the interhypostatic exchange. Relation in the proper sense cannot define Trinitarian being, because in this case there is the lending of hypostatic selfhood, which is not marked through accidents. In Trinitarian theology "relation" is used only as a logical tool. Still, divine presence in the world could be conceptualized through relations: a possibility, indicating that revelation is historically structured. In this respect, Photios radicalizes the ontological implications of Damascene's logical-analytical concept of "relation." Furthermore, following the view of revelation creationism, he transforms the Dionysian model of a dynamic cosmological hierarchy. The pillar of relations is now the hypostasis. Third, Photios underlines the role of the will in forming relations. Thereby he makes his contribution to the long tradition in Byzantine philosophy of conceptualizing the will of man and of Christ as an existential state.

2.3. Georgios Pachymeres

In his commentary on Aristotle's *Metaphysics* Georgios Pachymeres (1242–1310) – one of the most subtle exegetes of Aristotle in Byzantium – interprets "relation" exclusively as a logical concept, as is typical in the Byzantine tradition of textbook commentaries on Aristotle. Relation is a special case of the

16. Photios, *De spiritu sancti Mystagogiae liber* (Myst.), 8, PG 102, 289A.
17. *Amph.*, 75, 41–52.

category "quality" (τὸ ποιόν), in the following aspects:[18] 1) semantic complementariness ("double" is related to "half;" the acting - to the passive; the knowing - to the known); 2) accidence, connecting two beings (the one half is related to the other half and denotes an accidental property, which is a common species of both halves). Pachymeres examines cases, in which the category "relation" is ontologically independent. His analysis shows that when relation is a characteristic of an entirely standalone being, i.e. hypostasis, it is separate and does not merge with other qualitative and quantitative relations.

2.4. Gennadios Scholarios

In his commentary on the Aristotle's *Categories* Gennadios Scholarios (1400–1473) differentiates the predicative (κατὰ τὸ λέγεσθαι) from the ontological (κατὰ τὸ εἶναι) meaning of the category "relation." In both aspects the actual (πραγματικῶς) existence of a thing, of which the particular relation is predicated, is taken for granted. By "actual existence" Scholarios means energetic manifestation (ἐνεργείᾳ ὄν).[19] This category is neither identical with the essence, nor caused by it. As is well known, Aristotle defines "accident" as dependent being, which exists in something else.[20] Gennadios underscores that relation is a quite specific accident, as it is neither reducible to other accidents, nor is it a structural element of all other accidents. "Quality" and "relation" are not predicated of the essence in the same sense, because "relation" is dependent on "quality." When several subjects possess one and the same quality to a variable extent, they get into a relation with each other. But "quality" itself is not a relation and is not the cause of a relation.

On the level of predication relation is a genus, encompassing all partakers. In this sense each bearer of a relation is related to this genus by *a special relation*. So the *common relation* turns out to be the higher species of all special relations. The number of special relations is equal to the number of members. On the ontological level, however, relation is a single ontological entity (*substratum*), which is available in a multitude of substrates (ἐν δυσὶ μία).[21] Such polyadicity is not compatible with the concept of a static essence; relations have to do with the activity of an essence. When commenting on the relation between creator and creation - a relation postulated by human intellect and available only in the contingent world, and not in God - Scholarios gives a general explanation of the status of the relatives. These are not parts or substrates, but borders of the relation. It turns out that "relation" is an oscillation between extremes. Scholarios' speculation implies that a relation

18. Georgios Pachymeres, *Philosoph ia. Kommentar zur Metaphysik des Aristoteles*, ed. E. Pappa, Athen 2012, 41–42.
19. Gennade Scholarios, *Oeuvres Complètes*, ed. M. Jugie, VII, Paris 1936, 178.
20. *Ibid.*, 181.
21. *Ibid*, 199.

touches its subjects through an indiscrete convergence. This is valid for both potential and existential relations.

Scholarios considers the fact that the human soul is able to grasp the relatives in a single act of thought as an indication of the borderline status of relation.[22] Our soul conceives of the relatives as projections of a complex property, just as we think of whiteness and magnitude as two aspects of a white and big thing. In reality relation is a *communion* of beings, each of them existing self-dependently (δύο ἁπλῶς ὄντα). The conceptual framework of human reason does not allow for expressing the so formulated borderline status of relation through subject-attribute propositions.

Byzantine commentaries on the category "relation" accentuate dynamic extensibility as a key characteristic of the multitude of the created world. Byzantine creationism takes a stand against the cosmology of Origen, by insisting on the self-existence of creation and the high metaphysical value of unique single existence. When existence is conceptualized through the energy concept, relation is a metaphysical vector of the interaction.

3. *Relation by St. Maximos the Confessor*

3.1. Cosmological and Historical Aspects

The metaphysical synthesis of Maximos the Confessor (580–662) shows most clearly that the historization of the category "relation," depicted above, has an anthropological focus. This is a consequence of the radical Christ-centrism, dominating the thought of St. Maximus, for whom Incarnation is the ontological optimum of all creation. The content of human freedom for Maximos is much richer than for Dionysios. Not a mere return of creation to God is at stake, but the emergence of a new mode (τρόπος) of being, by which all creation enters into the hypostasis of Christ. As Christ is a man, it is exactly man, who has the capacity and responsibility of desiring and realizing this transition. That is why the purpose of history is the communion (κοινωνία) of every man with God. The movement towards this purpose is conceptualized through relations: ἐν σχέσει θεωρουμένη κίνησις.[23]

Constitutive for the metaphysical system of Maximos is the transition between three modes of creation, namely "emergence-movement-peace." This transition leads to the perfect revealing of God in human history. The eternal dynamic peace of the communion with God is seen as a new state of the world, which becomes possible because of divine love and man's free response to it. In order to reach this state, man has to freely offer the entire world to God as a gift. The divisions that mark the ontological borders of the world should be overcome so that the essential potential of each being is perfectly manifested. This overcoming takes place in the realizing of the essential potential

22. *Ibid.*, 199.
23. Maximus the Confessor, *Ad Marinum*, PG 91, 233A.

of creation and takes place in relations.[24] Maximos notes that "relation" is the pattern, in which man achieves the existence of God.

God creates through a "unifying relation" (κατὰ τὴν ἑνοποιὸν σχέσιν),[25] which is accessible for discursive knowledge, called by Maximos "natural contemplation." One should ask what the gnoseological status of this relation is. It cannot be a hypostatic union like the one of Christ's two natures: incarnation is non-relative, as divine and human natures are not united through a relation (σχετικὴ ἕνωσις) and their union is guaranteed by the Son's hypostatic acceptance of humanity.[26] Were the relation, through which God creates and maintains the world, of this kind, creation would be a multiple hypostasis.[27] Applicable is another mode of union, namely the communion of believers in the Christian church.[28] In the church the hypostasis of Christ is being actualized and there it lives within the mutual relations of the believers. Exactly this kind of relation is the object of the natural contemplation of creation. It provides access to God's being, although it cannot unveil God as such – either by essence, or by hypostasis.[29] This thesis is in strict correspondence with the argumentation of Photios, who demonstrates that the core of Trinitarian being is non-relative.

As for Dionysios, "relation" for Maximos is a prerequisite for the synergy of God and creatures within his providential care for the world. Each creature has a certain capacity for filling up with divine energy, which depends on its place in the cosmological hierarchy. Maximos does not conceptualize this type of relation according to any hierarchical scale of being. His concept is closer to the theoretical speculation of Gennadios Scholarios, for whom relation is reciprocal: relatives exchange potentiated essential energies. Besides, Scholarios' insistence that the relatives are the border of relation, is analogous to the role relations play in Maximos' theology: they bridge the gap between extremes. By "extremes" Maximos means not only the extreme values of a quality, but also the real and potential divisions, inequalities and contrasts in the contingent world. The partakers of these relations are often remote in time or place. By connecting divided sectors of the thinkable world, relations realize divine providence, leading creation to the dynamic peace of deification.[30]

---

24. In *Epistolae* (*Ep.*), PG 91, 513B. Maximos writes that unlike "difference" (διαφορά), relation always presupposes division. The system of relations is a negative of the matrix of overcoming the divisions.
25. *Myst.*, PG 91, 685 B; cf. *Myst.*, PG 91, 669A.
26. *Opuscula theologica et polemica* (*ThPol.*), PG 91, 200D.
27. Cf. *Myst.* VII, PG 91, 685AC.
28. *Myst.* 1, PG 91, 665D. The relation of faith, which constitutes the Church, is defined as simple and indivisible: τὴν κατὰ πίστιν ἁπλήν τε καὶ ἀμερῆ καὶ ἀδιαίρετου σχέσιν. It is not quite clear what Maximos means by "simple relation" in this case. Most probably this term denotes a relation, which is neither determined, nor dependent upon other relations. In the same way with "simple being" he denotes divine being, which is non-relative.
29. *Amb.* 74, PG 91, 1216B.
30. Cf. *Amb.* 74, PG 91, 1217AC.

The ontological principles of the essence are embedded in divine thoughts and are unknowable. Being is structured according to an unchangeable pattern and is in constant movement. This movement is not just an incidental disturbance of the peace of the essence,[31] but corresponds to the divine plan. And God constructs this plan not out of metaphysical necessity, but due to His love for the world. Having that in mind, no created essence is absolutely self-dependent: essence is relative, not only because it is caused, but also due to its dynamic existential realization.[32] The essential relativity results in the relations of co-existence that are not pre-determined, but develop as historical events. In these events man plays the central role.

3.2. Anthropological Aspects

The movement of the world towards God is mediated by man. This is why the category "relation" is an essential determinant of human existence and human knowledge: man internalizes relation, uniting the *logoi* of all created essences. The movement of human knowledge, as well as the movement of will, is defined by Maximos as "relation."[33]

In his work *Ambigua* Maximos conclusively demonstrates that the ontological function of "relation" to connect divided but mutually influenced beings, is compatible with human cognition. Being non-relative (ἄσχετος), God can be accessed, only if the level of contingent things is transcended, because all creatures are relative by essence.[34] When speaking of cognitive movement towards the non-relative God, Maximos does not mean that human intellect automatically ascends the cosmological hierarchy thanks to its natural intentionality. The striving for God, as Good and Truth, is innate in the human soul, but it is realized only if the activity of reason (λόγος) is synchronized with the divine knowledge, accessible for the intellect (νοῦς). Only then does understanding become a function of truth, and faith – of certain knowledge. This transformation of human cognitive powers traces out the gnoseological dimensions of deification (θέωσις).[35]

The internalizing of relations through the soul marks the transition to the new cognitive state. As Maximos explains, soul is the border of thought: it is a medium between the thinking agent (intellect) and that, which is thought. The activity of this medium historicizes knowledge, as the soul never reflects

31. *Ibid.*
32. *Ibid.*
33. Cf. τῶν ἄκρων σχέσις (Maximus Confessor, *De duabis Christi voluntatibus*, PG 91, 188B); Φρόνησις μέν ἐστιν σχέσις (*ThPol.*, PG 91, 21B), ἐν σχέσει γνωμικήν (*ThPol.*, PG 91, 172D).
34. At stake here is the overcoming of materiality, of material being and the notions, corresponding to it. Created being should be transcended, as it is *relative* and is grounded on relations.
35. For the deification of human nature in Maximos cf. G. Kapriev. "Die menschliche Natur in Christus nach Maximus Confessor und Johannes Damascenus," in: *Christus bei den Vätern*, ed. Y. de Andia, P. Hofrichter, Wien 2004.

again on that, which was once thought. Grasping an object is a unique movement of thought. From the moment this movement is completed, the subject of thought is always disposable. The intellect is able to activate this thought at any time, without an external activation of cognition from outside. As Maximos puts it, what is once thought of, enters the peace of thought forever. Due to the fact that everything exists in relation to something else, thinking makes the soul an interval (*intervallum*) between all relations in the world: in this sense it is the borderline of all relations.

In natural contemplation the cognitive movement is not initiated by man. Whereas sense perception enables the grasping of the properties of the world, natural contemplation reconstructs the relations among beings. It is some kind of actualization of divine foreknowledge for this world and of the movement towards the eschatological goal.[36] During of His earthly life, and especially on Tabor, Christ gave instructions as to what could be grasped "after Him" and "concerning Him."[37] In order to participate in the Christological event, man should be on the border and be a border between God and what is after Him.[38]

The process depicted by Maximos does not merely exemplify the ontology of the intellect. The dynamic peace in the eschaton is a state of the world, which is realized within the borders of individual human existence. In human mental and corporeal existence the extreme values of the world are preserved and overcome: borders penetrate each other (περιχώρησις τῶν ἄκρων) and the being of creatures is validated on a new level. Thus human thought is transformed in a unifying relation, encompassing everything, which is after God, and bringing everything to God.[39]

Striving towards divine love requires the cognitive achieving of all things.[40] At the same time, the soul should overcome the relations with the sensible; otherwise it would be ruined by the passions.[41] From a passive recipient, sense perception turns into a unifying relation between the "divided extremes." Imagination becomes subservient to reason, whereas reason, on its turn, opens up for the uncreated light. Thus the non-relative God becomes accessible to creation in His benevolence.[42] Through his acts in creation, God is the extreme of each relation.

The realization of the transition depicted is the task of practical philosophy. Purification of soul is needed, whereby the intellect is deified by the Holy Spirit. Maximos warns that the process is stochastic, and is not manageable by algorithms.[43] Of crucial importance is imagination. Although it

36. *Amb.* 74, PG 91, 1217D.
37. *Amb.* 36, PG 91, 1156B.
38. *Amb.* 74, PG 91, 1217C.
39. *Amb.* 76, PG 91, 1228D–1229A.
40. *Ep.*, PG 91, 401–404.
41. *Ep.*, PG 91, 392D.
42. *Ep.*, PG 91, 38B.
43. *Amb.* 78, PG 91, 1233A.

should be eventually overcome, it plays crucial role in tracing unifying relations in the fragmented world.[44] Practicing virtues is a relative exchange of energies between the opposing poles of the world.

Marriage will serve as our example. Man has the task to overcome sexual division and through marriage he bridges the gap (*intervallum*) between manhood and womanhood. Marital virtues strengthen this unifying relation and protect it from the destructive passions. Thus marriage becomes part of the hypostasis of Christ. At stake is not a mere natural relation, resulting from the desire of the eros. The ἀπάθεια, seen as the optimum of marital virtuousness, guarantees that the internalized relation is not subordinate to natural necessity, but rather a function of sense or cognitive intentionality. The energy of relation is transformed into a stable state of Christ-like human hypostasis. This state is called by Maximos "theological contemplation." This change corresponds for Maximos to the biblical topos of the third heaven. St. Paul witnesses that it is not possible for man to be lifted there. Maximos dares to claim that man himself becomes a heaven.[45]

Maximos develops a similar explanatory model of the historical validity of relations, when commenting on the intentional dimensions of participation in Christ's revelation. The addressing of the will towards its objects is an internal relation of the soul, bridging the extremes and realizing the natural desire for the Good. Man intentionally transforms his own existence in a relation, which confirms a certain individual position (προαιρετικὴ ἕξις).[46] The intentional relation develops into a stable state with the help of divine grace and moves beyond the borders of human nature. This is a divine gift for man.

The internalization of relations does not presuppose multiplicity of hypostatic selfhood: relation is in the ontological order of energy, and not of hypostatic identity, the latter being non-relative. Commenting on the Aristotelian categories, Byzantine philosophers insist, that habit and disposition are not relations in the proper sense, although they bear the characteristics of relations, i.e. manifest existential dynamic and hypostatic uniqueness. Maximos demonstrates that, when internalized, relation develops in a constant state of the person.

Summary

The analysis carried out in this text makes it clear, that the Aristotelian commentary tradition in Byzantium, at least as the category "relation" is concerned, follows the line of the metaphysical model, valid in this culture. The central place of Christ conditions the historical character of revelation, which gives importance exactly to that, which has been considered

44. *Ibid.*
45. *Amb.* 79, PG 91, 1237D.
46. *Amb.* 79, PG 91, 1237A.

secondary and inferior by neo-Platonism, namely individual existence and movement. The function of the category "relation" to indicate the hypostatic and energetic basis of causal interaction stems from the axiom that history is not moved by spontaneous actions or subjectively determined acts of will. On the contrary, history is a development of a program, embedded in the pillars of the contingent world. Each relation holds together divided things and the point of their dynamic convergence is the unity of Christ's divinity and humanity. The relatedness of the so construed concept of relation to human existence illustrates that the criterion for the scope and value of historical events is anthropological. At stake is human existence, in its most powerful manifestation according to the Trinitarian paradigm. This concept is not a precursor to the metaphysics of the person. The internalization of relation does not lead to the proclaiming of an absolute personal subject: it is seen as an indication that the profound base of each relation is God's love for creation. Philosophical thought is engaged in the ontology of encounter, which transcends the discrete conceptual structures and deals with borderline values.[47]

47. This text is an English version of my article "Die Kategorie 'Relation' als geschichtliches Strukturmoment in der byzantinischen Philosophie," which is to be published in: *Metaphysik und Geschichte. Festschrift für Prof. Dr. Günther Mensching*, hrsg. v. G. Kapriev, Sofia 2014.

The Neoplatonic Root of Angst and the Theology of the Real. On Being, Existence and Contemplation. Plotinus - Aquinas - Palamas

Nicholas Loudovikos

1. The Infinite, Contemplation and Angst

It is particularly urgent that we define our relationship with the real. The real, as the rational depth of the concrete being, where the greatest possibilities are flowing, has never really taken on the reassuring face of pagan divinity.[1] Any graduate of Kierkegaard's "school of possibility"[2] knows that all individual finitenesses are raised to forms of the infinite when existential angst crushes us, thus forcing us to search for the ultimate truth. Angst thus appears to be the practical school of contemplation, even when, as in Levinas, it concerns our resistance to the fraudulent attraction of the One for the sake of the communicative multiplicity of persons, for the sake of the "arbitrary absolute" of the human I and the communicative relationship which saves alterity from the dreadful fate of absorption into the One. Even then the "desire of the infinite,"[3] eats away at the seeker, as contemplation of the Good which simply reverses the poles of Neoplatonic transcendentality.

So, does contemplation have to be so closely linked to existential angst? In an essay, Jean Daniélou summarizes the relative Western tradition, writing of "une attitude contemplative."[4] It is not, therefore, only a matter of psychology, despite Kierkegaard's insistence. Because the contemplative attitude is a manifestation of a special contemplative life according to Daniélou, which life, in turn, has to do with the discovery of the interiority of the rational individual, because it is supposed that "C'est en Dieu que nous baignons

1. See G. W. Bowersock, *Hellenism in Late Antiquity*, University of Michigan Press 1990.
2. In his *Der Begriff Angst*. Neu übersetzt, mit Einleitung und Kommentar herausgegeben von H. Rochol, Philosophische Bibliothek, Meiner 1984.
3. E. Levinas, *Totalité et infini : essai sur l'extériorité*, Nijhoff, La Haye 1961, 268 : "Poser l'être comme extériorité, c'est apercevoir l'infini comme le Désir de l'infini [...]".
4. J. Daniélou, *La Trinité et le mystère de l'existence*, Paris : Desclée de Brouwer1968, 43.

quand nous rentrons à l'intérieure de nous-mêmes."[5] The abstract interiority of this enduring Augustinianism is simultaneously the trial and refreshment of anyone seeking the divine, Triune One. Or rather it is refreshment bound to the trial. A violent refreshment that thinks it discovers the "unity in nature" of God and Man (because of the "spirituality of our soul") and rushes towards an intellectual incursion into the divine interiority[6] which results in the possession of God, the only guarantee of the possession of the whole.[7] Such an incursion or possession, regardless of whether, in the end, it is a communion of persons (and there are many emphases on the communion of persons in this particular essay by Daniélou), is stippled with the painful particularization of the living, actual person, and is a diminution of real being. This defines the angst of his contemplation and the meagre joy of its achievement: the contemplative gaze, says Daniélou, is what brings us into the "births and goings forth" within the Trinity, which are the mysterious heart of existence.[8] Contemplation here, then, is an angst-ridden ersatz ontology, an imperfect union of a non-realistic being with its God Who is outside reality? This union is, in that case, a subtraction of the pragmatic and its associated angst, because it is, I think now clear that, within the limits of a particular philosophical and theological tradition, angst is not simply and always an existential symptom but is profoundly bound up with its ontology and the gaps in it.

2. Deficient Existence and the Angst of its Contemplation. Plotinus and Thomas Aquinas

Interiority is without question a valuable Platonic legacy, particularly as, in Plato himself (in the *Symposium* and elsewhere), it is not turned into psychologism. On the contrary, it is concern for the real Being – which for Plato is the soul – and its liberation, liberation of the authentic person from the bonds of the body and material life. Interiority, then, as simultaneous introversion and extroversion, an opening up of subject meaning to the outside, is already linked in Plato with ontology. Of course, in the final phase of his spiritual evolution, Plato attempts to retain some kind of bond of meaning towards the natural Being. In Plotinus, however, we have the full and absolute unfolding of the ultimate consequences of this ontology. Plotinian thought, according to Jaspers the archetype of every metaphysical and every philosophical mysticism, is a re-working of Platonic spiritualism upon

5. *Ibid.*, 30: "C'est en Dieu que nous baignons quand nous rentrons à l'intérieure de nous-mêmes".
6. *Ibid.*, 49 : "[...] ce Pére dans la familiarité duquel nous pouvons entrer".
7. *Ibid.*, 72: "Et il est sûr que dans le mésure ou nous possédons Dieu, nous possédons la plenitude".
8. *Ibid.*, 70.

the background of Stoic materialism,[9] the fundamental characteristic being the theory of emanations which classifies the entirety of beings both ontologically and axiologically in relation to the absolutely transcendent One. In contradistinction to Plato, it is precisely the One's transcendence (in which we may suppose if not Eastern at least Jewish influences – via Philo) and the quasi-identification of the reality of the emanation with that of the "fall"[10] which exacerbates monism to the full: in the end, the world is not the creation of God, but a falling away from Him.

This ontology leads, perhaps for the first time in the history of human thought with such clarity, to the differentiation between people's real existence in the here and now and their essence and its absolute definition of existence, as an ontological lack, as an irrevocable loss of being. A person is complete only in the realm of ideas, as pure soul, as spirit and part of a spiritual universe.[11] In the end, however, to this celestial person came "another person seeking to come into being and finding us there [...] foisting and adding himself upon the person that each of us was at first." The bad thing is that the added presence usually nullifies the activity of the original spiritual essence, making it "unconscious" in the phrase of Pierre Hadot.[12] The "birth" of a person, then, has to do with the profound angst of his division into a Being of essence and a Being of existence. In his existential being, a person, according to Plotinus, is no longer "everything:" real existence means loss and reduction of the Being, by definition particularized. The human soul itself is divided into a more divine soul (VI, 7, 5) and an earthly, "poised above" soul that uses the body. The function *par excellence* of corporeality, sensation, is also the result of the same insufficient "intellectual energy." The existence of a real being is therefore as a trace of life and trace of intellect (VI, 7, 15), the absence and the profound angst over the loss of real life. Real life is recourse to contemplation, without any possibility of making up the ontological lack in our existence: "the good man is he who lives in contemplation." So the

9. E. von Ivánka, *Plato Christianus. La réception critique du platonisme chez les Pères de l'Église.* Traduit de l'allemand par E. Kessler, révisé par R. Brague, J.-Y. Lacoste, Paris: Presses Universitaires de France 1990, 64.

10. *Ibid.*, 73.

11. *Enn.* VI, 4, 14. Henceforth, references will be incorporated into the text. I would also like to list a number of works which might assist in following the thinking behind this study, which, however, remains my own: A. Armstrong, *The Architecture of the Intelligible Universe in the Philosophy of Plotinus*, Amsterdam: A. M. Hakkert 1967; Idem, *Dualism Platonic, Gnostic and Christian. Plotinus amid Gnostics and Christians*, ed. D. Runia, Amsterdam, VU Vitgenerij: Free Iniv. Press 1984, 29–52; Idem, *The Apprehension of Divinity in the Self and Cosmos in Plotinus. The Significance of Neoplatonism*, ed. B. Harris, Norfolk, Virginia I. – S.F.N.S. Old Dominion University 1976, 187–197; P. Mamo, "Is Plotinian Mysticism Monistic?," *ibid.*, 199–211; H. Blumenthal, *Plotinus Psychology. His Doctrine of the Embodied Soul*, The Hague: M. Nijhoff 1971; J. Trouillard, *La Purification plotinienne*, Paris: Presses Universitaires de France 1955; K. H. Volkmann-Schluck, *Plotin als Interpret der Ontologie Platons*, Frankfurt 1957.

12. P. Hadot, *Plotin, ou la simplicité du regard*, Collection des Études augustiniennes. Série Antiquité 123, Paris ^{3}1989, 30.

angst of the loss of Being is transformed into the angst of contemplation: contemplation is also, here, despite the grandeur of its horizons, the radical exclusion of actual existing from the real life (VI, 7, 31). Contemplation means the denial of the existence, not only of subjectivism but of existing itself. And something else: contemplation is a tool to undermine our existence here, a way of excluding it from the possibility of becoming identical with its Being. The concept of nature, in any case, in which some scholars have seen an attempt to bridge the gap between body and soul, is, in Plotinus, prime proof of their ontologically absolute separation, and is more suited to the fallen character of actual existence.

So the "alterity" of existence, as a constituent part of selfhood must be done away with since, by its nature, it constitutes an estrangement from God.[13] Submerged in total transcendence, the One remains absolutely undifferentiated, neither knowing nor seeing itself (VI, 7, 39; VI, 7, 41) and there is no reason, no feeling, no knowledge of it – it does not even produce its own self (VI, 8, 10). Most of all, though, it does not desire us, does not reach out to us (VI, 9, 8). We desire it "of necessity" (VI, 9, 9); Plotinic eros, as Hadot perceptively remarks, is "feminine" (unlike the Platonic possessive, restless, impatient eros).[14] It is a profound passivity, a subtraction, a general expectation and readiness for a divine visitation. This passivity is, in any case, the deep characteristic of inadequate existence which becomes self aware: people are not self-governing, they are not masters of their own essence.[15] Their essence is elsewhere and lords it (tragically) over them. A person is actually a vacuum of essence, an ontological vacuum: our existence is a shadow, intersected by the nothingness of absence.[16] A strange precursor of the ontologies of existentialism, Plotinus continues: for people to gain control over their essence, all that is needed is for the chasm to deepen. We need to accept the nothingness of absence, the annihilation of our existence, as contemplation. Contemplation is the abandonment of happening and chance (VI, 8, 15) of the existence annihilated for the sake of the Good, which entirely expunges the particular physical existence, giving it a horizon of essence which is not now, however, what it was (VI, 8 13). We are masters of our essence only within the depths of the angst which is caused by the annihilation of our Being here in contemplation. The outlook is indeed bright, but actual beings have no part in it.

13. Cf. E. von Ivánka, *op. cit.*, 76.
14. P. Hadot, *op. cit.*, 76.
15. VI, 8, 12: "for the essence in us is one thing and we another. We are not masters of our essence, but essence in us is."
16. That similar concepts about Man have been projected by modern theologians (perhaps in ignorance of the fact that these are the positions of Plotinus) onto Fathers such as Gregory of Nyssa seems to me to be a mistake (particularly in view of Man's eschatological, ontological constitution).

It is, I think, abundantly clear that Greek thought, without the perspective of the Incarnation of the Word, would not have been able to proceed any further. Its greatness, in this case, coincides with the tragic impasse in which Neoplatonism found itself, which in the end brought about its exhaustion. This was caused by the ultimate effort to retain the truth of the Being and its stability. The tragic element lies in the fact that the survival of the Being is undermined by the sacrifice of particular individuals. The very rending of the Being and of existing is a magnificent, devastating movement of most profound, noble despair. Plotinus is extremely moving when he describes, almost deliriously, his philosophical paradise in the last tractate of the last *Ennead*. The individual is identified with the One, is refracted in the divinity ("one both"), finding it within it, it is identified with the Being, becomes the One beyond essence, the real Being: "it comes not to something alien but to its very self; thus detached, it is not in nothingness but in itself [...] it becomes something not of essence, but beyond essence, with which it engages" (VI, 9, 11). The denial of the individuals leads to the One beyond them, the soul becomes the manifestation of the One, which founds it by destroying it. The individual does indeed, find his supreme Being, but reduces to nothing the actuality of his existence. The achievement of Plotinus in providing the grounds for the eternality of the human individual is therefore undermined, despite its exceptional spiritual significance, by the reduction of his essential completeness.

But this is not the end of angst. Indeed, some of the most painful suspicions unfortunately begin just here. If the estrangement of the being from the One, either as emanation or fall, actually did take place at some time, does this not mean that the being was, by its very nature, already separate from the One? But if this is so, how then is real unity with the One ontologically possible? Is union with so many sacrifices through contemplation, real union, given the abandonment of the real being, necessary in order to achieve it? To put it more directly: how much room does Plotinian contemplation allow to the fanciful and particular narcissism of the philosophical eros? Although the questions are tormenting, we should nevertheless remember that the broad horizons opened up by Neoplatonism worked for the ancient world as the highest training for seeking likeness with the divine, even though this was so limited a possibility within the bounds of Neoplatonism itself.

I would like to attempt a single, delicate foray into Aquinas, the aim of which is to demonstrate how these Plotinic positions somehow became a permanent feature of Western thought. We shall look at Thomas' short essay *De ente et essentia*, which provides an overview of his positions on the matter.[17]

17. *L'être et l'essence = De ente et essentia*, Bibliothèque des textes philosophiques, Paris : Libr. J. Vrin [7]1982.

But first some general observations are in order, with the assistance of perhaps the greatest authority on Aquinas, Etienne Gilson. The existentialist reading of Aquinas that Gilson attempted and the fruitful discussion it engendered is familiar territory. What is of initial interest is the way in which Gilson understands and translates the Thomist terminology. He translates the term *ens* by the verb *be* and *esse* by exist.[18] Gilson considers that the *actus essendi* might, in the distinction between matter and form, be linked to the latter as the form of the species, in which case the whole of the particular Being has the function of matter. This implies the priority of existence over essence: the real Being is merely the existent Being. Existence has to do with the root of the real being, the existent Being is the only real being. But since only God is *ipsum purum esse*, every individual creature has as its limit the potential (in the philosophical sense) of its own Being, of which it manifests the existence. Gilson concludes that for Aquinas the essence of every particular *actus essendi*, which is not *ipsum purum esse*, it is precisely to be nothing but a particular being and not the absolute being. This means that the particular creature is defined as such by what it lacks.[19] The specific beings are creatures which, as in Plotinus, are characterized by fragmentation, the lack of universality. Existence means a particularized Being, fragmentary participation in the Being, exposure to nothingness, depending on the participation in pure existence (*actus*) or potential (*potentia*). In this way, sensible substances "can be ordered in a predicament." "One separated substance is like another with respect to their immateriality, but they differ one from another with respect to their grade of perfection according to how far each recedes from potentiality and approaches pure act."[20] Angels, therefore have more "*actus*" and less "*potentia*" and are therefore closer to pure being, while humans are at the lowest end of the scale of intelligent beings. This is because we have more potential and less act than any of the other spiritual beings, in such a way, indeed, as to require that material take part in our existence, i.e. we acquire a body. Although we have a soul as essence, because we have been thus created we are a compound species and severely restricted.[21] So our composite nature, as a condition of actual existence, means a reduced existence, loss of being, propinquity to nothingness. Created existence, (especially that of humans), is nothing other, by nature, than a falling away (as regards divine

18. E. Gilson, *Le Thomisme. Introduction à la philosophie de Saint Thomas d'Aquin*, 6th edition, Vrin ^{7}1982.
19. *Ibid.*, 178 : "En effet, l'essence d'un acte fini d'exister consiste à n'être que tel ou tel esse, non l'esse pur, absolu et unique dont nous avons parlé. L'acte d'exister se specifie donc par ce qui lui manque."
20. *De ente et essentia*, V.
21. Ibid. "Since, among intellectual substances, the soul has the most potency, it is so close to material things that a material thing is brought to participate in its existence: that is, from the soul and the body there results one existence in one composite thing, although this existence, as the existence of the soul, is not dependent on the body."

perfection), to the extent that in fact it extends to most dimensions of the actual. The full reality of the creation for Aquinas would simply be a totality of things, for some of which he would sometimes hesitate to use full ontological categories.[22] Actual existence, therefore, means a distance from the real Being. Participation in Being means a reduction of the existential completeness of creation for the sake of a spiritualistic *actus*. Existing, in general, means a lack of being, a reduction in essence. In Thomas, existence is the lack of universality, i.e. of pure existing. Conceiving it intellectually, he thinks of it as a "structure," bounded by its potentiality, i.e. excluding the infinite. It follows that ontic nature exists by definition as the opposite of the whole. For this reason, a philosophical kind of apophaticism is plainly present in Thomist thought, marking the innate and insurmountable weakness of the particular to exist in the mode of existence of the whole. Much later, existentialism itself would also include in its influences the proposition that we people do not possess pure existence. Of course Thomas differs from Plotinus as he allows participation in God to fulfil the creature's destiny, but, let us not forget, on the other hand, that he considers full divine contemplation in this life as impossible, precisely because of the present connection of the soul with a body; if, in order to achieve divine vision, the human mind must be "cut off" from its bodily existence "either by death or ecstasy," then the angst of the lost physical existence marks this sort of contemplation again.[23] The Aquinatian "logical" definition of existence is not necessarily philosophically wrong, but it is, as I think, simply inadequate, compared with its theological explanation, along with the theological understanding of participation, made by some representatives of the Greek Patristic tradition.

A brief reference to Heidegger might be sufficient to show the fate of the absorption of such positions into Western thought. Heidegger has been chosen because he attempted so insistently to deconstruct the traditional *cogito* on the one hand, and, on the other because he represents perhaps the most potent anti-Platonist of modern times, i.e. someone who attempted to undermine every ideal form with a timeless value, linking the truth not with a Being beyond the heavens but with a being (*Dasein*) profoundly finite in terms of time. In the light of the observations we have made so far, we can see another dimension, particularly as regards the issue of angst, which characterizes the access of the authentic *Dasein* into the spatio-temporal matrix. Heidegger tells us that the fundamental condition of us humans in the world is angst and what causes it is the world as such.[24] We have angst because of this being in the world (*in-der-Welt-sein*). Our angst opens up our *Dasein* as an individuated potential[25] and we have angst over precisely this potentiality. This angst evolves into angst in the face of death as the inevitable

22. E. Gilson, *op. cit.*, 177.
23. SCG III, 46, 2; ST I, 12, 11.
24. M. Heidegger, *Sein und Zeit*, 187.
25. *Ibid.*, 188.

culmination of this individuation – as Being towards Death, *Dasein* experiences angst[26] in the face of the ultimate nothingness of the world. Heidegger concludes: "Das Nichts, davor die Angst bringt, enthüllt die Nichtigkeit, die das Dasein in seinem Grunde bestimmt, der selbst ist als Geworfenheit in den Tod (The nothing which angst brings manifests the nullity which defines Dasein in its very basis, which itself is like projection into death)."[27]

Such a phrase could not have been written unless for centuries an ontology had been regularly absorbed which considered existence as lack of being, as a fall, as a reduction in essence.[28] The cosmological nothingness of the infinite potentialities revealed by the ontic-ontological difference, means the nullification of the actual *Dasein*; makes death manifest as the only prospect of its existence – i.e. the only way towards the meaning of the Being. Despite his anti-Platonism, Heidegger is here unable to escape Platonic transcendence. Death is the fate of the utmost reduction of the actual being, existence writhes in the ultimate angst, in this case, of its cosmological contemplation, without there being the slightest possibility of opening up the *Dasein* as such to the One, exactly as in Aquinas and Plotinus.

3. *The Real as Nature and Vision of God. Saint Gregory Palamas*

The issue with Hesychasm is that its absorption into scholarship was interrupted suddenly and early. The fall of the Empire and the resultant decapitation of the scholarship of the Greek nation in the 15th century, the terrible vicissitudes of the centuries-long, barbarous occupation and, thereafter, the impositions of the West and the brutal clashes over confessions forced the Eastern Church, for a long time, to put its energies into preservation and conservation. The Orthodox Church in Russia was unable to undertake the task, for the reasons described by Florovsky.

This prevented a real, in-depth dialogue between the victors of the Hesychast conflict, the Hesychasts, and those who were defeated, their, roughly-speaking, Westernizing opponents. There were two appalling consequences of this situation. In the first place, Hesychasm gradually gave the impression of real and substantive opposition to humanism, both classical and medieval and the natural, cosmological and, in part, metaphysical dimension of philosophy, whereas in fact it represented a drastic reacquisition, critique and transformation of all these (even though this was formulated largely through thinking and experience rather than in a historico-philosophical manner).

26. *Ibid.*, 266.
27. *Ibid.*, 308.
28. The human body is now emphatically absent from the reflections in *Sein und Zeit*. P. Ricoeur, noting this (*Soi-même comme un autre*, Paris: Seuil 1990, 378–379), observes that Heidegger has probably identified the given facts related ontologically to the body with the inauthentic human manner of existence. Is this, too, an unconscious link to the past which we are discussing?

It is therefore unfortunate, but true, that a good deal of obscurantism has crept in to Orthodox theology, especially in recent years, making it impossible to hold the potentially invaluable dialogue between Hesychasm and the human sciences and philosophy which would provide these with new horizons. The second disastrous effect is that, having already excluded any vibrant and meaningful communication between Hesychasm and philosophy and science in general, when, in recent years, a scholarly interpretation of Hesychasm was needed, what in fact occurred was the injudicious and unconscionable introduction of a truly foreign conceptual framework (or rather spiritual outlook) derived principally from the Neoplatonic tradition, which has interpreted Hesychasm in terms and ways which risk being at odds with its actual spiritual depths. Hesychasm thus becomes the monophysite, idealistic, closed "spirituality," embodying all the past moralism and legalism in a new, particular kind of ontological perspective, which I've called the will to power.[29] I therefore think it urgent that we work today to seek the authentic Orthodox criteria for an interpretation of Hesychasm, highlighting, at the same time, its vibrant topicality in the face of modern philosophical and anthropological demands. The first steps in this direction have, in fact, already been taken, but there is a long way still to go.

So with the prospect of the search for such criteria (somewhere between the insecure calcification of confessional, ideological positions and naïve, narcissistic theological euphoria) we are, in the first place, obliged to clarify the relationship of Palamism to Neoplatonism. The challenge of Endre von Ivanka[30] is a good start in this direction. Ivanka's arguments centre, of course, on the distinction between the One and the many which he observes in Palamas' thought, the attempt to describe the creation of the many and their return to the One, the union of the world and the One through the energies, and other related problems. In this way, Palamas is declared by Ivanka to be a Neoplatonist. This is far from being the case, however, as we shall see directly, though starting somewhere else. In accordance with the criteria of the present chapter, that starting-point can be the distinction in Palamas between essence and existence.

This distinction is, indeed, present in the work of Palamas and we shall study it in its main manifestations, on the one hand in *One Hundred and Fifty Chapters, Natural, Theological, Ethical and Practical* and, on the other, in the *Triads in Defence of those Living as Hesychasts in Sanctity.* In the chapters, then, the reasoning soul is considered to have life as its essence (31, 32, 33). The meaning of life here is not thought of only in its psycho-biological significance but also its metaphysical, as "giving life to the body attached" (30). Existence is described by Palamas, when alongside the notion of essence/life, he places "goodness" or "evil" as an existential quality, as potential, existent choice of

29. See my *Closed Spirituality and the Meaning of the Self...*, Athens 1999.
30. E. von Ivánka, *op. cit.*, 369–421.

the individual. In God, then, the identity of essence and existence is complete and this means that God has goodness "not as a quality but as essence" (34). In reasoning creation, existence underscores the potential of the individual to actualize his or her life/existence as "real life" (41), i.e. as existence in goodness which makes the particular person existentially universal. So Palamas' ontology is eschatological: existence is the possibility of free eschatological completion of the whole essence/nature in Christ. A rational person can either live really or be dead to the real life (45), depending on the eschatological mobilization of his existence, which is able to use its nature: "But we confess that our life, by cause and energy is the Son of God [...] Therefore our life [...] is nothing other than the Father, the Son and the Holy Spirit" (114). Existence is not by nature a fall and loss of being, but an eschatological opening of the essence/nature to the real Being. Existence is a gift of God and a way of perfecting nature, which is also a gift of God and not a falling away from Him. All of this, of course, demonstrates the profound absorption of the theology of Saint Maximus the Confessor which Palamas was able to achieve. Without the theology of the will of the former, this eschatology of existence in the latter would be impossible,[31] because it is the will which, as the fundamental existent factor, performs this eschatological opening of nature to its truth. This eschatological ontology of the actual natural person is what makes Palamas the very opposite of Neoplatonism.

Emphasis on this eschatological opening up of real existence is given by Palamas when, taking as his starting-point the "rapture" of Paul, he of necessity poses certain ontological questions (*Triads* 2, 3, 37). At the time of his rapture, the Apostle "was what? Not to be grasped by physical force or rather free of all physical force?" He was, answers Saint Gregory, the light with which he was unified. Through this light he "knew himself." He did not partake in the divine essence, but he did become uncreated by grace. Most importantly, however, he remained entirely himself; it was a case of the opening up of a particular person to eschatological likeness with God. What is fundamental here is that the specific person who was Paul, did not need to become "without form" in the Plotinian sense (*Enn.* VI. 9. 3). The real, natural existence of the person, not merely the intellect, but also the senses "bound together in the Spirit, will see together the invisible light, or better they will become altogether eternal (*συνδιαιωνίσουσι*) through this vision" (2. 3. 50). Before it gives a new dimension to ontology, this understanding of the human framework of body and soul, which will become together eternal through vision/participation, also reorientates theological gnosiology: this is now the end of philosophical "contemplation" and its angst. In the Platonic *Symposium* itself, for instance, there is indeed a bond between

31. I would refer the reader to the first chapter of the second part of my book *Closed Spirituality and the Meaning of the Self...*, Athens 1999: "The Theology of the Will as Transcendence of Naturalism in the Ontology of the Person and History."

the material and intellectual world, in the dynamic event of "birth in the good." But here, too, although we are brought to supreme beauty by beautiful bodies through beautiful souls and through being taught, the natural Being, having first played the role of the first "locus" of beauty and truth, is thereafter unable to be justified irrevocably and definitely within them, to remain together eternally with them. So, once its elevation to the One has been achieved, the body is abandoned, it is obliged to stay behind because it cannot also be presented to the One. How much more true is this in Plotinus, where perceptible beauty is for all intents and purposes ignored for the sake of inner beauty (V. 8. 2), and any staying together eternally is without meaning. (Of course, there remains, especially in Plato, the profound yearning that this might be so, and this is the enduring value of Platonic tradition in this respect).

And if Palamas is so severe towards apophaticism (concerning which every type of philosophical i.e. ultimately Platonic contemplation of the One is so proud) it is because the intellect as well as sensation and the body really take part in the vision, naturally "above feeling and mind" (2. 3. 25). The vision "is suffered," not contemplated and this means, above all, that not an intellectual apophaticism but communion beyond words is suffered (2. 3. 26) as a general passion of the *Dasein*, not as a Neoplatonic angst over the absent existence. Thereafter, of course, apophaticism is adopted, together with cataphatic theology, as a means of preserving, not merely as a way of acquiring, this eschatological, fulfilling opening up of existence. What connection, then, does Neoplatonic cognition (apophatic, of course) have with that of Hesychasm? Since here, instead of Neoplatonic contemplation, we have a new ontology!

Perhaps we would do well to rethink some of our criteria? Because, in his texts, Saint Gregory seems not to be concerned so much with the choice of one kind of apophaticism (of the essence or the person, for example) as to be interested in transcending apophaticism to the degree that this means "contemplation," i.e. what was in his own eyes an incomplete ontology. In the light of such observations, it is clear that an attempt must be made to make a real distinction between philosophical and theological apophaticism: apophaticism is not simply a phenomenon common to both theology and philosophy, and it is not possible to link the two together. The difference is precisely this: in the case of philosophy generally, apophaticism (where it really exists), means no possibility of complete ontology, whereas in theology it means *par excellence* the existence of such an ontology. This statement certainly seems provocative, and at some stage will deserve a separate and much fuller treatment. Philosophical apophaticism is structured as the ontological impossibility of real and complete communion with the One, and herein lies its spiritual depth. As such it deserves the deepest respect and is useful. But theological apophaticism (as a phenomenon which follows and does not precede participation beyond words in the uncreated) derives from and retains the opening up of ontology to the real, natural being and to its eschatological completion. Apophaticism here is a sign of the deep and real communion of the actual individual with his or her actual God (because this means the presence of divine energies, and, indeed, uncreated and divine ones). In this sense there are two features which we might say are fundamental for the structuring of this new "participatory" rather than apophatic, eschatological ontology of existence. First is the importance of the body and the soul's passible part. Indeed, in Barlaam's deprecation of the *Dasein* (2 .2 8 and particularly 11–13) there is a patent Neoplatonic echo which considers that attachment to the energies of the body and the passibility of the soul are darkness for the (rational) soul. Palamas, on the other hand, considers the body to be susceptible of deification and divine communion, since it already has "signified spiritual intentions" (2. 2. 10), it participates in prayer (2. 2. 16) through it the "energies of the Spirit" are put into action (2. 9. 22) and the fulfilling of the commandments is a joint action of the soul and body (2. 2. 20). Furthermore, Saint Gregory reacts (3. 3. 15) to Barlaam's Neoplatonic definition of impassibility as a necrosis of the passibility of the soul, by demanding a metathesis, a transformation, and not a dissolution of the soul's "passive" power of feeling and desiring. It is tempting here to recall the Stoics and their astonishing findings regarding the emotions and the psychophysiology of the feelings. With its central theme the concept of "deficiency" or "privation," Stoic theory came to the conclusion that it is not possible to remove the passibility of the soul from people. Reason itself is not merely divine, but is also a psychological function. And yet, despite these discoveries, natural man is to be rejected with even greater violence than before. The Stoic sage is in reality, "impassive," someone who has set at nought the passible part of his soul. Palamas is at the very opposite pole. Thus, the Hesychast father accepts into the Being all wisdom and all the profundity of the actual, indefinability and multiplicity, body and spirit, the complex and the unspoken, beauty and mystery, feeling and reason, suffering and emotion, light and darkness, material and history, love and hate, music and serenity, contemplation and communion, providing all of them with an eternal future in Christ, so long as they are "transposed" by being in the Church.

It really does require a powerfully Neoplatonic reading of Palamas not to discern the above points. That this Neoplatonic, or rather Origenian/Augustinian,[32] reading is a fact and that it unfortunately dominates the way in which Palamas' work is ignorantly perceived in the realm of Orthodoxy is beyond question. Any opposition to knowledge, unconscious or unabashed, any attack on philosophy, thinking or science per se, any depre-

32. There is an extensive study of this phenomenon in part one of my book *Closed Spirituality and the Meaning of the Self...*, Athens 1999: "The Meaning of Spiritual Being. Augustine and Symeon the New Theologian."

cation of art[33] and, finally, any monophysite devaluation of actual human existence usually has its roots, in modern times and in the Orthodox world, in a powerful unconscious Neoplatonization of Palamas' teaching. But according to Palamas, no tower of contemplation can be constructed upon an absence of real being. The last things are constructed only upon actual nature, in all its indefinable completeness, which is sanctified personally through the ascetic life. And it is not, of course, without significance that the mistaken trends mentioned above are usually followed (in practice though not so much in theory) by a certain bewilderment as regards ecclesiology.

Ecclesiology is, in fact, the second element in this anti-Neoplatonist existential eschatology, because it is in the mysteries that the vision of God is founded, in the Eucharistic manifestation of Christ,[34] not in the will to power of some deficient individual. And at this point Saint Gregory shows how profoundly he absorbed Symeon the New Theologian, Maximus the Confessor and, through the latter, Dionysius the Areopagite. In this particular instance, what Saint Maximus experienced very deeply, was deficient ontology, which also supposes Neoplatonic contemplation. This is why he sought to give an ontological foundation to anthropology, cosmology and his ascetic teaching, through ecclesiology, which he lived – entirely anti-metaphysically – as "Eucharistic ontology." The commotion created in some "traditional" theological circles in Greece by the mere mention of this term, which means the ecclesiastical actualization of eschatology as ontology, the possibility of the entire person being a member of the Church, is indicative of how strong the temptation of the Neoplatonic type of contemplation is in the religious psychology. In this sense, the Palamas vision of God is the end of angst-filled contemplation and the beginning of Being as an ongoing process of communion.[35] The Plotinic union, then, is not entirely real; we need a special psychoanalytic approach of this brilliant revery of the will, which, under the name of *amor intellectualis* manifests the noblest form of narcissism ever known in history. But Palamas is able to discriminate in these matters with remarkable clarity. There are two ways of ascent to the One, he says (*Refut.* IX, 11, 36). The first is that of the philosophers, which he calls "imaginative" precisely because it is only intellectual, without the body, which, as material, is abandoned. On the other hand, hesychast ascent is real, because it occurs through the Holy Spirit and because it involves "every kind of creation." People have to reach

33. From the distinguished H.-G. Beck, who considered Hesychast theology to be "iconoclastic" (*Von der Fragwürdigkeit der Ikonen*, Bayerische Akademie der Wissenschaften, Phil.-Histo. Kl. 1/1975, 1–4) through to a succession of art historians with A. Grabar at the head, Hesychast theology has been held responsible for interrupting the development of Byzantine art. This is not, in fact, the case. It was simply a process of assimilation which was interrupted prematurely because of historical conditions.
34. See, for example, *Hies* VII, 8; XXXVII, 10; XVII, 16, et al. See N. Loudovikos, *op. cit.*; *Homilies* VII, 8; XXXVII, 10; XVII, 16, et al.
35. See N. Loudovikos, *op. cit.*

God bearing with them the whole of the material creation, so that "the image of God will be complete." This is an astonishing transcendence of the whole of the relevant philosophical tradition. For Saint Gregory, the grace of the Spirit enters human existence only because it is uncreated; created grace cannot be united with it. The Spirit creates a mixing up of the whole of human existence, creating not only a new prospect of contemplation, but a new creation and transposing actual existence there.[36] The vision of the uncreated light is due to the alteration of the particular person into the body of Christ, not the other way round. This, in the final analysis is the difference between deficient Neoplatonic existence (even if it considers itself Christian) and real, full, ecclesiological existence: the former "contemplates," the latter "is." This is also the meaning of the sharp distinction between contemplation and communion with God, according to Palamas: "the saints do not merely contemplate, they also commune with the divinity, by grace" (*Refut.* VI. 12, 38).

Conclusion: From the Undermining of the Real to its Theology

One of the fundamental characteristics of ancient Greek thought is, in the opinion of Olof Gigon,[37] its unwavering adherence to the notion of the real/actual, what Greek philosophy called *physis* (nature). The deliberative treatment of nature on the basis of two other fundamental concepts, those of the *whole* and the *principle* gives us that most basic of philosophical categories, the Being. We must not forget that this last concept is bound up with the category of the *general,* which in ancient thought came absolutely before that of the particular, being a facet of the eternal.

It is precisely this steadfast adherence of the Greek spirit to the notion of nature as unalterable perfection of an essential core (as opposed to art or craft) which makes cohesion of the reality of the Being as of the initially general, unassailable and incontrovertible. The unshakeable stability of the Being (regardless of whether this is the Parmenides' Being or Heracleitus' Being-Becoming) became the object of innumerable philosophical efforts and is an invaluable contribution of Greek thinking to the world.

The philosophical sacrifices, however, were considerable and these undermined the achievement until it had to be abandoned, but in such a way that it could be retained in the end as a profound spiritual requirement. The ancient world collapsed with the gradual loss of certainty regarding the feasibility of access to the One and the uncertainty which this difficulty created as regards the texture, truth and actual identity of this supreme hypostasis.

36. See G. Mantzaridis, *Παλαμικά*, Θεσσαλονίκη: Πουρναρᾶ 1983, 175.
37. O. Gigon, *Grundprobleme der antiken Philosophie*, Bern & München: A. Francke 1959, I, 1; II, 3; II, 6; III, 1.

It left behind points of this grandiose contemplation and also the unrelenting angst of the ontological deficiency which undermines it, (even when the ideal of the "divine man" is not discernibly present as in, say, Aristotelian philosophy, the ideal of man as a citizen, which makes him a real being, also works as a way of excluding the natural person from the complete Being, depending on psycho-physical and racial features). Since then, the whole intellectual phenomenon known as philosophy, even when in more recent years it has turned its attention from the general to particular individuality, has involved the threat of existential alienation of the *existant* in the face of his actual incapacity to live for eternity together with the One and to become acquainted with what Kant calls "Selbstheit."[38]

In our own days, the need for a consciousness of their identity on the part of the modern Greeks has pushed some especially important thinkers towards establishing a continuum between ancient Greek and Christian epistemology while ignoring the continuum in the sphere of ontology. Indeed, a generous first interpretation of the connection seems clear: "contemplation" there, "vision" here; "ecstasy" there, "ecstasy" here; "One and many" there, "One and many" here; "communion" there, "communion" here, and so on and so forth. Perhaps there is a suggestion here that the "internal logic" of the ancient Greek epistemological position was such that their Christian "version" is a self-explanatory development of them? But in that case the sense is lost of the difference (or to be blunt, the chasm) which separates the two epistemologies in such a way that it cannot be bridged. The one, despite its profound nobility, despite its angst, remains in abeyance, undermining the actual individual in a bid to save the One, while the other transports the real person to the One in the Spirit. The chasm, or rather leap, is not due to our attempt to relativize the philosophical achievement; it is in fact due to the apocalyptic intervention of the Uncreated, which broadens the horizons to an extraordinary extent, without destroying anything at all.

So if there is any continuum at all between the two traditions, this might be found, oddly enough, in the sphere of ontology. In the sense that Christian ontology actualizes the most profound, unsatisfied desire of ancient philosophy, for the cohesion and unshakeable stability of the One, while not sacrificing real individuals. Besides, it demonstrates that the One is not merely transcendent, but also uncreated: the transcendent One of philosophy, which is also enclosed in a creation-centred way of thinking, is incapable of transposing the world to bring it closer. God, Who is uncreated, however, makes creation uncreated by grace.

38. Hegel's case not excepted, we would say. What is fundamental is the Absolute, which is made self-aware, not the *Dasein* as such, when the latter completes its self-advancement within history.

So we owe the preservation of the most precious philosophical dream to Patristic philosophy. It really is most extraordinary: we can, for the first time, have the whole Truth, the actual Truth about the Being itself, "dans une âme et un corps," as Rimbaud said[39].

39. This paper is a chapter 2, 2 of my *Closed Spirituality and the Meaning of the Self. Mysticism of Power and the Truth of Nature and Personhood* (Athens: Ellinika Grammata 1999), in Greek.

The First Origin, Thinking and Memory in the Byzantine Philosophy of the Late 13th and 14th Centuries: Some Historico-Philosophical Observations

Dmitry Makarov

1. An Allusion to a Neo-Pythagorean Source in the Theology of St. Gregory of Cyprus?

As Harry A. Wolfson noted in his time, discussing the theology of St. Cyril of Jerusalem, "[...] the doctrines which he tried to expound had, before they reached him, already gone through a process of philosophical reasoning; so whatever he says [...] reflects that background of philosophical reasoning."[1] It seems to us that from this standpoint one may look at an assertion from the recently published treatise by St. Gregory II of Cyprus (1241–1290), Patriarch of Constantinople (1283–1289), *An Antirrhetic against the Blasphemous Dogmas of Veccus which had been issued before the Author Ascended the Patriarchal Throne by the Grace of God.*[2] Here we read in the Ch. 5 that God the Father is "[...] the *originating* (πηγαῖα) *source* of Godhead, the natural *Beginning* (ἀρχὴ) and the *Root* (ῥίζα) of the Son and the Spirit [...]"[3]

1. H. A. Wolfson, "Philosophical Implications of the Theology of Cyril of Jerusalem," *Dumbarton Oaks Papers* 11 (1957) 1–19: 19.
2. According to Metropolitan Chrysostomos (Savvatos), the treatise in question was written between January 12th, 1283, and March 23rd, 1283 ; S. E. Chrysostomos Sabbatos, "Le 'Discours antirrhétique contre les blasphèmes de Bekkos' du patriarche Grégoire II de Chypre et son oeuvre intitulée 'Sur la procession du Saint-Esprit,'" in: J.-C. Larchet, éd., *La vie et l'oeuvre théologique de Georges/Grégoire II de Chypre (1241-1290), patriarche de Constantinople*, Paris 2012, 132, n. 11 (132–133); 145, n. 53. The target of St. Gregory's criticism was the Latinophile Patriarch John XI Veccus (Beccos) (1275–1282). From the secondary literature on his theological views see especially N. Γ. Ξεξάκη, *Ἰωάννης Βέκκος καὶ αἱ θεολογικαὶ ἀντιλήψεις αὐτοῦ*, Ἀθῆναι 1981.
3. Grégoire II de Chypre, "Discours antirrhétique contre les opinions blasphématoires de Bekkos," éd. par le hiérom. Th. Kislas sur la base des travaux préparatoires du métr. Chrysostomos Sabbatos, trad. par F. Vinel, ch. 5, in : J.-C. Larchet, éd., *La vie et l'oeuvre théologique de Georges/Grégoire II de Chypre...*, n. 2, 170.5.1–2.

Certainly, God the Father was said to be "the Origin and the Root" of both God the Son and the Holy Spirit in the 24th homily *Against the Sabellians, Arius and the Anomeans*,[4] which until recently was ascribed to St. Basil the Great and considered to be a part of his homiliary. But in 1990 the homily was reattributed to Apollinarius of Laodicea (CPGS [2243],[5] [2869], 3674).

Besides that, one may suggest another source, not as obvious as the aforementioned homily, but rather cryptic, having been used by Gregory of Cyprus. And, indeed, the word combination of ἀρχὴ καὶ πηγὴ καὶ ῥίζα τῶν πάντων can be seen in *The Exposition of the Things Mathematical Useful for Reading Plato* by the philosopher and mathematician, Theon of Smyrna (2nd century C.E.). As Theon puts it: "[...] according to the Pythagorean tradition, the numbers are *the beginning, the origin, and the root of everything*."[6] Might not this have been the case, evidenced by St. Gregory of Cyprus' hinting so elegantly about his acquaintance with some branches of Neopythagoreanism, as well as at a certain profit of this tradition for a human mind seeking after the truth?

St. Gregory's profound knowledge of ancient Greek philosophy cannot be called into question. It is not by chance indeed that Theodoros Alexopoulos has already underlined a typological affinity between his doctrine on the monarchy of God the Father, on the one hand, and Plotinus' teaching on the One (*Enn.* III, 8, 10)[7]. Alexopoulos' assumption will appear to be quite probable, if one takes into account the significance of the great Neoplatonist for Greek philosophy and science, but it may be hard to prove it unambiguously. On the other hand, John Whittaker has ascertained the fact of Barlaam the Calabrian (*ca.* 1290–1348) having cited from memory the two fragments from Syrian's *A Commentary to the Metaphysics of Aristotle* which were especially dedicated to Neopythagoreans (*In Metaph.* 166.3 ff. Kroll; 183.1 ff. Kroll).[8] The point in the both passages was just the absolute transcendence of the First Origin. This fact corresponds to Barlaam's thought about a concordance between those Neopythagorean teachings, on the one hand, and the treatise *On*

4. S. Basilii Magni *Homilia contra Sabellianos, et Arium, et Anomoeos*, PG 31, 609B.
5. With a characteristic note: "Apollinario Laodiceno attribuendum uidetur," in: M. Geerard, J. Noret, cura et studio, addiv. F. Glorie et J. Desmet, *Clavis Patrum Graecorum. Supplementum...*, Brepols, Turnhout 1998, 64. According to Manlio Simonetti (1990), the homily was written by an unknown follower of Apollinarius between 380 and 400 (*Ibid.*, 203). Cf. Н. И. Сагарда, *Лекции йо йаШролоїии, I-IV века*, Москва 2004, 642 and n. 4.
6. *Expositio* 17, 28–18, 2, Hiller. Italics are mine, D. M.
7. T. Alexopoulos, "Die Argumentation des Patriarchen Gregorios II. Kyprios zur Widerlegung des Filioque-Ansatzes in der Schrift 'De Processione Spiritus Sancti,'" *Byzantinische Zeitschrift* 104, 1 (2011) 1–39: 10–11. According to John Rist, the One was conceived by Plotinus as God, whereas the Mind (Nous) could sometimes be referred to as the *Second* God. See J. M. Rist, "Theos and the One in Some Texts of Plotinus," in: Idem, *Platonism and its Christian Heritage*, London: VR 1985, VII, 169– 180, esp. 179–180.
8. J. Whittaker, "The Pythagorean Source of Barlaam the Calabrian," in: Idem, *Studies in Platonism and Patristic Thought*, London: VR 1984, XIV, 155–158, esp. 156.

the Mystical Theology by Pseudo-Dionysius the Areopagite, on the other.[9] Interestingly enough, as John Whittaker has noticed, that the best manuscript containing the works of Syrian, i.e. *Paris. Coisl.* 161, originates from the 14th or 15th centuries. It formed a part of the library of the Great Laura on the Holy Mount Athos,[10] this fact being an additional proof of a certain acquaintance with neo-Pythagoreanism on behalf of both the Athonite monks and their adversaries. In a situation like this, our assumption concerning St. Gregory of Cyprus' possible cognizance of some neo-Pythagorean texts does not look highly improbable.

2. God as Thinking: On a Seeming Consonance between Barlaam the Calabrian and Theophanes of Nicaea

In the Sixth chapter of Barlaam the Calabrian's second treatise *On the Procession of the Holy Spirit, against the Latins* one is struck with such a phrase: "We affirm, then, that God conceives (νοεῖν) Himself [...]"[11].

Commenting on the passage in question, the prominent Greek historian of Byzantine philosophy, John Demetracopoulos, has adduced the only excerpt from St. Gregory of Nyssa's *On the Soul and Resurrection* which sounds as follows: "Godhead knows (γινώσκει) Himself; and the knowledge turns into love."[12]

The scholar suggested that this was "presumably" the only passage in the Fathers' writings, which touched upon the topic. But in the 14th century Theophanes III, Metropolitan of Nicaea,[13] wrote in his *Second Oration on the Taboric Light* (*ca.* 1369–1376) with a reference to St. Maximus the Confessor:

9. Ibid., 155–156. Barlaam is making a reference here to the 5th chapter of the *MT*, where God is described in extremely apophatic terms. So the Calabrian asserts that God is beyond any affirmation or negation, as existing in a way "transcendent to all" (literally "beyond everything," ἐπέκεινα τῶν ὅλων) (*MT* V, in: G. Heil, A. M. Ritter, hrsg., *Corpus Dionysiacum. Bd. II. De coelesti hierarchia. De ecclesiastica hierarchia. De mystica theologia. Epistulae*, Patristische Texte und Studien 36, Berlin, New York 1991, 149.1–150.9, esp. 150.5–9. On the Neopythagorean counterparts of the last formula see J. Whittaker, "ἐπέκεινα νοῦ καὶ οὐσίας," in: Idem, *Studies in Platonism and Patristic Thought*, n. 8, XIII, 91–104.
10. J. Whittaker, "The Pythagorean Source...," n. 8, 157 and n. 7 (a reference is made to the description of the Le fonds Coislin by Fr. Devreesse).
11. A. Fyrigos, a cura di, *Barlaam Calabro, Opere contro i Latini* II, Studi e Testi 348, Città del Vaticano 1998, 422.94.
12. S. Greg. Nyss., *De anima et Resurrectione Dialogus*, PG 46, 96C; J. A. Demetracopoulos, "Further evidence on the ancient, patristic, and Byzantine sources of Barlaam the Calabrian's 'Contra Latinos.' À propos de A. Fyrigos (ed.), Barlaam Calabro, Opere contro i Latini", *Byzantinische Zeitschrift* 96, 1 (2003) 104, n. 64.
13. Despite Theophanes' having not been canonized (on the reasons of such a development see D. Makarov, "Determining the Historical Context of Theophanes of Nicaea's Theological Propensities," *Phronema. Journal of St Andrew's Greek Orthodox Theological College* 28, 1 (2013) 29–52: 32–34, 51), he may be regarded as a teacher of the Church. It would mean that one ought to take his doctrinal views and philosophical statements into account as mostly authoritative for an Orthodox believer.

> [...] When thinking of God, one ought to consider His being according to His essence to be identical with His self-knowledge according to the essence (ταὐτὸν ἐπὶ Θεοῦ νοητέον τό τε κατ' οὐσίαν ὑπάρχειν καὶ τὸ γινώσκειν ἑαυτὸν κατ' οὐσίαν). And, indeed, knowing is the cogitative part of the knower's getting conformable to the known (τὸ γίνεσθαι [...] κατὰ τὸ γινωσκόμενον). But the essence of God is unique and simple, containing no otherness within itself. Besides that, it is totally Mind (νοῦς), and it is totally the Wisdom-in-itself (αὐτοσοφία), so that its being as the Mind and as the Wisdom-in-itself is identical to its being as such, the more so as the divine Maximus contends in the 82nd of his *Chapters on Theology*: "But God Himself, Who is total and unique, is Thinking according to His essence, whereas He, Who is total and unique, is essence according to His thinking."[14] In the case of God, therefore, His thinking and His essence are identical [to each other] [...] It follows that, as the essence of God is concerned, being [as such] is equal to its knowing itself (ταὐτὸν ἄρα ἔσται τῇ οὐσίᾳ τοῦ Θεοῦ τὸ εἶναι τῷ ἑαυτὴν γινώσκειν).[15]

It is self-evident that this view of St. Maximus the Confessor and of Theophanes of Nicaea, who tried to interpret this great Father in his own way, represents a much closer parallel to Barlaam of Calabria than the passage from St. Gregory of Nyssa.

Turning to St. Maximus' thought in its essence, one realizes that it was probably the Byzantine Palamite monk David Disypatos who came up with its most profound exegesis in the 14th century. Disypatos underscored[16] that God *is* Essence and Thinking and, therefore, He *possesses* both Essence and Thinking, but in a superessential (ὑπερουσίως)[17] and ineffable way. He is, then, neither Essence nor Thinking in our human understanding of these categories. It is due to His superessential mode of possessing this, first of all, and to the fact that the energies of God *are* the very Divine life, and not an analogue of any group of qualities which come together in a material substrate.[18] We tend to think that it is just this parallel from David Disypatos that enables one to better seize the Byzantine background and an implication of

14. S. Max. Conf., *Capita theologica et oeconomica* I, 82, PG 90, 1115C.
15. Γ. Θ. Ζαχαροπούλου, *Θεοφάνης Νικαίας (‡1380/1381). Ὁ βίος καὶ τὸ συγγραφικό του ἔργο*, Byzantine Texts and Studies 35, Θεσσαλονίκη 2003, 197.994–198.1010; cf. Χ. Σωτηρόπουλος, *Νηπτικοί και πατέρες των μέσων χρόνων*, Αθήνα 1996, 224.1033–1041, cf. ll. 1041–1048.
16. With a reference to S. Max. Conf., *Capita theologica et oeconomica* II, 3, PG 90, 1125D.
17. The notions "super-essentiality" and its cognates were introduced into Christian thought by the Areopagite (most likely, via Proclus). This notion is attested to in the *Corpus* no less than 4 times, whereas its cognate, the adjective "super-essential," is attested to about 117 times. See A. van den Daele, *Indices pseudo-Dionysiani*, Leuven 1941, 140.
18. Δ. Γ. Τσάμη, ed., *Δαβὶδ Δισυπάτου, Λόγος κατὰ Βαρλαὰμ καὶ Ἀκινδύνου πρὸς Νικόλαον Καβάσιλαν*, Byzantine Texts and Studies 10, Θεσσαλονίκη 1973, 62.28–64.28. There exists a Russian translation of the text, together with a scientific commentary by Dmitry Birjukov. See A. I. Solopov, D. S. Birjukov, eds., *Монах Давид Дисипат, Полемические сочинения. История и богословие паламитских споров*, Σμάραγδος φιλοκαλίας. Византийская философия 9, Святая гора Афон, Москва 2012, 188–192. On the Stoic origin of the teaching on the substrate

Theophanes' thought, despite the apparent affinity between our Metropolitan's line of reasoning and that of Aquinas' *Summa contra Gentiles* (SCG I, 46; III, 53).[19] I suppose that the implication under analysis may be that the Divine Mind might well be for Theophanes one of the energies of God, inextricably interconnected with the Divine essence due to the essence-energies *interpenetration*.[20] Certainly, such an interpretation of the identity between the Divine Mind and the Divine essence was unacceptable for Barlaam. So an assumption that Theophanes of Nicaea might have been influenced by the *Second treatise against the Latins* by Barlaam the Calabrian would be untenable, the more so as David Disypatos, being a prominent Palamite of the mid-14th century, came out with a severe criticism of Barlaam and Akindynos.

3. Theophanes of Nicaea, St. Gregory of Nyssa and Aristotle on Sensation and Memory: The Statement of the Problem

"What would be terrible is to lose one's memory [...]"[21] The idea expressed by the modern writer is not only topical for us; it was also worthwhile for the bearers of the Byzantine culture who held in high esteem human personality and each human being's uniqueness which was understood in the image and likeness of Christ, the Incarnate God-man. It is therefore quite natural, that in the harmonically well-balanced and attuned nature of human beings, one of important links turns out to be *the memory*. It is thus by analyzing Theophanes' conception of the memory and its faculties that we are going to finish our paper.

A small problem is that the corresponding speculations turn up in an anti-Palamite's putative speech, which opens the *Fourth treatise on the Light of Tabor*

---

and qualities see D. S. Birjukov's, 192, n. 85, where the following fragments are referred to: SVF I, 493; II, 318, 374, 376, 380.

19. SCG I, 46 [[...] evidenter apparet quod intellectus divinus nulla alia specie intelligibili intelligat quam sua essentia [...] non est in intellectu ejus aliqua species praeter ipsam divinam essentiam]; III, 53 [[...] Deo idem esse est quod intelligere [...]]; Г. И. Беневич, "Феофан Никейский. Между паламизмом и антипаламизмом; влияние Фомы Аквинского (по монографии И. Полемиса)," in: G. I. Benevich, D. S. Birjukov, eds., *Антология восточно-христианской богословской мысли: Ортодоксия и гетеродоксия*, Σμάραγδος φιλοκαλίας. Византийская философия 5, Москва, Санкт-Петербург 2009, V. 2, 576–577. In Marcus Plested's recent book one will find no mention of this example of affinity at all; M. Plested, *Orthodox Readings of Aquinas*, Oxford 2012, 89–95.
20. One of the most prominent Byzantine treatises where the topic of the interpenetration of the Persons of the Holy Trinity is penetratingly discussed is Nicephorus Blemmydes' *Another Syllogisms on the Procession of the Holy Spirit*. See M. Stavrou, ed., *Nicéphore Blemmydès, Œuvres théologiques*, Vol. II, Sources Chrétiennes 558, Paris 2013, 222–232. We've prepared a Russian translation of the text in our book: Д. И. Макаров, *Мариолоīия Феофана Никейскоīо в конт̄ексте визант̄ийской боīословской т̄радиции (VII - XIV вв.)*, Санкт-Петербург 2015, 298–302.
21. M. Frisch, *Man in the Holocene* (1979). Cited in our back translation from the Russian rendering of the novel in: M. Frisch, *Homo faber. Montock. Chelovek pojavljaetsja v epochu golocena. Sinjaja boroda*, Moscow 2004, 248.

(*ca.* 1369–1376).[22] Nevertheless, Theophanes never demonstrates any zeal to distance himself from those views of his theological opponent. Let us take as the first example the treatment of pronounced speech, or, to put it in a Stoic manner, of the pronounced word (λόγος προφορικός). Whoever might have authored the corresponding theory in the 14th century, it clearly reveals its Cappadocian and Palamite, but in the final analysis, Aristotelian origins.

> [...] a word, – in the construed anti-Palamite's words, – is a *symbol* of the movements of our soul (τῶν τῆς ψυχῆς κινημάτων).[23] First of all, the soul symbolically impresses (τυποῦσα) such a movement by the means of that stream of air, which issues from our mouth, and so brings this flow to *the sensation* of the listeners. Later on, the sense of hearing first perceives the current of air, which brings with itself *these impressions* (τοὺς τύπους), then [the sense] *wipes for itself* (ἀπομάττεται) these very *impresses* (τοὺς αὐτοὺς χαρακτῆρας), like a wax which receives a seal's imprint,[24] and hence (καὶ οὕτως) participates in the movements and thoughts (νοημάτων) of the first soul and grasps them. Now that the hearing has perceived *these impressions* (τοὺς τύπους), like the stream [had done this earlier], it immediately sends them off (ἀποβάλλεται [...] ῥαδίως), because of the flow being humid and easily dissolved (εὐδιάχυτον), whereas *the sensation*, as soon as it gets these *imprints*, instantly *transmits* (αὐτίκα παραπέμπειν) them to *the memory*,[25] since it is indispensable for the sensation to get free of *the impresses* already perceived,

22. I. D. Polemis, *Theophanes of Nicaea: His Life and Works*, Wiener Byzantinische Studien XX, Wien 1996, 15, 75. It is approximately in the same epoch, i.e. in 1375/1376, as we argue, that St. Philotheos Kokkinos, the pupil of Palamas and the instructor of Theophanes, wrote his *Two Treatises on the Taboric Light*; П. Янева, ed., *Филотей Кокин. De Domini luce. За Таворската светлина (editio princeps)*, София 2011; Д. И. Макаров, "Три заметки о датировке 'Двух слов о Свете Фаворском' св. Филофея Коккина," *Вестник Екатеринбургской Духовной семинарии* 1 (2013) 63–69.
23. See G. S. Zacharopoulos' n. 1 on p. 237 of his edition for St. Gregory of Nyssa's *Contra Eunomium*, XII, as the source of this expression and Theophanes' line of reasoning in general. Cf. "[...] The Creator of the logical nature gave us the word (τὸν λόγον) according to the measure of this nature, so as to enable us, through its agency, *to disclose the movements of our soul* (ἐξαγγέλλειν [...] τῆς ψυχῆς τὰ κινήματα);" S. Greg. Nyss., *Contra Eunomii libri duodecim. Liber XII*, PG 45, 989B; W. Jaeger, ed., *Gregorii Nysseni Opera I. Contra Eunomium libri...*, Leiden 1960, 294.18–20.
24. The source of this fragment was also detected by G. Zakharopoulos. It turned out to be a snatch from Elias' of Crete (late 11th –first quarter of the 12th centuries) commentaries to the orations of St. Gregory the Theologian. The text reads: "[...] it is impossible for the sight [...] to approach to a visible thing and *imprint in itself the impressions* (τοὺς τύπους [...] ἐκμάξασθαι) of what is immediately seen by the sight, if there is no lightened air. [These impressions] *are recorded in it, like in wax*, as if they were being delineated (διαγράφονται), and through the sight they *are transmitted to the memory* (τῇ τε μνήμῃ [...] παραπέμπονται) as well as to the common sense [of the soul];" Eliae metropolitae Cretae, *Commentarius in orationes S. Gregorii XIX...*, PG 36, 776B; note 2 (G. Zakharopoulos), 237 (cf. n. 15 *infra*). Cf. in the final analysis: Arist., *De anima* II, 12 424a 15–20 (a sensation is compared to wax); III, 1 425a 25–30 (on the common sense of a soul). On Elias of Crete see: М. М. Бернацкий, "Илия, митрополит Критский," *Православная энциклопедия* XXII, Москва 2009, 281.
25. On the contrary, those parallels from St. Basil the Great, which were adduced to this passage by G. Zakharopoulos, do not seem to be quite convincing, because the editor of Theophanes

> to recover its proper balance and to be ready to perceive other ones thereafter. The problem is that *any sensation* is able to perceive only a visible appearance of the perceptible things, until it comes into direct contact with them (μέχρις ἂν ἀτενῶς προσβάλλοι τοῖς αἰσθητοῖς). But when the sensation recedes from the contiguity (τῆς [...] συναφείας) and contact of such a kind, it thereby casts off (συναποβάλλεται) *the representations* (τὰς εἰκόνας) of the things perceived and passes them on to *the memory* (τῇ μνήμῃ), *so that these representations may be stored there, like in a storehouse* (ταμιείῳ).[26]

In this passage, like in many others, one can see clear traces of Theophanes' succession to the Iconophile theological and philosophical thought with its categorial apparatus. For example, in St. Theodore the Stoudite's *Letter 528* the concept "*impress*" (ὁ χαρακτήρ) designates the theandric Hypostasis of Christ, Which is depicted on the icon of the Lord (ἐν τῇ εἰκόνι).[27] This line of reasoning was to be continued in the 9th century by St. Photios of Constantinople's *Amphilochia* 231. Here we read that in course of the Incarnation the Hypostasis of Christ reveals to the human sight the traits (ὁ χαρακτήρ) of His human nature, which is united to His divinity in the uniqueness of the Hypostasis.[28] In Theophanes, in his turn, we may see the transfer of these Christological categories into the spheres of anthropology and philosophical psychology.

As for the structure of this reasoning in general, in G. Zakharopoulos' commentary those passages from St. Gregory of Nyssa's *Contra Eunomium,* which served as points of departure for Theophanes, are noted. More concretely, the idea of a stream of air being easily dissolved was reflected in the 12th book of *Contra Eunomium*, as well as the conception that the sense of hearing captured the meaning of the words spoken in the *memory* (τῷ μνημονικῷ) of a person who perceived other people's speech.[29]

---

relies too heavily on a supposed affinity between Theophanes' verb παραπέμπειν and St. Basil's formula παρακατέχω τῇ μνήμῃ; see Zakharopoulos' n. 3 on the p. 238 of his edition; PG 29, 2, 521B; PG 31, 200A. See the analysis *infra*.

26. Γ. Θ. Ζαχαροπούλου, *Θεοφάνης Νικαίας...*, 237.5–238.21. Cf. Χ. Σωτηρόπουλος, *Νηπτικοί...*, 252.8–24.
27. G. Fatouros, ed., *Theodori Studitae Epistulae. Pars altera textum epp. 71-564 et indices continens*, Berlin, New York 1992, 790.60–63. For the following analysis important is: V. Baranov, "Amphilochia 231 of Patriarch Photius as a Possible Source on the Christology of the Byzantine Iconoclasts," *Studia Patristica* LVIII (2013) 371–381, esp. 377–378.
28. See V. Baranov, "Amphilochia 231 of Patriarch Photius...," *passim*.
29. See especially: ὁ δὲ τῶν ῥηθέντων νοῦς *διὰ τῆς ἀκοῆς τῷ μνημονικῷ* τῆς τοῦ ἀκούοντος *ψυχῆς ἐγχαράσσεται*, εἴτε ἀληθὴς εἴτε διεσφαλμένος τύχοι; S. Greg. Nyss., *Contra Eunomii libri duodecim. Liber XII*, PG 45, 925B; W. Jaeger, ed., *Gregorii Nysseni Opera I...*, 239.29–240.1; n. 1 (G. Zakharopoulos) on the 237. See the whole fragment 924D–925B (239.6–240.1 Jaeger), especially the following note: "[...] nothing stable remains in a word after its being uttered [literally 'no hypostasis,' μηδεμιᾶς ὑποστάσεως];" Ibid. 924D (= 239.11–12 Jaeger); cf. 977AB (= 283.13–284.1 Jaeger). In the last snatch one may read: "[...] both the draught of the air [from outside] and the inner spirit [from inside] contribute to our pronunciation of words" (Ibid. 977A; 283.14–16 Jaeger). St. Gregory Palamas followed the tradition of St. Gregory of

But the Greek scholar did not take notice of the fact that such a formulation of the *memory-sensation* distinction is identical to St. Gregory Palamas' (*ca.* 1294–1357) differentiation between *sensation* and *imagination*. In fact, *sensation* is able to recognize and perceive (γνωστικὴ, [...] ἀντιληπτικὴ) only the things immediately present, whereas *imagination* (or phantasy, ἡ φαντασία) can do so also in relation to those absent in the immediate perception.[30] It looks as if Palamas was turning towards that tradition of Aristotle's psychology reception, which had found its reflection in the *Epitome of Logic* by Nicephorus Blemmydes (*ca.* 1197–1269). According to Blemmydes, *sensation* and *imagination* (ἡ φαντασία) belong to those cognitive faculties of our soul, which fall under the category of *irrational* (ἄλογοι).[31] He wrote: "*Sensation* is a concrete (partial) recognition of a thing present (ἡ τοῦ παρόντος μερικὴ γνῶσις) [...] *Imagination* is a concrete recognition of a thing absent."[32] All these tenets stem from Aristotle's thesis that " [...] sensation in its operation is directed towards [any] singular [thing]."[33]

As things stand now, one needs not suppose Theophanes' borrowing of Aquinas' slightly similar ideas about the cognitive and reminiscent faculties of the soul.[34]

In a word, Theophanes' passage in question clearly discloses its Aristotelian and Byzantine origins. According to Aristotle, the difference between *sensation* and *memory* lies in the fact that the former stays in the present, whereas the latter is oriented towards the past. This idea was brought forward, first and foremost, in one of the small Aristotelian treatises, to wit, *On Memory and Reminiscence*: "There can be no memory either of the future [...] or of the present, because the latter is comprehended with the *sensation*. For with the sensation we know neither the future, nor the past, but only the present, while the *memory* (ἡ [...] μνήμη) can be of the past only."[35] Elsewhere the Stagirite wrote that "[...] the *memory* is neither *sensation*, nor comprehension, but a trained habit or a condition of anything from these when a span of time has elapsed. And of the present there is no

---

Nyssa more or less strictly, when he denied the appropriateness for anthropology of one of the main Trinitarian analogies, i.e., that of the mind, word and spirit. For all these objects *are devoid of a hypostatic being*; Γρηγορίου τοῦ Παλαμᾶ *Συγγράμματα*, τ. 2, Θεσσαλονίκη 1966, 87.7–14; Γ. Δημητρακόπουλος, *Αὐγουστῖνος καί Γρηγόριος Παλαμᾶς. Τά προβλήματα τῶν ἀριστοτελικῶν κατηγοριῶν καί τῆς τριαδικῆς ψυχοθεολογίας*, Αθήνα 1997, 86. The influence on Theophanes of both SS. Gregories is more than probable.

30. Gregory Palamas, *The Homily on the Presentation of the Most Holy Virgin into the Temple* (BHG, 1095 = *Homily* 53), in: Σ. Κ. Οἰκονόμου, ed., *Τοῦ ἐν ἁγίοις πατρὸς ἡμῶν Γρηγορίου, ἀρχιεπισκόπου Θεσσαλονίκης, τοῦ Παλαμᾶ 'Ομιλίαι κβ...*, Αθήνησι 1861, 173–174.
31. Nicephorus Blemmida, *Epitome logica...*, III, 14, PG 142, 712D.
32. *Ibid.*, III. 16–17, PG 142, 713A.
33. Arist., *De anima* II, 5 417b 20.
34. But cf. *SCG*. II.80.6; *Ibid.* II.79.11: one's intelligence needs the imaginative, remindful and cognitive faculties (*imaginationis, memorativae et cogitativae virtutum*). Unlike the Byzantine authors treated *supra*, Aquinas distinguishes imagination from memory.
35. Arist., *De memoria et reminiscentia* 449b 10–15, Becker.

memory in the present [moment], [...] but *the present is* [perceived] *with sensation, the future is* [got] *with expectation, whereas the past is* [comprehended] *with memory.*"[36]

The raw material of the memory consists of the images or *phantasms* (φαντάσματα). Everything, which is kept in the memory like in a storehouse, exists as the *phantasms.* So the memory belongs to the same part of the soul as the imagination (ἡ φαντασία).[37] The affinity of this idea with Theophanes is probably not so striking, but it comes to the fore when we compare this Aristotelian teaching with the corresponding theories of Blemmydes and Palamas. Nevertheless, the following nuance of Aristotle's thought leaves no doubts as to the pedigree of Theophanes' conception of memory: "As a matter of fact, the originating motion ([both in the sensible things and in one's soul – D. M.] is being imprinted, as an *impression* of the object of sensation, the same way as [the impressions of] finger rings [are imprinted]."[38]

This "theory of the objects' impressions" seems to be borrowed by Theophanes from *On Memory and Reminiscence.* A scholar may be put on to this idea due to the systematic coincidences in the wording and categories, used by both authors in their descriptions of one and the same group of phenomena, to wit, the differences between one's immediate sensual perception of sensual objects, on the one hand, and one's memory about those very objects when they are absent in his or her perception, on the other hand. I think that, if a re-edition or a new translation of Theophanes' treatise is to be attempted, its future editor will have to indicate *On Memory and Reminiscence* and its presumably premeditated retelling by Theophanes in the *Index fontium.*

Last but not least, there exists even one more source for Theophanes' theory of perception. I mean the 15th and 16th chapters from Palamas' *The One Hundred and Fifty Chapters* (*ca.* 1349–1350):[39] "The formations (μορφώσεις) that occur in the senses arise from bodies but are not bodies, though corporeal, for they do not arise from bodies in an absolute sense (ἁπλῶς), but rather from the forms (τῶν [...] εἰδῶν)[40] which are associated with bodies.

36. Arist., *De memoria...* 449b 24–28: ἔστι μὲν οὖν ἡ μνήμη οὔτε αἴσθησις οὔτε ὑπόληψις, ἀλλὰ τούτων τινὸς ἕξις ἢ πάθος, ὅταν γένηται χρόνος. τοῦ δὲ νῦν ἐν τῷ νῦν οὐκ ἔστι μνήμη [...], ἀλλὰ τοῦ μὲν παρόντος αἴσθησις, τοῦ δὲ μέλλοντος ἐλπίς, τοῦ δὲ γενομένου μνήμη. Cf. *EN* IX, 1168a 13–14.

37. *Ibid.* 450a 22–23.

38. *Ibid.*, 450a 30–32: ἡ γὰρ γινομένη κίνησις ἐνσημαίνεται οἷον *τύπον* τινὰ τοῦ αἰσθήματος, καθάπερ οἱ σφραγιζόμενοι τοῖς δακτυλίοις.

39. Nr. 19, according to Rev. R. E. Sinkewicz (the dating is also his): R. E. Sinkewicz, "Gregory Palamas," in: C. G. Conticello, V. Conticello, eds., *Théologie byzantine et sa Tradition II (XIIIe-XIXe s.)*, Turnhout 2002, 144–145. According to a more recent research by John A. Demetracopoulos, the dating of this treatise should be transferred to the winter of 1347–1348; see Γ. Δημητρακόπουλος, *Αὐγουστῖνος καί Γρηγόριος Παλαμᾶς. Τά προβλήματα τῶν ἀριστοτελικῶν κατηγοριῶν καί τῆς τριαδικῆς ψυχοθεολογίας*, Ἀθήνα 1997, 110–115.

40. Cf. for example, Theodore of Smyrna's (late 11th–early 12th century) dubbing of the soul as "the place of the forms" (τόπος εἰδῶν); M. Trizio, "Ancient Physics in the Mid-Byzantine Period. The 'Epitome' of Theodore of Smyrna, Consul of the Philosophers Under Alexios I Komnenos (1081–1118)," *Bulletin de Philosophie Médievale* 54 (2012) 77–99: 85.

They are not themselves the forms of bodies but the *impressions* [or 'figures in relief,' D. M.] (τὰ ἐκτυπώματα) left by the forms, like *images* (οἷόν τινες εἰκόνες) inseparably separate from the forms associated with bodies. This is more evident in the case of vision and especially in the case of objects seen in mirrors."[41]

In the present consideration both Platonic language and imagery (the notions of "formations," "impressions" and such-like) come into notice. More than that, in the following, 16th chapter Palamas introduces one more specifically Platonic term from the theory of matter, i.e., ἐκμαγεῖα (Plat., *Tim.* 50c). And yet, I tend to believe that the Aristotelian epistemology, with its sharp distinctions between sensation, imagination and memory, represents the basic substrate of Theophanes' theory of knowledge, whereas certain influences of Plato, received by the metropolitan of Nicaea through the agency of Palamas' text, represent a superstructure of the theory in question. If one reads the 16th chapter of Palamas' *The One Hundred and Fifty Chapters*, one will get an impression that Theophanes studied the source carefully:

> *The imaginative faculty of the soul* (τὸ τῆς ψυχῆς φανταστικὸν), which in turn appropriates (προσοικειούμενον) these *sense impressions* (τὰ [...] ἐκμαγεῖα) from *the senses* (τῶν αἰσθήσεων), completely separates not *the senses* themselves but what we have called *the images* (τὰς [...] εἰκόνας) in them from the bodies and their forms. And it holds them stored there like *treasures* (θησαυρούς),[42] bringing them forward interiorly for its own use, one after another, each in its own time, even when a body is absent,[43] and it presents to itself all manner of things, objects of sight, hearing, taste, smell and touch.[44]

One can see that what Palamas assigned to one *imaginative faculty of the soul*, which was treated by him in a rather wide fashion, Theophanes related, in the fragment under analysis, to the two different powers of the soul, to wit, to the *memory* as the storehouse of the images of sensible objects, on the one hand, and to the *sensation* as such, on the other hand. Theophanes' theory had only indirect points of contact with the corresponding speculations of Aquinas (see n. 35 *supra*), but it reveals obvious Aristotelian and patristic origins instead (St. Gregory of Nyssa, St. Gregory Palamas). Most likely, Aristotle, Gregory of Nyssa and, probably, *Epitome of Logic* by Nicephorus Blemmydes, together with Elias of Crete's *Commentaries on the Orations* by St. Gregory the Theologian, had been attentively read by Theophanes (*ca.* 1315–1381)

41. R. E. Sinkewicz, ed., *Saint Gregory Palamas, The One Hundred and Fifty Chapters*, Toronto 1988, 98.15.4–11. The translation is also by R. E. Sinkewicz, *Ibid.*, 99.
42. Cf. the image of a storehouse in Theophanes.
43. R. E. Sinkewicz adduces a parallel from the 53rd Homily of Palamas: St. Gregory Palamas, *The Homily on the Introduction of the Virgin...*, 174.1–2; n. 31 (R. E. Sinkewicz) on the p. 101 of his edition of the *Chapters*.
44. R. E. Sinkewicz, ed., *Saint Gregory Palamas...*, 98.16.1–100.16.8. The translation is by R. E. Sinkewicz, *Ibid.*, 99–101.

in his younger years, which were contemporary with the first and second stages of the Hesychast controversy – (1334–1351),[45] and were periodically looked through later on. As for *The One Hundred and Fifty Chapters* by Palamas, it appeared when Theophanes was already a mature person. So he probably studied this writing and then developed his own version of the more or less "mainstream" Aristotelian epistemology, trying to combine Palamas' ideas with the notions and categories of the tradition of the Stagirite. This version not only bore the character of a compilation, but was also characterized by a rather high level of philosophical reflection and, by the same token, it was colored with a tendency to integrate different schools of Greek and Byzantine thought, be they Christian or "mundane" ones, into a coherent system. It is self-evident thereby that Aristotle bolstered Theophanes only insofar as the Stagirite's philosophical psychology did not contradict the Christian Revelation. The same can be said about St. Gregory of Cyprus' attitude towards his supposed Neopythagorean source. Contrary to this, in the anti-Latin treatises of Barlaam of Calabria only accidental affinities to the reasoning of Theophanes of Nicaea showed through. It was conditioned by the reverse correlation in his mind of the ancient Greek and, in general, any "mundane" philosophy, on the one side, and the Christian Revelation and its Tradition, on the other side, as compared to the representatives of the wide Palamite (Theophanes) and "proto-Palamite" (St. Gregory of Cyprus) branches of the latter Tradition[46].

45. I borrowed this periodization from A. Rigo, "Il Monte Athos e la controversia palamitica dal Concilio del 1351 al Tomo Sinodale del 1368. Giacomo Trikanas, Procoro Cidone e Filoteo Kokkinos," in: A. Rigo, a cura di, *Gregorio Palamas e oltre. Studi e documenti sulle controversie teologiche del XIV secolo bizantino*, Orientalia Venetiana XVI, Firenze 2004, 1–177, 2.

46. The research was conducted with the generous help of the Russian National Fund of Humanities, the project No. 15-03-00665 "The Variety of Humanism and of Its Ways: The Intellectual Legacy of Late Byzantium, Thirteenth to Fourteenth Centuries".

Manuel II Palaiologos Between Gregory Palamas and Thomas Aquinas

Ioannis Polemis

I. The case of the "Dialogue with a Muslim"

Manuel II Palaiologos' position towards the doctrinal views of Gregory Palamas has not been clarified yet. R.-J. Loenertz characterized the learned emperor as a reluctant Palamite, a view shared by H.-G. Beck,[1] while J. A. Demetracopoulos has recently argued that Manuel, although a moderate Palamite, made an ample, though not expressedly admitted, use of the writings of the great Scholastic theologian Thomas Aquinas which had been translated into Greek by his close friend and collaborator Demetrios Kydones.[2] The purpose of the present paper is to examine the evidence concerning the doctrinal position of the late Byzantine emperor provided by his extensive treatise *Dialogue with a Muslim*, which records the dialogues he had with a Muslim scholar, the so-called muterizes, while campaigning in Asia Minor in 1391.

The fourth book of that treatise deals with the problem of the participation of creatures in the divinity. Muterizes asks the emperor "how it is possible that mortal men who are plenty of evil passions participate in God who is immortal and beyond all passion?"[3] The emperor answers that

> all beings participate in God, some in this particular way, some in another, some in a greater, some others in a lesser extent, depending on the manner of their nature and composition. However, not even the angels, who come first after God himself, are in a position to participate in

1. H.-G. Beck, *Kirche und theologische Literatur im byzantinischen Reich*, Munich 1959, 748. The edition of the Letter of Manuel to Alexios Iagupes, where the Palamite teachings were discussed, by Ch. Dendrinos was not available to me.
2. J. A. Demetracopoulos, "Palamas Transformed. Palamite Interpretations of the Distinction between God's 'Essence' and 'Energies' in Late Byzantium," in: *Greeks, Latins, and Intellectual History 1204-1500*. Edited by M. Hinterberger, C. Schabel, Bibliotheca 11, Leuven, Paris: Walpole, MA 2011, 327–341. See also Idem, "Pope Benedict XVI's Use of the Byzantine Emperor Manuel II Palaiologos' 'Dialogue with a Muslim muterizes:' The Scholarly Background," *Archiv für mittelalterliche Philosophie und Kultur* 14 (2008) 264–304.
3. E. Trapp, *Manuel II. Palaiologos. Dialoge mit einem "Perser,"* Wiener Byzantinistische Studien II, Wien 1966, 46, 18–19.

> God's essence. But even the mystic ointment is not given to all people in a perfect manner by the inapproachable God who is beyond all participation, being above everything else; I am referring to the divine graces, through which man may come into contact with God. Even saintly men are not able to get those graces in a manner surpassing their own nature.[4]
>
> They participate in incorruption in a manner befitting their corruptible nature; that depends on their cleanness and their preparedness to receive the holy grace. God gives as much as our vessels are able to contain. The divine love is given to us in accordance with our own beauty which shines through our own virtues, in an ineffable manner, which cannot be grasped by any human mind. As soon as God dwells inside us, attracted by our own beauty (God may permit me to speak in this way), he fills his own house and adapts himself to our own peculiarities; in this way he permits us to enjoy his true beauty; I am not referring to his own nature but to the graces belonging to that nature: wisdom, prudence, sanctity, blessedness and all other gifts resembling those ones. However, we may not partake in his essence; anyone partaking in his essence will be destroyed or will become a new God. This is the case with the powers of the creatures: a being coming into contact with something superior will be conquered by it and will be transformed into the essence of what is mightier, unless it is completely destroyed, being unfitting for communicating with what surpasses it. If this is so, how is it possible for a creature which is perishable to come into contact with something uncreated and imperishable without being destroyed? Therefore, as I said, we partake of the natural gifts of God but not of his nature. God is good, wise and blessed, but his essence is beyond those things; he is beyond whatever we may catch with our mind or name or compare with a certain example, being unintelligible and unnameable. That is what concerns the way of our participation in God.[5]

In the passage quoted above the dependence of Manuel Palaiologos on the writings of Gregory Palamas is more than evident. The basic tenet of Manuel's theory is that there is a distinction between God's essence and his energies. The view that wisdom and blessedness are to be considered divine energies is characteristic of Gregory Palamas, who points out that God is beyond his goodness:

> whatever is good, is to be found in God, or rather God is identical with that and beyond that. Whatever one is able to discover in God is good,

4. At this point a slight deviation of Manuel from the Palamite doctrine is to be observed. Palamas insisted that the mystic union of those initiated into the mysteries of the divine contemplation is taking place in a supernatural way; see, e.g., *Triads* 3, 1, 28, in: *Γρηγορίου τοῦ Παλαμᾶ Συγγράμματα. Α΄ Λόγοι Ἀποδεικτικοί. Ἀντεπιγραφαί. Ἐπιστολαὶ πρὸς Βαρλαὰμ καὶ Ἀκίνδυνον. Ὑπὲρ ἡσυχαζόντων.* Ἐκδίδουν B. Bobrinsky, Π. Παπαευαγγέλου, J. Meyendorff, Π. Χρήστου, Θεσσαλονίκη 1988, 641, 4–17. However, that deviation may be explained as due to the use of a somehow different terminology by Manuel.
5. E. Trapp, 47, 13–38 (as footnote 3 above). All translations are mine.

> or rather goodness and a goodness surpassing goodness itself. Life is also to be found inside God, or rather he is identical to life, since life is something good and life is goodness. Wisdom is to be found in God too, or rather he is identical to wisdom, since wisdom is something good and wisdom is goodness. The same applies to eternity, blessedness and whatever good may one discover. The goodness of God is not to be identified with that goodness which may be grasped by the inspired mind of those who think and speak through a tongue which is moved by the spirit. That goodness is beyond these, being unintelligible and ineffable; it is not to be distinguished from that supreme simplicity which is beyond nature. There is a certain goodness, surpassing goodness itself. Our creator, the Lord of the universe may be understood and named, only because he is all goodness and beyond goodness; his essence is identical to his goodness.[6]

Palamas argues that goodness and blessedness are energies of God, though God himself is beyond his energies, and that the names of God refer to his uncreated energies, not to his essence, to which no name can be applied.

Manuel Palaiologos repeats this theory in the ninth book of the *Dialogue with a Muslim*:

> We gain a glimpse of the God who is beyond all beginning not through what is inside him but through what encircles him. That is a passage of a great theologian.[7] [...] Knowledge of God comes to men indirectly. The power of God which brings into completion the result of its energies is manifested through his visible energies; through that power the nature of God which is unintelligible to men becomes manifest to men to a certain extent. The way we apply certain names to God is also indirect. The names of God do not refer to his essence which is beyond the power of our mind; a drop of water is nothing compared to the great ocean, but that comparison cannot adequately describe the distance separating our mind from God's essence. We call him creator, but that name does not refer to his essence; even man's essence cannot be described by that name, much less the essence of God. He is also called wise, good, light etc.; we call him wise because of his power giving wisdom to men; we call him good because he has a power making men good; he is called light because of his power enlightening the human soul; the same applies to all other names. That power, or rather energy, which is named by us, through its various actions gives us a faint idea of the nature, to which it belongs. It is simple, although its results are various. God's nature or rather God's essence is named and grasped by us through that energy which is consubstantial with it; that energy is contained inside

6. *One Hundred and Fifty Chapters* 34, in: *Γρηγορίου τοῦ Παλαμᾶ, Συγγράμματα. Ε΄. Κεφάλαια ἑκατὸν πεντήκοντα, Ἀσκητικὰ συγγράμματα, Εὐχαί*. Ἐκδίδει Π. Κ. Χρήστου, Θεσσαλονίκη 1992, 52, 26–53, 20.
7. This is a passage of Gregory of Nazianzus frequently employed by Gregory Palamas; see, e.g., *Triads* 2, 3, 78, Χρήστου, 611, 25–27 (as footnote 4 above).

> the definition of the divine essence; the essence of God offers us the possibility to know her through that energy.[8]

We may compare that extract of the *Dialogue with a Muslim* with the following passage from the *Chapters* of Gregory Palamas:

> God is called nature of all beings, since they participate in him and they own their very existence to that participation; they do not participate in his essence – far from it – but in his energy. In this way God may be considered the foundation of the existence of all beings; he gives the various species their material shape, being the source of their form; he is also the source of the wisdom of all wise men; simply speaking, he is the source of all things. At the same time he is not a nature, being beyond nature; he is neither being, being beyond all beings, nor form, lacking a proper form, being above all forms.[9]

The same view is repeated in the *Triads*:

> God, being a supra-essential essence, is ineffable, unintelligible, and beyond our reach; we cannot participate in him. However, since he is also the essence of all beings, the life of all living creatures, and the wisdom of all wise men, and in one word, the foundation of the existence of all beings and the power giving them their beauty, God can be grasped by our mind; mortal beings can give him a name and participate in him.[10]

References to the Palamite theory concerning the distinction between God's essence and his energies in Manuel's work are not limited to books four and nine, where the problem is discussed extensively in a more systematic way, but are scattered all over his work. In book XVI we read that God is named after his own energies, and that the energy of the Holy Trinity is one and indivisible.[11] In book VII Manuel points out that "all those who accept and put into practice the advices of our Lord, are adopted by God in a mystic way. This becomes evident through their actions and through the powers of the Holy Spirit, which inhabit in them and come out of them, as if gushing out of a perennial spring."[12] It goes without saying that the powers of the Spirit are to be identified with the uncreated energies of God. In book X Manuel stresses once more that God is known through what is around him, not through what is inside him,[13] taking advantage of the passage by Gregory of Nazianzus he had mentioned in book IX. In book XX Manuel underlines that the heavenly powers participate in God's graces and through them they are able to transmit to us a faint picture of God, whose essence is unknown to

8. E. Trapp, 108, 39–109, 23 (as footnote 3 above).
9. *One Hundred and Fifty Chapters* 78, Χρήστου Ε΄, 79, 14–21 (as footnote 6 above).
10. *Triads* 3, 2, 25, Χρήστου Α,΄ 676, 26–30 (as footnote 4 above).
11. E. Trapp, 200, 12–37 (as footnote 3 above).
12. E. Trapp, 83, 12–15 (as footnote 3 above).
13. E. Trapp, 122, 8–9 (as footnote 3 above).

us.[14] The Palamite distinction is presupposed here, too. In the same book he tries to explain to muterizes why Christians venerate the icons of the saints: it is because they wish to honour the uncreated grace that dwells in them.[15]

How are we to interpret the constant employment of those Palamite theories by Manuel? In my view this is to be explained as a conscious attempt by the emperor to promote Palamism and at the same time to answer the objections of his anti-Palamite entourage. It is noteworthy that Manuel avoided discussing those doctrinal matters with his friend Demetrios Kydones in his copious correspondence with him. It is plausible that in composing his long *Dialogue with a Muslim* the emperor found the opportunity to settle his accounts with the anti-Palamites without taking the risk of openly attacking them.[16] The Palamites' theories are exposed as an integral part of the Orthodox doctrinal tradition, yet the emperor avoids pointing out their tendentious character. Under the cloak of a traditional genre of Byzantine antirrhetical literature, that of the polemic treatises against Islam, Manuel manages to disguise his true intention, which is the defense of the new official doctrine of the Byzantine church, i.e. Palamism.

II. Some evidence linking Manuel II Palaiologos with Thomas Aquinas: The case of the "Verses addressed to an atheist"

That does not mean that Manuel is a defender of all aspects of the hesychastic teaching. Manuel is an ardent defender of the value of Greek learning. He stresses the fact that *logoi* are a source of a pleasure for men,[17] proving himself an heir of the intellectual tradition of the early Palaiologian renaissance. His defense of the value of the *logoi* has a polemic tone; the emperor refers to the enemies of the *logoi*, who consider those unhappy men occupying themselves with them as engaged in useless play. He refrains from identifying those enemies of secular education with any known man or group of his time, but we will not be mistaken if we argue that those men are to be found among the monastic circles of late Byzantium. The fact that this letter is addressed to Nicholas Kabasilas, another leading representative of the defenders of secular education at the time, is not devoid of some interest. That

14. E. Trapp, 244, 6–9 (as footnote 3 above).
15. E. Trapp, 248, 42–249, 3 (as footnote 3 above).
16. I do not deny that Manuel's purpose was to refute the basic tenets of Islam as well; see Manuel II Palaiologos, *Dialoge mit einem Muslim.* Kommentierte griechisch-deutsche Textausgabe von K. Förstel, Würzburg 1993, XXVIII– XXXI.
17. *Letter* 67, 101–105, in: *The Letters of Manuel II Palaeologus.* Text, Translation and Notes by G. T. Dennis, Corpus Fontium Historiae Byzantinae VIII, Dumbarton Oaks, Washington D. C. 1977, 191: ἐκ περιουσίας δέ μοι εἴρηται ταυτὶ πρὸς τοὺς τοῖς λόγοις ὄντας ἐχθρούς. ποῦ γάρ, πρὸς Θεοῦ καὶ τῆς ἀληθείας αὐτῆς, ἢ πόθεν ὅλως παίζειν ἐστὶ τὸ περὶ λόγους πονεῖν; ἀλλ' ἡδονῆς τι μέρος καὶ οἱονεὶ τρυφή τίς εἰσι καὶ οἱ λόγοι, φασίν. It is noteworthy that a similar encomium of the *logoi* appears in Manuel Kalekas, *Letter* 16, 20–35, in: *Correspondance de Manuel Calecas.* Publiée par. R.-J. Loenertz, Studi e Testi 152, Città del Vaticano 1950, 189.

Manuel Palaiologos was unaware of the severe criticism of *logoi* undertaken by Gregory Palamas is impossible.

Manuel is far from expressing the official optimism of the Orthodox; he does not hesitate to curse his own life at the time of his trip to Northern Italy.[18] He even dealt with the possibility that a man of his times may be an atheist and composed a whole poem in order to persuade such a man to change his views.[19] That pessimistic view of contemporary reality is certainly not compatible with the hesychastic worldview. It is worth noticing that a contemporary of Manuel II Palaiologos, the pro-Latin scholar Manuel Kalekas, is happy to declare that those claiming that God did not exist were proved wrong, after the Turks were defeated near Ankyra in 1402.[20] Therefore, the poem of Manuel reflects a certain pessimistic mood of the inhabitants of what remained of the Byzantine Empire at the end of the 14th century. Even Demetrios Kydones, a man of a remarkably sober mood, does not refrain from employing the pessimistic exhortations of the pseudo-Platonic *Axiochus*, in order to underline the futility of all human endeavors.[21]

The subject of the *Verses addressed to an atheist* would suggest to somebody familiar with the relevant teaching of Thomas Aquinas that Manuel took advantage of the famous five arguments of the great Scholastic theologian proving the existence of God. This does not seem to be the case, however. At the very beginning of this poem Manuel points out that an atheist would admit

18. *Letter* 21, 23–28, G. T. Dennis 81 (as footnote 17 above): εἰ γὰρ ὑγιαίνοντες ἡμεῖς, οὐδὲν νοσούντων ἄμεινον διακείμεθα τῷ ἀπροσδοκήτῳ βληθέντες καὶ ἡμιθνῆτες νομιζόμενοι καὶ τοῦ ζῆν τῷ ἀπροσδοκήτῳ βληθέντες καὶ ἡμιθνῆτες νομιζόμενοι καὶ τοῦ ζῆν καταβοῶμεν συνεχῶς, τίς ἂν αὐτὸς παρὼν καὶ βλέπων καὶ ἀκούων ἐγένου χρονίοις προσπαλαίσας νοσήμασι καὶ μηδέπω γοῦν τελείως τούτων ἀπαλλαγείς; οὐδὲ γὰρ βιωτὸν εὖ φρονοῦσιν ἀνδράσιν μετὰ τὸν σκηπτὸν ἐκεῖνον. See also Manuel II Palaiologos, *Funeral Oration for his Brother Theodore*. Introduction, Text, Translation, and Notes by J. Chrysostomides, Corpus Fontium Historiae Byzantinae XXVI, Thessalonike 1985, 249, 12–14: Ἀλλ' οὐδὲ τὸ εὐεκτεῖν καὶ ὅσα καθ' αὑτὰ καλὰ περὶ πλείστου γένοιτ' ἂν ἡμῖν ἔτι. Πόθεν, οἷς γε μηδ' αὐτὸ τὸ ζῆν ἀγαθὸν ὅλως φαίνεται;
19. See the excellent edition of I. Vassis, "Οἱ ἀνέκδοτοι στίχοι 'Πρὸς ἄθεον ἄνδρα' τοῦ Μανουὴλ Β΄ Παλαιολόγου," *Βυζαντινὰ* 32 (2012) 37–100.
20. *Letter* 79, 5–10, in: R.-J. Loenertz, 281 (as footnote 17 above).
21. *Letter* 5, 49–54, in: Démétrius Cydonès, *Correspondance*. Publiée par R.-J. Loenertz, I, Studi e Testi 186, Città del Vaticano 1956, 27–28: τίς τῶν ἡλικιῶν ἐν ᾗ τις λύπης ἄνευ καὶ τοῦ δακρύειν διήγαγεν; ἀλλ' ἐν μὲν τῇ πρώτῃ δῆλον ὡς οὐδ' ἄνθρωποί τινές ἐσμεν καθαρῶς, ἀλλ' ὅσον προβατίοις ἡ φύσις καὶ ἀνθρώποις δίδωσι τότε. Παιδαγωγοὶ δὲ τὴν μετ' αὐτὴν ἐνοχλοῦσι καὶ πατὴρ ῥάβδῳ τὸν υἱὸν πέμπων εἰς διδασκάλου, καὶ τραχεῖ μὲν βλέμματι, ῥήμασι δὲ τραχυτέροις τὴν ἡδονὴν ἐξορίζων. ἡ δὲ μεταβολὴ τῶν τριχῶν πᾶσαν μὲν ἡδονὴν πᾶσαν δὲ ἄνεσιν περιτρέπει. Kydones seems to employ the following passage of *Axiochus* 366d–367a: Τί μέρος τῆς ἡλικίας ἄμοιρον τῶν ἀνιαρῶν; οὐ κατὰ τὴν πρώτην μὲν γένεσιν τὸ νήπιον κλαίει, τοῦ ζῆν ἀπὸ λύπης ἀρχόμενον; [...] ὁπόταν δὲ εἰς τὴν ἑπταετίαν ἀφίκηται πολλοὺς πόνους διαντλῆσαν, παιδαγωγοὶ καὶ γραμματισταὶ καὶ παιδοτρίβαι τυραννοῦντες [...] ἐπειδὰν δὲ εἰς τοὺς ἐφήβους ἐγγραφῇ καὶ φόβος χείρων ᾖ, τὸ Λύκειον καὶ Ἀκαδημία καὶ γυμνασιαρχία καὶ ῥάβδοι καὶ κακῶν ἀμετρίαι.

that there is no possibility of being created out of non-being;[22] that reminds us of the third argument of Aquinas, according to which: *Si igitur nihil fuit ens, impossibile fuit quot aliquot inciperet esse; et sic modo nihil esset; quod patet esse falsum.*[23] We might contend that the argument of Manuel constitutes a faint reminiscence of the relevant argument of the Scholastic theologian; however, extreme caution is needed. Going on, Manuel puts forward the question as to why God created the souls united with bodies, instead of creating them in a state free of all carnal passions; he answers that question arguing that this was impossible, since otherwise God would have chosen to create the souls united with bodies which is something inferior, instead of creating them without bodies which is something superior.[24] This is an argument employed by Aquinas in his *Summa contra Gentiles*:

> Si igitur animas creavit a corporibus separatas, oportet dicere quod hic modus essendi sit convenientior naturae earum. Non est autem ad ordinationem divinae bonitatis pertinens res ad inferiorem statum reducere, sed magis ad meliorem promovere. Non igitur ex divina ordinatione factum fuisset quod anima corpori uniretur. Praeterea. Non pertinet ad ordinem divinae sapientiae cum superiorum detrimento ea quae sunt infima nobilitare. Infima autem in rerum ordine sunt corpora generabilia et corruptibilia. Non igitur fuisset conveniens ordini divinae sapientiae, ad nobilitandum humana corpora, animas praexistentes eis unire: cum hoc sine detrimento earum esse non possit ut ex dictis patet.[25]

Aquinas wonders how it was possible that God created the souls without bodies and afterwards united them with their bodies, bringing them to an inferior status to their previous one. It is true that Aquinas discusses the theories of Origen concerning the preexistent status of the human souls, but his thought closely resembles that of Manuel. It is possible that the Byzantine emperor, in formulating his own arguments, took advantage of the argument of Aquinas in his *Summa contra Gentiles*,[26] which bears a certain similarity to his own view. If this is the case, then the *Verses addressed to an atheist* may reflect some contemporary Byzantine discussions sparked off by the theories of Thomas Aquinas.

---

22. Verses 3–5, in: I. Vassis, 55 (as footnote 19 above): εἰ γὰρ ἑτέρως εἶ φρονῶν, ἄκων ὁμολογήσεις,/ὡς ἔστι καὶ δι' οὐδενὸς ἐξ οὐδενός τε πρᾶγμα/γενέσθαι, ὅπερ ἄτοπον ἑκὼν ὁμολογήσεις.
23. *Summa theologiae I, Quaest. II, Artic. III.*
24. Verses 42–47, in: I. Vassis, 56 (as footnote 19 above): Τριῶν οὖν ἔξεστιν εἰπεῖν ἓν αἴτιον ὑπάρχειν/ἢ ὅτι δυνατὸν οὐκ ἦν ψυχὴν κτίσαι τὸν κτίστην/τῷ τρόπῳ ᾧ εἰρήκαμεν, σαρκὸς ἄνευ τουτέστιν,/ἢ ὅτι καὶ δυνάμενος ἴσως τοῦτο ποιῆσαι, ὅμως οὐχὶ πεποίηκε διὰ τὸ μὴ θελῆσαι/τῷ ἀντὶ τοῦ βελτίονος ἐκλέξασθαι τὸ ἧττον.
25. *Summa contra Gentiles II*, cap. 83.
26. It is worth noticing that in book IV of his *Dialogue with a Muslim* Manuel writes that Θεός ἐστιν ἡ θεία τρυφὴ καὶ μακαριότης καὶ διὰ τὴν εἰς Θεὸν κοινωνίαν καὶ οἱ θεῖοι καὶ μακάριοι τοῦτ' αὐτὸ γίγνονται (E. Trapp 48, 9–10, as footnote 3 above). That reminds us of *Summa contra Gentiles I*, cap. 101 (*Quod Deus sit sua beatitudo*).

On the other hand, in the *Verses addressed to an atheist* some traces of the Palamite teaching concerning the distinction between God's essence and his energies are to be found. Manuel argues that man cannot obtain an exact knowledge of God's nature, but at the same time he is able to grasp with his mind a faint outline of the divine.[27] That reminds us of the distinction between God's nature and his graces or energies introduced by Manuel in his *Dialogue with a Muslim*. Although not speaking clearly about that distinction, I think that this is what Manuel has in his mind.

III. Conclusion

The case of the emperor Manuel II Palaiologos is rather peculiar. While not refraining from having several contacts with the anti-Palamites of his empire, maintaining very close, even friendly, relations with them, at the same time he is not willing to sacrifice the new orthodoxy of the Byzantine church – Palamism, which was officially sanctioned under the auspices of his grand-father, the emperor John VI Kantakouzenos in 1351. It seems that despite his efforts not to alienate the pro-Western party, the emperor was sincerely convinced of the correctness of the Palamite doctrine concerning the distinction between God's essence and his uncreated energies. That can partly explain the purpose of his *Dialogue with a Muslim*: being a defense of Christian faith in general, at the same time the text is an eloquent vindication of the Palamite positions on the basic problem of the knowledge of God. Not wishing to hurt the feelings of his anti-Palamite friends, the emperor chose to present his own views on the subject in a treatise seemingly discussing a theme that has no connection with Palamism: that of the religion of Islam. At the same time, the possibility that Manuel took advantage of the writings of Thomas Aquinas both in the *Dialogue with a Muslim* and in his *Verses addressed to an atheist*, is not to be excluded.

27. Verses 152–156, in: I. Vassis 159 (as footnote 19 above): τὴν ἀκριβῆ γὰρ τῆς αὐτοῦ φύσεως καὶ τῆς γνώμης/λέγω μὴ δύνασθαι τινὰ τὴν ἔρευναν ποιεῖσθαι,/οὐ μὴν δὲ καὶ παντάπασιν ταύτας ἀλήπτους λέγω,/ὅτι σκιαγραφούμενον τοῖς νοῦν κεκαθαρμένοις,/μετρίως τε καὶ ἀμυδρῶς τὸ θεῖον, νῷ καὶ μόνῳ [...].

Demonstration (ἀπόδειξις) and Its Problems for St. Gregory Palamas: Some Neglected Aristotelian Aspects of St. Gregory Palamas' Philosophy and Theology

Constantinos Athanasopoulos

1. Demonstration in Aristotle: The problems

Perhaps the start of a discussion on the use of demonstration (*ἀπόδειξις*) in philosophy should be with Aristotle's *Posterior Analytics* (*Ἀναλυτικῶν Ὑστέρων*). Relevant discussion one can find also in *Prior Analytics* (*Ἀναλυτικῶν Προτέρων*), *Metaphysics* (*Μετὰ τὰ Φυσικά*), *De generatione animalium* (*Περὶ ζώων γενέσεως*) and in *De Anima* (*Περὶ ψυχῆς*).

In this work (*Posterior Analytics*), Aristotle starts his discussion by stressing that all learning and all teaching comes from knowledge already established, and this includes all sciences (mathematics included). He then attempts to chart a plausible description of how we acquire and how we achieve certainty in our knowledge of the world and in particular its mathematical qualities. Aristotle defines demonstration (*ἀπόδειξις*) as a process through which we acquire new knowledge (*ἐπιστήμη*) starting from things we already know: a) facts, b) meaning (i.e., what something means) or c) both (71b–72b). The first thing that we need to stress is that in demonstration, according to Aristotle, we proceed from things known to us (i.e., demonstration is deduction from what is necessary and known). In this way, these things that are taken as known are necessary and prior to our knowledge (i.e., what Aristotle calls *ἀρχαί*). *Ἀρχαί* are (necessarily) true (*ἀληθῶν*), primary (primitive, *πρώτων*), immediate (*ἀμέσων*, in time, i.e., there is no prior to them, *ἄμεσος* [...] *μὴ ἄλλη προτέρα*), more familiar to us (*γνωριμωτέρων*), prior to the conclusion (they have to be prior not only metaphysically but also according to their nature, i.e., they have to be more general and further from perception) and explanatory to the conclusion (*προτέρων καὶ αἰτίων τοῦ συμπεράσματος*, i.e., they must give a reason for why they are true via the middle term employed to connect the other two terms; the knowledge of this connective middle term basically is what we usually gain in a demonstration; see 71b19–25). They also relate to universals (73a–74a; 85b24). It is obvious that in such a system there cannot be a demonstrative knowledge of accidentals (things that are perishable or connected via relations that do not hold for all cases; see 74b–75b). It is also evident that in such a system there is an inherent difficulty in knowing whether one *knows* demonstratively or not (this depends on the knowledge one has for the things prior to demonstration and the things that demonstration is based upon: they have to be necessary and not of accidentals and they have to be considered – often without proof – as certain). In the same work (100a3–9), Aristotle claims that through perception we have memory and through many memories we have experience; through many experiences of a single thing, we can derive the universal that is applicable to this thing, and through the universal, the *ἀρχή* that we are going to use in demonstration (or work of art). While Aristotle (in the same work, 99b39–100a2), claims that many animals have this ability (to have perception and memory of things), understanding them and thus experience in the form that can be used in the production of universals (*ὑπόληψιν*) is limited to humans alone. This ability for experience in the form usable in universals is what makes humans able to form *διάκρισις* and draws humans to engage in theory and aesthetics (*De generatione animalium* 781b19–21).

Perhaps we can make more evident what Aristotle is thinking about here, if we use an example of how a biology scientist thinks about an animal. Let us use the example of panthers: suppose we wish to know if a panther (A) is a warm blooded animal (B) via demonstration (and not via catching one and testing its blood, because, for example, it is very difficult to catch one or they are very rare). What we need to do is to find out if panthers are mammals (D). If they are, then we can safely conclude that panthers are warm blooded animals, because we take it as an *ἀρχή* that all mammals are warm blooded animals and this *ἀρχή* provides us a reason to accept (B), once we affirm the connection (D). Note that the connection offered by (D) has to be necessary (in Aristotle's terminology: the middle has to be necessary, see *Posterior Analytics*, 75a13). Otherwise this will not work and demonstration will fail.

Difficulties with this form of reasoning have been discussed from antiquity (and surely were known to both Barlaam of Calabria and St. Gregory Palamas; I will discuss this issue further later on). Aristotle himself tries to deal with some of them in this work and in his *Topics*. The first has to do with the first principles (*ἀρχαί*) themselves. How do we come to know them? Since demonstration cannot show us how we come to know them, we have to accept them otherwise. The second has to do with the necessity of the middle term. In how many or what kind of demonstrations can we be certain that the middle term is necessary? Some may even claim that the necessity accepted here is impossible, because we do not know all the possible cases in which it is not necessary. How can we establish in this way its necessity? Aristotle believes that any answers to these two worries have to withstand attacks from scepticism, infinitely long explanations and circular reasoning (72b–73a).

Ultimately, Aristotle has to accept some kind of foundationalism, and today this move becomes more and more familiar in epistemology as a possible response to scepticism. But his foundationalism is more of an instrumental kind than a substantive one: Innatism is excluded and, as he has indicated, we do not arrive at *ἀρχαί* via demonstration from other more prior knowledge. Instead, Aristotle believes that we arrive at *ἀρχαί* via mental grasping of something that is evident through the process of *ἐπαγωγή*: we begin from observed individual cases and then through memory and accumulated experience we form (through intuition) the universal, which we will then use as an *ἀρχή*.

This *ἀρχή* for Aristotle can be either some form of propositional knowledge (i.e., raven (x) is black (w), I remember other ravens being black (t), so I conclude that *ravens are black* (y): the last proposition (y) is the *ἀρχή* that I will use for a demonstrative argument later on), or a concept (I recognise a black bird as a *raven*, due to my memory and experience of other such birds that other people called *ravens*). This concept I can then use in definitions, which acquire in Aristotelian epistemology a key role; they are important but not as important as demonstration, and not in the way of Plato's epistemology (for whom definitions caused some major epistemological worries) (*Posterior Analytics* II, 3–10). In Aristotle, *ἐπαγωγή* is the process (similar to contemporary inductive arguments) and *νοῦς* or *direct intuition* (perhaps this is the best translation here) is what goes through this process to arrive at *ἀρχαί* (note that it is not *λόγος* or reasoning), which also for Aristotle is important for *ἐπιστήμη* (99a–100b).

Note in relation to all this that *ἐπαγωγή* can be compared in terms of the intuitive work required in *τέχνη* or a skilled process like that employed by an artist; even though Aristotle himself thinks that the two are different: in *ἐπαγωγή* the problem solver hits upon a solution through sheer intelligence in direct insight and arrives at a universal. While the artist is arriving at a unique work of art that cannot be easily generalised nor can it be asserted as necessary (compare and contrast here Aristotle's *Nicomachean Ethics*, 1141a2–5; *Topics* 155b35–36; *Metaphysics* 1032a20 and 981a1–3; also read Groarke 2009, 335–337).

So, can we ascertain now whether Aristotle has solved the difficulties mentioned above via *ἐπαγωγή* and *νοῦς*? It seems that even though he has improved Plato's epistemology (which relied primarily on definitions) by admitting that demonstration together with definition can produce certain knowledge, he has only partially solved the problems mentioned above: by using an instrumental form of foundationalism and not a substantive one, he still needs to show how we recognise an *ἀρχή* as necessary in terms of the associated propositional knowledge and also something *necessarily* as falling in this or that concept (I recognise that my terminology here regarding "instrumental foundationalism" is idiosyncratic; but it is not far from relevant applications of similar terminology as in Jollimore 2005). In addition, he needs to answer satisfactorily how it is that we can recognise something as a universal; even though he does believe that direct intuition is most certain, sceptics (even of the ancient variety) often challenge "truths" arrived at in this way (and they have formulated specific arguments from antiquity to attack them). Ultimately he needs to prove that all science (or knowledge) is an enterprise that follows reason: *ἐπιστήμη δ' ἅπασα μετὰ λόγου ἐστίν* (100b10).

For Aristotle, to get clear and precise about demonstration is important, because it is through this that we can achieve a degree of certainty regarding our knowledge (*ἐπιστήμη*) of nature. In the above mentioned passages, Aristotle believes that through demonstration we arrive at *ἐπιστήμη* and he defines this as the knowledge of the cause of a specific event (or being) and of how this cannot be otherwise (71b10 and after), but because *ἐπιστήμη* is examining the universal and not the particular, knowledge of the exact characteristics of something that make it what it is cannot be arrived at through demonstration. For this reason, he claims that we can only know via *ἐπιστήμη* and demonstration (*ἀπόδειξις*) how something is (its Being), but not what its essence is. His reasoning here is complex and one should have in mind the relevant discussion in *Metaphysics* (cf. 995a15–20 and 1027a20).

Aristotle believes that the two (Being or that something exists, *τὶ ἐστίν* vs. its essence, i.e., its main characteristics that make it what it is – *τὸ τί ἦν εἶναι*) are different and demonstration cannot be used to arrive at the essence of something (92b4–20). In *Topics* (101b38), he claims that we can come close to the essence of a thing only through definition (which is discovered and not stipulated, so as to avoid circularity), a move, which even in Socratic terms, is susceptible to a sceptical attack (e.g., how are we certain that this discovery is the correct one?). This may be satisfactory for this *ad hoc* limited investigation, which he has to do in terms of knowledge gained in the natural sciences in the *Posterior Analytics*, and which, there, he finds is closer to mathematics. Aristotle thinks that one can, in this way, use universals drawn from observation of physical phenomena to gain such knowledge (note here that due to the complexity of his thinking in the above mentioned discussion in *Metaphysics*, Aristotle claims that ultimately we cannot be certain about how the world really is, since knowledge of the world as composite of matter and form is impossible, because matter is too unstable for absolute certainty), but he still has to show how his notion of necessity and explanation can be arrived at without an investigation into essences and how we use them to determine necessity and explanation (which we can then use in demonstration).

In terms of our panther example above, this means that we need to know what a panther's essence is prior to establishing what is necessary in terms of its characteristics (i.e., that a panther is an animal that can take the characterisation of a mammal for example and not the characterisation of a reptile). The *essence* here (in this example) provides the *possible* from which we will determine the *necessary* and this *essence* (*τὸ τί ἦν εἶναι*) can be provided by a definition (which for the sceptics is highly dubious). That mammals are warm blooded (an *ἀρχή* for our purposes) also means that we need to be certain that it is absolutely true; and unless we know all mammals (an impossibility, since we are still discovering new mammals), we cannot be certain about this. So, Aristotle's answers cannot be the perfect remedy for scepticism. Aristotle himself acknowledges this difficulty, when he states: "It is difficult to know whether one knows or not" (76a26). In general, for Aristotle *ἐπιστήμη* is indemonstrable, when it relates to first principles, and he also believes that only eternal relations (that have to do with universals) can be demonstrated: 71b16, 72a25–b2, 72b17–24, 76a16–21. However, he does define the demonstrative scientific knowledge in 71b9–13 and he does acknowledge that it is the most certain knowledge we can arrive at (he calls this *ἐπίσταςθαι ἁπλῶς* and he distinguishes this from the knowledge gained by the sophists or *κατὰ τὸ συμβεβηκός*). How is this possible? One possible answer may be that Aristotle follows some kind of an internalist or externalist justificationist agenda. But some have claimed that this may not be so (see Aydede 1998).

Now one may ask here: why bother with a theory that admittedly cannot ultimately be immune to sceptical doubt (even though it recognises that it considers total disbelief in scientific knowledge a serious error, see 72b5–10)? Here are some reasons: it may be the case that there are no other more plausible theories; it may be that any epistemological theory that is based only on what we observe cannot be satisfactory due to the transitory nature of what can be observed and the inherent lack in explanatory and predictive power of these observations. Something more theoretical is needed to predict and explain, and Aristotle's theory provides this power of prediction and explanation with less theoretical problems than all other theories on offer at his time. But still it may be that demonstration is good for only some sciences or where it can be applied with different sets of *ἀρχαί* in each science. Aristotle is not against this idea and indeed, in the above mentioned passages, he does accept that each science has its own set of *ἀρχαί* (75b36–76a31). In fact, Aristotle would agree that the way he describes the application of demonstration to produce new certainties from things already taken for certain makes demonstration most suited to mathematics (arithmetic), geometry and astronomy (76a37–76b12). The *ἀρχαί* in these sciences have all the characteristics that Aristotle outlined and connections for Aristotle in these disciplines can indeed take a necessary character. However, even there, one may object, we can have necessary connections (i.e., a connecting middle) that even though necessary, per Aristotelian requirements, may prove irrelevant to the problem to be solved or theory to be proved, see 75a13, 90a35). What do we do in these cases so as to guarantee that we will have new and certain knowledge based on truths that are relevant (producing relevant conclusions)? In addition, in the same work (*Posterior Analytics*) Aristotle maintains that each science has its own first principles, a position that complicates things even further and makes the application of whatever methodological certainties in the mathematical related sciences to other disciplines (such as theology) even more problematic.

2. *Medieval Philosophy: Reception and Understanding of the Problems*

It is by no accident that Medieval philosophers commenting on the *Prior* and *Posterior Analytics* (as reported in the Arabic commentaries, most notably al-Farabi and Averroes and other partially found third hand reports, such as James of Venice's early 12th century translation of commentaries produced by Alexander of Aphrodisias and Philoponus), tried to improve on Aristotle's theory of demonstration so as to find a most exact and demonstrable science and methodology, which would enable them to provide a stipulation fit for theological subjects of investigation (a protagonist in this regard could have been Richard Rufus of Cornwall, philosophical opponent of Roger Bacon and major influence on Duns Scotus; see Wood and Andrews, 1996). Thomas Aquinas, trying to improve on earlier such attempts (primarily Albertus Magnus' and Robert Grosseteste's epistemological theories) ends with his famous position on God being the only being where Essence and Existence (or Being and Essence in Aristotelian terms, see above) are not distinct; this makes God radically different from all created beings, where their essence is logically and metaphysically different from their existence, i.e., their essence allows them to exist in some sense without having real existence, i.e., they are perishable by definition (see *De Ente et De Essentia*, Chapter 4). This for Thomists solves the problem of necessary connections in terms of theology (since now existence of God is a tautology and you cannot get more certain than this) and guarantees (in the eyes of the Thomists) that demonstration in theology produces the most certain knowledge about God.

These famous stages in the development of demonstration did not take away anything from its appeal well into the modern age and we have examples of famous modern philosophers who tried to develop further our thinking about demonstration and its applicability in science (even though with rather problematic admissions for Aristotelians). It is worthy to note that Rene Descartes, even though critical of Aristotle, frequently used demonstration to prove his positions on light and more fundamental metaphysical theses (see for relevant examples in his *Letter to Mersene*, 27th May 1638, and in his *Rules for the Improvement of the Understanding*); John Locke thought that demonstration should be applied to moral reasoning; in his *Essay on the Understanding* he insists: "The precise, real essence of the things, moral words stand for, may be perfectly known; and so the congruity or incongruity of the things themselves be certainly discovered; in which consists perfect knowledge" (Book iii. ch. 11. sect. 16). In his peculiar way of connecting God to moral affairs, one could point to the fact that for Locke both theology and ethics are sciences in which demonstration should be freely applied. Indeed demonstration for these sciences is the most appropriate method of attaining certain knowledge. One could observe similar views in other modern philosophers (for example, Th. Reid, *Essays on the Intellectual Powers*, Essay vii., ch.1).

It is characteristic of the influence and fascination with Aristotle's theory of demonstration in the Middle Ages that most of the important authors in the middle and late periods of this era had something to say in terms of Aristotle's Theory of Demonstration. It is by no accident then, that Barlaam tried to incorporate his knowledge regarding the theory to his standpoints and intuitions in his own critique (which during the early phase of his debates with St. Gregory Palamas had to do with the *filioque*) and then proceeded to the way hesychastic practices developed in the late Byzantine Civilisation. I will now turn to what Sinkewicz and Ierodiakonou write about the nature of the debates on the issue of demonstration with possible replies from Palamas (on the basis of my brief examination of what I take to be Aristotle's theory of demonstration and Palamas' own writings). In this way, I hope Palamas' contribution on the use of demonstration will be more evident and usable for future work in the area.

3. The debate on Demonstration between Barlaam of Calabria (ca. 1290–1348) and St. Gregory Palamas (1296–1359) according to Sinkewicz and Ierodiakonou

To understand better the value of Palamas' contribution on the use of demonstration it is useful to examine two negative evaluations of his contribution and possible replies from Palamas. One could safely conclude that overall, the approach of both Sinkewicz and Ierodiakonou towards Palamas' contribution to the debates is a negative one: Sinkewicz thinks that Palamas had a very partial knowledge of the arguments contained in the treatises of Barlaam except one (see Sinkewicz 1982, 238), and also that either Palamas seriously misunderstood Barlaam's arguments or that he misunderstood Aristotle's theory about the use of demonstration (Sinkewicz 1982, 201–2). Ierodiakonou on the other hand claims that "Palamas' reasoning has a number of important flaws which are due to misinterpretation of specific aspects of Aristotle's logical theories" (Ierodiakonou 2004, 233).

It is important to stress that the debates about the use of demonstration in philosophical and theological reasoning took place primarily at the early phase of the discussions between Barlaam and Palamas and were related to the issue of what kind of reasoning and support to arguments could be admitted in the discussions between the Byzantine Orthodox and the Western Roman-Catholics to resolve the *filioque* issue (the Byzantine Orthodox could not accept this addition to the Creed and the Latin Roman-Catholic side insisted in upholding it). The discussion between the two protagonists started about the *filioque* (both were against it at the early phase, Barlaam changed his position after his departure from the Orthodox Church), proceeded into the area of appropriate methods for the investigation of theological truths (in this, i.e., how they tried to apply it in the realm of theological truths, they differed considerably) and ended with the debates about hesychasm. This aspect of the controversy is important for our purposes, since, at this early phase of the debates, the two protagonists were more concerned with criticising each other on the theoretical basis of their differences than with accusing each other of heresy. In this way, this early phase was more philosophical than the later phase. So, it would be useful for our examination into the philosophy behind the debates, if we examine in brief the claims of Sinkewicz and Ierodiakonou and offer some replies on the basis of our examination of Aristotle's thinking on demonstration and Palamas' use of the Aristotelian problems outlined above.

Sinkewicz justifies his claim about Palamas' poor knowledge of Barlaam's arguments by citing chronological evidence that points to the fact that only one of the *Antilatin Treatises* (AL5) was delivered to him on Mount Athos while all other treatises were reported to him through mutual friends and acquaintances. But even if we take Sinkewicz' chronological evidence at face value (and I have my reservations about this), he still needs to prove that indeed Palamas did not have in his command the main arguments presented in Barlaam's other works. Taking into consideration that the people who took the responsibility to be the messengers were friends with both Palamas and Barlaam and people who not only were intelligent and had full knowledge of the relevant arguments in the debates but also were never accused of reporting falsely the arguments employed, the importance for such a proof becomes even greater. From Sinkewicz's detailed discussion it is not conclusive that Palamas misunderstood, nor that he tried to misinterpret Barlaam. Their difference of opinion was real and understood by both. Both were against the *filioque* and the way the Latin Roman-Catholics tried to prove it; their difference of opinion concerned the use of demonstration in attaining certainty in science and philosophy and in particular in proving theological truths. Barlaam used demonstration in a strictly logical sense and tried to incorporate most of the Aristotelian intuitions contained in the Aristotelian logical works exclusively. Palamas showed a far greater understanding of the Aristotelian corpus and argued for a more liberal understanding of demonstration trying to overcome the inherent problems in Aristotelian logic.

I have argued elsewhere that the educated Byzantine philosopher of the time had a more complete command of the Aristotelian corpus than his western medieval colleagues and was able to compare and contrast the problems and the solutions proposed by Aristotle in his various logical, rhetorical and poetic works with great liberty and ease (Athanasopoulos 2010). In addition, the Byzantine scholar of the time had at his command more than thousand years of detailed commentaries and thus had a more rounded understanding of the relevant problems. I also argued in my previous work that, even when one considers the Aristotelian corpus itself, some of the most important logical and metaphysical Aristotelian problems found their solution in the rhetorical and poetic works of Aristotle. In this way, whoever had a fuller command of the Aristotelian corpus and its commentaries was not only more able to solve the problems inherent in some Aristotelian works, but also was able to use more liberally relevant Aristotelian terms and possible non-Aristotelian (but related to Aristotelian) terms that could be useful in the debates at hand.

It is doubtful that Barlaam had such a liberty and ease of reference and thus a command on Aristotelian intuitions so as to solve effectively the problems found in Aristotle's logical works. Even though we have a detailed record on the Byzantine Aristotelian scholar who was the teacher of Palamas, Theodoros Metochites (1290–1332), a famous Byzantine commentator on key Aristotelian and other ancient Greek mathematical and logical works, no such records exist for the teachers of Barlaam. It is important to note that Theodoros Metochites most probably imparted to Palamas some of his deep knowledge of the Aristotelian corpus as well as a more general knowledge of logical and mathematical problems and solutions (Ševčenko 1962; Bydén 2003). A characteristic of the legacy of this teacher (Theodoros Metochites) was his other famous student Nikephoros Gregoras (1295–1360), who became a famous Byzantine philosopher, mathematician and astronomer (among his many discoveries was the Gregorian Calendar, more than 200 years before its adoption by the West via Pope Gregory XIII); Gregoras also participated later in the debates (as a philosophical and theological opponent to Palamas). The influence of Theodoros Metochites on St. Gregory Palamas is still a largely unexplored area. What I would like to stress here is that most of Palamas' insistence on the ethical preparation for true illumination and his strong belief in upholding the true dogma of the Orthodox Church as a necessary condition for a true philosophical standpoint and as a plausible reply to the epistemological stalemate of scepticism on metaphysical truths was the result of the strong intellectual influence he received from his teacher (see Metochites 2002).

Proceeding further into Sinkewicz's argument in support of his claim that Palamas misinterprets Barlaam, it would be useful to consider his claim that Palamas considers Barlaam's views on the use of dialectic in the search for truths in an "absolute" sense, while Barlaam's intention was to use this in a more limited and relative sense (Sinkewicz 1982, 198). His argument here is that Barlaam's point about using dialectic as a useful tool to win arguments was not related to Palamas' more specific interest in searching and finding truth in theological matters. However, this attempt to vindicate Barlaam is rather suspicious, since, if one is to allow this kind of use of dialectic into all searches of truth (as is implied by Barlaam), he indirectly allows its application for theological truths as well (unless he explicitly excludes theological truths from any application of dialectic, which he is not explicitly admitting). Barlaam's rather vague remark about the use of dialectic in arguments, as Palamas is eager to note repeatedly, allows scepticism to creep into a realm where doubt should not be allowed. From Palamas' viewpoint an outright condemnation of dialectic would be the most certain way to exclude it from any consideration in the investigation of theological truths. This would be not only true to Palamas' insistence that theological truths need to be filled with certainty, but would also be true to the Aristotelian way of thinking about certainty in the epistemology of mathematical truths (which for Aristotle should be without any doubt, as we observed above in relation to his theory of demonstration).

Sinkewicz however, not only doubts Palamas' knowledge of Barlaam's arguments but proceeds into challenging Palamas' knowledge of Aristotelian logic as well. His key criticisms are related to a poor application of Aristotelian terminology and Palamas' poor understanding of the Aristotelian use of demonstration regarding unique realities (*μοναδικά*). In his first *Letter to Akindynos* (par. 9), Palamas puts forward the view that demonstration applied to specific unique realities such as God (which is a most certain reality), is a plausible Aristotelian move, because Aristotle rejected the use of demonstration in particulars on the ground that they have an uncertain character. Sinkewicz here (ibid, 198–199) is too eager to dismiss Palamas' admission as opposing or misinterpreting Aristotelian logic, without taking into full account Palamas' insistence that this unique reality (God) even though one (and thus to be considered as a particular in Aristotelian terminology) is more certain in its characteristics than any universal and thus, it should be admitted as an area for the application of demonstrative science. This is not only a correct application of Aristotelian logic in an area that was not existent nor possible at the time of Aristotle, but also was supported as a theological move by the many references in Church Fathers' writings that demonstration (*ἀπόδειξις*) should be used in the investigation of theological matters. One could find other areas in Sinkewicz's contribution where Sinkewicz seems too eager to support Barlaam and criticise Palamas, but here I will limit my critical discussion to the above mentioned points, which I consider most characteristic in his overall approach.

Ierodiakonou on the other hand makes some hasty critical statements about Palamas' arguments to conclude in the rather negative remarks mentioned above. She discusses three main areas where she finds that Palamas falls short regarding the dictates of a correct application of Aristotelian theory. She starts with Palamas' insistence that impression (*φαντασία*) cannot be involved in our investigations and syllogisms about God. She criticises Palamas here because, according to her, such an assertion cannot be admitted in the Aristotelian framework, due to the fact that Aristotle maintains in *De Anima* that all our thoughts, whatever they may be, are dependent on impressions (Ierodiakonou 2004, 234). Here, Ierodiakonou obviously conflates the Aristotelian conception about god with the Christian conception of God (such as the one found, for example, in the Areopagetic corpus). The two conceptions are radically different. The Aristotelian god is one with the world (in a metaphysical sense), while the Christian (in the Areopagetic tradition, which Palamas follows) is radically different (in a metaphysical-ontological sense). If Ierodiakonou was to apply the principle of charity in her Palamite reading, she would fully acknowledge the apophaticism inherent in the Palamite conception of God and would not find Palamas' claim about the complete lack of any impression in relation to God objectionable. She would also recognise not only that *De Anima* has some rather peculiar theses about impression (not found in other works) but also that the Aristotelian conception of god is not without theoretical problems itself (according to important commentators, Aristotle in *Metaphysics* 1074b did not have a conception of god as an agent of change in the world and indeed it was not a god in the traditional sense, but was only an appropriate theoretical device to close a theoretical gap in his system; see Elders 1972; Frede and Charles 2000). Further on, even when one considers the issue of whether the thought of god is dependent on an impression in the Aristotelian system, the Aristotelian god as an unmoved mover, eternal, unchanging and fully actual, without any knowledge of the external world nor a desire to acquire such a knowledge, engaged in self-contemplative thought (*νόησις νοήσεως*) is beyond any impression we can have about any other being in our world. So, from the above examination, we can easily see that, even in Aristotle's system, our thought of god is without any impression and this is exactly what Palamas wishes to maintain. So, it seems that Ierodiakonou here is too readily embracing her intuitions about the use of impressions in *De Anima* to properly engage in a plausible reading of Aristotle in terms of what Aristotle says about god and the impression we can or cannot have of it.

Her further logical intuitions about the use of universals in syllogisms and her conclusion that Palamas is misinterpreting Aristotle, when he claims that induction is necessary to find all the particulars that can be classified under one universal, seems also a too eager condemnation of Palamas, because her cited passages from *Posterior Analytics* (A31 88a11–17; B2 90a28–30), concern finding the particulars that relate to the cause and thus, connect the cause to the universal. However, again, if she was to apply the principle of charity in her evaluation of Palamas' arguments, she would find that Palamas' discussion in these arguments had to do with how we can achieve certainty with universals and Palamas just notes that in order to find the particulars which relate to the universal under which they are classified, in terms of causality, we need induction. Actually, Palamas here follows Aristotle and takes his reasoning a step further, because, as we saw above in the case of both *Posterior Analytics* and *De generatione animalium,* Aristotle accepts this: humans depend on memory regarding the instances of the particulars they have encountered to form the concept of the universal which they will use in demonstration and that this process resembles the inductive method. Aristotle actually follows a similar line of thought in *Prior Analytics* (II.23 and 14), where he mentions a syllogism that springs from induction (*ὁ ἐξ ἐπαγωγῆς συλλογισμός*) and he notes that this is not conclusive. Govier (in Govier 1987, 50–52) makes a similar point referring to the ancient commentaries on this point. Further evidence in support of this interpretation of Aristotle is provided in *Posterior Analytics* (II.16–17.98b32ff, 99a24ff), where Aristotle claims that the scientist must use first induction for the establishment of an ostensible definition to explain a thing's nature and then he must use demonstration to establish the effects of that nature to its species. Certainty is achieved only after the successful application of demonstration and not before this. In this way, I hope I have shown in some detail that Ierodaikonou's condemnation of Palamas as misinterpreting Aristotle both on the issue of impressionless god and on the issue of the use of universals and induction, are totally unfounded and without any support, if one wishes to adopt the principle of charity in terms of Palamas' arguments and a possible plausible reading of Aristotle when applied to the Christian (Areopagetic) concept of God.

Conclusions

From the above discussion, it can be concluded that Saint Gregory Palamas not only understood Barlaam's arguments and philosophical moves but he also identified key problems in Barlaam's thinking. Through a cursory discussion of some important problems on the application of demonstration in Aristotelian logical theory, we also found that recent claims that Palamas did not understand the nature of these problems in Aristotelian logic are not a charitable reading of Palamas' arguments and thus fall as too hasty and poorly supported by the available evidence. I hope in a future work, I will be able to present a more substantial analysis of the logic inherent in Palamas' arguments especially in terms of his development of earlier logical methods found in his teacher (Theodoros Metochites) and other important earlier commentators on the Aristotelian corpus.

Bibliography

Athanasopoulos, C., "Ousia in Aristotle's Categories," *Logique et Analyse* 53 (210) June (2010) 211–243.

Aydede, M., "Aristotle on episteme and nous: The Posterior Analytics," *Southern Journal of Philosophy* 36, 1 (1998) 15–46.

Bydén, B., *Theodore Methochites' Stoicheiosis Astronomike and the Study of Natural Philosophy and Mathematics in Early Palaiologan Byzantium*, Acta Universitatis Gothoburgensis 2003.

Elders, L., *Aristotle's Theology: A Commentary on Book [lambda] of the Metaphysics*, Assen: Van Gorcum 1972.

Frede, M., Charles, D., ed., *Aristotle's Metaphysics Lambda*, Oxford: Oxford University Press 2000.

Groarke, L., *An Aristotelian Account of Induction: Creating Something from Nothing*, McGill-Queen's Press, MQUP 2009.

Govier, T., *Problems in Argument Analysis and Evaluation*, Providence, R.I.: Floris 1987.

Ierodiakonou, K., "The Anti-Logical Movement in the Fourteenth Century," in: K. Ierodiakonou, ed., *Byzantine Philosophy and its Ancient Sources*, Oxford: Clarendon Press 2002, 219–235.

Jollimore, T., "Why is Instrumental Rationality Rational?," *Canadian Journal of Philosophy* 35, 2 (2005) 289–308.

Metochites, Th., *Ethikos - Peri Paideias*, critical edition by I. Polemis, Athens: Kanaki Publications 2002.

Sinkewicz, R. E., "The Doctrine of the Knowledge of God in the Early Writings of Barlaam the Calabrian," *Medieval Studies* 44 (1982) 181–242.

Ševčenko I., *Études sur la polémique entre Théodore Métochite et Niképhore Choumnos*, Bruxelles 1962.

Wood, R., Andrews, R., "Causality and Demonstration: An Early Scholastic 'Posterior Analytics,'" *The Monist* 79, 3 (1996) 325–356.

Authority and Tradition. The Case of Dionysius Pseudo-Areopagite in the Writing "On Divine Unity and Distinction" by Gregory Palamas

Mikonja Knežević

Gregory Palamas and Dionysius Areopagite – the issue on the relation between the two relevant and influential christian authors,[1] in the first place

1. "If a talented expert, with an extraordinary knowledge of the matter, would once want to write history of interpretations of Dionysius, it would, reflect a complete spiritual development of the Middle Ages" (see W. Völker, *Kontemplation und Ekstase bei Ps-Dionysius Areopagita*, Wiesbaden: F. Steiner 1958, 218). For the influence of *Areopagitica*, without which "the whole history of medieval misticism and philosophy would be incomprehensible" (Г. В. Флоровскiй, *Византiйскiе Отцы V–VIII*, Богословiе Отцевъ Церкви, Парижъ: YMCA-Press 1933, Heppenheim: Gregg Int. Publ. ʳ1972, 99), see: J. Meyendorff, "Notes sur l'influence dionysienne en Orient," *Studia Patristica* 2 (1957) 547–552; J. Kuhlmann, *Thomas von Aquin und Gregor Palamas als Dionysius-Erklärer. Theologiegeschichtlicher Vergleich*, Liber annualis 1966, Würzburg ²1968; S. Gersh, *From Iamblichus to Eriugena. An Investigation of the Prehistory and Evolution of the Pseudo-Dionysian Tradition*, Studien zur Problemgeschichte der antiken und mittelalterlichen Philosophie № 8, Leiden: Brill 1978; A. Louth, *Denys the Areopagite*, Outstanding Christian Thinkers, London, New York: Chapman 1989, ʳ2001; P. Rorem, *Pseudo-Dionysius. A Commentary on the Texts and an Introduction to their Influence*, New York, Oxford: Oxford University Press 1993; *Denys l'Aréopagite et sa postérité en Orient et en Occident. Actes du Colloque International, Paris, 21–24 septembre 1994*, édités par Y. de Andia, Études Augustiniennes. Collection Antiquité № 151, Paris : Institut d'Études Augustiniennes 1997 ; P. Rorem, J. C. Lamoreaux, *John of Scythopolis and the Dionysian Corpus. Annotating the Areopagite*, The Oxford Early Christian Studies, Oxford: Clarendon Press 1998; *Die Dionysius-Rezeption im Mittelalter. Kolloquium unter der Schirmherrschaft der S.I.E.P.M., Sofia, 8–11 April 1999*, hrsg. von T. Boiadjiev, G. Kapriev, A. Speer, Rencontres de Philosophie Médiévale, Turnhout: Brepols, Sofia: Lik 2000; J. McEvoy, *Mystical Theology. The Glosses by Thomas Gallus and the Commentary of Robert Grosseteste on De Mystica Theologia*, Paris: Peeters 2003; P. Rorem, *Eriugena's Commentary on the Dionysian Celestial Hierarchy*, Toronto: Pontifical Institute of Mediaeval Studies 2005; B. R. Suchla, *Dionysius Areopagita. Leben, Werk, Wirkung*, Freiburg am Breisgau, Basel, Wien: Herder 2008; S. Coakley, Ch. M. Stang, ed., *Re-thinking Dionysius the Areopagite*, Chichester, UK: Wiley-Blackwell 2009, etc. On the other hand, the influence of Palamas was particularly evident in the 20th century, while for Orthodox theologians it was, perhaps, even decisive. The reading of Palamas' *opus*, however, was mainly ideologically contaminated, both from the eastern and the western side; this issue requires a special study. For a litterature on Gregory Palamas, as well as for the chronology, editions and translations of his works, see: M. Knežević, *Gregory Palamas (1296–1357): Bibliography*, Belgrade: Institute for Theological Research 2012.

on the way that Palamas understood and interpreted areopagite writings, became particularly interesting since John Meyendorff, in his famous[2], although in many places problematic[3] study of Gregory Palamas, developed the thesis of the so called "christological corrective" (*correctif christologique*)[4] by which Palamas, allegedly, finally neutralized neoplatonic tendencies in the writings of a mysterious writer from the fifth century. According to Meyendorff, by this "christological corrective" Palamas finally gave the areopagite writings (yet another after Maximus the Confessor) a *christological* interpretation, thus refuting a closer and more consistent, as it appears[5], reading of the Areopagite as given by Barlaam the Calabrian. Moreover, Palamas thereby, Meyendorff even claimed, "came into such clear opposition to Dionysius that he had to resort to a forced and artificial exegesis of his thought, in order to avoid a direct attack on so venerable an authority," having done it to such an extent that his "christological corrective *completely* changed the structure of Dionysius's thought."[6] From the moment the the-

2. J. Meyendorff, *Introduction à l'étude de Grégoire Palamas*, Patristica Sorbonensia № 3, Paris: Éd. du Seuil 1959 = *A Study of Gregory Palamas*. Translated by G. Lawrence, Crestwood, New York: St Vladimir's Seminary Press ʳ1998.
3. A thorough critique of Meyendorff's reading of Palamas is given by J. Romanides, "Notes on the Palamite Controversy and Related Topics," *Greek Orthodox Theological Review* 6, 1 (1960–1961) 186–205; 9, 2 (1963–1964) 225–270. Romanides, in his extensive critical review questioned not only methodological assumptions of Meyendorff's approach to Palamas thought, but also pointed to the obvious textual abuses, all of that as a part of the project within the scope of which the theology of Palamas should have been presented as current, contemporary, and even relevant to modern philosophical streamings. Paradoxically but expectantly, Romanides's critique had very little receptiveness and was hardly ever, apart from some sporadic cases, seriously acknowledged: it seems that it suited the contemporary researchers, particularly those from the Orthodox ideological milieu, to repeat Meyendorff's constructions, considering thus Palamas as an "existentialist" and "personalist," rather than to undertake the (always serious and demanding) task of textual analysis. In a very concise form, but under a somewhat frightening atmosphere, Romanides repeated his objections against Meyendorff once again in: Ἰω. Σ. Ῥωμανίδης, "Ἀντί προλόγου," "Πρόλογος," "Δογματικοϊστορική Εἰσαγωγή," in: *Ρωμαῖοι ἤ Ρωμηοὶ Πατέρες τῆς Ἐκκλησίας. Γρηγορίου Παλαμᾶ ἔργα 1. Ὑπὲρ τῶν Ἱερῶς Ἡσυχαζόντων Τριᾶς Ά . Τόμος πρώτος.* Ἐπόπτης Ἐκδόσεως Ἰω. Σ. Ῥωμανίδης. Ἐπιμελήτρια Ἐκδόσεως Δ. Δ. Κοντοστεργιοῦ. Ἱστορικοδογματική Εἰσαγωγή ἀπό τόν Ἰω. Σ. Ῥωμανίδη. Μετάφραση ἀπό τήν Δ. Δ. Κοντοστεργιοῦ, Θεσσαλονίκη: Ἐκδοσεις Π. Πουρναρᾶ 1984, ²1991, 5–9, 11–33, 51–194, especially 5–6, 96–99. For further critiques of Meyndorff's thesis, see: J. Demetracopoulos, *Is Gregory Palamas an Existentialist? The Restoration of the True Meaning of His Comment on "Exodus" 3, 14: "Ἐγώ εἰμι ὁ ὤν,"* Athens: Παρουσία 1996.
4. J. Meyendorff, "Notes sur l'influence dionysienne en Orient," *Studia Patristica* 2 (1957) 547–552: 550.
5. Ἰω. Σ. Ῥωμανίδης, "Ἀντί προλόγου," in: *Ρωμαῖοι ἤ Ρωμηοὶ Πατέρες τῆς Ἐκκλησίας...*, Θεσσαλονίκη ²1991, 5–9: 6; cf. J. Romanides, "Notes on the Palamite Controversy and Related Topics," *Greek Orthodox Theological Review* 6, 1 (1960–1961) 186–205: 187.
6. J. Meyendorff, *Introduction à l'étude...*, Paris 1959, 262 = *A Study of...*, Crestwood, New York ʳ1998, 189 (italics are mine). In the English translation within the same sentence which I quoted, variations "Christocentric corrective" and "Christological corrective" are found. Formulation "Christological corrective" is, of course, found in other places of Meyendorff's study; cf. *Introduction à l'étude...*, 237, 284; *A Study of...*, 169, 206.

sis on "christological corrective" was presented – whether it was accepted as "thoroughly incontestable" ("völlig unbestreitbar"),[7] or it was contested with strong arguments[8] and at the same time characterized as "an illusion, a scholarly invention,"[9] or, again, accepted with a certain reserve and in a selective way[10] – it became a cause for the re-examination of relation between the mysterious Dionysius and Gregory Palamas. And yet, it seems to me that there is still a need for a more extensive study that would thoroughly examine *all* of Palamas' references to Dionysius and their interpretative credibility. Leaving aside this extensive and very challenging subject, I shall try in this short essay to deal with one issue only regarding the relation between Palamas and Pseudo-Dionysius and that reffering to the only one, short Palamas' writing, which I am to take as a "case study." Namely, I shall consider the way Palamas relates himself to the mysterious writer, who hid himself behind the name of the disciple of apostle Paul[11] (Acts 17:34), in his well known

7. A. M. Ritter, "Gregor Palamas als Leser des Dionysius Ps.-Areopagita," in: *Denys l'Aréopagite et sa postérité en Orient et en Occident. Actes du Colloque International, Paris, 21–24 septembre 1994*, édités par Y. de Andia, Études Augustiniennes. Collection Antiquité № 151, Paris: Institut d'Études Augustiniennes 1997, [565–]579.
8. J. Romanides, "Notes on the Palamite Controversy and Related Topics," *Greek Orthodox Theological Review* 9, 2 (1963–1964) 225–270: 249–257, and previously 236–249.
9. A. Golitzin, "Dionysius the Areopagite in the Works of Gregory Palamas. On the Question of a 'Christological Corrective' and Related Matters," *St. Vladimir's Theological Quarterly* 46, 2–3 (2002) 163–190 = *Scrinium* 3 (2007) 83–105[: 86, 102].
10. J. van Rossum, "Dionysius the Areopagite and Gregory Palamas: A 'Christological Corrective?,'" *Studia Patristica* XLII (2006) 347–353. Van Rosum talks of the "implicite," "silent," "even if unconscuous," "'corrective,'" which, again, really is "*christocentric*" and which is, in the first place, applied by Palamas to the Dionisyius' "*ambiguous ecclesiology*." Support for the thesis of the "ímplicite," "silent," "even if unconscious," but still "christocentric" Palamas' "'corrective,'" van Rossum finds in the famous Palamas' view on the "triadic nature" (ἡ τριαδικὴ φύσις) of man and his primacy over angels, which is presented in his *Physical and Theological Chapters*; cf. *Κεφάλαια ἑκατὸν πεντήκοντα φυσικὰ καὶ θεολογικά, ἠθικά τε καὶ πρακτικὰ καὶ καθαρτικὰ τῆς Βαρλααμίτιδος λύμης* 37–40, in: R. E. Sinkewicz, *Saint Gregory Palamas. The One Hundred and Fifty Chapters.* A Critical Edition, Translation and Study by R. E. Sinkewicz, Studies and Texts № 83, Toronto: Pontifical Institute of Mediaeval Studies 1988, 122–129. By the way, van Rosum here basically follows Ritter, who also finds a footing in the quoted place for the thesis on the "incontestability" of Palamas' "christological corrective," which – in a different ambience though – he calls "silent" ([...] eine – stillschweigende – Korretur [...]); see: A. M. Ritter, "Gregor Palamas als Leser des Dionysius Ps.-Areopagita," in: *Denys l'Aréopagite et sa postérité en Orient et en Occident...*, Paris 1997, 565–579: 577–578. (italics in the previous quotations are the author's)
11. That the very choice of the pseudonym in the case of the mysterious writer from the fifth century was not accidential at all, so that under its prysm – in other words, under the prysm of apostle Paul's teaching – one should interprete the whole *Corpus dionysiacum*, was exactly what Ch. M. Stang tried to show in his incentive study "Dionysius, Paul and the Significance of Pseudonym," *Modern Theology* 24, 4 (2008) 541–555. For the reasons of choosing exactly this pseudonym by the mysterious writer see also: A. Louth, *Denys the Areopagite*, London, New York 1989, ʳ2001, 10–11; P. Rorem, *Pseudo-Dionysius. A Commentary on the Texts...*, New York, Oxford 1993, 7; Ch. Schäfer, *The Philosophy of Dionysius the Areopagite. An Introduction to the Structure and the Content of the Treatise "On the Divine Names,"* Philosophia Antiqua XCIX, Leiden, Boston: Brill 2006, 170–171.

writing *On divine unity and distinction*,[12] otherwise the first part of a trilogy in which he tries to prove the theological relevance of the doctrine on energies. I shall pay special attention to the problem of *authority* comprehension; in that sense, a particular emphasis will be given to the thirty-third and thirty-fourth chapters of the writing in question, where Palamas, in an indirect, but quite explicit way, touches on the problem of *authorship* of which is today known as *Corpus Areopagiticum*.

In Palamas' writing *On divine unity and distinction* there exist sixty-seven explicit references to Dionysius the Aeropagite in total, out of which thirty-eight represent qualifications of his personality and his theological authority,[13] while the remaining twenty-nine represent references to different places from his writings or else general characterizations of some of his works. Dominant place is given to *On the divine names* – particularly its second chapter, from which Palamas explicitly draws twenty five quotations.[14] Of other quoted works there is *Letter 9* (*Titus, the hierarch*) which is quoted twice,[15] while, finally, in two other places, a general assesment of the course and goal of Dionysius' writing *De divinis nominibus* is given.[16] It is not necessary to emphasize that the largest number of quotations concerns Dionysius' thesis on unity and distinction in God, which was, together with the theme of angelic mediations in divine revelations, one of the key points of Palamas'

12. Γρηγορίου τοῦ Παλαμᾶ *Συγγράμματα*. Ἐκδίδονται ἐπιμελείᾳ Π. Κ. Χρήστου. Τόμος Β΄. Πραγματεῖαι καὶ ἐπιστολαὶ γραφεῖσαι κατὰ τὰ ἔτη 1340–1346. Προλογίζει Π. Χρήστου. Ἐκδίδουν Γ. Μαντζαρίδης, Ν. Ματσούκας, Β. Ψευτογκᾶς, Θεσσαλονίκη: Κυρομάνος [1966] ²1994, 69–95 [further: Συγγράμματα Β΄ [²1994]].

13. Seriatim: [*i*] Γρηγορίου Παλαμᾶ, *Περὶ ἑνώσεως καὶ διακρίσεως* 1, Συγγράμματα Β΄ [²1994] 69.1–2, 3–5; [*ii*] 2, 69.15; [*iii*] 3, 70.11; [*iv*] 5, 72.4–5; [*v*] 5, 72.13; [*vi*] 5, 72.13–18; [*vii*] 5, 72.20–21; [*viii*] 6, 73.14–55; [*ix*] 6, 73.22; [*x*] 7, 73.29; [*xi*] 7, 74.4; [*xii*] 11, 76.30; [*xiii*] 12, 77.25; [*xiv*] 13, 78.7; [*xv*] 16, 80.17; [*xvi*] 17, 80.26; [*xvii*] 17, 81.7; [*xviii*] 18, 81.22; [*xix*] 18, 82.5; [*xx*] 19, 82.30; [*xxi*] 19, 83.8; [*xxii*] 19, 83.12; [*xxiii*] 20, 83.23; [*xiv*] 20, 84.4; [*xxv*] 26, 87.19; [*xxvi*] 27, 87.32; [*xxvii*] 27, 88.11; [*xxviii*] 28, 89.3; [*xxix*] 28, 89.17; [*xxx*] 28, 89.22; [*xxxi*] 31, 92.2; [*xxxii*] 32, 92.20; [*xxxiii*] 32, 92.22–23; [*xxxiv*] 32, 92.25; [*xxxv*] 32, 92.26; [*xxxvi*] 32, 92.30; [*xxxvii*] 32, 93.8; [*xxxviii*] 33, 93.13.

14. Seriatim: [*i*] Γρηγορίου Παλαμᾶ, *Περὶ ἑνώσεως καὶ διακρίσεως* 2, Συγγράμματα Β΄ [²1994] 69.16–24; [*ii*] 2, 69.24–70.1–7; [*iii*] 2, 70.7–10; [*iv*] 3, 70.12–14; [*v*] 5, 72.18–22, 23–24; [*vi*] 6, 73.16–18; [*vii*] 6, 73.22–27; [*viii*] 11, 76.34–77.1–2; [*ix*] 11, 77.13–16; [*x*] 13, 78.11–15; [*xi*] 17, 80.26–28–81.1–2; [*xii*] 18, 81.23–24; [*xiii*] 18, 82.14–16; [*xiv*] 18, 82.21–25; [*xv*] 19, 83.5–7; [*xvi*] 26, 87.20–22; [*xvii*] 27, 87.32–33–88.1–5; [*xviii*] 27, 88.12–15; [*xix*] 27, 88.23–28; [*xx*] 28, 89.4–5; [*xxi*] 28, 89.29–30; [*xxii*] 29, 90.22–26, 29; [*xxiii*] 29, 91.2–4; [*xxiv*] 31, 92.13–16; [*xxv*] 32, 92.26–28. – By the way, a complete corpus of Palamas' works consists of the total of 444 direct quotations from the areopagite writings, out of which even 309 (around 70%) originate from the writing *On the divine names* – that is, of course, if one can rely on the index given in the complete works by Gregory Palamas edited under the conduct of Panayiotis Chrestou, and the concentration of J. Blackstone, "Reading Denys in late Byzantium: Gregory Palamas's Approach to the Theological Categories of 'apophasis' and 'union and distinction,'" in: E. Russell, ed., *Spirituality in Late Byzantium: Essays Presenting New Research by International Scholars*, Newcastle upon Tyne: Cambridge Scholars Publishing 2009, 45–53: 52, n. 10, this data was taken from.

15. [*i*] *Περὶ ἑνώσεως καὶ διακρίσεως* 5, Συγγράμματα Β΄ [²1994] 72.6–11; [*ii*] 17, 81.7–11.

16. [*i*] *Περὶ ἑνώσεως καὶ διακρίσεως* 27, Συγγράμματα Β΄ [²1994] 88.18–22; [*ii*] 32, 92.17–19.

reception of Areopagite,[17] the point that served him as an important haven for the foundation of his doctrine on the distinction of essence and energy in the divine being.[18]

Semantic aspects of Palamas' interpretation of the dionysian theory of unity and distinction – namely, the existence of more kinds of unity and distinction, the unplausibility of identification of the divine "energetic" distinctions with created beings, as well as proving that the multiplicity of energies does not abrogate the simplicity of God, and so on – will remain aside for now, and will be considered at some other time.[19] On this occasion, I shall, as I have already indicated, mainly turn to the places where Palamas refers to the value of authority *per se*, those places, namely, where Palamas with qualifications of the very personality of Dionysius wants to support Areopagite's – and then his own – theological standpoints.

For Palamas – and that can be read already in the introductory sentences of the writing – Dionysius Areopagite is an "immediate hearer of the voice of Christ's apostles" (αὐτήκοος γεγονὼς τῆς τῶν ἀποστόλων τοῦ Χριστοῦ φωνῆς), the one who "in accordance with it constantly practised himself in the whole science and language regarding the divine [matters]" (τῇ περὶ τὰ θεία συντόνῳ τε καὶ παντελεῖ σχολῇ καὶ γλῶτταν διαρκῶς γεγυμνασμένος), and, finally, the one who, "not without divine inspiration" (οὐδ' ἄνευ ἐπιπνοίας θείας), "was moved to present for the benefit of the latter [the doctrine of] divine unity and distinction, announcing to the wise the safest and the truest theology about them [*sc.* about divine unity and distinction]" (περὶ θείας ἑνώσεως καὶ διακρίσεως ἐκθέσθαι τοῖς ἔπειτ' ἐσομένοις λυσιτελῶς κεκινημένος, τὴν περὶ τούτων ἀσφαλεστάτην καὶ ἀληθῆ θεολογίαν τοῖς εὖ φρονοῦσι διετράνωσεν).[20] In the fifth chapter of the writing in question, Palamas says that Dionysius is "an authentic mystagogist more than anybody else in such [*sc.* theological] issues" (οὗτος γὰρ ἡμῖν εἴπερ τις τῶν τοιούτων ἀξιόχρεως

17. Cf. A. Louth, "The Reception of Dionysius in the Byzantine World: Maximus to Palamas," *Modern Theology* 24, 4 (2008) 585–599: 596.

18. On the significance of categories of unity and distinction for Gregory Palamas, see: A. Louth, "St Gregory Palamas and the Holy Mountain," in: D. Conomos, G. Speake, eds., *Mount Athos, the Sacred Bridge. The Spirituality of the Holy Mountain*, Oxford, Bern, Berlin, Bruxelles, Frankfurt am Main, New York, Wien: Peter Lang 2005, 49–67 = *Philotheos. International Journal for Philosophy and Theology* 7 (2007) 311–320: 319–320.

19. For this, see: Ἀ. Ράντοβιτς, *Τὸ μυστήριον τῆς Ἁγίας Τριάδος κατὰ τὸν ἅγιον Γρηγόριον Παλαμᾶν*, Ἀνάλεκτα Βλατάδων 16, Θεσσαλονίκη: Πατριαρχικὸν Ἵδρυμα Πατερικῶν Μελετῶν 1973, ²1991, 102–110. Also, in broad strokes: B. G. Bucur, "Dionysius East and West: Unities, Differentiations, and the Exegesis of Biblical Theophanies," *Dionysius* 26 (2008) 115–138; J. Blackstone, "Reading Denys in late Byzantium: Gregory Palamas's Approach to the Theological Categories of 'apophasis' and 'union and distinction,'" in: E. Russell, ed., *Spirituality in Late Byzantium...*, Newcastle upon Tyne 2009, 45–55. In regard to the study by Bogdan Bucur, it is symptomatic – for many things, i.e. – that its author, speaking of the dionysian theory of *unity* and *distinction* and the reception of that theory by Thomas Aquinas and Gregory Palamas, does not take *at all* into account Palamas' treatise named *On Divine Unity and Distinction*, and is almost solely focused on his *Physical and Theological Chapters*.

20. *Περὶ ἑνώσεως καὶ διακρίσεως* 1, Συγγράμματα Β΄ [²1994] 69.1–8.

μυσταγωγός), so that "from him as almost the first one [...] the Church was consecrated in the *elements of theology*" (καὶ παρ' αὐτοῦ σχεδὸν πρώτου [...] καὶ αὐτὰ σχεδὸν τὰ στοιχεῖα τῆς θεολογίας ἡ ἐκκλησία μεμύηται).[21] To the same effect is the whole course of the writing interwoven with a variety of affirmative attributes which are attributed to Dionysius, such as "θεοφάντωρ,"[22] "θεορρήμων,"[23] "θεηγόρος,"[24] "θεῖος ὑμνολόγος,"[25] "θείων ὑμνῳδῶν ἐξοχώτατος,"[26] "θεολόγος,"[27] while out of all of them, and with a high frequency of use in particular, the attribute "great" (μέγας) stands out. Exploiting the thought of the author he provided with such characterizations as "canon and light" (ὡς ἂν ἡμεῖς ταύτῃ κανόνι καὶ φωτὶ χρώμενοι) and "correctly interpreting the word of the *truth*" (ὀρθοτομοῦντες τὸν τῆς ἀληθείας λόγον),[28] Palamas will, as he himself says, be able to bring to that truth again those who fell away from it – naturally, if they themselves want to do so. And this enterprise of his would certainly be made possible by the fact that Dionysius thinks and speaks in the same way as "all those godbearers before him"[29] did – who, naturally, did not speak and think simply "by themselves, but following the sacred words" (οὐδ' αὐτοὶ παρ' ἑαυτῶν λέγοντες, ἀλλὰ τοῖς ἱεροῖς λογίοις ἑπόμενοι).[30]

Even from the very listing of these (for our modern ear) rather inappropriate qualifications, we can state that for Palamas they do not represent mere rhetorical adornments, nor just some flow of piety towards one great, as he considers him, authority from the past. For Palamas, the aforementioned qualifications have the importance of the first rate epistemological principle, which is evident even from the textual composition of the writing: the fact that Palamas quotes mentioned prerogations at the very beginning, undoubtedly points to the fact that they should have a function of one general epistemological premise – something like *premisa major* – from which one should conclude that what is said by the author to whom these prerogatives are attributed must inevitably be true. In the same sense, the distribution of attributes with the prefix god- (θεο-) throughout the whole writing serves as a constant reminder that the teachings coming from the author, who has these attributes, spring from the very divine revelation. Therefore, the fundamental gnoseological assumption, as well as the retreat point from which the conviction of the truthfulness of further conclusions is drawn, is

21. *Περὶ ἑνώσεως καὶ διακρίσεως* 5, Συγγράμματα Β′ [²1994] 72.13–17. In this, as in the other quotations from the writings of Gregory Palamas, italics are, of course, mine.
22. *Περὶ ἑνώσεως καὶ διακρίσεως* 33, Συγγράμματα Β′ [²1994] 93.13.
23. *Περὶ ἑνώσεως καὶ διακρίσεως* 7, Συγγράμματα Β′ [²1994] 73.29.
24. *Περὶ ἑνώσεως καὶ διακρίσεως* 7, Συγγράμματα Β′ [²1994] 74.4; 32, 92.26.
25. *Περὶ ἑνώσεως καὶ διακρίσεως* 32, Συγγράμματα Β′ [²1994] 94.20.
26. *Περὶ ἑνώσεως καὶ διακρίσεως* 32, Συγγράμματα Β′ [²1994] 94.22–23.
27. *Περὶ ἑνώσεως καὶ διακρίσεως* 32, Συγγράμματα Β′ [²1994] 92.25; 32, 93.8.
28. *Περὶ ἑνώσεως καὶ διακρίσεως* 32, Συγγράμματα Β′ [²1994] 92.25; 32, 93.8.
29. *Περὶ ἑνώσεως καὶ διακρίσεως* 2, Συγγράμματα Β′ [²1994] 69.15–16.
30. *Περὶ ἑνώσεως καὶ διακρίσεως* 19, Συγγράμματα Β′ [²1994] 83.4–5.

expressed by the affiliation to the *tradition* and, even more so, by the instance of (infallible and immediate) *authority*. Palamas' hermeneutics for its starting point has a view as follows: as Dionysius is an immediate hearer of the apostle's voice, what he talks of has an epistemological value of the first rate, as his words represent the derivative of hearing the immediate, apostolic experience (and knowledge) of the divine matters. Moreover, apart from this derived character - derived in so much as Dionisius receives it by the help of the apostle, and not directly from God - sayings by Dionisius also represent *direct* experience of the divine, to which Palamas' apposition "not without divine inspiration" (οὐδ' ἄνευ ἐπιπνοίας θείας)[31] undoubtedly directs us to. Hence, the dionysian theory of unity and distinction, having originated from the period when the opinion was directly inspired by the outpouring of the Holy Spirit, has a value and strength of an absolute and unquestionable axiomatic proposition, in other words, it is classified under the heading "general principles" (κοινῶν ἐννοιῶν) - that is, logical structures that reflect direct revelations of God to people.[32] The dionysian theories, thus, do not

31. *Περὶ ἑνώσεως καὶ διακρίσεως* 1, Συγγράμματα Β΄ [[2]1994] 69.4–5.

32. See: Χ. Ἀθ. Τερέζης, *Γρηγόριος Παλαμᾶς: Μεθοδολογικά. Ἡ θεωρία περὶ "ἑνώσεων-διακρίσεων,"* Ἀθῆναι: Ἴνδικτος 1999, 28. The expression "general principles" (κοιναὶ ἔννοιαι) I do not regard here in any other sense, but the Aristotelian one (although somewhat modified by Palamas), namely, that something is taken as "the beginning" of the proof; in other words, it is what Aristotle calls "general principles," "common standpoints" or simply "axioms" (ἀξιώματα) (Ἀριστοτέλους *Ἀναλυτικὰ πρότερα καὶ ὕστερα* | Aristotelis *Analytica Priora et Posteriora*. Recensuit brevique adnotatione critica instruxit W. D. Ross. Prefatione et appendice auxit L. Minio-Pluello, Scriptorum classicorum bibliotheca oxoniensis, Oxonii: e Typographeo Clarendoniano 1964, 1978, 1982, II.1.75a38–75b2, 76b10–16). It concerns, therefore, the matters which are comprehensive by their own nature and include, within the frame of Palamas' use of apodyctic syllogysm in theology, revealed truths as well - among others, those conveyed to us via "the disciple of apostle," Dionysius. Cf. Γρηγορίου Παλαμᾶ, *Β΄ Πρὸς Βαρλαάμ*, 54, in: *Γρηγορίου τοῦ Παλαμᾶ Συγγράμματα*. Ἐκδίδονται ἐπιμελείᾳ Π. Κ. Χρήστου. Τόμος Α΄. Λόγοι ἀποδεικτικοί. Ἀντεπιγραφαί. Ἐπιστολαὶ πρὸς Βαρλαὰμ καὶ Ἀκίνδυνον. Ὑπὲρ ἡσυχαζόντων. Ἐκδίδουν Β. Bobrinsky, Π. Παπαευαγγέλου, I. Meyendorff, Π. Χρήστου, Θεσσαλονίκη: Κυρομάνος 1962, [2]1988, 260–295: 291.28–29: "Κοιναὶ ἔννοιαι καὶ ἀξιώματα τὰ φύσει γνώριμα καὶ πᾶσιν ἀνωμολογημένα."

Two places from another Terezis' study of Gregory Palamas (Χ. Τερέζη, *Ἡ θέση τῆς ἑλληνικῆς φιλοσοφίας στήν Ὀρθόδοξη Ἀνατολή. Σπουδή στόν Ἅγιο Γρηγόριο Παλαμᾶ*, Φιλοσοφική καί θεολογική βιβλιοθήκη № 32, Θεσσαλονίκη: Πουρναρᾶ 1995, 94, 190) - sort of resemblance of some quotations presented here - were the inducement for a prominent Greek philosopher Γ. Ἀ. Δημητρακόπουλος, *Αὐγουστῖνος καί Γρηγόριος Παλαμᾶς. Τά προβλήματα τῶν ἀριστοτελικῶν κατηγοριῶν καί τῆς τριαδικῆς ψυχοθεολογίας*, Ἀθήνα: Παρουσία 1997, 98–100, to criticize Terezis for attributing to Palamas a sort of inherentistic theory, in other words, theory of innate ideas. Demetracopoulos, with good reasons, thinks that attributing this theory to Palamas has no textual confirmation - at least not where Terezis searches for it - up to Palamas' *Physical and Theological Chapters* and the influence of blessed Augustine - and even then in a quite unintentional and relaxed way. In his opinion, Terezis' interpretation "actually resembles more of a forced attempt to philosophize Palamas' teachings" (*op. cit.*, 98–99). Terezis' outstandingly pompous language and the use of difficult categorial apparatus during his analysis of Palamas' thought can actually lead us to the Demetracopoulos' assesment; on the other side, it is striking that Demetracopoulos proves that Palamas was not *sensu stricto* a philosopher (something that Palamas himself would have accepted with ease) almost under

represent subjective and, in some sense, arbitrary theoretical constructions, but are authentic and credible, not altering in any way theological truths which were revealed via Christ.[33]

On the whole, the very fact that Dionysius, according to Palamas, was the disciple of the apostle makes him the first rate *authority*, and thus an unerrable gnoseological criteria when the divine matters are concerned. This is, anyway, clearly testified by the very statement of Palamas that he would not use Dionysius' theology either less or more but as a "canon and light." Finally, the fact that the authority of Dionysius is taken as a starting assumption in consideration of the theological matters is most obvious, perhaps, in the place in which Palamas explicitly says that he takes Dionysius' *dicta* as "undemonstrable and self-evident principles" (ἐξ ἀναποδείκτων καὶ αὐτοπίστων ἀρχῶν)[34] – in other words, as axioms and unconditional propositions from which other conclusions are derived. They, thus, do not have further anagogic character, but represent the point of reference for each theological thesis that pretends to be credible. In short, Dionysius' testimonies, as "elements of theology" (τὰ στοιχεῖα τῆς θεολογίας),[35] "take up a place of credible and internally grounded epistemological criteria, both in terms of description of ontological relations, and the methodological derivations."[36]

Palamas' referring to the authority – and particularly due to the fact that the context of the whole story is dominantly theological – in the hermeneutical sense is quite plausible on its own and also legitimate to the very end. It matters, in a specific sense, if we evade the Enlightenment's somewhat ahistorical belief in the power of human reason, and if we, simultaneously, rehabilitate notions of tradition and authority, as, in the first instance at least, epistemologically neutral categories, ones that can have positive and negative foretoken[37] respectively. On that level, authority represents an instance which can lead us to the reaching of the truth, as it is founded on *cognitive and rational competence*, not on the force or superiority of the power which demands blind obedience and an "abdication of the mind" (*Abdikation der*

---

the imperative "to be or not to be" – that is, as if his "to be a philosopher" is dependent on how successful he would be in proving Palamas' "not to be a philosopher" – and "Byzantine philosophical sterility" *en bloc* at the same time. See: J. Demetracopoulos, *Is Gregory Palamas an Existentialist? The Restoration of the...*, Athens 1996, 38; Γ. Ἀ. Δημητρακόπουλος, *Αὐγουστῖνος καί Γρηγόριος Παλαμᾶς. Τά προβλήματα τῶν ἀριστοτελικῶν κατηγοριῶν...*, Ἀθήνα 1997, 101). Whatever the reason, Demetracopoulos within his exciting trilogy "Gregorius Palamas philosophus? I–III" (*op. cit.*, 55–63 [144–147], 77–79 [154], 94–104 [168–173]) presents valid arguments, which must be inevitably taken into account.

33. Χ. Ἀθ. Τερέζη, *Γρηγόριος Παλαμᾶς: Μεθοδολογικά...*, Ἀθῆναι 1999, 29.
34. *Περὶ ἑνώσεως καὶ διακρίσεως* 5, Συγγράμματα Β´ [²1994] 72.12–13.
35. *Περὶ ἑνώσεως καὶ διακρίσεως* 5, Συγγράμματα Β´ [²1994] 72.16–17.
36. Χ. Ἀθ. Τερέζη, *Γρηγόριος Παλαμᾶς: Μεθοδολογικά...*, Ἀθῆναι 1999, 31.
37. See: H.-G. Gadamer, *Wahrheit und Methode. Grundzüge einer philosophischer Hermeneutik*, in: Gadamer, *Gesammelte Werke*. Band 1. Hermeneutik I, Tübingen: J. C. B. Mohr (Paul Siebeck) [1960, ²1965, ³1972, ⁴1975, ⁵1986] ⁶1990, 281–290 [="Die Rehabilitierung von Autorität und Tradition"].

Vernunft) that would suspend every free opinion.[38] In short, when authority is based on knowledge, on cognitive insight and admittance that "[an]other may see a certain thing better than we ourselves can,"[39] then it is normatively justified and, together with tradition, represents an assumption of understanding.[40]

The problem, however, arises when referring to an authority and tradition gains a deformed shape, in the first place, by a neglecting or completely ignoring of the *critical* and *reflexive* note,[41] namely, the very critical distance the authority himself calls for, and which supposedly separates the notion of the authoritarian from the notion of the authoritative.

That the critical distance, at least in certain places, is lacking in Palamas during his treatment of Dionysius, is more than clear from the way he reacted when inviolable authority of this "archetypal Christian theologian" – whom Palamas "accepted unconditionally"[42] and followed ever since his early writings – was brought into question. And the authority of Dionysius, with the strength of the polemic context in which Palamas found himself, was questioned in an indirect, but quite explicit way in the thirty-third chapter of writing *On divine unity and distinction*, where Palamas endeavours to answer the question why none of the fathers from the first christian centuries referred to Dionysius' writings, his theory of unity and distinction, in particular. This, even in that time, old, but for Palamas certainly still disturbing, question was directed to him presumably by some of his oponents, which could be, possibly, concluded from the very way this "problem" was formulated: "Does *anyone* ask," says Palamas, "why the theologians after this revealer of God, who from the very beginning so zealously tried to teach on this distinction, *do not speak much of it* [...]"[43]– after which he strives to give a satisfying answer to this query, and, of course, to defend Dionysius, at any cost.

38. See: H.-G. Gadamer, *Wahrheit und Methode...*, in: Gadamer, *Gesammelte Werke.* Band 1. Hermeneutik I, Tübingen ^{6}1990, 284.
39. S. Radojčić, "Gadamerovo shvatanje tradicije," *Filozofija i društvo* 1 (2009) 71–91: 78.
40. See, for example: H.-G. Gadamer, "Wahrheit in den Geisteswissenschaften," in: Gadamer, *Gesammelte Werke.* Band 2. Hermeneutik II. Wahrheit und Methode. Ergänzugen. Register, Tübingen: J. C. B. Mohr (Paul Siebeck) [1986] ^{2}1993, 37–43: 39–40.
41. Reflection is, according to Gadamer, necessary for comprehension, and in the absence of it, one ends, as a rule, in an apologetic, "conducted reading." In other words, without a critical review – which, however, can never be absolute – there is no real comprehension. Cf. H.-G. Gadamer, "Reply to David Detmer," in: *The Philosophy of Hans-Georg Gadamer*. Edited by L. E. Hahn, Chicago: Open Court 1997, 287: "The stubborn clinging to prejudices or even the blind appeal to authority is nothing but the laziness to think."
42. J. Romanides, "Notes on the Palamite Controversy and Related Topics," *Greek Orthodox Theological Review* 9, 2 (1963–1964) 225–270: 250.
43. *Περὶ ἑνώσεως καὶ διακρίσεως* 33, Συγγράμματα Β΄ [^{2}1994] 93.13–16: "*Εἰ δέ τις διαποροίη, τοῦ θεοφάντορος τοῦτου διὰ τοσαύτης σπουδῆς θεμένου περὶ τῆς διακρίσεως διδάξαι ταύτης τὴν ἀρχήν, ὅτου χάριν οἱ μετ' αὐτὸν θεολόγοι μὴ πολὺν περὶ αὐτῆς πεποίηνται [...]*".

The way Palamas tries to give an answer to this more than justified objection is symptomatic and indicative by itself. If we look at those answers of his with valid prejudices, we would see that there is, in fact, more of circumvention, evading and displacement than the real answering to the aforementioned objection. Palamas, as quite often in his writings, appears full of self-confidence: we can, he says, "easily" (ῥᾴδιον) show that there are many places even in the works of the theologians "after" Dionysius where they theologize "in accordance" with Dionysius and "in similar words" with which Dionysius himself theologizes on distinctions in God – that is, on divine energies.[44] Apart from that, Palamas continues, not only theologians "after" Dionysius theologized as he had done, but that was also the case with the theologians who preceded him, as well as with "all the divine theologians from all ages in general."[45] In this very wide, we would say, corpus of thinkers who support Dionysius' – and then, not less importantly, his own – theological standpoints, Palamas includes apostles Paul and John as well as the Old Testament prophets Isaiah and Zachariah. More precisely, Palamas quotes the following places: 1. *Epistle to the Hebrews*, chapter two, the fourth verse, where the apostle Paul says that God bears witness not only by signs and wonders, but also by manifold *powers* and *gifts* of the Holy Spirit; 2. Two places from the *Book of Revelation*: firstly, chapter one, fourth verse, where together with the Father and the Son, *seven spirits against one Spirit* are included, which should, according to Palamas, signify innate energies of the Spirit. The second place from the *Book of Revelation* which Palamas refers to and interprets in the same sense is chapter five, verse six, where the apostle John speaks of a lamb with *seven horns* and *seven eyes*; 3. *Book of Isaiah*, chapter eleven, verses 1–3, where it is also spoken of the *seven spirits*, which, according to Palamas, represent again nothing else but uncreated divine energies; and finally, 4. *Book of Zachariah*, chapter four, verses 2–10 where the angel explains to the prophet, who saw seven lamps and seven pipes, that those are in fact *seven eyes* of the Lord which run to and fro through the whole earth – which should, in the same sense as the previously quoted places, signify "to the nature of God inherent providential progresses and energies" (τὰς φύσει προσούσας τῷ θεῷ προνοητικὰς προόδους τε καὶ ἐνεργείας).[46] And to make it all the more convincing, Palamas asserts that in his earlier writings against Barlaam and his followers, he showed that "witless" are those who do not accept the divine distinction concerned[47] – which should, according to him, offer by itself an additional answer to the quoted question.

Two things in this reply of Palamas are more than indicative. Firstly, all those who should try to find places in fathers "after" Dionysius – that is, in fathers of the first centuries – decisevely and explicitly presented dionysian

44. *Περὶ ἑνώσεως καὶ διακρίσεως* 33, Συγγράμματα Β′ [²1994] 93.16–20.
45. *Περὶ ἑνώσεως καὶ διακρίσεως* 33, Συγγράμματα Β′ [²1994] 93.20–23.
46. *Περὶ ἑνώσεως καὶ διακρίσεως* 33, Συγγράμματα Β′ [²1994] 93.23–94.10.
47. *Περὶ ἑνώσεως καὶ διακρίσεως* 33, Συγγράμματα Β′ [²1994] 95.1.

doctrine on unity and distinction in God, would be in great trouble. It seems that Palamas himself was aware of this, and that is the reason of his not saying that the *same* doctrine appears in these theologians, but the doctrine which is "in accordance" (συνῳδὰ) with it, being presented with "similar words" (τῶν οἰκείων λόγων).[48] Phrases "similar words" and "in accordance" are here of key importance; similarities and accordances between Dionysius and the fathers of the first christian centuries exist indeed, but "similar," as we well know, is not the "same" – either in terms of language, or the spirit and the choice of themes, and certainly not in terms of the way of formulating.

Secondly, it is symptomatic that Palamas himself, by the old and tested mechanism of displacement, actually *avoids* giving an answer to the real question, by shifting from proving that Dionysius' doctrine is present in the works of the fathers "*after*" him – which should have been proved actually – to proving that the doctrine on unity and distinction is also found in the thinkers *before* him, thus offering an extremely forced and artificial interpretation of the afore mentioned places from the Old and New Testament, an interpretation that could hardly leave an impression of deep convinction but in a few cases.

It seems that Palamas himself was aware of the fact that his answer to the posed question was not convincing, something which is obvious from the following, thirty-fourth chapter of the writing *On divine unity and distinction*, where he attempts to give a new answer – equally dissatisfying, in my opinion – to an objection with regard to the absence of referring to Dionysius' theory of "energetic" distinctions in the first christian centuries. Palamas now changes his polemic strategy: the absence of referring to this Dionysius' theory is a realistic one, but it is due, Palamas claims, to the external reasons. Namely, the fact that the theologians "after" Dionysius do not "particularly" (ἰδίᾳ)[49] deal with the theme of "energetic" distinctions – the word "particularly" is of importance here – is due to the thematic limits of their epoch, that is, to the fact that the central theme of the discussion in this era was the theme of the *hypostatic*, not of the *energetic*, distinction. As in those times, Palamas is convincing us, the theme of hypostatic distinction was a central one, and as it was disputed by the heretics, the defenders of the piety were fighting to prove it, trying to bring the truth of devoutness closer to the believers in a written form, so that the truth could be clearly discerned from the deception and from the lie of the irreverence.[50]

However, even for this subject, the fathers of the first centuries could have used the writings of Dionysius – had they been written then – and find places they could refer to,[51] but, as we know, they never did so, for their

48. *Περὶ ἑνώσεως καὶ διακρίσεως* 33, Συγγράμματα Β′ [[2]1994] 93.18–20.
49. *Περὶ ἑνώσεως καὶ διακρίσεως* 34, Συγγράμματα Β′ [[2]1994] 94.17–18.
50. *Περὶ ἑνώσεως καὶ διακρίσεως* 34, Συγγράμματα Β′ [[2]1994] 94.18–31.
51. Despite the fact that the issue of hypostatic distinction is not the *primary* aim of Dionysius' treatise *On the divine names*, as Palamas himself notices; *Περὶ ἑνώσεως καὶ διακρίσεως* 27, Συγγράμματα Β′ [[2]1994] 88.18–22. But, still, see quite explicitly: Τῷ συμπρεσβιτέρῳ Τιμοθέῳ

author had not been born yet, neither as a man, nor as a myth, nor as an author(ity) that was to influence the development of christian doctrine to a such great extent.

Thus, as we can relatively easily notice, Palamas misses a chance – the chance that was at his hand's reach – to critically re-examine certain inconsistences related to the "case of Dionysius" and thus – similar to the practice of some medieval authors[52] – to leave at least a trace of doubt concerning the personality of the author of areopagitic writings as well as this "premeditated forgery" of his (Florovsky). This is, in my opinion, due in the first place to Palamas' personal lack of readiness to make one critical step forward and so to *percieve* and *process* what plenty of facts were unequivocally pointing toward. And even if we must not demand from the medieval contemplative context what is possible for the later philological critical analysis, we may surely demand at least the possibility for *some* room to be left for a doubt and a critical reflexion, so that, in simple words, the already noticed fact that certain pieces from the puzzle are missing is at least *taken into account*. But, what is actually at issue here, and what seems to apply equally for any period of time or any contemplative context, is that diachronic inclination of man to close his eyes before the facts which undoubtedly lead him to a definite (unpleasant and psychologically disfunctional, as a rule) conclusion and, simultaneously with that, to postulate within the frame of a fictive description different *desiderata* as objective and even indisputable facts.

The authorship of Dionysius Areopagite, let us add, could have been questioned by Palamas not only on the basis of the previously quoted objection and the obvious external inconsistencies he himself had observed, but also on the basis of a so called *internal* analysis – in the first place, on the basis of the mind stream and the *language* of the dionysian corpus, which is in regards to these two parameters too far from the unaffected simplicity of the early

Διονύσιος ὁ πρεσβυτέρος *Περὶ θείων ὀνομάτων* 2, 5, *Patrologia Graeca* 4, 641D; *Corpus Dionysiacum I. De Divinis Nominibus.* Herausgegeben von B. R. Suchla, Berlin: Walter de Gruyter 1990, 128.8–13: "*Ἔστι δὲ καὶ διάκρισις ἐν ταῖς ὑπερουσίοις θεολογίαις, οὐχ ἣν ἔφην μόνον, ὅτι κατ' αὐτὴν τὴν ἕνωσιν ἀμιγῶς ἵδρυται καὶ ἀσυγχύτως ἑκάστη τῶν ἑναρχικῶν ὑποστάσεων, ἀλλ' ὅτι καὶ τὰ τῆς ὑπερουσίου θεογονίας οὐκ ἀντιστρέφει πρὸς ἄλληλα. Μόνη δὲ πηγὴ τῆς ὑπερουσίου θεότητος ὁ πατὴρ οὐκ ὄντος υἱοῦ τοῦ πατρὸς οὐδὲ πατρὸς τοῦ υἱοῦ, φυλαττόντων δὲ τὰ οἰκεῖα τῶν ὕμνων εὐαγῶς ἑκάστῃ τῶν θεαρχικῶν ὑποστάσεων.*" For this subject see also: S. J. Beggiani, "Theology at the Service of Mysticism: Method in Pseudo-Dionysius," *Theological Studies* 57 (1996) 201–223: 206–207; J. N. Jones, "The Status of the Trinity in Dionysian Thought," *Journal of Religion* 80 (2000) 645–657; J. Fisher, "The Theology of Dis/similarity: Negation in Pseudo-Dionysius," *Journal of Religion* 81 (2001) 529–548.

52. For the suspicions regarding the authorship of *Corpus Areopagiticum* in the ancient and the latter authors see: I. Hausherr, "Doutes au sujet du 'Divin Denys,'" *Orientalia Christiana Periodica* 2 (1936) 484–490; G. Makris, "Zwischen Hypatios von Ephesos und Lorenzo Valla. Die areopagitische Echtheitsfrage im Mittelalter," in: *Die Dionysius-Rezeption im Mittelalter...*, Turnhout 2000, 3–39. On the doubts about the authorship of the areopagite writings in the Byzantine world see my forthcoming essay titled: "'Dionysius ille quisquis fuerit.' Scholia on the 'Case, Areopagite.'"

christian epoch.[53] Striking similarities with neoplatonic writings Palamas could have comprehended relatively easily, as it is known for certain that he had been reading Plotinus[54] and Proclus, the latter of which was particularly known in the Byzantine world.[55] However, due to a lack of sufficient degree of critical reflection and not having the ability to overcome certain epistemological or, more precisely, "dogmatic blockades" (let us use one of Karl-Otto Apel's expressions), he chose, similarly to one of the authors of the *Prologue* for *Corpus Areopagiticum*,[56] to conclude that neoplatonic authors took the language and the ideas from "the disciple of apostle" Dionysius, rather than that Dionysius took the language and the ideas from them, in spite of the fact, that it would be assumed that the *holy fathers,* in thematic and terminological sense mainly *did not* follow "the disciple of apostle," while the *neoplatonists*, again, *did*, and in spite of the fact that Dionisius was *the only* christian author whose frame of mind and terminology so irresistably reminded of the neoplatonic school of thought, and in the first place of Proclus.[57]

Finally, if we want to approach the whole matter meticulously, we can say that, ultimately, it did not suit Palamas to call the issue of the authorship of areopagite writings into question, despite the numerous facts that should have led him to that. For, why snatch out of his own hand a powerful polemic

53. Г. В. Флоровскій, *Византійскіе Отцы V–VIII...*, Париж 1933, 95.
54. See: J. Demetracopoulos, *Is Gregory Palamas an Existentialist? The Restoration of the...*, Athens 1996, 21–25, 45–46; Ἰ. Ἀ. Δημητρακόπουλος, "'Υστεροβυζαντινὴ κοσμολογία. Ἡ κριτικὴ τοῦ Γρηγορίου Παλαμᾶ στὴ διδασκαλία τῶν Πλωτίνου καὶ Πρόκλου περὶ 'κοσμικῆς ψυχῆς,'" *Φιλοσοφία* 31 (2001) 175–191; 32 (2002) 111–132; Ἰ. Ἀ. Δημητρακόπουλος, "Γρηγορίου Παλαμᾶ, Κεφάλαια ἑκατὸν πεντήκοντα, 1–14: 'Περὶ κόσμου.' Κείμενο, μετάφραση καὶ ἑρμηνευτικὰ σχόλια," *Byzantiaka* 20 (2000) 293/5–348.
55. Cf. Χ. Ἀθ. Τερέζη, *Γρηγόριος Παλαμᾶς: Μεθοδολογικά...*, Ἀθῆναι 1999, 28.
56. Cf. *Patrologia Graeca* 4, 21D. This impossible scenario, according to which Proclus "literally quotes" (καὶ αὐταῖς δὲ ξηραῖς ταῖς λέξεσι) the "disciple of apostle" Dionysius Areopagite, was eventually adapted by H. Koch, "Proklos als Quelle des Pseudo-Dionysius Areopagita in der Lehre vom Bösen," *Philologus* 54 (1895) 438–454, who finally found out who actually quoted "literally" whom. Similar thesis is also found in 3, 13, *Patrologia Graeca* 4, 149–152, where, according to the scholiast, it seems that a complex terminology of the Council of Chalcedon and of the *Tomos* only follows Dionysius, and not the other way round, as in fact was the case.
57. In relation to Proclus' influence, I shall only mention two classical and well known studies that finally unmasked fascinating and almost fourteen centuries long – in some way – *manipulation*: H. Koch, "Proklos als Quelle des Pseudo-Dionysius Areopagita in der Lehre vom Bösen," *Philologus* 54 (1895) 438–454; J. Stiglmayr, "Der Neuplatoniker Proklos als Vorlage des sogenannten Dionysius Areopagita in der Lehre von Übel," *Historisches Jahrbuch* 16 (1895) 253–273, 721–748. However, these two studies not only dispersed apostolic aura of the author of *Corpus Areopagiticum*, but also in the same way – through joining to the philological one axiological diagnosis – dethronized *semantic* potentials of the writings concerned, with a consequence that they, especially in the philosophical sense, will be later characterized as a "forgery," and a "grotesque," not only in the part where Pseudo-Dionysius "literally quotes" Proclus, but also *en bloc.* This dethronization had great effects on the christian identity of the mysterious author and also on the christian content of his doctrine. For this, and, at the same time, for an example of overcoming such a position, see: Ch. Schäfer, *The Philosophy of Dionysius the Areopagite...*, Leiden, Boston 2006, 18–21.

weapon and remain without the patronage of the authority of apostle's own disciple for a doctrine he had to defend constantly and justify all over again?

At the very end, it should be said that Palamas, when the whole of his work is taken into account, is much more creative a thinker than one would discern from this episode. That can be seen on the basis of various interpretative factors. In the formal sense, we see it on the basis of the fact that in those places where he is not in full accordance with Pseudo-Dionysius, he simply does not mention him, nor does he try to follow him entirely and wholly. In terms of content, Palamas' creativity and a much higher degree of independence in regard to "Dionysius'" authority can be percieved from his further elaboration of the doctrine of energies, a doctrine that – still – can be found in earlier fathers only in less or more developed hints.[58] However, all this taken together will hardly confirm Meyendorff's thesis that Palamas performed a latent prestructuralization of Pseudo-Dionysius' thought – such boldness, as we have seen, he never had – certainly not to such a degree that the Areopagite's thought is "completely" changed, with the consequence that Palamas "in a number of issues undoubtedly contradicts Dionysius."[59] It is more likely that Palamas, being "open to the tradition" he belonged to, allowed to be changed on the part of that tradition, but also allowed himself to change that tradition, too – in the sense that within the scope of "a creative extension of ancient tradition,"[60] he further developed themes and possibilities that were implicitly present in Pseudo-Dionysius and other authors.[61] Hence, he undoubtedly overpasses the sterility of a "theology of repetition," having a sufficient degree of creativity to merit what was signified with a word ἀνάπτυξις – a term used by *Synodical Tome* of 1351 to characterize Palamas' theology, thus, as "a development" of doctrine on energies of Christ confirmed at the Sixth Ecumenical Council.[62]

58. See: Γ. Μαρτζέλου, *Οὐσία καὶ ἐνέργειαι τοῦ Θεοῦ κατὰ τὸν Μ. Βασίλειον. Συμβολὴ εἰς τὴν ἱστορικοδογματικὴν διερεύνησιν τῆς περὶ οὐσίας καὶ ἐνεργειῶν τοῦ Θεοῦ διδασκαλίας τῆς Ὀρθοδόξου Ἐκκλησίας*, Θεσσαλονίκη: Πουρναρά 1994; Ν. Ρ. Ξιώνης, *Οὐσία καὶ Ἐνεργείες τοῦ Θεοῦ κατὰ τὸν Ἅγιον Γρηγορίο Νύσσης*, Ἀθήνα 1999. – Cf. also V. Karayiannis, *Maxime le Confesseur. Essence et Énergies de Dieu*, Théologie historique № 93, Paris: Beauchesne 1993.
59. J. Meyendorff, "Notes sur l'influence dionysienne en Orient," *Studia Patristica 2* (1957) 547–552: 549.
60. G. Florovsky, "Saint Gregory Palamas and the Tradition of the Fathers," in: G. Florovsky, *The Collected Works*, ed. by R. C. Haugh, I–XIV. I: *Bible, Church, Tradition: An Eastern Orthodox View*, Vaduz: Buchervertriebsanstalt 1972, 1987, 105–120: 114.
61. A. Golitzin, "Dionysius the Areopagite in the Works of Gregory Palamas. On the Question of a 'Christological Corrective' and Related Matters," *Scrinium* 3 (2007) 83–105: 87. Cf. J. Blackstone, "Reading Denys in late Byzantium: Gregory Palamas's Approach to the Theological Categories of 'apophasis' and 'union and distinction,'" in: E. Russell, ed., *Spirituality in Late Byzantium...*, Newcastle upon Tyne 2009, 45–55[: 45].
62. See: *Συνοδικὸς τόμος κατὰ τῆς Βαρλαὰμ καὶ Ἀκινδύνου πλάνης τοῖς προτέροις κατ' αὐτῶν τόμοις ὁμόλογος. Ἐγένετο δὲ διὰ τοὺς ὕστερον ἀκολουθήσαντας τῇ τούτων πλάνῃ τόν τε χρηματίσαντα Ἐφέσου καὶ τὸν Γάνου, Γρηγορᾶν τε καὶ Δεξιόν, καὶ τοὺς αὐτοῖς συνυπαχθέντας*, in: Ἰω. Καρμίρης, *Τὰ Δογματικὰ καὶ Συμβολικὰ μνημεῖα τῆς Ὀρθοδόξου Καθολικῆς Ἐκκλησίας*, Τόμ. Α΄, Ἀθῆναι [2]1960, [r]Graz 1968, 374–410: 378; *Patrologia Graeca* 151, 722B3–4. For this topic see: Ж. К. Лар-

It is also worth mentioning that Palamas would not express such a devotion for Dionysius' authority only on the basis of his mere authoritativeness if in the writings that bore the name of the convert from the Areopagus there was not a "theological minimum,"[63] which would give legitimacy to their incorporation into christian tradition. In that sense, the hermeneutical principle advocated with regard to the dionysian writings by Vladimir Lossky,[64] which is contained in the referring of the apostle Paul to a Psalm of David – "one in a certain place hath testified" (Hebr. 2, 6) – certainly has its value, considering that it is entirely in the spirit of that famous Latin saying *Non quis, sed quid*, I am particularly fond of. According to this principle, in the final analysis, it is not important who the real author of aeropagite writings is – it is much more important *what* was testified, than *who* testified it, in the sense that if something is proper and true, it does not really matter who it comes from.[65] But, despite it all, there remains a question – the one that is surely motivating for consideration – would the "*quid*" of the writings that bear name of Dionysius Areopagite have been tackled to such an extent and had such an influence on the formation of Christianity had the illusion of their supposed "*quis*" been irrevocably broken before it became so dominant.

If we, now, from this episode, wish to come to the conclusion of a general type, it could be as follows. When chosing our authorities we must always be careful about two things, at least. Firstly, we must be careful in regard to *what* some authority says and to the *arguments* which he, contrary to our arguments, presents. Secondly, we must be cautious also in relation to the *one* who speaks, thus, towards the very *personality* of the authority, in the sense that even when we are convinced that what he says is indoubtedly correct, it can still remain hidden from us whether that authority really stays behind what he says – whether the issue is, if behind of what has been said really "hides" the author who we think is "hiding", or the issue is that some great or some alleged authorities just "hide" behind what they speak, while, actually, they stick to some totally diverse principles, fundamentally different from the ones they so eagerly preach.

ше, "Исихазам и Шести Васељенски Сабор. Има ли Паламистичко Богословље о Божанским енергијама основу у VI Васељенском Сабору?", in: *Свеши Григорије Палама у исшорији и садашњосши. Међународни научни симпосион: 650 година Саборског шомоса (1351–2001), 19–21. окшобар 2001*, ред. П. Пузовић, М. Васиљевић, Б. Брајовић, Србиње, Острог, Требиње: Духовна Академија Светога Василија Острошког 2001, 67–78/81.

63. Qualification I gave makes me closer to what says J. Pelikan, "The Odyssey of Dionysian Sprituality," in: *Pseudo-Dionysius. The Complete Works*. Translation by C. Luibheid. Foreword, Notes, and Translation Collaboration by P. Rorem. Preface by R. Roques. Introduction by J. Pelikan, J. Leclercq, K. Froehlich, New York: Paulist Press 1987, 8–23: 21–22, than, say, to less reserved estimations made by A. Golitzin, "'A Contemplative and a Liturgist': Father Georges Florovsky on the 'Corpus Dionysiacum,'" *St. Vladimir's Theological Quarterly* 43 (1999) 131–161: 140, note 35, 144, note 44 and A. Louth, "The Reception of Dionysius up to Maximus the Confessor," *Modern Theology* 24, 4 (2008) 573–583: 581, 582.

64. V. Lossky, *Essai sur la théologie mystique de l'Église d'Orient*, Foi vivante, Les Religions № 13, Paris: Éditions Montaigne 1944, [r]1990, 22–23.

65. Cf. Χ. Ἀθ. Τερέζη, *Γρηγόριος Παλαμᾶς: Μεθοδολογικά...*, Ἀθῆναι 1999, 27.

Nicholas Cabasilas and His Sacramental Synthesis

Milan Đorđević

This paper has the aim to question the notion of "synthesis" applied in the context of the Byzantine Christian philosophical tradition. The starting point of this process is the view according to which the traditionally argued systematic character of Byzantine philosophy in general should be understood as conceptual concentration around one particular philosophical issue and respectively one sphere of discussion, which thus generates a "point" or "center" of the philosophical synthesis and defines the paradigm of the philosophical research of the era. Within this process the theological and philosophical dimensions are being deepened and new relations between them are being achieved.[1] This conception will be adopted as the starting point for the following discussion in which I will try to show that the notion of synthesis cannot be completely exhausted with the process of conceptual explication, interaction and elucidation; on the contrary, it is possible to identify more complex synthetic patterns within the Byzantine Christian philosophical tradition, which have the potential to play a formative role at any stage of its further unfolding. In order to defend these claims and the corresponding approach, I will concentrate on the thought of a remarkable Byzantine intellectual of the 14th century, Nicholas Cabasilas, whose characteristic exposition and argumentation open new perspectives in approaching the Philosophy of Byzantium.

Being described as a "meditative Christian writer" concerned mainly with liturgical topics and as a "minor Aristotelian thinker," Cabasilas does not promise a lot, if we look for philosophical originality and systematic thinking. The fact that his main opus contains only two major works and a couple of sermons, treatises, letters and other smaller writings discourages us to look for any crucial contributions to the Byzantine philosophical and theological thought. And yet, literarily all "neopatristic" scholars without exclusion haven't missed to mention him as a key figure in the hesychastic movement of his time and to quote him as a supporter of their pro-palamite arguments. In parallel to this, the modern "antipalamites" are quite ambitious in their attempts to "depalamise" him and his thought, presenting

1. G. Kapriev, *Philosophie in Byzanz*, Würzburg 2005, 20.

him as a neutral and deeply ecumenically oriented intellectual, or even as an "criptoantipalamite" whose palamism was nothing more than a product of his alleged "opportunistic hypocricy."[2]

This ambiguity in Cabasilas' later reception coincides however with the attitude toward Cabasilas in the 14th century itself, in the time when he lived in Constantinople and Thessaloniki: all parties were trying to win him over to their side and to strengthen their position through having his name on the list of their supporters. But why would so many authors from the 14th century on try to win such a minor intellectual with a negligible bibliography to their side? Not to mention the fact that Cabasilas' sacramentology was accepted and praised even at the Council of Trent (1545–1562), for which the *Commentary of the Divine Liturgy* was translated in Latin in 1548.[3] So, what makes one author so suitable to be used as a by-the-way-argument in so many different contexts, but so rarely to be put in the focus of research activity (the number of the monographic researches of Cabasilas' thought is still unusually small)?

* * *

The thought of Nicholas Cabasilas represents one complex grid which embodies the central concepts of Christian philosophy in Byzantium. The liturgical-ascetic problem-sphere engraves the explicit structure of this grid, whereas the underlying philosophical concepts carry it, often in a fairly implicit manner. These concepts are employed by Cabasilas not only as tools for his liturgical exegesis or as means of constructing additional arguments for his claims, but in order to be ontologically activated, i.e. to achieve their final end. Cabasilas transforms these philosophical and theological concepts into liturgical realities, and thus places them in their most natural context – the only context in which they can fulfill their original discursive function.

The problem with approaching one such "synthesis" is that it cannot be treated in the same manner as the one achieved by Gregory Palamas for instance. Here we need another approach in comprehending the content and the function of the synthetic activity. If Palamas insisted on sharpening of the concepts and their concentration around his philosophical argument, at

2. J. Demetracopoulos, "Nicholas Cabasilas' Quaestio de Rationis Valore: An Anti-Palamite Defence of Secular Wisdom," *Byzantina* 19 (1998) 87–88; cf. Y. Spiteris, C. G. Conticello, "Nicola Cabasilas Chametos," in: *La théologie byzantine et sa tradition II*, ed. by C. G. Conticello, V. Conticello, Turnhout 2002, 315–322; G. Kapriev, *Philosophie in Byzanz*, 325–328. I have approached these issues in detail in my earlier monograph on Nicolas Cabasilas, a revised version of my doctoral dissertation defended at the Thomas Institute of the University of Cologne in 2011: Milan Đorđević, *Nikolas Kabasilas – ein Weg zu einer Synthese der Traditionen*, Recherches de Théologie et Philosophie médiévales – Bibliotheca, Paris, Leuven, Bristol CT: Peeters Publishers 2015. In this paper I offer further developments of some theses presented in the monograph.
3. P. Metso, *Divine Presence in the Eucharistic Theology of Nicholas Cabasilas*, Joensuu 2010, 5; cf. *Ibid.*, 137.

Cabasilas the accent shifts toward a softening of the strict conceptual structure of the exposition and puts its sacramental background to the fore. While in the first case the synthesized and explicitly philosophical concepts are "on the surface" and the sacrament is underneath holding them, in our case the sacrament comes to the fore and the concepts are underneath holding it.

The consequence of this characteristic of Cabasilas' thought is that here we cannot make a list of major philosophical topics and systematize them under the classical divisions: epistemology, cosmology, anthropology, Christology, etc. If we try to do this we won't be able to see its significance and we will righteously assess Cabasilas with attributes like "minor," "meditative," etc. The safest way to approach his thought leads then through an emphasizing of the most general concept of his thought: the sacrament and the way it functions in the lives of Christians. In order to accomplish this we must firstly abandon the usual distinction between Theology and Philosophy and begin treating this, for us, obviously theological concept in a philosophical manner. This first radical step brings us much closer to the Byzantine way of understanding the relation between these two activities, according to which all discursive theological activity was described through the term Philosophy, whereas Theology stayed as an expression for the non-discursive experience of contemplating God.[4]

After putting the emphasis on the sacramental synthetic field we will notice that all other applied concepts stay in relation to this one, but not so much supporting its validity (as the validity of a main argument), but simply and primarily "being there" as its inherent elements (coming out of it and having its purpose in it). The relation between the concepts and the field is ontological, rather than dialectical (in the conventional sense). For instance, when Palamas applies different philosophical concepts to the problem about the uncreated character of the Taboric light he does this in order to formulate valid arguments so that he can defend his central thesis. Indeed his arguments are related to the experience of God (Theology), they come out of it and try to describe it, but the context (field) within which they are applied to the problem is not the one of the "life in Christ," but the one of a philosophical controversy. Therefore the accent of Palamas' synthesis is on the shaping of precise and accurate arguments relating to the philosophical debate he is involved in, whereas the accent of Cabasilas' synthesis is on the integration of the already shaped concepts back in the most general sphere, relevant to every single Christian.[5]

The very structure of the main portion of Cabasilas' works resembles the foundation of the Christian life in general: the liturgy (*Exp.*), the sacraments

4. G. Kapriev, "Was hat die Philosophie mit der Theologie zu tun? Der Fall Byzanz", in: A. Rigo, ed., *Byzantine Theology and its Philosophical Background*, Turnhout 2011, 4–16.

5. Nicolas Cabasilas, *Vita* VI, 3–6. (Used edition : Nicolas Cabasilas, *La vie en Christ, Livres I–IV*, Sources Chrétiennes 355, éd. par M.-H. Congourdeau, Paris 1989 ; Nicolas Cabasilas, *La vie en Christ, Livres V–VII*, Sources Chrétiennes 361, éd. par M.-H. Congourdeau, Paris 1990)

(*Vita* I–V) and the ascetics (*Vita* VI–VII). In fact, Cabasilas succeeds in reducing Byzantine Christian philosophical thought to its most common and basic denominator, the "only thing needed:" the Divine love made available to creation in the sacramental life of the Church.[6] And he does this entirely on purpose. While the majority of classical Byzantine philosophers aim to expand the conceptual content of the tradition, he reduces it and goes down to the base, paying most attention to its precise place in the structure of the liturgy and the sacramental life of the Christians. Cabasilas in his method somewhat resembles a conceptual artist who focuses on the locating of the finished objects in the space and hence makes one such "installation" into a "functioning" piece of art. Still, there is a substantial difference, because Cabasilas does this according to the strict order defined by the very nature of the space in which he places his "objects."

In the case of Cabasilas the concepts don't concentrate around the core of the synthesis and stay there to guard it, but get "drown" into it, turned into it – still, without losing their essence and existence, but having achieved their ontological purpose. The way in which Cabasilas speaks about the central theme of his time, namely the *theosis* of the human person, is also way he treats the very λόγοι (concepts) he works with.[7] They exist exactly in order to be sanctified, to be transformed by the flames of the divine, inapprehensible light and, moreover, to begin radiating this same light themselves. This light that penetrates every single detail of Cabasilas' thought is the activity of the divine love, which is made accessible through their "drowning" in the all-uniting space of the sacrament of Christ.[8]

However, the "sacrament" here shouldn't be understood as a mystical meta-discursive reality which is above every concept and statement, as some higher form of knowledge superior to the rational and thus capable of guiding and directing it, but, on the contrary, as a synthetic space within which every philosophical concept receives its original discursive function. It is the common denominator of Christian Philosophy which is strictly immanent, although its subject matter (the mystical communion with God) entirely transcends human natural capacities.[9] Therefore the sacramental philosophy of Cabasilas must be distinguished from the transcendent sacramental reality itself. Within the sacramental discursive space the inherent oppositions of Christian philosophy are overcome and the multiplicity of byzantine philosophical problem-spheres and the interacting perspectives and concepts determining these problem-spheres are reduced and fulfilled. This often happens to a degree, at which point these particular concepts are not obvious

6. Nicolas Cabasilas, *Vita* VII, 109.
7. Cf. Nicolas Cabasilas, *Exp.* XXXVIII (Used edition : Nicolas Cabasilas, *Explication de la divine liturgie*, Sources Chrétiennes 4, éd. par S. Salaville, Paris 1967)
8. Nicolas Cabasilas, *Vita* IV, 7, 10, 26–27.
9. Cf. Nicolas Cabasilas, VII, 59–63.

in a given sacramental-philosophical context any more. They are not necessarily explicated as building blocks of arguments for an exact philosophical thesis directly deriving from them, still they are present there, but rather as "fulfilled" within the process of their dialectical "sacramentalisation" and "sanctification."

In this way Cabasilas succeeds at overcoming in his discourse the oppositions between the ascetic theology and the "school theology" (represented by the intellectuals close to the Emperors court and passionately criticized by the neopatristic scholars of the 20th century[10]); between the monastic asceticism and the lay piety of the city Churches; between the pro-western, latinophilic and the anti-western latinophobic intellectual currents. In Cabasilas one can find Byzantine Orthodoxy synthesized into a system valid for all Christians: laity, monks and clergy; educated and non-educated, philosophers and eremites; rich and poor; even politicians and businessmen. In the given context, he also makes a reference to the trending psychological topics such as stress and anxiety.[11]

In his major works Cabasilas revitalizes the stunted charismatic dimension of school theology and at the same time favors the philosophical and philological profundity of classical Greek education in the domain of ascetic theology.[12] He defends the role of secular wisdom for the accomplishing of the final end of human existence against the extreme voices coming from some of his monastic contemporaries,[13] and at the same time categorically rejects the idea that human intellectual power is superior to human willpower and thus supports the stand about the central role of asceticism for human perfection.[14] Cabasilas follows the pillars of Byzantine thought like Pseudo-Dionysius the Areopagite, Maximus the Confessor and Gregory Palamas on the majority of the topics he discusses, but he also consults Augustine, Anselm of Canterbury and Thomas Aquinas, whose philosophical and theological relevance appears to be neglected and even ignored by official Byzantine Orthodoxy.[15]

His writing *The Life in Christ* can actually be considered a sacramental guidebook of Byzantine philosophy and theology, reducing the whole diver-

10. Cf. J. Meyendorff, *Byzantine Theology: Historical Trends and Doctrinal Themes*, New York 1974, 62, 66; A. Schmemann, *The Historical Road of Eastern Orthodoxy*, Crestwood, NY 1977, 225–227.
11. Nicolas Cabasilas, *Vita* VII, 24–42.
12. Cf. M.-H. Congourdeau, "Introduction," in: M.-H. Congourdeau, éd., *N. Cabasilas, La vie en Christ, Livres I–IV, introduction, texte critique, traduction, et annotation*, Sources chrétiennes 355, Paris 1989, 11–67; R. E. Sinkewicz, "Christian Theology and the Renewal of Philosophical and Scientific Studies in the Early Fourteenth Century: The 'Capita 150' of Gregory Palamas," *Medieval Studies* 48 (1986) 334–351.
13. Nicolas Cabasilas, "*Quaestio de Rationis Valore*, ed. by J. Demetracopoulos," *Byzantina* 19 (1998) 55–57.
14. Nicolas Cabasilas, *Vita* VII, 100–101.
15. Cf. G. Kapriev, "Vier Arten und Weisen, den Westen zu bewältigen," in: A. Speer, P. Steinkrüger, ed., *Knotenpunkt Byzanz. Wissensformen und kulturelle Wechselbeziehungen*, Miscellanea Mediaevalia 36, Berlin 2012, 3–32.

sity of theological and philosophical topics to the "one thing needed" – the divine ecstatic love, from which these were primarily derived. The divine love is the source and fulfillment of every discursive activity, thus establishing the hierarchical structure of the system. The space within which the immanent presence and the activity of this love in the world is made possible, then, is the sacrament of Christ. Within it the system is being built and unfolded and, reversely, reduced back to the "one thing needed." The epistemological implications of Cabasilas' sacramentology are significant.

Cabasilas interprets the chronological order of the sacraments of the Church as mirrored in Christology: "He (Christ) descends in order that we could ascend [...]. What was last for him was made first for us."[16] As the order of the economy of salvation begins with the incarnation of the Logos, followed by his messianic activity and completed through his death and resurrection, the order of the sacraments begins with baptism (corresponding with the last stage of Christ economy), followed by the anointing (corresponding with the middle stage of Christ economy) and completed with the Eucharist (corresponding with the first stage of Christ economy). Here Cabasilas unites the famous Christological maxim of Athanasius: "God became human, so the man can become god,"[17] with the Pseudo-Dionysian claim about the simultaneous descending and ascending of the divine Eros[18] and thus places it in the particular sphere of the Church's sacramentality. Here it is possible even to establish a parallel to the doctrine of causality in Thomas Aquinas, to which Cabasilas was surely familiar with through his lifelong friend Demetrios Kydones, the famous translator of Aquinas in Greek.[19] The dialectical pattern of sacramental-erotic descending from the divine fullness and simplicity into the imperfection and plurality of the created world followed by the lifting of creation up to the starting point can be applied to the field of epistemology. In this exact pattern one can find the key for grasping the synthetic way of Cabasilas and its outstanding theological and philosophical significance, but also of the entire synthetic activity of the Christian philosophical tradition of Byzantium.

The carrying characteristic of this system is its inherent dynamism manifested through its capability to expand and contract. The starting point of the dialectical process is the contracted state in which the central concept of divine love is in the midst of the sacramental synthetic space and holds within itself the totality of the discursive content of the Christian faith. This is the territory of the two major commandments of the Scripture: the love

16. Nicolas Cabasilas, *Vita* II, 4.
17. Athanasius Alexandrinus, *De inc.*, 54, 3, PG 25, 192B.
18. Pseudo-Dionysius Areopagita, *Div. Nom.* IV, 14–16 (Used edition: Pseudo-Dionysius Areopagita, *De Divinis nominibus*, in: *Corpus Dionysiacum I*, hrsg. von B. R. Suchla, Patristische Texte und Studien 33, Berlin, New York 1990).
19. Thomas Aquinas, *Summa Theologiae* I, 5, 4 (Used edition: Thomas de Aquino, *Summa Theologica*, Heidelberg, Graz, Wien, Köln 1959).

of God and the love of neighbor, within which all the other commandments of the Law and the Prophets are found.[20] The discursive content of the faith is reduced to the core, where it dwells as fulfilled, but without losing its existence and significance. On the contrary, it is capable of exteriorizing itself in all its precision and complexity whenever there is a need for this.

This discursive content at this point has the quality of the notion of "dogma" in Saint Basil the Great, which denotes the secret, non-explicated teaching of the Church shared by the ensemble of the faithful participating in the sacramental life of the Church. On the other hand, the secret tradition ("dogma") can be declared publicly and thus become "preaching" ("kerygma") when a necessity obliges the Church to make its announcement.[21] Although this notion of "dogma" is secret, implicit and corresponds closely to the mystical metadiscursive reality, it is still placed within the field of the immanent and thus can express itself in terms of "kerygma."

When new unfamiliar concepts appear and start interacting with the system, the core releases the concepts that dwell within it, firmly keeping the bond with them and coordinating their activity. In this way the system interacts with the external concepts and assesses the issues generated through this interaction. Both the exterior and interior concepts are being impacted in this way: the new concepts are being adapted to the discursive order of the system and the old concepts are being viewed from a new perspective. This stage corresponds with the "unfolding" of the tradition, a notion introduced by Georgi Kapriev, through which he highlights the dynamic character of the tradition, thus escaping the risk of reducing it to "doctrinal development."[22]

The whole process is defined through the *bond* with the sacramental space, but it doesn't take place *within* it. The philosophical discussion is clearly distinguished from the sacramental practice, although it stays connected to it. The claim about the universal sacramentality of every single activity of the believing and practicing Christians[23] does not contradict this distinction: it can refer to the functional bond of the concepts with the sacramental reality, though not to their entering into its sacred space. The reason for this is entirely liturgically founded: its paradigmatic form is to be found in the relation between the liturgy of the catechumens and the liturgy of the holies. The external concepts stay outside the "sanctum sanctorum," until they are ready to "confess" the sacramental truth, i.e. until the orthodox form of their usage within Christian philosophy is found and articulated. This is, for instance, the stage of the "finished palamite synthesis," as it was

20. Mat. 22, 34–40.

21. Basil the Great, *De Spiritu Sancto* 27, PG 32, 188A–193A; cf. V. Lossky, "Tradition and Traditions," in: *In the Image and Likeness of God*, Crestwood, N.Y. 1985, 145–146.

22. G. Kapriev, *Philosophie in Byzanz*, Würzburg 2005, 20.

23. A. Kallis, "Sakrament - Ostkirchliche Theologie," *Lexikon für Theologie und Kirche* 8 (1999) 1445–1446; J. Meyendorff, *Byzantine Theology*, 191–193.

officially recognized by the councils in 1351 and 1368. Yet, at this stage the synthetic cycle is not yet completed.

The newly "converted" concepts should, analogically, be initiated in the "sanctum sanctorum" and receive their sacramental function. However, the initiation is not carried out in a manner of transferring them in a state of mystical silence and inactivity. The sacraments carry an important discursive dimension besides the mystical, which is expressed through words, gestures and symbols.[24] Within this dimension all new and old concepts are being applied, above all in hymnography and homiletics. These are predominantly constructed by the content coming from the Scriptures and the doctrinal and canonical acts of the Church Councils. The dense and explicit presence of complex and precisely exposed doctrinal content is a major formal characteristic of the Orthodox rite.[25] What is here of crucial importance, is that this textual dimension of the sacrament directly interacts with the expanded sacramental space, thus bringing all separate concepts together closer to the synthetic core. In contrast to the previous stage, this one takes place in the field of the sacrament and denotes the conceptual entrance into the "sanctum sanctorum."

At this point the sacramental discursive space contracts until it reaches the initial state of the reduction of all of its content to the central concept of divine love. The only thing that can be seen now is this concept that embraces all other concepts without assimilating them and radiating its light from the discursive space of the sacrament.[26] The closing words of *The Life in Christ* denote the climax of the philosophical synthesis of Cabasilas: "What would be then really worthy to be named 'life' if not love? Besides, the only thing that remains, when everything is taken away and that doesn't let the living ones to die is the life. Such is the love. And when in the forthcoming life everything gets abolished, as the apostle Paul says, only the love will remain and it will be sufficient for that life in Christ Jesus, our Lord, who deserves every eternal glory. Amen."[27] The primacy of love in the domains of ontology, anthropology, soteriology and eschatology applies to the domain of epistemology as well. Analogously, love is the only word left, it is the last resort of discursive thinking before the inexpressible experience of the ultimate mystical reality of communion with God. This is the final stage of "devolution" of the entire conceptual opulence of tradition, as well as an effective closure of the current synthetic cycle[28].

24. Nicolas Cabasilas, *Exp.* I.
25. G. Florovsky, "A Criticism of the Lack of Concern for Doctrine among Russian Orthodox Believers", ed. R. S. Haugh, *The Collected Works of Georges Florovsky, Vol. XIII, Ecumenism I: A Doctrinal Approach*, Belmont, MA 1976, 168–170.
26. Cf. Nicolas Cabasilas, *Exp.* XXXVIII.
27. Cf. Nicolas Cabasilas, *Vita* VII, 109.
28. Cf. G. Kapriev, *Philosophie in Byzanz*, 20.

This final stage of the synthesis of tradition should be once more clearly distinguished from the eschatological reduction of every historical reality to the fullness of the state of *theosis*. This state can be anticipated as theological (i.e. mystical, metadiscursive) knowledge achieved through the sacramental-ascetic experience. On the contrary, the "involution" achieved in Cabasilas has an iconic character and represents a discursive expression of this last form of knowledge. Indeed, Cabasilas writes exactly about the mystical experience of sacramental knowledge, which is beyond any rational expression, but the very activity he undertakes (the writing) is located entirely in the domain of rationality. On the other hand, as long as the sacrament denotes the domain of the encounter between finite and infinite, partial and perfect, crated and uncreated, it won't be possible to isolate rationality from sacramentality, but on the contrary, the former will be capable of being entirely penetrated by the later and will represent one of its constitutive elements.

* * *

The most significant achievement of Cabasilas is that he completes the synthetic cycle carried out by Gregory Palamas and enables it for further synthetic processes. Palamas' greatest success relates to the central phase of the synthesis, namely to the extraction of relevant arguments from the sacramental field and to their interaction with the external concepts and the issues generated within the debate of his time. The last enclosing step, however, is carried out far more efficiently by Cabasilas than by Palamas (in his late homilies). In this sense, Meyendorff was completely right in claiming that the thought of Cabasilas represents "palamite" theology at its purest.[29] Besides, what applies to "palamism" is to a significant degree applicable to the entire intellectual tendency often labeled as "Byzantine humanism," considering in fact that the sacramental discourse of Cabasilas includes a fruitful and unique reception of Ancient Greek and Medieval Latin philosophy.

The previously stated fact that Cabasilas was championed by all opposing sides – now and then – indicates that the dominant characteristic of his thought is common for all. His common acceptance should not be explained in the terms of a supposed selective reading of his works. One such thesis is based on an oversimplification and underestimation of both Cabasilas' contemporaries and modern researchers of his thought. Even more false would be to turn to the argument of the "imperfection of discursive thinking," according to which the apparent oppositions reconcile on some higher mystical level. In this way, the fundamental discursive dimension of Christian sacramentality is being denied, and respectively the actuality of its historical, natural, human dimension as well. The Christological implications of such an approach are profoundly questionable. Instead, it is much more sure

29. J. Meyendorff, *St. Gregory Palamas and Orthodox Spirituality*, Crestwood, N.Y. 1974, 131.

to look for reasons for the specific reception of Cabasilas within his own conceptual and dialectic framework.

The distinguishing and sharpening of the interacting internal and external concepts by Palamas, is followed by the integrating of the unfolded discursive content in the sacramental synthetic space and its gradual reduction to the core concept carried out by Cabasilas. Therefore, to read Cabasilas in the same manner as the tractates from the debate or the respective conciliar acts, means simply to miss the whole perspective of Cabasilas' thought. Indeed, some of the concepts present in Cabasilas were applied as arguments for opposing theses, but in Cabasilas they are released from their argumentative context, being adapted and directed to an entirely different end: to their ontological fulfillment.

Having exposed this extended conception of the synthesis of tradition, we can finally once more approach the disputed issue about the attitude of Cabasilas towards the philosophy of Gregory Palamas. Exactly by avoiding its basic terms, arguments and questions and reducing them gradually to the "one thing needed," Cabasilas actually confirms palamite philosophy in the most effective possible way. In this sense, the classification of Cabasilas in the party of the "antipalamites" is false, not because it is too radical, but on the contrary, because it is in fact not radical enough. The arguments of the antipalamites remain on the same conceptual plain with palamism. On the other hand, Cabasilas' position transcends the entire logic of the palamite-antipalamite debate and negates its very discursive framework: it's not the answers of the "palamites" that Cabasilas problematizes, it's in fact the questions of both palamites and the antipalamites, which are simply not actual in the sacramental discourse of Cabasilas.[30] Therefore, the synthesis completed by Cabasilas is not simply "the other side of the coin" in relation to "palamism," as it may seem[31], but it is the very coin as a whole, embodying in itself the fundamental stances of the entire hesychast philosophy and ultimately closing the actual synthetic cycle.

30. It is however essential to underline the fact that these questions were really never put by Palamas and the supporters of hesychasm, but precisely from their opponents, whereas Palamas was the one who answered them through adapting the ascetic discourse of the hesychasts to the opposing arguments and their discursive framework. Or, in other terms, Palamas played the key role in activating the appropriate conceptual content from the synthetic core of the tradition and applying it in the synthetic interaction between the external concepts and problems and the sacramental field. On the other hand, as it has been already discussed, the role of Cabasilas in this synthetic cycle concerns the stage of integration of the unfolded content within the sacramental field.

31. Cf. J. Meyendorff, *Byzantine Theology*, 108.

Scholarios vs. Pletho on Philosophy vs. Myth

Panagiotis Ch. Athanasopoulos

From the 14th century onwards, the ancient[1] dispute over the merits and demerits of Plato and Aristotle was rekindled[2] in Byzantium. In the 15th century, it developed into a theological–philosophical controversy,[3] the core of which was the question whether Aristotelianism or Platonism is more compatible with (or less distant from) the Christian religion. Thus, an ardent debate began, in which several great intellectual figures (such as Scholarios,[4] Pletho,[5] Bessarion[6] and George of Trebizond[7]) were involved. The issue had many facets, including the value of myth in philosophy. In this paper, I focus on the philosophical controversy between Scholarios and Pletho regarding the question of the value of Platonic myth as a means of detecting, exhibiting and teaching philosophical truths, with an emphasis laid on the undeclared sources used by the two opponents. Indeed, as will be shown, Scholarios heavily relied on Thomas Aquinas. In this respect, a significant part of this study falls under the editorial *Thomas De Aquino Byzantinus*[8] project, which aims to explore Byzantine Thomism; more specifically, the presence of Thomas in Scholarios' texts forms part of volume X of its Series altera (*Thomas de Aquino a Byzantinis receptus*).[9]

---

1. This controversy begins from the 1st century A. D. and continues at intervals in Byzantium.
2. Cf., e. g., Nicholas Cabasilas' mid–14th cent. reaction to Nicephoros Gregoras' radicalization of Theodore Metochites' Platonism and anti–Aristotelianism (J. A. Demetracopoulos, 1999, 111–116; 311–314).
3. B. Bydén, 2013, 158.
4. For Scholarios, see E. Trapp, H.–V. Beyer, R. Walther, 1976–1996 (from now on abbreviated as *PLP*), n. 27304; M.–H. Blanchet, 2008.
5. For Pletho, see *PLP*, n. 3630.
6. For Bessarion, see *PLP*, n. 2707.
7. For George of Trebizond, see J. Monfasani, 1976.
8. For the *Thomas de Aquino Byzantinus* project, see J. A. Demetracopoulos, 2012 and 2014b; cf. the websites of the Laboratory of Humanities, Faculty of Humanities and Social Studies, University of Patras (http://www.labarts.upatras.gr/dimitr/index1.html) and the Hellenic Institute, Royal Holloway, University of London (https://www.royalholloway.ac.uk/hellenic-institute//research/Thomas.htm).
9. *Loci diversi ex Thomae de Aquino scriptis graece translatis a nonnullis auctoribus Byzantinis aut explicite aut implicite laudati* (Simon Constantinopolitanus; Manuel Moschopoulos; Nilus

In 1439, on the sidelines of the Council of Ferrara–Florence, Pletho gave a famous lecture, which came to be traditionally known as *De differentiis* (*Περὶ ὧν Ἀριστοτέλης πρὸς Πλάτωνα διαφέρεται*). In this, Pletho argued for the inferiority of Aristotle to Plato, accusing the former of erring in eighteen issues out of his intemperate wish to differentiate himself from Plato. Pletho's writing, unsurprisingly, caused major reactions. In 1443/44, Scholarios refuted it in his *Contra Plethonis difficultates de Aristotele* (*Κατὰ τῶν Πλήθωνος ἀποριῶν ἐπ' Ἀριστοτέλει*) where he defended both the philosophical method and doctrine of Aristotle.

This refutation was dedicated to Constantine XI Palaeologos, as was meant to be the fulfillment of the author's promise to the emperor.[10] Scholarios declares that his intention was not to depreciate Pletho or even prevent any reader from being affected by Pletho and despising Aristotle; for, Aristotle's value is well established.[11] He also clarifies that he does not even seek any praise for defending Aristotle.[12] His motive, he says, was that Pletho surpassed everybody in insolence[13] and unlawfulness, by unleashing accusations against Aristotle.[14] This deserved an answer, which would show Pletho's ignorance of Aristotle's views. Besides, to Scholarios, Pletho should have declared his predilection for Plato without despising Aristotle; after all, everyone engaged in philosophy does likewise.[15] Scholarios declares that he holds both Plato and Aristotle in equally high esteem[16] and that both philosophers committed several errors, because they searched for truth on the basis of their own minds, when the light of truth had not yet shined on earth.[17] At this point, Scholarios seems to reproduce Thomas Aquinas' view of the limited character of the human capacity of knowing the truth concerning divine things on the basis of the *lumen rationis*.[18] As has been shown,[19] Scholarios reproduces this doctrine later on in his writing.

Cabasilas; Nicolaus Cabasilas; Manuel Corinthius; Prochorus Cydones; Demetrius Cydones; Manuel Calecas; Joseph Bryennius; Marcus Eugenicus; Macarius Macres; Manuel II Palaiologus; Georgius Scholarius – Gennadius II; Georgius Gemistus cognomine Pletho; Bessarion; Matthaeus Camariotes et al.).

10. Scholarios, *Contra Plethonis difficultates de Aristotele*, 1, l. 5–2, l. 3.
11. *Ib.*, 2, l. 3–8.
12. *Ib.*, 2, l. 13–14.
13. *Ib.*, 2, l. 20–22.
14. *Ib.*, 2, l. 25–26.
15. *Ib.*, 3, l. 28–31.
16. *Ib.*, 4, l. 26–29.
17. *Ib.*, 4, l. 30–32.
18. On Aquinas' distinction between *lumen rationis* and *lumen fidei*, see, e. g., *SG* I, 3, 2; *ST* I^{a}, q. 32 a. 1 co. and ad 1.
19. J. A. Demetracopoulos, 2004, 169–170 (Appendix II).

Thomas, *SG* I, 3, 2	**Scholarios, *Contra Plethonis difficultates de Aristotele*, 4, l. 30–32**
Est autem in his quae de Deo confitemur duplex veritatis modus. Quaedam namque vera sunt de Deo quae omnem facultatem humanae rationis excedunt, ut Deum esse trinum et unum. Quaedam vero sunt ad quae etiam ratio naturalis pertingere potest, sicut est Deum esse, Deum esse unum, et alia huiusmodi; quae etiam philosophi demonstrative de Deo probaverunt, ducti naturalis lumine rationis.	ἐς δὲ ἀλήθειαν οὐκ ὀλίγα καὶ ἄμφω τὼ ἄνδρε ἐξαμαρτεῖν, ἅτε τοῦ τῆς ἀληθείας φωτὸς μήπω ταῖς τῶν ἀνθρώπων ψυχαῖς ἐπιλάμψαντος.

As early as the preamble, Scholarios begins his attack with irony, arguing that even Pletho himself could benefit, should he actually pay attention to Aristotle's supporters who had exhibited "τὴν συγκεκαλυμμένην ἐκείνου σοφίαν".[20] As will be shown, Scholarios, when referring to Aristotle's interpreters, implies not only himself, but also some authors whom he would call upon to defend Aristotle. Among them, Thomas Aquinas has a prominent place.

Still, Scholarios does not restrict himself to defending Aristotle. He also tries to show that Plato was inferior to him: ἢ καὶ Πλάτωνα αἰτιῷτό τις ἂν ἐν πολλοῖς, μεταφοραῖς τισι καὶ τύποις τὰ δόγματα ἐπικαλύπτοντα, εἰ βούλοιτο ἐπὶ τὸ χεῖρον ἀκούειν, καὶ οὐ μόνον ἐς ἐπιστήμην, ἀλλὰ καὶ ἐς ἀρετὴν καὶ φύσιν παρανομεῖν τῳ δόξειεν ἂν τῇδέ πῃ σκοπουμένῳ.[21] This accusation is directed against Plato's habit of using metaphorical language (allegories, symbolisms and myths), which, to Scholarios, renders philosophical doctrines more obscure than clear. According to Scholarios, this practice is an unlawful detriment to science, ethics, and natural philosophy. Scholarios goes on by stating that philosophical language does not need any adornment; so, the *lingua obscura* of Aristotle suits the philosopher, while the ornamented language of Plato fits *par excellence* the poet.[22] This Scholarian rejection of Plato's usage of myth is not based only on Aristotle's *Metaphysics*[23] but also on Thomas Aquinas' *Commentary* on *Metaphysics*:[24]

20. Scholarios, *op. cit.*, 8, l. 19–22.
21. *Ib.*, 8, l. 22–25.
22. *Ib.*, 8, l. 22–29.
23. Aristotle, *Metaphysica* 1000a5–22. Apart from the passages cited in this paper, many passages from the *corpus aristotelicum* expressing a critical stand concerning myth in philosophical and scientific inquiry are traceable (see, e. g., *De caelo* 284a18–23; *Historia animalium* 578b23; 579b2–7; 597a4–9; 605a2–6; 756b3–8; *Mirabilium auscultationes* 839a8–11; *Politica* 1311b40–1312a6).
24. Thomas Aquinas, *Sententia Metaphysicae,* lib. I, lect. 15 n. 7; lib. III, lect. 11 n. 3. Cf. n. 6: Si vero aliquis velit de his inquirere secundum veritatem fabulis occultatam, immanifesta est. Ex quo accipitur quod Aristoteles disputans contra Platonem et alios huiusmodi, qui

Aristotle *Metaphysica* 1000a5–22	Thomas Aquinas *Sententia Metaphysicae,* lib. I, lect. 15, n. 7	Scholarios *Contra Plethonis difficultates de Aristotele*, 8, l. 22–29
Οὐθενὸς δ' ἐλάττων ἀπορία παραλέλειπται καὶ τοῖς νῦν καὶ τοῖς πρότερον, πότερον αἱ αὐταὶ τῶν φθαρτῶν καὶ τῶν ἀφθάρτων ἀρχαί εἰσιν ἢ ἕτεραι. Εἰ μὲν γὰρ αἱ αὐταί, πῶς τὰ μὲν φθαρτὰ τὰ δὲ ἄφθαρτα, καὶ διὰ τίν' αἰτίαν; Οἱ μὲν οὖν περὶ Ἡσίοδον καὶ πάντες ὅσοι θεολόγοι μόνον ἐφρόντισαν τοῦ πιθανοῦ τοῦ πρὸς αὐτούς, ἡμῶν δ' ὠλιγώρησαν (θεοὺς γὰρ ποιοῦντες τὰς ἀρχὰς καὶ ἐκ θεῶν γεγονέναι, τὰ μὴ γευσάμενα τοῦ νέκταρος καὶ τῆς ἀμβροσίας θνητὰ γενέσθαι φασίν, δῆλον ὡς ταῦτα τὰ ὀνόματα γνώριμα λέγοντες αὐτοῖς· καίτοι περὶ αὐτῆς τῆς προσφορᾶς τῶν αἰτίων τούτων ὑπὲρ ἡμᾶς εἰρήκασιν· εἰ μὲν γὰρ χάριν ἡδονῆς αὐτῶν θιγγάνουσιν, οὐθὲν αἴτια τοῦ εἶναι τὸ νέκταρ καὶ ἡ ἀμβροσία, εἰ δὲ τοῦ εἶναι, πῶς ἂν εἶεν ἀΐδιοι δεόμενοι τροφῆς)· – ἀλλὰ περὶ μὲν τῶν μυθικῶς σοφιζομένων οὐκ ἄξιον μετὰ σπουδῆς σκοπεῖν· παρὰ δὲ τῶν δι' ἀποδείξεως λεγόντων δεῖ πυνθάνεσθαι διερωτῶντας τί δή ποτ' ἐκ τῶν αὐτῶν ὄντα τὰ μὲν	Dicit ergo primo, quod dicere species esse exemplaria sensibilium et mathematicorum eo quod huiusmodi causas participent, est dupliciter inconveniens. [...] Alio modo quia est simile metaphoris quas poetae inducunt, quod ad philosophum non pertinet. Nam philosophus ex propriis docere debet. Ideo autem hoc dicit esse metaphoricum, quia Plato productionem rerum naturalium assimilavit factioni rerum artificialium, in quibus artifex ad aliquid exemplar respiciens, operatur aliquid simile suae arti. **lib. III, lect. 11, n. 3** Deinde cum dicit "qui quidem", excludit solutionem poetarum theologorum [...] Circa primum considerandum est, quod apud Graecos, aut naturales philosophos, fuerunt quidam sapientiae studentes, qui deis se intromiserunt occultantes veritatem divinorum sub quodam tegmine fabularum, sicut Orpheus, Hesiodus et quidam alii: sicut etiam Plato occultavit veritatem philosophiae	ἢ καὶ Πλάτωνα αἰτιῷτό τις ἂν ἐν πολλοῖς, μεταφοραῖς τισι καὶ τύποις τὰ δόγματα ἐπικαλύπτοντα, εἰ βούλοιτο ἐπὶ τὸ χεῖρον ἀκούειν, καὶ οὐ μόνον ἐς ἐπιστήμην, ἀλλὰ καὶ ἐς ἀρετὴν καὶ φύσιν παρανομεῖν τῳ δόξειεν ἂν τῇδέ πη σκοπουμένῳ· ἀλλ' αὐτός τε Πλήθων δικαίως Πλάτωνι χρῆται καὶ ἡμεῖς οὕτω χρώμεθα· καίτοι τὸ μὲν ἀσαφὲς Ἀριστοτέλους σοφῷ, τὸ δὲ Πλάτωνος ἐπικεχρωσμένον ποιητῇ μάλιστα, ὡς ἂν μὴ λέγω χείρονι ἐπιτηδεύματι, πρέπον ἔστιν εἰπεῖν.

tradiderunt suam doctrinam occultantes sub quibusdam aliis rebus, non disputat secundum veritatem occultam, sed secundum ea quae exterius proponuntur.

ἀΐδια τὴν φύσιν ἐστὶ τὰ δὲ φθείρεται τῶν ὄντων.	sub mathematicis, ut dicit Simplicius in *Commento "Praedicamentorum"*. [...] Si enim per fabulas veritas obumbretur, non potest sciri quid verum sub fabula lateat, nisi ab eo qui fabulam confixerit.

Further, Scholarios' addition "ὡς ἂν μὴ λέγω χείρονι ἐπιτηδεύματι" conceals an interesting aspect of the conflict. In ch. 2 (*Περὶ ἡγεμόνων τῶν βελτίστων λόγων*) of Book I of his *Laws,* Pletho categorizes the "leaders", whom one can rely on, in order to find the truth, into four groups (from the minor to the major "leader"[25]): "ποιηταί, σοφισταί, νομοθέται, φιλόσοφοι."[26] This classification, as has been shown,[27] in all probability derives from Plutarch.[28] Pletho enriches Plutarch's list by adding the "sophists". Moreover, in Pletho's view, Jesus Christ and the Christian leaders[29] are included among the sophists, since they are accused of: (a) using absurdities, by which they deceive the more illiterate people,[30] and (b) formulating pseudo-"revelations."[31] Pletho even accuses Jesus and Christians as being "charlatans,"[32] which is the worst type of sophist,[33] and proposes capital punishment for "sophists" in general: burning at the stake![34]

Scholarios had read Pletho's *Laws* and understood the anti-Christian character of Pletho's attack on Aristotle,[35] as Scholarios himself declares in the end of the *Contra Plethonis difficultates de Aristotele*.[36] Considering all these, it is plausible to assume that Scholarios' phrase "ὡς ἂν μὴ λέγω χείρονι ἐπιτηδεύματι" reveals his intention to respond to Pletho's attack against Christ and Christians; Scholarios does not blame Plato for "sophistry," but for something even worse: "poetry," substantiating his accusation on the basis of Plato's utilization of myths.

Subsequently, Scholarios explains that he is not so eager to repudiate Plato as to despise him simply because of his linguistic style; neither does

25. See J. A. Demetracopoulos 2014a, 206.
26. Pletho, *Leges* I, 2, 28, l. 1–2.
27. J. A. Demetracopoulos, *l. c.*
28. Plutarch, *Amatorius* 763B10–C6.
29. J. A. Demetracopoulos, 2004, 25; *Id.*, 2014a, 210–211.
30. Pletho, *op. cit.*, I, 2, 34, l. 26–36, l. 1.
31. *Ib.*, I, 2, 34, l. 13–17.
32. J. A. Demetracopoulos, 2014a, 210–211.
33. Pletho, *op. cit.*, I, 2, 36, l. 1–13.
34. *Ib.*, III, 31, 126, l. 10–12.
35. J. A. Demetracopoulos, *op. cit.*, 218, n. 221.
36. Scholarios, *op. cit.*, 114, l. 17–27.

he consider that Plato has argued anything "γελοῖον" or "μειρακιῶδες."[37] Besides, it was as difficult for Plato as it was for Aristotle to comprehend the truth of beings - and even the same is true for Scholarios' era.[38] Here Scholarios again reflects Thomas Aquinas.[39]

Thomas Aquinas *SG* I, 3, 2	Scholarios *Contra Plethonis difficultates de Aristotele*, 8, l. 32–34
Est autem in his quae de Deo confitemur duplex veritatis modus. Quaedam namque vera sunt de Deo quae omnem facultatem humanae rationis excedunt, ut Deum esse trinum et unum. Quaedam vero sunt ad quae etiam ratio naturalis pertingere potest, sicut est Deum esse, Deum esse unum, et alia huiusmodi; quae etiam philosophi demonstrative de Deo probaverunt, ducti naturalis lumine rationis.	Χαλεπὸν γὰρ ἦν καὶ αὐτῷ Πλάτωνι καὶ παντὶ ἀνθρώπῳ μετ' Ἀριστοτέλους αὐτὴν λαβεῖν τὴν τῶν ὄντων ἀλήθειαν, καὶ νῦν δὲ οὐχ ἧττον χαλεπόν ἐστι.

This brief negotiation in the Preamble is merely Scholarios' warning shot before the main attack, which follows in the first Part of his treatise. In this Part, Scholarios starts from Pletho's claim that Aristotle did not consider "τὸν πάντων βασιλέα Θεὸν δημιουργὸν τοῦ παντὸς εἶναι, ἀλλὰ τοῦ οὐρανοῦ μόνον κινητικόν."[40] Scholarios unfolds his thought by addressing the issue of the origin of Plato's wisdom. He notes that Plato superseded Anaxagoras' and Pythagoras' theological knowledge thanks to his journey to Egypt, where "πολλὰ τῆς ἱερᾶς ἀληθείας ἐδέξατο σπέρματα."[41] Plato's journey to Egypt[42] is a tradition that goes back to the time of Cicero at least.[43] Scholarios[44] appeals to the testimony of Jerome,[45] Plutarch,[46] Xenophon[47] and Plato himself.[48] As

37. *Ib.*, 8, l. 29–32: οὔτ' οὖν διὰ τοῦτο Πλάτωνος ὀλιγωροῦμεν ἢ συκοφαντεῖν προαγόμεθα, οὔτε δι' ἅ φησι καθάπαξ ἄμοιρα ἀληθείας, φαύλως πεφιλοσοφηκέναι τοῦτον ἀποφαινόμεθα, καὶ γελοῖόν τι ἢ μειρακιῶδες φρονῆσαί τε καὶ εἰπεῖν.
38. *Ib.*, 8, l. 32–34.
39. Thomas Aquinas, *SG* I, 3, 2.
40. Scholarios, *op. cit.*, 10, l. 17–19.
41. *Ib.*, 12, l. 10.
42. For the place of Egypt in Plato's thought, see, e. g., L. Brisson, 1987, 153–168; J. McEvoy, 1993, 245–275.
43. Cicero, *De re publica* I, 16, 10–18; *De finibus* V, 87, 3–5.
44. Scholarios, *op. cit.*, 12, l. 6–10.
45. Jerome, *Epistula* 53 (Ad Paulinum Presbyterum), 2, 443, l. 6–13.
46. Plutarch, *Solon* 2, 8, 1–4; *De Iside et Osiride* 354D9–E3.
47. Xenophon (?), *Epistula* 1, 31–35.
48. Cf. Plato, *Philebus* 18B6–C3; *Timaeus* 21C4–D3; 21E1–7; *Critias* 113A3–B2; *Phaedrus* 274C–275D; *Politicus* 290D6–E3; *Leges* 656D1–4; 660B2–C1; 747B6–D1; 799A1–2; 819A8–B2; *Epinomis* 986E6–987A7.

regards Scholarios' reference to Plutarch and Xenophon, it seems that his source is Theodoret of Cyrus:[49]

Theodoret of Cyrus *Graecarum affectionum curatio* II, 24, 1–25, 5	Scholarios *Contra Plethonis difficultates de Aristotele*, 12, l. 6–10
Χρόνῳ δὲ ὕστερον καὶ ὁ Πλάτων τήνδε τὴν ἀποδημίαν ἐστείλατο· καὶ τοῦτο λέγει μὲν ἐν τοῖς *Παραλλήλοις* ὁ Πλούταρχος, λέγει δὲ καὶ Ξενοφῶν ὁ Γρύλλου, ἐν οἷς πρὸς τὸν Σωκρατικὸν Αἰσχίνην ἐπέστειλε· γράφει δὲ ὧδε· "Αἰγύπτου γὰρ ἠράσθησαν καὶ τῆς Πυθαγόρου τερατώδους σοφίας· ὧν τὸ περιττὸν καὶ μὴ μόνιμον ἐπὶ Σωκράτει διήλεγχεν ἔρως τυραννίδος, καὶ ἀντὶ διαίτης λιτῆς Σικελιῶτις γαστρὸς ἀμέτρου τράπεζα." Τοιαῦτα περὶ τοῦ Πλάτωνος ὁ Ξενοφῶν ἔγραψεν, ὅτι τῆς Σωκράτους διδασκαλίας ὑπεριδών, τὴν τερατώδη Πυθαγόρου σοφίαν ἐζήλωσε καὶ Διονυσίῳ τῷ Σικελίας τυράννῳ ξυνῆν, Συρακουσίας ἀπολαύων χλιδῆς· ἔφη δὲ αὐτὸν καὶ τῆς Αἰγυπτίων ἐρασθῆναι σοφίας.	Πλάτων δὲ σπουδαιότατος τῶν πρὸ αὐτοῦ πάντων γεγενημένος καὶ ἅμα ἐκ τῶν Ἀναξαγόρου καὶ Πυθαγόρου ἀμυδράς τινας τῆς ὑψηλοτέρας ἀληθείας ἐμφάσεις δεξάμενος, πλεύσας εἰς Αἴγυπτον, ὡς Ἱερώνυμος λέγει καὶ Πλούταρχος καὶ πρὸ αὐτῶν Ξενοφῶν καὶ αὐτὸς δ' ὑπὲρ ἑαυτοῦ, ἐκεῖθεν πολλὰ τῆς ἱερᾶς ἀληθείας ἐδέξατο σπέρματα.

This is strengthened by the fact that, subsequently, Scholarios utilizes Theodoret again (see *infra*, 408–411).

Scholarios goes on by arguing that, according to Plato, the human agent, apart from the things that can be reached by means of the light of human reason, is capable of receiving some divinely inspired truth.[50] It seems that Scholarios has here in mind Thomas Aquinas:[51]

Thomas Aquinas *SG* I, 3, 2	Scholarios *Contra Plethonis difficultates de Aristotele*, 12, l. 10–14
Est autem in his quae de Deo confitemur duplex veritatis modus. Quaedam namque vera sunt de Deo quae omnem facultatem humanae rationis excedunt, ut Deum esse trinum et unum. Quaedam vero sunt ad quae etiam ratio naturalis pertingere potest, sicut est Deum esse, Deum esse unum,	Ἐδόκει γὰρ αὐτῷ μὴ τοσαῦτα μόνον εἰδέναι τοὺς ἀνθρώπους δύνασθαι, ὅσα ἂν ὑπ' ἀλλήλων ὠφεληθεῖεν, ἢ αὐτοὶ ἐπινοήσειαν οἴκοθεν, τῷ συμφυεῖ τῆς ἑαυτῶν διανοίας φωτὶ χρώμενοι, ἀλλὰ δύνασθαί τι καὶ ἱερὸν εἰς τὸν ἀνθρώπινον καταπέμπεσθαι νοῦν.

49. Theodoret of Cyrus, *Graecarum affectionum curatio* II, 24, 1–25, 5.
50. Scholarios, *op. cit.*, 12, l. 10–14.
51. Thomas Aquinas, *l. c.*

et alia huiusmodi; quae etiam philosophi demonstrative de Deo probaverunt, ducti naturalis lumine rationis.

Scholarios then states that Plato, although aware of the truth, did not offer it in its pure form to the people. On the contrary, even though Plato expresses his contempt for poets, he combined the truth with the doctrines of some poets (such as Musaeus, Linus, Hesiod, Homer, and Orpheus). However, according to Scholarios, he should have kept the truth pure and unaltered, especially since he knew that Moses is by far older than the earliest Greek poet, i.e. by more than a millennium.[52] Scholarios' reference to these poets in conjuction with his reference to the time of Orpheus, Linus, and Musaeus and his dating of Moses a thousand years prior to the Greek poets makes it evident that Scholarios' source is Theodoret again:[53]

Theodoret of Cyrus *Graecarum affectionum curatio* II, 49, 1–50, 9	Scholarios *Contra Plethonis difficultates de Aristotele*, 12, l. 14–25
Ταῦτα δὲ οὐκ ἀδολεσχῶν διεξῆλθον, ἀλλὰ σαφῶς ἐπιδεῖξαι βουλόμενος, ὡς Ὀρφεὺς γενεᾷ μιᾷ πρεσβύτερος ἐγεγόνει τῶν Τρωϊκῶν. Λῖνος δὲ καὶ Μουσαῖος ἀμφὶ τὰ Τρωϊκὰ ἐγενέσθην, καὶ Θάμυρις μετὰ τούτων, καὶ Φιλάμμων ὡσαύτως. εἰ τοίνυν τούτων μὲν κατὰ τὸν Πορφύριον ὁ Μωϋσῆς πλείοσιν ἢ χιλίοις πρεσβύτερος ἔτεσιν, οὗτοι δὲ παλαιότατοι τῶν ποιητῶν ἐγένοντο –μετὰ γὰρ τούτους καὶ Ὅμηρος καὶ Ἡσίοδος ἐγενέσθην, καὶ οὗτοι δ' αὖ πάλιν Θαλοῦ καὶ τῶν ἄλλων φιλοσόφων πολλοῖς ἔτεσιν ἀρχαιότεροι, καὶ οἱ ἀμφὶ Θαλῆν τῶν μετ' αὐτοὺς πεφιλοσοφηκότων–, τί δήποτε μὴ τούτους πάντας καταλιπόντες πρὸς Μωϋσέα τὸν τῆς θεολογίας ὠκεανὸν μεταβαίνομεν, "ἐξ οὗπερ," ποιητικῶς εἰπεῖν, "πάντες ποταμοὶ καὶ πᾶσα θάλασσα;"	ὅθεν οὐ μόνον Αἰγυπτίων τοιαῦτα ἀπώνατο, ἀλλὰ καὶ τοῖς παρ' Ἕλλησι ποιηταῖς αὐτός τε πολλὰ πείθεται καὶ τοῖς ἄλλοις οὕτω ποιεῖν συμβουλεύει, ὡς ἱερά τινα καὶ θεῖα προτιθεῖσι διδάγματα, Μουσαίῳ τε δηλονότι καὶ Λίνῳ περὶ τὰ Τρωικὰ γενομένοις, καὶ Ἡσιόδῳ καὶ Ὁμήρῳ ὕστερον τούτων ἀκμάσασι, καὶ Ὀρφεῖ γενεᾷ μιᾷ ταῦτα προειληφότι, καίτοι ἄνευ εἰκότων καὶ ἀναγκαίων λέγειν αὐτούς φησιν. [...] Μωσέα μὲν ἀρχαιότερον εἰδότα τῶν παλαιοτέρων ποιητῶν πλεῖν ἢ χιλίοις ἔτεσι, τῆς δὲ ἐκείνου θεολογίας καὶ τῆς αὐτῶν φλυαρίας πολὺ τὸ διάφορον ἐγνωκότα [...]

In Scholarios' view, Plato should have kept the truth he received from Moses unaltered and abstain from mixing it with the "nonsense" (*λήρους*) of the poets, i.e. the myths.[54] This *en bloc* rejection of myth has a long tradition

52. Scholarios, *op. cit.*, 12, l. 14–25.
53. Theodoret of Cyrus, *op. cit.*, II, 49, 1–50, 9.
54. Scholarios, *op. cit.*, 12, l. 33–37.

in the ancient and early Byzantine Christian literature.[55] However, this utilisation of the word *λῆρος per se* in conjunction with Scholarios' reference to (a) Plato's fear of telling the truth and (b) the influence of Moses' theology on Plato's texts[56] indicates that Scholarios has once again drawn material from Theodoret:[57]

Theodoret of Cyrus
Graecarum affectionum curatio
I, 60, 1–61, 3

Ταῦτα ἐν τῷ *Τιμαίῳ* περὶ τῶν ποιητῶν ὁ Πλάτων εἴρηκε καὶ προσέταξεν Ὁμήρῳ καὶ Ἡσιόδῳ καὶ τοῖς ἄλλοις ποιηταῖς μυθολογοῦσι πιστεῦσαι καὶ οὐκ ᾐδέσθη φάναι, ὅτι ἄνευ εἰκότων καὶ ἀναγκαίων ἀποδείξεων λέγουσι, καὶ ταῦτα κωμῳδῶν ἀλλαχοῦ τὰ παρ' ἐκείνων λεγόμενα, ὡς ἐν ἑτέρῳ δὴ χωρίῳ σαφῶς ἐπιδείξομεν. Εἰ δὲ τοῖς τοὺς λήρους ἐκείνους μυθολογοῦσι καὶ τοὺς αἰσχροτάτους διαπλάττουσι μύθους πιστεύειν ὁ Πλάτων παρακελεύεται καὶ μηδεμίαν αὐτοὺς ἀπόδειξιν ἀπαιτεῖν [...]

II, 32, 1–43, 4

Ἀλλ' ὅμως καὶ ταῦτα παρ' Αἰγυπτίων μεμαθηκώς, οἳ παρ' Ἑβραίων μαθήματά τινα τῆς ἀληθείας παρέλαβον, παρέμιξε τοῦ πλάνου τῇ θεολογίᾳ τινὰ καὶ τῶν Διονυσίων καὶ Θεσμοφορίων τὰ δυσαγῆ παραδέδωκεν ὄργια, καὶ οἷόν τινι μέλιτι περιχρίσας τὴν κύλικα, τὸ δηλητήριον πόμα τοῖς ἐξαπατωμένοις προσφέρει. Ταὐτὸ δὲ τοῦτο καὶ Πλάτων πεποίηκεν· ἀξιάγαστα γὰρ αὐτοῦ τῷ ὄντι τὰ περὶ τοῦ ὄντος ἐν τῷ *Τιμαίῳ* ξυγγεγραμμένα. [...] Τίς οὖν οὕτω φιλαίτιος καὶ μεμψίμοιρος, ὡς νεμεσῆσαι τοῖς εἰρημένοις καὶ μὴ πᾶσαν αὐτοῖς προσμαρτυρῆσαι ἀλήθειαν; Τὸ γὰρ ὂν ἀεὶ γενέσεώς ἐστιν ἁπάσης ὑπέρτερον, τὸ δὲ γινόμενον, ἀλλοιώσεις παμπόλλους ἐπιδεχόμενον, εἰκότως ἔφη οὐδέποτε εἶναι. [...] Εἰκότως οὖν ἄρα 'οὐκ ὄντα' ὠνόμασε τὰ γινόμενά τε καὶ ἀλλοιούμενα. Καὶ τῷ *Κρίτωνι* δὲ διαλεγόμενος ὁ Σωκράτης ἕνα πάντων ὀπτῆρά φησιν· [...] Ὁρᾶτε, ὦ ἄνδρες, ὅπως ἐν τούτοις ὁ Πλάτων καὶ ὁ Σωκρά-

Scholarios
Contra Plethonis difficultates de Aristotele, 12, l. 33–13, l. 6

Ἀλλ' εἴτε δεδιὼς τὰς ὑποψίας τοῦ ὑπερόριον σοφίαν ἐς Ἕλληνας μετακομίσαι, εἴτε καὶ βουλόμενος Ἑλληνισμόν τινα μεταπεπλασμένον ἐνστήσασθαι, εἴτε καὶ οὕτω κρίνων κακῶς, οὐ πάντα ἐπείθετο Μωϋσεῖ, ἀλλὰ τῷ καθαρῷ τῆς ἐκείνου θεολογίας πολλὰ τῶν ποιητικῶν συνεκέρασε λήρων, οὐκ ἂν εἴη ῥᾴδιον ἀποφήνασθαι. Τοῦτο μέντοι γε δῆλόν ἐστιν, ὅτι Πλάτωνι τὸ πρὸς τοὺς ἄλλους διαφέρον ἐν ταῖς περὶ τοῦ ὄντος γνώμαις καὶ αὐτοῦ Θεοῦ καὶ τῆς τῶν ὄντων παραγωγῆς ἐκ τῆς ἱερᾶς προσεγένετο τοῦ Μωσέως διδασκαλίας· ὡς δὲ καὶ τὰ περὶ τῆς ἀθανασίας τῆς ψυχῆς πρώτῳ Πλάτωνι διὰ Μωσέα βέλτιον ἢ τοῖς ἄλλοις ἀπ' αὐτοῦ τε καὶ πρὸ αὐτοῦ φιλοσόφοις διώρισται· ὡς δὲ καὶ τὰ περὶ τῆς ἀιδίου Τριάδος, ἥτις ἐστὶ τἀγαθὸν καὶ νοῦς καὶ ἡ τοῦ παντὸς ψυχή, ὡς Πλωτῖνος καὶ Νουμήνιος τὰ τοιαῦτα εἰς Πλάτωνα ἀναφέρουσι.

55. Cf., e. g., Tatian, *Oratio ad Graecos*, 21, 1, 1–2, 8; 34, 2, 4–9; 40, 1, 1–10; Hippolyte of Rome, *De universo*, fr. 1, l. 1–6; Georgius Monachus, *Chronicon Breve*, 110, 113, l. 34–46.
56. Scholarios, *op. cit.*, 12, l. 33–13, l. 6.
57. Theodoret of Cyrus, *op. cit.*, I, 60, 1–61, 3; II, 32, 1–43, 4; II, 70, 1–79, 3; II, 85, 1–86, 2. See also II, 114, 1–115, 3; V, 67, 1–2.

της τὸν τῶν οὐκ ὄντων θεῶν ἐξήλασεν ὁρμαθὸν καὶ μόνον τῶν ὅλων τὸν πρύτανιν αἰδεῖσθαι καὶ φοβεῖσθαι παρεκελεύσατο, διδάσκων ὡς, εἴποτε πλειόνων ἐμνήσθη θεῶν, διὰ τὸν ἐξηπατημένον τῶν Ἀθηναίων ὅμιλον τοῦτο ποιῆσαι προσηναγκάσθη. Εἰ γὰρ δὴ καὶ ταῦτα δεδρακὼς ὁ Σωκράτης οὐ διέφυγε τὴν τοῦ κωνείου φιάλην, τί οὐκ ἂν ἔπαθεν, εἰ προφανῶς ἠρνήθη τὸν πολὺν ἑσμὸν τῶν θεῶν; Καὶ τοῦτο δῆλον ὁ Πλάτων πεποίηκεν, ἐν οἷς πρὸς Διονύσιον ἔγραψεν. [...] Πῶς ἄν τις σαφέστερον τὸν οἰκεῖον ἐπιδείξειε σκοπόν; Γυμνὴν γὰρ ἔδειξεν, ἣν εἶχε περὶ τῶνδε τῶν ὀνομάτων διαφοράν, μονονουχὶ λέγων· "τῆς τῶν πολλῶν εἵνεκα δόξης τὸ πληθυντικὸν ὄνομα περὶ τοῦ Θεοῦ τίθημι, τὰς ἐξηπατημένας προλήψεις τῶν πολιτῶν ὑφορώμενος· σπουδαίως γὰρ ἐπιστέλλων καὶ θαρρῶν τῷ τε κομίζοντι καὶ τῷ δεχομένῳ τὰ γράμματα, ἑνικῶς τὸν Θεὸν ὀνομάζω καὶ τοῦτον ἀρχὴν ποιοῦμαι τῶν λόγων." [...] Ἀλλ' ὅ γε ἐν τούτοις ἀκριβῶς οὕτω θεολογήσας, ἐν ἄλλοις, ἢ τοὺς πολλοὺς ὀρρωδήσας ἢ τῷ ὄντι γε ἀγνοήσας, πολλῶν ἐποιήσατο μνήμην θεῶν καὶ πολλὴν ἐνεργάζεται τοῖς ἐντυγχάνουσι λώβην. Ἀνθ' ὅτου δὴ οὖν, ὦ φίλοι, τὸ θολερὸν καὶ γεῶδες ἀρυόμεθα νᾶμα, καὶ μὴ τὴν πηγὴν ἐκείνην ζητοῦμεν τὴν διαυγῆ καὶ διαφανῆ, ἐξ ἧς οὗτος λαβὼν τῆς θεολογίας τὰς ἀφορμάς, τὸ ἰλυῶδες αὐτοῖς καὶ γεῶδες ἀνέμιξεν;

II, 70, 1–79, 3

Ἐφ' ἑτέραν τοίνυν μέθοδον διδασκαλίας τραπήσομαι καὶ δείξω τὸν Πλάτωνα καὶ τοὺς μετ' ἐκεῖνον ἐκ τούτων μὲν τῶν θείων ἀνδρῶν[58] τῆς θεολογίας σεσυληκότας τινά, τοῖς δὲ σφετέροις ἐντεθεικότας ξυγγράμμασιν. Καὶ γὰρ ὁ Πλάτων, ἐν οἷς πρὸς Κορίσκον ἐπέστειλε, καὶ τάδε προστέθεικεν· [...] Ταῦτα, ὦ φίλοι ἄνδρες, τοῦ Πλάτωνός ἐστι δόγματα. Ἀλλὰ τούτων τὰ μὲν ἀξιέπαινα καὶ τῆς ἀποστολικῆς καὶ προφητικῆς διδασκαλίας ἐχόμενα, τὰ δὲ τῆς Ἑλληνικῆς μυθολογίας κυήματα. [...] Ὀνόματος μὲν γὰρ ψιλοῦ μεταδέδωκε τοῖς δικάζειν πεπιστευμένοις, καὶ μέντοι καὶ τοῖς τὴν θείαν εἰκόνα ὡς οἷόν τε τετηρηκόσιν ἀκήρατον· φύσει δὲ Θεὸν τὸν ἀεὶ ὄντα καὶ κατὰ ταὐτὰ καὶ ὡσαύτως ἔχοντα μόνον εἴωθεν ὀνομάζειν. [...] νῦν δέ γε ἀρκέσει δηλῶσαι, ὡς ὁ φιλόσοφος οἶδε τὸν τοῦ παντὸς ἡγεμόνα καὶ αἴτιον καὶ τὸν τοῦ αἰτίου πατέρα· [...] Ὁρᾶτε, πῶς ὀρρωδοῦντες καὶ δεδιότες τὰ τῆς ἀληθείας προσέφερον δόγματα καὶ αἰνιγματωδῶς, οὐ σαφῶς, ἐκήρυττον τὴν ἀλήθειαν, τὸν τῶν πολλῶν ὑφορώμενοι πλάνον;

II, 85, 1–86, 2

Αὐτίκα τοίνυν τὴν Πλάτωνος διάνοιαν ἀναπτύσσοντες, καὶ ὁ Πλωτῖνος καὶ ὁ Νουμήνιος τρία φασὶν αὐτὸν εἰρηκέναι ὑπέρχρονα καὶ ἀΐδια, τἀγαθὸν καὶ νοῦν καὶ τοῦ παντὸς τὴν ψυχήν, ὃν μὲν ἡμεῖς "Πατέρα" καλοῦμεν, "Τἀγαθὸν" ὀνομάζοντα, "Νοῦν" δέ, ὃν ἡμεῖς "Υἱὸν" καὶ "Λόγον" προσαγορεύομεν, τὴν δὲ τὰ πάντα ψυχοῦσαν καὶ ζωοποιοῦσαν δύναμιν "Ψυχὴν" καλοῦντα, ἣν "Πνεῦμα ἅγιον" οἱ θεῖοι προσαγορεύουσι λόγοι. Καὶ ταῦτα δέ, ὡς ἔφην, ἐκ τῆς τῶν Ἑβραίων φιλοσοφίας τε καὶ θεολογίας σεσύληται.

Thus, Scholarios concludes: Plato following Moses and mixing up the revealed truth with the views of the so-called "divine" – according to the Greeks – poets, argued that the world is created and consists of the same matter throughout.[59] This view – although widespread – is in all probability derived from Eusebius of Caesarea's *Praeparatio Evangelica*:[60]

Eusebius of Caesarea ***Praeparatio Evangelica*** **XV, 6, 1, 1–4**	**Scholarios** ***Contra Plethonis difficultates de Aristotele*, 14, l. 12–16**
Μωσέως γενητὸν εἶναι τὸν κόσμον ὁρισαμένου ποιητήν τε καὶ δημιουργὸν τοῖς ὅλοις τὸν θεὸν ἐπιστήσαντος τοῦ τε Πλάτωνος τὰ ἴσα Μωσεῖ φιλοσοφοῦντος [...] **7, 4, 1–3** ἔτι ὁ μὲν Πλάτων πάντα τὰ σώματα, ἅτε ἐπὶ μιᾶς ὁμοίας ὕλης θεωρούμενα, βούλεται τρέπεσθαι μεταβάλλειν τ' εἰς ἄλληλα [...]	Ταύτῃ τοίνυν τῇ ἱερᾷ τοῦ Μωσέως διδασκαλίᾳ Πλάτων ἑπόμενος, οὐ μὴν δ' ἀλλὰ καί τισι τῶν παρ' Ἕλλησιν ἐνθέων, ὡς αὐτοί φασι, ποιητῶν, γενητὸν εἶναι τὸν κόσμον τίθησι καὶ ὕλην αὐτῷ ὑποτίθησι παντὶ τὴν αὐτήν, οὐχ ἑτέραν μὲν οὐρανῷ, ἑτέραν δὲ τοῖς ἐν γενέσει καὶ φθορᾷ πράγμασι.

It is at this point that Scholarios focuses on the Aristotelian method and points out that the Stagirite, once a disciple of Plato, "πρὸς τὴν τῆς φιλοσοφίας ἐπιμέλειαν ἦλθεν," but he did so in his own, distinct way.[61] True,

58. Presumably, Moses is included in these divine men.
59. Scholarios, *op. cit.*, 14, l. 12–16.
60. Eusebius of Caesarea, *Praeparatio Evangelica* XV, 6, 1, 1–4; 7, 4, 1–3.
61. Scholarios, *op. cit.*, 14, l. 35–36: Ἀριστοτέλης δέ, ὁμιλητὴς γενόμενος Πλάτωνος, οὐκ ἀπὸ τῆς αὐτῆς τῷ διδασκάλῳ γνώμης πρὸς τὴν τῆς φιλοσοφίας ἐπιμέλειαν ἦλθεν.

Aristotle owes gratitude to Plato, and it is Aristotle himself who points out that we should owe gratitude to those who help us in the quest for truth, offering the example of the composers Timotheus and Phrynis. In this case, Scholarios names his source: "ἐν ἐλάττονι ἄλφα τῶν *Μετὰ τὰ φυσικά*."[62] Nevertheless, a closer examination reveals that he utilizes Thomas' *Commentary* on *Metaphysics*:[63]

Aristotle *Metaphysica* 993b11–19	Thomas Aquinas *Sententia Metaphysicae*, lib. II lect. 1 n. 16	Scholarios *Contra Plethonis difficultates de Aristotele*, 14, l. 36–15, l. 4
Οὐ μόνον δὲ χάριν ἔχειν δίκαιον τούτοις ὧν ἄν τις κοινώσαιτο ταῖς δόξαις, ἀλλὰ καὶ τοῖς ἐπιπολαιότερον ἀποφηναμένοις· καὶ γὰρ οὗτοι συνεβάλοντό τι· τὴν γὰρ ἕξιν προήσκησαν ἡμῶν· εἰ μὲν γὰρ Τιμόθεος μὴ ἐγένετο, πολλὴν ἂν μελοποιίαν οὐκ εἴχομεν· εἰ δὲ μὴ Φρῦνις, Τιμόθεος οὐκ ἂν ἐγένετο. τὸν αὐτὸν δὲ τρόπον καὶ ἐπὶ τῶν περὶ τῆς ἀληθείας ἀποφηναμένων· παρὰ μὲν γὰρ ἐνίων παρειλήφαμέν τινας δόξας, οἱ δὲ τοῦ γενέσθαι τούτους αἴτιοι γεγόνασιν.	Est autem justum ut his, quibus adjuti sumus in tanto bono, scilicet cognitione veritatis, gratias agamus. Et ideo dicit, quod "iustum est gratiam habere, non solum his, quos quis existimat veritatem invenisse, quorum opinionibus aliquis communicat sequendo eas; sed etiam illis, qui superficialiter locuti sunt" ad veritatem investigandam, licet eorum opiniones non sequamur; "quia isti etiam aliquid conferunt nobis." Praestiterunt enim nobis quoddam exercitium circa inquisitionem veritatis. Et ponit exemplum de inventoribus musicae. Si enim non fuisset Timotheus qui multa de arte musicae invenit, non haberemus ad praesens multa, quae scimus circa melodias. Et si non praecessisset quidam philosophus nomine Phrynis, Timotheus non fuisset ita instructus in musicalibus.	Καίτοι γὰρ Πλάτωνι χάριν εἰδώς, ἅτε συνεργῷ γενομένῳ πρὸς τὴν θεωρίαν τῆς ἀληθείας, τοῦτο μὲν ἐξ ὧν καλῶς τε καὶ ἀληθῶς πεφιλοσόφηκεν ἀφορμὰς δεδωκότι τῆς ἀληθείας, τοῦτο δὲ καὶ ἐξ ὧν ἐπλανήθη ἀφορμὰς γυμνασίου παρασχομένῳ, καθὼς αὐτός φησιν ἐν ἐλάττονι ἄλφα τῶν *Μετὰ τὰ φυσικά*, ὅπου καὶ παραδείγμασι τοῖς εὑροῦσι μουσικὴν κέχρηται, Τιμόθεον καὶ πρὸ τούτου Φρύνιν τινὰ ὀνομάζων·

As is evident, Scholarios' text contains words which are absent from Aristotle's text, but which occur in Aquinas'.

62. *Ib.*, 14, l. 36–15, l. 4; Aristotle, *Metaphysica* 993b11–19.
63. Thomas Aquinas, *Sententia Metaphysicae*, lib. II lect. 1 n. 16.

Scholarios keeps accusing Plato of having combined elements from Pythagorean philosophy, the revealed truth of Moses and the poetic myths, which resulted in supporting views without proof and confusing the sciences with each other. By contrast, Aristotle defined the boundaries of each science and attributed to each its own logical methods (e. g., the natural ones to physics, the mathematical ones to mathematics, and so on).[64] This is what he did for theology, too.[65] Thanks to this approach, Aristotle avoided Plato's mistakes, i.e. to conceal the truth about God under myths, as the poets did, and introduce mathematics to philosophy.[66] The background to this passage is Thomas' *Commentary* on *Metaph*ysics.[67]

Thomas Aquinas *Sententia Metaphysicae,* lib. III lect. 11 n. 3	Scholarios *Contra Plethonis difficultates de Aristotele,* 15, l. 32–35
Circa primum considerandum est, quod apud Graecos, aut naturales philosophos, fuerunt quidam sapientiae studentes, qui deis se intromiserunt occultantes veritatem divinorum sub quodam tegmine fabularum; [...] sicut etiam Plato occultavit veritatem philosophiae sub mathematicis, ut dicit Simplicius in *Commento "Praedicamentorum."* [...] quia scilicet veritatem, quam intellexerunt, taliter tradiderunt, quod eis solum possit esse nota.	Καὶ οὔτε, καθάπερ οἱ ποιηταί, ὑπό τινι μύθων περικαλύμματι τὴν περὶ τῶν θείων ἀλήθειαν συνεκάλυψεν, οὔτε καθάπερ Πλάτων ὕστερον, ὑπὸ τοῖς μαθηματικοῖς τὴν τῆς φιλοσοφίας λαμπρότητα συνεσκίασεν, ὥστ' αὐτῷ μόνῳ τὴν ἀλήθειαν γινώσκεσθαι δύνασθαι...

Plato's errors had this result: none, except himself, could understand the truth Plato offered. Thus, even Plato's followers couldn't agree on the interpretation of his concealed meanings.[68] On the contrary, Aristotle chose his own way in philosophical enquiry, as he himself states "ἐν βῆτα τῶν *Μετὰ τὰ φυσικά*". There Aristotle states his preference for the philosophical quest which is based on proofs, and accuses those who follow Hesiod's method, i. e. those who speak through myths.[69] Here again the background is Aristotle's text,[70] but Scholarios' source is Thomas' *Commentary* on *Metaphysics.*[71]

64. Scholarios, *op. cit.*, 15, l. 11–20.
65. *Ib.*, 15, l. 25–27.
66. *Ib.*, 15, l. 32–35.
67. Thomas Aquinas, *op. cit.*, lib. III lect. 11 n. 3.
68. Scholarios, *op. cit.*, 15, l. 34–16, l. 1.
69. *Ib.*, 16, l. 1–13.
70. Aristotle, *op. cit.*, 1000a9–22.
71. Thomas Aquinas, *l. c.*; *ib.*, n. 5; n. 6.

Aristotle
Metaphysica
1000a9–22

Οἱ μὲν οὖν περὶ Ἡσίοδον καὶ πάντες ὅσοι θεολόγοι μόνον ἐφρόντισαν τοῦ πιθανοῦ τοῦ πρὸς αὑτούς, ἡμῶν δ' ὠλιγώρησαν (θεοὺς γὰρ ποιοῦντες τὰς ἀρχὰς καὶ ἐκ θεῶν γεγονέναι, τὰ μὴ γευσάμενα τοῦ νέκταρος καὶ τῆς ἀμβροσίας θνητὰ γενέσθαι φασίν, δῆλον ὡς ταῦτα τὰ ὀνόματα γνώριμα λέγοντες αὑτοῖς· καίτοι περὶ αὐτῆς τῆς προσφορᾶς τῶν αἰτίων τούτων ὑπὲρ ἡμᾶς εἰρήκασιν· εἰ μὲν γὰρ χάριν ἡδονῆς αὐτῶν θιγγάνουσιν, οὐθὲν αἴτια τοῦ εἶναι τὸ νέκταρ καὶ ἡ ἀμβροσία, εἰ δὲ τοῦ εἶναι, πῶς ἂν εἶεν ἀΐδιοι δεόμενοι τροφῆς)· ἀλλὰ περὶ μὲν τῶν μυθικῶς σοφιζομένων οὐκ ἄξιον μετὰ σπουδῆς σκοπεῖν· παρὰ δὲ τῶν δι' ἀποδείξεως λεγόντων δεῖ πυνθάνεσθαι διερωτῶντας τί δή ποτ' ἐκ τῶν αὐτῶν ὄντα τὰ μὲν ἀΐδια τὴν φύσιν ἐστὶ τὰ δὲ φθείρεται τῶν ὄντων.

Thomas Aquinas
Sententia Metaphysicae,
lib. III lect. 11 n. 3

Dicit ergo, quod "sectatores Hesiodi, et omnes, qui dicebantur theologi, curaverunt persuadere solis sibi, et nos alios spreverunt"; quia scilicet veritatem, quam intellexerunt, taliter tradiderunt, quod eis solum possit esse nota. Si enim per fabulas veritas obumbretur, non potest sciri quid verum sub fabula lateat, nisi ab eo qui fabulam confixerit. Ii igitur Hesiodistae prima rerum principia "deos" nominaverunt; et dixerunt, quod illi de numero deorum, qui non gustaverunt de quodam dulci cibo, qui vocatur nectar vel manna, facti sunt mortales; illi vero qui gustaverunt, facti sunt immortales.

n. 5

Si enim intelligantur ista verba secundum quod sonant, nullius efficaciae esse videntur.

n. 6

Si vero aliquis velit de his inquirere secundum veritatem fabulis occultatam, immanifesta est. Ex quo accipitur quod Aristoteles disputans contra Platonem et alios hujusmodi, qui tradiderunt suam doctrinam occultantes sub quibusdam aliis rebus, non disputat secundum veritatem occultam, sed secundum ea quae exterius proponuntur.

Scholarios
Contra Plethonis difficultates de Aristotele,
16, l. 1–13

Ὅτι δὲ τὴν τοιαύτην ἀπεστράφη ὁδόν, αὐτὸς ἐν βῆτα τῶν *Μετὰ τὰ φυσικὰ* δείκνυσι, τοὺς περὶ Ἡσίοδον αἰτιώμενος, λέγοντας τοὺς μὲν μὴ γευσαμένους τοῦ νέκταρος καὶ τῆς ἀμβροσίας θεοὺς θνητοὺς γεγονέναι, τοὺς δὲ γευσαμένους ἀθανασίας τυχεῖν. Εἰ γὰρ ταῦτα γνοίη τις, φησί, κατὰ τὸν ἦχον μόνον τὰ ῥήματα, οὐδὲν δραστηριότητος ἔχουσιν· εἰ δὲ κατὰ τὴν ὑπ' αὐτοῖς ἐγκεκρυμμένην ἀλήθειαν, οὐδὲν ἂν σαφὲς ἀποφαίνοιντο, ἐκείνοις μόνοις οὔσης ταύτης γνωρίμου. Καὶ τοῦτο τῆς κατὰ Πλάτωνος διαλέξεως καὶ τῶν ἄλλων πρὸ αὐτοῦ φιλοσόφων οἶμαι εἶναι Ἀριστοτέλει ἀπολογίαν, ὅτι μὴ πρὸς τὴν ἐνδομυχοῦσαν ἀλήθειαν, ὡς ἂν αὐτοὶ φαῖεν, ἀλλὰ πρὸς τὰ ἔξωθεν οὑτωσὶ καὶ φανερῶς προτεινόμενα τὰς διαλέξεις ποιεῖσθαι προήχθη, τὴν φιλοσοφίαν εἰλικρινῆ καὶ ἁπάσης ἀσαφείας καὶ ἀμφιβολίας ἀπηλλαγμένην τοῖς ἀνθρώποις παραδοῦναι βουλόμενος.

Scholarios has not ceased his attack yet. Thus, he unleashes another onslaught against Plato and everyone who utilizes myths, stating that most of the time they blatantly lie and argue contrary to logic.[72] On the other hand, Aristotle does not offend the beliefs of the Greeks, neither does he legislate on their behalf nor does he define the truth on the basis of mere possibility (*εἰκότα*).[73] To support his argument, Scholarios cites: (a) *Metaphysics* 1074b13–14, where Aristotle exhibits the views "τῶν ἀρχαίων καὶ τῶν πολλῶν" regarding *κεχωρισμένα εἴδη*, and (b) *Metaphysics* 1074a14–17, where Aristotle deals with immovable principles.[74] Especially, as regards the interpretation of the first citation, Scholarios takes into account not only Aristotle's text but also Thomas' *Commentary* on *Metaphysics*:[75]

Aristotle *Metaphysica* **1074b13–14**	**Thomas Aquinas** *Sententia Metaphysicae,* **lib. XII lect. 10 n. 20**	**Scholarios** *Contra Plethonis difficultates de Aristotele,* **16, l. 19–21**
Ἡ μὲν οὖν πάτριος δόξα καὶ ἡ παρὰ τῶν πρώτων ἐπὶ τοσοῦτον ἡμῖν φανερὰ μόνον.	Tertio comparat id quod ostensum est de substantiis separatis, ad opiniones antiquas, et ad opiniones vulgares, quae de his suo tempore habebantur, ibi, "tradita autem sunt."	Ἐν γὰρ τῶν *Μετὰ τὰ φυσικὰ* Λ,[76] τὰ περὶ τῶν κεχωρισμένων εἰδῶν ταῖς τῶν ἀρχαίων καὶ τῶν πολλῶν παραβάλλων δόξαις καὶ συνᾴδοντα δείξας, ἐπάγει·

According to Scholarios, Aristotle accepts any truth acquired through logic, but recognizes that there is another, higher sort of truth: the truth revealed to those possessed by deity, i.e. the seers (*μάντεις*).[77] Still, Aristotle is aware that the philosopher's duty is to prove things by means of logic;[78] so, he leaves myths to the poets and divinations to the seers.[79] Obviously, in Scholarios' view, Aristotle is the first one to make the true transition from myth to logic.

72. Scholarios, *op. cit.*, 16, l. 14–17: Τὰ πλεῖστα γὰρ αὐτῶν οὐκ ἐπικεχρωσμένον ἔχουσι τὸ ψεῦδος, ἀλλὰ καὶ ἔνδοθεν πολὺ τὸ [πολὺν τὸν edd.: correxi] παράλογον ἔχει, καὶ ὅπως ἂν ἐξετάζοιτο, τῷ λόγῳ φανερῶς εἰσιν ἐναντία. Cf. Plato, *Epistula* 7, 340D6–341A3: Οἱ δὲ ὄντως μὲν μὴ φιλόσοφοι, δόξαις δ' ἐπικεχρωσμένοι, καθάπερ οἱ τὰ σώματα ὑπὸ τῶν ἡλίων ἐπικεκαυμένοι [...]
73. Scholarios, *op. cit.*, 16, l. 17–19.
74. Aristotle, *op. cit.*, 1074a14–17: Τὸ μὲν οὖν πλῆθος τῶν σφαιρῶν ἔστω τοσοῦτον, ὥστε καὶ τὰς οὐσίας καὶ τὰς ἀρχὰς τὰς ἀκινήτους [καὶ τὰς αἰσθητὰς] τοσαύτας εὔλογον ὑπολαβεῖν (τὸ γὰρ ἀναγκαῖον ἀφείσθω τοῖς ἰσχυροτέροις λέγειν).
75. Thomas Aquinas, *op. cit.*, lib. XII, lect. 10, n. 20.
76. Scholarios, *op. cit.*, 16, l. 19–21: Ἐν γὰρ τῶν *Μετὰ τὰ φυσικά* Λ [λ' edd.: correxi], τὰ περὶ τῶν κεχωρισμένων εἰδῶν ταῖς τῶν ἀρχαίων καὶ τῶν πολλῶν παραβάλλων δόξαις καὶ συνᾴδοντα δείξας, ἐπάγει...
77. *Ib.*, 16, l. 24–26: Ὥστε καὶ μείζω τινὰ ἀνάγκην ἀληθείας οἶδε τοῦ φαινομένου εὐλόγου, ἣ τοῖς ἐπίπνοις ὑπὸ τοῦ θείου ἐνδίδοται.
78. *Ib.*, 16, l. 26–29.
79. *Ib.*, 16, l. 29–31.

Finally, it was time for Scholarios to reveal what he approves with respect to the two philosophers. As regards Aristotle, Scholarios praises this twofold approach concerning the truth: on the one hand, Aristotle admits that there is a sacred truth, which is greater than that of logic.[80] And this view is emphasized[81] by Scholarios. On the other hand, Aristotle uses logical methods, in the cases where logic is necessary and applicable.[82] As regards Plato, Scholarios praises the fact that Plato yields somewhat to the truth, i.e. does reveal some aspects of the truth. Nevertheless, Plato neither yields in the way he should nor does he distinguish where the sacred or divine truths are found. Therefore, he largely mixes the sacred and divine sayings with philosophical issues.[83] Plato is superior to all other writers in terms of elaborate language but inferior to Aristotle in the aspect of doctrine and the practicing of dialectics and the other philosophical methods.[84]

Of course, Scholarios knows that Aristotle's philosophical method – although the most appropriate – caused (and still causes) antipathy to many. Even Aristotle was aware of this. Aristotle, Scholarios says, addresses all of them in the end "τῶν *Μετὰ τὰ φυσικὰ* τοῦ δευτέρου," indicating that not every learner enjoys the same teaching method. Those who are imaginative prefer mathematics, whereas those equipped with weaker intellects prefer to be taught by means of examples from the *sensibilia*. Others prefer the testimony of an old authority, whereas others cannot follow thorough investigation or meticulous expositions, because they consider this a haggle (*μικρολογία*).[85] As has been shown[86] on the basis of Scholarios' rather awkward, Latin-influenced style and the content and wording of his text, this exposition of the various sorts of learners is directly and exclusively based on Aquinas' *Commentary* on *Metaphysics*.[87]

Aristotle *Metaphysica* 994b32–995a14	Thomas Aquinas *Sententia Metaphysicae*, II, 5, 4	Scholarios *Contra Plethonis difficultates de Aristotele*, 17, l. 23–35
Αἱ δ' ἀκροάσεις κατὰ τὰ ἔθη συμβαίνουσιν· ὡς γὰρ εἰώθαμεν οὕτως	Deinde cum dicit "alii vero" hic ostendit quomodo homines in consideratione veritatis propter con-	Αὕτη τοίνυν ἡ τῆς κατ' Ἀριστοτέλη φιλοσοφίας ὁδός, καίτοι

80. *Ib.*, 16, l. 37–17, l. 2: Ἡμεῖς δὲ Ἀριστοτέλη τοῦ μὲν ἱεράν τινα ἀλήθειαν εἶναι ὁμολογεῖν, καὶ ταύτῃ μείζω τινὰ ἀνάγκην τῆς ἀπὸ τοῦ λόγου προσμαρτυρεῖν οὐ μεμφόμεθα, καὶ αὐτοὶ τοιαύτην τινὰ δόξαν ἔχοντες.
81. Emphasis is laid by means of litotes (*οὐ μεμφόμεθα*) and the use of additional *καί* (*καὶ αὐτοί*).
82. Scholarios, *op. cit.*, 17, l. 2–6.
83. *Ib.*, 17, l. 6–10.
84. *Ib.*, 17, l. 10–13.
85. *Ib.*, 17, l. 23–35.
86. J. A. Demetracopoulos, 2012, 122.
87. Thomas Aquinas, *op. cit.*, lib. II lect. 5 n. 4.

ἀξιοῦμεν λέγεσθαι, καὶ τὰ παρὰ ταῦτα οὐχ ὅμοια φαίνεται ἀλλὰ διὰ τὴν ἀσυνήθειαν ἀγνωστότερα καὶ ξενικώτερα· τὸ γὰρ σύνηθες γνώριμον. Ἡλίκην δὲ ἰσχὺν ἔχει τὸ σύνηθες οἱ νόμοι δηλοῦσιν, ἐν οἷς τὰ μυθώδη καὶ παιδαριώδη μεῖζον ἰσχύει τοῦ γινώσκειν περὶ αὐτῶν διὰ τὸ ἔθος. Οἱ μὲν οὖν ἐὰν μὴ μαθηματικῶς λέγῃ τις οὐκ ἀποδέχονται τῶν λεγόντων, οἱ δ' ἂν μὴ παραδειγματικῶς, οἱ δὲ μάρτυρα ἀξιοῦσιν ἐπάγεσθαι ποιητήν. Καὶ οἱ μὲν πάντα ἀκριβῶς, τοὺς δὲ λυπεῖ τὸ ἀκριβὲς ἢ διὰ τὸ μὴ δύνασθαι συνείρειν ἢ διὰ τὴν μικρολογίαν· ἔχει γάρ τι τὸ ἀκριβὲς τοιοῦτον, ὥστε, καθάπερ ἐπὶ τῶν συμβολαίων, καὶ ἐπὶ τῶν λόγων ἀνελεύθερον εἶναί τισι δοκεῖ. διὸ δεῖ πεπαιδεῦσθαι πῶς ἕκαστα ἀποδεκτέον, ὡς ἄτοπον ἅμα ζητεῖν ἐπιστήμην καὶ τρόπον ἐπιστήμης· ἔστι δ' οὐδὲ θάτερον ῥᾴδιον λαβεῖν.

suetudinem diversos modos acceptant: et dicit, quod quidam non recipiunt quod eis dicitur, nisi dicatur eis per modum mathematicum. Et hoc quidem convenit propter consuetudinem his, qui in mathematicis sunt nutriti. Et quia consuetudo est similis naturae, potest etiam hoc quibusdam contingere propter indispositionem: illis scilicet, qui sunt fortis imaginationis, non habentes intellectum multum elevatum. Alii vero sunt, qui nihil volunt recipere nisi proponatur eis aliquod exemplum sensibile, vel propter consuetudinem, vel propter dominium sensitivae virtutis in eis et debilitatem intellectus. Quidam vero sunt qui nihil reputent esse dignum ut aliquid eis inducatur absque testimonio poetae, vel alicuius auctoris. Et hoc etiam est vel propter consuetudinem, vel propter defectum iudicii, quia non possunt diiudicare utrum ratio per certitudinem concludat; et ideo quasi non credentes suo iudicio requirunt iudicium alicuius noti. Sunt etiam aliqui qui omnia volunt sibi dici per certitudinem, idest per diligentem inquisitionem rationis. Et hoc contingit propter bonitatem intellectus iudicantis, et rationes inquirentis; dummodo non quaeratur certitudo in his, in quibus certitudo esse non potest. Quidam vero sunt qui tristantur, si quid per certitudinem cum diligenti discussione inquiratur. Quod quidem potest contingere dupliciter. Uno modo propter impotentiam complectendi: habent enim debilem rationem, unde non sufficiunt ad considerandum

βελτίστη οὖσα, πολλοῖς γέγονέ τε καὶ νῦν ἐστιν ἐπαχθής· πρὸς οὓς αὐτὸς ἀπολογούμενος ἐν τέλει τῶν *Μετὰ τὰ φυσικά* τοῦ δευτέρου, δείκνυσιν ὅπως ἐν τῇ μαθήσει τῆς ἀληθείας οὐ τὸν αὐτὸν τρόπον ἀσμενίζονται πάντες τῆς διδασκαλίας. Οἱ μὲν γάρ, φησί, τῷ τοῖς μαθήμασιν ἐντετράφθαι καὶ δι' ἀσθένειαν μὲν κρίσεως, δραστηριότητα δὲ φαντασίας, πάντα βούλονται σφίσιν ὑπὸ τοῖς μαθηματικοῖς προτίθεσθαι λόγοις· οἱ δὲ δι' ἀδυναμίαν νοήσεως παράδειγμά τι τῶν αἰσθητῶν ἐπιζητοῦσι πρὸς ἑκάστην ἀπόδειξιν· οἱ δὲ τῶν παλαιῶν τινος μαρτυρίαν· οἱ δὲ πρὸς τὴν σὺν ἀκριβείᾳ πάντων ἔρευναν ἀπεχθῶς ἔχουσιν, οὔτε δυνάμενοι παρακολουθεῖν καὶ ἄλλως μικρολογίαν εἶναι τὸ πρᾶγμα οἰόμενοι, καθ' ὁμοιότητα τῶν ἐν ταῖς ἀπαιτήσεσι τῶν χρεῶν, ὀργιζομένων τοῖς καὶ τὰ ἐλάχιστα εἰσπραττομένοις· ἀνελευθέρους γὰρ καὶ ἀκαίρους καὶ φειδωλοὺς τοὺς τοιούτους ἀποκαλοῦσιν.

> ordinem complexionis priorum et posteriorum. Alio modo propter micrologiam, idest parvorum ratiocinationem. Cujus similitudo quaedam est in certitudinali inquisitione, quae nihil indiscussum relinquit usque ad minima. Imaginantur autem quidam, quod sicut in symbolis conviviorum non pertinet ad liberalitatem, quod debeant etiam minima computari in ratiocinio, ita etiam sit quaedam importunitas et illiberalitas, si homo velit circa cognitionem veritatis etiam minima discutere.

To Scholarios, Aristotle did what is the philosophers' duty: he precisely defined and distinguished the sciences from each other and determined the issues of each science, according to the necessity of logic. Neither Plato nor anyone else did so. True, sometimes Aristotle accepts axioms of earlier philosophers or common beliefs and in some cases utilizes examples. Nevertheless, these are just details which simply help him to manifest the truth, depending on the audience.[88]

Here ends the subject, and Scholarios continues arguing on the juxtaposition of Aristotle with Plato, regarding the perpetuality and the creation of the world.[89] However, Scholarios will, occasionally, refer once again to the use of myths by Plato and the poets.[90] In this case the background is *Metaphysics* 1000a9–22 of Aristotle, but Scholarios, as expected, draws again from Thomas' *Commentary* on *Metaphysics*:[91]

Aristotle ***Metaphysica*** **1000a9–22**	**Thomas Aquinas** ***Sententia Metaphysicae,*** **lib. III lect. 11 n. 3**	**Scholarios** ***Contra Plethonis difficultates de Aristotele*, 20, l. 21–25**
Οἱ μὲν οὖν περὶ Ἡσίοδον καὶ πάντες ὅσοι θεολόγοι μόνον ἐφρόντισαν τοῦ πιθανοῦ τοῦ πρὸς αὑτούς, ἡμῶν δ' ὠλιγώρησαν (θεοὺς γὰρ	Deinde cum dicit "qui quidem," excludit solutionem poetarum theologorum. [...] Circa primum considerandum est, quod apud Graecos, aut na-	Εἴρηται δὲ καὶ ὅτι ἐν τοῖς *Μετὰ τὰ φυσικὰ* τὰ αὐτὰ περί τε Πλάτωνος καὶ τῶν θεολόγων καλουμένων ἀπελο-

88. Scholarios, *op. cit.*, 18, l. 3–18.
89. *Ib.*, 18, l. 19 sqq.
90. *Ib.*, 20, l. 21–25.
91. Thomas Aquinas, *op. cit.*, lib. III lect. 11 n. 3; n. 5.

ποιοῦντες τὰς ἀρχὰς καὶ ἐκ θεῶν γεγονέναι, τὰ μὴ γευσάμενα τοῦ νέκταρος καὶ τῆς ἀμβροσίας θνητὰ γενέσθαι φασίν, δῆλον ὡς ταῦτα τὰ ὀνόματα γνώριμα λέγοντες αὐτοῖς· καίτοι περὶ αὐτῆς τῆς προσφορᾶς τῶν αἰτίων τούτων ὑπὲρ ἡμᾶς εἰρήκασιν· εἰ μὲν γὰρ χάριν ἡδονῆς αὐτῶν θιγγάνουσιν, οὐθὲν αἴτια τοῦ εἶναι τὸ νέκταρ καὶ ἡ ἀμβροσία, εἰ δὲ τοῦ εἶναι, πῶς ἂν εἶεν ἀΐδιοι δεόμενοι τροφῆς) – ἀλλὰ περὶ μὲν τῶν μυθικῶς σοφιζομένων οὐκ ἄξιον μετὰ σπουδῆς σκοπεῖν· παρὰ δὲ τῶν δι' ἀποδείξεως λεγόντων δεῖ πυνθάνεσθαι διερωτῶντας τί δή ποτ' ἐκ τῶν αὐτῶν ὄντα τὰ μὲν ἀΐδια τὴν φύσιν ἐστὶ τὰ δὲ φθείρεται τῶν ὄντων.

turales philosophos, fuerunt quidam sapientiae studentes, qui deis se intromiserunt occultantes veritatem divinorum sub quodam tegmine fabularum, sicut Orpheus, Hesiodus et quidam alii: sicut etiam Plato occultavit veritatem philosophiae sub mathematicis, ut dicit Simplicius in *Commento "Praedicamentorum."* Dicit ergo, quod sectatores Hesiodi, et omnes, qui dicebantur theologi, curaverunt persuadere solis sibi, et nos alios spreverunt; quia scilicet veritatem, quam intellexerunt, taliter tradiderunt, quod eis solum possit esse nota.

n. 5

Si enim intelligantur ista verba secundum quod sonant, nullius efficaciae esse videntur.

γήσατο ποιητῶν, ὅτι ὁ μὲν ἦχος αὐτῶν οὐδὲν δραστηριότητος ἢ πιθανότητος ἔχει, ἡ δὲ ὑπ' αὐτοῖς συγκεκαλυμμένη διάνοια αὐτοῖς μόνοις γινώσκοιτ' ἂν ἀκριβῶς, ἕτερος δὲ οὐδεὶς ἂν εἰδείη.

Let us now turn to Pletho's reaction in his *Contra Scholarii pro Aristotele obiectiones* (*Πρὸς τὰς Σχολαρίου ὑπὲρ Ἀριστοτέλους ἀντιλήψεις*), which was composed between 1443/44 and 1449. Pletho dedicated a whole chapter to defend Plato's usage of myths.

Pletho focused on Scholarios' idea that Aristotle's obscure language suits the philosopher, while Plato's ornamented language fits *par excellence* to the poet.[92] Pletho wonders how this is possible, since the philosopher, because of his love for the people, has the duty to clarify the deep meanings of philosophy and make them more comprehensible.[93] According to Pletho,[94] myth is reasonable, provided it does not contain "nonsense" (which is the case with poets' use of it), but philosophical knowledge in a form simple and appropriate for those who cannot reach its deeper meanings. So, Plato, in order to free *φιλομυθία* from being stuck on poetic myths, produced certain beneficial myths of his own regarding the divine matters, which are beneficial both for the wise and for those who are ignorant of philosophy.[95]

92. Quoted by Pletho, *Contra Scholarii pro Aristotele obiectiones*, 6, l. 8–10.
93. *Ib.*, 6, l. 11–17.
94. *Ib.*, 6, l. 17–19.
95. *Ib.*, 6, l. 21–24: Ἀπάγων γὰρ τὸ τῶν πολλῶν φιλόμυθον τῆς τῶν ποιητικῶν μύθων μοχθηρίας, αὐτὸς ἑτέροις μύθοις εὐαγέσι τισὶν ἔδωκέ τι ἐννοεῖν καὶ τούτοις τῶν θείων οὐ πάνυ τοι

Apart from this beneficial - according to Plato and Pletho - use of the myth, it is obvious that philosophy is a privilege of the few,[96] whether they are the philosopher-kings of Plato's *Republic* or the rulers of his *Laws* or the wise men in Pletho's *Laws*.[97]

Once Pletho demonstrates the usefulness of Plato's conception of myth, he starts his counter-attack, stating that obscure language in philosophy does not benefit the wise men, because they are obliged to toil for something that ought to have been more easily comprehensible, while the ignorant would not benefit either, because ambiguity would confuse them.[98]

Subsequently, Pletho remarks that his criticism regards some clear Aristotelian views, whereas Scholarios uses some obscure points of Aristotle's writings as a pretext, in order to offer an odd interpretation of the clear ones.[99]

Pletho's brief answer should not be seen as superficial; it focuses on the core of the debate. Pletho answers as a defender of the allegorical interpretation[100] of myth. He also points out Scholarios' use of Thomistic material and blames Scholarios of appealing to some irrelevant material from Aquinas.[101] As has been shown,[102] Pletho refers here to the Thomistic distinction of the source of knowledge into "natural light of reason" (φυσικὸν φῶς τοῦ λόγου) or "natural light of the mind" (φυσικὸν φῶς τοῦ νοῦ) and "light of divine revelation" (φῶς τῆς θείας ἀποκαλύψεως) or "light of divine knowledge" (φῶς τῆς θείας ἐπιστήμης). Nevertheless, Pletho makes this statement in the course of his dealing with Scholarios' reference to Aristotle's *Metaphysics*;[103] there, Scholarios defended his view that Aristotle considered "εἶναί

ἀλλότριον, ἵν' οἵ τε σοφοὶ ὁμοῦ καὶ οἱ πολλοὶ ἀπόναιντό τι αὐτοῦ. Pletho, when referring to the charges against the *φιλομυθία* of the people, may have had in mind Aristotle's *Metaphysica* 982b19–21 (ὁ φιλόμυθος φιλόσοφός πώς ἐστιν· ὁ γὰρ μῦθος σύγκειται ἐκ θαυμασίων).

96. See e. g. Plato, *Respublica* 494A4: Φιλόσοφον μὲν ἄρα, ἦν δ' ἐγώ, πλῆθος ἀδύνατον εἶναι.
97. Pletho, *Leges* I, 2, 28, l. 16–27: Παρὰ δὲ νομοθετῶν τε καὶ φιλοσόφων μᾶλλον ἤπερ τινῶν ἄλλων ἀνθρώπων πύθοιτ' ἄν τίς τι ὑγιὲς περὶ τῶν τοιούτων. [...] οἵ τε φιλόσοφοι τὴν ἐν τοῖς οὖσιν ἀλήθειαν κεφάλαιον εὐδαιμονίας ποιούμενοι, καὶ ταύτην πρὸ πάντων ἂν χρημάτων διώκοντες, εἰκότως ὡς μάλιστα, εἴπερ τινὲς ἄλλοι ἀνθρώπων, καὶ τυγχάνοιεν ἂν αὐτῆς. Ἀλλὰ δὴ ἡ τῶν πολλῶν φύσις ἀσθενεστέρα περὶ τὴν τῶν μεγίστων γνῶσίν τε καὶ κτῆσιν ἢ ὥστε τυγχάνειν ἂν τοῦ περὶ αὐτὰ ἀκριβοῦς.
98. Pletho, *Contra Scholarii pro Aristotele obiectiones*, 6, l. 24–26.
99. *Ib.*, 6, l. 26–30.
100. The allegorical interpretation of myth is rooted in ancient times. For the contemporary tendencies in myth interpretation, see A. Gkartziou, 2005, 1–16.
101. Pletho, *op. cit.*, 17, l. 17–22: Καὶ σὺ τὰ Ἀριστοτέλους ἅπαντα ἐπεληλυθὼς βιβλία καὶ οὐδ' ὁτιοῦν ἐν αὐτοῖς πρὸς τὸ σοὶ σπουδαζόμενον συμβαλλόμενον εὑρών, ἀλλὰ καὶ ἃ ᾠήθης εὑρηκέναι, τούτων ἐκ μὲν τῶν πλειόνων καὶ ἐλεγχόμενος αὐτὸς ἀντὶ τοῦ ἐλέγχειν, τοῖς δ' αὐτὸς προστιθεὶς οὐδὲν ἑπόμενον, ἔστι δ' ἃ καὶ τῶν Θωμᾶ ἐνείρων οὐκ ἐν καιρῷ, ἀλλὰ τηνάλλως μακρολογῶν [...]
102. J. A. Demetracopoulos, 2006, 307–308.
103. Pletho, *op. cit.*, 17, l. 10–13 = Scholarios, *op. cit.*, 38, l. 1–3: Ὡς, εἰ καὶ δυνατόν ἐστι λέγειν, ὅτι ἐν τοῖς διαπεπτωκόσι τῶν *Μετὰ τὰ φυσικά* ἴσως τι εἴρηκε περὶ τῆς πρώτης ἀρχῆς πλατύτερόν τε ὁμοῦ καὶ σαφέστερον, διαπεπτωκέναι δὲ πολλὰ λέγουσί τέ τινες καὶ πιθανόν ἐστι.

τινα ἀρχὴν ποιητικὴν τοῦ παντός."[104] This probably indicates that Pletho had also identified Scholarios' use of Thomas' *Commentary* on *Metaphysics*, although this presupposes that he somehow had access to Scholarios' own translation of this commentary. Anyway, Pletho was well acquainted with Thomas' works, since Demetrios Cydones, the most significant of Thomas' Greek translators, was in all probability Pletho's teacher[105].

To sum up:

1) Scholarios developed his views on the use of myth in philosophy on the basis of Aristotle's and Thomas Aquinas' opinions, as is indicated by the reception of Aristotle's *Metaphysics* and Thomas' *Commentary* on *Metaphysics* in Scholarios' text. As regards the reception of Thomas, Scholarios utilized his Thomistic material freely, i.e. in some cases he translates *verbatim*, in others he paraphrases, in others he sums up Thomistic material, while in other passages reminiscences or locutions of Thomas' text are spotted. In fact, the extended use of Thomas' *Commentary* on *Metaphysics* is not something unfamiliar to Scholarios, since he himself has noted the use of Thomas' works in his *Compendium* of Thomas' *SG*: Οἷς[106] πᾶσι σχεδὸν ἡμεῖς ἐνετύχομεν, ὀλίγοις μὲν τοῖς ἑρμηνευθεῖσιν ὑπ' ἄλλων[107] πρότερον εἰς τὴν Ἑλλήνων φωνὴν [...][108] Apart from this, several works of Scholarios directly show his admiration for the famous Dominican. It will suffice to refer to the *Compendium SG* and the *Compendium ST* I^{a} II^{ae}, the Greek translation of *De ente et essentia* and the associated *Commentarium* of Armandus de Bellovisu, and last the Greek translation of Thomas' *Commentarium in De Anima* of Aristotle.

But why did Scholarios choose to utilize Thomas Aquinas? In Scholarios' era Thomas' *œvrue* was very well known in Byzantium[109] thanks to the Greek translations[110] of some of his works by Demetrios[111] and Prochoros[112] Cydones. The high rank of Aristotle's work in Thomas' thought on the one hand and Scholarios' Aristotelianism on the other led him to carefully study Thomas. In fact, as J. A. Demetracopoulos has noted, Scholarios' philothomism and anti-Plethonism are in all probability closely connected,

104. Scholarios, *op. cit.*, 37, l. 33–34.

105. For this issue, see J. P. Mamalakis, 1939, 43–45, 185–186; J. A. Demetracopoulos, 2004, 30.

106. I.e. Thomas' *opera*.

107. I.e. by Demetrios and Prochoros Cydones.

108. Scholarios, *Compendium SG*, 2, l. 2–4. For some useful data regarding the reception of Thomas' work by Scholarios, see P. Tavardon, 1983, 57–74; J. A. Demetracopoulos, 2002, 117–171; *Id.*, 2006, 276–341.

109. J. A. Demetracopoulos, 2012, 111–123.

110. For the Greek translations of some of Doctor Angelicus' works, see S. G. Papadopoulos, 1967; *Id.*, 1974, 274–304 (a summary of 1967); G. Podskalsky, 1977, 173–230; J. A. Demetracopoulos, 2010, 822–826.

111. For Demetrios Cydones, see S. G. Papadopoulos, 1967, 78–90; *PLP*, n. 13876; F. Tinnefeld, 1981, 4–74; A. Fyrigos, 2004, 32–37, 60–72.

112. For Prochoros Cydones, see S. G. Papadopoulos, 1967, 90–97; *PLP*, n. 13883; C. Triantafyllopoulos, 2012, 414–424; J. A. Demetracopoulos, (forthcoming), cap. VII, § 2 (Der byzantinische Thomismus).

since, in Scholarios' view, Aristotelianism is much more compatible with Christianity.[113]

2) It is known that Scholarios had translated Thomas' *Commentary* on *Metaphysics,* but, unfortunately, this translation is permanently lost, because its codex unicus,[114] preserved in the library of Escorial, was burnt during the fire of 1671.[115] In all probability, when Scholarios was composing his text against Pletho, his translation was on his desk. Therefore, the Thomistic passages spotted in Scholarios' text can contribute to a partial restoration of Scholarios' lost translation.

3) Scholarios' usage of Theodoret and Eusebius reveals the inner core of the Scholarios–Pletho debate. Scholarios had identified the anti–Christian character of Pletho's text[116] and foresaw that this controversy would cause the resurfacing of the old debate between Christianity and paganism. Thus, he had recourse to some fundamental writings of the polemical literature of ancient Christianity, in order to draw arguments against Pletho's paganism. As regards Theodoret, it should be mentioned that Scholarios extracted some passages from his *Graecarum Affectionum Curatio,* which are preserved in *Par. Gr.* 1289, ff. 195^{v}–197^{v}.[117] In the context of his anti–pagan polemics, Scholarios had recourse to Origen's *Contra Celsum*, too.[118]

Bibliography

Primary sources

Cicero, *De finibus bonorum et malorum*, in: T. Schiche, *M. Tulli Ciceronis scripta quae manserunt omnia*, Fasc. 43, Lipsiae 1915.

113. J. A. Demetracopoulos, 2002, 167–168.

114. For the codex, see G. De Andrès, 1968, 112, codex n. 252 (Δ. IV. 8).

115. For the results of the fire of 1671 in general, see G. De Andrès, 1968, 7–12 (Prologue).

116. Cf. Scholarios' statement in *Ad exarchum Josephum de Gemisti Plethonis libro et contra multorum deorum cultum*, 156, l. 2–4: Ἐκεῖνός τε γὰρ θρασύτερον ἐπῄει τῷ φιλοσόφῳ, πολλὴν εἰδὼς ἐκ τῆς ἐκείνου φιλοσοφίας καὶ ὧν ἀντέστη τῷ Πλάτωνι συνηγορίαν τῇ δόξῃ τῆς ἀληθείας [i.e. Christian faith] προσγινομένην. See also: J. A. Demetracopoulos, 2004, 34.

117. These *Excerpta* are listed in the index of this ms. under the title *κβ'. Σημειώσεις ἀναγκαῖαι ἐκ τοῦ βιβλίου τοῦ μακαρίου Θεοδωρίτου* (sic) *ἐπισκόπου Κύρου.* For a description of this ms., see H. Omont, 1886, 288–289. For the *editio princeps* of these *Excerpta*, see: P. C. Athanasopoulos, forthcoming.

118. See J. A. Demetracopoulos, 2014a, 217 (and n. 218). – Incidentally, a new critical edition of Scholarios' text is badly needed. First of all, in several cases the text suffers from the choice of wrong writings and errors in accentuation. Secondly, the text division does not correspond to its content, which means that this division must be reconsidered. Thirdly, there is almost no *apparatus fontium*, since in more than 100 pages of text, the editors have noted just three (!) sources (ad 20, l. 32–33; 44, l. 8; 95, l. 5–6). Nevertheless, in less than 20 pages of Scholarios' text we spotted undeclared sources in several cases (see Appendix below) – not to mention Scholarios' abundant references to Plato, Aristotle, and Pletho.

This paper presents a part of the results of postdoctoral research prepared within the scope of Byzantine Philosophy at the University of Patras, Greece.

Cicero, *De re publica*, in: C. F. W. Mueller, *M. Tulli Ciceronis scripta quae manserunt omnia*, Part 4/v. 2, Lipsiae 1890.

Eusebius, *Praeparatio Evangelica*, in: K. Mras, *Eusebius Werke*, v. 8: *Die Praeparatio evangelica*, Die griechischen christlichen Schriftsteller 43. 2, Berlin 1956.

Georgios Gemistos Plethon, *Leges*, in: C. Alexandre, *Pléthon, Traité des lois*, Amsterdam 1966 (Paris [1]1858).

Georgios Gemistos Plethon, *Contra Scholarii pro Aristotele obiectiones*, in: E. V. Maltese, *Contra Scholarii pro Aristotele obiectiones*, Lipsiae 1988.

Georgios Gemistos Plethon, *De differentiis*, in: B. Lagarde, "Le *De differentiis* de Pléthon d'après l'autographe de la Marcienne," *Byzantion* 43 (1973) 312–343.

Georgios Monachos, *Chronicon Breve*, in: J.-P. Migne, *Patrologiae cursus completes. Series Graeca*, v. 110, Paris 1863, coll. 41–1260.

Hippolyte of Rome, *De Universo*, in: W. J. Malley, "Four unedited fragments of the *De Universo* of the Pseudo-Josephus found in the *Chronicon* of George Hamartolus (Coislin 305)," *Journal of Theological Studies* 16 (1965) 15–16.

Homer, *Iliad*, in: D. B. Monro, T. W. Allen, *Homeri opera*, v. 1–2, Oxford 1978 ([1]1902).

Jerome, *Epistula* 53 (*ad Paulinum Presbyterum*), in: I. Hilberg, *S. Eusebii Hieronymi opera* (Sect. I, Pars I: Epistularum Pars I), *CSEL* 54, Vindobonae–Lipsiae 1910, 442–465.

John, in: E. & E. Nestle, B. & K. Aland, J. Karavidopoulos, C. M. Martini, B. M. Metzger, *Novum Testamentum graece*, Stuttgart [27]1993, 247–319.

Origen, *Contra Celsum*, in: M. Borret, *Origène. Contre Celse*, Sources chrétiennes 132 (v. 1), 136 (v. 2), 147 (v. 3), 150 (v. 4), Paris 1967 (v. 1), 1968 (v. 2), 1969 (v. 3–4).

Paul, *I Epistula ad Corinthios*, in: E. & E. Nestle, B. & K. Aland, J. Karavidopoulos, C. M. Martini, B. M. Metzger, *Novum Testamentum graece*, Stuttgart [27]1993, 441–472.

Scholarios, *Ad exarchum Josephum de Gemisti Plethonis libro et contra multorum deorum cultum*, in: L. Petit, X. A. Siderides, M. Jugie, *Γενναδίου τοῦ Σχολαρίου ἅπαντα τὰ εὑρισκόμενα - Œuvres complètes de Gennade Scholarios*, v. 4, Paris 1935, 155–172.

Scholarios, *Contra Plethonis difficultates de Aristotele*, in: L. Petit, X. A. Siderides, M. Jugie, *Γενναδίου τοῦ Σχολαρίου ἅπαντα τὰ εὑρισκόμενα - Œuvres complètes de Gennade Scholarios*, v. 4, Paris 1935, 1–116.

Scholarios, *Compendium Summae contra Gentiles*, in: L. Petit, X. A. Siderides, M. Jugie, *Γενναδίου τοῦ Σχολαρίου ἅπαντα τὰ εὑρισκόμενα - Œuvres complètes de Gennade Scholarios*, v. 5, Paris 1931, 1–338.

Scholarios, *Compendium Summae Theologiae I[a] II[ae]*, in: L. Petit, X. A. Siderides, M. Jugie, *Γενναδίου τοῦ Σχολαρίου ἅπαντα τὰ εὑρισκόμενα - Œuvres complètes de Gennade Scholarios*, v. 6, Paris 1933, 1–153.

Scholarios, *Translatio Commentarii Thomae in Aristotelis De Anima*, in: L. Petit, X. A. Sideridès, M. Jugie, *Γενναδίου τοῦ Σχολαρίου ἅπαντα τὰ εὑρισκόμενα - Œuvres complètes de Gennade Scholarios*, v. 6, Paris 1933, 327–581.

Scholarios, *Translatio Thomae De ente et essentia et Commentarium*, in: L. Petit, X. A. Sideridès, M. Jugie, *Γενναδίου τοῦ Σχολαρίου ἅπαντα τὰ εὑρισκόμενα - Œuvres complètes de Gennade Scholarios*, v. 6, Paris 1933, 154–321.

Tatian, *Oratio ad Graecos*, in: E. J. Goodspeed, *Die ältesten Apologeten*, Göttingen 1915, 268–305.

Theodoret of Cyrus, *Graecarum Affectionum Curatio*, in: P. Canivet, *Théodoret de Cyr. Thérapeutique des maladies helléniques*, v. 1–2, Sources chrétiennes 57, Paris 1958.

Xenophon, *Epistulae*, in: R. Hercher, *Epistolographi Graeci*, Amsterdam 1965 ([1]Paris 1873), 788–791.

Thomas Aquinas, *Summa Theologiae*, in: *Sancti Thomae Aquinatis opera omnia iussu impensaque Leonis XIII P. M. edita*, v. 4–5, Romae 1888–1889.

Thomas Aquinas, *Sententia Metaphysicae*, in: corpusthomisticum.org (Textum Taurini 1950 editum).

Thomas Aquinas, *Summa contra Gentiles*, in: corpusthomisticum.org (Textum Leoninum emendatum ex plagulis de prelo Taurini 1961 editum).

Secondary Literature

Athanasopoulos, P. C., "Scholarii 'Excerpta' ex Theodoreti Episcopi Cyrensis 'Graecarum Affectionum Curatione': Editio Princeps," *Revue des études byzantines* 73 (2015). (forthcoming)

Blanchet, M.-H., *George-Gennadios Scholarios (vers 1400-vers 1472). Un intellectuel orthodoxe face à la disparition de l'empire byzantin*, Archives de l'orient chrétien 20, Paris 2008.

Brisson, L., "L'Égypte de Platon," *Les études philosophiques* 2/3 (1987) 153–168.

Bydén, B., "'No prince of perfection': Byzantine anti-Aristotelianism from the patristic period to Pletho," in: D. Angelov, M. Saxby, eds., *Power and Subversion in Byzantium. Papers from the 43rd Spring Symposium of Byzantine Studies, Birmingham, March 2010*, Publications of the Society for the Promotion of Byzantine Studies 17, Aldershot 2013, 147–176.

De Andrès, G., *Catalogo de los codices Griegos desaparecidos de la Real Biblioteca de el Escorial*, El Escorial 1968.

Demetracopoulos, J. A., *Νικολάου Καβάσιλα Κατὰ Πύρρωνος. Πλατωνικὸς φιλοσκεπτικισμὸς καὶ ἀριστοτελικὸς ἀντισκεπτικισμὸς στὴ βυζαντινὴ διανόηση τοῦ 14ου αἰῶνα* (with an English Summary: *Nicholas Cabasilas' "Contra Pyrrhonem." Introduction, Critical Edition, Modern Greek Translation, Philosophical Analysis, and Historical Context*), Athens 1999.

Demetracopoulos, J. A., "Georgios Gennadios II Scholarios' 'Florilegium Thomisticum'. His Early Abridgment of Various Chapters and Quæstiones of Thomas Aquinas' 'Summae' and His anti-Plethonism," *Recherches de théologie et philosophie médiévales* 69, 1 (2002) 117–171.

Demetracopoulos, J. A., *Ἀπὸ τὴν ἱστορία τοῦ βυζαντινοῦ θωμισμοῦ: Πλήθων καὶ Θωμᾶς Ἀκυινάτης*, Αθήνα 2004.

Demetracopoulos, J. A., "Georgios Gemistos-Plethon's Dependence on Thomas Aquinas' 'Summa Contra Gentiles' and 'Summa Theologiae'," *Archiv für mittelalterliche Philosophie und Kultur* 12 (2006) 276–341.

Demetracopoulos, J. A., "Latin Philosophical Works Translated into Greek," in: R. Pasnau, ed., *The Cambridge History of Medieval Philosophy*, II, Cambridge 2010 (revised edition 2014), 822–826.

Demetracopoulos, J. A., "Thomas Aquinas' Impact on Late Byzantine Theology and Philosophy: The Issues of Method or 'Modus Sciendi' and 'Dignitas Hominis'," in: A. Speer, P. Steinkrüger, hrsg., *Knotenpunkt Byzanz*, Miscellanea Mediaevalia 36, Berlin, New York 2012, 333–410.

Demetracopoulos, J. A., "The Influence of Thomas Aquinas on Late Byzantine Philosophical and Theological Thought: À propos of the Thomas De Aquino Byzantinus Project," *Bulletin de philosophie médiévale* 54 (2012) 101–124.

Demetracopoulos, J. A., "Hermonymos Christonymos Charitonymos' *Capita decem pro divinitate Christi:* A posthumous Reaction to Plethon's anti-Christianism," in: J. Matula, P. R. Blum, eds., *Georgios Gemistos Plethon: The Byzantine and the Latin Renaissance*, Olomouc 2014a, 143–259.

Demetracopoulos, J. A., "Commission VIII: Byzantine philosophy. Section II: Thomas de Aquino Byzantinus," *Bulletin de philosophie médiévale* 56 (2014b), forthcoming.

Demetracopoulos, J. A., "Die Philosophie des 15. Jahrhunderts," in: G. Kapriev, hrsg., *Grundriss der Geschichte der Philosophie. Begründet von Fr. Überweg, Die Philosophie des Mittelalters*, I.1. *Jüdische und byzantinische Philosophie/Byzantinische Philosophie*, Basel 2014, cap. VII, § 2 (Der byzantinische Thomismus). (forthcoming)

Fyrigos, A., "Tomismo e antitomismo a Bisanzio (con una nota sulla 'Defensio S. Thomae adversus Nilum Cabasilam' di Demetrio Cidone)", in: A. Molle, ed., *Tommaso d'Aquino († 1274) e il mondo bizantino*, Venafro 2004, 27–72.

Gkartziou, A., "Οι μίτοι του μύθου: σύγχρονες οδοί ερμηνείας του αρχαίου ελληνικού μύθου," in: Κ. Μπουραζέλης–Μ. Στεφάνου, επιμ., *Μύθος μετά λόγου. Διάλογοι για την ουσία και τη διαχρονική αξία του αρχαίου ελληνικού μύθου. Πρακτικά του συμποσίου Ἁγιος Κήρυκος, Ικαρία 17-20 Ιουνίου*, Αθήνα 2005, 1–16.

Omont, H., *Inventaire sommaire des manuscrits grecs de la Bibliothèque Nationale*, I: Ancien Fonds frec, Paris 1886.

Mamalakis, J. P., *Γεώργιος-Γεμιστὸς Πλήθων*, Texte und Forschungen zur byzantinisch-neugriechischen Philologie 32, Ἀθῆναι 1939.

McEvoy, J., "Platon et la sagesse de l'Égypte", *Kernos* 6 (1993) 245–275.

Monfasani, J., *George of Trebizond. A Biography and a Study of his Rhetoric and Logic*, Columbia Studies in the Classical Tradition 1, Leiden 1976.

Papadopoulos, S. G., *Ἑλληνικαὶ μεταφράσεις θωμιστικῶν ἔργων. Φιλοθωμισταὶ καὶ ἀντιθωμισταὶ ἐν Βυζαντίῳ. Συμβολὴ εἰς τὴν ἱστορίαν τῆς βυζαντινῆς θεολογίας*, Ἀθῆναι 1967.

Papadopoulos, S. G., "Thomas in Byzanz: Thomas–Kritik in Byzanz zwischen 1354 und 1435," *Theologie und Philosophie* 49 (1974) 274–304.

Podskalsky, G., *Theologie und Philosophie in Byzanz. Der Streit um die theologische Methodik in der spätbyzantinischen Geistesgeschichte (14/15 Jh.), seine systematischen Grundlangen und seine historische Entwicklung*, Byzantinisches Archiv 15, München 1977.

Tavardon, P., "Georges Scholarios: un thomiste byzantin?," *Βυζαντιακά* 3 (1983) 57–74.

Tinnefeld, F., *Demetrios Kydones. Briefe*, I.1, Bibliothek der griechischen Literatur 12, Stuttgart 1981.

Triantafyllopoulos, C., "The Thomist Basis of Prochoros Kydones' anti–Palamite treatise 'De essentia et operatione Dei' and the Reaction of the Byzantine Church," in: A. Speer, P. Steinkrüger, hrsg., *Knotenpunkt Byzanz. Wissensformen und kulturelle Wechselbeziehungen*, Miscellanea Medievalia 36, Berlin, New York 2012, 411–430.

Trapp, E., Beyer, H.-V., Walther R., *Prosopographisches Lexikon der Palaiologenzeit*, I–XIX, Wien 1976–1996.

Websites

www.corpusthomisticum.org
www.labarts.upatras.gr/dimitr/index1.html
https://www.royalholloway.ac.uk/hellenic-institute//research/Thomas.htm

Appendix

Some undeclared Sources in Scholarios' *Κατὰ τῶν Πλήθωνος ἀποριῶν ἐπ' Ἀριστοτέλει*

This table of undeclared sources in Scholarios' text provides data in three columns: (i) reference to Scholarios' text, (ii) Scholarios' undeclared sources spotted, and (iii) an indication (in the form of *crux*) whether each spotted passage constitutes (wholly or partially) a quotation or a paraphrase of the source–text. As stated above, this paper focuses on the Scholarios-Pletho debate regarding the use of myth in philosophy; so, this Table regards the pages of Scholarios' work, which refer to this issue. Besides this, Scholarios utilizes several undeclared sources, mostly from Aquinas' *Commentary* on *Metaphysics*. Therefore, the following table is not exhaustive;[119] more sources are to be found.

	Scholarios *Contra Plethonis difficultates de Aristotele*	**Undeclared source**	**Verbatim/ Paraphrase**
1	4, l. 30–32	Thomas Aquinas, *SG* I, 3, 2	
2	8, l. 22–29	Thomas, *Sententia Metaphysicae* lib. I lect. 15 n. 7; III lect. 11 n. 3 (cf. n. 6)	+
3	8, l. 32–34	Thomas Aquinas, *SG* I, 3, 2	
4	12, l. 6–10	Theodoret of Cyrus, *Graecarum Affectionum Curatio* II, 24, 1–25, 5	
5	12, l. 10–14	Thomas Aquinas, *SG* I, 3, 2	
6	12, l. 14–25	Theodoret of Cyrus, *Graecarum Affectionum Curatio* II, 49, 1–50, 9	+
7	12, l. 33–13, l. 6	Theodoret of Cyrus, *Graecarum Affectionum Curatio* I, 60, 1–61, 3; II, 32, 1–43, 4; 70, 1–79, 3; 85, 1–86, 2 (cf. 114, 1–115, 3; V, 67, 1–2)	+
8	14, l. 12–16	Eusebius of Caesarea, *Praeparatio Evangelica* XV, 6, 1, 1–4; 7, 4, 1–3	+
9	14, l. 36–15, l. 4	Thomas Aquinas, *Sententia Metaphysicae* lib. II lect. 1 n. 16	+
10	15, l. 32–35	Thomas Aquinas, *Sententia Metaphysicae* lib. III lect. 11 n. 3	+
11	16, l. 1–13	Thomas Aquinas, *Sententia Metaphysicae* lib. III lect. 11 n. 3; n. 5; n. 6	+
12	16, l. 19–21	Thomas Aquinas, *Sententia Metaphysicae,* lib. XII lect. 10 n. 20	+
13	17, l. 23–35	Thomas Aquinas, *Sententia Metaphysicae* lib. II lect. 5 n. 4	+
14	20, l. 21–25	Thomas Aquinas, *Sententia Metaphysicae* lib. III lect. 11 n. 3; n. 5	+

119. For example, Scholarios, *Contra Plethonis difficultates de Aristotele*, 21, l. 9–14 = Thomas Aquinas, *ST* I^{a}, qu. 1, art. 5 ad 1 (cf. J. A. Demetracopoulos, 2006, 310–311).

Byzantine Thinking and Iconicity: Post-structural Optics

George Arabatzis

1. Introduction

The issue, here, despite the title, is not about history of philosophy, but, an occasion, on the basis of some historical experiences, to seize the opportunity for a study of a particular arrangement of relationships between "images" and "discourses" or the description of a state of things about images and discourses. By "Byzantine iconicity" is meant nothing other than the perceptual-cultural frame where matters of cultural interest were translated into images. In other words, the images were used to appease some major discomforts or key contradictions of this precise cultural context. The term "Byzantine" refers to an order that is not limited strictly to a single historical context but concerns more general cultural dispositions; the more general use is expressed by the term "Byzantinism," which, in the first place, is employed to demarcate a political order where practices of concealment, verbosity, hypocrisy, deceit, bureaucratic arrangement, full moral and political discrimination, inconsistency between reasons and intentions, and words and things are paramount. By extension, the term "Byzantinism," besides the denotation of the longstanding political behavior of the court of Constantinople, may be applied to other moments of political history in other places and with different actors.[1]

2. Itineraries of Byzantinism

2.1. The Literary Byzantinism

There is, however, another use of the term Byzantinism, signifying the normal literary life in the long term (*longue durée*). In this context, some observations made by the French intellectual and writer Julien Benda are highly

1. In this regard, Byzantinism is a version of political "machiavellianism;" see A. B. Bozeman, *Politics and Culture in International History*, Princeton: Princeton University Press 1989, 298–356.

enlightening.[2] In his view, the great literatures have great moments and these usually are the initial ones. Ancient tragedy, for example, stands for such initial greatness in regards to the history of the theater. The grandiose moments are nonetheless not meant to last, but the end of the initial greatness does not mean the completion of the general literary life. The literary activity goes on and the ensuing literature, though it lacks the magnificence of the beginnings, is not devoid of literary quality and sublimity. The normal, so to speak, in the long European literary life, for Benda, is modeled on Alexandrian literature, which is also the prototype of Byzantine literature. Thanks to the Byzantines, Alexandrian literature achieved a prolonged literary life of a thousand years. Byzantinism, Benda says, in the western world, finds in Alexandrian literature the basic standards of literature. Literary Byzantinism is consequently philologism or pedantry.

Some of the characteristics of literary Byzantinism which Benda recognizes in French literature and philosophy of his time (i.e. the middle of the 20th century) are the following: (a) the creation of a group or an elite of scribes who practice precisely this philologism, and (b) the formation of an ambiguous relationship with intellectualism. Point (b) needs further clarification: literary Byzantinism is an intellectualist approach insofar as it rejects any enthusiastic (*en-theos* = inspired or possessed by God) rupture with tradition, in the face of which it adopts a formal attitude of reproductive knowledge. On the other hand, pure intellectualism and its ideas are rejected by literary Byzantinism since they would render problematic the "esoteric knowledge" of Byzantinist scholars and hinder their lyrical idealism, their hermeticism and sophistication that constitutes a first order evidence of such a "literature for litterateurs."

2.2. The Philosophical implications of Byzantinism

Julien Benda recognizes, for example, a shift to Byzantinism in the interpretation of Husserl's phenomenology by Emmanuel Levinas. Pursuing Benda's criticism, the "face" in Levinas constitutes a paradoxical excess of the problem of transcendental reduction because it allows, in the context of philosophical sciences, to posit Ethics in the place of Ontology as the first such science. The ethics of the faces of other people combines freedom with moral obligation. The gaze of others is not reducible to the desire of the subject to objectify and, at the same time, is a very rigorous means of enforcing morality in interpersonal relationships. The gaze of the Other is apt to give birth to an original feeling of guilt even in circumstances where no culpable act is performed, in contrast for example to the analysis of the guilty gazing in Sartre's *Being and Nothingness*.[3]

2. J. Benda, *La France byzantine ou le triomphe de la littérature pure*, Paris : Gallimard 1945.
3. J.-P. Sartre, *Being and Nothingness. An Essay on Phenomenological Ontology*, translated by H. E. Barnes, New York: Simon and Schuster 1956, 347–353.

Does all that delimit a new perception of Byzantine iconicity? For George Steiner, in our times, the name of a single agglomeration is not sufficient to record a phenomenon similar to that of Alexandria or Byzantium and our era is perhaps to be known as the era of journalists and scribes exercising in the public space.[4] Otherwise, would Byzantine iconicity perhaps mean the development of a new onto-theology,[5] i.e. metaphysics in the long term, meaning not this or that particular metaphysics but the "forgetfulness of Being" described by Martin Heidegger as a relation between borrowed knowledge, fear, faith, dogmatism and lack of grounded expression?

2.3. Philosophy and Thinking

The distinction here between philosophy and thinking follows a new imperative that was laid out by Martin Heidegger (occasionally commenting upon Kierkegaard), marking a turn in his philosophical career.[6] The name of Kierkegaard places us in the heart of iconicity since he was the philosopher that located first the anguish generated by the ethico-aesthetic.

According to Kierkegaard, the ethico-aesthetic opposes directly the cosmological argument for the existence of God. In particular, there are two possibilities as to the relations between ethics and aesthetics: (a) aesthetics is moral (dandyism); (b) aesthetics is counter-moral (as in the close relations between literature and the representation of evil). Kierkegaard unites the two, ethics and aesthetics, in the belief that this has already happened, under the pressure of Christianity; modernity is ethico-aesthetic. Very explicit in this regard is the first part of his book *Either/Or* (1843), and especially the chapter "The Immediate Erotic Stages or the Musical Erotic."[7] Kierkegaard notes that the happy idea of the world of the Ancient Greeks consists in two conjunctions: (1) an aesthetic material finds its deserving representative (the epic poetry comes across Homer), and (2) the aforementioned representative happens to wish for that specific material. It is of no use, says Kierkegaard, for aesthetics to focus on form and thus Mozart's *Don Giovanni* is great art, like the Ancient art, but in a different manner. The difference is not perceptible if one insists on the formal analysis because this latter does not guarantee the perception of such a difference.

The distinction between idea and form is metaphysical and for Kierkegaard it is the repetition of older metaphysical polarities. Kierkegaard's analysis concludes in the following way: sensibility is the proper quality of modern aesthetics, unknown to the Ancient world. This position seems

4. G. Steiner, *Le sens du sens*, Paris : Vrin 1988, 47.
5. M. Heidegger, *Identity and Difference*, translated by J. Stambaugh, New York: Harper and Row 1969.
6. M. Heidegger, *What is Called Thinking?*, translated by J. Glenn Gray, New York: Harper and Row 1968.
7. S. Kierkegaard, *Either/Or*, Part I, Edited and Translated by H. V. Hong and E. H. Hong, Princeton: Princeton University Press 1987, 45–135.

unlikely and in order to understand it, Kierkegaard says, one must contemplate the category of the most approximate, the most familiar. His audacious thesis is that Christianity introduced sensibility in the modern world and this happened through positive opposition. By opposing sensibility, Christianity transformed it into Principle, Force and System. Positive opposition is thus complementary to the opposed. Yet, the philosophical audacity here is only semi-successful since opposition gives birth to the opposed but this time in a new sense. Sensibility in the Ancient world was a psychological phenomenon and not a properly spiritual one and the Platonic idea of the harmony of the soul corresponds to this sense of sensibility. Ancient sensibility was life and pleasure to which the gods also wished to partake. Greek gods do not exemplify but represent the tendencies that already exist in humans. It is Christianity that posited the idea of representation-exemplarity. The exemplified sensibility in Christianity as rupture with harmony (and, thus, a break up with the cosmological argument) is followed by a number of contradictions, principally the one between religious language (asceticism) and music (rhythm). Music in particular, for Kierkegaard, signifies a return of the demonic against the hegemonic ambitions of religious language.

2.4. Byzantine iconicity and education

The aestheticization of ethics performed by Byzantinism creates an extended cut in the social body separating from one side the aesthetically aware and, on the other, the aesthetically ignorant. Moreover, this aestheticization results in a new aesthetical categorical imperative expressed in an exemplary manner by the German word *Bildung*. The categorical imperative of aesthetic morality means that the masses of citizens should be informed and educated aesthetically, in an attempt to democratize aesthetics. Here arises the aesthetic and teleological problem of the images as pure representation, beyond their so-called value-neutrality and objectivity. The question is, also, that of the criticism of the intentional look that is promoted by the phenomenological perspective. The image is, in phenomenology, an observational and invisible power within a framework of meta-representational, radical differences of imitation, accountable for a finite consciousness. The gaze may imply the passivity of the spectator but the overcoming of the distinction in imagination means that the sensible must give way to an all embracing visible and invisible. The critique of onto-theology is greatly indebted to Levinas's contribution[8] about the indestructible and non-reducible moral obligation generated from the face. The person is not an element of the representation but a morally decisive encounter with Being. The infinite occasion for a face-to-face encounter stands for the infinity of interpretations, analogous to the infinity that is stemming from the face of the other man.

8. See R. Bernet, "L'un-pour-l'autre chez Sartre et Levinas," in : *Philosopher en français*, edited by J.-Fr. Mattéi, Paris : PUF 2001, 83–94.

Is the thinking about face iconoclastic? One witnesses here the return of the anxiety about representation. The presence of the face can be detached from the distinction between form and presence. Does the reference to form mean some return to naturalistic Aristotelianism, contrary to facial nominalism? Can morals be separated from metaphysical wisdom? The interpersonal love in Levinas borrows elements from the vocabulary of obedience (present as well in the troubadour poetry or in Spinoza's politico-theological); does this imply that the facial project is axiological? Is the image ultimately proved to be only one more key trick? Do images carry with them the love of this world together with the concern for human solidarity?

2.5. Iconicity and the look of history

The artist's eye in the painting of Velázquez' *Las Meninas* follows a disorderly representation and makes evident the epistemic system of representation in the classical era.[9] An approach to Byzantine iconicity according to gaze can be justly regarded as "Eurocentric." The aesthetic is a solely European matter and Kant, already, has warned that the German autonomy of aesthetics constitutes a philosophical transgression since the ancient Greeks were seeing aesthetics as sensibility, i.e. belonging to the world of the senses.[10] On the other hand, modern media and modern images aim to manipulate the perception of the infinite and the universality of culture. Already in Schiller, aesthetics appears to be a form of resistance against the bureaucratic-administrative class.[11] The widely shared poetic morality in iconicity shows that psychological depth is not only of the individual. Consequently, the individual utilitarianism cannot seek universality. The perception of the pictures for the masses, strongly promulgated in our culture, is nothing but the imitation of the same, i.e. the perpetuation of itself.

9. M. Foucault, *The Order of Things*, London: Routledge 2002, 3–18. The phenomenon of the suture of the human gaze to images is due to the voyeuristic option of seeing without being seen. In the images of television, for example the look of the news presenter right into the eyes of the viewer marks, as it has been said, the warrant of truth. The presenter's look into the eyes of the viewer constitutes some first order evidence: "She is there," says the spectator about the presenter, "I see her speaking to me."

10. I. Kant, *Critique of Pure Reason*, translated by W. S. Pluhar, Indianapolis: Hackett 1996, 74. To this, one can relate Kierkegaard's positions about the ethico-aesthetic. Furthermore, faced with the functionalism of the new representational technologies, aesthetics appears as a modern asceticism, as the current refuge from the dominant world-vision based on simulation. The images thus are distinguished into conformist representations and images of resistance. The anti-utilitarianism of the latter may be regarded either as ethical or as poetic, i.e. as ascetic or ecstatic (roughly, a difference like the one between Bresson and Fellini in cinema or Latour and Rubens in painting).

11. F. Schiller, *On the Aesthetic Education of Man: In a Series of Letters*, edited and translated by E. M. Wilkinson and L. A. Willoughby, Oxford: Clarendon Press 1967.

2.6. The structural homology between images and thinking

Pierre Bourdieu writes that Panofsky's study about the structural homologies between Gothic architecture and scholastic thinking constitutes one of the greater challenges addressed to positivism.[12] Positivism claims that meanings are already posited, well before the recognition of facts themselves, creating thus a sort of vicious cycle. In order to surpass this cycle, one has to study the *modus operandi* of structures by transcending the mixture of dogmatism, empiricism, mysticism and positivism that characterizes the immediate intuition of events. The objects under scrutiny are constructed and not empirically given and their comprehension is achieved in spite of phenomena.

Iconology is proved to be indispensable because, in any other case, the sense of an icon as expression of a meaning or an iconographic programme would be reduced solely to the consciousness of its creator. An image would say nothing more than what its creator manifestly would desire to express. The meaning of the work would be exhausted either in its iconographical inspiration or in the philosophical or aesthetical ideas of its craftsman. Such an interpretation of the image would be exclusively allegorical. The collective creation of medieval works of art is a valid hypothesis for research to the measure that one refers to the expression of ecclesiastic thinking. Yet, this thinking is formed by individuals. The collective and the individual are related through the concept of *habitus*. The content of *habitus* is alien to the consciousness of collectivities as well as individuals. Its manifestation need not be intentional in any particular subject.

To understand the iconological *habitus*, one must read the symptoms of the process of synthetic intuition according to Bourdieu. Thus, the distinction between iconology and iconography consists in the following characteristics: iconography is included in positivism as the image of individuality while iconology refers to the history of style. The structural iconology, as Bourdieu visions it, consists in the negation of the positivist collection of small-scale facts. Structural iconology discovers the meaning of a sequence of which positivism has little to say. The sense of a sequence is found not in the search for a *zeitgeist* but by locating iconological correspondences or structural homologies in relation to a *modus operandi*.

Thus, for example, the development of Gothic art coincides with the retreat of education from monasteries and their mystical and anti-dialectic tradition and its transfer to the scholastic universities with their rationalism and ordered knowledge. Yet, if *habitus* is the genetic grammar of attitudes,

12. P. Bourdieu, "Postface," in: E. Panofsky, *Architecture gothique et pensée scolastique, précedée de L'abbé Suger de Saint-Denis*, Paris : Minuit 1967, 133–167. The idea of a structural homology of linguistic origin may be found in seminal state in Max Weber when he addresses the issue of elective affinities (*Wahlverwandtschaft*). Unfortunately, metaphysics had absorbed everything about these symbolic relations and the research on elective affinities was limited by positivist factualism.

how is one to explain such an innovation? There is no possibility to refer either to the conversion of reflexive consciousness or to the evolution of distinct essences. One should imagine here the interplay of internalized forms and solutions to concrete problems that, though in the limits of the initial sequence, can transform the various stages of action into small moves that introduce variations into the sequence. In sum, this is a game of name-giving and randomness.

In the name of anti-teleological principles, one discovers here a higher teleology. Intentionality is in fact double, simultaneously functional and formal, and questions each time the rationality of the production of meaning. The ethico-aesthetic replaces the weak philosophical generalizations. In the medieval world, the category of the ethico-aesthetic consists in the categories of asceticism and aestheticism or the Church as destiny and the sense of the theological-aesthetical sublime.

2.7. Structuralism and Byzantinism

The concept of structure had aspired to assess in a decisive way the relationship between ideal and material culture. One must admit that, in the context of a more traditional view, these two remained, more or less, in a state of dissension. The interpretation or explanation of the cultural world tends to one or the other direction. In particular, the transition from the material to the symbolic and ritual level, though a matter of daily practice in every culture, constitutes a huge problem for the cultural logic. What the everyday life reconciles, the mind never ceases to divide. Structuralism presented a way leading from the ideality to "reality" through the notion of the unconscious adoption and the difference established within independent practices. One may speak here of a symbolic realism and its understanding, though accused of being solely synchronic, is, in fact, highly historical; yet, its logic is not that of the historical flow of events but concerns larger sections of historicity. The structuralism focuses on cultural content as distinct from individualistic and functional approaches. A certain use of structuralism in an attempt to comprehend the Byzantine world was made by Evelyne Patlagean.[13] The distinguishing similarities and differences push, however, the structuralism to face some difficult problems in order to adjust the theory to data arising from specific cultural contexts. Thus, structuralism may once have appeared almost as a speculative philosophy, quite far from what it really is. The adepts of structuralism tried to exclude the question of intentionality from their analysis and this preoccupation hurt in some degree the popularity of the movement. The issue of intentionality was wrongly identified with that of social subjectivism, although intentionality is a phenomenon that aspires to universality in the physical world. The thesis that intentionality is an

13. E. Patlagean, *Structure sociale, famille, chrétienté à Byzance : IVe-XIe siècle*, London : Variorum Reprints 1981.

exclusively mental fact misses the point as to the character of intentionality and the nature of the mental. In both cases, the connection of intentionality with the world of nature constitutes equally a challenge and a fundamental insight; this problem proves to be philosophically crucial. In particular, the issue of intentionality has the advantage of raising the problems of the past and the present in a way that the first appears subordinate to the constitutive force of the present and to the issues of the moment.

For example, what is the "Byzantine past?" It's largely a product of Eurocentrism and it is not difficult to follow the action of the western centers of power playing around it. The hard part is to clarify what constitutes the Byzantine past. The question of the Byzantine Ego or Byzantine subjectivity can't be overlooked. In particular, the question of Byzantine cultural heritage can't be separated from that of the subjectivities of the modern world. The question is how the interpretative margins of the Byzantine Ego can be led towards an interpretive center in a time of decentered self and dissemination. In this perspective, the question of power must be extended towards the generalized intentionality. The problem of the origins and action is part of this stage of interrogation. The study of processes opposes here the universality of concepts. In particular, intentionality as a natural and/or as a social force is at times an important part of cultural assessment. Despite contrary claims, the causative imperatives cannot be omitted even in this case; understanding is not opposed to causation.

In the Byzantine world the concept of person/personality played an important role. However, on the moving ground of person-centrism, positivity has to face some unanswered questions. The modernist distinction of sciences aiming at positivity does not coincide necessarily and in a fertile way with person-criticism; the person-centered study of Byzantine culture failed to reach the stage of person-criticism (due also to the fact that the issue of gender was greatly ignored). The research must initiate the discussion about the alternative historicity of the Byzantine world. Byzantine historicity in itself is an alternative one as is evidenced by the popular literature that has developed around it. The remains of the past as fragments and ruins, as relics and recollections, are becoming the subjects of discussion and confrontation. The desire for the alternative is strong in some parts of the population that is not satisfied by the value-neutrality of science, which is suspected as malevolent. In addition, the desire for the knowledge of the past may lessen due to the high esteem that a large number of people, fairly or unfairly, have for the achievements of progress. In the immediate consciousness, the domain of the past does not cover more than three generations and during this time, the improvement of the general standard of life entails a belief in progress.[14] In many ways, this belief is not erroneous. However, the notion of progress fails to reduce the anguished presence of time and the concerns that this last

14. R. Hoggart, *The Uses of Literacy: Aspects of Working-Class Life*, London: Penguin 2009.

topic raises. These can be exploited in an institutional manner and, perhaps, this is the reason for the conflicting versions of the past and the subsequent thirst for the alternative.

Close to the notion of progress, after Kant, appears, in an increasingly central manner, the idea of critical philosophy. The critical relationship with truth is controversial: on the one hand, criticism argues that truth is the product of contextualized meanings and, on the other, it posits that it is realistically accessible. Particular attention has been given by criticism to aesthetics and its expressions and, in this regard, it has placed a heavy burden on the perception of culture and its representations. The Critical Theory of Frankfurt, more specifically, denies the positivity, which emerged from the Enlightenment and insists instead on its negative aspects, particularly as a source of terrorist reason and domination. The Critical Theory defends new forms of emancipation against the oppressive practices of the social totality and the individual consciousness. In this perspective, the Critical Theory follows the Nietzschean analysis of the artificial character of consciousness and its historic origins. Another point of the Critical Theory is the avoidance of the crystallization of the past into ideology; this requires from the researcher a particular cultural attitude of self-observation and attention, in order to avoid the historical serialization as self-evident and to surpass the aura of established sciences that participate in the fixation of the commonsensical idea of historical progression. Moreover, technological products are not independent from the above stated ideological process but on the contrary they are parts of it. However, there is still the danger of the absolute relativization of the historical past and the general acceptance of the present, which is no less ideological as it is subject to manipulation (for instance, by the media) and to control. The concepts that are strongly related to culturalism like "truth" or "origin" are made conditional and the region of textual cultures and their interactive processes become autonomous. In any case, it is doubtful whether one can dispense of the active Ego and, in the case of the Byzantine world, the need for a deep understanding of the Byzantine Ego. The Byzantine Ego is the key issue for the critical interpretation of the Byzantine world, and iconicity forms a crucial part of the question.[15]

3. *Three post-structural grids of interpretation*

3.1. History, reason, analysis

Since this paper is an attempt to comprehend the perception and thinking in a world such as Byzantium, it would be quite appropriate to try to establish the legitimacy of such an effort. The historian of medieval philosophy, Alain de Libera, has examined the question and tried to delimit the relevant

15. See G. Arabatzis, "La perception philosophique du sujet byzantine," in : *Marges de la philosophie byzantine*, ed. G. Arabatzis, Athens : Kardamitsas 2013, 77–91.

epistemic field, starting with the actuality of modern philosophy's divisions and in particular the division between analytic and continental philosophy.[16] The initial step of his analysis is the desire for and the prerogative of a semantic-conceptual holism. This approximation of words as terms and concepts is very similar to the analytic use of common language. Yet, the effort is right away inhibited by the Analytic critique, which refutes any idea of approximation between philosophy and the history of philosophy considered as a "culture of commentary." Even more, the "Analytics" believe that the "Continentals" are aiming at the identification of philosophy with the history of philosophy and this has two additional unhappy consequences: (i) the passivity of the philosophical-scholar, unacceptable for a state of democratic affairs and (ii) the textocentrism, which alienates philosophy from the world of clear argument and debate.

In contrast, the debate and the active philosopher are guaranteed in the Analytic framework, which posits for the philosophical interlocutors the status of "fellow philosophers." Here, de Libera questions the democratic nature of this arrangement since the fellow philosophers are only those that practice philosophy in a given geographical and mental area – in brief, the Anglo-Saxon area. This idea of how to do philosophy corresponds to a philosophical market that favors some very determined interests of economic character. In fact, says de Libera, the choice of fellow philosophers is made on the basis of criteria that surpass largely the philosophical debate; these criteria are (a) the establishment of a selective philosophical canon of works and (b) the elimination of all publications that are not conformed to the above canon. The situation is quite medieval as to this point.

The continental philosophy, in turn, cannot be for de Libera anything other than the product of the Analytic exclusion since it is considered by the Analytics as a melodramatic philosophy in its intellectual rivalries and it is systematically under-qualified by them on the argumentative level. Continental philosophy is criticized by the Analytics for being based on syncretism and association of ideas. This Analytic stand is said to be ahistoric contrary to Continental philosophy's historicism but in fact it is very historical since it promotes the historicism of the Analytic hegemony. The question is not without reminding of the ways that Byzantine philosophy was and still is underestimated by the tenants of western medieval philosophy.

Against this practice of exclusion, de Libera is defending the position of a reasonable or commonsensical relativism. In his work as an historian of (medieval) philosophy, he sees no contradiction between his initial holism and the atomism of truths. Holism and atomism are both instruments in the service of the historian of philosophy. For that reason, he accepts a certain trans-temporality of the philosophical debates throughout history and admits that terms may be co-extant during the historical evolution. The

16. A. de Libera, *L'art des généralités. Théories de l'abstraction*, Paris : Aubier 1999, 610–636.

task is described as the epistemic contextualization of situated philosophical problems. The use that de Libera makes of episteme is quite distinct from Foucault's; in order to establish his method, de Libera appeals to the notion of "Question-Response Complexes," (borrowed from R. G. Collingwood) or "Structures" in a broad sense. The historian of (medieval) philosophy is engaged in an imaginary debate with past philosophers in order to delimit their proper philosophical problems. The use of QRCs is quite independent from the various theories of truth and the only truth-proof caution here is the principle of non-contradiction, the supreme philosophical *dignitas*. A second caution of primordial importance consists in avoiding any kind of historical under-determination where apparently similar philosophical responses may seem to answer irrelevant initial philosophical problems. The heart of the matter is the effort to demarcate successfully the relevant in every historical case QRC even if the problems posited by past philosophers are to be proven in the end fake. The historian of philosophy is certainly at the end of the line a historian.

Thus, de Libera proposes a form of philosophical archeology in a non-foucaultian idiom.[17] The way to carry through this task is to make an appeal to the idea of the trans-historic but not permanent validity of the terms-concepts. The aim of his method is to insert in the philosophical canon new areas of philosophical interest like Arabic-Muslim medieval philosophy (and, also, the Byzantine philosophy).

The problem with de Libera's position is not its relativism but its commonsensism about the notion of time. In brief, he sees history as granted and in that he is quite remote from the Foucaultian idea of history as rupture and indeterminate variation.

3.2. Foucault's challenge to medieval studies

If Byzantinism is a sort of medievism then it constitutes a transposition of Kantian transcendental idealism into medieval studies and a criticism of the theory of truth of *adaequatio*.[18] The historian of medieval philosophy Van Steenberghen saw the overall medieval thinking as an introduction to Thomas Aquinas. After Aquinas a progressive decline follows until the final disaster brought about by modernism. Etienne Gilson also, though he had a profound knowledge of modern philosophy, considered that no important progress had been made in metaphysics post Aquinas; Aquinatian metaphysics was the only complete metaphysics. Thus, the post-structural approach to medieval thinking is necessarily paired with a critique of Thomocentrism. Alain de Libera combined a new valuation of Arab philosophy with a critique of medieval philosophy's Eurocentrism. It becomes more and more evident

17. *Ibid.*, 630.
18. Ph. W. Rosemann, *Understanding Scholastic Thought with Foucault*, New York: St. Martin's Press, The New Middle Ages 1999, 1–20.

that a renewed interest is directed to peripheral philosophies in the place of the dominant scholasticism and concerns more marginal philosophers. Special attention is also given to the material conditions of the production of philosophy; the medieval commentary is thus viewed as a kind of work in progress.

Foucault has placed his "historical" research under the auspices of Nietzsche, viewing positively the negative critique of Nietzsche by Wilamowitz-Moellendorf. Wilamowitz had accused Nietzsche of cultivating a kind of philology of the future (*Zukunfstphilologie*) in the form of philological dilettantism. If the religious is sublime how can someone distinguish it from the ethico-aesthetic?[19] This last idea is seen in a dual manner as separation from the Self and as a *totaliter alter*. It is a thematization of the distinction between sign and resemblance that came about in the 17th century (producing an archeological rupture), which made necessary the philosophy of Hobbes. The Foucaultian approach focuses on particular events and not facts leaving aside the particular intellectual struggles and fractional treaties. Foucault's God is the God of events and not the God of the philosopher who stands in expectation of possible *theophanies*. Forgetfulness is nothing more than a kind of extensive expectation. Discourse is transcending meaning as well as language. Foucault is advancing two kinds of historical relation: genealogy and archeology. Archeology is not in search of principles but of historical *a prioris*. Genealogy, on the other hand, in the capacity of variation, is an alternative to dialectics where any event is referring to a singular usurpation, to a unique accident. The genealogy of religion, concerning the monotheistic religions, refers to the interpretation of texts and God's perspective is related to a philosophy of space not time. The effort to secularize time during the 19th century has been successful but not the corresponding effort about space. Foucault is undertaking a hetero-typology of discursive locations, distinct, due to their realism, from utopias. Amidst them there are spaces, secularized or not, like the Biblical desert. The desert is the location of *theophanies*, the paradigmatic space of the *totaliter alter*, a space apart from ethico-aesthetic nature, the desert of the mind. Would there be any onto-theological relation between the desert and the Kantian sublime? What would be here the proper place of transgression? These are questions that have to do with the strong presence and the attraction exercised on Foucault by negative theology or mysticism even as para-philosophy. Yet, the concept of the self as location and not as subject or essence is quite different from any para-philosophy. Is the self an auto-transcending entity? For Foucault, the detachment from the self is at the same time a re-constitution of the self, a kind of secular sanctity.[20]

19. Th. R. Flyn, "Partially Desacralized Spaces: the Religious Availability of Foucault's Thought," in: *Michel Foucault and Theology. The Politics of Religious Experience*, eds. J. Bernauer and J. Carrette, Aldershot: Ashgate 2004, 143–155.

20. See J. Bernauer, "The Prisons of Man: an Introduction to Foucault's Negative Theology," *International Philosophical Quarterly* 27, 4 (1987) 365–380.

The Foucaultian conception about the crucial importance of *parrhesia* accompanies his idea of philosophy as philosophical behavior. This is something quite different from a university specialization. Foucault sees classical rationalism as profound Christianization and not the contrary. Foucault's *parrhesia* stems from multiple sources and among them Cynical philosophy and asceticism. Foucault opposes the idea of political theology as an exercise in obedience and in that he is Anti-spinozist. He also wishes to detach himself from the Enlightenment's tale about the Dark Ages and the dawn of rationalism. The Hebrew image of God as pastor consists in the practice of obedience that makes demands of particular forms of knowledge and subjectivity since the pastor must be aware not only of the general truths of faith but, also, of the partial truths of every soul. To this imperative correspond some practices of confession and self-control, a technology of the self, aiming at a special kind of subjectivity where the location of truth is the soul. One is confessing the content of his soul and puts it under continuous scrutiny in order to mortify his ancient self. Self-torture, asceticism and renouncement of the self were greatly promoted under the light of obedience during the Christianization of classical West.[21]

Parrhesia is presented by Foucault as an antidote to the confessional style. *Parrhesia* exists also in Christianity, in the frame of asceticism inherited by the Cynical philosophy. This *parrhesia* consists in declaring truth in a different manner from prophecy as well as from the discourse of the *phronimos*. Criticism is preferred over flattery and the moral duty over interest. The Cynic is a parrhesiast, being an autonomous personality; the Cynic is an apostle of truth. Revolt, art and Christianity are forms of *parrhesia*. The difference between pagan and Christian mysticism is also due to the fact that Christians demand for a totally other world. Cynic asceticism meets Platonic metaphysics but in none of them appears the concept of obedience. Obedience to the Other man and the completely Other world are opposed to each other. The ultimate question is that of the construction of a totally different world.

Foucault is not abandoning the concept of obedience by distinguishing two fears, the believer's and the unbeliever's. *Parrhesia* may be the expression of the pure and the noble, related to love and to belief in God but, also, can be the sign of arrogance, shamelessness and impiety; the frame of Foucaultian reflection is in any case anti-humanist. Is it for that reason a part of negative theology? In any case, he was the one who made such a comparison in a text on Maurice Blanchot;[22] Foucault's theology is negative as to the deification of man through intellectualism but not in the form of a negative anthropology as is the case with Sartre. The Nietzschean death of the God implies the death of human subjectivity.

21. See J. Delumeau, *Le catholicisme entre Luther et Voltaire*, Paris : PUF 1971.
22. M. Foucault, *La pensée du dehors*, Paris : Fata Morgana 1986.

Would that mean a re-deification of God? Man's deification was accomplished in the historical and not the supernatural level, demystifying thus the sacred history of man. Negative theology comes neither from the subject nor from science. Human science means that man is limited as well as temporary. Man will thus vanish like a trace on the sand by the sea, erased by the waves. Foucault's philosophy is a historicism without a human subject, the perception of a critical turn of the religious-mystical formation of the self. Foucault demanded for the relativization of any particular anthropology and the negation of individuation.

3.3. Byzantine iconicity and onto-theology

Hegel's aesthetics and his claim about the "end of art" still determine our ideas on the artistic phenomenon and coincide with the modern hegemony of Aesthetics (with a capital A to signify the "orthodoxy" of the modern aesthetics after Winckelmann).[23] Until recently, aesthetic thinking was operating through a series of conceptual pairs, considered eternally valid, like space and time, matter and form, design and color. Aesthetics introduced the difference between image and substance, where the first testifies, somehow, for the second, a characteristic not only of Hegel but also of a line of thinkers like Vasari and Winckelmann, but also Kant, Cassirer or Panofsky. One tries to construct a kind of archeology of the aesthetic concepts, focusing primarily on the visual arts and thus turns to Plato and Aristotle to discover if it is in them that the idealistic idea of the image has its roots. The *Republic* seems to be the text par excellence where the idea is construed on the grounds of the difference between images and substance. However, the question of the division between the original and the derivative in Plato is not sufficient for defending the above difference and does not allow us to consider Plato as an iconoclast since in him the imitation does not concern the picture in general, but the masking of the ontological. There is a positive mimesis in Plato and iconic negativity concerns rather the narration. In addition, Plato's images require some extra artificiality in order to appear as they truly are. His criticism concerns rather the trompe-l'oeil paintings that tend to usurp the place of their models; only in this case the image becomes an idol and pairs with the doctrine of *ut pictura poesis*.

Aristotle, for his part, underscores that men take pleasure from images exactly as they are having fun by learning easily. Therefore, one confronts the notion that artistic imitation has a real epistemological value. A beautiful image is like a beautiful metaphor, it posits the thing represented in the sight of the beholder. The Aristotelian *mimesis praxeôs* may be a kind of representation of the action, something that would mean identifying the praxis with *poiesis* like in Plutarch, since it is in Plutarch that one can witness the theory

23. See P. Rodrigo, *L'étoffe de l'art*, Paris : Desclée de Brouwer 2001. This part of the paper is inspired by Rodrigo's analysis.

of *ut pictura poesis.*[24] Aristotle has a rather different conception of mimesis, a presentation of nature and action, some sort of world making. Nothing in the Aristotelian theory of the image reminds us of the knowledge by kinds (*eidètikè*).[25] Regarding his interpretation of *leukographein*,[26] this technique does not signify the primacy of drawing over color, as was thought rather hastily by classical aesthetics (Winckelmann); there is nothing in Aristotle that would make us believe that he speaks particularly of drawing. By emphasizing the artistic importance of mono-colored painting, Aristotle emphasizes rather the importance of the materiality and not the ideality of the artwork.

Thereafter comes the idea of objectivity in art. The question of objectivity itself is raised because of the differences introduced by the classic aesthetics that produced, as already mentioned, a series of bifurcations such as form and content, ideality and materiality, subjectivity and objectivity. One must rather consider the materiality that informs the logic of the artwork and transcends every eidetic classification. The image is neither the ghost of a thing nor an idol. On the level of concrete expression, the color cannot be a simple supplement to the drawing or the ornament of the logical structure that is the drawing, as Kant thought by considering the color in paintings as a *parergon*. The slicing of the total aesthetic experience into formless sensations and a priori forms makes Aesthetics a metaphysics of representation. Goethe and Lessing were able, at least partially, to overcome the aesthetic essentialism as well as the idealizing speculative Aesthetics. Lessing, in particular, was in a position to defend, contrary to Winckelmann, the autonomy of artwork. Hegel has distorted the meaning of the Lessingian critique by presenting it as a traditional aesthetic residue in order to preserve Winckelmannian idealism. Hegel therefore falls within the logic of the representation as shown above and thus the image in him conforms to the idea of objectivism in Art; Hegel was committed to this notion of representation by following the Neoplatonists (of the Renaissance) and in ignorance of the true positions of Plato and Aristotle. Art, neither as imitation nor as transposition of an art form to another (*ut pictura poesis*), but in its concrete materiality, constitutes a critique of objectivity.

What is particularly challenged here is the transformation of aesthetics into Aesthetics or the formation of an aesthetic orthodoxy with its conceptual arsenal that was established in and by German idealism. What characterizes the philosophical content of this orthodoxy is the idea that artistic quality becomes a discursive genre. Hence, aesthetic orthodoxy is a philosophy based on a logical fallacy that claims that the works of art are the subjects of a special significance, that of Aesthetics. However, the analysis of meaning in art is no different from the analysis of other areas of significance, and only

24. Plutarch, *De Glor. Athen.*, 345C–F.
25. Aristotle, *De Anima*, III, 3 and 7–8.
26. Aristotle, *Poetics*, VI, 1450 a38–b4.

an analysis of aesthetic quality (i.e. the style) must be of importance here. In a famous note in the *Critique of Pure Reason*, Kant advised, already against Aesthetics: "The Germans are the only people who at present use this word to indicate what others call the critique of taste. At the foundation of this term lies the disappointed hope, which the eminent analyst, Baumgarten, conceived, of subjecting the criticism of the beautiful to principles of reason, and so of elevating its rules into a science. But his endeavors were vain. For the said rules or criteria are, in respect to their chief sources, merely empirical, consequently never can serve as determinate laws a priori, by which our judgment in matters of taste is to be directed. It is rather our judgment, which forms the proper test as to the correctness of the principles. On this account it is advisable to give up the use of the term as designating the critique of taste, and to apply it solely to that doctrine, which is true science – the science of the laws of sensibility – and thus come nearer to the language and the sense of the ancients in their well-known division of the objects of cognition into *aistheta kai noeta*, or to share it with speculative philosophy, and employ it partly in a transcendental, partly in a psychological signification."[27] It is true, however, that in his third critique, Kant has revised its initial rejection with particular emphasis on the question of communication in art and hence on the question of aesthetic categorization. His analysis is made for three specific purposes: (1) to refute the errors of the logic of esthete idealism, (2) to preserve the autonomy of the work of art in its concrete existence, and (3) to disclose oneself on the conceptual equivalents of the mysterious and original emotion of art.

One should examine Byzantine iconicity, first in its relation with onto-theology. Charles Barber, writing about Byzantine icons assumes the aesthetic dynamism of the metaphysical bipolarities.[28] The icon plays the role of a force simultaneously visioning and invisible. The visual economy is structured around the activities of "making visible" in an essentially post-representational frame. The conditions of iconicity are those of a donation to a finite consciousness, and the visual model implies thus an intentionality that is opposed to mimesis. The gaze appears offensive, involving the impotence of the facing spectator. The division between the sensible and the intelligible images undertaken by the criticism of onto-theology, according to Barber, must give rise to an operation of *perichoresis*.[29] The exchange between visible and invisible, operated in contrast to the division between sensible and intelligible, would preferably be on the basis of the opposition between the created and the uncreated. The critique of onto-theology owes much to the contribution of Levinas to an idea of moral obligation that is immutable and irreducible, stemming from the human face. The face is not

27. I. Kant, *Critique of Pure Reason*, translated by J. M. D. Meiklejohn, London 1855, 44, note.
28. Ch. Barber, *Figure and Likeness. On the Limits of the Representation in Byzantine Iconoclasm*, Princeton-Oxford: Princeton University Press 2002.
29. Ch. Barber, "Defacement," *The Yearbook of Comparative Literature* 56 (2012) 104–115.

a representative unit but illustrates the otherness and the morally decisive encounter with it. To be within the limits of a face-to-face is the evidence for what is essentially concealed and produces nothing but an infinite hermeneutics, which equals the infinity manifested in the human face. For Barber, Jean-Luc Marion suppresses the iconic economy that has been established by the Byzantine iconophiles and thus Marion assumes the position of an iconoclast.[30] Barber marks a return to the anxieties of Byzantine thinking about the representation of Jesus and consequently refers to the Letter of Eusebius of Caesarea to the sister of Constantine the Great, Constantia. Eusebius is worrying about the consequences of the iconic representation of Christ and, especially, in regard to the dual, human and divine, nature, which does not fail to produce a dilemma: does not the representation of Christ on the painted surface mean a clear reduction to humanity alone? And, similarly, doesn't this announce a step away from everything that makes the sublimity of the idea of God? Would it not, then, be something akin to the pagan idolatry? The Patriarch Nikephoros (9th century) will respond to these anxieties by borrowing much from the Aristotelian philosophy of representation. To refute the possibility of an image of Christ is docetism or the inability to clearly define what is visible and what is invisible about the two natures. The physical appearance in this case is not imaginary but a dynamic actuality of representation. The painted face of Christ, departing from metaphysical bipolarity, points to the duality of the icon itself. The presence of the face is the presentation of its formal features, an unexpected impact of naturalized Aristotelianism. Nikephoros speaks of the form as vision and purity, a donation made not to humans (the phenomenological donation) but to God. The painted humanity of Christ is, thus, generic and individualized. If, for Levinas, the view of each face is primarily a moral event, the iconic face of a saint, according to Barber, is a form of metaphysical wisdom. The Other man through otherness plays in the register of the accessible and inaccessible. Thus, the call of the face proves to be doubly problematic, as differentiating solipsism and solipsistic difference. The Levinasian reference to face claims a trans-subjective love but connotes also a language of submission. That is because the other of the given face is ever more distant and lost in the difference between axiology and facticity. The icon in this manner becomes a device that is clearly abandoning the invisible Christ and ultimately, according to Marion, produces only trivialities. Thus for Marion, the very possibility of pictorial reality disappears and, therefore, any occasion for a real face-to-face. The iconophile, then, on the contrary, worships what is visually present.

30. Ibid.

3.4. Some characteristics of iconicity in Byzantine intellectualism

To outline some trends of iconological intellectualism in Byzantium, it would be reasonable to first form a classification of typical writers of this current. Among these, the names of Michael Psellos and Michael of Ephesus seem suitable for a first approach.[31] It is obvious that a comprehensive treatment of the issue is nothing other than a *desideratum* of the research. The establishment of a research direction in the relevant study is necessary because the data are so far rather confused. Michael Psellos and Michael of Ephesus, despite the fact that they are almost contemporary, are very different philosophical personalities. Manuel Chrysoloras, in later times, i.e. during the Renaissance, will summarize and transpose the Byzantine iconological spirit. All three define the scope of what may be called "Byzantine iconological intellectualism."

Psellos, in his treatise on the ideas of Plato, has, for the most part, effectuated a "montage" or "collage" of fragments from Plotinus's *Ennead* V, 9 but in the text that comes from his own hand he says that he will approach the world of non-platonic ideas not in the traditional method of vision, but by thoroughly guessing. One could call it a method of divination in reference to the theurgic practices of the Neoplatonists. The divination method is also a direct reference to Plato's dialogue *Phaedrus*, which marks a reform of the rigidness of the *Republic* in poetic matters as well as on the level of an enlarged rationality. The objective in the *Phaedrus* is to transform the exile of the poetic non-rational element by acknowledging its divine "*mania*," a term which, in Greek etymology, according to Plato, is close to the word "*manteia*" (= divination). The Psellian term *katamanteuomenos* has perhaps the meaning of an inward movement, a penetration to the action of divination itself so that the term acquires a reflective and intuitive character. It would be natural, therefore, to consider that the Psellian perspective on ideas is distinctively subjectivist, close perhaps to what is called today a "philosophy of the mind." The icon, therefore, for Psellos, in its pure form, namely the "*theôria*" (from the Greek verb *oran* = to see) of ideas, involves a mental image, a very distinct approach from Plato where the paradigm of vision is used to designate a separate world. Psellos appears thus as a mental psychologist according to a first approach to his iconology.

Michael of Ephesus, in his commentary on Aristotle's *Parts of animals* uses the image of childbirth as a paradigm of the biological relation of humans to the animal world. If Psellos is the iconographer of inland landscapes, Michael of Ephesus's philosophy becomes manifest through his naturalistic example. The epistemic use of the image of birth is based on the Aristotelian theory of vision as the purest of all sensations. Vision, thus integrated into the optics of the position "according to nature," binds us to the natural world

31. For the subsequent analysis, see G. Arabatzis, *Βυζαντινή Φιλοσοφία και Εικονολογία* [= *Byzantine Philosophy and Iconology*], Athens: Kardamitsas 2012, 155–174.

but at the same time, as episteme, takes us away from it and places man in the position of the observer. The iconological consequences of this approach point to a mimetic iconography of reality, a faithful reproduction, within the limits of the scientific ideas of the time. In addition, mimesis in Michael of Ephesus is directly related to the possibility of emotional arousal because the image of the internal organs of the human body gives rise to an instant movement of repulsion. Mimesis, therefore, is directly related to the production of emotions. At the same time, Michael of Ephesus demands for an attitude of emotional detachment in order to control, scientifically and in each case, the emotions of the observer. The fact that both the commentary of Michael of Ephesus and the original by Aristotle are not addressed to the scientist but the man of general culture means that the emotional distancing concerns the man of the generic culture that acquires thus a better perspective for an understanding of the state of things. Mimesis, episteme and emotivism are the main axes of iconology in Michel of Ephesus. The difference here with Psellos is evident.

Manuel Chrysoloras worked for several years in the West, especially in Italy, with no solely cultural objectives but also for the good of his Byzantine homeland. The western milieu of the first Renaissance, into which the Byzantine scholar was literally propelled, was already secularized on the iconological level. The world-vision of Chrysoloras was patriotically oriented, aiming at a reconciliation of Rome with Constantinople, if not on the spiritual level, at least on the question of the filiation between the two states. The Christian empire could combine the two traditions of Byzantium and the West, in fact already intertwined throughout history. Therefore, on the iconological level, Chrysoloras tried to combine the rhetorical tradition of the Byzantine iconic discourse (manifested, for example, in the genre of *ekphraseis*) and the original Aristotelian moralism with the theory of the creative artist, already progressing in the West, which is alien to the artistic anonymity prevalent in the empire of the East. As the rhetoric *ekphrasis* in Byzantium called for a writer, also visual art, according to Chrysoloras, asked for a creator. The literary paradigm allows precisely for the introduction of the theory of the creator in iconography. The theory did not meet only theoretical purposes but also political ones, as stated above, amidst the effort of reaching a successful reconciliation between East and West. For this reason, and also because of the gradual depreciation of Byzantine intellectuals in Italy, Chrysoloras's theory has not attracted the attention of scholars until very recently. From the point of view of general iconology, the position of Chrysoloras shows the progressively extensive dimensions that the Byzantine iconology can assume.

The three ideal types of iconology mentioned here (Michael Psellos, Michael of Ephesus, Manuel Chrysoloras) point to the limits of intellectualism in Byzantine iconology. The difference between Byzantine iconography and iconology should be emphasized: the first is philosophical while the second is para-philosophical. This view, however, can only be a temporary one. The distinction is part of the idea of an expanded rationality, of the dialectic between philosophy and non-philosophy and between philosophy and institutionalized parallel traditions, which call now for more philosophical attention.

3.5. Concluding remarks

The position of images in the grid "speech, communication, power" in Byzantine iconicity appears as a question of great historical weight. Byzantine iconicity, then as now, addresses the many and manifests also its Byzantinism, i.e. the separation of an aesthetic elite from the rest of population, a cleavage that works deeply and divisively, turning the ideal of aesthetics against the many. In the new technology-governmental model, the old function of pictures does not seem to be maintained, while the general idea of "raw life" is promoted. This provides, however, a new context for a new occasion to understand Byzantine iconicity for cultural purposes.

Index nominum

A

B

C

D

E

F

G

H

I

J

K

L

M

N

O

P

Q

R

S

T

U

V

W

X

Y

Z

Georgi Kapriev, DSc, is a graduate of the Sofia University "St. Climent Ohridski" University in philosophy. He has specialized in Cologne and Paris. He is a member (2002–2012 president of the Commission "Byzantine Philosophy") of the International Society for Study of the Mediaeval Philosophy (S.I.E.P.M.), of the Society for Study of the Philosophy of the Middle Ages and Renaissance in Germany (GPMR) and a co-founder of the European Graduate School for Ancient and Mediaeval Philosophy (EGSAMP).

He was a visiting professor at the University of Cologne in 2005/6 and 2013 and a visiting lecturer at the universities of Amsterdam, Bari, Berlin, Bonn, Bochum, Cologne, Hannover, Karlsruhe, Lausanne, Lecce, Münster, Würzburg, Zürich etc.

He is the author of 19 books and editor of 21 editions. Editor-in-chief of www.philosophia.bg . Co-editor of: *Archive for Mediaeval Philosophy and Culture*, *Bibliotheca Christiana*, *Christianity and Culture*, etc. He translates from Latin, Ancient Greek, German and Russian.

Dušan Krcunović is Docent for the Philosophical Anthropology and Modern Directions in Ontology at the Faculty of Philosophy in Nikšić (University of Montenegro). In 2010 he supported his doctoral dissertation *The Problem of Creation in Plato's "Timaeus" and St. Basil's "Hexaemeron"* (in print) at the Deparment of Philosophy, at the Faculty of Philosophy in Nikšić.

Dušan Krcunović is an autor of of several articles on ancient philosophy, cosmology and philosophical anthropology, published in Serbian. He is Editor-in-chief *of Luča. Journal for Philosophy and Theory of Culture and Society*. Currently he prepares a book entitled: *Epimetheus: A Secret Hero of Philosophical Anthropology*.

Torstein Theodor Tollefsen is professor in philosophy at the Department of Philosophy, History of Art and Ideas and Classical Languages at the University of Oslo. His main interest is in late antique and early Byzantine Christian Philosophy, especially cosmology, metaphysics, and the doctrine of icons. He has published articles on the Cappadocians (especially on St. Gregory of Nyssa), Dionysius the Areopagite, and St. Maximus the Confessor, and two books in the Oxford Early Christian Studies series: *The Christocentric Cosmology of St. Maximus the Confessor*, Oxford 2008, *Activity and Participation in Late Antique and Early Christian Thought*, Oxford 2012. His most recent publication is the article "Christocentric Cosmology" in the *Oxford Handbook on Maximus the Confessor*, ed. P. Allen and B. Neil, Oxford 2015. He has recently completed a draft for a new book on St. Theodore the Studite: *St. Theodore the Studite and the Philosophy of Images.*

ILARIA RAMELLI is Full Professor of Theology and K. Britt endowed Chair at the Graduate School of Theology, SHMS (Angelicum University), the director of international research projects, Senior Visiting Professor of Greek Thought (Harvard and Boston University), Senior Research Fellow in Religion (Erfurt University), and Visiting Research Fellow (Oxford University). She earned two MAs, a PhD, a postdoctorate, and two Habilitations to Full Professor and has been Young Researcher in Late Antiquity, Professor of Roman Near Eastern History, and Fellow in Ancient Philosophy (Catholic University Milan, 2003–present), as well as Senior Visiting Professor of Church History and Senior Research Fellow in Ancient and Patristic Philosophy (Durham University). She has been elected Fellow of the Royal Historical Society. She is a member of many directive and scientific boards of scholarly series and journals and of numerous international scholarly associations, and regularly serves as a peer reviewer for prestigious scientific series and journals, and as a scientific consultant in tenure/hiring evaluations for outstanding Universities, as well as in advanced research funding for international scholarly Foundations. She has taught courses and seminars, delivered invited lectures, and held senior research fellowships and senior visiting professorships in numerous (including topmost) Universities in Europe, North America, and Israel, and has never interrupted an intense scholarly activity for over two decades. She has received many academic prizes and has authored numerous books, articles, and reviews in leading scholarly journals and series, on ancient philosophy, especially Platonism and Stoicism, patristic theology and philosophy, early Christianity, and the relationship between Christianity and classical culture.

DMITRY BIRIUKOV got his MS in physics, BA in Religious studies, and C.sc. in philosophy in St Petersburg, Russia. Now he is pursuing his PhD at the University of Padova, Department FISPPA (Philosophy), Italy. He is a research supervisor of a Scientific and Educational Centre of Problems of Religion, Philosophy and Culture at the State University of Aerospace Instrumentation and an academic secretary and researcher at the Institute for History of Christian Thought at the Russian Christian Academy for the Humanities in St Petersburg. He is an executive editor and editorial board member of the "Byzantine Philosophy" series, guided by the St Petersburg State University Press and the Russian Christian Academy for the Humanities Press (15 volumes have been issued). Also he is a board member of a number of Russian theological and philosophical journals. His area of studies is Byzantine philosophy, especially the problem of universals in this philosophy, Byzantine Platonism, the Palamite and Arian debates.

JOHANNES ZACHHUBER is Professor of Historical and Systematic Theology at the University of Oxford and a Fellow of Trinity College, Oxford. He holds a DPhil from the University of Oxford (1997) and a Dr. theol. habil. from Humboldt University, Berlin (2011). His research interests lie in late ancient theology and philosophy as well as modern theology. Major publications include *Human Nature in Gregory of Nyssa* (2000), *Theology as Science in Nineteenth-Century Germany* (2013), and *Individuality in Late Antiquity* (ed. with A. Torrance, 2014).

José María Nieva is an Associate Professor of Ancient Philosophy at the Department of Philosophy of the University of Tucumán (Argentina). He is the autor of *Ver en el no-ver: Ensayo crítico sobre el De Mystica Theologia de Dionisio Areopagita* (Tucumán, EUNT 2010), and of several articles concerning Dionysius the Areopagite and other Platonic and Neoplatonic thinkers.

Filip Ivanović was born in Podgorica (Montenegro) in 1986. He earned his PhD from the Department of Philosophy and Religious Studies of the Norwegian University of Science and Technology in Trondheim, with a thesis entitled *Love, Beauty, Deification: The Erotic-Aesthetic Soteriology of Dionysius the Areopagite and Maximus the Confessor*. As for previous education, he holds BA and MA degrees from the Department of Philosophy of the University of Bologna. Among his publications are the edited volume *Dionysius the Areopagite between Orthodoxy and Heresy* (2011) and the monograph *Symbol and Icon: Dionysius the Areopagite and the Iconoclastic Crisis* (2010), as well as several other journal articles and book chapters. As organizer or speaker he participated at over twenty international conferences and symposia in Argentina, UK, Greece, Spain, Israel, etc. In 2010 he was a guest fellow at the Centre for the Study of Antiquity and Christianity of the University of Aarhus, and in 2013 he spent a semester in Athens as a fellow of the Onassis Foundation, with affiliation to the Norwegian Institute and the National Hellenic Research Foundation. He is a member of a number of professional and academic associations, including *Société Internationale pour l'Étude de la Philosophie Médiévale*, *International Society for Neoplatonic Studies*, and *Association Internationale d'Études Patristiques*. His areas of interest include Greek and Byzantine philosophy, patristics, and Christian studies.

Basil Lourié, b. 1962, PhD (2002), and Dr habil. (2008) in Philosophy (St. Petersburg State University), the Editor-in-Chief of *Scrinium: A Journal of Patrology, Critical Hagiography, and Church History*, Senior Research Fellow of the St. Petersburg State University of Aerospace Instrumentation.

Vladimir Cvetković, PhD, is an independent researcher based in Göttingen, Germany, Germany. He is also a non-residential research fellow of the Institute of Philosophy and Social Theory of the University of Belgrade, Serbia. Previously he conducted research and taught at the universities of Aarhus (Denmark), St Andrews (UK), Oslo (Norway), Belgrade and Nis (Serbia). His research interests include Patristics and Byzantine tradition, especially Gregory of Nyssa and Maximus the Confessor, as well as Modern Orthodox theology. He is the author of a monograph on Gregory of Nyssa and time, and of more than fifty scholarly articles on various topics published in English, Serbian, French, Romanian, Bulgarian and Greek.

Gorazd Kocijančič (1964) is Slovenian philosopher, poet and translator. He is author of four books of poetry: *Your Names* (Društvo SKAM, 2000), *Thirty Steps and We're Gone* (LUD Literatura, 2005), *Certamen spirituale* (Študentska založba, 2008) and *Primož Trubar Is Leaving Ljubljana* (Študentska založba, 2012). His book of essays *Tistim zunaj: Eksoterični zapisi 1990–2003* (*To Those Outside: Exoterical Writings 1990–2003*) won the Rožanc National Award. Kocjančič's translation of the collected works of Plato garnered him the Sovre Award, while his poetry book *Primož Trubar zapušča Ljubljano* received the Prešeren Foundation Award (2013). Kocijančič was one of the collaborators in the publication of the Standard Slovenian translation of the Bible, as well as an editor for the translation of the bilingual Diels-Kranz collection *Fragmenti predsokratikov* (*Fragments of the Pre-Socratics, 2012*). He translated in Slovene and annotated numerous patristic works (*Thoughts of the Greek Fathers on Prayer*, 1993; *The Wisdom of the Desert*, 1994; *Apostolic Fathers*, 1996; *Gregory of Nyssa: Life of Macrina, Dialogue On the Soul and Resurrection*, 1996; *Logos in Defence of the Truth: Selected Writings by the Early Christian Apologists*, 1998; *Maximus the Confessor: Selected Works*, 2000). His last work is translation of the complete works of Dionysius the Areopagite (2009) and of Boethius' *Consolation of Philosophy* (2012). His writings have been translated into English, German, Czech, Serbian, Polish, Italian and Russian. Currently he is working on his own philosophical system: the first, ontological part, was published in 2009 under title *Razbitje. Sedem radikalnih esejev* (*Being torn apart. Seven radical essays*), second part in 2011 (*Erotics, politics, etc. Three essays on the soul*).

Uroš T. Todorović, PhD, is a theorist of Byzantine and Modern art, iconographer and artist, and his area of research includes Byzantine art, Modern art, Theology and Philosophy. He was born in Jagodina, Serbia, and grew up in Belgrade where he began his studies in sculpture. He migrated to Australia at the age of twenty and completed his studies there, expanding his interests significantly and acquiring a number of university qualifications. His doctoral research brought him to Greece in early 2007. In 2012 he successfully defended his doctoral thesis entitled *The Diachronic Character of Late Byzantine Painting: The Hermeneutics of Vision from Mistra to New York*. In his thesis he examined the influence of Late Byzantine painting on the work of three major 20th century abstract painters: Vasily Kandinsky, Kazimir Malevich and Mark Rothko. His research was supported by scholarships from the University of Sydney (2006), Kostas and Eleni Ourani Foundation (2007) and Alexander S. Onassis Foundation (2008). His postdoctoral research was supported by National and Kapodistrian University of Athens and Alexander S. Onassis Foundation (2013). His undergraduate studies in theology were supported by the Holy Synod of the Church of Greece (2008–2012). At Athens University he began his second doctoral research concerning the theology of the Pre-iconoclastic period and its relationship to certain aspects of Byzantine art. He is fluent in English, Greek and Serbian and he can also speak Russian and Persian. His professional experience covers the fields of iconography, painting, sculpture, conservation of cultural heritage, translation and teaching. His artworks have been exhibited at a number of significant exhibitions in Australia and Greece. In 2009 The City of Athens Cultural Centre hosted his most recent solo exhibition of drawing and painting, entitled Mystagogy. There are two publications about his painting: *Mystagogy* (in English and Greek - 2009) and *Byzantine Memories* (in Greek - 2009). Most recently, he has written extensive texts on Byzantine art for the *Great Orthodox Christian Encyclopedia (Μεγάλη Ορθόδοξη Χριστιανική Εγκυκλοπαιδεία)*, published under the auspices of the Ecumenical Patriarch of Constantinople Bartholomew and the the Archbishop of Athens and all Greece, Hieronymus. His biography and iconographical artworks are included in the same Encyclopedia.

Slobodan Žunjić (1946), Associate Professor of ancient Philosophy at the University of Belgrade (1990–1997) and Adjunct Professor of Philosophy at the University of Rhode Island (1999–2007) is mostly engaged in research of ancient, Byzantine and modern philosophy. He specialized in ancient philosophy at the University in Tubingen, where, as a fellow of the Humboldt Foundation, he studied the unwritten doctrines of Plato, under the supervision of Hans Kraemer. He obtained his PhD degree at the University of Belgrade in 1985, with a thesis entitled *The Concept of One in Aristotle's Metaphysics*. He is the author of more than twenty books on ancient, Byzantine and modern philosophy, such as: *The History of Serbian Philosophy*, Belgrade 2014 (in Serbian), *Philosophy and its Language*, Belgrade 2013 (in Serbian), *Logic and Theology: The Dialectic of John of Damascus in Byzantine and Serbian Philosophy*, Belgrade 2012 (in Serbian), *Services to Mnemosyne: Critical Appraisals of Contemporary Philosophy*, Belgrade 2007 (in Serbian), *Die serbische Philosophie heute*, hrsg. M. Djuric und S. Zunjic, München 1993, *Martin Heidegger and National Socialism*, Novi Sad 1992 (in Serbian), *Aristotle and Henology*, Belgrade 1988 (in Serbian), etc.

Scott Ables, BA, MDiv, MSt, is currently a third year DPhil student at the University of Oxford. The title of his thesis is: *The Purpose of Perichoresis in the Oikonomia and Theologia of John of Damascus*. His current research seeks to situate John of Damascus in his eighth century Syro-Palestinian historical context. He has published several articles on John of Damascus.

Ivan Christov is an Associate Professor at the Faculty of Theology, Department of Historical and Systematical Theology, and also a Director of the *Center for Advanced Studies of Patristic and Byzantine Spiritual Heritage* at Sofia University. His research interests are in the field of Ancient philosophy and its transformation in Medieval philosophy and Christian theology.

Ivan Christov obtained MA in St. Petersburg University in 1986 (thesis on the *Hexaemeron* by John the Exarch) and developed PhD on the tradition of the Greek *Hexaemeron* in the same university in 1991. His academic specialization includes visits to Pontificio Istituto Orientale (Rome), University of Oxford (All Souls College), and Ostkirchliches Institut (Regensburg).

The main academic activities of Ivan Christov are related to the publication of philosophical and theological classics. Within the context of a national effort to join the common European traditions and values he initiated an academic bilingual edition of Aristotle in six volumes (of which two volumes have already come out). Among his other publications are *On the Soul and the Resurrection* of St. Gregory of Nyssa (bilingual), the *Five Theological Orations* by St. Gregory of Nazianzus, *On the Celestial Hierarchy, On the Ecclesiastical Hierarchy* and the *Letters* by St. Dionysius the Areopagite, *Fragments of the Palamitic Debates* by an uncertain author. He also took part in the edition of the *Corpus Areopagiticum* in the Old Slavonic translation by Isaias of Seres (*Monumenta linguae Slavicae dialecti veteris*, t. LV 4.1-3, t. LV 5, 2012-2013). Related to his editorial work are his publications on the formation of Old Slavonic philosophical language and development of lexical and terminological databases: a Greek-Latin-Old Slavonic database of the medieval translations of Aristotle (172 philosophical terms), a database of Isaija of Serres' translation of the *Corpus areopagiticum* (41543 records), a Greek-Old Bulgarian database of general lexics (17711 records) and a Greek-Church Slavonic database (30746 records).

Ivan Christov is a member of the international boards of three academic journals and four international societies in philosophy and Christian theology.

Smilen Markov (Varna, 1980) made his PhD at the University of Cologne with a book *Die metaphysische Synthese des Johannes von Damaskus. Historische Zusammenhänge und Strukturtransformationen* (Brill, 2015). At present he is assistant professor in Christian philosophy and Byzantine theology at the Faculty of Theology of the University of Veliko Turnovo. Dr. Markov has also given seminars on Byzantine personalism, urban studies and systematic theology. At the Universities of Cologne and Lausanne he did research on the Aristotelian reception in the early Byzantine period. Smilen Markov is the author of more than 20 articles in the field of Medieval and Byzantine philosophy in Bulgarian, English, German, Russian and Italian. He is a member of the S.I.E.P.M., in which he coordinates the section "The Aristotelian corpus in Byzantium between the 9th and the 15th centuries – readings and traditions". Dr. Markov is an editor in *Philosophia: An Electronic Journal for Philosophy and Culture.*

Nicholas Loudovikos is a Greek theologian, priest, psychologist, author and professor. He was born in Volos, Greece in 1959. He studied Psychology and Education at the University of Athens, Theology at the University of Thessaloniki, Philosophy at the University of Sorbonne in Paris, Philosophy and Roman Catholic Theology at the Catholic Institute of Paris, Philosophy and

Protestant Theology at the University of Cambridge (England). He received a PhD in 1989 from the Faculty of Theology of Aristotle University of Thessaloniki. The title of his dissertation was: *The Eucharistic Ontology in the Theological Thought of St. Maximus the Confessor.*

He has worked as a researcher at the Tyndale House (Cambridge) and has taught and lectured at the Centre for Advanced Religious and Theological Studies (CARTS) of the Department of Theology at the University of Cambridge, at Durham University, as well as at other Universities and Research Centres. Today he is a Professor of Dogmatics and Philosophy at the University Ecclesiastical Academy of Thessaloniki, a Visiting Professor at the Institute for Orthodox Christian Studies at the University of Cambridge, and an Honorary Research Fellow at the University of Winchester, UK. Fr.

Nikolaos Loudovikos is member and co-secretary (Orthodox) of the Saint Irenaeus Joint Orthodox-Catholic Working Group.

Fr. Loudovikos has published the following books: *A Eucharistic Ontology: Maximus the Confessor's Eschatological Ontology of Being as Dialogical Reciprocity*, Brookline, Mass.: Holy Cross Orthodox Press 2010, *Theopoiia. The Postmodern Theological Quest*, Athens: Armos 2007, *Psychoanalysis and Orthodox Theology. On Desire, Catholicity and Eschatology*, Athens: Armos, 2006, *Orthodoxy and Modernization. Byzantine Individualization, State and History in the Perspective of the European Future*, Athens: Armos 2006, *Theological History of the Ancient Hellenic Philosophy. Presoccratics, Socrates, Plato*, Athens: Pournaras Publishing 2003, *The Apophatic Ecclesiology of the Homoousios. The Ancient Church Today*, Athens: Armos 2002, *Closed Spirituality and the Meaning of Self*, Athens: Ellinika Grammata 1999, etc.

Dmitry Igorevich Makarov (1977) is Dr. of sciences in philosophy (2006), a winner of a special award of the Russian Academy of Sciences in Moscow for a historical monograph written by a young historian (2003), a winner of a prize of St Seraphim of Sarov Foundation for educational activities (2006). He is the head of the Department of general humanities at the Urals State Conservatoire named after M. P. Mussorgsky (since 2014) and a professor of the Department of Biblical Theology of the Yekaterinburg Orthodox Seminary, Russia. After defending his doctoral thesis on Theophanes of Nicaea (2006) he additionally trained at the Leuven Catholic University (2007), read lectures at the Charles University (Prague, 2013) and at the St Petersburg Ecclesiastical Academy (2012). He took part in a number of international scientific conferences, including the 20th (Paris, 2001) and the 21st (London, 2006) International Congresses of Byzantine Studies, the International Conference "The Image of the Perfect Christian in Patristic Thought" (Lviv, Ukraine, 2009), etc. He is expected to take part in the second meeting of the Society of Orthodox Philosophers in Europe (near Fulda, Germany, June 2015). He has authored two books (in Russian): *Anthropology and Cosmology of St. Gregory Palamas as Reflected in his Homilies* (St Petersburg: The Oleg Abyshko

Publishing House, 2003); *Theophanes of Nicaea's Mariology within the Context of the Byzantine Theological Tradition, Seventh to Fourteenth Centuries* (St Petersburg: The Oleg Abyshko Publishing House, 2015), and a number of articles in *Byzantion, Byzantinoslavica, Studia Patristica, Scrinium, Phronema, Parrhesia, Vizantijskij Vremennik* (Byzantina Chronika, Moscow) etc. in Russian, English and Czech which were out in different countries (Russia, U.S.A., Belgium, Australia, Czech Republic, Bulgaria, Ukraine etc.). His page at Academia.edu is: https://uralconsv.academia.edu/DmitryMakarov.

IOANNIS POLEMIS was born in 1966. After graduating from the Athens University, where he studied Classics, he pursued his studies at Oxford, where he wrote his thesis on Theophanes of Nicaea, a Byzantine bishop of the late XIV century, under the supervision of C. Mango. He received his D.Phil. in 1991. He began his teaching at the University of Thrace (1995–1998) as an assistant professor of Byzantine Literature. In 1998 he was appointed assistant professor of Medieval Greek Literature at the University of Thessalonike. He is currently professor of Byzantine Literature at the Athens University. Except for his book on Theophanes of Nicaea (*Theophanes of Nicaea: His Life and Works*, Wiener Byzantinistische Studien XX, Wien 1996), Polemis has published several works of Theodore Metochites, a scholar of the early XIV century. His other books include a monograph on Theodore Dexios (*Theodori Dexii, Opera omnia*, Corpus Christianorum. Series Graeca 55, Turnhout-Leuven 2003), and an edition of several texts dealing with the Palamite controversy (*Theologica Varia Inedita saeculi XIV*, Corpus Christianorum Series Graeca 76, Turnhout 2012). In 2014 his edition of the funeral orations of Michael Psellos (*Michael Pselli, Orationes funebres, vol. I*, Bibliotheca scriptorum Graecorum et Romanorum Teubnerianna, Berlin/Boston 2014) came out.

CONSTANTINOS ATHANASOPOULOS, PhD, FHEA, is an Associate Lecturer and a Research Associate at the Open University and a Tutor in Philosophy at the University of Glasgow. He has published many related papers in Greece, Germany, UK, Russia, Poland, Romania and Portugal and two books on Byzantine Philosophy and Byzantine Civilisation in Greece (one is with the Hellenic Open University); he is a co-editor in *Divine Essence and Divine Energies: Ecumenical Reflections on the Presence of God in Eastern Orthodoxy*, edited by C. Athanasopoulos and C. Schneider, James Clarke & Co, 2013. He is currently editing a collection of papers read at the International Conference on the Philosophy and Theology of St Gregory Palamas, which took place in March 2012 in Greece (Thessaloniki, Veroia and Holy Mt Athos).

MIKONJA KNEŽEVIĆ (1978), Docent for the Byzantine Philosophy at the Faculty of Philosophy in Kosovska Mitrovica, graduated at the Faculty of Philosophy in Nikšić, University of Montenegro, in 2001. In 2008 he supported his doctoral dissertation on Gregory Palamas at the Deparment of Philosophy, Pedagogy and Psychology (Section: Philosophy) at the Faculty of Philosophy of National and Cappodistrian University in Athens. He is an autor of the book *Njegoš and Hesychasm*, Belgrade: Institute for Theological Research 2015 (in Serbian) as well as of two ehxaustive international bibliographies: *Maximus the Confessor (580–662): Bibliography*, Belgrade: Institute for Theological Research 2012 and *Gregory Palamas (1296–1357): Bibliography*, Belgrade: Institute for Theological Research 2012. He has also published several articles on byzantine philosophy and theology in Serbian and English. He translates from English, Greek and German language. Dr Knežević is a vice president of the *Philosophical Society of Montenegro* and Operative editor of *Luča. Journal for Philosophy and Theory of Culture and Society*. He is also a member of International Association of Greek Philosophy and a member of Editorial Board of different scientific journals in Serbia, Montenegro and Bulgaria (*Smisao: Journal of the Department for Humanities of the Matica Srpska; Recueil de Travaux de la Faculté de Philosophie de la Université de Priština; Theologikon. The Annual of the Center for Systematic Theology; Philosophia: An Electronic Journal for Philosophy and Culture*).

Milan Đorđević (Skopje, 1981) is a docent of Philosophy and Psychology at the Faculty of Theology of the University of Skopje. He got his PhD at the University of Cologne, his MA in Philosophy at the University of Sofia and has finished his bachelor studies in Theology at the University of Skopje. His research interests are in the field of the byzantine philosophy and the orthodox christian theology. He is author of research papers published in the *Archive for Medieval Philosophy and Culture* (Sophia), the *Yearbook of the Faculty of Orthodox-Christian Theology of the Faculty of Theology in Skopje* and in theologically oriented periodicals in Macedonia and Bulgaria. His dissertation *Nicholas Cabasilas – One Way toward a Synthesis of the Tradition* has been published by Peeters (Belgium) in 2015.

Panagiotis Ch. Athanasopoulos, PhD, is a post-doc researcher at the Laboratory of Humanities, University of Patras and a research collaborator of the "Thomas de Aquino Byzantinus" international research project (2007-). His Doct. Diss. (*Hippolytus' De Antichristo – A Critical Edition*, Ioannina 2013) was prepared at the Department of Philology, University of Ioannina. His interests include Christian Literature and Greek and Latin Medieval Philosophy.

George Arabatzis, Associate Professor of Byzantine philosophy of the University of Athens, studied philosophy in Paris, France. A Scholarship holder of the French Government, he obtained his Ph.D. with honors from the École de Hautes Études en Sciences Sociales and he made a post-doctoral research in the University of Torino, Italy, with a grant from the Italian Government. From 1998 to 2012, he was a researcher at the Research Centre on Greek Philosophy of the Academy of Athens. He has been a Visiting Scholar-Research Fellow at the Princeton University, the University of Texas at Austin, the University of Helsinki, the University Charles in Prague, the University of

Jassy, Romania, etc. He gave lectures in the above universities and other ones and taught philosophy at the Aristotle University of Thessaloniki, at the Post-graduate programme in Philosophy of the University of Athens, at the Greek Open University, at the University of Peloponnese and at the École de Hautes Études en Sciences Sociales. He has participated in Greek and International Conferences and he is a member of Greek and International Philosophical Societies. His research is focused on Byzantine philosophy, its Ancient Sources and its modern perception. He has notably published: *Éthique du bonheur et orthodoxie à Byzance (IVe–XIIe s.)*, avec une préface de André Guillou, Paris, Éd. P. Belon, 1998, coll. "Textes. Documents. Études" No. 4 – *Paideia and Episteme in Michael of Ephesus. In Part. Anim. 1,3–2,10*, Athens, Research Centre on Greek Philosophy of the Academy of Athens, 2006 (in Greek with an English Summary) – *Byzantine Philosophy and Iconology*, Athens, 2012 (In Greek with an English summary). He has edited the volumes: *Studies on Supernaturalism*, Berlin, Logos Verlag, 2009. – *L'actualité de la pensée byzantine*, Byzantinische Forschungen, XXXI, 2013 (Adolf M. Hakkert, Amsterdam). – *Marges de la philosophie byzantine*, Athens, Kardamitsas, 2013.

HERE
ENDS THE BOOK,
THE WAYS OF BYZANTINE
PHILOSOPHY,
EDITED AND PROLOGUED
BY MIKONJA KNEŽEVIĆ,
WITH THE BLESSING OF BISHOP MAXIM
OF WESTERN AMERICAN DIOCESE;
THIS EDITION IS LIMITED TO
1000 COPIES AND WAS PUBLISHED
IN ALHAMBRA, CALIFORNIA,
IN COLLABORATION WITH THE
FACULTY OF PHILOSOPHY IN
KOSOVSKA MITROVICA, PRINTED
AT THE INTERKLIMA-GRAFIKA PRESS
IN VRNJCI, SERBIA,
OWNED BY
KYR LJUBIŠA ČEPERKOVIĆ,
REALIZED BY
SEBASTIAN PRESS
IN LOS ANGELES, CA ,
AND FINISHED
ON THE 13TH DAY
OF OCTOBER,
IN THE YEAR OF THE
LORD 2015.